UNDERSTANDING
THE AMERICAN PAST

AMERICAN HISTORY AND ITS INTERPRETATION

Boston, Toronto

Understanding the American Past

Written and Edited by

EDWARD N. SAVETH

Little, Brown and Company

For
BETTY

Published simultaneously in Canada
by Little, Brown & Company (Canada) Limited

PRINTED IN THE UNITED STATES OF AMERICA

Introduction

MANKIND always needs perspectives, and never more than
when it has just emerged from some shattering convulsion.
After the smoke, clangor, and anguish of the First World War,
when Europe and America had been too intensely occupied with
day-to-day problems of survival to dare look behind or ahead,
thoughtful people felt an overmastering thirst for the instruction
of History. Campaigns, massacres, the fall of empires, the Armistice,
the insoluble problems of reconstruction, had meant everything;
then in December, 1922, the globe stood awaiting the disclosures
of Tutankhamen's tomb, the lessons to be gathered from the treasures buried with an Eastern potentate two thousand, three hundred
years earlier. From the speeches of Wilson, Lloyd George, and
Poincaré, and from the soul-searing debates over boundaries, repa-
rations, and armaments, men turned with a sense of rescue to
H. G. Wells's *Outline of History* and the companion surveys of
humanity's long past. To use Daniel Webster's image, the mariners
tossed at sea under long days of storm and driving wrack seize the
first moment of calm to get their bearings from the eternal stars.

Once more mankind has partially emerged from a period of terrible storm. Once more it needs to study the compass and turn its
glasses upon Arcturus. Mr. Saveth's collection of interesting and
penetrating essays on American history, and his discerning survey
of historical writing in the United States, will help reflective readers
to gain their bearings. It is a commendable service, for the citizens
of no country need a better understanding of their past than do
Americans.

It has been too much the tendency of Americans, indeed, to
underrate both their history and their historians. They evaluate too
lightly the immense mass and complexity of our three hundred and
fifty years of past experience, from the time when North America

became a priceless stake in the struggles of European Powers to the time when the United States found itself the political guide, shield, and arbiter of Western civilization. They underrate equally the thoughtfulness, the philosophic breadth, and the analytical subtlety which our best historians, especially of the twentieth century, have brought to the study of American experience. The adventurous qualities of our national Odyssey were always plain. Even George Bancroft could do justice to that side of the story. But the full richness of the tapestry we had woven was not clear until students of politics had dealt in critical terms with the problems involved in the rise of our great organized state; until psychologists had probed the American mind in different periods of growth; until sociologists had studied the heterogeneities of our social evolution, and economists the interrelations of material factors with other elements; until students of literature had shown how well our writers (whatever their aesthetic deficiencies) had mirrored the national soul and mind. Readers of this volume will catch some glimpses of the true importance and value of our continental heritage.

American experience has always been an epitome of much world experience. Our struggle against raw savage nature reflected and epitomized mankind's long struggle against forest, desert, and beast. In one sense the United States is the first European nation, for it is the first nation in which the blood of all European peoples has mingled. Yet in other respects a great deal of our American history is unique. We have carried forward a unique experiment in the forging of democracy; in the adjustment of capital and labor, and the subordination of both to government; and above all, in the development of a spirit of free experiment under conditions of liberty and fair equality of opportunity. No country has a story better worth reading than America's. Mr. Saveth's volume is a feast in itself; to discerning readers it will be but the antepast to a still richer feast which they can find for themselves.

ALLAN NEVINS

Columbia University
May 10, 1954

Contents

Introduction
    BY ALLAN NEVINS   v

Historical Understanding in Democratic America
    BY EDWARD N. SAVETH   3

I. *The American Mold*

The Puritan Tradition
    BY SAMUEL ELIOT MORISON   67

The Virginians
    BY CARL BRIDENBAUGH   80

The Declaration of Independence
    BY JULIAN P. BOYD   94

Mercantilism and the American Revolution
    BY LAWRENCE A. HARPER   101

Radicals and Conservatives after Independence
    BY OSCAR AND MARY F. HANDLIN   115

The Spirit of the Constitution
    BY CHARLES A. BEARD   128

George Washington: Administrator
    BY LEONARD WHITE   144

Alexander Hamilton: Nation Maker
    BY REXFORD G. TUGWELL AND JOSEPH DORFMAN   158

Thomas Jefferson: Anti-totalitarian

    BY A. WHITNEY GRISWOLD   178

The American People in 1800

    BY HENRY ADAMS   190

II. *Sectional Conflict and Civil War*

Pre-Civil War Sectionalism

    BY FREDERICK JACKSON TURNER   217

William Leggett and Jacksonian Democracy

    BY RICHARD HOFSTADTER   227

The Impact of the Revolutions of 1848 on American Thought

    BY MERLE CURTI   242

The Reactionary Enlightenment

    BY LOUIS HARTZ   259

John Brown

    BY ALLAN NEVINS   285

Political Processes and Civil War

    BY ROY F. NICHOLS   303

Lincoln and the Governance of Men

    BY JAMES G. RANDALL   315

III. *Forces in America to the First World War*

Tom Watson and the Negro

    BY C. VANN WOODWARD   339

Henry Villard: Entrepreneur

    BY THOMAS COCHRAN   360

Karl Marx and Samuel Gompers

    BY JOHN R. COMMONS   376

Kansas
BY CARL L. BECKER 384

The Business Attitude toward the Spanish-American War
BY JULIUS W. PRATT 406

The California Progressive
BY GEORGE E. MOWRY 422

How We Got Into World War I
BY WALTER MILLIS 435

IV. *Our Times*

Middle Western Isolationism
BY RAY ALLEN BILLINGTON 451

The Third-generation American
BY MARCUS L. HANSEN 472

Franklin D. Roosevelt and the New Deal
BY ERIC F. GOLDMAN 489

Roosevelt and His Detractors
BY ARTHUR SCHLESINGER, JR. 514

The "Sitting Ducks" of Clark Field
BY LOUIS MORTON 529

American Character
BY HENRY S. COMMAGER 552

Notes 565

Index 593

UNDERSTANDING
THE AMERICAN PAST

Historical Understanding in Democratic America

by

EDWARD N. SAVETH

The real historians are those who love history for its own sake, who love it when they are old as when they were young. . . . To them history is a profession, a profession worthy of its hire, and in itself a sufficient reward for the hardest efforts. [JOHN SPENCER BASSETT: *The Middle Group of American Historians.*]

SOME years ago, Carl Becker wrote an article which he called "What We Didn't Know Hurt Us A Lot." [1] It is in the spirit of Becker's title that this book about American history and American historical writing is offered the general reader. In a world divided between democracy and dictatorship, with history an avowed weapon in the struggle between these two systems, we Americans must have fuller knowledge of our democratic heritage and its advantages over the ways of totalitarianism. We need to know more American history than the drab data presented to a captive classroom audience in the average textbook; more than the flashy fragments of our heritage to be found among the slashing sabers and perturbed petticoats of the historical novels.

One of the purposes of this volume is to promote broader knowledge of American history, while telling something of the historian and his art. We have adopted this dual approach because of general unawareness of the historian's role in American society. Actually, the historian's is a very heavy responsibility because in telling us what we were in the past, he is bound to influence our conceptions of what we are now and will be tomorrow. It is true that relatively few people read history. But as Guy Stanton Ford, former Executive

Secretary of the American Historical Association, has said, the historian's delving filters through to all quickly enough, with the result that "in the homelands of dictatorship it is history and the social sciences that have first been brought to heel. . . ." [2] The meaning that the historian discovers in the past is of crucial importance both in the Iron Curtain countries where the historian's formulations are controlled and in the democratic world where they are not.

Synthesizing American history and American historical writing (historiography), this book has as its central theme the meanings which historians have discovered in the past. The balance of the introduction describes the more significant understandings of American history evolved between the publication of the first volume of George Bancroft's *History of the United States from the Discovery of the American Continent* in 1834 and the present — a theme which is continued in the prefaces to the historical selections reprinted herein. The selections are descriptive of major events and developments in American history as told by some of our outstanding historians. They offer the reader, if not a history of the United States, then insight into the nature of American development based upon accounts of some of the more significant aspects of our history. The selections provide, in addition, a rich and varied sampling of American historical writing.

Before attempting to trace the course of American historical interpretation, something ought to be said about my own conception of historical understanding. The latter I have found to be conditioned by the impact upon the historian of the world in which he lives, and also by the development of his art. This, I realize, is not all there is to it by any means. Historical understanding is, in addition, a highly individual matter — an analysis of which ought to place greater stress than was possible in an essay of this length upon the individual historian and his unique perceptions. Historical understanding in democratic America is an adventure of the unfettered human intellect, which is the most powerful force in the universe. And because at least part of the power of the free mind in democratic society is rooted in its unpredictability, the course of historical understanding, from Bancroft's day to our own, has been rather difficult to sketch — particularly on a canvas as limited as ours.

Therefore, what has been attempted in the succeeding pages is an outline of certain of the major trends in the writing of American history, and since this has not been attempted before for a general audience, I hope it will serve a useful purpose.

JEFFERSON-JACKSON AND FEDERALIST-WHIG

Characteristic of American writings on history, throughout most of the nineteenth century, was the multi-volume narrative embracing a relatively large segment of the American past. Overwhelmingly political in tone, nineteenth-century historical writing reflected, even as it did not define, our major political traditions: the Jefferson–Jackson and the Federalist–Whig. But while it was fairly common for the American historian during the nineteenth century to orient his conception of the American past around one or the other of these political perspectives, he was frequently insistent upon the impartiality of his approach.

Accordingly, when George Bancroft — who deserves more than anyone to be called the father of American historical writing — published in 1834 the first volume of his *History of the United States from the Discovery of the American Continent*, Whiggish George Ticknor politely chided the historian by saying "you are not made by your talents or affectations, by your temperament or your pursuits, to be either the leader or the tool of demagogues." [1] Ticknor saw Bancroft's *History* as a formidable political weapon for the party of Jacksonian democracy and, in effect, it was.

To Bancroft, however, the political preference his work proclaimed was less contrived by the author than inherent in the subject matter of American and world history. Graduating from Harvard in 1819, Bancroft then went to study in Germany, where he was impressed by two major historiographic traditions, both of which are reflected in his *History*. From the early scientific historians of the Continent, Bancroft received a belief in the progressive thrust of history toward perfection, in accordance with some pre-ordained Divine scheme of which God was the cause and history the consequence. From the European romantic historians Bancroft derived the idea of history as the revelation of the unique genius of a people — genius which, for the most part, found expression in their political institutions. Combining these two heritages, Bancroft wrote history geared to the conviction that the United States, a late development of civilization, was also its finest flowering; that the institutions of American democracy were the fruition of a Divine plan and the American people its consecrated agents.

If "the popular voice," as Bancroft hazarded on July 4, 1826, "is the voice of God," it was inevitable that he view the political movement led by Andrew Jackson as advancing the American people toward the goal of his historical teleology.[2] No wonder, then, that he wrote history that was, in the words of Professor Jameson, "redolent of the idea of the new Jacksonian democracy — its exuberant confidence, its uncritical self-laudation, its optimistic hopes."[3] At the same time, Bancroft denied that his work was anything but objective. When Leopold von Ranke referred to the *History* as "the best book written from the democratic point of view," Bancroft replied: "If there is democracy in history, it is not subjective but objective. . . ."[4]

Bancroft's understanding of the American past in the political tradition of Jefferson and Jackson was continued by James Schouler, whose *History of the United States Under the Constitution* began chronologically with the Constitutional convention and extended through the Civil War and Reconstruction periods.

As the nineteenth century advanced, however, the political orientation characteristic of Bancroft's and Schouler's work yielded to a predominantly Federalist–Whig approach even as the temper of the country became predominantly Republican. The first three volumes of Richard Hildreth's *History of the United States of America* were published in 1849, and from the "advertisement" in the beginning of the first it was apparent that this was a work which was very different in tone from Bancroft's. "Of centennial sermons and Fourth of July orations, whether professedly such or in the guise of history," Hildreth wrote with Bancroft in mind, "there are more than enough. It is due to our fathers and ourselves, it is due to truth and philosophy, to present for once, on the historic stage, the founders of our nation unbedaubed with patriotic rouge. . . ." Hildreth, according to Arthur Schlesinger, Jr., aspired toward an impartial historical narrative. At the same time, Schlesinger observes, Hildreth's "immense temperamental preference for experience over theory, his New England background and training, and his utilitarianism, caused him to prefer Hamilton's practical achievements to Jefferson's theories." [5]

The Federalist-Whig orientation was characteristic, too, of a large body of "popular history" designed to appeal to the general public. The "folk heroes" of these popular mid-nineteenth-century books, according to Merle Curti, "were not, by and large, champions of democracy, that is, of the rights and interests of the plain people." Despite the professed devotion of the authors to accuracy and nonpartisanship, Curti continues, "The Federalist–Whig view . . . informed their writing." [6] The same might also be said of the most widely read American history textbooks in the forty years before the American Civil War. [7]

Hermann Eduard von Holst's *Constitutional and Political History of the United States*, a long-winded, dry-as-dust, eight-volume review of the political aspects of the slavery controversy, published between 1876 and 1892, also supported the Federalist-Whig understanding. In von Holst's opinion, those Americans in the post-Civil War era who opposed slavery, state rights, Jeffersonianism, and the Democratic Party, acted in accord with the "Times-Spirit" of the age. [8] But the Times-Spirit was, in essence, what von Holst believed it to be, and again we have the case of an historian identifying his own point of view with a trend he believed to be inherent in the historic process. [9]

James Ford Rhodes, in the *History of the United States from the Compromise of 1850*, [10] tried to avoid this kind of fault by rejecting any philosophy of history as likely to prejudice his findings. Indeed, against the dangers of bias in history, he erected the bulwarks of "diligence, accuracy, love of truth, impartiality." [11] Rhodes, in fact, did make great strides toward relative objectivity in treating the issues surrounding the American Civil War and he made a fairer statement of the cause of the South than von Holst had done. However, when Rhodes in the eighth volume of his *History* dealt with labor disturbances in the anthracite fields of Pennsylvania, he wrote as a Republican and as a former businessman whose sympathies were entirely with the mine operators and against the miners. The latter, Rhodes observed, were mainly Irishmen who acted in accordance with a hereditary bent toward "strong drink and carousing . . . robbery and murder." [12]

Despite the overwhelming preoccupation of the nineteenth-century historian with politics, there were intrusions of nonpolitical themes — occasionally in the volumes of Bancroft and Schouler and, more frequently, in those of Rhodes. Nevertheless, the appearance in 1883 of John Bach McMaster's *History of the People of the United States*[13] represented a new departure in American historical writing in so far as its primary aim was "to describe the dress, the occupations, the amusements, the literary canons of the times; to note the changes of manners and morals; to trace the growth of the human spirit. . . ."[14] Large, sprawling, and formless, and American social history has ever since retained this characteristic, McMaster's work was not thesis-drawn; indeed the historian, in the interest of impartiality, presented evidence on both sides of controversial questions, so that the reader might draw his own conclusions. At times, this is rather skillfully done and we can almost see the historian weighing his data in an effort to achieve a balanced point of view. On the other hand, there are occasions when the scales tip rather obviously and it is the opinion of McMaster's biographer, Eric F. Goldman, that the *History of the People* is oriented toward Republican-capitalist America of the late nineteenth century and voted for McKinley, even as Bancroft's volumes had voted for Jackson.[15] This was true, too, of the textbooks McMaster wrote for elementary and secondary school use, and which achieved wide distribution.[16]

The Profession of Historian and the Science of History

Until the last two decades of the nineteenth century, American history had been written by men who were not trained particularly for the task. Indeed, the prevailing conception of history was as a branch of literature. This is not said in depreciation of any of the nineteenth-century historians we have mentioned, nor of others like Francis Parkman, William Hickling Prescott, and John Lothrop Motley whom we have not. Actually, it is to the credit of the nineteenth-century man of letters, turned historian, that he wrote good history in such a manner as to appeal to a large popular audience.

How the personnel involved in the writing of American history altered between 1880 and 1910 is apparent in a comparison, as to background and preparation, of the contributors to the eight-volume *Narrative and Critical History of America*, which appeared under the editorship of Justin Winsor between 1884 and 1889; and the authors of the American Nation Series which Albert Bushnell Hart edited between 1904 and 1907. Of the former, only one had received graduate training in history; of the twenty-four authors in the latter series, all but two had done graduate work.[1] By 1884, professionalization had advanced to the point at which the American Historical Association, guild of the country's professional historians, was founded. Eleven years later, the *American Historical Review* began publication.

The advent of the professional historian, of course, did not make obsolete all that had gone before. There was, indeed, a certain amount of vigor in the histories written by early nineteenth-century historians that is responsible for some still being read today. Moreover, the best of the amateurs anticipated the professionals in their judicious use of sources, and in many instances their approach to history was intelligent and creative. Although from 1890 to the present the professionally-trained historian has dominated American historiography,[2] we must not lose sight of the fact that a retired businessman, James Ford Rhodes, made the first fairly successful attempt at a relatively impartial treatment of the Civil War; that a young engineer, John Bach McMaster, produced the first significant history of American society; that a former clergyman, Edward Eggleston, early conceived of American history as the record of the culture of the American people: their ideas, customs, and beliefs;[3] that today the historical writings of Bernard De Voto, the late Mark Sullivan, and the late Frederick Lewis Allen meet exacting professional standards.

With the professionalization of history, the subject approached the status of a science. This was caused in part by the impact of Darwin and Spencer on American thought and the consequent vogue of "scientism"; in part by the influence of the German masters, who in the latter nineteenth century trained the first generation of professional historians — American facilities for such training being extremely limited.[4]

"Scientific history," as it evolved in the late nineteenth century, was a term of two meanings. First, it implied strict faithfulness to the written record of the past. The scientific historians were bound to find fault with certain of the practices of the historian-freebooters of an earlier era. For example, Jared Sparks, greatest of the early American historical editors, between 1834 and 1837 published twelve volumes of *The Writings of George Washington* in which he made omissions without indicating them, corrected Washington's spelling and sentence structure, and in many other ways improved his English. Not only that: Sparks had been enjoined by Justice Washington, who loaned him the manuscripts, "to avoid giving offense to the writers [of letters to Washington] or their famileis [*sic*] by publishing any which have a reference to the state of parties, and alluding to particular indeviduals [*sic*] by name." And Sparks replied: "I am fully aware of the delicacy you mention, and trust my judgment will guard me against any indiscretion." [5]

Scientific historiography would tolerate none of this. Strict faithfulness to the letter and punctuation of historical documents was to be the rule from now on. The same scrupulous care was exercised in getting at the facts of history. Subjects were investigated in depth rather than breadth and a gap in research was to be bridged neither by guess nor intuition. As extensive digging revealed a widening range of historical sources, and as historical monographs proliferated, the historian was forced to narrow his scope. The huge chunks of the American past which the nineteenth-century narrative historian bit off yielded to well-chewed morsels published as monographs by university presses or as articles in academic journals.

The last significant effort in the old tradition of nineteenth-century narrative historiography — that is in the pattern of Bancroft, Hildreth and Rhodes — was by Edward Channing, who, in his *History of the United States* (the first volume of which appeared in 1905), announced his intention of exploring American history "from the discovery of America to the close of the nineteenth century." [6] Nor did subsequent historians attempt anything as all-embracing as Channing's plan to treat "the growth of the nation . . . as one continuous development from the political, military, institutional, industrial, and social points of view." [6] Narrative histories now in process include Allan Nevins's *Ordeal of the Union* and Lawrence H. Gipson's *The British Empire Before the American Revolution.* The temporal span embraced by both of these histories is a great deal smaller than what Channing hoped to cover.[7]

As scientific historians dug deep and narrow shafts into the American past, it was apparent to John Spencer Bassett, writing in 1916, that history had become less a "thing of human activities to be dressed in flowing robes and with due attention to the harmonies," than it had been with the more style-conscious historians of the early nineteenth century. Bassett observed that "in proportion to the population history is less-read today by voluntary readers than it was a hundred years ago. None of our historians command the same degree of respect from the public that men like Bancroft . . . and Sparks commanded in their day."[8] Bassett found it difficult to name a historian who earned his living by writing history — and although he may have been overstating the case, the consequences of the impact of scientific history were, in general, as he had indicated.

But from the point of view of the scientific historian, his lay readership might well have been considered expendable. After all, if history was a "science," then why should the historian worry, any more than the physicist and chemist did, about appealing to the "generally interested," as distinct from those who were professionally concerned? In the academic world of the late nineteenth century, in which the scientism of Darwin and Spencer was dominant and in which history was bidding for its place in the curriculum on the basis of its alleged scientific character, the historian felt that he had larger fish to fry in attempting to discover the laws of history. What historian, said Henry Adams, with a "spark of imagination . . . can have helped dreaming of the immortality that would be achieved by the man who should successfully apply Darwin's method to the facts of human history"?[9]

THE COMPARATIVE METHOD AND THE TEUTONIC HYPOTHESIS

This introduces the second conception of scientific history: the belief that there were historical laws which would become apparent to the scholar in the course of patient pursuit of facts. Searching for law in history, the American historian of the late nineteenth century was guided in his probings by the comparative method, the technique of which they acquired in the seminars of their European masters. The latter, in turn, had taken over the comparative method from the philologists, who had used it to trace word relationships. Even as similarity between words offered a clue to their common origin, resemblances between political institutions, it was believed, were indicative of their having sprung from a common source.

Fifty years earlier, Bancroft had learned at Göttingen that history was an evolving and interrelated pattern. Now, in the late nineteenth century, the thread of evolution was alleged to be in the racial characteristics of the Aryan peoples in their various homelands. English and Continental historians, notably Edward Augustus Freeman and G. L. von Maurer, on the basis of apparent institutional resemblances, traced English and German political institutions to the ancient Teutonic tribes who roamed the German forests in Tacitus's day and before — and to even more remote origins in some "common primaeval brotherhood" of the Aryan peoples. It was maintained by these historians that the Aryans, in their original homeland, had developed a common language, mores and institutional pattern. Upon their dispersal, a segment of the Aryans, according to the Teutonists, went to Greece, where they comprised the nucleus of Greek civilization; another segment went to Rome and forged the Empire's grandeur. But the pick of the Aryans were supposed to have migrated to Germany where, in the depths of the Black Forest, the Aryo-Teutonic peoples developed the basis of political institutions common to Germany, England, and the United States.

The Teutonic hypothesis received its fullest development in the United States during the 1880's at the Johns Hopkins Graduate School, which was under the direction of Herbert Baxter Adams, lately returned from studies at Heidelberg under Johann Bluntschli and Max von Erdmannssdorffer. Adams, like other American disciples of the Teutonic hypothesis, believed with Freeman that the United States was another homeland of the Aryan peoples; that even as the Teutonic "seeds" had been transplanted from Germany to England by the Anglo-Saxon invaders of England during the sixth century, so these same "seeds" were introduced into America by the Anglo-Saxon Puritans. At this point, the Teutonic hypothesis was joined by the social Darwinist argument which had the transplanted Aryan seed "germinating" into the institutions of the New England town, the governments of the New England states, and finally into our national Constitution — culmination of "Aryan" political evolution.[1]

Herbert Baxter Adams's paper on the "Germanic Origins of New England Towns" was a model of such theorizing. According to Adams, the ancient Teutons had evolved in their councils and village moots "the seeds of self-government, of commons and congresses." In the German forest was developed "the single head of the state, the smaller council . . . and the general assembly of the whole people," nuclei of the institutions of Holland, Germany, New England and the United States. These little communes, said Adams — reflecting the influence of Darwin and Spencer as well as Freeman — were "the germs of our state and national life . . . the primordial cells of the body politic." The historian should treat the United States, Adams urged, "as an organism of historic growth, developing from the very protoplasm of state-life."[2]

This understanding of American history was also taught by Moses Coit Tyler[3] and Andrew D. White at Cornell[4]; by John W. Burgess at Columbia[5]; and by Albert Bushnell Hart at Harvard.[6] In addition, the Teutonic hypothesis was given expression in the popularly-written histories of John Fiske which, unlike the work of the academicians, did reach the general public.[7]

Thus, the first generation of American scientific historians found meaning in the American past in the light of the belief that acquired characteristics were inherited; that "race" was not only a biological phenomenon but a cultural and political determinant. These concepts, borrowed from the natural sciences and joined by the comparative method and the Teutonic hypothesis, convinced many professional historians that the new realm of meaning they had discovered in the American past was truly scientific as contrasted with what they regarded as the unscientific preconceptions of earlier historical writing. But what actually did happen is that the professional historian, at the end of the nineteenth century, in the name of science, committed the historian to the kind of prejudices to be found in the writings of their predecessors.

For example, the superiority of the Anglo-Saxon and Protestant American, which almost all the earlier nineteenth-century historians accepted pretty much on faith, now found "scientific" confirmation. In the books of John Fiske, the line of historical evolution reaches upward from the Aryan to the Protestant nations of England, Holland, Germany, and the United States.[8] The scientific historian, like his predecessor, did not lose sight of God's role in the determination of events. God, it is true, was no longer the active agent intervening in the affairs of men that He was in Bancroft's volumes. But He still presided over the ordered Spencerian universe of John Fiske, whose history, with the battalions of Protestantism and Anglo-Saxonism in the van, evolved in accordance with a Divine plan.[9]

Further, the Teutonists strengthened the trend toward conservatism in American historical writing — toward the Whig–Republican understanding of the American past which had come to dominate late nineteenth-century American historiography. To such an extent did this school of history believe that political institutions were products of historical evolution, and therefore inviolate, that the Teutonists were inclined to resist the idea of change in the American political and economic structure.[10] Finally, aggressive nationalism, which was certainly no newcomer to American historical writing, found expression during the latter nineteenth century as the historian, amidst nationalist and imperialist rivalries of the day, argued the necessity for American expansion in terms of the superiority of the original Aryan inheritance, its perfection on this continent, and the mission of the American (Aryan, Anglo-Saxon, and Protestant) beyond our borders.[11]

Although the Teutonic hypothesis and the comparative method were believed to have constituted the basis of an historical science, there are obvious fallacies in both. First, the theory of the historical evolution of the Aryan peoples, as developed by Freeman and his American disciples, was more fairy tale than history. Second, resemblances between institutions separated widely in time and place, which these historians professed to discover, were more apparent than real and, in addition, provided no sure proof of the common origin of political forms. Third, the Social Darwinist conviction that there existed biological analogies in history is without foundation.

However, despite the fact that the Teutonic hypothesis and the use the Teutonists made of the comparative method can be shown to be demonstrably false, faith in scientific method in historiography need not be weakened. Indeed, the progress in historical understanding between 1890 and the present — and I use the word "progress" deliberately — has been within the framework of the scientific approach. Without equating history with the physical sciences, it should be realized that in both the investigator is constantly modifying, rejecting, and finding new understandings. And even as much of the natural science of the nineteenth century has been outmoded, this is also true of the history written in that period. And if a particular approach can be shown to be demonstrably false, this should not cause the historian to abandon the empirical or scientific method. The latter remains, in the words of Charles A. Beard, "the only method that can be employed in obtaining accurate knowledge of historical facts, personalities, situations, and movements. The scientific method is, therefore, a precious and indispensable instrument of the human mind." [12]

THE FRONTIER HYPOTHESIS

Despite the great vogue among historians of the Teutonic hypothesis,[1] there was even in the 1890's some dissent from it — which was to grow stronger, as time passed, until the theory became completely unacceptable.[2] In 1893 a young instructor at the University of Wisconsin named Frederick Jackson Turner told a meeting of the American Historical Association that historians were paying too much attention to the Germanic origins of American institutions and too little to the American factors involved.[3]

Born in the almost frontier community of Portage, Wisconsin, Turner came East, after attending the University of Wisconsin, to study under Herbert Baxter Adams. But he was not too much influenced by Adams, and we can almost imagine him listening with one ear to Adams's exposition of the principles of Teutonism — and meanwhile thinking back to the scenes he most loved, and later described in an autobiographic letter:

I spent my youth in a newspaper office in contact with practical politics, and in a little town at "The Portage," Wis., over
which Marquette had passed. There were still Indian (Winne-
bago) tepees where I hunted and fished, and Indians came in
to the stores to buy paints and trinkets and sell furs. Their
Indian ponies and dogs were familiar street scenes. . . . As
the local editor and leader of his party, my father reported
the community life, the problems of the farmer, the local news
(which I helped to "set up") . . . harmonized the rival tongues
and interests of the various towns of the county, and helped
to shepherd a very composite flock. My school fellows were
all these varied classes and nationalities, and we all "got on
together" in this forming society. . . .

Is it strange that I saw the frontier as a real thing and experienced its changes? . . . My mother's ancestors were preachers! Is it strange that I preached of the frontier?[4]

Turner, particularly in his earlier writings, shared some of the
ideas of the Teutonists. He was, like them, a social evolutionist and
on more than one occasion resorted to the use of biological
analogy in history.[5] Turner, however, was less concerned with the
remote sources of racial and ancestral history than with uniquely
American influences. His mentors were not the German and
English historians who so impressed Herbert Baxter Adams and
John W. Burgess, but rather his undergraduate teacher at the University of Wisconsin, Professor W. F. Allen, who was influential in
motivating Turner's thinking about the role of the West in American
historical development. Turner, too, was less interested in recon-
structing the political life of the ancient Teutons than he was in
quantitative data illustrative of the American scene to be found in
*Scribner's Statistical Atlas of the United States Showing by Graphic
Methods Their Present Condition and Their Political, Social and
Industrial Development,* which was published in 1885, and the
Compendium of the Eleventh Census, 1890.[6]

Not a great stylist, Turner wrote little and that little seemed to
come hard. That the frontier theme was a stimulant to his prose,
however, is indicated by the fact that his *Significance of the Frontier
in American History* is both a classic of American historiography and
one of the most influential essays ever written by an American
historian. In it, Turner offered not only an explanation of American

development based on the role of the frontier, but an expression, as well, of rising Western regional consciousness against the East and of the groundswell of mass discontent that demanded, in the depression days of 1893, institutional accommodation to environmental change.

In 1893, Turner was writing of what he considered to be a bygone era in American history. He cited the aforementioned 1890 report of the Superintendent of the Census to prove that the unsettled part of the West had been so broken into that a frontier line could hardly be said to exist.

"This brief official statement," according to Turner, "marks the closing of a great historic movement. Up to our own day American history has been in a large degree the history of the colonization of the Great West. The existence of an area of free land, its continuous recession, and the advance of American settlement westward, explains American development."

Having stated this thesis, Turner went on to affirm what most of the Teutonists would never grant: that behind political institutions and modifications in them were, not the forces of race and historic continuity, but changing environmental conditions. "The peculiarity of American institutions is the fact that they have been compelled to adapt themselves to the changes of an expanding people — to the changes involved in crossing a continent, in winning a wilderness. . . ." The phenomenon of change, Turner concluded, would not drop out of American life despite what was regarded as the end of the frontier process. New social frontiers would have to be sought, Turner seemed to be saying between the lines of this essay — and, more explicitly, in subsequent writings — by way of response to "the stubborn American environment" and "its imperious summons to accept its conditions." [7] It is not accidental that Franklin Delano Roosevelt's early statement of the principle of the welfare state, as opposed to laissez-faire, drew in part upon Turnerian conceptions. [8]

Turner may not have been a prolific writer, but he was undeniably provocative. When he first addressed his colleagues on the significance of the frontier, it is true that Turner's hearers did not fall like tenpins before the bowling ball of his argument. However, in a relatively short time, the frontier hypothesis attracted a rather wide following among American historians. This was true, particularly, of the younger men in the profession who were stimulated by Turner's ability as a teacher first at Wisconsin and then at Harvard. And the pull toward the frontier hypothesis was all the stronger because with the Teutonic theory becoming more patently sterile, the profession offered little in the way of an alternative thesis.

Another reason for the attractiveness of the frontier hypothesis was the fact that, like the Teutonic theory, it stressed that democracy was born and nurtured in a forest environment. The American historian played his role in the development of the myth that people and institutions are somehow purified in a wilderness environment and vaguely corrupted in cities. Herbert Baxter Adams's account of the "Germanic Origin of New England Towns" has the ancient Teutons, in the cool shadows of the Black Forest, building their *tun* near some rapid-flowing stream, and developing therein the seeds of the political system that made America great. The frontier hypothesis, also, assigned to democracy a forest birth, alleging that the wilderness bred individualism and egalitarianism. Consequently, in accepting Turner, the historians were in keeping with a tradition that went back to Jefferson's conception of democracy as an agrarian phenomenon, and before him to Rousseau and Montesquieu.[9]

Finally, adherence to the frontier hypothesis aligned the historian with the politically progressive forces of the late nineteenth and early twentieth century without his having to run the risk of being dubbed an extremist. The implications of the Turner thesis were Jeffersonian and Jacksonian, not Marxian. Even conservatives could take comfort in a theory that derived "rugged individualism" from the frontier experience.[10] Charles A. Beard has said that "although Turner did not invent the phrase 'rugged individualism' he did in effect . . . identify it with the frontier spirit. . . . Wittingly or not he fortified the [conservative] teachings of Sumner in economics and sociology and of Burgess in political science."[11]

HISTORY AND SOCIETY

History, stated Turner in 1910, should "hold the lamp for conservative reform"; it should not merely preserve "curios for the . . .

museum." [1] This present-minded approach to the past was coupled with Turner's avowed use of a thesis, or frame of reference — the frontier — in the light of which he developed his understanding of American history. There was, however, by no means unanimous support among the historical guild of the principle of thesis-shaped history, and of Turner's belief that history should be viewed from the "vantage-ground of present developments." [2]

The objectivists among American historians who based their position upon Leopold von Ranke's belief that it was the task of the historian merely to describe "how it was in the past," as well as the advocates of thesis-written history, were agreed that historical narratives ought to be based on facts "established and classified to the fullest extent possible at the present moment." [3] But once the facts were established, what was the historian to do with them? On this issue professional opinion divided.

Some held it to be sufficient for the historian merely to establish a factual foundation. According to George Burton Adams: "To furnish materials for later builders, may be a modest ambition; but it is my belief that in our own field of history, for a long time to come, the man who devotes himself to preliminary labors, will make a more useful contribution to the final science, or philosophy of history, than he who yields to the allurements of speculations and endeavors to discover in the present state of our knowledge, the forces that control society. . . ." [4] A variant of the objectivist position was suggested by Albert J. Beveridge who claimed that "facts when justly arranged interpret themselves." [5]

But, countered the proponents of thesis-shaped history, the so-called "objective" historian would still have to select his facts, generally with some synthetic principle in mind. Even Rhodes — who said "the object of history is to tell a story and leave philosophy to others," and aimed to "get rid so far as possible of all preconceived notions and theories" — nevertheless did discriminate among the materials of history, utilizing some rather than others. [6] Was not a point of view implicit in such selection?

James Harvey Robinson and Carl Becker, who, *circa* 1905, promulgated the idea of "the New History," believed that it was neither possible nor desirable for the historian to be objective. History, they believed, ought to be made to serve the current interests of society and the latter should guide the historian both in the selection of a subject and in the handling of materials. The New History had, in addition, a frank political tone. "The time has come," said Robinson, "when the present shall turn on the past and exploit it in the interests of advance" — which was the equivalent of inviting the historian to enlist his discipline in the battalions of political insurgency.[7]

The followers of Turner and the disciples of the New History may have been bold in their statement of the present political uses of history, but they were not the first to make history serve political ends. This is apparent in the see-sawing of American historiography between the Jefferson–Jackson and Federalist–Whig points of view throughout most of the nineteenth century. Moreover, the fact that the New History formally struck at the standard of objectivity does not mean that only its disciples wrote history that was not objective. Our discussion of the nineteenth-century narrative historians is indicative of how little the protestations of truth and objectivity that adorned their prefaces carried over into their work as a whole. And while Robinson spoke approvingly of history as an instrument of political progressivism, a few years earlier conservative historians like John Fiske and John W. Burgess — from the high ground of avowed impartiality — had been using history to prove that William Jennings Bryan, the Populists, and the Socialists could not possibly be right in what they advocated.[8]

BEARD'S *Economic Interpretation of the Constitution*

More by implication than by direct statement, the principle of the New History found expression in Charles A. Beard's *Economic Interpretation of the Constitution* (1913). In 1894, Beard had left his home near Spiceland, Indiana, where his father was one of the town's leading and wealthiest citizens, to attend DePauw University. The conservatism of the young Charles A. Beard, probably taken over from his father, was somewhat shaken at DePauw by his teacher, Colonel James Riley Weaver — a Civil War veteran of Republican predilections who, in a small Middle Western Methodist institution, had Beard reading the *Communist Manifesto* and *Das Kapital*.[1]

After graduating from DePauw, Beard spent two years abroad in Germany and England. He worked with reform and labor elements in Britain, and became so prominent in British Labor Party circles that J. Ramsay MacDonald considered him for a post in a labor government, the advent of which MacDonald optimistically thought was nearer than it actually was.[2]

Beard, however, returned to America, took his doctorate at Columbia and began teaching there. A number of influences went into the shaping of his ideas. There was, of course, the background of his European experience, of old Colonel Weaver, and of his father William Beard — whose influence, if traceable, would be of extraordinary interest. He came abreast, too, of the burgeoning American reformism of the early twentieth century and the ideological expression given it by Oliver Wendell Holmes, Roscoe Pound, John Dewey, and Arthur F. Bentley.[3] The last was but one of a number of legal and political scholars who had come to regard law and politics less as ideological abstractions, than as rooted in group conflict and group interest.[4]

Beard, too, was heir to the random if not consistent use of the economic interpretation by writers, thinkers, and politicians in the American past. In *An Economic Interpretation of the Constitution,* Beard acknowledged his indebtedness to James Madison; but there were a number of others — John Adams, Daniel Webster, John C. Calhoun, and Richard Hildreth — who recognized economic realities for what they were.[5]

Several books which were published within a few years of *An Economic Interpretation of the Constitution* could not have failed to impress Beard: E. R. A. Seligman's *Economic Interpretation of History;*[6] a Marxist treatise by one of Turner's former students, Algie M. Simons,[7] which was a crude anticipation of Beard's thesis on the Constitution; and J. Allen Smith's *The Spirit of American Government,*[8] which was written in the tradition of Jeffersonian liberalism and argued that the Constitutional Convention was constituted overwhelmingly of members of the commercial and propertied classes who sought to protect and further their economic interests.[9]

Beard, of course, had read Turner, and early in *An Economic Interpretation of the Constitution* he pointed to the frank recognition that Turner and his school gave material forces in history.[10] However, Beard well knew that he could go only so far in establishing Turner and the Turnerians as precedents. Turner, it is true, as early as 1894, had stated that a number of studies of "natural economic groupings" in American history would be of fundamental importance in promoting understanding of political history. However, the Turner theory was essentially sectional, distilling class conflicts and economic tensions into an all-embracing conception of the "frontier" and "section" which, in a sense, obscured them. Beard extricated these economic and class forces from what amounted to sectional obfuscation, and made them determining in historical sequences. In so doing, he advanced an interpretation of history which reflected the spirit of the industrial age even as Turner, in a sense, harked back to an earlier agrarian one.

Beard, in explaining the origins of our most significant political institution, the Constitution of the United States, dropped the theme of democracy's forest birth. Beard, unlike Turner and unlike the Teutonists, abandoned the romantic notion of the mystical blending of man and nature that allegedly resulted in the flowering of democracy. To Beard, in 1913, political forms were shaped by man's material interests, a theme which had all the romance of bookkeeping.

In fact, something like bookkeeping was involved as Beard scoured the records of the Treasury Department in order to discover the public-security holdings of the men who framed the Constitution, and then made further inquiry into their financial biographies.[11] And, all the while, Beard had this hypothesis in mind: if you were to find, he wrote, that "men owning substantially the same amounts of the same kinds of property were equally divided on the matter of adoption or rejection — it would then become apparent that the Constitution had no ascertainable relation to economic groups or classes, but was the product of some abstract causes remote from the chief business of life — gaining a livelihood." But, on the other hand, if you discovered "that substantially all of the merchants, money lenders, security holders, manufacturers, shippers, capitalists, and financiers and their professional associates are to be found on one side in support of the Constitution and that substantially all or a major part of the opposition came from the non-slaveholding farmers and the debtors — would it not be pretty conclusively demonstrated that our fundamental law was not the product of an abstraction known as 'the whole people' but of a group of economic interests which must have expected beneficial results from its adoption?" [12]

Investigations of the sort that Beard conducted into the economic affairs of the founding fathers were then quite popular in America. The time was 1913, and political Progressivism was at flood tide. Woodrow Wilson was in the White House, a reform Democrat whose election had been made possible by the bolt of the Progressive faction from the Republican Party. For a decade before the publication of *An Economic Interpretation of the Constitution,* Americans had been reading in their magazines of large circulation the revelations of muckraking journalists whose stock in trade was the exposure of the depredations of Big Business and of the corrupt relationship between business and politics.[13] Therefore, the ground was well prepared for the reception of Beard's book, which, despite the formidable apparatus of its scholarship, had the tang of a muckraking document.[14] Beard, in effect, was exposing the economic interests behind the Constitution, the American holy of holies. This was scholarship — and also scandal. Small wonder that conservative Americans like William Howard Taft and Nicholas Murray Butler attacked the book while Progressives, despite Beard's claim to neutrality in politics, seized upon Beard's thesis as both ammunition for, and affirmation of, their cause.[15]

Yet it cannot be said, definitely, that *An Economic Interpretation of the Constitution* was designed, in the writing, to serve the Progressive cause—which was what James Harvey Robinson wanted the New History to do. Beard insisted that the book was above the political battle,[16] and one might reasonably conclude that a book written in a style so painstakingly chaste was designed as a scholarly contribution and not as a political tract. But Beard did tell Eric Goldman: "How did I arrive at my economic interpretation? . . . Well, I did read the writings of the Fathers, hundreds of them, hundreds of pages of economic emphasis. And I *was* writing in 1913, when reformers were filling the air with shouts of 'who gets what?' " Also, the argument from style can prove the other side of the coin, in so far as its studied objectivity and restraint permitted the book to speak with an authority that the propaganda missives did not have. "It was," Beard further told Goldman, "something to have a thousand footnotes and James Madison join the chorus, wasn't it?"[17] And yet those who see Beard's work, *circa* 1913, as exemplifying the teachings of the New History will find a better basis for their argument in Beard's *Contemporary American History*, which was published in 1914.[18]

THE BROADENING FRAMEWORK OF HISTORY — TO WORLD WAR I

In addition to the frontier hypothesis and the economic interpretation, other approaches employed by historians in the pre-World War I period broadened and deepened their perceptions of the American past. In 1891, Nathaniel Southgate Shaler's *Nature and Man in America* stressed the importance of geographic influences in American history, a point of view which also found expression in the series of volumes edited by Archer B. Hurlburt entitled "Historic Highways." Ellen C. Semple, American disciple of the German anthropo-geographer, Ratzel, made bold use of geographic determinism in her *American History and its Geographic Conditions* (1903).

Before the First World War, the recording of our economic history, as distinct from the economic interpretation of history, grew in importance. The Carnegie Corporation underwrote large-scale explorations of the history of American commerce, industry, and transportation in accordance with a plan of study formulated in 1902 and entitled "Contributions to American Economic History." As part of this project, John R. Commons and his associates prepared a multi-volume *Documentary History of American Society* (1910–1911), and a pioneer *History of Labour in the United States*, the first two volumes of which appeared in 1918.

There were also incipient beginnings in the field of social history. McMaster's first volume had been published as early as 1883, and by 1900, Edward Eggleston, speaking before the American Historical Association, called for the abandonment of "drum and trumpet history," in favor of the "history of culture, the real history of men and women."[1] The disciples of the New History talked a great deal, even if they wrote rather little, about the history of American society.

In part, this was a conscious reaction against earlier political emphases — and in part, also, because, in their opinion, history ought to illuminate present social problems. Finally, Carl Becker, in the spirit of the New History, suggested that the historian expand his vistas by drawing upon such fields as archaeology, psychology, anthropology, geography, economics and sociology, in order to enhance his understanding of the American past.[2]

These developments were accompanied by an increasing maturity of viewpoint, manifest particularly during the first two decades of the twentieth century, in the historian's approach to the American Revolution — an event so fraught with patriotic implications that its handling was a true test of emancipation from narrow nationalist prejudices. Already, in 1891, Professor James F. Jameson observed that Americans were beginning "to look at our characteristics and modes of life with an externality of view unknown to the previous generation"; and that our historians, in keeping with this trend, "have become more critical and discriminating, have learned more nearly to look upon the course of American history with an impartial eye."[3]

A contribution of monumental character to a broader understanding of the colonial period of American history, and incidentally to understanding of the American Revolution, was the work of Herbert Levi Osgood, whose three volumes on *The American Colonies in the Seventeenth Century* were published between 1904 and 1907, while another four on the colonies in the eighteenth century appeared posthumously in 1924. Osgood's work not only surpassed Bancroft's in depth of research, but, along with another young scholar named Charles McLean Andrews, placed colonial development within the framework of British imperial policy. Too many historians, stated Andrews, had lost sight of the fact "that the colonists were members of a great colonial empire, [and] were subject to an elaborate colonial administration that existed, as it were, outside of themselves."[4]

As for the American Revolution itself, Osgood in 1887 considered it "but an episode in the development of the English colonial system and the law which governs it."[5] Bancroft would have been shocked by Osgood's conclusion that "there is no proof that Parliament intended to overthrow the constitutional rights of the colonists. . . . There was nothing that can be called tyrannical or unconstitutional in the plans of Grenville, Townshend or Lord North." [6]

Despite an early interest in economic theory, Osgood's scholarly but rather ponderous and dull volumes dealt almost entirely with the political and constitutional aspects of the relationship between England and the colonies. To a lesser extent, Andrews's work, both early and late, slighted the economic aspects of the tie binding the American colonies and the mother country.[7] It remained for George Louis Beer to develop an understanding of the economics of imperial policy, "to describe and explain the origins, establishment, and development of the British colonial system up to the outbreak of the disagreements that culminated in the American Revolution; to analyze the underlying principles of British colonial policy in so far as they found expression in the laws of trade and navigation." [8]

Arthur M. Schlesinger's *Colonial Merchants and the American Revolution, 1763–1776*, which was published in 1918, placed primary emphasis upon the interests and attitudes of a specific economic group. A year before the Schlesinger study, Clarence W. Alvord's *The Mississippi Valley in British Politics* appeared as a contribution of the frontier school to our maturing historical viewpoint concerning the American Revolution. Alvord saw the British ministers concerned less with Boston and New York than with the Western transmontane region. To Alvord, the Revolution was culmination of "two series of events, one Eastern and one Western, which had for years run parallel, so closely interwoven that any attempt to understand the one without a knowledge of the other must inevitably fail. If historians would interpret rightly the causes of the American Revolution . . . they must not let their vision be circumscribed by the sequence of events in the East." [9]

Jameson's own provocative study of *The American Revolution Considered As a Social Movement* did not appear until 1926 — but it was further evidence of that maturity of historical viewpoint about which the author had spoken earlier. Unfortunately, in the 1920's, when these newer attitudes concerning the War for American Independence began to replace the traditional ones in textbooks, it was apparent from the kind of opposition they provoked that the "externality" of the historian's point of view was not shared by certain vocal segments of the population who insisted that the historians were betraying this country to the British Empire.[10]

The framework of the study of history in the pre-World War I period was broadened not only by newer interpretive emphases, but also by a wider range of source materials and their greater availability. Almost all early-nineteenth-century historians, except for the very wealthy, complained about how difficult it was to get materials upon which to base their narratives. Jared Sparks observed that there were but seven libraries in the United States "in which a whole stock of books relating to America may not be ranged in the corner of a single case." [11] By the time of the American Civil War, because of the efforts of historical editors like Hezekiah Niles, Jonathan Elliot, Peter Force, Lyman C. Draper, and Sparks himself, increasing quantities of historical materials bearing upon national development became available. In addition, sixty-five local historical societies had been founded in every state east of Texas except Delaware, in addition to those in the District of Columbia and in the Territory of New Mexico. Finally, many state governments authorized publication of materials pertinent to their own historical development.[12]

To an increasing extent, in the later nineteenth century, the historian was indebted to the patient work of editor and librarian. More and more historical societies were founded, not only on the state level but in towns and counties as well. And since the establishment of local historical societies was confined to no single state or region, one of the consequences of this development was that the dominant New England emphasis in American historiography — resulting from the fact that much of our national history was written by New Englanders from sources relating to the history of New England — began to diminish. Pronouncement of the Turner thesis had served to stimulate a broadened interest in history, particularly in the states of the Middle West, which was manifest in the professionalization and improvement of previously established state historical societies, as well as in the founding of new ones.[13] Of special significance was the organization in 1907 of the Mississippi Valley Historical Society and the founding, eight years later, of the *Mississippi Valley Historical Review.*

The South, largely because of the destructive impact of the American Civil War, had lagged behind the Midwest in the compilation of sources and in the writing of its local history[14] — although there did appear between 1903 and 1907 a twenty-volume coöperative history series entitled "The South in the Building of the Nation." In this early period, however, the foremost contribution to the historiography of the South was made by non-Southerners — Herbert Baxter Adams, who was born in New England and founded The Johns Hopkins Graduate School (where the political institutions of Southern states were studied along with those of the rest of the country according to the principle of the Teutonic hypothesis) and William A. Dunning, the New Jersey-born historian, who at Columbia specialized in the history of the Reconstruction.[15] Ulrich B. Phillips, who was to distinguish himself in the regional history of the South, was a student of Dunning's at Columbia, and by 1918, when Phillips's *American Negro Slavery* appeared, it was apparent that the latter had taken over not only the careful research techniques for which Dunning was known but also Dunning's dim view of the capacities and potentialities of the American Negro.

On the Pacific Coast, the most significant compilation was prepared under the general supervision of Hubert Howe Bancroft, the first volume of whose *The Native Races of the Pacific States of North America* appeared in 1875. Aided by a staff of research assistants and writers, Bancroft ground out volume after volume on the history not only of Washington, of Oregon, and of California but also of Central America, of Mexico, of the Mountain States and the states of the Southwest.[16]

THE CONTINUING "RENAISSANCE"

So much had been going on in American historiography that in 1922 Schlesinger's *New Viewpoints in American History* spoke of an historical "renaissance."[1] The 1920's, characterized by great creativity in the artistic and literary fields, were none the less productive in historiography. However, even as the literary renaissance of the 1920's had roots — as Maxwell Geismar points out — in the work of earlier writers such as Stephen Crane and Jack London, so the sources of historical creativity reached back to the New History movement and beyond.[2]

In the pattern of the New History, Carl Becker's *The Declaration of Independence* (1922) was the first, and somewhat belated, fruit of the movement's concern with the relationship between ideas and social progress. The influence of the New History was apparent, too, in the first four volumes of the "History of American Life" series which appeared in 1927 under the editorship of Schlesinger, Carl Becker, and Dixon Ryan Fox and which represented an attempt to write American social history on a scale comparable to the treatment of American political development in the earlier American Nation series.

As in any historical series, the volumes in this one tend to be of uneven merit. In some, the data of social history seem to drone on endlessly while the chapters of intellectual history, at times, seem more sandwiched in than properly integrated with the overflowing materials of American social evolution. This criticism, the usual one made of the series, is more applicable to some volumes than to others, and there are a few to which it does not apply at all. Such criticism, too, ought to be measured against Professor Schlesinger's defense of the series, advanced before the American Historical Association in December 1936, when he called attention to the truly pioneering task confronting him and the other editors when they undertook this large-scale investigation into a hitherto little-explored field.[3]

The New History was not the only development in American historiography to realize some of its potential in the 1920's. Additional volumes in the "Contributions to American Economic History" project of the Carnegie Corporation were published — notably Percy Bidwell and John Falconer, *History of Agriculture in the Northern United States* (1925); and Victor S. Clark, *History of Manufactures in the United States* (1929). In 1928 the *Journal of Economic and Business History* began publication, while the study of the history of American business, which its professional sponsors attempted to separate from economic history, was given impetus by the establishment of a chair in business history at Harvard University (awarded to N. S. B. Gras), and the launching of the *Bulletin of the Business Historical Society* in 1926.

Provincialism in historiography, which has traditionally manifested itself in accounts of American development centered in the
contribution of a particular section (New England) or a particular
people (New Englanders), was further weakened in the 1920's.[4]
An aspect of this was an immoderate, iconoclastic, and altogether
unfortunate attack upon the puritans and the puritan tradition by
certain historians, the most prominent of whom was James Truslow
Adams, who should have known better; and the brilliant defense
of the puritans by Samuel Eliot Morison and Kenneth Murdock.[5]
(The literary counterpart of this historiographic controversy was the
clash between Stuart Pratt Sherman, who took up the cudgels for
the puritan and the Anglo-Saxon, against Ludwig Lewisohn, whose
conception of the United States, as a culturally pluralistic nation,
included not a little derogation of the Puritan heritage).[6]

More constructively, however, Frederick Jackson Turner in 1925
stressed the importance of a sectional approach to the understanding
of American history — a thesis which had been hinted at in his
earlier writings and which promoted consciousness of sectional
influences other than that of New England.[7] Herbert E. Bolton,
indebted in part to the earlier work of H. H. Bancroft, began
rewriting early American history with particular stress upon the
role of non-English elements, especially the Spanish.[8] Marcus L.
Hansen, in 1927, revealed the possibilities offered by immigration
as a field for historical research. Even as Bolton directed the attention of the historian to the richness of Spanish and Mexican archives
and out of his patient investigation evolved a new perspective upon
the American past, so Hansen, by rescuing the neglected area of
immigration from the amateur and the jingoist, helped pave a new
road to historical understanding.[9]

Another aspect of the continuing historical renaissance of the
1920's was Richard Shryock's developing interest in the history
of American medicine.[10] And Joseph Schafer, who in 1920 had
become Superintendent of the State Historical Society of Wisconsin,
launched the systematic and intensive exporation of local history
that was to be the unfinished *Wisconsin Domesday Book.*[11]

Far more influential than the work of any of the historians thus
far mentioned, in impact both upon the general public and perhaps

upon the historical guild, were Charles and Mary Beard's *Rise of American Civilization* and Vernon L. Parrington's *Main Currents in American Thought*, which were published in the late 1920's. The Beards gave the impression of having abandoned the rigid economic determinism which had characterized Charles Beard's earlier work on the Constitution. They now stated: "The heritage, economics, politics, culture, and international affiliations of any civilization are so closely woven by fate into one fabric that no human eye can discern the beginnings of its warp and woof. And any economic interpretation, any political theory, any literary criticism, any aesthetic interpretation which ignores this perplexing fact, is of necessity superficial." [12] Nevertheless, the stress of *The Rise of American Civilization* is upon the role of economic and class factors in the entire field of American history; in the manner of a large, powerfully written, and erudite interpretive essay.

A similar approach was employed by Parrington, in whose *Main Currents in American Thought*, economic forces are made to serve as cultural determinants. From his colleague at the University of Washington, J. Allen Smith, and also from Turner and Beard, Parrington derived the basic thesis of his work. His conception of the pragmatic value of ideas, particularly in the service of political radicalism, Parrington got from John Dewey and the proponents of the New History. In the preface to *Main Currents*, which apart from his doctoral dissertation was the only book Parrington wrote, the author had described originally his approach to history as "radical rather than conservative, Jeffersonian rather than Federalistic." [13]

The importance and influence of the work of the Beards and of that of Parrington cannot be underestimated. These historians, undoubtedly, explained a great deal about the American past. But even as some contributors to the "History of American Life" series may be charged with extracting too little meaning from the materials of history, so the Beards and Parrington might be said to have derived too much. Their books give the impression of wrapping up the subject of American history — an impression that became more widespread as these volumes, published in prosperity's heyday, attracted an increasing number of uncritical readers in the depression. Many people who read these books in the gloomy atmosphere of breadlines, and *Triple-A Plowed Under,* were willing to grant that there were aspects of American intellectual and general history which were either linked remotely or totally unrelated to economic and class forces. But, in admitting this much, the tendency was to add that although Parrington and Beard were not without their faults, they had revealed the mainsprings of American development and what did not fit their theses could be dismissed as trivia. Also, a not unimportant factor in overcoming the doubts one had about these books was that Parrington and the Beards were forceful writers who all but overwhelmed the reader with the strength of their expression. And in those days of joblessness and despair, it was rather easy to be overwhelmed by the going-over Parrington and Beard gave the standpatters throughout American history.

In stressing the determining role of economic and class forces in history, Beard and Parrington approached a Marxian analysis. But the resemblance between these historians and the Marxists was more apparent than real. To be a Marxist required acceptance of the dialectics of historical materialism which would doom capitalism and build socialism on the ruin. Beard did not go along with this, nor did Parrington in any of the latter's published writings.

It should be observed here that Marxism, as an ideology, was to find rather few adherents among American historians, despite its being all the rage in some intellectual circles in the 1930's. Louis M. Hacker was to be one of the editors of a short-lived *Marxist Quarterly* (1936–1937), an intellectual organ of the Marxists dissenting from the Stalinist position. Stalinist historiography is best represented in the work of Philip S. Foner, who writes mainly in the field of labor history, and in that of Herbert Aptheker who specializes in Negro history.

It is the conclusion of David S. Bowers, expressed in the authoritative *Socialism in American Life,* that no significant contribution to the Marxist philosophy of history, apart from the "revisionism" of Sidney Hook and Max Eastman, has been made in America.[14] The fact is that although during the depression decade American historians were to rewrite large segments of American history in the light of economic interpretation, they took their cue from Beard and Parrington, rather than from Marx, Lenin, Stalin, and Trotsky.

DEPRESSION TRENDS

The impact of the economic interpretation of American history was apparent particularly in the 1930's in the historian's approach to the Reconstruction Period in the South. Earlier in the century, William A. Dunning and his disciples had conceived of Reconstruction mainly in political terms. Their understanding of what had happened was mainly as follows: Radical Republicans, bent upon maintaining political predominance and punishing the white South, used carpetbagger, scalawag, and Negro as instruments of sectional subjugation. The Reconstruction governments were regarded by Dunning and his students as epitomizing graft, corruption, and misrule — the consequence of Northern mendacity and the innate political incapacity of the Negro. Reconstruction, thus characterized, ended, much to the satisfaction of these historians, with the restoration of "white supremacy" in the South by 1876.[1]

This point of view, developed by Dunning and his students, was also the theme of Claude Bowers's dramatically written *The Tragic Era* which was published in 1928 and reached a wide audience. Also, in that year, Ulrich B. Phillips identified "The Central Theme of Southern History" as the effort to keep the South "a white man's country." [2]

To some extent, this pattern of understanding had been challenged by the work of Arnett[3] and Simkins[4] in the 1920's. Even earlier, James W. Garner and C. Mildred Thompson manifested some awareness of the importance of economic forces in Reconstruction.[5] But it was not until the 1930's, because of the stress which the studies by Woodward,[6] Bond,[7] Wharton,[8] Shugg,[9] and Beale[10] placed upon the social and economic aspects of the Reconstruction process, that a newer viewpoint emerged. The South, according to these historians, had not been unduly punished by the victorious North. The Radical Reconstructionists, it was contended, aimed less at the castigation of the defeated South than toward the preservation of the political power of the Republican Party and with it the high tariffs that the Northern industrialists wanted. True, at least one prominent Radical Republican leader, Thaddeus Stevens, recognized that the political power granted the Negro would prove in the long run inadequate unless the latter was given an economic competence derived from the divided estates of the plantation aristocracy. But the bulk of the Republicans, mindful of the precedent involved in property division, was unwilling to go along with Stevens's proposal.

This newer viewpoint of the Reconstruction process was less condemnatory of the Radical governments in the Southern States. Corruption, it was pointed out, was not confined to the Southern legislatures with their large Negro representation, but was characteristic as well of the state governments outside the South, and of the national government in which the Negro featured hardly at all. Legislatures North and South, it was contended, were corrupted alike by unscrupulous business interests anxious to obtain privileges through bribery. Moreover, the enhanced budgets of the Radical governments — which Dunning and his students had attributed to dishonesty and pilfering — were now said to be mainly the result of expenditures for schools and social services, which up until this point had been sadly neglected. The subsequent "Bourbon restoration" governments, it was indicated, were able to economize — that is, if they did economize — at the expense of these services. Finally, it was shown that measures taken by these "Bourbon lily-white" governments to disenfranchise the Negro were turned against the poorer white elements in the population also; that "all-white" rule in the South meant upper-class rule, as well. Thus did the historian's research into the economic realities of Reconstruction alter his understanding of a controversial era in American history.

Extensive use of the economic interpretation of history, in the 1930's, coincided with the coming to maturity in the depression decade of a generation of historians who, by birth and background, were more likely to be what Charles A. Beard called "asphalt flowers" than products of a rural upbringing.[11] As such, they were inclined to think more in terms of the urban and industrial rather than the rural and frontier influences upon American development. There was, as Blake McKelvey has pointed out,[12] an accelerated interest in urban history beginning with the publication in 1933 of Arthur M. Schlesinger's *The Rise of the City*. A subsequent article by Schlesinger argued that "the city, no less than the frontier, has been a major factor in American civilization." [13]

Thus, in the depression decade, the city loomed as a challenge to the frontier hypothesis. In 1928, Charles A. Beard claimed that Turner, in making the frontier and the wilderness central to American development, had placed insufficient stress upon urbanization and industrialization, class and economic forces.[14] Five years later, Louis Hacker disputed Turner's belief that the American social experience, because of the presence of the frontier, was unique. On the contrary, said Hacker, American development was not very different from that of other Western European capitalist countries.[15]

Turner was not without defenders — the more prominent of whom were Avery Craven, F. L. Paxson, and Joseph Schafer. These men carried on in the conviction, expressed by Craven, that "the constant exposure of institutions to the influence of free land on a frontier was a unique experience in national history." And the influence of the frontier, Craven believed, even in the 1930's was something to reckon with. "The American farmer is still far from a peasant in temper, regardless of material conditions. The American millionaire has acted in a rather unique way with his millions. The democratic dogma is something even quite distinct from European democracy as it rises out of the great rural American regions. The average American is still far more sectionally conscious than he is class-conscious. And American history must avoid a completely urban-industrial viewpoint if it is to remain true to the facts of two centuries and more of rural dominance. The process by which we reached complexity is still more significant as a historical fact than the mere conditions reached at the end of that process." Craven, very much *en rapport* with the structure of agrarian society in the West and South, criticized Hacker sharply for seeing American history from the point of view of New York's Lower East Side.[16]

But there were, during the 1930's, certain criticisms made of the Turner thesis to which a mere declaration of faith in the pervasive influence of the frontier was by no means an adequate reply. Such criticism, for the most part, centered mainly in Turner's conception of the frontier as a "safety valve" for Eastern workers in depressed times, when they allegedly migrated to the West. (A line of criticism, incidentally, which was not unrelated to the concern of the 1930's with the problem of economic opportunity.) In 1935 and 1936, Carter Goodrich and Sol Davison together,[17] and Murray Kane separately,[18] showed by meticulous research that the wage earner, in bad times, did not go West. It was difficult for him to do so, it was pointed out, because the worker was not trained as a farmer and was otherwise unfamiliar with the conditions of frontier existence. Moreover, the move West generally involved expenses beyond the pocketbook capacity of the unemployed worker. Whatever influence the frontier had upon American life, it did not serve, these scholars believed, as a safety valve whereby industrial workers, upon losing their jobs, spilled out upon the land. Also, in 1936, Fred Shannon showed how even the enactment of the Homestead Act, which made land available to the *bona fide* settler free of cost, still failed to make the West attractive to the "labor surplus." [19] Finally, Goodrich and Davison, while concluding that no great number of industrial workers became homesteaders, nevertheless subscribed to the principle of the safety valve in so far as they believed that Western lands proved attractive to some of the Eastern farm population that otherwise would have gone to the cities for factory jobs. But Fred Shannon, in 1945, assailed even this modified version of the safety-valve theory, arguing that the frontier, after the 1840's, was not even an outlet for potential wage earners.[20]

Not all criticism of the frontier hypothesis in the 1930's centered in the safety valve concept and its relationship to economic opportunity. Turner's contention that democracy was a wilderness-grown product was disputed by Benjamin Wright Jr., who viewed democratic development in America as more the result of an over-all nineteenth-century trend than as a consequence of the impact of the frontier. Wright, in refutation of Turner's belief that the West was a source of democracy and political innovation, showed how the constitutions of the Western states were imitative of those of the East — including the politically undemocratic features of the latter.[21]

Even as not all criticism of the frontier hypothesis in the 1930's was centered in its economic aspects, neither did the economic interpretation of American history sweep everything before it. Late in the decade of the 1930's, certain American historians became increasingly aware of the role of propagandist, psychological, and leadership influences upon the course of historical events. James G.

Randall in 1937 departed from current economic emphases in Reconstruction historiography and affirmed many of the earlier attitudes of the Dunning school.[22] And while Parrington and Beard, in the economically booming 1920's, wrote books that were prophetic of the depression-bound 1930's, so in the depression decade Allan Nevins, Thomas Cochran, and Louis Hacker had in preparation volumes and articles premised upon theses concerning American capitalism which were anticipatory of the better times, economically, to come in the 1940's.

BUSINESS HISTORY

In 1940, Dixon Ryan Fox, a brilliant historian lost to his craft first by his elevation to the presidency of Union College and then by his untimely death, took a long look at the undermining of the safety-valve theory and told an audience at Union College that the Turner doctrine tended to encourage defeatism; that too many false prophets were proclaiming that the disappearance of free frontier land meant the disappearance of opportunity. On the contrary, said President Fox, the word frontier meant merely "the edge of the unused." In the arts and sciences and in business, argued Fox, the challenge remains.[1]

The challenge of business enterprise, to which Fox called attention, was the subject of considerable re-examination by American historians beginning in 1940. In that year appeared Allan Nevins's distinguished biography of John D. Rockefeller which was to a considerable extent an erasure and redrawing of the portrait presented by Ida Tarbell in her muckraking *History of the Standard Oil Company* (1904). Miss Tarbell had berated Rockefeller for his business ethics, monopolist tactics, and exploitation of the American people. This conception of Rockefeller was carried forward in a variety of historical and journalistic works and in 1934 Matthew Josephson rated Rockefeller high in the company of the *Robber Barons*.

With the appearance of John T. Flynn's *God's Gold* in 1932, there was some modification of this traditional stereotype. Now, in 1940, Nevins argued that Rockefeller's business ethics ought to be judged in the perspective of his times — being no worse and perhaps better than those of his competitors; that monopoly was inevitable in the oil business; that Rockefeller was less exploiter than benefactor of the American people by making available to them the benefits of large-scale production. Rockefeller, as depicted by Nevins, was less "robber baron" than creative personality — an "industrial states-man" who accomplished significant feats of business organization.[2]

Louis Hacker's *Triumph of American Capitalism* was also pub-lished in 1940. An account of capitalist development to the end of the nineteenth century, this book, like most of Hacker's work, is undeniably provocative. At the same time, at least one critic notes a schizophrenic quality about the volume: seeing it as a Marxist treatment of American history and a paean of praise for the cre-ativity, achievement, and fundamentally democratic character of laissez-faire industrial capitalism.[3]

Finally, and once again in 1940, the subject of business history was given more orthodox treatment in a paper read before the American Historical Association by Thomas Cochran. The latter placed great stress upon research in business history, particularly corporate history, in its relationship to the broader pattern of social development.[4] In so doing, he presented before the historical guild the point of view of the business-history specialist, which until then had been expressed mainly in the *Bulletin of the Business Historical Society*.

The historian's heightened interest in the businessman and the business system paralleled the rediscovery by certain intellectuals of values in American society that they had previously neglected. As Hitler's blitz hit France, Archibald MacLeish assailed those whom he called the "irresponsibles" — because of their failure to make Americans conscious of the aspects of their unique heritage which were antithetical to fascism.[5] The cry was taken up by Lewis Mum-ford[6] and Carl Becker,[7] among others[8] who, deploring the "art for art's sake" formulations of the 1920's and the class-oriented approach of the 1930's, would emphasize American values and the American democratic and libertarian traditions. It is in this atmosphere that the businessman's stock in American intellectual circles began to go up.

(Previously, incidentally, the businessman had been little noticed; and he was, on the whole, a not very popular figure in the American novel, as the readers of William Dean Howells's *The Hazard of New Fortunes* (1885); Theodore Dreiser's *The Financier* (1912); and Sinclair Lewis's *Babbitt* (1922) can testify. True, there were more favorable accounts by Booth Tarkington in *The Plutocrat* (1927) and Sinclair Lewis in *Dodsworth* (1929), but the depression did not add to the popularity of the businessman and the business system among novelists. However, in the 1940's, Harrison Smith in the *Saturday Review of Literature* and John Chamberlain in *Fortune* insisted that it was the task of the novelist to write about good and positive forces in American life rather than bad and negative ones — that the businessman as part of the American scene was deserving of more generous treatment than he had thus far received.[9])

In a sense, the intellectual's concern with the impact of business upon national life was overdue. As Henry Commager has said, American society is unique for the separation that has grown up between the businessman and the writer.[10] The historian, in the past decade, has made a significant contribution toward bridging this gap. He did so by pursuing these main lines of inquiry into the area of business history (1) the individual corporate study which N. S. B. Gras, at Harvard, had been insisting, for a quarter of a century and more, was basic in business history;[11] (2) by full-length biographies of businessmen such as Mr. Nevins's study of Rockefeller; (3) by studies of the behavior of men in business situations such as William Miller's *Men in Business*;[12] (4) by exploring the relationship between business and government — best represented by the series of volumes sponsored by the Social Science Research Council; [13] (5) by presenting large syntheses, centering on the over-all relationship between business and society, like Cochran and Miller's *The Age of Enterprise*[14] and E. C. Kirkland's brief treatment of *Business in the Gilded Age*;[15] (6) by accounts of the relationship between business and intellectual development, such as Curti's chapter entitled "Business and the Life of the Mind." [16]

THE CONSERVATIVE AND THE LIBERAL TRADITIONS

With "Babbitt and Robber Baron . . . being given a much more dispassionate, even friendly, treatment," remarked a participant in the 1951 convention of the American Historical Association, "the winds of historical doctrine are now veering decidedly into the conservative quarter." [1] We will recall that in the last decade of the nineteenth century American historiography was predominantly conservative in emphasis. However, mainly because of the influence of Turner, Beard, and the New History, the profession became committed predominantly to liberalism.

So much was this the case that Samuel Eliot Morison, in his presidential address before the American Historical Association on December 29, 1950, stated that "fifty years ago, it was difficult to find any general history of the United States that did not present the Federalist-Whig-Republican point of view, or express a very dim view of all Democratic leaders except Cleveland. This fashion has completely changed; it would be equally difficult today to find a good general history of the United States that did not follow the Jefferson-Jackson-F.D. Roosevelt line." In Morison's opinion, "there has been altogether too much of this" in so far as the "present situation is unbalanced and unhealthy, tending to create a sort of neo-liberal stereotype. We need a United States history written from a purely conservative point of view. . . ." [2]

This does not mean that in recent years the historical guild in the United States has lacked professing Republicans. In the last years of his life, James Truslow Adams was very critical of the New Deal, and complained bitterly that the cost of supporting a bureaucracy was diminishing his royalties. On Election Day, 1952, a letter in the Herald Tribune by an authority on early American civilization, Professor Thomas Jefferson Wertenbaker, denied that the New Deal and the candidacy of Adlai Stevenson were in the Jeffersonian tradition. T. Harry Williams has stated that Lincoln would have been "amazed and amused" by the "professional thinkers of the New Deal and their doctrinaire tendencies." [3] Charles A. Beard was very much opposed to some aspects of the Roosevelt administration, and so is that admirable historian-ecologist, James C. Malin. [4]

At the same time, a certain amount of Republican allegiance among American historians does not add up to a pattern of historical writing in the Federalist-Whig-Republican tradition. At the outset of his excellent study of American liberalism, Eric F. Goldman shows how difficult it is to arrive at a definition of "liberalism," and it is equally difficult, perhaps more so, to define "conservatism." [5] A certain amount of confusion on this level is part of our heritage from the political history written during the nineteenth century, in which the historian made apparent his political convictions in the course of the narrative but made no real attempt at definition. It is only recently that scholars, notably Clinton Rossiter, have begun to grapple with the problem of defining our political traditions.[6]

Rossiter seems to feel that the liberal and conservative traditions in America have a great deal in common — a conclusion, however, which Merrill Jensen does not hesitate to dispute.[7] In historiography, it is apparent that there is not a little overlapping between the liberal and conservative traditions, even as they have elements of separateness, and it is difficult to tell at times where one begins and the other breaks off. Bancroft and Schouler, for example, are within the so-called liberal tradition of American historiography. But Schouler had his doubts about the possibility of making good citizens out of Irish laborers;[8] and Bancroft, in later life Ambassador to Germany, manifested a rather illiberal admiration for Bismarck and the Junkers.[9] On the other hand, much that a conservative historian like Richard Hildreth has written could be claimed for the liberal tradition.[10]

In like manner, certain understandings of the American past which are interpreted generally as serving the liberal tradition and which, in effect, have been laid claim to by the liberals, could easily form part of a conservative frame of reference. Hofstadter and Beard remind us that the well-worn conservative principle of rugged individualism is implicit in Turner's frontier hypothesis.[11] In the 1930's, the Beards' view of the Civil War as the inevitable consequence of the conflict between Northern industrialists and Southern planters found ready acceptance among those whose views were to the left of center, who hailed the Beards' understanding of the American Civil War as "the second American Revolution" and eagerly anticipated yet a third American Revolution. At the same time, the Beardian view of the Civil War as an irrepressible class conflict also has been embraced by historians who are by no means liberal in their defense of the civilization of the antebellum South. In their scheme of things, the view that the Civil War was inevitable provides justification for the adamant branch of pro-slavery Southern opinion in the 1850's.[12] Under these circumstances, and in view of the enigmatic character of Beard's political behavior, one would hesitate before committing Beard and his views to one or the other of our political traditions even if we were sure of our definitions.

Similarly, the historian's interest in "Babbitt" and "Robber Baron" does not imply of necessity a conservative commitment on the former's part. The fact that Joseph Dorfman has revealed that Jacksonian democracy had significant roots in the aims and aspirations of the business community, does not make a conservative of Dorfman. Much that has been done by way of historical rehabilitation of the businessman, was accomplished by historians whose work and political conviction fall within the Jefferson-Jackson-FDR tradition.

And what of the businessman? Do we place him in the liberal or the conservative fold? Schlesinger, Jr., in *The Age of Jackson* sees the businessman as a predatory figure sacrificing the well-being of the larger community to his own selfish interests. Handing over the businessman to the conservatives, Schlesinger places the salvation of the Republic in the hands of the liberals who, from the days of Jackson to those of Roosevelt, stepped in to repair the damage to society's structure caused by the greed of the businessman.[13] Chester M. Destler seems to share this point of view in an article minutely documenting the anti-social behavior of American businessmen in the post-Civil War era.[14]

Other historians are less willing to exclude the businessman from the liberal tradition. Thus, Dorfman and Bray Hammond have revealed business as a motive force behind Jacksonian democracy.[15] Cochran and Miller,[16] like Hacker,[17] hold that the growth of political democracy is intimately tied to the burgeoning of the free enterprise business system in the late nineteenth century.

Although the American historian has attempted no over-all treatment of the American conservatism and has made only feeble attempts to grapple with a definition, in the last decade there was some interest in individuals and events considered generally as being within the conservative tradition. Nathan Schachner wrote an appreciative biography of Alexander Hamilton[18] and there were two sympathetic studies of John C. Calhoun by Margaret Coit and Charles M. Wiltse,[19] and one of John Randolph by Russell Kirk.[20] Coit, Wiltse and Kirk, as does Avery Craven,[21] write with warm understanding of the statesmen of the Old South and with not a little sympathy for the values of pre-Civil War Southern society. Adrienne Koch and William Peden reduced John and John Quincy Adams to a useful one volume;[22] Leonard D. White revealed the amazingly vitalist character of the principles and administrative policies of *The Federalists*,[23] and Leonard Labaree surveyed *Early American Conservatism.*[24] Henry Adams received a great deal of attention, while even his irascible brother, Brooks, found a biographer of sorts.[25]

Somewhat disappointing from the point of view of the development of Henry Cabot Lodge as a conservative figure is the biography of Lodge by John Garraty.[26] On the other hand, the difficulties involved in attempting to place a key personality within our ill-defined political traditions are indicated in Eric Goldman's review of John Blum's *The Republican Roosevelt.*[27]

But these studies spotlighted more than they floodlighted the American conservative tradition,[28] and the conservative synthesis which Morison[29] hoped for, and which Schlesinger, Jr.,[30] felt was necessary for the proper functioning of the two-party system, did not emerge.

The Challenge to Economic Determinism

Despite the undoubted influence of the economic interpretation of history upon historical writing in the 1930's, very few American historians were economic determinists in the narrow sense. Beard, himself, although coming very close to economic determinism, balked at the label.[1] Similarly, there was less a downright commitment by most historians who were influenced by Beard to the principle of economic determinism than there was general awareness on their part of the importance of economics, among other factors, in historical sequences. While historians, in recent years, have been more inclined to quarrel with the kind of simple relationship that Parrington found between ideas and economic status,[2] the general idea of the role played by economic forces in historical sequences was not eclipsed with the end of the depression decade even as it did not begin with the depression, either. C. Vann Woodward, writing in 1951, still conceived of the Civil War Reconstruction periods as had Beard in 1928, that is, "as a revolution — the Second American Revolution." [3]

Even so, there gradually appeared a shift away from economic emphases during the 1940's. For one thing, the economic interpretation of history seemed to have outlived its usefulness in the arsenal of liberal reformism. There is, it is true, nothing inherently liberal in the economic interpretation of history, which has in the past been used on occasions by historians who wrote in the Federalist tradition[4] — for instance, Richard Hildreth; but, more frequently than not, use of economic determinism implied a generally liberal outlook on the part of the historian.

The rise of Hitler to power and the growing Nazi menace hit the traditional economic determinism of American liberalism in a very tender spot. Since the end of World War I, liberals and liberal historians had been pointing to the futility of American intervention and book after book was written asking why we fought and tracing the role of economic interest in our involvement. Never again, these volumes reiterated, as did the leading journals of liberal opinion, would the American people be trapped into going to war.[5]

But Hitler's marching armies changed all this. Liberals now spoke in terms of the morality, not the economics, of resistance to fascism — as they smarted under MacLeish's attack on "the irresponsibles" and at the same time rallied to his banner. While off to one side, Charles A. Beard was heard to mutter angrily, "So now it's all morals and no economics and we rally behind the leader. And just what Roosevelt do we rally around — the Roosevelt who is going to keep us out of war by Lend-Lease or the Roosevelt who knows full well that Lend-Lease is the sure path to war?" [6]

Indicative of the trend toward moral emphases was the fact that whereas the Beards in 1928 found the Civil War inevitable in terms of an irrepressible class conflict between Northern industrialists and Southern plantation-owners, Schlesinger, Jr., in 1949 wrote of the war being inevitable, not in terms of economics, but because of the moral issue posed by slavery.[7] Hacker, in 1948, addressing the Conference on American History sponsored by the University of Pennsylvania, began in this vein: "I should start out by saying . . . that a materialistic interpretation of politics is untenable. This is the Marxian analysis. . . ." [8]

But war and fascism were not the sole causes of the historian's de-emphasis of the economic approach. The American historian has always been influenced by developments in other fields: the Teutonists by the philologists; Turner by the geographers and atlas makers; the disciples of the New History by John Dewey; Beard by Seligman and possibly by Marx; and so on. Since the late 1930's, influences from the other social sciences, particularly sociology and psychology, had been streaming in upon the historian. The historical guild manifested increasing awareness of the work of Durkheim, Freud, Mosca and Pareto; of the role of irrational and emotional forces in history and the propagandistic techniques employed in bringing them into play.[9]

The historiography of the American Civil War, always a sensitive weather vane to the winds of historical doctrine, registered the altered emphasis. Before Schlesinger, Jr., substituted morality for economics as foundation for the belief that the Civil War was inevitable, the analysis by the Beards had been under attack from other directions. It was pointed out by a growing number of historians in the 1930's and 1940's that there were between the economic systems of the North and South elements of reconcilability as well as conflict and that the former probably outweighed the latter. For example, Avery Craven and James G. Randall, conscious of the role of fanaticism and propaganda in political movements here and abroad, insisted that the war did not emerge out of the diverse interests of economic classes, but was brought about by hotheads and fanatics, like the abolitionists in the North and the fire-eaters in the South, who, with very little material at stake, were none the less hell-bent for war. As clever propagandists, said Craven and Randall, these extremist if minority elements on both sides of the Mason and Dixon line were able to inflame sectional passions to a point where compromise, which might have been brought about by sensible and responsible men of property, became impossible.[10]

POLITICAL HISTORY, MILITARY HISTORY AND THE INDIVIDUAL'S ROLE

It is curious how, in the 1940's, political history, military history, and the individual's role seemed to take a new hold on the historian's imagination. Influenced by the New History, the historian had been striving to emancipate himself from what he considered to be the overemphasis of nineteenth-century historiography upon any single one of these forces. Now, in relatively recent years, the historian seemed to be returning to what he had earlier rejected. Was historiography, then, following the repetitive cycle that is vulgarly attributed to history?

Not at all. Politics, which in the 1930's tended to be the tail to the economic kite, emerged in the historiography of the next decade as having a determining force of its own. But the new political history differed from what nineteenth-century historians wrote. Its chief proponent, Roy F. Nichols, described it as "a new species of political history which would borrow from the fields of social anthropology and social psychology to secure deeper understanding of the intricacies of human behavior." [1]

This revived interest in political history is not unrelated to the rise of a great federal bureaucracy and the problems incidental to its administration; the trend toward increased governmental centralization; and the lurking fear of a dictator. No wonder, then, when the dull gray of the depression was pierced by the gunfire of World War II, that the drift was back to political history. It was Pendleton Herring's observation that contemporary preoccupation with "political history, in explicit or implicit terms" was motivated by the crisis of our times, which made imperative the exploration of "the phenomenon of political power which, in the United States, operates through democratic institutions." [2] William T. Hutchinson, to combat the threat of totalitarianism, urged the study of constitutional history.[3] Finally, Charles A. Beard in *The Republic* reaffirmed the high esteem in which he had always held the Constitution with the rather deep-seated conviction that in a troubled world the political guarantees offered by our basic document are mankind's best hope.[4]

Similarly, the enormously increased influence of the military upon modern life has rekindled the historian's interest in military history. Not only are historians restudying the tactics and strategy of old wars and battles, but as a consequence of the impetus provided by the armed forces they are systematically chronicling the military

operations of World War II.[5] Samuel Eliot Morison, who is both
Jonathan Trumbull Professor of American History at Harvard and
a Rear Admiral on the retired list of the naval reserve, is writing
with the aid of a staff of assistants a fourteen-volume series on the
United States Navy's role in World War II. Under the supervision of
the Chief Historian of the Department of the Army, Kent Roberts
Greenfield, an estimated ninety-six volumes on the history of the
Army and the Air Forces in World War II will be written. The
Marines, too, have made a beginning on their history.[6] (Really, it
was not so very long ago that Edward Eggleston stated before the
American Historical Association that historians ought not concern
themselves too much about wars and military history; that it was
the purpose of history "to teach . . . the wisdom of diplomacy, the
wisdom of avoidance — in short, the fine wisdom of arbitration, that
last fruit of human experience." [7])

The new military history, however, manifested a great deal more
awareness than did the old of the interrelationships between military and social phenomena. This is particularly apparent in the conception of military history held by T. Harry Williams,[8] who is concerned with the relationship between politics and command. The
Social Science Research Council, the Twentieth Century Fund, and
the Carnegie Foundation, in approaching the study of military history, are specifically concerned with the impact of the military machine upon civilian life.

Contemporary stress upon problems of political leadership and
awareness of the leader's role in crisis situations have caused the
historian to focus increasingly upon the individual's place in history.
This trend bore an undeniable relationship to the general world
political situation at a time when, as Sidney Hook remarked in 1943,
"interest in the words and acts of outstanding individuals had flared
up to a point never reached before, when the fate of the world
seemed to rest upon the decisions of individual leaders, dictatorial
or democratic." [9] Certainly the individual did not become in the
historiography of the 1940's what he was a century earlier to George
Bancroft, a giant striding across the stage of history and kicking
the props around. On the other hand, the individual did emerge
from the great mass of social and economic detail under which the
historian had submerged him in the two preceding decades.

Projected upon this background, if not emergent therefrom, are the multi-volume, biographical accounts of the lives of prominent Americans — a form of historical writing which has become increasingly popular in recent years. Indeed, such works are the successors in the heavyweight division of American historiography to the ponderous narrative histories that characterized nineteenth-century historical writing. At present, Dumas Malone is doing a study of Jefferson in four or five volumes, of which two have been published. The late Douglas S. Freeman portrayed Robert E. Lee in four, with another three volumes devoted to Lee's lieutenants. Mr. Freeman, indefatigable in life, published five volumes of a larger work on George Washington — and there still remained to Freeman at the time of his death the task of covering Washington's career through the Presidency and into retirement. Irving Brant is doing a similarly detailed treatment of the life of James Madison — a full three volumes having brought the author only to the year 1800. James G. Randall planned to devote five volumes to what the reviewers like to call a "potentially definitive" biography of Lincoln, but death stayed his hand after the publication of the third. Frank Freidel, who has published two volumes of a projected six on Franklin Delano Roosevelt, threatens to out-heavy the heavyweight biographical historians and start a new division. Mr. Freidel is a young man and a rapid and careful worker. But in view of the task that lies ahead of him, one can only wish him godspeed.

The reason for the inordinate length of these biographical treatments is that they embrace the times as well as the life of the individual with which they are dealing. Needless to say, it is proper for the biographer to see his subject in relationship to the period in which he lived. Indeed, this is an essential of good biography. At the same time, one of the problems posed by these volumes and, in fact, by the writing of biography generally is the extent to which the materials normally available to the historical investigator or biographer enable him to delineate character and explore motivations. For example, clues to the subconscious and irrational elements in human behavior are rarely included in the sources usually accessible to the historian and, when they are, tend to be vaguer, more misleading, and more fragmentary than the general run of historical evidence. That is why most historical biography written within a Freudian framework has not been particularly successful.

For thirty years and more, historians have cast occasional glances in the direction of psychology and psychoanalysis in the expectation that these sciences would contribute to historical understanding, particularly in the realm of biography. Thus, in 1922, when Freudianism as a literary trend invaded Greenwich Village and penetrated into Chicago's Bohemian hinterland, Clarence W. Alvord found his "attitude toward the history problem . . . undergoing considerable change. I am becoming," he wrote, "more and more an adherent of the psychological school of historians." [10]

In that same year, however, Schlesinger's *New Viewpoints* found the psychological and psychoanalytic approach so little developed that he did not include it within the scope of his discussion. [11] Between the publication of *New Viewpoints* and the appearance of Sidney Ratner's "The Historian's Approach to Psychology" (1941) [12] a great many psychoanalytic hours went by without much having been done by way of a psychological or psychoanalytic interpretation of history. Historians, it is true, manifested increased awareness of the psychological impact of propaganda; but any relatively rare psychoanalytical interpretation that was attempted, such as the psychologist L. P. Clark's *Lincoln: A Psycho-biography* (1933) tended to be pretty much off base.

Ratner, a dozen years ago, took his colleagues to task for their neglect of the psychoanalytic approach. "Fruitful investigation by controlled psycho-analytic methods," Ratner wrote, "might have been made by Parrington, for instance, of the impetus given by the frustration of a Samuel Adams, a Thomas Paine, and an Abraham Lincoln through poverty or marital unhappiness to their embarking on a political career. He might also have explored the relationship between Alexander Hamilton's glorification of *Machtpolitik* and the desire for power he derived, in part, from the illegitimacy of his birth. Inconsistencies like Hamilton's defense of the Constitution and his criticism of the class basis of agrarian radicalism could have been explained in terms of rationalization as employed by Pareto and Freud."

But one might ask Ratner by what "controlled psychoanalytic methods" the historian is to proceed? And is the evidence available for procedure in this direction? With regard to the latter point, it should be granted that in the case of Alexander H. Stephens, the Confederate leader, the data did permit his biographer, Rudolph von Abele, to turn in a fairly creditable performance.[13] But the mass of material bearing upon Stephens's emotional life is a relative rarity among the sources of biography. "Freudian psychoanalysis is one thing," wrote the late James G. Randall, "and the transference of Freudian psychoanalysis to biography without adequate biographical or historical basis is a very different thing."[14] It is true, as Schlesinger, Jr., points out, that the historian ought to try to see his materials in the light of the contributions of Max Weber, Pareto, and Freud — but in the case of a possible Freudian approach, one wonders whether the very nature of historical evidence limits its value.[15]

INTELLECTUAL HISTORY

In the past ten years and more, the exploration of American intellectual development has consumed an ever-increasing share of the professional historian's attention.[1] The beginning of American intellectual history goes back to the post-Civil War era and Moses Coit Tyler's desire "to help American civilization to be a success" by reaffirming American ideals amidst what he considered to be the crass materialism of the gilded age. Obviously inspired by the dynamic role assigned the idea in Buckle's *History of Civilization in England,* Tyler frequently stated his belief in the ideological motivation of American history. However, his approach to the study of ideas in America was primarily biographical, centering in the life and work of mainly literary figures. While Tyler did not succeed in his pronounced purpose of revealing the inner spirit of the American people, he did provide a useful and scholarly recapitulation of aspects of American intellectual development.[2]

Early in the present century, the New History stressed the idea both as an expression of historic processes, and as a force in history. While in the books of Becker, Parrington, and Beard, which betrayed the New History's influence, intellectual history became more than the mere literary phenomenon that Tyler had made it out to be, this conception of American intellectual development was also not without limitations. The New History, conceiving of ideas in terms of the relationship they bore to social and economic forces, was only incidentally concerned with inner creative processes.

While the decade of the twenties yielded syntheses such as those by the Beards and Parrington, smaller segments of American intellectual development were explored through the traditional scientific methods. Such examination was encouraged by the establishment of outlets for the publication of investigations of this type: the *New England Quarterly* in 1928; the *Columbia Studies in American Culture* in the 1930's; the *William and Mary Quarterly* in 1944 and the *American Quarterly* in 1949. Thus, a bibliographic backlog was established upon which later comprehensive surveys were to be built.

Merle Curti's *Growth of American Thought* (1943) differed from Parrington's approach in so far as it was centered less upon the individual than upon the stream of thought. His scope as to sources, too, was much broader than Parrington's, extending from dime novels to metaphysics — all of which was placed within context of the socio-economic background in recognition of the instrumental role of ideas that was Curti's heritage from John Dewey and the New History.

Less all-embracing were the syntheses of Ralph Barton Perry[3] and Ralph H. Gabriel.[4] These authors, intent upon exploring the nature of the American democratic faith, centered their inquiries in specific aspects of our intellectual history which they held central to democratic development. Also, somewhat more selective was Henry Steele Commager's *The American Mind*, which was "not concerned . . . with abbreviated histories of American philosophy or religion, sociology or economics, politics or law, but with ideas that illuminate the American mind and ways of using ideas that illustrate the American character."[5]

No other field of historical research offers such challenging opportunities for integration between history and the other fields of knowledge as does the relatively little-developed area of intellectual history. Here the interdisciplinary barriers are at their lowest and the historian is in a position to respond to the widest range of intellectual stimuli.

SYNTHESIS AND *Kulturgeschichte*

Thought, or the idea, was also a point of integration for the historian desirous of penetrating to the *geist* of American history or of finding syntheses of the varied manifestations of our civilization. The Puritan historians, "the Lord's Remembrancers," synthesized their work about the idea of a chosen people acting out God's will in the New England wilderness.[1] The belief in a chosen people, with a separate national destiny over which God presided, was made to apply by certain nineteenth-century American historians, notably Bancroft, to the American people as a whole.[2] Later in the past century, particularly in the volumes of Alfred Thayer Mahan, author of *The Influence of Sea Power on History*, this was translated into the belief in a national and racial mission beyond our borders and formed part of the rationale of imperialism.[3]

Implicit in the conception of history working out in accordance with a Divine plan was the notion of progress. Addressing the American Historical Association in 1886, when he was eighty-six years old, George Bancroft found both progress and God's will apparent in history.[4] When the old man spoke of the laws of progress in history, it is doubtful whether he had Darwin and Spencer in mind. Darwinian and Spencerian influences were apparent, however, in the work of John Fiske, the most widely read historian of the 1890's, whose volumes spoke of the inherent necessity for progress in history in accordance with a vast evolutionary scheme which reflected the spirit of late nineteenth-century science, but was presided over, nevertheless, by God.[5]

On the other hand, the first hundred pages or so of the first volume of Henry Adams's *History of the United States during the Administrations of Jefferson and Madison* (perhaps the finest example of *Kulturgeschichte* in American historiography), are somewhat less certain of progress in America and, in particular, of democracy's ability to meet the challenge of the American environment. And, by 1910, when Adams's *Letter to American Teachers of History* appeared, the author thought that he had discovered synthesis in American and world history too, in the retrogressive principle of the second law of thermodynamics. Kelvin's law of the dissipation of mechanical energy, according to Adams, predestined both the physical universe and society to a progressive loss of energy and to inevitable degeneration and decay which, according to Adams's computations, would be particularly apparent following the year 1921.[6]

Other historians, as we have seen, discovered different synthetic principles: in racial and biological determinism (the Teutonists); in the influence of the frontier (Turner); the evolution of a national state (Burgess); the triumph of freedom over slavery (von Holst); in class conflict (Beard); in Marxism (Hacker).[7] In the 1940's, with the nation at war, historians seemed particularly interested in synthesis about a particular conception of the American type, as if trying to determine what it was that distinguished us, as a people, from our enemies. Thus, for the purpose of gaining "insight into national behavior" Arthur Schlesinger explored "why the American has come to what he is, how he reacts instinctively to life, wherein he differs from other peoples." [8] This theme also attracted James Truslow Adams, whose *The American* was published in 1943; and certainly Henry Commager was not unmindful of it in the chapters he devoted to "The Nineteenth-century American" and "The Twentieth-century American" in his notable volume *The American Mind*.[9]

As has been indicated, multi-volume syntheses of relatively large periods of American history by individual historians are more characteristic of nineteenth- than twentieth-century American historiography. At present, large-scale approaches to American history are attempted mainly through historical series: the American Nation Series, the History of American Life, Chronicles of America, the Economic History of the United States, and the Library of Congress Series in American Civilization. Written by many hands, these series cover more of the field of American history than an individual historian could be expected to encompass working alone. On the other hand, there is bound to be, in a series of volumes, a certain amount of unevenness. And there is always danger in an historical series of the substitution of mere coverage of the field for a broad synthetic viewpoint.

There have been relatively few exponents of *Kulturgeschichte* among American historians. The latter, for the most part, have taken a more limited view of history than did Professor J. H. Breasted when he spoke of *Kulturgeschichte* as "the whole range of human life [treated] as a symmetrical whole" and as "the very lifeblood of history." [10] In Europe, *Kulturgeschichte*, with its stress upon the economic, social and cultural and its concentration upon the life of the people, developed as a protest against political emphases in historiography. Beyond that, however, even as the political historians sought synthesis in the emergence and development of the national state, the disciples of *Kulturgeschichte* looked for unity in the mass psyche of specific historic periods which, like a diapason, penetrated into every phase of human activity. Generalizing thus, the proponents of *Kulturgeschichte* were on less solid ground than they were in their extension of the realm of history beyond the narrowly political.[11]

Accordingly, when Karl Lamprecht's argument for *Kulturgeschichte*, entitled *Moderne Geschichtswissenschaft*, appeared in English translation in 1905 under the title *What Is History?*, it was apparent that there was much in it that paralleled or influenced the New History, particularly in the latter's break with the political emphasis of nineteenth-century American historiography. On the other hand, American historians have been a great deal less willing (and this speaks well for their judgment) to follow Lamprecht in attempting to penetrate into the psyche of specific historic periods. Lamprecht had tried to do this in his *Deutsche Geschichte*, which described the primitive period of history as "symbolic," the early Middle Ages as "typical," the later Middle Ages as "conventional," the Renaissance and the enlightenment as "individualistic," the age of romanticism and the industrial revolution as one of "subjectivism" and the most recent period as characterized by "nervous tension" (*Reizbarkeit*).[12]

Something like this attempt to define historic periods psychologically, was essayed by Brooks Adams in *The Law of Civilization and Decay*.[13] Also, Henry Adams wrote of the Middle Ages as a primarily "imaginative" and "artistic" era, even as the nineteenth and twentieth centuries impressed him as being characteristically "economic," and a degeneration from a previous higher form.[14] In recent years, the Beards in *The American Spirit* (1942) attempted to describe "the interior aspects of civilization in the United States since 1776," but they were not too successful.[15] On the other hand, the more narrowly-defined study by Oscar Handlin of Boston's immigrant community in the early nineteenth century, an analysis in the pattern of Emile Durkheim's conception of "the internal constitution of the social milieu," is a more successful example of what might be described as *Kulturgeschichte*.[16] Handlin's study, sharply defined geographically and chronologically, is representative of the tendency of *Kulturgeschichte* to find expression in recent American historiography in local or regional history as if the historian, within a relatively limited theater of operations, could explore more conveniently the multiform aspects of social behavior.[17]

Kulturgeschichte, interpreted as folk history, has had an interesting renaissance in recent years in local and regional history and in the few good histories we have of immigrant groups.[18] It has been stimulated by such volumes as T. C. Blegen's *Grass Roots History*, with its application of the widest possible range of interpretation to regional and local developments;[19] by magazines like *American Heritage*;[20] and by the publications of local and state historical societies.[21] In addition, there has been a conscious effort to bring "folk history" to the people who made it and are making it. The Social Science Research Council has even fathered a manual for the amateur interested in assisting in the writing of regional and cultural history,[22] and an effort has been made to make regional history attractive to Everyman by altering the format of state and local historical publications to give them more popular appeal.[23]

Certainly, a revitalized local history movement has been one of the more significant historiographic developments of recent years. At the same time, a certain amount of catering to an amateur and antiquarian approach to the oddities of regional behavior has been contributory to the atomization of our history. And we are mindful of the injunction of Dixon Ryan Fox that social history unless "collected about a synthetic principle, becomes . . . a synonym for miscellaneous or nondescript."[24]

RELATIVISM AND OBJECTIVISM

It is apparent from our survey thus far that different schools of historical interpretation have found dissimilar configurations in our history. At the same time, while historians continue to disagree in their understandings of the American past, there has been steady progress in the development of the historian's methodology between Bancroft's day and our own. Despite this undeniable technical advance, the question remains whether the historian, in his forays into the past, is grasping at the appearance rather than the reality of historical truth. Consequently, a survey of the understandings which historians have evolved of the American past must also include a discussion of the feasibility of attaining real historical understanding at all.

Certainly, no yes or no answer can be given to this question, which has been debated sporadically throughout much of the history of American history. In recent years, the reports of the Commission on the Social Studies of the American Historical Association of 1932 and 1934 stressed the uncertainty and contingency of all historical knowledge, the "narrow land of rational certainty, relative, conditional, experimental." [1]

With knowledge of the past relative, as these reports contended, to the historian's perception of it, Charles A. Beard, who exerted not a little influence in drafting the recommendations, urged historians to approach their materials with a thesis or frame of reference in mind. At the same time, Beard would not have the historian abandon a scholarly approach, nor a search for "particular facts that may be established by the scientific method." [2] Practically the same conclusions concerning the nature of historical knowledge and the need for a frame-of-reference approach were advanced by the Committee on Historiography of the Social Science Research Council in 1946, under the chairmanship of Merle Curti. [3]

Of course, not the entire profession is committed to the conclusions of the Beard and Curti committees. In recent years, historical relativism and frame-of-reference history have been sharply attacked by Chester M. Destler, [4] James C. Malin, [5] Samuel Eliot Morison, [6] and Edward C. Kirkland, [7] among others. In general, these critics score relativism and history written in terms of a thesis or frame of reference as contrary to the first aim of the historian, which is to describe without prejudice what happened in the past. The relativists, in turn, assert that history has never been written "objectively" and without prejudice; that many historians, while loud in their protestations of objectivity, are nevertheless obviously prejudiced — a conclusion which tends to be justified by parts of this discussion.[8]

The strongest objection to approaching history in terms of a frame of reference is that the historian might become the prisoner of his assumptions. But if the historian is willing to test and modify his thesis in terms of the evidence, this danger is to some extent transcended. Indeed, the relativist might possibly find common ground with the objectivist insofar as the former strives to refine his thesis in the hot fire of historical evidence — working within a relativistic framework toward the objectivist goal of "explaining the event exactly as it happened." Regardless of whether the conflict between relativism and objectivism is reconcilable in the broader philosophical sense, it may be possible practically for the historian to utilize the best elements of both systems in attempting to explain the past.[9]

Similarly, the ability of the historian to come "nearer the fortress of certainty and actuality" to "even occupy a part of that fortress, shrouded as it is in the fog of history," [10] may derive less from dogmatic commitment to either relativism or objectivism or to any one of the many interpretations of American history that we have discussed. "System," Schlesinger, Jr., reminds us, "is never a substitute for insight. . . . Historians must face the sad fact that theirs is essentially an art — as personal as the painter's intuition or the doctor's diagnosis, and, like both, dependent upon innate capacities operating in conjunction with wide, firsthand experience." [11] Guided by his art and an acquired or innate sense of judgment (there is no *chemin royale* to either), the historian must pick his way among the facts and theories of history toward the achievement of a synthesis satisfactory to him and able to withstand the critical comment of his colleagues.

HISTORICAL UNDERSTANDING AND THE PRESENT CRISIS

Historians are divided in their views of the role history should play in the present conflict between democracy and communism. Proclaiming the "relativity of all history," Conyers Read, in his presidential address before the American Historical Association in December 1949, invited the profession to enlist under the relativist banner and avowed that historians can afford less than ever before "a neutral attitude toward the main issues of life. . . . We must assert our objectives, define our ideals, establish our own standards and organize all the forces of our society in support of them. . . ."[1] A year later, Samuel Eliot Morison, in his presidential address before the same group, while pointedly rejecting relativism, urged historians to write the kind of history that would make a man want to fight for his country; to stress the positive rather than negative values in American civilization; to avoid debunking revered historic figures and to render unto the American folk their heroes.[2]

On the other hand, Merle Curti, in his presidential address before the Mississippi Valley Historical Association, expressed disapproval of the readiness with which Read would commit the historian to the exigencies of the present crisis.[3] In the years to come, there can be little doubt that one of the more significant problems confronting the historical guild in America will be the conflict between the traditional freedom of the historian and mounting pressure upon him to serve the needs of democratic society in the cold war.

Historians have always reflected in their work, some more than others, the impact of the world in which they live. The frank invitation to their colleagues by Read and to a lesser extent by Morison to enlist in the struggle between democracy and communism is by no means an innovation if we remember James Harvey Robinson's battle cry earlier in the century. Ordinarily, however, there has been in the past and there are now a sufficient number of historians more sensitive than their fellows to the needs of the hour and, in a sense, no blowing of trumpets is necessary to get at least a partial mobilization. True, the American people must be brought to a greater awareness of their traditions, as was stated in the beginning of this introduction. But it would be unfortunate if they were acquainted with only one aspect of their many-sided heritage.

Above all, in enlisting Clio's aid in the preservation of democracy in the mid-twentieth century, we must be ever on guard against the regimentation of historiography (and needless to say Read and Morison are no advocates of this), that would bring American historians to a position approaching the status of the profession behind the Iron Curtain where, according to the expert opinion of Bertram Wolfe, in speaking of Soviet historiography, "there are no

individual viewpoints or private judgments or pluralistic approaches.
. . ." One of the tests of a successful mustering of Clio's support
against communism is the professional and public attitude toward
the historian of good faith who, in conscience, desires to pursue his
art for the sake of his art and for no other reason. In the struggle
of the free world against the slave, the historian also serves who
seeks truth objectively in accordance with the high standards of
his profession. Continuing free inquiry accompanied by professional
responsibility is the American alternative to the historian following
a "line" or "official viewpoint" about the past.

In America, unlike Russia, there is no monistic and state-deter-
mined understanding of the American past; that is, the past has no
official meaning. In our survey of American historiography between
Bancroft's day and our own, the many understandings that have
evolved reflect the diversity of democratic society. It is true, undoubtedly, that in the technique of the cold war, a specific line
about the past can have great propagandistic value and one should
not underestimate the service to the Communist cause rendered by
what Leon Trotsky once called "the locomotive of history"— since
streamlined by Stalin and Malenkov. However, for us to adopt anything like a standardized version of the American past, for democracy to devise a historical locomotive of its own, would be a
confession of weakness in addition to overlooking the fact that the
diversity of democratic historiography is itself a source of strength.

The varied pattern of American historiography, now as in the
past, does not permit of easy summation. It is difficult, therefore,
to present the reader at the conclusion of this survey with a "where
historians now stand" analysis. At the same time, some such account-
ing is necessary.

There are approximately 7500 professional historians, the vast
majority of whom earn their basic income from teaching, not writing. Most of what they write is published in professional journals
and by university presses. Much of the output of the professional
historian has little appeal to the general public. But the heavily foot-
noted article, or book which the historian writes mainly for other
historians is, for the most part, the backbone of professional achievement

A lesser amount of historical writing reaches the general public through the medium of the trade book and the magazine article. Inevitably, in trade books and articles, the writing improves and the subject is, as a rule, less specialized and of more general interest. The opinion, sometimes expressed by reviewers, that good historical writing went into eclipse with the advent of the scientific school in the late nineteenth century is not entirely true. This judgment is based largely upon the fact that the scholarly monographs are not read and are not designed to be read by the general public. But the output of Nevins, Morison, Commager, and Schlesinger among the older historians, and Goldman, Handlin, Hofstadter, and Schlesinger, Jr., among the younger men, is evidence that the art of good historical writing in our times is by no means dead.

The American historian today is less of a public figure than he was in the past. Two of our Presidents, Theodore Roosevelt and Woodrow Wilson, were historians. Bancroft was a cabinet member and an ambassador. We have no comparable representation in the government today, although Walter Johnson, Arthur Schlesinger, Jr., and Bernard DeVoto were in the entourage surrounding Adlai Stevenson in the latter's unsuccessful bid for the presidency in 1952. In the lower echelons of government service, except for the military historians, historians have been eclipsed by the how-to-do-it people: economists, sociologists, political scientists, and others who have specific skills which government bureaus can make use of. There is, of course, some sprinkling of historians in the departments, in the Library of Congress and in the National Archives.[4]

Ideologically, the historian is a hard man to pinpoint. Before an attempt is made to do so, it should be pointed out that by far the more numerous of the profession are research scholars primarily, who are not too much concerned with interpretation and meaning and who, if they have larger ideological convictions, do not necessarily express them in their work. It should be realized, too, that while the preceding pages have been devoted to tracing the course of historical understanding, they do not answer the question as to how deeply a particular understanding penetrates the body of professional opinion.

If generalizations must be made about the ideological climate of the American historical profession today, the following is my impression. Politically, the American historian is predominantly committed to liberalism, and those who think otherwise mistake the professional wish for the professional deed.[5] There is not a little dissatisfaction among historians with the liberal orientation, in part because it has been overdone and also because it is lacking in answers to current problems. But American conservatism is a creed that is not yet formulated. The profession gives the impression of being ready, at times even eager, to shift its political orientation without there being anything for it to shift to.[6] Peter Viereck, preaching conservatism, is a prophet not without honor but without the kind of documented and seasoned argument that is likely to appeal to the American historian.

In the historian's contemporary quest for understanding, he reaches beyond the economic interpretation of history and toward an interdisciplinary approach. Even as the conventional college course in American history shows signs of yielding to one in American studies or American civilization, so the historian, despite some strong dissenting voices, seems committed to borrowing from allied fields. And yet, while recognizing the importance of an interdisciplinary approach in principle, not too many historians practice it. Moreover, Professor Richard Hofstadter, a brilliant young historian and advocate of the broadest possible approach to history, is himself rather uncomfortable in using some of the wider angles. Exploring the causes of the Spanish–American War, Hofstadter ventures into what he describes as "the high and dangerous ground of social psychology." On this terrain, Hofstadter aserts, "we historians are at a great disadvantage; we are inexpert psychologists, and in any event we cannot get the kind of data for this period which would satisfactorily substantiate any psychological hypotheses. However, we have little other choice than to move into this terrain whenever simple rationalistic explanations of national behavior leave us dissatisfied."[7]

The historian, as we have seen, in the World War II era has shown increased interest in moral values. In a sense, this is by no means a new trend: the historian has always written in the light of certain moral assumptions. This was true, for instance, of Beard, whose belief in the importance of economic motivations in men's lives was also in its way a moral decision. At the same time one wonders what the effect of the search for morality in history will have upon the historian's striving for objectivity. Truth in history is difficult to come by and historical research is less likely to illumine moral than other issues. The argument between Nevins and Destler[8] over the morality of business practice, between Dumond and Owsley[9] over whether the abolitionist crusade was a good or evil thing are, essentially, arguments over moral conviction and incapable, therefore, of easy resolution.

Finally, the historian's moral conviction might easily blind him to certain obvious realities. The late Professor James G. Randall detested war. But the moral judgment that war is evil, ought not to have pushed him to the conviction that war is avoidable. It is one thing for Randall to criticize from the vantage of 1950 the men of 1850 by saying that if they had behaved differently the Civil War would not have come. But 1950 is not 1850, and the alternatives to war which scholars are capable of framing in their studies almost a century after the event, may have been less apparent and less feasible to participants.[10] The historian is on solid ground in rejecting categoric economic determinism. At the same time, the historian should be wary of moral judgments which, by their nature, may be subjective and almost wish-fulfilling.

Despite some concern with moral values, the American historian is relatively unaffected by the intellectual's revived interest in religion. True, the "Christian Understanding of History" was the subject of a presidential address by Kenneth Scott Latourette before the American Historical Association in 1951,[11] and Reinhold Niebuhr's *Irony of American History* is geared to the author's belief in the limitation of man and of the historian as products of history.[12] But neither Latourette nor Niebuhr are American historians. Similarly, the resignation that one finds in the work of the English historians, Arnold Toynbee[13] and Herbert Butterfield,[14] before the imponderables of history, and their subsequent turning to God, has little echo among American historians. Perhaps mindful of the allusions to God in nineteenth-century American historiography, the contemporary American historian is a rationalist and convinced of the value of scientific method in the understanding of the past.

It is true that our survey of a century and a quarter of American historical interpretation has revealed the historian's understanding of the past as less permanent than shifting, less fixed than kaleidoscopic. And while at the end of this introduction we can offer no fixed formula for historical understanding, at the same time one hundred and twenty-five years of historical interpretation does not add up to relativistic chaos either. Between Bancroft's day and our own the art of the historian has advanced — and progress in the realm of historical understanding has been made in terms of reason rather than faith. The overwhelming majority of American historians are unwilling to surrender the belief that they have the power to "differentiate between historical narratives that are *better grounded or more reliable than others*";[15] that it is within their professional competence to judge one understanding of an incident in history superior to another.

True, ultimate historical understanding evades the seeker. Perhaps it always will. Nevertheless, the historian as a consequence of the open-minded and rationalistic exploration of the past, and the clash of opinion surrounding his views, will come closer to the reality that he aspires to describe. And although the final goal might elude him, in the process of rational striving to achieve it both democracy and the historian's art will be advanced.

The selections which follow are descriptive of some of the highlights of American history and illustrative of certain of the trends in American historical interpretation discussed in this introduction. These selections are historic rather than historiographic, having to do with events in American history rather than with the art of historical writing and interpretation as such. Each selection, however, expresses a point of view about the event being described — which is related in the editor's prefaces to other understandings of the incident and to the general pattern of historical understanding set forth in this survey.

Needless to say, in this attempted synthesis of American history and historiography, large segments of both have had to be omitted. Because of spatial limitations, many historians whose work merits inclusion have had to be excluded. However, for what we have been unable to bring within the covers of this volume, the reader may compensate by delving deeper into the literature of American history while remembering Thomas Jefferson's remark to John Adams: "A morsel of genuine history is a thing so rare as to be always valuable." [16]

I should like to express my deep gratitude to Professor Allan Nevins, Professor Eric F. Goldman and Professor Richard Hofstadter, who read this introduction and offered helpful suggestions. Needless to say, I am responsible for any errors of fact and interpretation.

E. N. S.

I
The American Mold

The Puritan Tradition

by

SAMUEL ELIOT MORISON

["The English and Religious Background," from *The Puritan Pronaos: Studies in the Intellectual Life of New England in the Seventeenth Century* (New York, 1936), pp. 5–17, 20–24. Reprinted by permission of New York University Press.]

A quarter of a century ago, recalled Samuel Eliot Morison in 1950, his was almost a lone voice "crying in the wilderness against the common notion of the grim Puritan painted by J. Truslow Adams and other popular historians of the day; the steeple-hatted, long-faced Puritan living in a log cabin and planning a witch-hunt or a battue of Quakers as a holiday diversion. That picture has given way to one of the jolly Puritan sitting in a little frame house furnished with early American furniture, silverware and pewter, one arm around a pretty Priscilla and the other reaching for a jug of hard cider." [1]

The Puritan, undeniably, has had his ups and downs in American historiography. He was revered by early American historians, most of whom were New Englanders, until Charles Francis Adams in 1894 attacked the tradition of filiopietism among American historians and stated that "the earlier times in New England were not pleasant times in which to live; the earlier generations were not pleasant generations to live with." [2] *This was also the verdict of Brooks Adams, who stressed the religious and political intolerance of the puritans.* [3] *This point of view was elaborated upon during the debunking of puritanism that went on in the 1920's, characteristically in the work of James Truslow Adams who, incidentally, before the appearance of his* The Founding of New England *in 1921, had been a stanch defender of the puritans.* [4]

The following selection is less a defense than an explanation of puritanism and the significance of the puritan tradition. It is also an example of the writing of the master stylist among living and contemporary historians. Morison's is not a self-consciously ornate or decorative prose, but involves instead a nicety of expression which serves to illuminate the narrative. For Morison, the perfection of style is at the same time a refinement of meaning — reminding one of another writer of sparkling historical prose, Carl Becker, who maintained "that in literary discourse form and content are two aspects of the same thing." [5]

Samuel E. Morison is Jonathan Trumbull Professor of History at Harvard.

NEW ENGLAND differed from the other English colonies in that it was founded largely for the purpose of trying an experiment in Christian living. This statement is self-evident to anyone who has read extensively in the literature of the times, both puritan writings and writings of their enemies. It has, of course, been challenged by people so superior in intellect that they can give you the essence of an era without the labor of reading the sources. We have all been told that the dynamic motive of settling New England was economic, though expressed in a religious jargon. Doubtless the idea of bettering their condition in life was present in a very large number of early New Englanders: the spirit of adventure must also claim a share; but no one who has delved deeply into the origin and history of the New England Colonies can, by any fair application of the rules of evidence, deny that the dynamic force in settling New England was English puritanism desiring to realize itself. The leaders, whom the people followed, proposed like Milton to make over a portion of the earth in the spirit of Christian philosophy: a new church and state, family and school, ethic and conduct. They might and did differ among themselves as to the realization of these high and holy aims; but a new City of God was their aim.

Until 1630, New England was anybody's country; the little band of Pilgrims who landed at Plymouth Rock ten years earlier were too few and isolated to have leavened any large lump of people hostile or indifferent to their point of view. But once the Massachusetts Bay Colony was founded, the fate of New England was sealed. In ten years' time, fifteen or twenty thousand people came over under puritan leaders; and three new colonies, Connecticut, Rhode Island, and New Haven, had been founded to contest with Massachusetts Bay the rivalry for divine favor and godly living.

Who were these puritans, and what did they propose to do? They were a party in the Church of England that arose in Elizabeth's reign, with the purpose of carrying out the Protestant reformation to its logical conclusion, to base the English Church both in doctrine and discipline on the firm foundation of Sacred Scripture; or, in the words of Cartwright, to restore the primitive, apostolic church "pure and unspotted" by human accretions or inventions. Religion should permeate every phase of living. Man belonged to God alone: his only purpose in life was to enhance God's glory and do God's will; and every variety of human activity, every sort of human conduct, presumably unpleasing to God, must be discouraged if not suppressed.

English puritanism, though essentially a religious movement, had its political and economic aspects. In their search for the original pattern of the Christian church in the apostolic age, the puritan leaders did not agree. They were divided into the Presbyterians, who thought that the primitive church was governed by a series of representative assemblies or synods; and the Congregationalists, who insisted that there never had been a unified church, only churches: each individual congregation should be a democracy of the "visible saints," of those admitted to full communion upon satisfactory evidence that they were God's elect. New England was founded by Congregationalists, the more democratic wing; and the latent democratic principle in their polity proved, humorously enough, an exceptionally heavy cross for the autocratically inclined parsons to carry. But whether Congregational or Presbyterian in its polity, puritanism appealed to the average Englishman's anti-clericalism. It gave the layman a larger part in the local church than he had enjoyed since the Roman emperors became Christian.

Puritanism also had its economic side. I do not hold to the thesis of Max Weber and Troeltsch, that puritanism arose as a justification for usury; *i.e.,* for taking interest on loans. In New England certainly, the Church was no respecter of persons, and the spectacle of Robert Keayne, the profiteering merchant of Boston, having to stand up in meeting and take a tongue-lashing from the Reverend John Cotton for infringing the puritan code of business ethics, would have warmed the heart of Father Coughlin. The Weber thesis, as restated by R. H. Tawney, accords better with the facts, as observed in New England. Puritanism was unascetic; it came to terms with this world. Under the medieval church you could only approach perfection (short of Heaven) by withdrawing from this world and entering the priesthood or a monastic order. But puritanism taught that a man could serve God quite as effectually in his chosen calling, as by entering the sacred ministry; that a farmer or merchant who conducted his business according to Christian ethics was more agreeable in the sight of God than one who withdrew from the world and escaped his social responsibilities by a celibate or monastic life. This doctrine of the calling, that you could serve God by nobly fulfilling a function determined by the conditions of this world, and thus prove your right to an easy place in the next world, was probably the main reason why puritanism appealed to the rising middle class, the nascent capitalists of the sixteenth and seventeenth centuries. Puritanism was essentially a middle-class movement. It was far too exigent in its moral demands ever to be popular with earthy-minded peasants, or with the nobility and the very rich, who saw no point in having money if you could not do what you liked with it.

In its attitude toward love, puritanism had more in common with Judaism than with medieval Christianity or Jesuit piety. Puritanism did not hold with asceticism or celibacy. The clergy married young and often; their church offered no monastic retreat for men who were too much troubled by women. Milton's invocation "Hail, wedded love!" in Paradise Lost (iv. 750) expresses the puritan ideal very neatly; and William Ames, the puritan casuist, implies in his *de Conscientia* that women have a right to expect something more from their husbands than mere duty. "Increase and multiply," the oldest of God's commands, was one that the puritans particularly enjoyed obeying — or some of us would not be here. Continence was a moral ideal on which due weight was laid; abstinence was not a superior virtue, confounded with chastity, but was in conflict with the purpose of creation. Married men who came out to New England were bluntly told to send for their wives or return to them. It was easier to obtain a divorce in New England in the seventeenth century than in old England; for the puritans, having laid such store on wedded love, wished every marriage to be a success.

On its intellectual side, which mainly concerns us, puritanism was an enemy to that genial glorification of the natural man, with all his instincts and appetites, that characterized the Renaissance, and the great Elizabethans. Shakepeare's

> What a piece of work is man! how noble in reason! how infinite in faculties! in form and moving how express and admirable! in action how like an angel! in apprehension how like a god!

is the antithesis of puritanism, which taught that natural man was wholly vile, corrupt, and prone to evil; that he could do no good without God's assistance; that he thoroughly deserved to broil in hell for all eternity, and would do so if he did not grasp the hand of grace proffered him by a merciful God, through Jesus Christ.

Predestination, one of the cardinal doctrines of Calvinism, was not stressed by the New England puritans; Michael Wigglesworth does indeed touch on it when he consigns the *reprobate* infants (not the *unbaptized* infants as is commonly said) to the "easiest room in hell"; but after reading some hundreds of puritan sermons, English and New English, I am about ready to deny that the New England puritans were predestinarian Calvinists. John Cotton indeed was wont to "sweeten his mouth with a bit of Calvin" before retiring (rather a sour bedtime confection, one would think), but in general the New England puritans quoted their revered Ames and Perkins and the church fathers much more than they did Calvin; and John Harvard had more volumes in his library by St. Thomas Aquinas than by St. John of Geneva. The puritan sermons assume (when they do not directly teach) that by Virtue of the Covenant of Grace, and through the efforts of the churches, salvation lay within reach of every person who made an effort; Christ helped those who helped themselves. Fatalism is completely wanting in the New England view of religion or of life. The karma of Buddhism implied a blind, meaningless universe; a poor joke that God played on humanity in one of his idle or sardonic humors. But the puritans, like the Jews, regarded this earth and humanity as a divine enterprise, the management of which was God's major interest; they were God's people and their God was a living God, always thought of as intensely concerned with the actions and characters of people and nations.* Each individual was a necessary item in a significant and divinely ordered cosmos. God has a personal interest in me, and has appointed work for me to do. If I am incapable of receiving his grace, it is unfortunate; but if that is God's will, who am I to complain? Yet while there's life, there's hope; and at any time before death my risen Lord may whisper in my heart that I am of the blessed ones elected by his Father to salvation.

It is generally supposed that puritanism hampered intellectual and artistic activity; and there is some truth in this charge. Puritanism banned three forms in which the English excelled: the drama, religious music, and erotic poetry. Just why it banned the drama is still a matter of debate among the professors. Was it that the drama was supposed to lead to immorality, or because it amused people too much? Or simply because a number of the church fathers, like Chrysostom, had thundered against the pagan drama of their day? Whatever the reason, the puritan war on the theater was hideously successful. There is no stranger phenomenon in literature than the swift rise of the English drama to a high zenith between 1580 and 1611, with Marlowe and Shakespeare; and its equally swift decline a few years after the death of Shakespeare. But it was not the puritans alone who killed the theater. Their theological enemies, Bishop Laud and the high churchmen, were equally responsible. James I liked a good show as much as anyone and, as long as he reigned, the English theater had court patronage; but Bishop Laud took charge of the conscience of Charles I, and discouraged the King from patronizing the drama, as an object unworthy of a Christian monarch's support. Deprived both of middle-class and court patronage, the English theater had no audience left but the sort that attends burlesque shows today; and the English theater became not much better than burlesque shows. It was the puritans, to be sure, who

* B. H. Streeter, *The Buddha and the Christ* (1932), p. 51 *et passim.*

closed the theaters; but one imagines that by 1642 the managers welcomed the closure, as it saved them from losing more money.

Although puritanism had nothing against music as such, the puritans injured music by taking it out of the churches. Religious exercises were stripped down to the bare rudiments of the days when early Christians met in secret, and would not have dared to play an organ, even if the organ had been available. Consequently instrumental music, like the other beautiful incidents with which the medieval church had enriched religious expression, was done away with for want of scriptural sanction, and because it was supposed to make the worshiper dreamy. To secular music (as Dr. Percy Scholes has shown in his recent work) the puritans had no objection; Oliver Cromwell kept an orchestra at his court, and the first Italian opera to be played in England was produced under his Protectorate, and by puritans.* A few musical instruments were brought out to New England, and more were ordered in the latter part of the century. There was "no law agin' it," but music was not a form of activity that the English puritans cared much about, or were willing to make much effort to maintain in the New World.

I do not propose to hide the puritans behind the excuse that there was no room or opportunity for these things in a pioneer community. The German Moravians who came to Pennsylvania in the early eighteenth century maintained high musical standards because they believed that music was worth making some effort to keep up. And the puritans transplanted high educational standards for the same reason. Hard as colonial Americans worked, they, or some of them, had a certain leisure and surplus to devote to things of the spirit; and it depended entirely on their set of values what things of the spirit, if any, they chose to cultivate.

While the puritan wrote off certain cultural activities such as the drama, and failed to do much for others, such as music, he was stimulated by his faith to an intellectual activity that was conspicuous in other English colonies by its absence. The alternative to a puritanically controlled intellectual life, in new settlements, was

* Percy A. Scholes, *The Puritans and Music in England and New England* (Oxford University Press, 1934).

intellectual vacuity; the emphasis was on acquiring an estate. The "best people" were engaged in growing tobacco or sugar cane, or trading with the natives; there was no incentive to lead a life of the spirit, no market for books, or audience for a play. At about the same time as the founding of New England, four other important English colonies — Virginia, Bermuda, Maryland, Barbados — and some lesser island plantations, were established. Virginia by 1660 had a population almost equal to that of the whole of New England; and for wealth, Barbados was not far behind; neither was a puritan colony. Yet, whoever heard of a Virginian play in the seventeenth century, or a Barbadian love lyric? Or, indeed, a Virginian literature of any sort, between the death of the first settlers and the eighteenth century? Where is the devotional poetry we might expect from Maryland, a Catholic colony? Why did not the scenic beauties of "still-vext Bermoothes," which at second hand lend such grace to Shakespeare's *Tempest,* inspire some native Bermudian to song, or prose? And even in Mexico and Peru, where an enormously wealthy governing class existed almost a century before New England was founded, and whither learned ecclesiastics were constantly emigrating, almost a century elapsed before any native intellectual life developed. The seventeenth century was the great age of Mexican and Peruvian literature; Don Pedro de Peralta Rocha Barnuevo y Benavídes, the savant of Lima, was almost contemporary with Cotton Mather — and Don Pedro was very much the same sort of indiscriminate and omniscient pedant as Don Cotton.* But New England, within ten years of the founding of Massachusetts Bay, had a vigorous intellectual life of its own, expressed institutionally in a college, a school system, and a printing press; applied in a native sermon literature, poetry, and history. What is more, this life did not perish with the founders: it deepened and quickened as the century grew older, developing a scientific side. For in puritanism, New England had a great emotional stimulus to certain forms of intellectual life.

A humanist New England would doubtless have provided a pleasanter dwelling place, and a more sweet and wholesome stream to swell the American flood, than puritan New England. But there was

* Irving A. Leonard, "A Great Savant of Colonial Peru," *Philological Quarterly,* XII (1933), 54–72; note especially the estimate of him on p. 63.

no such alternative. Humanism is a tender plant, depending on a stable and leisured society, and on a nice adjustment of human relations, that cannot bear transplanting. As already noted, in a new country the natural alternative to intellectual puritanism is intellectual vacuity; and for a very good reason, that the mere physical labor of getting a living in a virgin country is so great as to exhaust and stultify the human spirit, unless it have some great emotional drive. That, I take it, explains why in the non-puritan colonies the humanist tradition of Elizabethan England shriveled and died; and why those colonies had to wait a century or more before they had any intellectual life worthy of the name. In South Carolina, we are told, the French planters of the end of the seventeenth century brought their Montaignes, and Montaigne is perhaps the best representative in old-world literature of a kindly, reflective, and disciplined humanism; yet the soil was unpropitious, and the humanist tradition perished. Puritanism, on the contrary, throve under conditions of vigor, hardship, and isolation; hence the New England colonies were able almost immediately to create and support a distinct way of life that showed an unexpected vigor and virility long after English puritanism had been diluted or overwhelmed. The intellectual alternatives for New England, then, were not puritanism or humanism, but puritanism or that overwhelming materialism that we find in the typical newly settled region, whether it be English, French, Spanish, or Dutch.

Again we have a paradox. Puritanism in New England preserved far more of the humanist tradition, than did non-puritanism in the other English colonies. For the grammar schools and the college fostered a love of *literae humaniores:* Cicero, Virgil, Terence, and Ovid; Homer, Hesiod, and Theocritus. It was no small feat to keep alive the traditions of classical antiquity in a region that had never known the grandeur that was Rome, the glory that was Greece. The New England schools and colleges did just that; and handed down a priceless classical tradition to the eighteenth and nineteenth centuries — only to see it mangled and thrown aside by the professional educators and progressive pedagogues of our own day and generation. The classics flourished in New England under puritanism, and began to decay when puritanism withered.

The reason why the puritans nourished classicism, while rejecting other aspects of Renaissance humanism, was their concern for the education of posterity. Massachusetts Bay, New Haven, Connecticut, and even Rhode Island were ruled both in church and state by men who had attended the British universities and the English grammar schools. A careful combing of lists of emigrants reveals that at least one hundred and thirty university alumni came to New England before 1646. This does not seem a very impressive total; but the entire population of New England in 1645 was not greater than 25,000, and probably less, which means that there was on the average one university-trained man to every forty or fifty families — a far larger proportion than there is in the United States or in Great Britain today. In addition there was a large but indeterminate number of men who had had a sound classical education in the English grammar schools, and therefore saw eye-to-eye with the university men on intellectual matters. These Oxford and Cambridge alumni, moreover, had an influence all out of proportion to their numbers. They were not concentrated in the seaports, but scattered all over the country, on the frontier and in country villages as well. Although they did not monopolize the political ruling class, since most of them were parsons, and as such ineligible to office, they did constitute an intellectual ruling class. Their standards were accepted by the community, and maintained in the college that they founded, largely for the purpose of perpetuating all that they understood by civilization. The intellectual life of New England was determined by the top layers of society; it was no proletarian cult welling up from the common people. *Accepted* by the community, not *imposed* on it, I say; for men of education were the chosen leaders of the puritan emigration. Deprived ministers or discontented country gentry gathered groups of neighbors, friends, and parishioners, emigrated in the same ship, and settled in the same place. They were the shepherds to whom the people looked for guidance and inspiration, on whose spoken words they hung, and whose written words they perused eagerly. . . .

No subject of popular interest today, even economics, can compare in pervasiveness with the theology of the seventeenth century. Perhaps we can faintly grasp what theology meant to the people in those days if we imagine all parsons, priests, and rabbis turned out of our modern places of worship, and their places taken by economists who every Sabbath brought you the latest news from the Almighty in Washington, D.C., and told you just how you could escape taxes, or get a share of the divine (federal) bounty.

The puritans were the extreme wing of the Protestant party in the English universities, and the losing wing. They came to New England because they had lost every bout since 1570, when their great champion Cartwright had been expelled from his college fellowship and his chair of divinity at Cambridge. Until the reign of James I they thought that at least their theology was safe, since the Thirty-nine Articles of the Church of England were predominantly Calvinist; but James I discerned the anti-monarchical implications of puritanism, high-church theologians began to interpret the Thirty-nine Articles in a reactionary manner, and through court influence puritans were expelled or excluded from posts of honor and emolument in the universities, as in the government. This state of things, coming to a head in the years 1629–1634 with persecution, started the great puritan migration to New England. The educated men who organized and led this exodus brought with them a deep and lively interest in religion. The religious point of view dominated the intellectual life of New England for over a century, almost until the contest with England began.

A secondary intellectual interest in the Oxford and Cambridge of 1600 was poetry. All English schoolboys and college students were trained to write Latin and Greek verse; and at every marriage, birth, or death in the Royal Family, the choice wits of Oxford and Cambridge got out *epithalamia, gaudia,* or *threnodia* celebrating the happy or lamentable event in hexameters or elegiacs. It was an era of religious poetry, mostly by university-trained men — Spenser, Milton, Donne, Quarles, George Herbert, and, later, Cowley and Dryden. This tradition and, to a surprising extent, the amorous poetical fashion of Elizabeth's reign crossed to New England, together with other things of which the stricter puritans did not approve. For New England puritanism, like the Anglican Church of the Restoration, was a *via media;* a middle course between what Cotton Mather called the "Rigid and High-flown Presbyterians"* and the rigid sectaries and separatists. It never formally

* *Magnalia Christi Americana* (1702), book vii, 4–5.

separated from the Church of England, as Roger Williams passionately believed it should. And New England puritanism had to make terms with humanity, because it was in a responsible position. It has often been observed that political responsibility sobers down a fanatic, although of late the examples to the contrary are possibly more frequent. When the emigrant puritans found themselves in a position of power in the New England colonies, they were neither so rigid nor so fanatical as one would suppose from the pamphlets they had written when out of power; and so in England itself, when the Civil War brought the puritans on top.

It is not, then, correct to judge the puritans, as many writers have done, by the fanatical pamphlets of William Prynne, the Martin Marprelate tracts, and the writings of Richard Baxter. When in power they soon learned that no layman, however sincerely religious, could be expected to give all his waking moments to thoughts of God; that he must be given opportunity for earning a living, and for reasonable recreation, or, as they called it, "seasonable merriment." There was much opportunity for love and laughter in colonial New England, though not as much as there should have been. Thus, the puritans forbade the observance of Christmas, because of the pagan revelry that merry England had inflicted on the day of Christ's Nativity; but they established Thanksgiving Day which took its place; and now we have both Thanksgiving Day and Christmas. They abolished May Day, which in Elizabethan England was far from being the innocent schoolchildren's holiday that it is now; but instead they got two holidays in spring and early summer: election day and the college commencement, which soon took on the character of a Flemish kermis. Toward the end of the century, after a new cheap and fiery beverage, rum, had been invented, they attempted to regulate the liquor traffic; but they never attempted or even suggested a complete prohibition of all alcoholic beverages. Indeed, it might be agreed that puritan restrictions on purely physical enjoyment tended to stimulate intellectual life; that a good many people who in England would have lingered in a tavern, carousing and singing songs, stayed at home and wrote prose and poetry, or argued over the fine points of the last sermon, and picked flaws in their parson's theology!

I must ask you to keep in mind the small and thinly populated area of which we are speaking. The estimates of the United States Census Bureau give the New England colonies 17,800 people in 1640; 106,000, at the end of the century. As a basis of comparison, Virginia and Maryland combined had about the same population as New England from 1660 to the close of the century. Boston, the largest town in the English colonies, had about 7,000 people by 1690. It would be absurd to expect so thinly populated and isolated a province to produce poets of the caliber of Milton and Dryden, or prose writers equal to Lord Clarendon and John Locke. We must remember what is to be reasonably expected of a community of 25,000 to 100,000 people, agricultural for the most part, having no leisure class, or ready means of wealth, or method of conserving inherited property. New England was a poor country, even by the standards of the day, struggling with a niggardly nature for livelihood, subject to the constant tendency of the frontier to reduce humanity to a dead level of ambition and intellect. Under such circumstances we should not expect anything very great, original, or creative; for no new colony, since those of ancient Greece, has been able, during the period of adjustment to a new environment, to equal the intellectual achievement of its mother country. [The puritans were] a small group of people striving manfully, even heroically, to achieve an ideal — an ideal not merely religious, though permeated by it; an ideal of transmitting a civilization, and of planting in the New World the very vines whose fruit they had enjoyed in the Old. As New Englanders themselves were wont to say, "Despise not the day of small things."

The Virginians

by

CARL BRIDENBAUGH

["Training the Ruling Class." From *Seat of Empire, the Political Role of Eighteenth-Century Williamsburg.* (Williamsburg, Virginia, 1950), pp. 3–17. Reprinted by permission of Colonial Williamsburg.]

From the top layer of the social hierarchy in Virginia there emerged during the eighteenth century a group of statesmen including such figures as George Washington, Thomas Jefferson, Patrick Henry, George Mason, George Wythe, Peyton Randolph, James Madison and John Marshall, who were among the ablest public men to appear at any time in American history. These men left a permanent imprint upon our national life.

A great deal of fiction along with historic fact has come down to us concerning the origin of these early Virginians. As early as 1896, Philip Bruce's Economic History of Virginia, in the Seventeenth Century, *while rejecting the romantic notion of the Cavalier origin of Virginia's upper class, nevertheless maintained that there are many evidences that a large number of immigrants were sprung from English families of substance."* [1] *John Fiske's* Old Virginia and Her Neighbors *stressed the importance of Cavalier immigration to Virginia between 1649 and 1660.* [2]

From the researches of Thomas Jefferson Wertenbaker, it is apparent that very many of the first families of Virginia in the eighteenth century, perhaps most of them, were descendants from those who but two generations earlier had wrested their huge domains from the savage and the wilderness, accomplishing this feat frequently with very little to sustain them but hardiness, tenacity, and good fortune. [3] *However, apart from the question of the precise origin of the Virginia aristocracy, there had emerged, by 1750,*

*as James Truslow Adams reminds us, a "class so wealthy, so power-
ful, its members so bound to one another by marriage and other
ties, and so intrenched in influence with the various authorities as
to set them apart in quite a different way from that which in the
moderate distinctions of wealth had operated earlier."* [4]

*In the following selection, Carl Bridenbaugh, who is Margaret
Byrne Professor of History at the University of California, describes
the process whereby this class was trained to govern. Many aspects
of the political schooling of the Virginia aristocrat were undeniably
undemocratic — but it was colonial Virginia's solution to the problem
of how to bring about the desirable result described by John Tyler
when he said: "good and able men had better govern than be
governed."*

*Virginia is Bounded by the Great Atlantic Ocean to the East,
by North Carolina to the South, by Maryland and Pennsylvania
to the North, and by the South Sea to the West, including California.*
                        —THOMAS LEE TO THE BOARD OF TRADE, 1750

A S LAND-HUNGRY Virginians like Thomas Lee faced westward
from their Tidewater lands in 1750 and succeeding years, the
sheer immensity of the extent of the Old Dominion fired their im-
aginations and supplied a fillip to their activities. Expansion was in
the air. All the people of the colony, Tidewater Tuckahoe and back-
country Cohee alike, were infected with the virus of empire building. Although we may smile at Colonel Lee's inflated limits, we
must admit that east of the Mississippi River Virginia could lay
valid claims to a princely domain of 359,480 square miles — a territory three times the size of King George's British Isles! As it existed
at the close of the War for Independence, the commonwealth was
still larger than all of New England with Delaware tossed in for
good measure.

In population as well as size Virginia led all the colonies. It contained nearly twice as many inhabitants in 1776 as Massachusetts,

or Pennsylvania, or Maryland, or North Carolina. The Old Dominion's population — white and black, free and slave — was equal to five sixths of that of New England, and it composed one fifth of all the people in the colonies.

By the standards of the eighteenth century this oldest, largest, and most populous colony was properly regarded by Britons as the prime link in the great chain of empire. It furnished the Mother Country with a valuable and much needed staple — tobacco — and in return absorbed ever-increasing quantities of British manufactures. Unwavering loyalty to the king was the constant boast of Virginians, who took pardonable pride in the remarkable stability of their society and of their government.

As early as 1700 a pattern of life had been established which made Virginia throughout the century, like Connecticut, a land of steady habits. Verily, its political history before 1750 makes dull reading! No rebellion broke out after Bacon's fiasco of 1676; no foreign enemy ever crossed her boundaries; no rift in the social fabric ever threatened the security of the colony's ruling class.

Let us begin with the people. Tidewater Virginia presented the unusual spectacle of a whole society devoting its energies to the production of a single crop — "that chopping herbe of hell, tobacco." Cultivation of the soil absorbed the attention of nearly all the inhabitants — rich, middling, and poor, white or black — and nearly all lived on some kind of a farm. That in the whole colony there was no town of consequence astonished visitors in these years. The essence of eighteenth-century Virginia was its *rural quality*. And yet, with a few significant exceptions, most colonial Americans were farmers and rustic in their outlook. What was it then that made Virginia's society different? What was there about the Old Dominion that produced within the space of half a century a galaxy of statesmen who, for sagacity, ability, courage, political insight, and absence of provincialism, could challenge any other country or period of history to produce their equals? The answer, in all probability, may be discovered in the plantation way of life and in the system of government that was evolved to meet the needs of this society.

The plantation differentiated Virginia agriculture from that of other communities in old England or the Northern and Middle colonies. The plantation made the Chesapeake society unique. Unlike the traditional American farm, a tobacco estate was virtually a little society in itself. Out of the thousands of acres owned by well-to-do planters, only small areas were actually cleared and under cultivation at one time; most of their lands were still forest. Moreover each large holding was usually divided into several units in order to secure more efficient production: one would contain the "mansion house" where dwelt the owner and his family; others, similarly composed, were operated by overseers or leased by white tenant farmers.

Each unit, or "quarter," had its gang of ten to thirty slaves who performed the heavy work in the fields or at the barns and outbuildings. Contrary to commonly accepted belief, the number of Negroes seldom reached three hundred, even on very large plantations; throughout the whole Tidewater region the average planter owned only eight or ten slaves. Rounding out the population of the plantation were a few white indentured servants, who customarily performed the tasks requiring highly skilled artisans, although here and there one found a "country-born" slave possessing some facility at a trade.

Among the great plantations of Virginia was Nomini Hall, Potomac River seat of Councilor Robert Carter. As the visitor approached it, either by boat up Nomini Creek or by carriage down the long lane impressively flanked by towering poplars, this great estate resembled nothing so much as a tiny village set down in an area carved from the surrounding woodlands. The great mansion of the type so well known to the modern tourist achieved its commanding appearance from the many dependent buildings clustered around it. Four structures — the brick schoolhouse, the washhouse, the coach house, and the stable — formed a square of which the mansion was the center. Stretching westward from the great house were the kitchen, bakehouse, dairy, storehouse, and other small buildings which created the illusion of "a little handsome street." Near the tobacco and corn fields, behind a row of trees which screened them from the main quadrangle, were the rude cabins in which the slaves were quartered.

Perhaps a hundred and fifty souls, black and white, comprised the community at Nomini Hall. Its owner, Robert Carter, presided over this large "family" like some patriarch out of the Old Testament. By virtue of his planning and management — his rule, if you will — the yearly endeavors of the community were a success or a failure. He determined the lands to be cultivated each season, what crops should be planted, how many hogs should be raised, and every other activity on the plantation. It was he who arranged for shipment and sale of the crops when they were harvested, and it was he who made the outside purchases necessary for the little village throughout the coming year. The coopers who fabricated the tobacco casks, the smiths who forged the iron work and shod the horses, as well as the miller who ground the corn and wheat at Nomini Creek dam — all came under his direct surveillance. He also had to look after the health and clothing of his Negro workers. Over his slaves he possessed by law the power of life and death; his white servants were virtually serfs until the expiration of their indentures; his tutors, overseers, clerks, and other white employees were subject to his control and to the plantation routine and discipline. In consequence, the management of a plantation called for something more than mere business acumen or a knowledge of current agricultural methods.

Such a plantation was in reality a tiny, practically self-sufficient society. Mere listing of the quantities consumed by Robert Carter's dependents for the single year 1773 causes astonishment: "27,000 Lb. of Pork, and Twenty Beeves, 550 Bushels of Wheat, besides Corn — 4 Hogsheads of Rum and 150 Gallons of Brandy."

This society existed, for the most part, little influenced by the outside world. A man could live a long time on an estate like Nomini Hall without becoming aware of the colonial government at Williamsburg, let alone that of His Majesty the King in London.

Nowhere did the eighteenth century provide a more thorough schooling in the management of practical affairs and in the handling of people than on these Tidewater plantations where young Virginians were reared. Early did they develop an awareness of their privileged status; early did they acquire the habit of command. They came into manhood prepared and expecting to rule; it was a birthright bred in their bones and nourished on plantation fare. These traits were, moreover, nicely blended with a formal education in the classical tradition at the plantation school. Though they lived amid rural surroundings, the Virginia gentry displayed a striking urbanity; they were never rustics. To reach maturity in one of these little tobacco societies was to be exposed to a superb elementary training in the difficult art of governing people. One must seek the genesis of the great Virginians of the Revolutionary Era on the plantation; two indispensable crops were there produced: tobacco and leaders.

Here the very conditions of life forced upon gentlemen a careful cultivation of those arts so essential to men who propose to lead others — the outward appearance of a leader, an erect bearing, horsemanship, an easy dignity, self-assurance sometimes verging on arrogance, and that prime capacity of reaching decisions quickly.

Born to rule, reared to rule, the generality of these men — as Francis Walker Gilmer, a leading literary figure of Jefferson's day, readily admitted — acquired their culture and learning from conversation rather than from books. Although the majority of the planters were a highly sociable folk who had developed conversation and the external graces to a fine art and who regarded the outdoor life of action as the only good life, the best of these barons of the Tidewater also passed much of their time in reading. Few men of their time were better informed than Virginians on such subjects as history and politics. In Virginia, remarked the observant Duc de La Rochefoucauld-Liancourt, "a taste for reading is more prevalent among the gentlemen of the first class than in any other part of America, but the common people are, perhaps, more ignorant than elsewhere." Some of this first class assembled libraries whose contents included the wisdom of the ages upon the important subject of government. On their shelves were the standard works of Plutarch, Harrington, Sidney, Locke, and the rest, well worn from much reading. For them this study became a necessity, and in their greatest statesmen we perceive immediately the noteworthy combination of the active and the practical with the scholarly and the contemplative that is so refreshingly startling upon first encounter and a matter for amazement and admiration thereafter. Ruling over their own acres was their first lesson in statesmanship; the plantation was their primer of politics.

In the middle of the eighteenth century, perhaps less than three hundred families were seated on plantations in Tidewater Virginia like the one at Nomini Hall. This group formed a parochial aristocracy whose ranks were apparently even more difficult to enter than those of the English gentry. For over half a century "gentlemen of the best families and fortunes" had been consciously coalescing into an exclusive ruling class based principally upon the possession of great tracts of land. In part they achieved their desire to perpetuate their families and their power by legal enactments requiring their estates to descend to their eldest sons, who in turn were forbidden to alienate any inherited lands. These were the famous laws of *primogeniture* and *entail* passed in 1705. The ranks of the gentry were further consolidated by carefully planned intermarriages among the great families, since in good eighteenth-century fashion family plans always took precedence over dictates of the heart. The fruits of these arrangements forcibly struck all visitors: "an aristocratical spirit and principle is very prevalent in the laws, policy and manners of this Colony," observed Josiah Quincy Jr. of Boston, while on a tour of the seaboard in 1773.

Thus privileged by law and carefully selected — one almost says bred — through intermarriage, these Virginians wore an air of assurance and pride of place, exhibited a haughtiness and condescension toward their inferiors, and studiously cultivated the attitudes of leaders — characteristics all of an aristocratic order. Such qualities prevailed among the patrician families of the Old Dominion — Burwells, Byrds, Carters, Corbins, Fitzhughs, Harrisons, Lees, Ludwells, Nelsons, Pages, Randolphs, Robinsons, Tayloes, and their kin. These people were not aristocrats on the make; they were already made, and they and the rest of Virginia knew and admitted it.

The luxuriously furnished great plantation houses that once studded the banks of the Potomac, the Rappahannock, the York, and the James combined with an elaborate elegance of dress on the part of the residents to keep the leading Virginia families in a constant state of emulation with each other. These were their badges of distinction. Regardless of the costs, Tidewater grandees steadily increased their votive offerings to the cult of magnificence. Ostentation was intended to impress — and it did. Dazzled by the conspicuous baronial splendor of the great families of the plantation country, a traveler of the 1760's exclaimed: "In most articles of life a great Virginia planter makes a greater show and lives more luxuriously than a country gentleman in England, on an estate of three or four thousand pounds a year."

Perennially writers emphasize the close resemblance of Tidewater Virginia to the country life of old England. The Chesapeake and Atlantic highways, as well as the tobacco trade, they assert, bound the planters irrevocably to the Mother Country, and, moreover, the Virginians themselves voluntarily, nay eagerly, sought, as John Donne had said, "to make this land . . . the suburbs of the Old World." From a cursory glance this contention seems true. There was much indeed about the tobacco plantation that resembled the seat of an English squire. Much more important than the fact itself was the belief of Virginians that they were living in the manner of the English squirearchy.

Actually these men were more American than they knew. Not until threats of the application of naked power by the British authorities came in the 1760's did they begin to sense how far they had diverged from the English norm in thought and in deed. In 1765 Virginians sincerely protested their loyalty to their king — *but it was a loyalty of their own defining.* Loyalty to their own class and tradition — to Virginia, as they would have put it — was their transcending loyalty. As early as 1759 an English parson named Andrew Burnaby had shrewdly taken the measure of the rulers of the Old Dominion. He noted that the public character of the Virginians corresponded with their private one: "they are haughty and jealous of their liberties, impatient of restraint, and can scarcely bear the thought of being controuled by any superior power. *Many of them consider the colonies as independent states, unconnected with Great Britain,** otherwise than by having the same common king, and being bound to her with natural affection." This is precisely the position taken by Thomas Jefferson in 1774 in his famous *Summary View.* Sentiments like these are redolent of the American soil. Here we have a native growth; there is nothing English in it.

The first gentlemen of Virginia were, in reality, a working aristocracy. As we have seen they had to be experts in agriculture, know

* The italics are mine. — C. B.

something of elementary manufacturing, display business talents, and act in many executive capacities. To the community they owed, in addition, a political obligation. This at the very least implied service on the parish vestry.

The vestry had been brought into existence in connection with the establishment of the Church of England as the state church, and was designed to serve as the lay body whose duty it was to look after the ecclesiastical affairs of the local area called the parish. In each parish this body was made up of twelve of "the best Gentlemen of the Country." Until 1676 the vestrymen and church wardens had been elected, but thereafter the vestries filled their own vacancies and became exclusive bodies. The principal church duties of the vestrymen were erecting and maintaining the church building and the chapels of ease in the parish, handling funds, and engaging the minister.

But it was in its political and social, rather than its ecclesiastical capacity, that the parish achieved its greatest importance. As the smallest unit of government in Virginia, it came closest to the every-day life of the people. The vestry publicly published all laws pertaining to servants, slaves, morals, and vital statistics; it posted notices about lost property, stray animals, runaway servants, and the docking of entails; it announced all the governor's proclamations. Of first importance to everyone was the power of the vestry to apportion among the freeholders their shares of the tithes, or taxes, for the support of the church as well as the county and colony levies. The care of the parish poor also devolved upon this body of gentlemen, who were authorized to lay taxes for their support. Often, also, where no county or provincial authority interposed, vestries assumed the initiative for erecting ferries, opening roads, and founding schools.

To the planter, fresh from unchallenged authority over his own little patriarchal domain, the occasional meeting of the vestry served as the vital second step of his political training. Here he sat with eleven other planters who were his equals and determined what was best for the middling and inferior folk of the parish. Membership in vestries had become virtually hereditary by 1750, and collectively the vestrymen made up a sort of panel from which Virginia's rulers were drawn. Government was their business quite as much as the raising of tobacco because their birth, place, wealth, education, practical training, and frequently intelligence, fitted them to rule.

Membership on a vestry board was a local honor highly prized, and its meetings were unusually well attended. During George Washington's years of service as a vestryman of Truro Parish, 1763–1774, thirty-one meetings were held. He missed only eight, and these for such valid reasons as sickness, attendance at the House of Burgesses, and absence from the county.

Like the management of a great plantation, membership on the vestry was regarded as a prerogative of the aristocracy. Here in Virginia's smallest unit of local government, public servants were self-appointed and, with the passage of years, increasingly tended to act independently of the people. The average Virginian knew at first hand about taxation without representation because of his annual experience with the local vestry. On the other hand, vestries generally performed their duties to the parish faithfully, though hardly efficiently, and always of course, without charge. Whatever its weaknesses, and there were many, the parish vestry became the great nursery for Virginia's statesmen.

The only other governmental unit of which the majority of Virginians of the eighteenth century were aware was the county. Here again the people were witnesses to rule by the rich, the well born, and the *responsible* few. The royal governor at Williamsburg was authorized by law to appoint eight justices of the peace in each county, although in 1769 their numbers ranged from seven to twenty-four per county. Only members of the upper class ever received these coveted appointments to membership in the squirearchy, which, as in England, symbolized social recognition and opened the way to political preferment. When a vacancy occurred in any county, the justices submitted three names from which the governor made his choice. Thus, like the vestry, the county justices tended to become a self-perpetuating group.

If a Virginia justice of the peace took his duties seriously, as was often the case, he paid heavily for the honor, because the office was both burdensome and time-consuming. Acting as a local magistrate he heard both civil and criminal small causes. From his decision an appeal might be taken to all the justices sitting as a full bench at the county court. Each month, on a day specified by law, four or more justices met regularly at the county courthouse to record deeds and probate wills, to hear civil suits to the value of twenty-five shillings or two hundred pounds of tobacco, and to try criminal cases not involving the death penalty.

Court day was a gala occasion, and the sessions were always well attended because Virginians liked few things better than a lawsuit. At Leesburg, seat of Loudoun County, in December 1774, Nicholas Cresswell listened to "a great number of litigious suits. The people seem to be fond of Law. Nothing uncommon for them to bring suit against a person for a Book debt and trade with him on an open account at the same time. To be arrested for debt is no scandal here."

Surpassing judicial duties in importance, however, were the executive and administrative burdens saddled on the county officials by the Assembly, which passed laws and cavalierly left their administration to local authority. The court made up the list of titheables, apportioned and collected the colony's taxes as well as the taxes for county activities. Opening and maintaining highways, erecting bridges, superintending ferries, regulating tobacco warehouses, licensing taverns, and conducting elections all came within the purview of the justices. Often, too, where provincial legislation was lacking, the court passed ordinances governing runaway servants or slaves and other local matters.

Frequently, as one would expect, county officials were snowed under by this avalanche of duties. Viewed from almost any angle the Virginia system of county government appeared inefficient. The justices were amateurs, more often than not ignorant of law and government and devoid of any inclination to read up on it. Since they were unpaid, their sole incentives were honor and the public service. Many, like Richard Bland, Edmund Pendleton, George Mason, Richard Henry Lee, and Patrick Henry, worked hard at their jobs; others proved mere time-servers, often lazy and incompetent, who, being appointed for life, unfortunately could not be removed.

Cumbersome and inept as the county court came to be, this institution was, nevertheless, well suited to the temper and to the grievances of the people of Virginia. Justice was rendered upon a person-to-person basis. Decisions were governed by the unwritten custom of the community which guaranteed the citizen protection against the routine tyranny of the modern judicial system wherein the observance of the letter of the law not infrequently throttles the spirit that gives it life. Everyone who could attended at the courthouse when the justices convened. Business and sociability competed with the rendering of justice on such occasions. Sooner or later virtually every freeholder came to know who the judges were and to have a pretty good idea whom he desired among the gentry to represent him as a burgess at Williamsburg.

Notwithstanding the rural isolation in which they lived, Virginia freeholders, or small property owners, were politically alert, and they would travel great distances to exercise the franchise. After 1762 anyone possessing twenty-five acres and a house, or fifty acres of uncleared land, could vote in the election of burgesses. It is not generally realized that the right to vote was not only as widely conferred in Virginia as in the Middle and New England colonies, but more widely exercised. In Virginia elections one white in eleven took part as compared with one in fifty in Massachusetts. Of course it must be noted that Virginians had no vote or voice in local matters at all, whereas the New England town meeting provided a great forum for the political training of the average man.

The primary political and social fact of eighteenth-century Virginia was rule by a class. The gentlemen of Virginia believed implicitly in the right of their class to rule; the proper business of the gentry was politics. Election laws stated that freeholders should choose "the best men of the country," and custom decreed that only members of the upper class were selected. True, the gentlemen vied with each other for freeholders' votes, and, in defiance of the law, treating with liquor before the sheriff opened the polls was so common a practice that Colonel Robert Munford, burgess from 1765 to 1775, openly scored the abuse in a three-act satire of a county election called *The Candidates*, written in the early seventies. In 1774 at Alexandria, when Colonel George Washington and Major Charles Broadwater were elected burgesses, they "gave the populace a Hogshead of Toddy . . . [and] in the evening the returned Member [Mr. Washington] gave a Ball to the Freeholders and Gentlemen of the town." Aristocrats who, like Robert Wormeley Carter and

James Madison, "never ask'd but one man to vote" for them, generally failed of election. Even "the best gentlemen," it appears, had to "familiarize" themselves "among the People" by the "corrupting influence of spiritous liquors and other treats having a like tendency," since to the voters there were gentlemen and gentlemen.

In theory, power in colonial Virginia proceeded from the top downward — from the king to the governor to the Assembly to the county and ultimately to the parish. By the time it seeped through these several layers of authority and acted upon the individual it was pretty throughly diluted. Viewed from the bottom upward, it is clear that the parish and the county enjoyed virtual autonomy. Only once a year, when taxes and quit rents on land were collected or occasionally at election times and at militia musters, did Virginians become aware, even, of the government at Williamsburg. Whether in the Tidewater or in the Piedmont, they all lived in the country. To them government was largely an abstraction, except the county court and the vestry, where the rule of gentlemen whom they knew by name was personal and easygoing. Local aristocrats usually were "the best people," and their trusteeship was accepted and approved by the lower classes who were entirely willing to leave colony matters to their betters. What went on in London was upon the whole a matter of indifference to them, although to the gentry it was a vital matter, especially if it impinged on their political status.

A striking instance of the ready assent of the common people of Virginia to rule by the first gentlemen and their confidence in this leadership occurred in 1774 when Benjamin Harrison was setting out to represent his colony at the First Continental Congress. A number of "respectable, but uninformed inhabitants" of the neighborhood waited upon him, and their spokesman said: "You assert that there is a fixed intention to invade our rights and privileges; we own that we do not see this clearly, but since you assure us that it is so, we believe the fact. We are about to take a very dangerous step, but we confide in you, and are ready to support you in every measure you shall think proper to adopt."

By the time a gentleman of the Tidewater came to be elected to represent his county in the House of Burgesses at Williamsburg, he had been exposed to an unsurpassed opportunity to school himself in what might be called the art and mystery of governing people. Commencing with control over his personal servant as a little boy, he gradually assumed more and more authority on the plantation; at maturity he took his "hereditary" seat on the parish vestry; soon thereafter he advanced to the office of justice of the peace. Many youthful planters held these offices in their early twenties and, on the thresholds of their careers, acquired at first hand a priceless apprenticeship in executive, administrative, and judicial work. If they were serious and curious like Robert Carter, Thomas Jefferson, and others, they employed the leisure time afforded by plantation life in supplementing their practical experience with the study of history and public law. Intellectual exercise never attracted the bulk of the gentry, but to the cream of the ruling class, to its thinkers and leaders, it appealed mightily. They became the great statesmen of the Old Dominion. Ideals of self-government and home rule were inculcated in these Virginians by the actual facts of their existence, while in their libraries they found the historical precedents for their position and worked out a theory on which they could base their course of action if their position should ever be threatened.

The Declaration of Independence

by

JULIAN P. BOYD

["Backgrounds," reprinted by permission of Princeton University Press from *The Declaration of Independence* (Princeton, 1945), pp. 1–5.]

The Declaration of Independence, cornerstone document of American freedom, has been the subject of varying historical interpretation. Some anti-Jeffersonian historians, like von Holst, are plainly suspicious of it as the product of French influence and, therefore, external to the Anglo-Saxon legal tradition.[1] On the other hand, historians with a broader viewpoint, such as James Schouler, have paid hearty homage to it.[2]

More recently, the trend among historians is toward better understanding of the document in terms of the ideas that enter into it and the evolution of its text. Although the historiography of the Declaration begins with Hazelton's full account,[3] Becker's treatment with its stress upon literary qualities of the Declaration is a major historiographic contribution.[4] More recently, Julian P. Boyd, Librarian at Princeton, has added to our knowledge of the Declaration by studying the evolution of its text. The following selection from Boyd's volume is indicative of the multiple sources from which the Declaration of Independence was derived.

IN A broad sense, the author of the Declaration of Independence was the American people.* Its great object was to formulate the

* In this brief analysis of the text of the various drafts of the Declaration I have leaned heavily upon Mr. Carl Becker's excellent study, *The Declaration of Independence: a Study in the History of Political Ideas* (2d ed., New York,

principles of government in such a way as to justify rebellion, and the subject of government, as John Adams pointed out, was a subject discussed daily at almost every fireside in America on the eve of the Revolution. If, as Jefferson intended, the Declaration was "an expression of the American mind," he was in this sense the inspired amanuensis of the people. Like that other wide-ranging intellect of the eighteenth century, Benjamin Franklin, he was ever ready to acknowledge his derivative authorship, even when the felicity of his prose, the clarity of his expression, and the daring of his ideas combined to stamp the product of his pen as indubitably and singly Jeffersonian. Thus, as author of the far-reaching legal reforms in Virginia by which "every fibre would be eradicated of ancient or future aristocracy; and a foundation laid for a government truly republican," Jefferson, far from claiming sole authorship of this liberating system of laws, paid high tribute to his coadjutors George Mason and George Wythe.* Thus also did he respond to the busy efforts of a New England Federalist, Timothy Pickering, who early in the nineteenth century endeavored "to show how little was his merit in compiling" the Declaration.† What Pickering sought to prove was that Jefferson had contributed nothing original, nothing distinctively new, nothing solely Jeffersonian to the great apologia

---

1942) and I wish to acknowledge an indebtedness which all readers of this book must feel and which in my case is very great. I have also found John H. Hazelton's *The Declaration of Independence: Its History* (New York, 1906) an indispensable source of information.

* Marie Kimball, *Jefferson: the Road to Glory* (1943), p. 227–228.

† Pickering made a very precise copy of the Richard Henry Lee copy at Washington on February 26, 1805 (now in the Massachusetts Historical Society), and doubtless his intention even at that date was the same as that stated in the above quotation, which was made in a letter to Henry Lee, May 3, 1811; Hazelton, *op. cit.*, p. 481–484. Indeed, as early as 1802 the Federalists endeavored to rob Jefferson of the credit of authorship of the Declaration; "Buckskin," in the *Virginia Gazette and General Advertiser* for Sept. 15, 1802, declared "It is a fact, no less true than it will be surprising to the people of America, after the repeated and positive assertions to the contrary, that the present Chief Magistrate of the United States was not the draftsman of the Declaration. . . . That gentleman, it is true, reported to Congress what had been prepared by the Committee of which he (as first named) was a chairman." When the *Richmond Enquirer* published on June 20, 1806, the copies of the Declaration and the Virginia Constitution that Jefferson had sent to George Wythe, it prefaced these documents with the statement that "The federal assertion that Mr. Jefferson was not the author of this celebrated declaration, has long since been refuted, or else these papers would have furnished the most abundant refutation."

of the American Revolution. What he actually accomplished was to give Jefferson the opportunity to state the things that might have remained unspoken but for Pickering's gratuitous efforts.

The Fourth of July oration delivered at Salem by Pickering in 1823, almost two decades after he had set out to depreciate Jefferson's claim to authorship, quoted a letter from John Adams to the effect that the Declaration contained no idea, "but what had been hackneyed in Congress for two years before."* Indeed, Adams had added, the substance of it was to be found in the Declaration of Rights of 1774 and "in a pamphlet, voted and printed by the town of Boston, before the first Congress met, composed by James Otis, as I suppose, in one of his lucid intervals, and pruned and polished by Samuel Adams." If by "the substance of it" Adams meant the nature and purpose of government, he was engaged in laboring the obvious, a forgivable trait in the aged statesman who had been called by Stockton of New Jersey "the Atlas of American Independence." But the obvious as uttered by Pickering and the obvious as stated by the venerable statesman of Braintree had two very distinct connotations. Adams may have been a trifle querulous, but Pickering was acting upon a definite purpose that he had stated so early as 1811. When he said that the Declaration contained only hackneyed ideas, he meant it as criticism, thereby exposing himself to the obvious response: the greatness of the Declaration lay in the very fact that it expressed what Adams himself had said was in the minds and hearts of the people.

Jefferson made such a response. "Pickering's observations, and Mr. Adams' in addition . . .," he wrote to Madison, "may all be true. Of that I am not to be the judge. Richard Henry Lee charged it as copied from Locke's treatise on Government. . . . I know only that I turned to neither book nor pamphlet while writing it. I did not consider it as any part of my charge to invent new ideas altogether and to offer no sentiment which had ever been expressed before." † The important task (as Jefferson further wrote May 8, 1825, to Henry Lee) was "Not to find out new principles, or new

* *Letters of Members of the Continental Congress*, E. C. Burnett, ed., I, 515–516.

† *Writings of Jefferson*, P. L. Ford, ed., X, 266. The letter is dated August 30, 1823.

arguments, never before thought of, not merely to say things which had never been said before; but to place before mankind the common sense of the subject, [in] terms so plain and firm as to command their assent, and to justify ourselves in the independent stand we [were] impelled to take. Neither aiming at originality of principle or sentiment, nor yet copied from any particular and previous writing, it was intended to be an expression of the American mind. . . . All its authority rests then on the harmonizing sentiments of the day, whether expressed in conversation, in letters, printed essays, or the elementary books of public right, as Aristotle, Cicero, Locke, Sidney, etc." *

Thus did Jefferson share his authorship with the American people and thus did he identify the harmonizing sentiments of the day with concepts of government which had an ancient and diverse lineage. The idea that men were born equal, that they were possessed of certain inherent and unalienable rights, that these rights included life, liberty, and the pursuit of happiness, that it was the duty of government to protect and preserve these rights, that the government which did not do so could be abolished — this was an idea familiar not only to those who had written "elementary books of public right," but also to every pamphleteer, every lawyer, every minister of the gospel, almost every American subject of George III in the epochal year 1776. Indeed, as one historian has put it, some of the American writers at the time of the Revolution "were acquainted with practically all of the exponents of the idea [of fundamental law] from Sophocles to Blackstone." † But John Locke, whose two treatises on government appeared in 1690, is generally accepted by historical and legal scholarship as the great fountainhead of Revolutionary thought in America.‡ He, too, like Jefferson, drew from many springs and was drawn from for many purposes. Even Thomas Hobbes, whose great *Leviathan* stood at the other pole from Locke, thought "all men are born equal, but by Nature Free," which, from an exponent of absolutism, was even more than

* *Ibid.*, VII, 407.
† Charles F. Mullett, *Fundamental Law and the American Revolution*, p. 7.
‡ Mr. Becker's work contains a masterly analysis of the natural-rights philosophy and of the American view of the nature of the British constitution. See also Randolph G. Adams, *Political Ideas of the American Revolution* (Durham, 1922).

Jefferson could put into the Declaration. The Revolutionary dialecticians employed ideas from whatever source bore authoritative weight, whether it was Aristotle or Cicero among the ancient writers; or Grotius, Pufendorf, Vattel, Burlamaqui, and Montesquieu among the Continentals; or Hooker, Hoadley, Locke, Sidney and Buchanan in the great stream of English libertarian thought.*

What was new and revolutionary in the Declaration was the fact that here, for the first time, a political society formally declared the purpose of the state, enumerated some of man's natural rights, and affirmed the right of revolution. But this innovation was the act of a free people, not an invention of Jefferson. Even Jefferson's inclusion of "the pursuit of happiness" as an indefeasible right does not warrant the assumption that this was a new philosophy of government, distinctively Jeffersonian and distinctively American. "Samuel Adams and other followers of Locke had been content with the classical enumeration of life, liberty, and property; but in Jefferson's hands the English doctrine was given a revolutionary shift," wrote V. L. Parrington in his *Main Currents in American Thought*. "The substitution of 'pursuit of happiness' for 'property' marks a complete break with the Whiggish doctrine of property rights that Locke had bequeathed to the English middle class, and the substitution of a broader sociological conception. . . ." In this view, in which Parrington seems to project his own preference for human rights over property rights and with which others have concurred, Jefferson's selection of the broader phrase is given a greater emphasis than even the all-inclusive doctrine of the right of revolution. The idea that happiness is the end of government is an ancient one, and it was embraced by Richard Bland, John Adams, James Otis, James Wilson, Alexander Hamilton, George Mason, and a host of other contemporaries of Jefferson, to say nothing of Burlamaqui, Wollaston, Beccaria, Bolingbroke, and a friend of Thomas Hobbes, John Hall — who, in *The Grounds and Reasons of Monarchy Considered,* published in 1651, identified the pursuit of happiness as a natural right in these words: "My natural liberty, that is to say, to make my life as justly happy and advantageous to me as I can, he [the monarch] can no more give away from me than my understanding and eyesight, for these are privileges which God and Nature hath

* Mullett, *op. cit., passim.*

embued me with, and these I cannot be denied, but by him that will deny me a being." Another merging of the philosophy of happiness with liberal political thought in the eighteenth century stems back, indeed, to Leibnitz's theory of human perfectibility, which was applied by Christian Frederick von Wolff in his elaborate eight-volume *Jus Naturæ Methodo scientifica pertractatum* (Frankfurt, 1740–1748); von Wolff, in turn, was digested, drawn upon, and popularized by Emerich de Vattel, whose *Law of Nations* was a political manual for John Adams, James Wilson, Thomas Jefferson and many other Revolutionary statesmen. John Adams did not consider the matter open to question as being a novel theory of government: "Upon this point all speculative politicians will agree, that the happiness of society is the end of government, as all divine and moral philosophers will agree that the happiness of the individual is the end of man. From this principle it will follow that the form of government which communicates ease, comfort, security, or, in one word, happiness, to the greatest number of persons, and in the greatest degree, is the best." Jefferson only indicated in the Declaration certain unalienable rights and *among these* were life, liberty, and the pursuit of happiness. He knew the long history of the concept of natural rights and the varying enumerations that had been made by classical writers. Like Adams, he chose the inclusive term rather than the narrow word "property." That he differed with Locke in the choice of this phrase is infinitely less important than that he and the people for whom he spoke grounded their Declaration upon Locke's great justification of revolution. For revolution, in both the Jeffersonian and the Lockian sense, is merely the ultimate means of pursuing happiness, whereby the people may "institute new Government, laying its foundation on such principles and organizing its powers in such form, as to them shall seem most likely to effect their Safety and Happiness." This assertion, indeed, was a new declaration among nations, and the convictions that led to it had been long in maturing. Precisely one hundred years before Jefferson justified revolution by "the Laws of Nature and of Nature's God," Philip Ludwell (a great-grandfather of the Virginian who moved the resolution of independence) declared on June 28, 1676, that Bacon's rebellion was "contrarie to the Law of God or Man." But Philip Ludwell spoke for the seventeenth century and Hobbes and Filmer; his great-grandson, with Jefferson, moved in the tradition of Locke, Bolingbroke and Vattel.*

This is not to imply that Jefferson was guilty of plagiarizing the works of the classical authors on the subject of government. Some have seen similarity of phrase in the Declaration and in the second treatise by Locke; others have seen parallels between it and a passage in James Wilson's pamphlet, *Considerations on the Nature and Extent of the Legislative Authority of the British Parliament*. But even if Jefferson had "copied from any particular and previous writing," even if he had used an identifiable model — and his colleagues in Congress would have agreed as to the excellence of Locke — the most that would be proved by this is that he had failed to be original in an enterprise where originality would have been fatal. The greatness of his achievement, aside from the fact that he created one of the outstanding literary documents of the world and of all time, was that he identified its sublime purpose with the roots of liberal traditions that spread back to England, to Scotland, to Geneva, to Holland, to Germany, to Rome, and to Athens. In the fundamental statement of national purpose for a people who were to embrace many races and many creeds, nothing could have been more appropriate than that the act renouncing the ties of consanguinity should at the same time have drawn its philosophical justification from traditions common to all.

* Parrington, *op. cit.* (New York, 1927), p. 343–344; Ray Forrest Harvey, *Jean Jacques Burlamaqui* (Chapel Hill, 1937), pp. 106–140; Gilbert Chinard, *Thomas Jefferson: The Apostle of Americanism* (Boston, 1939), p. 71ff.; but *cf.* H. L. Ganter, "Jefferson's 'Pursuit of Happiness' and Some Forgotten Men," *William and Mary Quarterly*, 2d ser., XVI, (1936), 422–34, 558–85. Locke used the phrase "pursuit of happiness" at least three times, though not in a political context. The quotation from John Adams is given in Harvey, *op. cit.*, p. 118; that from John Hall is quoted by E. A. Beller in the *Huntington Library Quarterly*, (1943), VI, 212; that from Philip Ludwell is in the *Virginia Magazine of History* and Biography, (1894), I, 178. I am indebted to Dr. John H. Powell of the University of Delaware for drawing my attention to the relationship of Vattel, von Wolff, and Leibnitz, an area of study that has been explored by Albert de Lapradelle in the introduction to Charles G. Fenwick's translation of the 1758 edition of Vattel's *Law of Nations* (vol. III, Carnegie Institution of Washington, 1916). The statement of Adams, quoted above, is almost a paraphrase of the following by Vattel: "'The end or aim of civil society is to procure for its citizens the necessities, the comforts, and the pleasures of life, and, in general, their happiness; to secure to each the peaceful enjoyment of his property and a sure means of obtaining justice; and finally to defend the whole body against all external violence." *Ibid.*, p. 13.

Mercantilism and the American Revolution

by

LAWRENCE A. HARPER

[From *The Canadian Historical Review*, XXIII (March 1942), 2–15. Reprinted by permission.]

Historians disagree concerning the role of the mercantilist system in causing the American Revolution. George Bancroft's account of the relationship between mercantilism and the American Revolution was expressive of the influence of the free-trade principles toward which he was favorably inclined in the 1840's. It was Bancroft's conclusion that the Navigation Acts and the mercantilist system were exploitative of the colonies, without the latter receiving any reciprocal advantages, and that the Acts were therefore a primary cause of the American Revolution.[1]

Some dissent from this point of view was registered by Mellen Chamberlain in 1889. The latter, while supporting Bancroft's conclusion, nevertheless saw the colonies deriving some economic benefit from the markets guaranteed them under the operation of the mercantilist system.[2] In 1907, George Louis Beer's original researches in the British Foreign Office caused him to conclude that under the mercantilist system the American colonies occupied a relatively favored economic position.[3]

In 1935, Louis Hacker, taking an economic view of the American Revolution as a conflict between English merchant capitalism and nascent colonial capitalism, reached a conclusion not unlike Bancroft's concerning the influence of the Navigation Acts. According to Hacker, "The blows aimed at colonial merchant capitalism through the strengthening of the Acts of Trade and Navigation, the promulgation of the Proclamation Line of 1763 and the passage of the Currency Act of 1764, precipitated the crisis in imperial-colonial relations; and merchant capitalists (whether land specula-tors or traders) were soon converted from contented and loyal subjects into rebellious enemies of the crown." [4]

Hacker was challenged by Charles McLean Andrews, who argued, as did Beer before him, that the colonists derived substantial bene-fit from the operation of the mercantilist system — particularly because of the protection, credit, and market that the mother country offered. It was Andrews's further conclusion that the con-stitutional rather than the economic issue was the critical one fol-lowing 1770. [5]

Like Andrews, Oliver M. Dickerson's study of the Navigation Acts in relationship to the Revolutionary crisis sharply distinguished between the regulatory aspect of the mercantilist system and the attempt to use the acts of trade as revenue-producing devices. According to Dickerson: "there would have been no American Revolution had the navigation and trade system as it existed be-fore 1763 been permitted to operate after that date in the way in which it had heretofore functioned — free of all revenue-producing implications." The latter, Dickerson maintains, were made necessary by the extravagances of George III and the corrupt elements sur-rounding him. [6]

Lawrence Henry Gipson does not disagree essentially with this conclusion. On the other hand, he is more charitable toward the King and his ministers. Gipson sees a real need by the Crown for additional revenues because of the debt incurred by England during the French and Indian Wars, and also for financing imperial ad-ministration. States Gipson: "The mounting Anglo-French rivalry in North America from 1750 onward, the outbreak of hostilities in 1754, and the subsequent nine years of fighting destroyed the old equilibrium, leaving the colonials after 1760 in a highly favored position in comparison with the taxpayers of Great Britain. Attempts on the part of the Crown and Parliament to restore by statute the old balance led directly to the American constitutional crisis, out of which came the Revolutionary War and the establishment of American independence. . . ." [7]

In the following selection, Lawrence A. Harper of the University of California presents his understanding of the role of mercantilism in the American revolutionary crisis, based on a long-time and exhaustive study of the problem.

T HE TERM "mercantilism" is one of those words which have different meanings for different people. On the one hand, George Louis Beer claimed that English mercantilism was a well-balanced system designed for the benefit of the colonies as well as the mother country, and on the other, Sir William Ashley declared that the regulations of English mercantilism were either pious formulas nullified in the actual world of commerce by fraud and evasion, or merely a codification of commercial habits which would have been followed in any case. For reasons which have been explained more fully elsewhere* we shall reject Beer's claim that there was no exploitation and accept the statements of the mercantilists themselves that they planned to exploit the colonies for the benefit of the mother country. We shall deny the Ashley view that there was no actual regulation and conclude from more recent studies of the evidence that the English laws did regulate trade and commerce.

These two conclusions provide us with a working definition of English mercantilism in its colonial aspects. It had as its purpose, exploitation; and as its means, regulation. Both phases of the problem, exploitation *and* regulation, are important. To understand the relationship of mercantilism and the Revolution we must not only analyze the extent to which the colonists were exploited but also consider the skill with which they were regulated.

An analysis of how the colonists were exploited is no easy task, as anyone knows who has struggled with the many statutory ambiguities involved. The calculations involved in estimating the burdens placed upon the colonial economy are complicated. They call for arithmetical computations involving duties, preferences, or drawbacks of such odd amounts as one shilling tenpence and $16/75$ of a twentieth of a penny per pound of tobacco. They run afoul of complicated analyses of costs and close decisions about the inci-

* L. A. Harper, *The English Navigation Laws* (New York, 1939), chap. XIX.

dence of taxation. The answer required some thousands of hours of WPA and NYA labor in tabulating the necessary data and hundreds more in analysing and correlating them, the details of which have been compressed [herein].* All that can be attempted here is to state the conclusions and indicate the grounds upon which they are based. We can, however, simplify our analysis of the mercantilist code which exploited the colonies by dividing it into four parts: first, the basic provisions concerning the trans-Atlantic trade; second, the supplementary measures restricting manufactures; third, the subsidiary rules with reference to the American trade; and fourth, the much discussed measures enacted after the French and Indian War.

In examining the first part, we find that the basic provisions concerning the trans-Atlantic trade placed a heavy burden upon the colonies. By means of the Navigation Acts, England attempted both to keep foreign vessels out of the colonies and to enable English merchants to share in the more profitable parts of the trans-Atlantic trade. The enumeration of key colonial exports in various Acts from 1660 to 1766 and the Staple Act of 1663 hit at colonial trade both coming and going. The Acts required the colonies to allow English middlemen to distribute such crops as tobacco and rice and stipulated that if the colonies would not buy English manufactures, at least they should purchase their European goods in England. The greatest element in the burden laid upon the colonies was not the taxes assessed. It consisted in the increased costs of shipment, transshipment, and middleman's profits arising out of the requirement that England be used as an *entrepôt*.

The burdens were somewhat lightened by legislation favoring the colonies, but not as much as is usually alleged. The suppression of tobacco production in England, for example, was comparatively unimportant to the colonies, since the great quantities of colonial tobacco re-exported caused its price to be determined by a world rather than by an English market. Moreover, the motive was not goodwill for the colonists but fiscal, since the heavy revenues

* L. A. Harper, "The Effect of the Navigation Acts on the Thirteen Colonies" (in *The Era of the American Revolution*, ed. by Richard B. Morris, New York, 1939).
Subsequent footnotes in Professor Harper's article had to be omitted here because of their great length. — Editor.

derived from tobacco could be collected more easily at the water-front than upon the farm. Likewise, although colonial shipbuilders and shipowners approved the clauses of the Navigation Acts which eliminated Dutch rivals, they did not need such protection. They had managed to carry cargoes and to build ships which could be sold in the world market before the laws were enacted and they continued to do so after the Revolution. The fact is that colonial shipowners suffered, directly, and colonial shipbuilders, indirectly, under the Navigation Acts — since other clauses enabled English shipowners (as contrasted with American) to carry 80 per cent of the trade between the British Isles and the Thirteen Colonies whereas they carried only 20 per cent after the Revolution.

Similarly the drawbacks, bounties, and tariff preferences, of which we are so often reminded, did not materially offset the burdens placed upon the trans-Atlantic trade. The drawbacks paid by English customs authorities on foreign products re-exported to the colonies should not be listed as a benefit to the colonies. There would have been no duties to be drawn back except for the requirement that the colonists purchase their European goods in England. The portion of the duties which England retained, while less than it might have been, was obviously greater than nothing at all. Likewise, *bounties paid upon English manufactures exported* to the colonies were of advantage to the English producer, who received them whether his goods were exported to the colonies or anywhere else, rather than of benefit to the colonial consumer who otherwise would, and often did, buy competitive European goods.

On the other hand, however, the bounties paid upon colonial products were of real advantage to the colonies. They sustained the growth of indigo in South Carolina, did much to foster the development of naval stores in North Carolina, encouraged the lumber industry in New England, and at the end of the colonial period averaged more than £65,000 a year for the Thirteen Colonies alone. Similarly the preferences granted colonial products were beneficial in so far as they operated. Although they had no effect upon such commodities as tobacco and rice and their effect upon other commodities is somewhat uncertain, colonial raw silk, naval stores, and lumber definitely benefited. Yet the total sum represented by such preferences was never great and it is doubtful wheither the benefit the Thirteen Colonies thus derived amounted to even one-twentieth of that obtained by the British West Indian planters, who, in the year 1773 alone, pocketed £446,000, thanks to a preferential rate which enabled their sugar to hold the English market despite a five-shilling-per-hundred-weight differential in price.

The uncertainties underlying many of our calculations do not permit an exact statement, but judging from calculations for the year 1773, it would seem that after all proper allowances have been made for bounties and other preferences, the net burden imposed upon the Thirteen Colonies by the restraints upon the trans-Atlantic trade was between two million and seven million dollars a year. In these days of astronomical budgets such figures do not seem especially impressive, but the annual per capita burden represented by the lower estimate would come close to meeting all the expenses of operating the national government during Washington's administration, in addition to paying the current expenses of government, have raised in twelve years (from 1790–1801) a sum sufficient to pay both the domestic and foreign debt incurred by the United States Government during the Revolutionary War.

When we turn to the second part of our discussion, the supplementary measures restricting manufacture, we find a difference of opinion concerning the effect of English restrictions upon manufacturing wool, hats, and iron. The earlier tendency was to dismiss the regulations as immaterial, but recently some have swung the pendulum to the other extreme and argue that the restraints were very important. Neither extreme appears to accord with the facts. In the case of hats, proximity to the source of supply of furs and the comparatively simple process of manufacturing had led to the development of an industry, which appears to have been injured by the legislation. But the hat industry played only a minor part in the total economy. Woollen manufactures were, of course, much more important, but there is much evidence to indicate that here the English prohibitions had little material effect. The colonies found that they were handicapped by an inadequate supply of good wool when they tried to develop homespun goods at the time of the Revolution — and even as late as 1791 Hamilton found that an adequate supply of labor was one of the chief stumbling blocks to his program for encouraging industry. It required an embargo, a war, and a protective tariff before large-scale woollen manufacturing began to develop, and it did not pass beyond the household stage until many years after being freed of English mercantilism — which, incidentally, had never forbidden the manufacture of homespun for domestic use or local distribution.

In the case of iron manufactures the British legislation encouraged the development of pig and bar iron and tried to discourage the manufacture of more advanced forms, but in both respects the influence of the legislation is doubtful. Because of the proximity of iron ore to forests America had a great advantage in producing crude iron, before coke replaced charcoal, and probably did not need legislative encouragement. With such an advantage in producing crude iron it was only natural that some more advanced iron articles would be produced in the colonies, whatever thoroughgoing mercantilists might dream about having the crude iron sent over to England and having it returned in the form of pots, pans, and other manufactures.

The various disallowances of colonial laws which were intended to foster colonial manufacturing further illustrate the English intention of discouraging it, but, despite that intent, English mercantilism as a whole probably had a greater tendency to promote than to hinder colonial industry. The colonies' most dangerous industrial competitors were in many respects not the English, but the Dutch, the Germans, and other Europeans — to say nothing of the natives of India — against whose competition the provisos of the Staple Act of 1663 provided a very useful tariff barrier. Moreover, the large sums which mercantilism withheld from the colonies reduced their available cash, and probably forced many colonists to use homespun or other American products instead of buying British.

The third point of our inquiry into colonial exploitation by England should not detain us long. Until the Molasses Act of 1733 the inter-American trade had been left virtually alone except for the requirement that the English colonies trade in English or colonial ships. Even after 1733, the prohibitive duties on foreign sugar, molasses, and rum were usually evaded. Such evasion required bribery, fraud, or concealment, which probably served as a mildly protective tariff in favor of the British sugar islands, but the prices quoted in the Thirteen Colonies for sugar, molasses, and rum do not indicate that the legislation had any radical effect upon the trade.

The fourth part of our inquiry — that relating to the period after 1763 — is a different matter. The researches of Schlesinger and others have demonstrated how the British measures of that period aroused the resentment of the merchants, who unleashed an avalanche of agitation which soon went beyond their control. The agitation was not directed toward revolution at first, but agitation by its very nature promotes conditions favorable for revolution — and revolution followed as a natural sequence. Yet, conceding all the irritation thus aroused, we must still face the questions: Were the measures unduly exploitive? Did they fundamentally upset the economic equilibrium? Were they fatal ills which would inevitably lead to the death of the Empire, or merely minor upsets which the Empire might have recovered — granted otherwise favorable conditions and good luck?

In reviewing the period it does not seem fair to blame British mercantilism for prescribing regulations which were demanded by the circumstances of the time. The British currency and land policies seem to fall under this category. The restrictions upon paper money undoubtedly distressed those who lacked funds, but they merely affirmed a truth which Americans had to learn from sad experience — that in the eighteenth century at least, no political alchemy could transmute paper into gold. Similarly the Proclamation of 1763 and the Quebec Act of 1774 essentially concerned imperial problems and American imitation of the policy after independence was not mere flattery but a tribute to its inherent soundness. The measures disappointed those who had hoped to acquire fortunes from land speculation, but what else could the British have done? Neither they nor the United States Government after them could allow private individuals to stir up trouble by moving into Indian territory before the way had been prepared for settlement by negotiations which extinguished the Indians' claims to the area. In view of the British debt it was merely good fiscal policy to charge for the land, and the prices and terms of sale proposed by the British mercantilists seem very reasonable when compared with the prices and terms adopted by the Federal government after 1787. And what solution did the Thirteen States themselves find for the conflicting claims to the territory west of the Alleghenies except to create a new governmental unit?

To one who frankly does not profess to be an expert on the point, it is difficult to understand how British mercantilism discriminated materially against the colonists. It is true that in the maneuvering for land grants, British interests sometimes clashed with colonial interests, but we hear fully as much about clashes between different colonial groups. Both the small frontiersmen and the big speculators were charged more for land than they were accustomed to pay, but it was not as much as they were to be charged by the United States Government thereafter. In the readjustments which accompanied the establishment of the new policies the fur traders of the Thirteen Colonies suffered somewhat because of the machinations of British opponents but their loss was not great, and in any event by the Revolutionary period trade in furs formed only a negligible fraction of the colonial economy.

The pre-Revolutionary taxation measures, however, are a different matter, and one for which British mercantilism must bear full responsibility. Yet in analyzing the figures we find that the average annual revenue raised by the Sugar Acts, the Townshend Acts, and all the other taxes collected in the Thirteen Colonies by the British government amounted to only 31,000 pounds. This sum barely exceeded the indirect taxes which were collected on colonial merchandise passing through England. Moreover, both the taxes collected indirectly in England and directly in the colonies failed to equal the bounties which the British government was paying to the colonies — to say nothing of the advantages which they were deriving from preferential duties on their shipments to England. More interesting still, calculated on an annual per capita basis, the taxes collected during the Revolutionary period directly in the colonies and indirectly in England, totaled less than one seventh of the taxes assessed at the beginning of the century.

Yet even though the amount of taxation was not great, we must consider the possibility that the form of its assessment detrimentally affected colonial interests. The Tea Act, for one, definitely injured the illicit trade in tea by so reducing the price of the legal article that it lessened, if it did not eliminate, the profit from smuggling. However unfair smugglers may have thought them, such tactics can hardly be said to have injured the economy of the country — especially since tea was not a pivotal commodity.

Molasses, the rum which was made from it, and the provision trade which accompanied it, however, were vital factors in colonial economy, and historians have often called attention to their importance in such books as *Rum, Romance, and Rebellion,* by Charles W. Taussig, published in 1928. The Sugar Act of 1764 served notice that the British Government intended to make its regulations effective when it lowered the duty on foreign sugar and molasses and prohibited the importation of foreign rum entirely. The provisions concerning sugar and rum were comparatively immaterial since no great quantities were imported, but the duty of threepence per gallon on molasses was another matter, since literally millions of gallons came from the foreign West Indies. Many feared that the trade could not bear a tax of threepence per gallon, and in response to their pleas the duty was reduced in 1766 to one penny per gallon and the tax was assessed on both British and foreign molasses. The excitement aroused by these taxes leads one to look for evidence of the havoc which they wrought in trade, but an examination of the wholesale prices of molasses does not disclose any noticeable change attributable to the legislation. And if we carry our investigations further we find that the tax which the Federal Government placed and kept upon imports of molasses after 1790 almost equaled the threepence per gallon placed upon foreign molasses in 1764 and materially exceeded the one penny duty retained after 1766. In brief, whatever the connection between rum and romance, the statistics of colonial trade disclose no correlation between rum and rebellion.

Insofar as the statistics can be followed, the correlation between wine and rebellion is much closer. The Sugar Act of 1764 had also placed a duty upon wines, which gave those imported by way of Britain a preferential rate of three pounds per ton. The preference was not sufficient to enable the English to capture the trade in Madeira wine, but it enabled them to gain a flourishing trade in port, which previously had been negligible. Yet such an infringement of colonial taste hardly seems to justify a revolt — especially when we note that the quantity involved was not large, and that by the post-Revolutionary period Americans preferred port and other wines to Madeira.

Thus, an analysis of the economic effects of British mercantilism fails to establish its exploitive aspects as the proximate cause of the Revolution. The only measures which afforded a sufficient economic grievance were the *entrepôt* provisions of the Navigation Acts, which governed the trans-Atlantic trade. They helped to create a fundamental economic unbalance, but cannot be connected directly with the Revolution. The colonists had lived under them for more than a century without desiring independence and even in the Revolutionary period with few exceptions the *entrepôt* provisions were accepted as the mother country's due for the protection which she afforded. In fact, the official representatives of the colonies were willing to guarantee the British commercial system provided that the measures of political taxation were withdrawn. If there were any inexorable economic forces which were inevitably drawing the colonies toward revolution, they are hard to detect and the colonists were unaware of them.

Anyone who maintains that the Revolution resulted from the inevitable clash of competing capitalisms must reckon with several points: That burdens upon the trans-Atlantic trade were proportionately greater at the beginning of the eighteenth century than in 1776; that the restraints of the land and currency policies were basically the same as those prescribed by the Federal government; and that after 1766 the taxes laid on molasses by Britain were less than those imposed by the United States after 1790. He should also explain why the surplus colonial capital alleged to be bursting its confines did not venture into the manufacturing enterprises which the law did not prohibit; why the colonists did not finance their own middlemen in England; and, finally, why they did not pay their debts. If by a clash of expanding capitalism is meant that colonists with money were irritated because their freedom of action was restrained by outside regulation, one must immediately concede that the charge is justified; but such colonial resentment seems more properly classified as a political rather than an economic factor. It is merely an old point dressed in new garb, and was better expressed by John Adams when he declared that the American Revolution began when the first plantation was settled.

When we turn, however, from the economic effects of mercantilism to its regulatory aspects, we are faced with a different story. We can establish a direct correlation between mercantilism and the Revolution. Although earlier English regulations had been reasonably satisfactory, the regulatory technique of the British government under George III was pitifully defective. As a mother country, Britain had much to learn. Any modern parents' magazine could have told George III's ministers that the one mistake not to make is to take a stand and then to yield to howls of anguish. It was a mistake which the British Government made repeatedly. It placed a duty of threepence per gallon on molasses, and when it encountered opposition, reduced it to one penny. It provided for a Stamp Act, and withdrew it in the face of temper tantrums. It provided for external taxes to meet the colonial objections and then yielded again by removing all except one. When finally it attempted to enforce discipline, it was too late. Under the circumstances, no self-respecting child — or colonist — would be willing to yield.

Moreover, British reforming zeal came at a very bad time. The colonists were in a particularly sensitive state due to the postwar deflation and the economic distress which accompanied it. The British also attempted to exert unusual control at a time when the removal of the French from Canada had minimized the colonists' dependence upon Britain. Most important of all, the reforms followed one another too rapidly.

In social reform, irritation often is to be measured not so much by what a regulation attempts to achieve as by the extent to which it changes established habits. The early history of English mercantilism itself offers a good illustration of the point. Bitter complaints came from Virginia and Barbados when tobacco and sugar were first enumerated because those colonies had become accustomed to conditions of comparatively free trade, whereas few or no complaints were heard from Jamaica, which had developed under the restrictive system. The mercantilist system was geared for leisurely operation and before George III's reign succeeded by virtue of that fact. Its early restraints led to Bacon's rebellion in Virginia, but fortunately for the mother country the pressure against New England was deferred until the next decade when it, too, led to an explosion in the form of revolt against Andros. These uprisings were separated both geographically and chronologically, so that neither attained dangerous proportions, and both were followed by a reasonably satisfactory settlement of at least some of the colonial grievances.

During the Revolutionary era, however, the tempo of reform was not leisurely. Doubtless all the colonists were not irritated by any one British reform, but each individual had his own feeling of grievance which enabled him to agree fervently with the complaints of others against British policy and thus add to the heated tempers of the time. The politician who objected to the political implications in taxation reforms found an audience in the land speculators and frontiersmen who complained that the colonists were being deprived of the reward of their blood and suffering by the Proclamation of 1763 and the Quebec Act of 1774. Debtors and inflationists chimed in to tell of the iniquities of the Currency Act; lawyers and printers could not forget the threat to their interests in the Stamp Act. On Sundays the preachers thundered against the dangers of popery in Quebec and voiced their fear that Britain planned to establish an Anglican Church in the colonies. The merchant was always ready to explain not merely how harmful British taxes were to colonial economy, but how irksome were the new administrative rules and regulations. Such chronological and geographical barriers as existed were overcome and a community of antagonisms was maintained by the Committees of Correspondence and other agitators, but such revolutionary forces could not have succeeded if the different elements of the colonies had not recently experienced a mutual sense of grievance.

In short, many of the misunderstandings which have arisen in connection with mercantilism and the American Revolution have grown out of the failure to distinguish between the two phases of mercantilism: exploitation and regulation. The fact that the colonists were exploited by English mercantilism does not necessarily mean that mercantilism caused the American Revolution. Economic forces are not magnets which inexorably move men in predetermined patterns. For better or for worse, men try to regulate their economic as well as their political destiny. A large part of governmental activity consists in attempting to mold economic conduct and to minimize the friction which results from clashes or constraints. English mercantilism was such an attempt. It succeeded rather well in minimizing friction until 1764. For the next decade it bungled badly, and the penalty was the loss of the Thirteen Colonies.

Radicals and Conservatives after Independence

by

OSCAR AND MARY HANDLIN

["Radicals and Conservatives in Massachusetts after Independence," from the *New England Quarterly*, XVII (September 1944), 343–355. Reprinted by permission.]*

In the 1940's, Charles A. Beard's argument that the movement for the Constitution had its inception in the economic interests of the early American upper class was amplified in the work of Merrill Jensen. The latter extended Beard's thesis about the framing of the Constitution back into the so-called "critical period," roughly from the conclusion of the Revolutionary War until the assembling of the Constitutional Convention. According to Jensen, government under the Articles of Confederation was not the hopeless fiasco that conservative historians like John Fiske had made it out to be.[1]

Under the Articles of Confederation, asserted Jensen, there was a reasonable amount of stability and prosperity for the generality of the population which was satisfied to let the form of government remain as it was. Like Beard before him, Jensen sees the Constitutional Convention as a class movement brought about by a minority of the population to further their economic interests. The minority, contends Jensen, consisted of "conservatives" who, between 1776 and 1789, were bent upon frustrating the egalitarian tendencies of the radicals.[2]

The Handlins are plainly dubious about this thesis; at least insofar as it applies to Massachusetts. To begin with, they deny the

* This note was written in the course of a study of the role of government in American economy, under the auspices of the Committee on Research in Economic History of the Social Science Research Council.

continuity of "radicalism" and "conservatism" between 1776 and 1789. Secondly, they deny that social groupings in the American population were as well-defined as Beard and Jensen said they were. Finally, the Handlins are less inclined than Beard and Jensen to regard political behavior as motivated by economic status.

The Handlins have written a dissenting note rather than a repudiation of the Beard and Jensen thesis. The same verdict might apply, as well, to the work of Robert E. Thomas in criticism of Beard's An Economic Interpretation of the Constitution.[3]

Oscar Handlin is Associate Professor of History at Harvard.

S TUDENTS of the American Revolution soon become aware that a division of opinion existed among those who sustained the patriot cause. Thirty-five years ago, Carl Becker discovered, in an acute analysis of New York politics before independence, that the brightly colored picture of conflict between colony and empire concealed the subtler shadowings of a significant cleavage among the Americans themselves. The fight against England was involved with and related to an internal struggle for power.[*]

Since 1909, careful research has explored the nature of the domestic divisions and their connection with the causes of the revolt against the mother country. These studies found that in New England, by and large, two groups contested the control of the struggle with Britain. The merchants and their allies in the dominant economic group in the colonies, harried by the new direction of British colonial policy, turned for assistance against England to elements lower in the social scale, to "their natural enemies in society." [†] Men of substance and property, concerned primarily with the adjustment of their own grievances, they calculated on limiting the nature of the conflict and moderating its pace, and were ever apprehensive lest, in the excitement of the contest, the machinery of

[*] *Cf.* Carl L. Becker, *History of Political Parties in the Province of New York, 1760–1776* (Madison, 1909).

[†] A. M. Schlesinger, *Colonial Merchants and the American Revolution, 1763–1776* (New York, 1918), p. 307.

state slip into the hands of those whose aid they courted. More cautious and more moderate as the crisis approached, more aware of the benefits of remaining within the empire, the group contained a substantial number who would not tolerate the course of events that precipitated the break, and so became Tories. But though thus split at the crucial moment into moderates and loyalists, the merchants and their satellites had, during the preceding fifteen years, on the question of relation to the mother country, acted as a coherent conservative party.

Against them were arrayed elements which saw in the Revolution a strategic opportunity for wresting political power and privilege out of the hands of the groups which had dominated colonial government since the beginning of the century. The urban artisans and laborers, the small farmers, the frontier settlers, under-represented and underprivileged, aggrieved against England on their own score, used collaboration with the conservatives as a lever with which to earn power in the state. With only a slight stake in the old order, these had little patience with moderation and, in addition, found their main chance in the dilemma of the merchants. Anxious to precipitate the issue, extremists in their demands, they were the radicals.*

The validity of this interpretation of the period before the Revolution is not so open to question as is the thesis that this same party division persisted beyond 1776. Mr. Becker himself set the theme for such question in the epilogue of his study:

> . . . The differentiation of loyalist and revolutionist had not yet been completed before the beginning of new party alignments are [sic] to be observed. . . . These new alignments were merely the revival, in a slightly different form, of the fundamental party divisions which had existed from the time of the stamp act. The fear of British oppression was transformed into the fear of oppression by the national government, while the demand of the unfranchised classes for recognition . . . was to find its ultimate answer only in the achievements of Jefferson and Jackson.†

* The general position is summarized in Curtis P. Nettels, *Roots of American Civilization* (New York, 1938), pp. 621 ff.
† Becker, pp. 274 ff.

This concept, pushed further, implicitly and explicitly, by successive writers, has entered into much of the newer historical thinking on the early national period, and has recently been restated by Merrill Jensen, who found the same division into radicals and conservatives after as before 1776:

> The basic social forces in colonial life were not eliminated by the Declaration of Independence. There was no break in the underlying conflict between party and party representing fundamental divisions in American society.*

The thesis that revolutionary parties continued into the post-revolutionary era supplies a comfortable link with their putative descendants of the end of the century. But whatever the nature of the connection of Federalists and Democratic Republicans with conservatives and radicals, the two decades after 1775 present problems which cannot be solved in terms of this simple explanation. A re-examination of this thesis even from the material in commonly available sources and standard accounts reveals serious deficiencies. As applied to Massachusetts, at least, it is misleading and inaccurate, and fails to explain the most significant developments in the twenty years between the outbreak of war and the emergence of the parties of Jefferson and Hamilton. It cannot account reasonably for the activities of the leading personalities in the State between 1775 and 1795; it does not square with the political reactions of the State's economic groups; it leaves no place for the changes in class structure and composition; and it cannot explain the impact of new issues.

How can the significant statesmen of the period be fitted into a consistent two-party system that reaches back before 1774? † By 1790, Hancock and Bowdoin had emerged as leaders of two opposing groups; by 1797 Gerry and Samuel Adams had become Republicans of sorts while John Adams was a Federalist of sorts. Yet on the

* Merrill Jensen, *The Articles of Confederation: An Interpretation of the Social-Constitutional History of the American Revolution, 1774–1781* (Madison, 1940), p. 7.

† In this and succeeding paragraphs, reference is made, in the absence of other citations, to biographical accounts in the *Dictionary of American Biography* and Alden Bradford, *Biographical Notices . . .* (Boston, 1842).

revolutionary issues, on the questions arising out of relations with England, they had taken identical, radical, positions. And what was true of the brightest luminaries was likewise true of the lesser, younger lights; Pickering and Sullivan, Strong and Austin divided later, but on revolutionary questions they had been united.

Nor was this a surface unity only, concealing fundamental differences under the pressure of an emergency which demanded cooperation. For even the crisis did not create concord everywhere. Although all the persons here mentioned were radicals, there were conservatives before independence, and the course of the struggle heightened rather than abated differences. In the Continental Congress until 1776, for instance, there was a division over the extent of legitimate British authority and over the measures proper to meet the coercive acts. But here all the Massachusetts delegates acted together. In Philadelphia all New Englanders seemed to shine as democrats; John Adams was a radical fully as "arch" as Sam when compared with Galloway, Dickinson, or even Jay.*

But if all those prominent after 1775 were radicals, were there no conservatives in Massachusetts before that date? The question answers itself. The closest Bay approximations to Jay and Dickinson were Hutchinson, Bernard, and Oliver, the respectable established merchants of the provincial metropolis. There were some merchants, particularly those like Hancock and Bowdoin from newly risen families, who were radical for individual reasons.† There were others like John Andrews who chose independence when the issue was clearly drawn.‡ But the most prominent and the most important cherished the advantages which came from their position in the British trading system, and preferred unity with the mother country.§

In Massachusetts, sooner than elsewhere, the conservatives perceived the true character of the struggle. They had of course organ-

---

* Cf. Schlesinger, pp. 244, 410 ff., and 433; Nettels, p. 646; Becker, p. 253; and Jensen, pp. 118 and 127.

† For Hancock, cf. Schlesinger, p. 103 ff.; and John Adams, *Works* . . . (Boston, 1850), II, 215–216.

‡ For Andrews, cf. the long footnote in Schlesinger, p. 434; also p. 281 ff.

§ Cf. in general, C. M. Andrews, "Boston Merchants and the Non-Importation Movement," *Publications* of the Colonial Society of Massachusetts, *Transactions, 1916–17* (Boston, 1918), XIX, 159 ff.

ized to resist the trade laws after 1763.* But they did not, as did their kind in New York and Pennsylvania, pursue the chimerical hope of tempering or controlling the radicals. There were no moderates in Massachusetts, no Friends of Liberty and Trade to counterbalance the Sons of Liberty. The conservatives knew the potential power of those beneath them in the social scale, feared it, and would have no truck with it. By 1766 the most prominent were already distrustful. Three years later, Governor Bernard noted that he has "the generality of respectable Men on his Side," while in New York "they are more generally against Government." †

After 1770, as prosperity returned, many more refused any longer to participate in the protest movement. Their minds were made up earlier than those of the New York conservatives who eventually became Tories but still participated in the Third Provincial Congress in 1776. Long before, the loyalist character of Massachusetts conservatives was clear; their conversion "occurred earlier than in the other provinces." ‡

When the break came, the most prominent emigrated. The Hutchinsons, Vassalls, and Brattles went, and with them more than two hundred others in 1775 alone.§ Some were induced to stay by diverse personal considerations. But in either case, they played no part in the politics of the new state. Among those who remained, the very loyalty to the mother country, the conviction of her ultimate success, would have kept them out of politics at least until the peace, even had they been able to efface the taint of their toryism. The original division between radicals and conservatives in Massachusetts could therefore not have persisted beyond 1775.‖ By then

* Schlesinger, 60 ff.

† Edward Channing and A. C. Coolidge, *Barrington-Bernard Correspondence* . . . (Cambridge, 1912), p. 142; Schlesinger, p. 92. The evolution of policy in New York is carefully traced by Becker, pp. 86 ff., 112 ff., 195, and 264.

‡ *Cf.* Andrews, XIX, 243; Schlesinger, pp. 240–257, 260, and 604; Becker, pp. 207 and 274; and Virginia D. Harrington, *New York Merchant on the Eve of the Revolution* (New York, 1935), pp. 348–349.

§ *Cf.* Schlesinger, p. 604; and Lorenzo Sabine, *Biographical Sketches of the Loyalists of the American Revolution* . . . (Boston, 1864), I, 25. There are more complete lists in James H. Stark, *Loyalists of Massachusetts* . . . (Boston, 1910); and in Justin Winsor's *Memorial History of Boston* (Boston, 1881), III, 175 ff.

‖ *Cf.* A. E. Morse, *Federalist Party in Massachusetts to the Year 1800* (Princeton, 1909), p. 11.

the only participants in the struggle for independence were the radicals. The other side disappeared completely, either physically or by a withdrawal from politics. All the subsequent divisions and alignments originated from within the once united radical party.

Those who maintain that the same divisions were always present and persisted unchanged rest their case upon the contention that the break with England was not, after all, the true test of radicalism and conservatism, that opposing ideas of the nature of the state and divergent social attitudes determined fundamental party groupings which emerged into the open, once the obscuring issue of independence was cleared away.* If actions are an index to men's ideas — and in this period they supply almost the only available index — such a dichotomy cannot be established for the leading figures. The state constitution of 1780 and Shays's Rebellion, issues laden with social import, failed to split the prominent men in the State; the two Adamses, Hancock and Bowdoin, Gerry and Strong, shared the same attitudes. Even the antagonisms raised by the Federal Constitution failed to produce a lasting and open break among these men. The objections to the document, as summarized by Mrs. Warren, were limited and largely met by the proposed amendments. In any case, immediately after ratification, Strong and Gerry, the delegates who had refused to sign at Philadelphia, were both co-operating with groups which had fought bitterly for adoption. It is quite revealing in this respect to find the Ames brothers, who later divided so sharply, both welcoming the new instrument of central government.†

The rare occasions on which social ideas were formally expressed

* For example, Jensen, pp. 10 and 57.
† It is unnecessary here to review the controversy between Beard and Libby. Even the former would acknowledge that, in 1790, "the Federalist-Republican schism" was not yet "clearly developed." Gerry was not a Republican until after 1796 (cf. Charles A. Beard, Economic Origins of Jeffersonian Democracy [New York, 1915], pp. 10 ff., 43, 62, and 73). For the state of parties in 1790, cf. the illuminating letter by Gerry to Bowdoin, June 25, 1790, Massachusetts Historical Society Collections, Seventh Series (Boston, 1907), VI, 196. Cf. also Charles Warren, "Elbridge Gerry, James Warren, Mercy Warren and . . . the Federal Constitution in Massachusetts," Massachusetts Historical Society Proceedings (Boston, 1932), LXIV, 162; and Charles Warren, Jacobin and Junto . . . (Cambridge, 1931), p. 44. On the state constitution, cf. H. A. Cushing, History of the Transition from Provincial to Commonwealth Government in Massachusetts (New York, 1896).

fail to furnish a firm basis for party divisions. When John Adams did outline a system of government in 1776, he was, at the same time, condemned for being too popular and too aristocratic.* A period which could take him for the author of *Common Sense* could hardly have been aware of deep party differences, based on ideas of the state.† Nor does the historian's perspective simplify the task of pigeonholing Adams on the basis of such divisions; any attempt to do so must produce contradictions. In a recent work, for instance, the Braintree lawyer appears at least six times as a conservative, eight times as a radical, and on one page, actually as a radical in the text and as a conservative in its footnote.‡ At the root of this confusion is the inescapable fact that specific instances of party division must either be drawn from questions arising out of the imperial problem,§ or be created by anticipating party affiliations which arose twenty years later, identifying those who became Federalists as conservatives and those who became Democrats as radicals.‖

But even if one disregards the affiliations of individual men as aberrations, and focuses attention upon broader social groupings, the thesis of continuous party development still does not conform to the actual alignment of the social classes in the Commonwealth.

The notion that the radical and conservative parties persisted beyond independence rests upon the assumption that Massachusetts society throughout this period remained divided into two coherent and consistent parts, the merchants on one side, the artisans and farmers on another. This assumption is untrue. The misconception that "the masses in the towns and on the frontier" voiced the same economic and political demands has fathered numerous errors.¶ That they had worked together for independence was no omen of future collaboration. On such vital questions as price-fixing, com-

---

* *Cf.* Patrick Henry to Adams, May 20, 1776, in Adams, *Works*, IV, 201 ff.; also IV, 193 ff.

† *Cf.* Adams, II, 507 ff.

‡ Jensen, pp. 13, 57, 90, 144, 167, and 173; 44, 46, 52, 62, 65, 83, 95, and 118; 85.

§ *Cf.* Jensen, pp. 41, 55, 59, 88, 89, and 115.

‖ That is clearly the case, for instance, when it is said of John Adams in 1775 "that while he was a conservative, he was never really a Federalist" (Jensen, p. 85).

¶ Jensen, p. 10; Nettels, p. 660.

modity control, and representation in the General Court, urban areas — artisans and laborers included — were bitterly hostile to the country sections.*

Far from acting automatically with the farmers, the artisans and other elements frequently supported the merchants against the agriculturalists. Thus the commercial towns rejected the Constitution of 1778 and accepted that of 1780 almost unanimously. Revere and the mechanics meeting at the Green Dragon applied the pressure that helped swing the ratifying convention of 1788 in favor of the Federal Constitution. And Bowdoin was congratulated on his election in 1786 by a committee of manufacturers and tradespeople as well as by a committee of merchants.† In the very nature of the case, the merchants were not numerous enough to control the State or even the towns in which they lived without the support of substantial numbers drawn from the "masses."

It is not proper to speak even of the farmers as a single coherent unit. Various factors — nearness to market, character of husbandry, and length of settlement — often more important in this period than the common roots in the soil, created serious divisions and struggles for control even within purely agricultural towns. Unsettled conditions of government sometimes permitted "Poor People, that had no whare Else to go" and had pitched "upon the ungranted Lands," to oust from the town meeting not the remote land speculator or money investor, but the settled inhabitants who also tilled the soil.‡ Furthermore, the farming regions in the state rarely acted together; against the unanimity of the commercial towns on the two state constitutions, for instance, the agricultural communities offered only diversity. The vote on the ratification of the Federal Constitution also reveals a striking division among the rural towns. Those close to urban areas tended to favor it, but Worcester County opposed it,

---

* On the question of representation, for instance, Plymouth pointed out that the Constitution of 1778 would "opperate to the disadvantage of the Towns bordering on the Sea Coast whenever any Commercial Question may be agitated" (Massachusetts Archives, CLVI, 426).

† Cf. Massachusetts Historical Society Collections, Seventh Series (Boston, 1907), VI, 50–53; and Winsor, III, 196.

‡ Cf. Hancock petitions, Massachusetts Archives, CLXXXI, 102 and 206.

while Berkshire, Hampshire, Bristol, Essex, and the Maine counties show no meaningful pattern at all.*

Social mobility complicated the realignment of the various groups in the revolutionary years and made difficult the perception of interests or the delineation of policy. Emigration created great gaps in the trading communities. While the statistical evidence is fragmentary, other indications, no less valuable, point to a substantial displacement.† Of the nineteen persons mentioned by Andrews as prominent in the Merchants' Club in Boston between 1764 and 1770, for instance, only two remained through the Revolution; one had left in 1768, two had died before 1775, one was insane, and fully thirteen had become Tories.‡ Even the merchants who stayed found their position shaken by changes in the total economic setting. Depreciation presented serious problems to all creditors. The closing of the port of Boston transformed all the conditions of trade, and the old order never returned, for independence ended the State's role in the British trading system. Such men as Bowdoin and Jonathan Jackson lost heavily until the end of hostilities. The position of the old established merchants was difficult to maintain without resorting to new and unestablished methods.§

Into the vacuum created by emigration and by the lack of adaptability of the old merchants, there rushed a host of newcomers. Some were traders from the outlying towns. Others rose from petty retailing, or even from off the farms. Still others were enterprising young men who saw and seized opportunities. Privateering shipowners,

---

* Cf. the map plotted from the votes as given in *Debates and Proceedings in the Convention of the Commonwealth of Massachusetts Held in the Year 1788, and Which Finally Ratified the Constitution of the United States . . .* (Boston, 1856). For other interpretations, cf. R. A. East, "Massachusetts Conservatives in the Critical Period," in *Era of the American Revolution,* edited by R. B. Morris (New York, 1930), p. 365; O. G. Libby, *Geographical Distribution of the Vote of the Thirteen States on the Federal Constitution, 1787–1788* (Madison, 1894), p. 12 ff.; S. B. Harding, *The Contest over the Ratification of the Federal Constitution in the State of Massachusetts* (New York, 1896), pp. 99–100. The broad shadings in Libby's general map tend to minimize the diversities.

† The figure in R. A. East's *Business Enterprise in the American Revolutionary Era* (New York, 1938), note 24, pp. 219–220, is far too low. Almost four times as many left in 1775 before the act of banishment there cited. *Cf.* also note 15, *supra.*

‡ *Cf.* Andrews, XIX, 164.

§ *Cf.* Winsor, IV, 154 ff.

and aggressive newcomers with contacts in the government that assured profits from speculation, contracting, and the purchase of loyalist property, all thrived in a fluid economy which often bewildered the traditional merchant.*

It is not surprising, then, to find the new men ever more important in all the activities of the Commonwealth. Again, statistical evidence is indecisive. If rough quantitative measurements can serve further to substantiate conclusions from social and political data, one can point to the high percentage of newcomers among the purchasers of loyalist estates.† But more important, all the social and political evidence points in the same direction. Revolutionary conditions produced the new merchant, so different in experience, origins, and interests that in 1785 the Senate, stronghold of property and wealth, actually refused to permit the return of the banished Tories because of "the clamours of a few who have plundered their Effects," although the more popular House had agreed.‡ North Shore traders like Cabot, whom straitened family finances had driven from a Harvard hall to a ship's cabin; former mechanics and the sons of mechanics like Gorham and Christopher Gore; former ship captains like Mungo Mackay in Boston; the tanner Timothy Dexter in Newburyport; William Gray, son of a shoemaker in Salem; and, in the West, poor newcomers like Theodore Sedgwick and John Chandler Williams were the characteristic figures of the new era.§

* Cf. East, Business Enterprise, chapter II.

† Using as a test election or appointment by the town meeting to any town office or committee between 1758 and 1774 (cf. Boston Town Records, 1758–1777, Record Commissioners' Reports [Boston, 1886, 1887], vols. XVI and XVIII), a comparison, on the same basis, of ninety-one Suffolk County absentees for whom agents were appointed with those who acquired their estates reveals that 48 per cent of the absentees had held office as compared with only 27 per cent among the purchasers. (The absentee lists are given in Massachusetts Historical Society Proceedings, Second Series, X [Boston, 1896], 162 ff.)

‡ Cf. J. F. Jameson, editor, "Letters of Stephen Higginson, 1783–1804," Annual Report of the American Historical Association, 1896 (Washington, 1897), I, 727.

§ Cf. East, Business Enterprise, p. 65; Stephen W. Williams, Genealogy and History of the Family of Williams (Greenfield, 1847), p. 43; M. C. Crawford, Famous Families of Massachusetts (Boston, 1930), I, 160–161; Winsor, III, 191; and Volume of Records Relating to the Early History of Boston, containing Miscellaneous Papers, Record Commissioners' Report (Boston, 1900), XXIX, 272 and 289.

In these circumstances, to assume a continuous development of a merchant class is to argue that membership in an economic group automatically and immediately shapes political and social points of view. Certainly, in this transitory period when all the problems of government were new, such oversimplification falsifies a complex and involved process. Even excluding such prominent individual deviators as Hancock and Gerry, the merchants needed time to acquire and consolidate control, and even to become conscious of their own identity and interests in the unclear, rapidly changing, and confused condition of the state's economy. The young, the strangers, the newly risen, needed time to discover that they were a class, to sever old ties and establish new ones, to ascertain their interests and discover how to protect them.

The confusion and complexity of the reactions of new social groupings to new problems was evident on many levels of state policy. Nowhere did colonial experience furnish a simple precedent. Rarely was status in 1775 a determining influence, for the status of every group changed continually under the pressure of new conditions and of the very acts of government. In the economic sphere, the decades of paper-money controversy offered no guide to the mazes into which Revolutionary finance plunged the state. Those who had repeatedly sought the cure-all of an adequate circulating medium found the presses, once started, uncontrollable. While everyone scampered for safety, the flood of paper converted many hard-moneyed men into proponents of official inflation and many soft-money men into defenders of the sanctity of contract. In the realm of state government, when the Province Charter of 1691 proved ineffective, some who had defended it in 1775 found attractions in the idea of a new state constitution which they had once fought, while some of those who had earliest demanded a constitution became the bitterest foes of that adopted. Finally, many who had at first opposed centralizing tendencies most vigorously were persuaded by the exigencies of a defenseless commerce after independence that a greater measure of authority had to be vested in the national government.

The groupings which emerged from these issues were not simple. Most important, the groupings on any one issue were not coterminous with those on another. Certainly there were not two clear-cut camps. Where, then, were the extensions of the old radical and conservative parties?

Later, there came a time when the parties of Jefferson and Hamilton attempted to establish a pre-revolutionary ancestry. But it certainly was not theirs legitimately. The new forces which arose in the two decades after Lexington were the products of the problems of those years. The key to their understanding must be sought in the economic and social conditions in which they evolved. The mossy conception of two-party continuity, smooth-seeming and attractive at first sight, has pre-empted the most fertile areas of our thinking and prevented the growth of more fruitful interpretations.

The Spirit of the Constitution

by

CHARLES A. BEARD

[The selection from Charles A. Beard's *The Supreme Court and the Constitution* (New York, 1912) is used with the permission of Miriam Beard Vagts and The Macmillan Company. Copyright 1912 The Macmillan Company.]

Between 1912 and 1914 Charles A. Beard published three books: An Economic Interpretation of the Constitution of the United States, Contemporary American History, *and* The Supreme Court and the Constitution. *Together, these volumes illustrate a maverick quality about Beard's thinking that defies categorization.*

What was Beard's relationship to political progressivism in these years? The answer to this question will not be fully revealed until a much-needed biographical study is made. There can be no doubt that his Economic Interpretation of the Constitution *gave comfort if not commitment to the progressive cause. According to Morton White, Beard's* Contemporary American History *aligned him more definitely with the progressives than did the aforementioned volume.[1] But Beard's* Supreme Court and the Constitution *appeared at a time when progressives, angered by illiberal decisions by the courts on matters affecting legislation for the social welfare and for the regulation of industry, were arguing that it had not been the intent of the framers of the Constitution to grant to the judiciary the right to review legislative acts.*

Beard emphatically denied this conclusion. But his refutation of the progressive position derived from those premises in Beard's book on the Constitution that political progressives of both parties in 1913 were likely to find appealing. It was precisely because the Founding Fathers wanted an additional legal safeguard for property rights, argued Beard, that they implied judicial review of legislation by the courts. One is inclined to wonder at the kind of aid Beard's scholarship was rendering contemporary political progressivism by arriving at an anti-progressive conclusion based on a typically progressive view of the American Constitution.[2]

We have reprinted this selection from one of Beard's lesser-known books because it is a convenient summary of the underlying argument of his more familiar Economic Interpretation of the Constitution. *Along with the trenchant economic analysis it offers, the selection reveals Beard's respect for the Constitution and its framers. True, the latter were not motivated by abstract principles of right and justice, but Beard considered their creativity to have been none the less remarkable for having its origins in self-interest.*

The late Professor Beard was one of America's most distinguished historians and publicists.

THOSE who hold that it was not the intention of the framers of the Constitution to establish judicial control of legislation make much of the opposition aroused by the sporadic attempts of a few state courts to exercise such a control prior to 1787. Dean Trickett cites the cases and exclaims: "These then are the precedents!" Mr. Boudin cites them and also exclaims: "Such were the state 'precedents,' and such was the temper of the people at the time of the Philadelphia convention met to frame the Constitution of the United States." The only trouble with this line of argument is that it leaves out of account the sharp political division existing in the United States in 1787 and the following years.

The men who framed the Federal Constitution were not among the paper-money advocates and stay-law makers whose operations in state legislatures and attacks upon the courts were chiefly responsible, Madison informs us, for the calling of the convention. The framers of the Constitution were not among those who favored the assaults on vested rights which legislative majorities were making throughout the Union. On the contrary, they were, almost without exception, bitter opponents of such enterprises; and they regarded it as their chief duty, in drafting the new Constitution, to find a way of preventing the renewal of what they deemed "legislative tyranny." Examine the rolls of the state conventions that ratified the Constitution after it came from the Philadelphia convention, and compare them with the rolls of the legislatures that had been assailing the rights of property. It was largely because the framers of the Constitution knew the temper and class bias of the state legislatures that they arranged that the new Constitution should be ratified by conventions.

The makers of the Federal Constitution represented the solid, conservative, commercial and financial interests of the country — not the interests which denounced and proscribed judges in Rhode Island, New Jersey and North Carolina, and stoned their houses in New York. The conservative interests, made desperate by the imbecilities of the Confederation and harried by state legislatures, roused themselves from their lethargy, drew together in a mighty effort to establish a government that would be strong enough to pay the national debt, regulate interstate and foreign commerce, provide for national defense, prevent fluctuations in the currency created by paper emissions, and control the propensities of legislative majorities to attack private rights.

It is in the light of the political situation that existed in 1787 that we must inquire whether the principle of judicial control is out of harmony wth the general purpose of the Federal Constitution. It is an ancient and honorable rule of construction, laid down by Blackstone, that any instrument should be interpreted, "by considering the reason and spirit of it; or the cause which moved the legislator to enact it. . . . From this method of interpreting laws, by the reason of them, arises what we call equity." It may be, therefore, that the issue of judicial control is a case in equity. The direct intention of the framers and enactors not being clearly expressed on this point, we may have recourse to the "reason and spirit" of the Constitution.

As Blackstone shows by happy illustration the reason and spirit of a law are to be understood only by an inquiry into the circumstances of its enactment. The underlying purposes of the Constitution, therefore, are to be revealed only by a study of the conditions and events which led to its formation and adoption.

At the outset it must be remembered that there were two great parties at the time of the adoption of the Constitution — one laying emphasis on strength and efficiency in government and the other on its popular aspects. Quite naturally the men who led in stirring up the revolt against Great Britain and in keeping the fighting temper of the Revolutionists at the proper heat were the boldest and most radical thinkers — men like Samuel Adams, Thomas Paine, Patrick Henry, and Thomas Jefferson. They were not, generally speaking, men of large property interests or of much practical business experience. In a time of disorder, they could consistently lay more stress upon personal liberty than upon social control; and they pushed to the extreme limits those doctrines of individual rights which had been evolved in England during the struggles of the small landed proprietors and commercial classes against royal prerogative, and which corresponded to the economic conditions prevailing in America at the close of the eighteenth century. They associated strong government with monarchy, and came to believe that the best political system was one which governed least. A majority of the radicals viewed all government, especially if highly centralized, as a species of evil, tolerable only because necessary and always to be kept down to an irreducible minimum by a jealous vigilance.

Jefferson put the doctrine in concrete form when he declared that he preferred newspapers without government to government without newspapers. The Declaration of Independence, the first state Constitutions, and the Articles of Confederation bore the impress of this philosophy. In their anxiety to defend the individual against all Federal interference and to preserve to the states a large sphere of local autonomy, these Revolutionists had set up a system too weak to accomplish the accepted objects of government; namely, national defense, the protection of property, and the advancement of commerce. They were not unaware of the character of their handiwork, but they believed with Jefferson that "man was a rational animal endowed by nature with rights and with an innate sense of justice and that he could be restrained from wrong and protected in right by moderate powers confided to persons of his own choice." Occasional riots and disorders, they held, were preferable to too much government.

The new American political system based on these doctrines had scarcely gone into effect before it began to incur opposition from many sources. The close of the Revolutionary struggle removed the prime cause for radical agitation and brought a new group of thinkers into prominence. When independence had been gained, the practical work to be done was the maintenance of social order, the payment of the public debt, the provision of a sound financial system, and the establishment of conditions favorable to the development of the economic resources of the new country. The men who were principally concerned in this work of peaceful enterprise were not the philosophers, but men of business and property and the holders of public securities. For the most part they had had no quarrel with the system of class rule and the strong centralization of government which existed in England. It was on the question of policy, not of governmental structure, that they had broken with the British authorities. By no means all of them, in fact, had even resisted the policy of the mother country, for within the ranks of the conservatives were large numbers of Loyalists who had remained in America, and, as was to have been expected, cherished a bitter feeling against the Revolutionists, especially the radical section which had been boldest in denouncing the English system root and branch. In other words, after the heat and excitement of the War of Independence were over and the new government, state and national, was tested by the ordinary experiences of traders, financiers, and manufacturers, it was found inadequate, and these groups accordingly grew more and more determined to reconstruct the political system in such a fashion as to make it subserve their permanent interests.

Under the state constitutions and the Articles of Confederation established during the Revolution, every powerful economic class in the nation suffered either immediate losses or from impediments placed in the way of the development of their enterprises. The holders of the securities of the Confederate government did not receive the interest on their loans. Those who owned Western lands or looked with longing eyes upon the rich opportunities for speculation there chafed at the weakness of the government and its delays in establishing order on the frontiers. Traders and commercial men found their plans for commerce on a national scale impeded by local interference with interstate commerce. The currency of the states and the nation was hopelessly muddled. Creditors everywhere were angry about the depreciated paper money which the agrarians had made and were attempting to force upon those from whom they had borrowed specie. In short, it was a war between business and populism. Under the Articles of Confederation populism had a free hand, for majorities in the state legislatures were omnipotent. Anyone who reads the economic history of the time will see why the solid conservative interests of the country were weary of talk about the "rights of the people" and bent upon establishing firm guarantees for the rights of property.

The Congress of the Confederation was not long in discovering the true character of the futile authority which the Articles had conferred upon it. The necessity for new sources of revenue became apparent even while the struggle for independence was yet undecided, and, in 1781, Congress carried a resolution to the effect that it should be authorized to lay a duty of 5 per cent on certain goods. This moderate proposition was defeated because Rhode Island rejected it on the grounds that "she regarded it the most precious jewel of sovereignty that no state shall be called upon to open its purse but by the authority of the state and by her own officers." Two years later Congress prepared another amendment to the Articles providing for certain import duties, the receipts from which, collected by state officers, were to be applied to the payment of the public debt; but three years after the introduction of the measure, four states, including New York, still held out against its ratification, and the project was allowed to drop. At last, in 1786, Congress in a resolution declared that the requisitions for the last eight years had been so irregular in their operation, so uncertain in their collection, and so evidently unproductive, that a reliance on them in the future would be no less dishonorable to the understandings of those who entertained it than it would be dangerous to the welfare and peace of the Union. Congress, thereupon, solemnly added that it had become its duty "to declare most explicitly that the crisis had arrived when the people of the United States, by whose will and for whose benefit the federal government was instituted, must decide whether they will support their rank as a nation by maintaining the public faith at home and abroad, or whether for the want of a timely exertion in establishing a general revenue and thereby giving strength to the Confederacy, they will hazard not only the existence of the Union but those great and invaluable privileges for which they have so arduously and so honorably contended."

In fact, the Articles of Confederation had hardly gone into effect before the leading citizens also began to feel that the powers of Congress were wholly inadequate. In 1780, even before their adoption, Alexander Hamilton proposed a general convention to frame a new constitution, and from that time forward he labored with remarkable zeal and wisdom to extend and popularize the idea of a strong national government. Two years later, the assembly of the state of New York recommended a convention to revise the Articles and increase the power of Congress. In 1783, Washington, in a circular letter to the governors, urged that it was indispensable to the happiness of the individual states that there should be lodged somewhere a supreme power to regulate and govern the general concerns of the confederation. Shortly afterward (1785), Governor Bowdoin, of Massachusetts, suggested to his state legislature the advisability of calling a national assembly to settle upon and define the power of Congress; and the legislature resolved that the government under the Articles of Confederation was inadequate and should be reformed; but the resolution was never laid before Congress.

In January, 1786, Virginia invited all the other states to send delegates to a convention at Annapolis to consider the question of duties on imports and commerce in general. When this convention assembled in 1786, delegates from only five states were present, and they were disheartened at the limitations on their powers and the lack of interest the other states had shown in the project. With characeristic foresight, however, Alexander Hamilton seized the occasion to secure the adoption of a recommendation advising the states to choose representatives for another convention to meet in Philadelphia the following year "to consider the Articles of Confederation and to propose such changes therein as might render them adequate to the exigencies of the union." This recommendation was cautiously worded, for Hamilton did not want to raise any unnecessary alarm. He doubtless believed that a complete revolution in the old system was desirable, but he knew that, in the existing state of popular temper, it was not expedient to announce his complete program. Accordingly no general reconstruction of the political system was suggested; the Articles of Confederation were merely to be "revised"; and the amendments were to be approved by the state legislatures as provided by that instrument.

The proposal of the Annapolis convention was transmitted to the state legislatures and laid before Congress. Congress thereupon resolved in February, 1787, that a convention should be held for the sole and express purpose of revising the Articles of Confederation and reporting to itself and the legislatures of the several states such alterations and provisions as would when agreed to by Congress and confirmed by the states render the Federal Constitution adequate to the exigencies of government and the preservation of the union.

In pursuance of this call, delegates to the new convention were chosen by the legislatures of the states or by the governors in conformity to authority conferred by the legislative assemblies.* The delegates were given instructions of a general nature by their respective states, none of which, apparently, contemplated any very far-reaching changes. In fact, almost all of them expressly limited their representatives to a mere revision of the Articles of Confederation. For example, Connecticut authorized her delegates to represent and confer for the purpose mentioned in the resolution of Congress and to discuss such measures "agreeably to the general principles of Republican government" as they should think proper to render the Union adequate. Delaware, however, went so far as to provide that none of the proposed alterations should extend to the fifth part of the Articles of Confederation guaranteeing that each state should be entitled to one vote.

It was a truly remarkable assembly of men that gathered in Philadelphia on May 14, 1787, to undertake the work of reconstructing the American system of government. It is not merely patriotic pride that compels one to assert that never in the history of assemblies has there been a convention of men richer in political experience and in practical knowledge, or endowed with a profounder insight into the springs of human action and the intimate essence of government. It is indeed an astounding fact that at one time so may men skilled in statecraft could be found on the very frontiers

---

* Rhode Island alone was unrepresented. In all sixty-two delegates were appointed by the states; fifty-five of these attended sometime during the sessions; but only thirty-nine signed the finished document.

of civilization among a population numbering about four million whites. It is no less a cause for admiration that their instrument of government should have survived the trials and crises of a century that saw the wreck of more than a score of paper constitutions.

All the members had had a practical training in politics. Washington, as commander in chief of the revolutionary forces, had learned well the lessons and problems of war, and mastered successfully the no less difficult problems of administration. The two Morrises had distinguished themselves in grappling with financial questions as trying and perplexing as any which statesmen had ever been compelled to face. Seven of the delegates had gained political wisdom as governors of their native states; and no less than twenty-eight had served in Congress either during the Revolution or under the Articles of Confederation. There were men trained in the law, versed in finance, skilled in administration, and learned in the political philosophy of their own and all earlier times. Moreover, they were men destined to continue public service under the government which they had met to construct — Presidents, Vice-presidents, heads of departments, justices of the Supreme Court, were in that imposing body. They were equal to the great task of constructing a national system strong enough to defend the country on land and sea, pay every dollar of the lawful debt, and afford sufficient guarantees to the rights of private property. The radicals, however, like Patrick Henry, Jefferson, and Samuel Adams, were conspicuous by their absence from the convention.

As Woodrow Wilson has concisely put it, the framers of the Constitution represented "a strong and intelligent class possessed of unity and informed by a conscious solidarity of interests." * They were not convened to write a Declaration of Independence, but to frame a government which would meet the practical issues that had arisen under the Articles of Confederation. The objections they entertained to direct popular government, and they were undoubtedly many, were based upon their experience with popular assemblies during the immediately preceding years. With many of the plain lessons of history before them, they naturally feared that the rights and privileges of the minority would be insecure if the principle of majority rule was definitely adopted and provisions made for

* *Division and Reunion*, p. 12.

its exercise. Furthermore, it will be remembered that up to that time the right of all men, as men, to share in the government had never been recognized in practice. Everywhere in Europe the government was in the hands of a ruling monarch or at best a ruling class; everywhere the mass of the people had been regarded principally as an arms-bearing and tax-paying multitude, uneducated, and with little hope or capacity for advancement. Two years were to elapse after the meeting of the grave assembly at Philadelphia before the transformation of the Estates General into the National Convention in France opened the floodgates of revolutionary ideas on human rights before whose rising tide old landmarks of government are still being submerged. It is small wonder, therefore, that under the circumstances, many of the members of that august body held popular government in slight esteem and took the people into consideration only as far as it was imperative "to inspire them with the necessary confidence," as Mr. Gerry frankly put it.*

Indeed, every page of the laconic record of the proceedings of the convention preserved to posterity by Mr. Madison shows conclusively that the members of that assembly were not seeking to realize any fine notions about democracy and equality, but were striving with all the resources of political wisdom at their command to set up a system of government that would be stable and efficient, safeguarded on one hand against the possibilities of despotism and on the other against the onslaught of majorities. In the mind of Mr. Gerry, the evils they had experienced flowed "from the excess of democracy," and he confessed that while he was still republican, he "had been taught by experience the danger of the levelling spirit." †
Mr. Randolph, in offering to the consideration of the convention his plan of government, observed "that the general object was to provide a cure for the evils under which the United States labored; that, in tracing these evils to their origin, every man had found it in the turbulence and follies of democracy; that some check therefore was to be sought for against this tendency of our governments; and that a good Senate seemed most likely to answer the purpose." ‡ Mr. Hamilton, in advocating a life term for Senators, urged that "all

* Elliot's *Debates,* vol. V, p. 160.
† *Ibid.,* vol. V, p. 136.
‡ Elliot's *Debates,* vol. V, p. 138.

communities divide themselves into the few and the many. The first are rich and well born and the other the mass of the people who seldom judge or determine right."

Gouverneur Morris wanted to check the "precipitancy, changeableness, and excess" of the representatives of the people by the ability and virtue of men "of great and established property — aristocracy; men who from pride will support consistency and permanency. . . Such an aristocratic body will keep down the turbulence of democracy." While these extreme doctrines were somewhat counterbalanced by the democratic principles of Mr. Wilson, who urged that "the government ought to possess, not only first the force, but second the mind or sense of the people at large," Madison doubtless summed up in a brief sentence the general opinion of the convention when he said that to secure private rights against majority factions, and at the same time to preserve the spirit and form of popular government, was the great object to which their inquiries had been directed.*

They were anxious above everything else to safeguard the rights of private property against any leveling tendencies on the part of the propertyless masses. Gouverneur Morris, in speaking on the problem of apportioning representatives, correctly stated the sound historical fact when he declared: "Life and liberty were generally said to be of more value than property. An accurate view of the matter would, nevertheless, prove that property was the main object of society. . . . If property, then, was the main object of government, certainly it ought to be one measure of the influence due to those who were to be affected by the government." † Mr. King also agreed that "property was the primary object of society";‡ and Mr. Madison warned the convention that in framing a system which they wished to last for ages they must not lose sight of the changes which the ages would produce in the forms and distribution of property. In advocating a long term in order to give independence and firmness to the Senate, he described these impending changes: "An increase of population will of necessity increase the proportion of those who will labor under all the hardships of life and secretly sigh

* *The Federalist*, no. 10.
† Elliot's *Debates*, vol. V, p. 279.
‡ *Ibid.*, vol. V, p. 280.

for a more equal distribution of its blessings. These may in time out-number those who are placed above the feelings of indigence. According to the equal laws of suffrage, the power will slide into the hands of the former. No agrarian attempts have yet been made in this country, but symptoms of a levelling spirit, as we have understood have sufficiently appeared, in a certain quarter, to give notice of the future danger." * And again, in support of the argument for a property qualification on voters, Madison urged, "In future times, a great majority of the people will not only be without land, but any other sort of property. These will either combine, under the influence of their common situation, — in which case the rights of property and the public liberty will not be secure in their hands, — or, what is more probable, they will become the tools of opulence and ambition; in which case there will be equal danger on another side."† Various projects for setting up class rule by the establishment of property qualifications for voters and officers were advanced in the convention, but they were defeated. On account of the diversity of opinion that prevailed, agreement was impossible, and it was thought best to trust this matter to the discretion and wisdom of the states.

Nevertheless, by the system of checks and balances placed in the government, the convention safeguarded the interests of property against attacks by majorities. The House of Representatives, Mr. Hamilton pointed out, "was so formed as to render it particularly the guardian of the poorer orders of citizens," ‡ while the Senate was to preserve the rights of property and the interests of the minority against the demands of the majority.§ In the tenth number of *The Federalist,* Mr. Madison argued in a philosophic vein in support of the proposition that it was necessary to base the political system on the actual conditions of "natural inequality." Uniformity of interests throughout the state, he contended, was impossible on account of the diversity in the faculties of men, from which the rights of property originated; the protection of these faculties was the first object of government; from the protection of different and unequal

---

* Elliot's *Debates,* vol. V, p. 243.
† *Ibid.,* vol. V, p. 387.
‡ Elliot's *Debates,* vol. V, p. 244.
§ *Ibid.,* vol. V, p. 203.

faculties of acquiring property the possession of different degrees
and kinds of property immediately resulted; from the influence of
these on the sentiments and views of the respective proprietors en-
sued a division of society into different interests and parties; the unequal distribution of wealth inevitably led to a clash of interests in
which the majority was liable to carry out its policies at the expense
of the minority; hence, he added in concluding this splendid piece of
logic, "the majority, having such coexistent passion or interest, must
be rendered by their number and local situation unable to concert
and carry into effect schemes of oppression"; and in his opinion it
was the great merit of the newly framed Constitution that it secured
the rights of the minority against "the superior force of an interested
and overbearing majority."

This very system of checks and balances, which is undeniably the
essential element of the Constitution, is built upon the doctrine that
the popular branch of the government cannot be allowed full sway,
and least of all in the enactment of laws touching the rights of property. The exclusion of the direct popular vote in the election of the
President; the creation, again by indirect election, of a Senate which
the framers hoped would represent the wealth and conservative interests of the country; and the establishment of an independent judiciary appointed by the President with the concurrence of the Senate — all these devices bear witness to the fact that the underlying
purpose of the Constitution was not the establishment of popular
government by means of parliamentary majorities.

Page after page of *The Federalist* is directed to that portion of
the electorate which was disgusted with the "mutability of the public councils." Writing on the presidential veto, Hamilton says:

> The propensity of the legislative department to intrude
> upon the rights, and absorb the powers, of the other depart-
> ments has already been suggested and repeated. . . . It
> may perhaps be said that the power of preventing bad laws
> included the power of preventing good ones; and may be used
> to the one purpose as well as the other. But this objection will
> have little weight with those who can properly estimate the
> mischiefs of that inconstancy and mutability in the laws which
> form the greatest blemish in the character and genius of our
> governments. They will consider every institution calculated

to restrain the excess of law-making and to keep things in the same state in which they happen to be at any given period, as more likely to do good than harm; because it is favorable to greater stability in the system of legislation. The injury which may be possibly done by defeating a few good laws will be amply compensated by the advantage of preventing a number of bad ones.

When the framers of the Constitution had completed the remarkable instrument which was to establish a national government capable of discharging effectively certain great functions and checking the propensities of popular legislatures to attack the rights of private property, a formidable task remained before them — the task of securing the adoption of the new frame of government by states torn with popular dissensions. They knew very well that the state legislatures, which had been so negligent in paying their quotas under the Articles, and which had been so jealous of their rights, would probably stick at ratifying such a national instrument of government. Accordingly they cast aside that clause in the Articles requiring amendments to be ratified by the legislatures of all the states; and advised that the new Constitution should be ratified by conventions in the several states composed of delegates chosen by the voters. They furthermore declared — and this is a fundamental matter — that when the conventions of nine states had ratified the Constitution the new government should go into effect so far as those states were concerned. The chief reason for resorting to ratifications by conventions is laid down by Hamilton in the twenty-second number of *The Federalist*: "It has not a little contributed to the infirmities of the existing federal system that it never had a ratification by the people. Resting on no better foundation than the consent of the several legislatures, it has been exposed to frequent and intricate questions concerning the validity of its powers; and has in some instances given birth to the enormous doctrine of a right of legislative repeal. Owing its ratification to the law of a state, it has been contended that the same authority might repeal the law by which it was ratified. However gross a heresy it may be to maintain that a party to a compact has a right to revoke that compact, the doctrine itself has respectable advocates. The possibility of a question of this nature proves the necessity of laying the foundations of our national government deeper than in the mere sanction of delegated authority. The fabric of American empire ought to rest on the solid basis of the consent of the people. The streams of national power ought to flow immediately from that pure original fountain of all legitimate authority."

Of course, the convention did not resort to the revolutionary policy of transmitting the Constitution directly to the conventions of the several states. It merely laid the finished instrument before the Confederate Congress with the suggestion that it should be submitted to "a convention of delegates chosen in each state by the people thereof, under the recommendation of its legislature, for their assent and ratification; and each convention assenting thereto and ratifying the same should give notice thereof to the United States in Congress assembled." The convention went on to suggest that when nine states had ratified the Constitution, the Confederate Congress should extinguish itself by making provision for the elections necessary to put the new government into effect. "What they (the convention) actually did, stripped of all fiction and verbiage," says Professor Burgess, "was to assume constituent powers, ordain a Constitution of government and of liberty, and demand the *plébiscite* thereon, over the heads of all existing legally organized powers. Had Julius or Napoleon committed these acts, they would have been pronounced *coups d'état*. Looked at from the side of the people exercising the *plébiscite,* we term the movement revolution. The convention clothed its acts and assumptions in more moderate language than I have used, and professed to follow a more legal course than I have indicated. The exact form of procedure was as follows: They placed in the body of the proposed Constitution itself a provision declaring that ratifications by conventions of the people in nine states (commonwealths) should be sufficient for the establishment of the Constitution between the states (commonwealths) so ratifying the same. They then sent the instrument entire to the Confederate Congress, with the direction, couched in terms of advice, that the Congress should pass it along, untouched, to the legislatures of the commonwealths, and that these should pass it along, also untouched, to conventions of the people in each commonwealth, and that when nine conventions should have approved, Congress should take steps to put the new government into operation and abdicate.

Of course the mass of the people were not at all able to analyze the real character of this procedure. It is probable that many of the members of the convention itself did not fully comprehend just what they were doing. Not many of them had had sufficient education as publicists to be able to generalize the scientific import of their acts." *

After the new Constitution was published and transmitted to the states, there began a long and bitter fight over ratification. A veritable flood of pamphlet literature descended upon the country, and a collection of these pamphlets by Hamilton, Madison, and Jay, brought together under the title of *The Federalist* — though clearly a piece of campaign literature — has remained a permanent part of the contemporary sources on the Constitution and has been regarded by many lawyers as a commentary second in value only to the decisions of the Supreme Court. Within a year the champions of the new government found themselves victorious, for on June 21, 1788, the ninth state, New Hampshire, ratified the Constitution, and accordingly the new government might go into effect as between the agreeing states. Within a few weeks, the nationalist party in Virginia and New York succeeded in winning these two states, and in spite of the fact that North Carolina and Rhode Island had not yet ratified the Constitution, Congress determined to put the instrument into effect in accordance with the recommendations of the convention. Elections for the new government were held; the date March 4, 1789, was fixed for the formal establishment of the new system; Congress secured a quorum on April 6; and on April 30 Washington was inaugurated at the Federal Hall in Wall Street, New York.

* Burgess, *Political Science and Constitutional Law*, vol. I, p. 105.

George Washington: Administrator

by

LEONARD WHITE

["George Washington As An Administrator," from *Boston University Law Review*, XXIV (June 1944), 145–156. Reprinted by permission.]

*George Washington is a much revered figure in American histori-
ography. The cult of adulation began with Parson Mason L. Weems,
whose* Life of Washington *was published in 1800 and became one
of the most popular books ever written in America. Weems invented the cherry-tree legend and his biography includes, in keeping
with its over-all tone, an account of the entrance of its saintly hero
into heaven.*[1]

*Subsequent early nineteenth century biographers, John Mar-
shall,*[2] *Jared Sparks*[3] *and Washington Irving,*[4] *were reverential
and venerative, without, of course, including the kind of nonsense
put into print by Weems and consumed avidly by the American
public. Nevertheless, typical of the orientation of these biographies
was John Marshall's opinion of Washington: "No man has ever appeared upon the theatre of public action, whose integrity was more
incorruptible, or whose principles were more perfectly free from
the contamination of . . . selfish and unworthy passions. . . ."*[5] *In
1889 we find Henry Cabot Lodge writing of Washington as "very
great and wise and pure. . . ."*[6]

*In private life Washington was a plantation owner; in politics,
a Federalist and a conservative. Consequently, for historians writing
in the Federalist-Whig-Republican tradition Washington became,
as he did for the country as a whole, a symbol of conservatism. Thus
Henry Cabot Lodge, himself a pillar of conservatism if not of reac-*

tion in the United States Senate, presents Washington as a hard-headed businessman who "meant to have his due no matter how trivial." [7] *Approximately the same viewpoint is present in William R. Thayer's* George Washington, *which was well received in an era when Presidents Coolidge and Hoover were paying tribute to Washington as a successful man of affairs.* [8]

As for the liberal historians, they were content to leave Washington and his enormous prestige to the conservatives. Reluctant to attack the American demigod, it is interesting that Claude Bowers in his Jefferson and Hamilton *elects to build up Jefferson at the expense of Hamilton — not Washington. It was only the exigencies of the isolationist debate preceding American entrance into World War II which caused historians to challenge the political capital isolationists were making of the "Farewell Address."* [9]

With the advent of the New Deal, Jefferson replaced Washington as conservatism's patron saint. It was Jefferson, not Washington, who as the historic personality standing for state rights, low taxes, economy and passivity in government, could be best identified as opposed to the centralizing tendencies of the New Deal. [10] *In addition, historical studies of Washington in the last decade by Curtis Nettels,* [11] *Charles Ambler,* [12] *and Douglas S. Freeman* [13] *have attempted, as far as the material permits, to present Washington less as an isolationist, conservative, and businessman and more in terms of his career as Revolutionary leader, democrat, and internationalist.*

There is yet another perspective from which the career of Washington can be studied profitably. Brooks Adams was one of the few historians who early manifested awareness of the importance of administrative processes. In his fascinating Introduction to The Degradation of the Democratic Dogma, *Adams paid homage to Washington's ability as an administrator without attempting to tell the story in detail.* [14] *In the 1940's, as we have seen, there was a quickening of interest on the part of historians in political and administrative history; and Leonard D. White, Professor of Political Science at the University of Chicago, began writing a history of public administration in the United States of which two volumes have now been completed. It is interesting how the particular focus of Professor White's investigation adds a new dimension to our understanding of Washington, which is not too clearly discernible in the traditional pattern of Washington historiography.*

WHEN Washington took the oath of office on April 30, 1789, he entered upon an office the nature of which was described only by certain sentences in an untried Constitution. When he returned on foot to his house in Philadelphia on March 4, 1797, after attending the inauguration of John Adams, he left an office upon which his character and personality had made an indelible impress. It is a curious circumstance that Washington's abilities as an administrator have never been explored, although he was the first and one of the ablest executives ever to hold the office of President.

I propose to analyze Washington's administrative career, first by describing the qualities of mind and personality which contributed to his administrative success; second by examining his experience before he became President; and third by observing what may be called his administrative techniques, leading at the close to an evaluation of Washington as a chief executive. His methods as administrative head of the government reflected faithfully the quality of his mind and the lessons of his previous experience. To these we now turn.

WASHINGTON'S PERSONALITY AND CHARACTER

In his early twenties Washington was ambitious for public notice; and at the same time he was filled with a sense of personal responsibility to serve the commonwealth. He entered the military service in 1751 at the age of nineteen and served through the French and Indian Wars to 1760. At the age of twenty-four (May 14, 1775) he wrote (but did not send) this letter to his brother, John.

> The Gen'l. [Braddock] has appointed me one of his aids de Camps, in which Character I shall serve this Campaigne, agreeably enough, as I am thereby freed from all commands but his, and give Order's to all, which must be implicitly obey'd.

I have now a good oppertunity, and shall not neglect it, of forming an acquaintance, which may be serviceable hereafter, if I can find it worth while pushing my Fortune in the Military way.*

In August, 1755, he referred in another letter to "what at present constitutes the chief part of my happiness, i.e. the esteem and notice the Country has been pleas'd to honour me with." In 1758 he wrote Colonel Thomas Gage (who was later to enrage the inhabitants of Boston):

> I wou'd now, altho' I think modesty will scarcely permit me to ask it, beg the favour of you to mention me to Gen'l Forbes (if you are acquainted with that Gentleman:) I mean not, Sir, as one, who has favors to ask of him; on the contrary, having entirely laid aside all hopes of preferment in the Military line, (and being at present induced to serve this Campaign from abstract motives purely laudable.) I only wish to be distinguished in some measure from the general run of provincial Officers, as I understand there will be a motley herd of us! This, I flatter myself, can hardly be deemed an unreasonable request, when it is considered, that I have been much longer in the Service than any provincial officer in America.†

This youthful anxiety for public notice was later absorbed into a mature sense of personal duty to take a part in public affairs, a feeling which remained one of Washington's deepest motivations.

This concern for *res publica* was a part of the tradition of the Virginia aristocracy, shared by many of Washington's contemporaries. Few, if any, however, shared his extraordinary balance and perspective. The essence of this notable aspect of his character, which was to carry him through many difficult moments, is expressed in an almost incidental observation written in 1797: ". . . the more combined, and distant [,] things are seen, the more likely they are to be turned to advantage." Only rarely was this balance upset by momentary bursts of anger and passion.

---

* *Writings of George Washington* (Fitzpatrick, ed.), I, 124. All quotations from Washington are from this collection, unless otherwise noted.
† *Ibid.*, II, 176–177.

Not far removed from his capacity to see things in their distant relationships was his dominant sense of order. Whether as a military leader, a plantation manager, or a chief executive, the necessity of order and system was ever present in his mind. He began the habit of writing memoranda to himself at the age of seventeen, and followed it consistently whenever the need arose. "System," he wrote in 1797, "to all things is the soul of business." One of his first cares after becoming President was to arrange the hours of the day, and the days of the week, to protect his time; otherwise, as he wrote his friend David Stuart, "I could not get relieved from the ceremony of one visit before I had to attend to another. . . ."

Throughout his life Washington had the capacity to reach decisions and to follow them through; he could "get things done." As President he recognized that it was impossible for him alone "to perform all the great business of the State," but he did not intend the affairs of the Republic to suffer by inattention on the part of his associates. Shortly after he became President he wrote to his department heads:

> Let me impress the following maxim upon the executive officers. In all important matters, deliberate maturely, but execute promptly and vigorously and do not put things off until tomorrow; which can be done and require to be done today. Without an adherence to these rules, business will never be done, or done in an easy manner, but will always be in arrears, with one thing treading upon the heels of another.*

He took his own responsibilities as head of the administrative machine seriously, and imposed upon himself the same close attention to business which he expected from others. Jefferson later described Washington's central administrative position in a revealing passage.

> . . . He was always in accurate possession of all facts and proceedings in every part of the Union, and to whatsoever department they related; he formed a central point for the different branches; preserved an unity of object and action among them; exercised that participation in the suggestion of affairs which his office made incumbent on him; and met himself the due responsibility for whatever was done.†

* H. L. Ritter, *Washington as a Business Man*, p. 210.
† *Works of Thomas Jefferson* (Federal ed.), IX, 311.

In short the principal personal qualities which made Washington an able administrator were: a strong sense of duty, sublimating an early ambition; balance and perspective; order and system; energy in accomplishment; and, it should be added, a character of the highest integrity. His unswerving devotion to the highest standards of conduct appeared in all his public acts and statements, and although Jefferson and Adams might entertain an unflattering opinion of his intellect, none could fairly escape from acknowledging the grandeur of his character.

WASHINGTON'S EXPERIENCE IN ADMINISTRATION

In his first inaugural address, Washington observed that he was "unpracticed in the duties of civil administration." He brought to his new office, however, not only a promising pattern of human qualities, but a range of experience which made the new task relatively easy. Two separate aspects of his life before 1789 seem especially significant in forming his administrative talents: his experience as a plantation manager, and his experience as a military commander.

The former is not to be despised. The number of persons whom Washington supervised at Mount Vernon was greater than the number required to carry on any of the embryonic departments at the seat of government in his day. There remains a fascinating page from his instructions to his plantation manager which reveals a perfect sense of good management:

. . . There is much more in what is called head work, that is in the manner of conducting business, than is generally imagined. For take two Managers and give to each the same number of labourers, and let these labourers be equal in all respects. Let both these Managers rise equally early, go equally late to rest, be equally active, sober and industrious, and yet, in the course of the year, one of them, without pushing the hands that are under him more than the other, shall have performed infinitely more work. To what is this owing? Why, simply to contrivance resulting from that forethought and arrangement which will guard against the misapplication of labour, and doing it unseasonably. . . .*

* The Writings of George Washington, XXX, 175–176, footnote 4.

As a Virginia planter Washington's energy, system, and sense of planning and timing made him one of the best known "gentleman farmers" of his region. The management lessons he learned here were relevant to his vastly expanded duties as the chief executive of the national business.

Washington's experience as a military commander, both in the French and Indian War and in the Revolutionary War, was his second guide to civil administration. As commander in chief from 1775 to 1783 he struggled not only with the organization of an army, but with a dilatory Congress, with thirteen discordant colonial-state governments each vital to the maintenance of the army, with jealous and ambitious officers, and with a motley crew of foreign adventurers who came seeking military glory. It would be hard to imagine a commander in chief called upon to do so much with such slender resources and with such faulty civil organization to give him support.

From these hard and often threatening years in the army, Washington gained experience which he put to work as President. Here he became convinced of the utter necessity of an active and effective executive power. He would never subject any future military or civil leaders to the vacillation and indecision which he had endured. Here he became versed in the art of dealing with a representative assembly and sensed the necessity of supplying it with executive leadership. Here he was impressed with the dangerous strength of provincial loyalties and with the overriding necessity of building up a national organism as rapidly as local patriotism would permit. The delicacy of this balance between center and circumference was deeply engraved upon his mind; in 1788 he wrote to the absent Jefferson, ". . . infinite circumspection and prudence are yet necessary in the experiment."

In the army, too, he learned the basic techniques of large-scale management. The relationship between responsibility and authority, unity of command, the rules of delegation, the function of a staff, the necessity for training, the forms of co-ordination and the details of timing, all were an essential part of his life as commander in chief. Here it was that he devised one of his favorite formulas, describing administration as like a clock, every part of which was essential to the whole. Here it was too, that he confirmed the personal habits of leadership and attention to detail which he was to carry with him to the Presidency.

No better single illustration of the administrative lessons learned by Washington from army experience can be cited than his grasp of the nature and functions of a military staff. The essential character of such a staff has never been more clearly put than in this passage from one of the President's letters:

> . . . The variegated, and important duties of the Aids of a Commander in Chief . . . require experienced Officers, men of judgment, and men of business, *ready pens* to execute them properly, and with dispatch. A great deal more is required of them than attending him at a Parade, or delivering verbal orders here and there; or copying a written one. They ought if I may be allowed to use the expression, to possess the Soul of the General; and from a *single* Idea given to them, to convey his meaning in the clearest and fullest manner. This, young men unacquainted with the Service and diffident, would not do; be their abilities what they may.*

Finally we may note in passing another element of Washington's education in civil administration. As a member of the Virginia House of Burgesses for fifteen years he became familiar with the affairs of one of the principal colonies, and accustomed to thinking about and deciding issues of government. As president of the Constitutional Convention in 1787 he listened to all the debates of that eminent body, an unrivaled school for statesmen. The concept of vigorous executive leadership which he had already acquired in the army must have been powerfully confirmed as the Convention molded into final form the office which he was destined to occupy.

We may venture, then, to assert that Washington came to his duties as chief executive both with qualities of mind and with a type of experience which forecast success in administration. He had not been a governor, but he had sat in the Virginia House of Burgesses from 1760 to 1775. He had not had broad commercial experience, but he was a large plantation owner, producing for the English market and buying abroad. He had been engaged in large land operations in New York and in the West. Although he had never been abroad, he had seen more of America than had most Americans. In

* *Ibid.*, XXXVI, 373–375.

short, as much as any of his fellow citizens he knew the problems of public management as they presented themselves in the eighteenth century.

WASHINGTON'S ADMINISTRATIVE TECHNIQUES

We may now examine more closely some of Washington's administrative techniques as President. It is important to grasp firmly at the outset that he always saw administration in the framework of his grand objectives, and did not hesitate to make administrative decisions buttress these great ends. Washington desired above all to create a broad base of public support for the new general government. In the field of administration he sought to create respect and support for the new regime in many ways. He was extremely careful about the character of his appointments to public office. He sought men of standing in their community to speak and act for the new government. He selected local men to serve as field agents in the Federal revenue services rather than seeking more abruptly to make a nation by creating a public service indiscriminately intermingled. He was shrewdly careful to place contracts for building the first ten cutters for the coast guard all the way from Portsmouth, New Hampshire, to Charleston, South Carolina. In his own cabinet, he found a place for Massachusetts, New York, and Virginia, and in the Supreme Court for other states.

The office of President itself he sought to surround with dignity. In his own personality Washington was reserved and somewhat aloof; an easy congeniality did not come naturally to him. His personality coincided with his considered view concerning the character of the office he held. His own choice of official title was, "His High Mightiness, the President of the United States and Protector of their Liberties"; fortunately a less "high-toned" formula was devised. In his public appearances on state occasions, Washington rode in a coach drawn by four horses, followed by his official family in other coaches. On other occasions, however, he could be seen riding alone on horseback, around the Battery in New York, or in the streets of Philadelphia, or walking from place to place unattended. In order, in his own words, "to preserve the dignity and respect that was due to the first Magistrate," he decided to give dinners only to "official characters and strangers of distinction," and to accept no invitations. When he visited Massachusetts in 1789 on his first tour, gouty John Hancock, then governor, waited in vain for Washington to call upon him first; Hancock quickly had to sacrifice his pride in the face of rising popular indignation and was carried, gout and all, to pay his respects to the President of the United States.

As chief executive, Washington grasped firmly the reins of leadership. Although deferential to Congress, he laid out the main lines of public policy for its consideration. He went further and drafted bills which embodied his recommendations and which were handed to Federalist members to introduce. His cabinet heads were in and out of Congress freely, especially in the early years. Within the administration he kept close watch on matters large and small. All important letters were sent from the department heads to his home for inspection; they were returned on the next day. Initiative came both from the President and from the department heads, notably Hamilton; decisions were invariably those of the President. He allowed his department heads little margin for delay; there are many instances in which he asked for an opinion, and named the next morning for its delivery. Regularly before he left the seat of government he asked for schedules of business to be cleared prior to his departure; nothing was left at loose ends. Indolent officials received sharp letters from him, inviting them to attend to their public duties; to Woodbury Langdon, Commissioner of Loans for New Hampshire, he wrote, ". . . If any circumstances should be incompatible with your immediate and steady attendance, it is proper you should resign the Office." In short, Washington did not hesitate to assume an active leadership both toward Congress and within the administration; he quickly became the central pivot around which the whole machine moved. It was neither Theodore Roosevelt nor Woodrow Wilson who invented the concept and practice of executive leadership.

Washington was not, however, a "lone wolf." He had confidence in his own judgment, but he preferred to instruct his judgment by the views of others. The habit of consultation was deeply ingrained; it had been a regular part of his military life, and it led to the early formation of the cabinet. "I am anxious, always," he once wrote to

Hamilton, "to compare the opinions of those in whom I confide with one another; and those again (without being bound by them) with my own, that I may extract all the good I can." His principal adviser from 1789 to his death was Alexander Hamilton; others whom he often consulted were Jay, Jefferson (to 1793), Randolph (to 1796), Madison, and C. C. Pinckney. He was sometimes upset when such powerful figures disagreed in their advice.

This observation suggests a comment on how Washington made up his mind. He was more accustomed to asking for advice than to receiving unsolicited opinions, although Jay and Hamilton occasionally gave him uninvited, but not unwelcome, opinions. He preferred to secure advice in writing. His mind was deliberative, rather than argumentative; he was at a loss to argue effectively with Jefferson, for example, and often lapsed into silence. He withheld action until the last moment. As a rule no one knew his decision until it was publicly announced; this practice especially prevailed in his nominations and appointments. The process of making up his mind was apparently a solitary one, in which, to use his own phrase, he sought "the more combined, and distant" view. Certain it is that a decision once made was settled. Indecision and vacillation were not a part of Washington's mind, and ambiguity was not a part of his method.

Washington had great capacity to deal with details, and although he recognized that a military commander or a civil executive ought not to bother with details, he never succeeded in getting rid of them. Appointments, great and small, were brought to his desk, and no collector of customs, surveyor of revenue, captain of a cutter, or keeper of a lighthouse was commissioned except after personal consideration by the President. He signed the contracts for building each lighthouse, and took time to enjoin economy in the choice of materials. He asked Jefferson whether in the new Federal city on the Potomac there ought to be any wooden houses, and whether "stoups" ought not to be prohibited absolutely. Later he wrote the district commissioners, "I wish . . . that so much of the stone walls, on which the railing in the Street is to be placed, as shall appear above the pavement . . . should be of freestone hewed." Although Washington complained of the mass of these details, we may suspect that at heart he enjoyed dealing with them. His administrative principles and his personal predilections fell at war with each other, and principle yielded.

Although he expected Hamilton, Jefferson, and Knox to manage their departments on their own responsibility, along the lines which he had approved, they submitted to his decision a mass of details which today would appear indefensible. In financial matters, however, the delegation of details was nearly complete; Washington was unfamiliar with these operations and Hamilton was their master. In foreign affairs, the delegation was less complete, since the details often involved issues which the President could not avoid. In military affairs, it was still less complete; this was the area of Washington's own personal competence. In planning the new Federal city, effective delegation was at its lowest point, due to personal strife among the district commissioners and between them and Pierre L'Enfant.

WASHINGTON'S CONTRIBUTION AS AN EXECUTIVE

The administrative events of Washington's two terms can be quickly summarized. His first task was to organize the departments and put the machine in motion. For some months Washington occupied the unique and peculiar position of being a president without possessing a government. But within a year a full-fledged system had been set up and was at work. The departments had been created; the revenue service was fully established; the army had been regularized; the postal service had been taken over; the members of the foreign service of the United States had been appointed and had taken their stations; the Federal courts were fully organized with marshals and district attorneys in every part of the Union; the system of registration and clearance of vessels was in order; in short, a paper constitution had become a working government.

Public administration is a complex of relationships, all of which had to be fixed by the first President. To establish these was a second great contribution of George Washington. He was deeply conscious of his role as precedent maker. "Many things which appear of little importance in themselves and at the beginning," he once wrote, "may have great durable consequences from their having been established at the commencement of a new general government. It will be much easier to commence the administration, upon a well adjusted system, built on tenable grounds, than to correct errors or alter inconveniences after they shall have been confirmed by habit." By the close of his administration he had established the major network of relationships upon their permanent foundations: the connections between the President, the Senate, and Congress; between the President, the State Department, and foreign ministers to the United States; between the chief executive and the heads of departments; between the executive branch and the courts; between the President and the governors; between the departments and their field services; and among the departments themselves. These were years of precedent making — precedent making which could not be avoided, and it is not strange that Washington felt "an anxiety for the Community that every new arrangement should be made in the best possible manner." One proof of Washington's administrative insight is that the general pattern of official relationships which he worked out still prevails.

Certainly the most dramatic domestic event of his administration was the challenge to the power of the Federal government to enforce its own revenue laws. This challenge was raised by the whisky-distilling farmers of western Pennsylvania and came to a climax in the Whisky Rebellion. Washington organized an impressive demonstration of the power of the new general government to defend itself. In a contemporary letter he declared, ". . . Neither the Military nor Civil government shall be trampled upon with impunity whilst I have the honor to be at the head of them." * Never again, short of the Civil War, was there a serious defiance of the administrative measures of the Federal government.

Upon the new system of administration set in motion in 1789 had to be impressed a character and an ideal. To it Washington imparted ideals of integrity, impartiality, and competence which were to stand intact for forty years, and which remain even today as standards to be cherished, although not fully restored from the mid-century orgy of spoils politics. These ideals were not the least of his contributions.

Washington never formulated a systematic statement of the func-

* *The Writings of George Washington* (Fitzpatrick, ed.), XXXII, 161.

tions and appropriate qualities of a chief executive.* That he had a firm grasp of the essentials of conducting affairs which he put to daily use cannot, however, be doubted by anyone who reads his letters and his public papers. The first President was a thoroughly competent administrator, with a sure understanding which permitted him to establish in eight years an office of major importance, with settled relationships to Congress, to the departments of state, and to a public which had to be taught that the head of a state can be powerful without endangering liberty. In his daily administrative tasks he was systematic, orderly, energetic, solicitous of the opinions of others but independent in his own judgment, insistent upon facts and deliberation but decisive, intent upon general goals and the consistency of particular actions with them. Less inventive than Hamilton, he was not brilliant but steady; he balanced different courses of conduct against each other in the recesses of his own mind rather than in argumentation with his associates; always sensitive to public reaction, he never swerved from the decisions which his intelligence and conscience dictated. His principal failure was his inability to maintain the unity of his cabinet in the face of the bitter conflict between Hamilton and Jefferson; his principal success was to plant in the minds of the American people the model of a government which commanded respect by reason of its integrity, energy, and competence.

* "With me," wrote Washington, "it has always been a maxim rather to let my designs appear from my works than by my expressions." (*Writings of George Washington*, Fitzpatrick ed., XXXVI, 113, December 21, 1797). Small comments as follows: "Whether Washington, like his successors, was in possession of any definite opinions as to the powers of the Presidency at the date of his entry into that office, or whether he formulated any theory as to the Chief Magistracy during his subsequent years in the service cannot be conclusively determined. . . . Being essentially a man of deed and not of contemplation, a man for whom facts and not abstractions had an attraction, he was preoccupied with the problem of putting into successful operation the product of the Philadelphia Convention." Norman J. Small, *Some Presidential Interpretations of the Presidency*, p. 13. Parrington thought so little of Washington's contribution to the thought of his time that he did not include him in his *Main Currents in American Thought*.

Alexander Hamilton: Nation Maker

by

REXFORD G. TUGWELL AND
JOSEPH DORFMAN

[From *Columbia University Quarterly*, XXIX (December 1937), 209–226. Reprinted by permission.]

That there are fewer books about Alexander Hamilton than Thomas Jefferson can be accounted for in part by the predominantly Jefferson-Jackson-FDR orientation of American historical writing in the past half-century. Jefferson, too, is undoubtedly a more attractive personality, which helps explain his appeal — as does the fact that Jefferson is our democratic philosopher par excellence. *Yet, as Dorfman and Tugwell indicate, "It is only fair to remember, however much we may deprecate Hamilton's distrust of the people, that Jefferson had an equal distrust of the majority rule which has become the instrument above all others on which modern democracy relies. It is also fair to remember that Jefferson maneuvered to become President and so was often less than single-minded in his devotion to this country's good. . . . Jefferson's weakness for political preferment was certainly matched by Hamilton's ambition for place and money, and by his degeneration into reaction after retirement from office."* [1]

In recent years historians, in writing about Hamilton, have presented him less in the pattern of defender of the rich and well-born — which is the way the Jeffersonian historian Claude Bowers saw him — than in the role of state maker. [2] *Like most so-called new viewpoints in American historical writing, this is not entirely orig-*

inal. Henry Cabot Lodge's biography of Hamilton, which was pub-
lished in 1886, has a similar emphasis; while Charles A. Beard, in
stressing the economic motivations of the Founding Fathers, paid
homage to their achievement — particularly Hamilton's.[3] *Hacker,*
in 1947, maintained that "Hamilton's reading of his times and of the
future of America was that of the wise statesman. Over bitter parti-
san opposition, he was able to establish the country's public and pri-
vate credit on a secure footing; and by doing so was able to secure
the stability and economic growth of the United States." [4]

Nevertheless Beard, in 1948, deplored the fact that the very men-
tion of Hamilton's name "still arouses choking emotions in the
bosoms of all 'right thinkers' who confine their knowledge and inter-
est to the Anti-Federalist tradition . . . without stopping to inquire
what would have happened to the Republic if Hamilton had never
lived or whether the Constitution would have been firmly estab-
lished if he had not drawn to it a powerful understanding. . . ." [5]

Naturally, the question arises as to what brought about this
changed attitude toward Hamilton in the historiography of the past
decade. Undeniably, greater appreciation of Hamilton coincided
with the economic prosperity of the 1940's. At the same time, it
should be observed that the booming economy of the 1920's pro-
duced no comparable transformation in the historian's attitude,
despite the fact that Hamilton's name, coupled with Andrew Mel-
lon's, was then on everyone's lips. Today, the favorable reception
given Hamilton can be accounted for largely in terms of the histori-
an's quickening interest in politics and statecraft, in which Hamil-
ton excelled.

However, the selection reprinted below was written in a period
when America was depression-bound, by Tugwell and Dorfman,
both of whom were pro-New Deal. And while ultimate historical ob-
jectivity might be difficult, perhaps impossible, to achieve, the fol-
lowing selection is indicative of how fair-minded scholars, regard-
less of personal proclivities and the climate of contemporary
opinion, arrived at a remarkably sound evaluation of the achieve-
ment of a highly controversial figure. This selection is the first half
of a two-part article, the second section of which deals with Hamil-
ton's career after his retirement from office when, in the words of

Allan Nevins, Hamilton's "best work had all been done; his cruelest errors remained to be committed." [6]

Rexford Guy Tugwell is a former government official and is now Professor of Political Science at the University of Chicago. Joseph Dorfman is Professor of Economics at Columbia University.

A GREAT deal has been made of the unusual circumstances surrounding Alexander Hamilton's birth and early training — more than is warranted. There seems now something exotic about a West Indian boyhood; but there was nothing exotic about it in Hamilton's time. The West Indies were then simply other British colonies, and rather more important ones than any on the mainland except perhaps Virginia, and relations with them were closer than those which existed among any but the nearest neighbors in what later became the states. They had the same difficulties with Britain, too, except that their disputes had a more sensible outcome than our own. If the Barbadian model had been followed on the continent our history might still have been linked to that of the British Empire, and might, in consequence, have been less filled with controversy over obvious issues. At any rate, Hamilton did not arrive in the mainland colonies unaware of what was going on here; in fact, he came from an environment more mature in constitutional ideas than the one to which he came. Then too, part of his boyhood was spent in the Danish islands, and they, also, contributed something to his political orientation.

He was precocious. At twelve he was managing a considerable mercantile establishment in Christianstadt and had a start on a formal education which was pursued with ease and rapidity, after he came to New York in 1772, at a New Jersey boarding school and at King's College. But he was not only precocious, he was clever and attractive, qualities which gained him alliances with the great families of the colony, furnished scope for his talents, and perhaps led indirectly to his tragic death in 1804. A man of genius could hardly have chosen, in all the years of our history, a span of life in which opportunity would be so generous. And Hamilton took advantage of all that was offered. For he had intense ambitions, too.

It might be thought strange that a poor provincial boy should seem to have been born equipped with aristocratic notions, which included not only approval of monarchy and distrust of democracy, but also a thorough conviction, apparent in every measure he sponsored in his life, that wealth was a badge of virtue and that successful traders were the natural protectors of society. But in reality this was a natural outcome of his circumstances. The people with whom he was thrown during his early years were planters and merchants and it was to this class that he belonged. They were, moreover, West Indian planters and merchants. What this means can only be understood against the background of over a hundred years of precariously maintained white prestige in tropical islands where Negro life is lush — as lush as the vegetation which always reburies human clearing in spreading greenery. A careless tide of color has been kept back by increasingly savage efforts as the years have passed. The gay and shiftless blacks are not wholly immune to provocation either, as several slave revolts prove; and a careless attitude toward life in general can easily extend to an utterly casual extinction of the master class. West Indians, as a consequence, breathe fear as they breathe the heavy perfume of their flowers and it does something irretrievable to their natures. They are incapable of viewing men as equal; they are incapable of viewing the lower classes as men at all, really. At least Hamilton had difficulty in doing so; and his utmost concession to a widened franchise had attached to it a heavy property qualification — the distinction between slave and master on the estate.

The famous difference between Hamilton and Jefferson in these matters, which has been thought to be so important in our history, can, to the extent to which it is true, be explained in these terms. One might not think so who went to look at Monticello, for Jefferson appears to have had, to a fuller degree than Hamilton, all the appurtenances of that planter life, to have lived on the sufferance of his black slaves, and to have been raised in a far more aristocratic fashion. But this similarity was altogether on the surface. Jefferson had the instincts of the small planter and the artisan. He liked to do things with his own hands and in a small way. Furthermore, in his part of Virginia there was more ease of relationship between master and slave than the Deep South or even the Tidewater ever knew. Jefferson looked forward to the elimination not only of slavery but of poverty as a whole. Even at that time freed slaves were not unknown; and to be black was not thought to be beastly.* A surge of color was not engulfing everything; it was a white man's country, too. There were farmers as well as planters.

Then, too, Jefferson met the world out of a background of more settled gentility than Hamilton could with that question concerning his birth forever intruding. Hamilton came well recommended, a brilliant lad with upper-class manners but with no family and small funds. He had his way to make. He had to prove his right to the aristocratic connections he sought. Jefferson needed no recommendation. He moved naturally in a well-known circle. He could afford the eccentricities of the rich and well-born. He could even afford to be a democrat.

It would be easy to exaggerate the part King's College had in shaping Hamilton. He went there, in the first place, because Princeton would not have him. Why King's should have been willing to put up with his demands for irregularity, we do not know. He wanted to study mostly by himself and to syncopate his course. Perhaps this was easier from King's having, besides Myles Cooper, who was president, only two other instructors, Samuel Clossy (who taught mostly in the Medical School) and John Vardill, who was an assistant tutor. This lack of personnel made the instruction primitive at best and such busy overseers may have been glad for a bright lad who needed no driving. It must be remembered that the course was not professional and could only be considered preprofessional for prospective clergymen. Clossy taught the classics and natural philosophy and Vardill was his assistant. Cooper gave lectures in composition, disputation, theology, and moral philosophy. Prevailing institutions, conduct, ways of thinking were given elaborate jus-

* Jefferson, of course, felt that blacks were "inferior." He could hardly have felt otherwise in his time. But he felt that Virginia was changing her cultivation from tobacco (which was by then a losing crop), to foodstuffs, a kind of farming to which whites were held to be better adapted. He thought that after emancipation the Negroes should be exported. In the West Indies no such shift was or could be contemplated.

tification. Students were expected to regard them as having been formed by the operations of natural law; they therefore exemplified right reason and self-evident truth. Revelation was made some use of in tight places but slavery, private property, business gain, and royal prerogative were easily justified in a moral philosophy which relied extensively on Old Testament ethics and the natural law teachings of Grotius and Pufendorf.

But Hamilton always went directly into any intellectual enterprise, seizing on its core and throwing aside the nonessential covering, no matter how many layers of it there might be. His was a mind with power and he used it with economy. As a result he got over ground with incredible rapidity. This was true of him at every age. It appears in his student memoranda (some of which could and did serve for others' texts) just as it did in the greatest of his state papers later on. It was a scarcely human force, this devouring mind. And he was able to implement it early with a swinging balanced prose, tuned to the contemporary style, but growing more direct as he grew older, and strangely effective in spite of its formality. He must have given that fine old Tory, Myles Cooper, some bad moments even before the one we have record of in which Hamilton's hatred of masses on the loose triumphed over his detestation of an old gentleman who would hide in an attic from a mob.* Cooper thought Hamilton was urging the crowd to pull him out of his retreat and he called out "Don't believe him," before he dodged out at the back.† But the young man was telling his inferiors how to behave toward gentlemen; he was not inflaming passions.

At King's College sides were being taken. This could hardly have been avoided even in an institution which dedicated its students to disciplines as remote as possible from contemporary politics — remote, that is, except in the sense of supporting the *status quo*. These were stirring times in America. The English were bearing down on their colonies; the Navigation Acts were being enforced; smuggling was being more strictly controlled; and Parliament was

---

* Cooper ridiculed the notion that a stripling like Hamilton was the author of some of the sharpest strictures on the utterances of himself and fellow loyalists. John C. Hamilton, *Life of Alexander Hamilton* (Boston, 1879), I, 74.
  † *Ibid.*, p. 100.

imposing duties on colonial imports. Everything was heading up to the first constitutional crisis of Hamilton's experience — that in which the colonists separated overseas parliament from overseas king and denied the authority of the one while they affirmed their loyalty to the other. This was the issue so sharply dramatized by the Boston Tea Party when Hamilton had been two years on the mainland. And it was the issue which had its logical constructive protest in the setting up of an American parliament of sorts — the Continental Congress. The movement was not a popular one — not at this stage. It was men of large property who were framing petitions then, denying the right of the English Parliament to tax "without representation" or to regulate business enterprise without the consent of colonial assemblies who were chosen by and of the propertied folk. These petitions were being addressed to the British king by substantial and loyal subjects. They ventured to inform His Majesty that true liberty meant protecting the fruits of talent and industry and that, as things were, talent and industry were at the mercy of legislative despots. There were other loyalists too, of course, who for years in New York, once fighting got under way, appeared to have chosen the winning side, but who, in this preliminary stage, were on the defensive. They fell back on the theory that the English regulations, however trying, must be put up with or there would be no respect for authority. The argument was hot. Both sides, as is usual, cited learned works in natural law and moral philosophy and appropriated the favor of Deity.

But official King's College never wavered. It stood against rebellion. Vardill had long been writing in defense of Church and Crown. Later, in 1773, he went to England to be ordained, was appointed Regius Professor of Divinity and Natural Law at King's. Instead of returning, however, he joined what we would now call the intelligence service, using his colonial knowledge in the British interest. Clossy, disgusted with the outbreaks in the colony, returned to England in 1774. In the following year Cooper, after asserting that "open disrespect to government" sprang from unprincipled minds, and rebellion, even if successful, would lead to the country's ruin, was forced to take the unceremonious leave which caused Hamilton to make his first public appearance.*

* A *History of Columbia University* (New York, 1904), p. 46.

That young man, still a student, took his stand, as his teachers did, on the eternal natural laws, "written on the whole volume of human nature itself"; but these laws led him to the conclusion that the repugnant Parliamentary regulations were null and void. He said that the love of power was natural to men, and if taxation by the representatives of property were denied, then civil society must end. This was so because men by contract form society to protect their property and thus their liberty. Loyalist writers answered that taxes were already laid by representatives of the nation — to be a representative a legislator need not be chosen by all: witness the case of the English masses who had no franchise. Hamilton quickly admitted the principle that a property qualification was essential. He could see that artisans would be dependent on their masters in selecting representatives. In America the propertied class was in the position of the English masses; they had no representatives because they selected none.*

So the argument ran. But verbal exchanges at length lost their dramatic value and violence seeped through the brick-lined alleys and washed up to the walls of King's. Instruction came to an end, hurried by a shower of stones. The instructors departed with discretion, conservative to the end and, so far as we know, unabashed by the rough refutation of their doctrine. Hamilton was left undecided as to what he ought to do. He thought of going back to his mother's people where his younger brother was; he still had the funds which would have seen him through to his degree. He used them, finally, to equip a company of state militia, and so got the customary commission. This was the beginning of several years of action, of life in camp and on the march which ended, as Hamilton's jobs always did, in a thinking task. He became an aide to Washington through some brilliant maneuvering, partly his own and partly that of some well-placed friends. It became clear, after a bit, however, that Washington's aides were merely that. When the General dared to rebuke him for tardiness one day he drew himself up, stared at the commander in chief and said: "I am not conscious of it, Sir; but since you have thought it necessary to tell me so, we

---

* "The Farmer Refuted," 1774, *Works of Alexander Hamilton* (Lodge, ed.; New York, 1904), pp. 88–92, 119–120. Unless otherwise specified, all references are to this edition of Hamilton's works.

part." * And they did, too. The twenty-four-year-old lieutenant colonel demanded a field assignment and got it, ultimately, under Lafayette, with whom he served with distinction until after Yorktown.

Between Yorktown and the peace there were two years. That time was sufficient for the driving youth to become a father (he had married General Schuyler's daughter), a member of the bar, and a delegate to the Continental Congress. All was confusion then in public life; but all was clear in Hamilton's mind. The government had no resources because it had no taxing power; the Treasury was empty and the fatal twins of borrowing and begging had been used until "not worth a Continental" had become a permanent and expressive phrase, indicative of the furthest degradation. Crooks operated hand in hand with Congress, playing games with declining dollars, and disgusting honest folk. Hamilton's genius for penetrating analysis never shone so brightly as during this time of trial. The thing to do, he saw, was to temporize, to try for help from France, but above all to establish the principle of Federal authority. When he wrote the reply of Congress to the objections Rhode Island made to Federal assessment, he went straight to the issue: that position, he said, "would defeat . . . all the purposes of the Union." He went further, in a burst of honesty, to say, "The truth is that no Federal Constitution can exist without powers that, in their exercise, affect the internal policy of the component members." †

With these words there began one fundamental constitutional controversy which has persisted throughout our history. The convention which liquidated in compromise the weary corruption of the Continental Congress failed to provide a solution when complete settlement was possible; we had a civil war which, as force always does, missed the mark; and, because of it, we have had only a crippled power to meet recurring economic crises since. Entangled with it, there grew up the issue of independence for the executive, legislative, and judiciary branches for which not even Hamilton found the right solution until too late. He consented to compromise once too often and found that his political enemies could, after traduction, deny even a cabinet officer the privileges of the floor of Con-

* To Philip Schuyler, February 18, 1781, Works, IX, 232.
† "Report on Impost Duty," 1782, Works, II, 183.

gress; and there was thus started a career of legislative blackmail which has not yet been stopped — has, indeed, grown worse with the multiplication of governmental duties and the increase in the size of Congress.

These questions developed their critical phases through the fourteen years between Hamilton's leaving the army and his retirement from the Treasury. As far as he himself was concerned they opened with the reading of philosophy and the study of law, proceeding through the great constitutional debates to the establishment of a permanent fiscal policy and ending their creative uniqueness with the "Report on Manufactures" which permanently established the tariff on our continent. Through it all — and this is one of the curious characteristics of Hamilton — he wrote as though the responsibilities of statecraft had continuous control of his mind. Most men grow into the recognition of greatness gradually and become conscious of the weight of every word and action only after learning the hard lessons of public office. Not so with Hamilton. When he was young he approached serious questions with a strange gravity; when he was more mature, he met them without compromise and with undiminished vigor. During his years in public office he was not on the side which created difficulties with well-to-do citizens who can be so savage at the betrayal of their class, and so his courage was never tested in that way; but there were occasions when a little withholding of intention, a tenderness of statement, a shift in the directness of action might have helped. These he seldom used; and for Madison, who knew how to use them all, he developed a contemptuous understanding.

The pre-law reading of Rousseau and Hobbes must have set up some lively conflicts in his mind. We have now only the remote residue of the state papers with which to judge the course of his progress in theory.* Certainly his profession of "democracy" at this time was sufficiently verbose. He inveighed against the imposition of an "aristocracy of wealth," but close examination indicates that the injustice in this was deplored on behalf of a democracy of property owners. This is, of course, a severe modification of Rousseau. There is a characteristic passage in which he makes clearly the point that a gov-

* Pay-Book of the State Company of Artillery commanded by Alexander Hamilton, in John C. Hamilton's edition of the *Works* (New York, 1850), I, 4.

ernment where a chamber of superior wealth is created to check the assembly chosen by the propertied, irrespective of the size of holdings, must surely end in convulsions.* Somewhat earlier than this he had been much more extreme; indeed the following, written when he was just under eighteen,† displays a faith not justified by later writings or acts; it was probably not thoughtfully meant even then: "All men have one common original: they participate in one common right. No reason can be assigned why one man should exercise any power or pre-eminence over his fellow creatures more than another. . . ."

But this was one of the first of the controversial papers. Hamilton quickly learned the arts of understatement and the amenities of consistency. For a man who wrote and said so much he was remarkably sure-footed. Most importantly, perhaps, he became more and more direct and pragmatic. He was never profound in spite of erudition. Even this "Full Vindication," early as it was, paid only lip service, so to speak, to so-called theory. When he really got down to business he wanted to know whether what was proposed (opposition to parliamentary taxation of colonial commerce) had also the "sanction of good policy." He put it this way: "To render it agreeable to good policy three things are requisite. First, that the necessity of the times requires it; secondly, that it be not the probable source of greater evils than it pretends to remedy; and lastly, that it have a probability of success." And this was the outline of his whole argument after obeisance to "plain and indisputable principles." ‡ Hamilton is not the first or last young intellectual to begin by reference to vague principle and to win simplicity only by struggle with himself. But he was certainly fast in finding his métier. His evolution is perfectly illustrated in this first document.

He was not yet free of his entangling alliances, of course. One of his most serious appeared in "The Farmer Refuted" (but only one year later) when he wrote the much-quoted sentences: "The sacred rights of mankind are not to be rummaged for among old parchments or rusty records. They are written, as with a sunbeam, in the whole volume of human nature, by the hand of the Divinity it-

* To Gouverneur Morris, May 19, 1777, *Works*, IX, 71–72.
† "A Full Vindication," 1774, *Works*, I, 6.
‡ *Ibid.*, p. 14.

self, and can never be erased or obscured by mortal power." This eloquence might be forgiven any youth of nineteen except Hamilton; and even for him it must be said that he was arguing with a prominent clergyman before an upper-class audience likely to be impressed by respectful references to nature and the Deity. But the body of this thirty-five-thousand-word tract is legalistic argument and precise statement of the economic conditions for a successful American policy. Of these last the most prophetic was the declaration that American independence would come simply through recognition of our resources, geography, extent, and the like factors which became the real basis of his later statesmanship and which have dominated our policy from that day to this.*

As the war progressed and Hamilton worked closer and closer to the centers of power his faith even in a democracy of property owners faded. There were dissensions in the Congress and in the state governments themselves; and worse yet, there was the disrupting quarrel between them. State rights were supreme and no general direction was available even for the war. Quotas for revenue assigned to the various colonies were repudiated at will; military appointments were used to placate small-town politicians; militia levies were local and temporary. Gross corruption and inefficiency were everywhere. No orderly mind could contemplate the surrounding chaos except with revulsion. Those who had whatever authority could be wrested from local politicians used their powers in ways which seem peculiar to us now. Hamilton was so outraged once that he publicly denounced members of Congress who used their offices for private profit; and he made a savage attack on Samuel Chase. Here was the case of a prominent and respectable citizen — he was afterward a Justice of the Supreme Court — who thought it not unworthy to get profit for himself at the public expense.† This kind of thing, said Hamilton, was ruining the country.

It is difficult to remember sometimes, as such incidents come to light, that there was a certain contemporary justification. Mercantilism was orthodox. It was made to seem quite legitimate to trade with the enemy if by doing so a favorable money balance was secured; and with such doctrines abroad the private side lines of office

* To the great trouble of laissez-faire statesmen of all parties and factions.
† "Publius," 1778, Works, I, 199–209.

holders seemed thoroughly innocent.* Hamilton shared at least the mercantilist bias for monetary balances even though his gorge rose against the private adaptation of the mercantilist lack of scruple as to the source of the funds themselves. He believed that the public credit must be secured at all costs; depreciation of the currency could lose the struggle faster than armies could win it. When he was twenty-two he began to show that special talent for finance which enabled him to dominate the fixing of the new nation's fiscal policy. He wrote letters containing financial schemes not only to his military superiors and to acquaintances in Congress, but also to Robert Morris, the current strong man of finance. This had consequences, for Morris recognized his talent and afterward was influential in furthering his ambitions. The one idea which dominated this early letter writing was the conviction that whatever scheme was adopted for financial regeneration (and he was flexible about that) it must be a sort which would be profitable to the financial and business classes. It was this profit which would tie them to the government. Every scheme he worked out had this as a feature. He knew his times; he knew human nature as well as Adam Smith did; and he did bulwark his government eventually with selfish and respectable support.

It has been noted that all the forces which impinged upon Hamilton tended to reinforce an aristocratic bias already sufficiently strong when he left the West Indies. Another of these forces was the study of law into which he plunged after Yorktown, for it was English law. Still another was the conditions he met as a beginning practitioner. He was a penniless man with high connections and family standards hard to meet; he had to make money. Furthermore, he was surrounded by a speculative group who were just then beginning the exploitation of Western lands and enterprises. Among these were William Duer, afterward a great entrepreneur, and Aaron Burr, grandson of Jonathan Edwards, son of a Princeton president, and later to be Hamilton's executioner. These and others were seeking to found fortunes; Hamilton joined in the game.

The fiscal ideas detailed in the papers written during his army years and just after exhibited close reasoning and mature restraint.

* It is well to say that laissez-faire believers could find reasons also.

His ideas shifted somewhat when it came to detailed scheming, although he held closely to the mutual support between business and government. He saw that the depreciation of the currency which had taken place so far was not caused altogether by its excessiveness; the moneyed people had found depreciation profitable. This led him to the conclusion that these same motives could be used for a reverse effect. He suggested that a bank under government auspices but controlled by private stockholders with limited liability should be chartered, and no other established during its lifetime. The model was the Bank of England; but he went much further than the original in linking public business and private profit. In his last plan the general government and the states were to deposit with it their specie and the proceeds of foreign loans. It was not only to perform the functions of discount and deposit, but to coin money, issue paper currency, and have allotted to it all the contracts for supplying the fleets and armies. Its notes were to be acceptable in payment of all public duties.

In this scheme the increased issues of paper over specie reserves would make possible loans to the government for which the customary market interest of 8 per cent would be paid. Furthermore this additional paper, by creating business prosperity, would increase the amount of taxes which might be levied and so render the public debt secure. Since people are influenced by such things, the name of the new currency was to be changed. Even if the war should be lost, England would retain the bank because of its manifest advantages, and the shareholders would not be endangered. Of course, the support of the moneyed classes would be forthcoming only if a solid confederation, vigorous administration, and a permanent military force were established.

Similarly, bounties to promoters of domestic enterprise would be beneficial along with tariffs and other favors. Those who demanded that the sovereign should leave trade absolutely alone were running counter to the teachings of experience and common sense. Such views had arisen from the antipathy to war-time price fixing and from the misreading of Hume's "Essay on the Jealousy of Commerce." But neither Hume, "that ingenious and sensible thinker," nor any other authority questioned that government interposition

was one of those moral influences often necessary to rectify an un-
favorable balance of trade and to restore commerce to the natural,
invariable laws of profitable activity.*

But the most important function of import duties was to supply
funds for backing the public debt which might in this way be made
fully negotiable; and if it were it could then serve as a circulating
medium and as capital. Incidentally this would also allow its holders to incorporate as a bank. The national debt might turn out to be
a blessing for a further reason: the masses would be forced to work
harder in order to pay the necessary taxes. Thanks to popular maxims, he thought, we labor less than any people of Europe. About the
public debt he had strong views always; he suggested seriously the
joining of army discontent with that of the public creditors; but
Washington felt that such attempts would cause convulsions.† Still
Washington was learning to respect and trust the younger man.
Robert Morris, also, was impressed and it was through his urging
that Hamilton became Receiver of Continental Taxes for New
York State, an officer whose thankless duty it was to collect Federal
requisitions. The pay was scarcely more than nominal; but it furnished a connection with national finance and with Morris which
later developed toward the secretaryship of the Treasury.

One of Hamilton's biographers quite lost his restraint when he
came to discuss the events of 1787; he called it "the wonderful
year." ‡ It was all of that. It was then, above all, that Hamilton had
his way with his country. That we have a Constitution at all and
are a union instead of an association of jealous neighbors, we may
well owe to him more than to any other single person. Many other
individuals were involved, but none had his determination and certainty. In 1786 under Washington's auspices at Mount Vernon,

---

* Hamilton, on this particular point, himself misread Hume, although there
were arguments in Hume which might have been used (Hume, *Political Dis-
courses* [Edinburgh, 1752], pp. 82–84). He had read Adam Smith and even had
prepared a commentary for his own perusal, but it would not have suited his
purpose to cite Smith, whose only clear exception to the doctrine of free trade
was the Navigation Acts.

† To James Duane, 1780, "Continentalist," 1781, 1782, "Report on Impost
Duty," to Robert Morris, 1780, 1781, to Washington, February 7, 1783, April,
1783, to Governor Clinton, May 14, 1783; *Works*, I, 233–237, 261, 267–270; II,
189; III, 319–387; IX, 312–313, 332–337, 341.

‡ Henry Jones Ford, *Alexander Hamilton* (New York, 1920).

Commissioners from Maryland and Virginia met for certain commercial negotiations. The discussion there disclosed a need for more general agreement and the Virginia Legislature appointed commissioners to meet those who might be appointed by other states. The intention was clear enough; several sovereign states were to try for mutual accommodation in interstate trade. But Hamilton took the opportunity, small though it was, to pursue his controlling purpose — the establishment of union. He could manage the preliminary concurrence of New York because the city's merchants had grievances; he could even become a delegate himself because the meeting seemed to Governor Clinton relatively unimportant. In fact it was unimportant, except that it opened a narrow door through which Hamilton could go. Only five states were represented; but there were others also from which demands for the regulation of trade were beginning to come. Using this as his lever, Hamilton suggested a further meeting. He did it in the vaguest of terms (this on the advice of Edmund Randolph of Virginia), going gently, smoothly forward; nevertheless the recommendations adopted by the meeting for a convention to meet in Philadelphia in 1787 did say that one object was to be the rendering of the "Constitution of the Federal Government adequate to the exigencies of the union." * But even this was softened. The delegates were not to have plenary powers. Everything would afterward have to be ratified.

Nevertheless the West Indian adventurer had really stirred the British lethargy, had disturbed the predilection for local advantage, the resisting dislike for organization and control. The strategy was moving. Yet much had to be given away. Sometimes it seemed that nothing would be left. He foresaw the long struggle involved in the legislative compromise. But he had come to love his country deeply. He did not, it is true, respect her intelligence greatly. He thought her beautiful but not wise. Others, including Jefferson, would think her wise rather than adorable, however, and so rather more than compensate for Hamilton's strange infatuation. The Constitution would turn out to have a queer mixture of democratic conviction and aristocratic noblesse. Hamilton acted rather as though he were appointing and instructing executors to protect and shelter her after his death. He was doubtless inclined to limit unduly the qualifica-

* "Address of the Annapolis Convention," 1786, Works, I, 335–339.

tions for executors; but there were fundamental principles of power involved. The source of the mandate we cannot now approve; Hamilton preferred to ignore some parts of his nation which seemed to him unbeautiful or unruly; we now take her whole and find her mandate in a majority quite unselected. But we still have not remedied those limitations on the executors of our forefathers' will, as our nation develops, which Hamilton would have struck away in the beginning in so far as they interfered with the expansion of the money economy.

The peace of 1783 had given the country no ease. Public creditors were clamant; commercial rivalries had become so intense that the extreme recourse of conciliation had been attempted at Mount Vernon; the states had refused to be assessed except as it suited their selfish plans; there had been armed risings in New England and forcible suspension of the courts to prevent foreclosures. So in forming the Constitution arrangements were consented to, even fought for later, which none of the Fathers believed to be wise and which have been a torment ever since. To this even the policy of private profit from public ventures for the sake of establishing a self-interested protector class is not an exception. If it was desired to have businessmen profit from the establishment of union this was never for the sake of the businessmen but always in the interest of union. Hamilton has often been said to have been an aristocrat, and he was; he has often been said to have been something less than a genuine democrat, and this is true. But his was a genuinely national loyalty, not a class or a local identity. He was looking for strength for his nation and he got it where he could find it.

Hamilton had in mind, when he came to the Convention, a modification of the model furnished by the British Government of that time. He seems, for instance, to have wanted a hereditary monarchy with so much power that no advantage would ever be found in securing more. In this way corruption would be made impossible — a consideration of great weight to one who had had an intimate experience with the Continental Congress. He thought, also, that the setting up of a House of Lords for the wealthy would create a permanent interest in the state from which honors came and would furnish a check on the probable radicalism of a House of Commons.

For this last he had, he thought, enough evidence in the paper-money habits of the state legislatures, their readiness to pass debt-staying laws and the like. Wealth indicated enlightenment; the propertyless were irresponsible. A substantial property interest indicated the practical focus for political power; it was solidly rooted in resource and it commanded active defense. This was the clue to the securing of permanence for the infant nation.

There was more to this argument. In fact, Hamilton was inclined to elaborate it beyond necessity. Liberty could be defined best as freedom to acquire and keep wealth; it followed from this, of course, that equality was nonsense. There must always be the rich and the poor, nobles and commons, creditors and debtors. The advance of industry and commerce would only widen these disparities; wealth would become more concentrated and virtue would be its graceful appendage. All this might be deprecated as a departure from strict republican principle, but it could not be prevented. It was inherent in a human nature which was self-interested and especially so in pecuniary affairs. If the influence of the wealthy, moreover, should be circumscribed by law, they would secure the same effect by corruption. What is inevitable may as well be called virtuous. Another aspect of the same situation was that too much democracy would, through the rise of demagogues, lead to a despotism which must be less intelligent than that of the wealthy. In pursuing this thought, Hamilton used the authority of Hume's Tory history; it was shown there that the bribery of Parliament by the Crown was, under the circumstances, a wise way of maintaining an equilibrium. It brought out the dominant traits of self-interest and ambition but it secured their energies for the public benefit.

In effect, the whole lesson of history was that "popular" government could not last long and that while it did last it made misery. What he was getting at was that America would be wisest to set up a President and a Senate chosen for life by an electorate restricted to considerable property holders, and to center most of the power in these as against the necessary Chamber of Commons or small property holders — the "turbulent people." But he felt that even this would scarcely be enough; the states would have to be reduced to administrative units of the central government and within each there would need to be placed a representative of the national authority with veto power over its legislative assembly.* On the whole Hamilton's scheme, basing itself on the belief that economic power could never center in the people, in workers and small farmers, would withhold from them a political power which they would certainly use irresponsibly and center it in the wealthy who would use it with decorum.

If all this seems inconsistent with his way of thinking in the early days of the Revolutionary War, it can only be said that with the most reasonable of us there are times when we succumb to plausible theories which seem to commit us to beliefs we never really have. In 1782, which was not far removed from the time of his youthful obeisances to Rousseau, he had written in one of his reports to Morris that on the matter in question (inducing the New York Legislature to meet its Federal obligations), he would do what he could but that that would not be much until the whole system of government had been changed. "The inquiry," he said of the legislature, "constantly is what will please, not what will benefit the people. In such a government there can be nothing but temporary expenditure, fickleness and folly." † This was the way his convictions ran and ran consistently. The people could not be trusted even to look after themselves. And when it came to setting up a permanent government for the new nation, his earlier tentatives in the direction of democracy were dropped. This was a serious matter and a practical one. Playing with theories was out of place.

Hamilton was not too well pleased by the final draft of the Constitution. He feared especially the vast powers of the states and would have located the reservoir of sovereignty, if he could, in the Federal government, a fault which he went some way toward remedying later on when, in one of his remarkable overnight memoranda, he developed full-blown the doctrine of implied powers. But fearful as he was, he knew that great gains had been made and he labored with characteristic energy to secure ratification. It was a bitter and prolonged fight. The arguments he used were those which came out

* "Propositions for a Constitution of Government," and speeches in the Federal Convention, *Works*, I, 347–428.
† To Robert Morris, August 13, 1782, *Works*, IX, 273.

of his now settled convictions. This Constitution would cause land values to rise; funds would come out of hiding; industry would prosper. The essentials of property protection and security of contracts and persons had been gained. The courts were firmly rooted and wealth need hide no longer. The rich and the well-born had been committed to the country's future. When New York voted, he knew at last that the symbol of his adoration was enshrined; the holy of holies, moreover, was reasonably removed from vulgar disturbance; at thirty-three his life's work was done.

Thomas Jefferson:
Anti-totalitarian

by

A. WHITNEY GRISWOLD

["Jefferson's Republic: The Rediscovery of Democratic Philosophy." Reprinted from the April 1950 issue of *Fortune* Magazine by special permission; copyright 1950 *Time Inc.*]

We have already pointed out how, far more than Hamilton, the many-sided Jefferson has attracted historians to his career. (Interestingly, Hamilton's latest biographer complains that the "present standard editions of Hamilton's Works . . . *disclose a considerable number of errors in transcription, in attributed dates, and in elisions of pertinent sections."* [1] *The same can be said of the earlier editions of Jefferson's writings. A project is now under way, however, for a "complete Jefferson" in upwards of fifty volumes.* [2] *Nothing like this is contemplated for Hamilton.)*

Between 1943 and the present, three "comprehensive" biographies of Jefferson either have been completed or are in process. Nathan Schachner, in 1951, published two large-size volumes on Jefferson; Mary Kimball has produced thus far two volumes that bring Jefferson's career to 1784; Dumas Malone also has published two volumes of a projected four-volume treatment that will probably stand as the outstanding Jefferson biography of our times.

Yet each of Jefferson's most recent biographers sees him differently. To Mrs. Kimball, Jefferson is always the idealized Virginian. Professor Malone, while less laudatory of his central figure, is no less appreciative. Professor Malone's treatment focuses about a "core" of consistency that the author believes characterized Jefferson throughout his career; while Mr. Schachner, who sees small virtue in consistency, permits his Jefferson to have a more erratic line of development.

In the following selection, A. Whitney Griswold, President of Yale University and formerly professor of history there, sums up an aspect of Jefferson's thinking which is particularly meaningful for us today.

JEFFERSON'S case against totalitarianism, though scattered through his voluminous papers and correspondence and never summed up in a formal essay, is one of the most definitive ever stated in history. In American history it is the most definitive. Jefferson's opposition to absolutism in any form, on any pretext, was as thoughtful as it was uncompromising. No matter what the motives or premises supporting it, whether idealism or efficiency, Jefferson opposed it *à outrance*. From the moving prologue of the Declaration in 1776 to the yet vivid epilogue in the letters he was writing in 1826, he asserted the capacity of human nature to achieve both freedom and order without resort to coercion — and, per contra, the impossibility of achieving either by means of coercion. "I have no fear, but that the result of our experiment will be, that men may be trusted to govern themselves without a master," he wrote apropos of the Constitution. "Could the contrary of this be proved, I should conclude, either that there is no God, or that he is a malevolent being." Did the republican form of government lack the energy to preserve itself? On the contrary, he believed it "the strongest government on earth . . . the only one where every man, at the call of the law, would fly to the standard of the law, and would meet invasions of the public order as his own personal concern. Sometimes it is said that man cannot be trusted with the government of himself. Can he, then, be trusted with the government of others? Or have we found angels in the form of kings to govern him? Let history answer this question."

History has answered it, to our satisfaction, in the negative. And it is being answered in Jeffersonian language, in such current — and representative — essays in democratic philosophy as James Bryant Conant's *Education in a Divided World,* Bertrand Russell's *Authority and the Individual,* David E. Lilienthal's *This I Do Believe,* and Vannevar Bush's *Modern Arms and Free Men.* Conant speaks for them all when he pleads that we use our educational system as the instrument of self-government and self-improvement — the alternative to paternalism and coercion — for which Jefferson intended it. It is the heart of Russell's warning against "too much tendency towards authority, and too little care for the preservation of initiative" in modern society. And, of course, it is the heart of Jefferson's entire thought.

That thought is compressed into axioms in the Declaration. It is spelled out more fully in the Bill of Rights. As soon as Jefferson (then Minister to France) received a full report of the work of the Federal convention he wrote Madison to urge the adoption "of a bill of rights, providing clearly, and without the aid of sophism, for freedom of religion, freedom of the press, protection against standing armies, restriction of monopolies, the eternal and unremitting force of the habeas corpus laws, and trials by jury in all matters of fact triable by the laws of the land." Madison had come away from the convention persuaded by Hamilton and James Wilson that a Bill of Rights was unnecessary and that it might prejudice the Constitution's chances of adoption. Jefferson converted him, and, in the process, once more transmitted his powerful influence from the realm of thought to the realm of action. The first thing Madison did after taking his seat in the House of Representatives in the First Session of the First Congress of the United States was to propose a group of amendments embodying his friend's ideas. We have so long taken these first ten amendments for granted that it may be difficult for us to see in them the irreducible minima of democracy. Yet take away one of them, or any significant part of one, and the dictator's boot is through the door.

It is not so much the originality of the Bill of Rights as the emphasis Jefferson placed upon it that is remarkable. It was not original. One by one its component principles had accumulated in the body of the English common law. Many were stated in the English Bill of Rights of 1689. Virginia had adopted its world-famous Bill of Rights in 1776; Jefferson himself was author of the seminal Virginia Act for Establishing Religious Freedom, passed in 1785; and by 1789 eleven states had bills of rights appended to or incorporated in their constitutions. But Jefferson counted the protection of these rights, together with a representative legislature, as one of the two "essentials constituting free government" — far too important to be omitted from the Constitution of the United States. A national bill of rights would prevent defections among the states — "A brace the more will often keep up the building which would have fallen, with that brace the less." It would put a "legal check" into the hands of the judiciary . . . "a body, which, if rendered independent and kept strictly to their own department, merits great confidence for their learning and integrity." This consideration, which Jefferson told Madison carried great weight with him, is exceptionally interesting in the light of Jefferson's subsequent quarrels with John Marshall and his general reputation of hostility to the Supreme Court. It suggests that while he relied on the court to safeguard the Bill of Rights, he was also counting on the bill to ensure a long-run democratic tendency on the part of the court. History has borne out the acumen of this thought. The principal attacks upon our civil liberties have come from the legislative, not from the judicial branches of our government; and in the long run the principal defense of them has been made by the Supreme Court. The court's vested responsibility for our civil liberties has kept it anchored to democratic fundamentals through all kinds of political weather.

Jefferson's full thought on the subject of civil rights goes much deeper than the materialistic laissez-faire doctrine with which he is sometimes associated. The purposes of society, he held, did not require "a surrender of all our rights to our ordinary governors." There were "certain portions of right not necessary to enable them to carry on an effective government, and which experience has nevertheless proved they will be constantly encroaching on, if submitted to them . . . there are also certain fences which experience has proved particularly efficacious against wrong, and rarely obstructive of right, which yet the governing powers have ever shown a disposition to weaken and remove. Of the first kind, for instance, is freedom of religion; of the second, trial by jury, habeas corpus laws, free presses."

If the tyranny of the legislature was "the most formidable dread at present," the tyranny of the executive would come in its turn. It did not matter. With the first ten amendments added to the Constitution, the foundations of free government were secure. But his thoughts had even deeper springs. The "rights" of which he spoke, and the "fences" with which he surrounded them, were not ends in themselves: they were means to ends. The human race had been endowed with a moral sense. This moral sense inclined men to sociability as well as to independence. To permit the moral sense to spread and accrue to the benefit of society as a whole, it must be given freedom to develop at its source, in the individual. This was the wellspring of Jefferson's opposition to absolutism and his championship of the Bill of Rights. It comes clearly into focus in a summary of his political theory that he wrote out for his friend du Pont in 1816:

> I believe . . . that morality, compassion, generosity, are innate elements of the human constitution; that there exists a right independent of force; that a right to property is founded in our natural wants, in the means with which we are endowed to satisfy these wants, and the right to what we acquire by those means without violating the similar rights of other sensible beings; that no one has a right to obstruct another, exercising his faculties innocently for the relief of sensibilities made a part of his nature; that justice is the fundamental law of society; that the majority, oppressing an individual, is guilty of a crime, abusing its strength, and by acting on the law of the strongest breaks up the foundations of society; that action by the citizens in person, in affairs within their reach and competence, and in all others by representatives, chosen immediately and removable by themselves, constitutes the essence of a republic; that all governments are more or less republican in proportion as this principle enters more or less into their composition; and that a government by representation is capable of extension over a greater surface of country than one of any other form.

It is this moral quality that makes democracy a political philosophy, not a mere ideology. It is this that has enabled it to survive the changing circumstances from Jefferson's time to ours. It survives in an industrial age because it is at bottom moral rather than economic. Jefferson's agrarianism was a timely expression of his theory of property, which rested upon his major premise concerning the moral sense. He believed that a right to property was "founded in our natural wants," a biological corollary to the rights to life and liberty with which it was associated. Before the moral sense could flourish, even though protected from tyranny by the Bill of Rights, society must guarantee to each individual the opportunity to satisfy his elemental physical needs. The improvement of this opportunity within prescribed social limits — enjoyment of the property right "without violating the similar rights of other sensible beings" — developed the responsibility of the individual, to the benefit of society. Property, in this sense, was another means to an end. The concrete form of property universally in demand at that time and apparently inexhaustible in supply was land. Thus Jefferson's essentially moral theory of property assumed the contemporaneous shape of a doctrine identifying family farming with democracy, and a public policy favoring the interests of the small landholder.

No sooner had he signed the Declaration of Independence in 1776 than he hastened back to Virginia to abolish the laws of primogeniture and entail. At the same time he proposed a law appropriating to every landless citizen of the state fifty acres "in full and absolute dominion." These fundamentally democratic principles, designed to equalize economic opportunity, have carried through our public land laws from the Ordinance of 1785 (of which Jefferson wrote the first draft) and the Homestead Act and its amendments to the Farmers Home Administration and cognate agricultural agencies of today.

Nor did Jefferson imprison them in an agrarian mold. As President he foresaw the day when "an equilibrium of agriculture, manufactures, and commerce" would be desirable, and as political philosopher he provided for it:

> Whenever there is in any country, uncultivated lands and unemployed poor, it is clear that the laws of property have been so far extended as to violate natural right. The earth is given as a common stock for man to labor & live on. If for the encouragement of industry we allow it to be appropriated, we must take care that other employment be provided to those excluded from the appropriation. If we do not, the funda-

mental right to labor the earth returns to the unemployed. It is too soon yet in our country to say that every man who cannot find employment but who can find uncultivated land shall be at liberty to cultivate it, paying a moderate rent. But it is not too soon to provide by every possible means that as few as possible shall be without a little portion of land. The small landholders are the most precious part of a state.

Here is a moral preamble to the social-security legislation of recent years, an unmistakable projection of the principle of equal opportunity from the agrarian into the industrial and every other economic sphere. The earth as a common stock with equal opportunity for every man to labor and live on it — this was a far cry from the freebooting individualism of the later nineteenth century. So was Jefferson's advocacy of an antimonopoly amendment, a constant and specific theme in his correspondence with Madison in 1788 and 1789. Our efforts to control monopoly in the interest of small business and individual enterprise are faithful reflections of his moral, socially oriented individualism applicable to the whole economy and not confined to any part of it.

Equal opportunity: this, in the fullest meaning of the phrase, is the key to Jefferson's social thought as it was to his economic. And the instrumentality for making equal opportunity real was education. Every child should go to school, and society should make it possible for everyone, regardless of social or economic "status," to pursue his education as far as his intellectual capacities enabled him. This was Jefferson's corollary to popular sovereignty. It was the means whereby the people could not only instruct themselves in the intelligent use of the franchise but also could produce their leaders and teachers in every sphere of life. It was the *sine qua non* of a truly mobile, classless society.

It is impossible to exaggerate the importance of education in Jefferson's scheme of things. The time and thought he lavished on his own studies, on prescriptions of curricula for his friends and relatives, on his bills for promoting public education in Virginia, and, as founder, on the University of Virginia, speak for themselves. They form one of the richest themes in his voluminous papers and correspondence. Since we are interested in his political philosophy, we must not miss the significance he attached to education in that sphere. It was, he said, "the most certain, and the most legitimate engine of government." His speeches and letters abound in such categorical statements as, "I think by far the most important bill in our whole code, is that for the diffusion of knowledge among the people. No other sure foundation can be devised, for the preservation of freedom and happiness"; and, "I know of no safe depository of the ultimate powers of the society but the people themselves; and if we think them not enlightened enough to exercise their control with a wholesome discretion, the remedy is not to take it from them, but to inform their discretion by education"; and again — a sentence that leaps to life against the Iron Curtain — "if a nation expects to be ignorant and free, in a state of civilization, it expects what never was and never will be."

We have given more than lip service to these precepts, as is proved by our development of the most comprehensive system of public and private education in the world. But it is only recently that we have begun to think about the precepts as Jefferson did, to find in them a practical, democratic alternative to paternalism and coercion. We still allow too many of our children to slip through the mesh, especially in underpopulated rural and overcrowded industrial areas. Within our schools and universities our efforts at quality have a long way to go to catch up with our quantitative achievement. But we are beginning to perceive, as our education in democratic political philosophy progresses, that education "is indispensable to the maintenance and growth of freedom of thought, faith, enterprise, and association." These phrases, from the report of the President's Commission on Higher Education in 1947, are evidence of the galvanizing of good, old-fashioned American doctrine into a program of action.

To the Bill of Rights, equal economic opportunity, and education, Jefferson coupled one further link in his chain of democratic political theory. This was — to cite his summary of 1816 once more — "action by the citizens in person, in affairs within their reach and competence, and in all others by representatives, chosen immediately and removable by themselves." This, he said, was "the essence of a republic," and we would certainly call it the essence of a democracy.

Jefferson left no doubt as to how he applied this principle. He would first admit all citizens to the process of government by giving them the franchise. Then he would keep them actively engaged in it by maintaining the greatest possible diffusion of power and responsibility throughout the state. He advocated universal suffrage ahead of his time, and in the pure sense of the word, he was a better federalist than Hamilton. In his *Notes on Virginia,* written in 1781, he declared that the "influence over government must be shared among all the people," and in the model constitution he drew up for Virginia in 1783 he gave the franchise to "all free male citizens, of full age, and sane mind" upon a year's residence in the country. It is true that his era, and most of his colleagues, did not go as far as he did in this respect, possibly because they lacked his faith in the corollary of universal education. But there can be no doubt of his own mind. The very import of the term *republic,* he wrote John Taylor in 1816, was "that governments are more or less republican, as they have more or less of the element of popular election and control in their composition; and believing, as I do, that the mass of the citizens is the safest depository of their own rights and especially, that the evils flowing from the duperies of the people, are less injurious than those from the egoism of their agents, I am a friend to that composition of government which has in it the most of this ingredient."

But it was not enough merely to give everyone the vote. The actual process of government, from the local village and town up through the county, state, and national levels, should be so organized as to "divide it among the many, distributing to every one exactly the functions he is competent to. . . ."

It is by dividing and subdividing these republics from the great national one down through all its subordinations, until it ends in the administration of every man's farm by himself; by placing under every one what his own eye may superintend, that all will be done for the best. What has destroyed liberty and the rights of man in every government which has ever existed . . . ? The generalizing and concentrating all cares and powers into one body, no matter whether of the autocrats of Russia or France, or of the aristocrats of a Venetian senate. And I do believe that if the Almighty has not decreed that man shall never be free (and it is a blasphemy to believe it), that the secret will be found to be in the making himself the depository of the powers respecting himself, so far as he is competent to them, and delegating only what is beyond his competence by a synthetical process, to higher and higher orders of functionaries, so as to trust fewer and fewer powers in proportion as the trustees become more and more oligarchical. . . . Where every man is a sharer in the direction of his ward-republic, or of some of the higher ones, and feels that he is a participator in the government of affairs, not merely at an election one day in the year, but every day; when there shall not be a man in the State who will not be a member of some one of its councils, great or small, he will let the heart be torn out of his body sooner than his power be wrested from him by a Caesar or a Bonaparte.

It is here that appearances are most unfriendly to Jefferson — and to democracy — in the modern state. Concentration and centralization seem to be the order of the day. In the United States, monopoly in business and industry has conjured up monopoly in labor and in agriculture, and the struggle among these great pressure groups has involved the government as the ally of monopoly in particular while it attempts to restrain monopoly in general. How can political power and responsibility be diffused in the face of such a trend? We may maintain our civil liberties, guarantee equal opportunity in the minimal terms of economic security, and make everyone a voter. But can we make every man a "participator" in the Jeffersonian sense? Democratic political philosophy posits this as our goal. What are our chances of attaining it?

In the first place, despite the trend toward concentration, our economy remains the most competitive, and our society, particularly in its organizational forms, the most diversified and mobile in the world; and in that competition and diversity there is still great scope for individual initiative. If, says James B. Conant in a homely illustration, "a man is a skilled worker, the employee of a large concern, a member of a union, an important dignitary in a fraternal order, the natural leader of his immediate neighbors for political purposes, we should have to place him not in one social pattern, as in the case of the soldier in time of war, but in at least half a dozen.

And since most social patterns tend to have an explicit top and bottom, we may speak of his position in each. To the extent that it may be high in one and low in another the complexities increase and the whole situation may defy description." It may indeed defy description, but it also defies totalitarianism in a thoroughly Jeffersonian fashion.

In the second place, while the trend toward centralization has in some ways diminished the vitality of the old geographical units of self-government familiar to Jefferson, the last quarter-century has witnessed a proliferation of new economic and social units as capable of operating on democratic principles as the towns and counties. Would Jefferson have been prepared for this development or something like it? It is easy to infer as much from his oft-repeated maxims, "The earth belongs to the living," and "As new discoveries are made, new truths disclosed, and manners and opinions change with the change of circumstances, institutions must advance also, and keep pace with the times." But even in the old-fashioned form, local government is not dead. On the contrary, the grants-in-aid policy has brought many a local agency to life, and — always given the desire to do so — its powers of resuscitation are capable of saving rather than exterminating many more. Vivid proof of the possibility has been furnished by the Soil Conservation Service, in which we find government ending "in the administration of every man's farm by himself" in an almost literal fulfillment of Jefferson's prescription.

Most impressive of all the omens, however, is our general rediscovery of democratic philosophy, and our use of it as an instrument of public policy. Everywhere Americans are arguing as they have not argued since Jefferson's time "that the nature of the democratic state requires that some sort of action should be or should not be taken," not just in books but in the preambles to public law and the directives of public policy; in the Truman doctrine, the Marshall Plan, and the North Atlantic Pact; in the reports of the President's Committees on Civil Rights and Higher Education; in the Employment Act of 1946 and the subsequent Economic Reports of the President, committing us not to full employment on any terms, but to maximum employment under a system of free enterprise in business and family farming in agriculture; in Supreme Court decisions such as *McCollum* vs. *Board of Education* (1948) specifically citing Jefferson, maintaining his "wall of separation" between church and state. The argument is summed up in the introduction to the Hearings before the House Judiciary Subcommittee on the Study of Monopoly Power in 1949:

> The weight of opinion seemed to place the safeguarding of political freedom in the first position. . . . The motive of protecting not only free enterprise but free political institutions was stressed by one witness after another as peculiarly important in the present disturbed state of the world.

When Americans argued like this in the last quarter of the eighteenth century, the result was a federal democracy that has lasted to the third quarter of the twentieth. Jefferson called this polity a "republic." The renewal of the argument today suggests a very real possibility that when the totalitarian wave of the present has receded, to join all the totalitarian waves of the past, the foundations of Jefferson's republic will still be standing.

The American People in 1800

by

HENRY ADAMS

["Popular Characteristics," from *History of the United States of
America During the First Administration of Thomas Jefferson*
(New York, 1889), I, 41–74.]

Henry Adams devoted the first six chapters of his History of the
United States of America *during the Jefferson and Madison Administrations to an analysis of American life in the year 1800. Introducing a
primarily political history, these chapters which take up "Physical
and Economical Conditions," "Popular Characteristics," "Intellect
of New England," "Intellect of the Middle States," "Intellect of
the Southern States," and, finally, "American Ideals" are not too
well integrated with the bulk of the nine-volume narrative.[1] Nevertheless, the author had an over-all purpose in mind which was served
by including them.*

*In writing of the United States between 1800 and 1817, Adams
was attempting to trace "linear progress" or "at least progression" in
American history between these two dates.[2] Nature and mental
outlook, Adams felt, made for a certain amount of inertia in
American society in the year 1800. "The task of overcoming popular
inertia in a democratic society was new," [3] Adams added, "and
seemed to offer peculiar difficulties." However, by 1817, science and
invention had dragged society forward despite the resistance of the
populace and the physical environment. By that time, "the traits of
American character were fixed; the rate of physical and economical
growth was established." [4]*

*Conquest of the physical environment was not the only challenge
confronting American democracy. Both the first and the last parts
of Adams's* History *ended with the historian asking questions.
Adams said of the Americans of 1815, "they were intelligent, but*

*what paths would their intelligence select? They were quick, but
what solution of insoluble problems would quickness hurry? They
were scientific, and what control would their science exercise over
their destiny? They were mild, but what corruptions would their
relaxations bring? They were peaceful, but by what machinery were
their corruptions to be purged? What interests were to vivify a
society so vast and uniform? What ideals are to ennoble it? What
object, besides physical content, must a democratic continent aspire to attain? For the treatment of such questions, history required
another century of experience."* [5]

Adams, personally, was a great deal more pessimistic about some
of these answers than was the History, which, with its nagging
doubts, was published between 1889 and 1891. In the novel Democracy which Adams published anonymously in 1880, he presented the American system of government as easy prey to political
corruption. Later in life, his pessimism deepened. "The Rule of
Phase Applied to History," which Adams wrote in 1909, spoke of
retrogression rather than progression history — a theory which he
grounded "scientifically" in Lord Kelvin's second law of thermodynamics.

(Kelvin, in the middle of the nineteenth century, had postulated a
universe which was progressively declining in energy. Despite the
fact that by 1909 the second law of thermodynamics was regarded
by most physicists as outmoded, Adams nevertheless seized upon
it as providing confirmation for his dismal view of the future. In a
universe that was declining in energy, Adams argued, thought also
was a form of energy and mankind was losing the ability to respond creatively to the challenge offered by the environment. Perhaps by 1921, certainly no later than 1924, Adams computed,
thought would have reached the limit of its possibilities — and beyond that date the world and mankind was destined to sink deeper
into the morass.[6])

T HE GROWTH of character, social and national — the formation of men's minds — more interesting than any territorial or
industrial growth, defied the tests of censuses and surveys. No

people could be expected, least of all when in infancy, to understand the intricacies of its own character, and rarely has a foreigner been gifted with insight to explain what natives did not comprehend. Only with diffidence could the best-informed Americans venture, in 1800, to generalize on the subject of their own national habits of life and thought. Of all American travelers President Dwight was the most experienced; yet his four volumes of travels were remarkable for no trait more uniform than their reticence in regard to the United States. Clear and emphatic wherever New England was in discussion, Dwight claimed no knowledge of other regions. Where so good a judge professed ignorance, other observers were likely to mislead; and Frenchmen like Liancourt, Englishmen like Weld, or Germans like Bülow were almost equally worthless authorities on a subject which none understood. The newspapers of the time were little more trustworthy than the books of travel, and hardly so well written. The literature of a higher kind was chiefly limited to New England, New York, and Pennsylvania. From materials so poor no precision of result could be expected. A few customs, more or less local; a few prejudices, more or less popular; a few traits of thought, suggesting habits of mind, — must form the entire material for a study more important than that of politics or economics.

The standard of comfort had much to do with the standard of character; and in the United States, except among the slaves, the laboring class enjoyed an ample supply of the necessaries of life. In this respect, as in some others, they claimed superiority over the laboring class in Europe, and the claim would have been still stronger had they shown more skill in using the abundance that surrounded them. The Duc de Liancourt, among foreigners the best and kindest observer, made this remark on the mode of life he saw in Pennsylvania: —

> There is a contrast of cleanliness with its opposite which to a stranger is very remarkable. The people of the country are as astonished that one should object to sleeping two or three in the same bed and in dirty sheets, or to drink from the same dirty glass after half a score of others, as to see one neglect to wash one's hands and face of a morning. Whiskey diluted with water is the ordinary country drink. There is no

settler, however poor, whose family does not take coffee or chocolate for breakfast, and always a little salt meat; at dinner, salt meat, or salt fish, and eggs; at supper again salt meat and coffee. This is also the common regime of the taverns.

An amusing, though quite untrustworthy Englishman named Ashe, who invented an American journey in 1806, described the fare of a Kentucky cabin:

> The dinner consisted of a large piece of salt bacon, a dish of hominy, and a tureen of squirrel broth. I dined entirely on the last dish, which I found incomparably good, and the meat equal to the most delicate chicken. The Kentuckian eat nothing but bacon, which indeed is the favorite diet of all the inhabitants of the State, and drank nothing but whiskey, which soon made him more than two-thirds drunk. In this last practice he is also supported by the public habit. In a country, then, where bacon and spirits form the favorite summer repast, it cannot be just to attribute entirely the causes of infirmity to the climate. No people on earth live with less regard to regimen. They eat salt meat three times a day, seldom or never have any vegetables, and drink ardent spirits from morning till night. They have not only an aversion to fresh meat, but a vulgar prejudice that it is unwholesome. The truth is, their stomachs are depraved by burning liquors, and they have no appetite for anything but what is high-flavored and strongly impregnated by salt.

Salt pork three times a day was regarded as an essential part of American diet. In the *Chainbearer,* Cooper described what he called American poverty as it existed in 1784. "As for bread," said the mother, "I count that for nothing. We always have bread and potatoes enough; but I hold a family to be in a desperate way when the mother can see the bottom of the pork-barrel. Give me the children that's raised on good sound pork afore all the game in the country. Game's good as a relish, and so's bread; but pork is the staff of life. . . . My children I calkerlate to bring up on pork."

Many years before the time to which Cooper referred, Poor Richard asked: "Maids of America, who gave you bad teeth?" and supplied the answer: "Hot soupings and frozen apples." Franklin's question and answer were repeated in a wider sense by many writers, but none was so emphatic as Volney:

> I will venture to say [declared Volney] that if a prize were proposed for the scheme of a regimen most calculated to injure the stomach, the teeth, and the health in general, no better could be invented than that of the Americans. In the morning at breakfast they deluge their stomach with a quart of hot water, impregnated with tea, or so slightly with coffee that it is mere colored water; and they swallow, almost without chewing, hot bread, half baked, toast soaked in butter, cheese of the fattest kind, slices of salt or hung beef, ham, etc., all which are nearly insoluble. At dinner they have boiled pastes under the name of puddings, and the fattest are esteemed the most delicious; all their sauces, even for roast beef, are melted butter; their turnips and potatoes swim in hog's lard, butter, or fat; under the name of pie or pumpkin, their pastry is nothing but a greasy paste, never sufficiently baked. To digest these viscous substances they take tea almost instantly after dinner, making it so strong that it is absolutely bitter to the taste, in which state it affects the nerves so powerfully that even the English find it brings on a more obstinate restlessness than coffee. Supper again introduces salt meats or oysters. As Chastellux says, the whole day passes in heaping indigestions on one another; and to give tone to the poor, relaxed, and wearied stomach, they drink Madeira, rum, French brandy, gin, or malt spirits, which complete the ruin of the nervous system.

An American breakfast never failed to interest foreigners, on account of the variety and abundance of its dishes. On the main lines of travel, fresh meat and vegetables were invariably served at all meals; but Indian corn was the national crop, and Indian corn was eaten three times a day in another form as was salt pork. The rich alone could afford fresh meat. Ice-chests were hardly known. In the country fresh meat could not regularly be got, except in the shape of poultry or game; but the hog cost nothing to keep, and very little to kill and preserve. Thus the ordinary rural American was brought up on salt pork and Indian corn, or rye; and the effect of this diet showed itself in dyspepsia.

One of the traits to which Liancourt alluded marked more distinctly the stage of social development. By day or by night privacy was out of the question. Not only must all men travel in the same coach, dine at the same table, at the same time, on the same fare, but even their beds were in common, without distinction of persons. Innkeepers would not understand that a different arrangement was possible. When the English traveler Weld reached Elkton, on the main road from Philadelphia to Baltimore, he asked the landlord what accommodation he had. "Don't trouble yourself about that," was the reply; "I have no less than eleven beds in one room alone." This primitive habit extended over the whole country from Massachusetts to Georgia, and no American seemed to revolt against the tyranny of innkeepers.

"At New York I was lodged with two others, in a back room on the ground floor," wrote, in 1796, the Philadelphian whose complaints have already been mentioned. "What can be the reason for that vulgar, hoggish custom, common in America, of squeezing three, six, or eight beds into one room?"

Nevertheless, the Americans were on the whole more neat than their critics allowed. "You have not seen the Americans," was Cobbett's reply, in 1819, to such charges; "you have not seen the nice, clean, neat houses of the farmers of Long Island, in New England, in the Quaker counties of Pennsylvania; you have seen nothing but the smoke-dried ultra-montanians." Yet Cobbett drew a sharp contrast between the laborer's neat cottage, familiar to him in Surrey and Hampshire, and the "shell of boards" which the American occupied, "all around him as barren as a sea-beach." He added, too, that "the example of neatness was wanting"; no one taught it by showing its charm. Felix de Beaujour, otherwise not an enthusiastic American, paid a warm compliment to the country in this single respect, although he seemed to have the cities chiefly in mind: —

American neatness must possess some very attractive quality, since it seduces every traveller; and there is no one of them who, in returning to his own country, does not wish to meet again there that air of ease and neatness which rejoiced his sight during his stay in the United States.

Almost every traveler discussed the question whether the Americans were a temperate people, or whether they drank more than the English. Temperate they certainly were not, when judged by a modern standard. Every one acknowledged that in the South and West drinking was occasionally excessive; but even in Pennsylvania and New England the universal taste for drams proved habits by no means strict. Every grown man took his noon toddy as a matter of course; and although few were seen publicly drunk, many were habitually affected by liquor. The earliest temperance movement, ten or twelve years later, was said to have had its source in the scandal caused by the occasional intoxication of ministers at their regular meetings. Cobbett thought drinking the national disease; at all hours of the day, he said, young men, "even little boys, at or under twelve years of age, go into stores and tip off their drams." The mere comparison with England proved that the evil was great, for the English and Scotch were among the largest consumers of beer and alcohol on the globe.

In other respects besides sobriety American manners and morals were subjects of much dispute, and if judged by the diatribes of travelers like Thomas Moore and H. W. Bülow, were below the level of Europe. Of all classes of statistics, moral statistics were least apt to be preserved. Even in England, social vices could be gauged only by the records of criminal and divorce courts; in America, police was wanting and a divorce suit almost, if not quite, unknown. Apart from some coarseness, society must have been pure; and the coarseness was mostly an English inheritance. Among New Englanders, Chief Justice Parsons was the model of judicial, social, and religious propriety; yet Parsons, in 1808, presented to a lady a copy of *Tom Jones*, with a letter calling attention to the adventures of Molly Seagrim and the usefulness of describing vice. Among the social sketches in the *Portfolio* were many allusions to the coarseness of Philadelphia society, and the manners common to tea parties. "I heard from married ladies," said a writer in February, 1803, "whose station as mothers demanded from them a guarded conduct — from young ladies, whose age forbids the audience of such conversation, and who using it modesty must disclaim — indecent allusions, indelicate expressions, and even at times immoral innuendoes. A loud laugh or a coarse exclamation followed each of these, and the young ladies generally went through the form of raising their fans to their faces."

Yet public and private records might be searched long, before they revealed evidence of misconduct such as filled the press and formed one of the commonest topics of conversation in the society of England and France. Almost every American family, however respectable, could show some victim to intemperance among its men, but few were mortified by a public scandal due to its women.

If the absence of positive evidence did not prove American society to be as pure as its simple and primitive condition implied, the same conclusion would be reached by observing the earnestness with which critics collected every charge that could be brought against it, and by noting the substance of the whole. Tried by this test, the society of 1800 was often coarse and sometimes brutal, but, except for intemperance, was moral. Indeed, its chief offense, in the eyes of Europeans, was dullness. The amusements of a people were commonly a fair sign of social development, and the Americans were only beginning to amuse themselves. The cities were small and few in number, and the diversions were such as cost little and required but elementary knowledge. In New England, although the theater had gained a firm foothold in Boston, Puritan feelings still forbade the running of horses.

> The principal amusements of the inhabitants, said [Dwight] are visiting, dancing, music, conversation, walking, riding, sailing, shooting at a mark, draughts, chess, and un-happily, in some of the larger towns, cards and dramatic ex-hibitions. A considerable amusement is also furnished in many places by the examination and exhibitions of the superior schools; and a more considerable one by the public exhibitions of colleges. Our countrymen also fish and hunt. Journeys taken for pleasure are very numerous, and are a very favorite object. Boys and young men play at foot-ball, cricket, quoits, and at many other sports of an athletic cast, and in the winter are peculiarly fond of skating. Riding in a sleigh, or sledge, is also a favorite diversion in New England.

President Dwight was sincere in his belief that college commence-ments and sleigh-riding satisfied the wants of his people; he looked upon whist as an unhappy dissipation, and upon the theater as im-moral. He had no occasion to condemn horse racing, for no race course was to be found in New England. The horse and the dog existed only in varieties little suited for sport. In colonial days New England produced one breed of horses worth preserving and developing — the Narragansett pacer; but, to the regret even of the clergy, this animal almost disappeared, and in 1800 New England could show nothing to take its place. The germ of the trotter and the trotting match, the first general popular amusement, could be seen in almost any country village, where the owners of horses were in the habit of trotting what were called scratch-races, for a quarter or half a mile from the door of the tavern, along the public road. Perhaps this amusement had already a right to be called a New England habit, showing defined tastes; but the force of the popular instinct was not fully felt in Massachusetts, or even in New York, although there it was given full play. New York possessed a race course, and made in 1792 a great stride toward popularity by importing the famous stallion "Messenger" to become the source of endless interest for future generations; but Virginia was the region where the American showed his true character as a lover of sport. Long before the Revolution the race course was commonly established in Virginia and Maryland; English running horses of pure blood — descendants of the Darley Arabian and the Godolphin Arabian — were imported, and racing became the chief popular entertainment. The long Revolutionary War, and the general ruin it caused, checked the habit and deteriorated the breed; but with returning prosperity Virginia showed that the instinct was stronger than ever. In 1798 "Diomed," famous as the sire of racers, was imported into the state, and future rivalry between Virginia and New York could be foreseen. In 1800 the Virginia race course still remained at the head of American popular amusements.

In an age when the Prince of Wales and crowds of English gentlemen attended every prize fight, and patronized Tom Crib, Dutch Sam, the Jew Mendoza, and the Negro Molyneux, an Englishman could hardly have expected that a Virginia race course should be free from vice; and perhaps travelers showed best the general morality of the people by their practice of dwelling on Virginia vices. They charged the Virginians with fondness for horse racing, cockfighting, betting, and drinking; but the popular habit which most shocked them, and with which books of travel filled pages of description, was the so-called rough-and-tumble fight. The practice was not one on which authors seemed likely to dwell; yet foreigners like Weld, and Americans like Judge Longstreet in "Georgia Scenes," united to give it a sort of grotesque dignity like that of a bullfight, and under their treatment it became interesting as a popular habit. The rough-and-tumble fight differed from the ordinary prize fight, or boxing match, by the absence of rules. Neither kicking, tearing, biting, nor gouging was forbidden by the law of the ring. Brutal as the practice was, it was neither new nor exclusively Virginian. The English travelers who described it as American barbarism might have seen the same sight in Yorkshire at the same date. The rough-and-tumble fight was English in origin, and was brought to Virginia and the Carolinas in early days, whence it spread to the Ohio and Mississippi. The habit attracted general notice because of its brutality in a society that showed few brutal instincts. Friendly foreigners like Liancourt were honestly shocked by it; others showed somewhat too plainly their pleasure at finding a vicious habit which they could consider a natural product of democratic society. Perhaps the description written by Thomas Ashe showed best not only the ferocity of the fight but also the antipathies of the writer, for Ashe had something of the artist in his touch, and he felt no love for Americans. The scene was at Wheeling. A Kentuckian and a Virginian were the combatants.

Bulk and bone were in favor of the Kentuckian; science and craft in that of the Virginian. The former promised himself victory from his power; the latter from his science. Very few rounds had taken place or fatal blows given, before the Virginian contracted his whole form, drew up his arms to his face, with his hands nearly closed in a concave by the fingers being bent to the full extension of the flexors, and summoning up all his energy for one act of desperation, pitched himself into the bosom of his opponent. Before the effects of this could be ascertained, the sky was rent by the shouts of the multitude; and I could learn that the Virginian had expressed as much beauty and skill in his retraction and bound, as if he had been bred in a menagerie and practised action and attitude among panthers and wolves. The shock received by the Kentuckian, and the want of breath, brought him instantly to the ground. The Virginian never lost his hold. Like those bats of the South who never quit the subject on which they fasten till they taste blood, he kept his knees in his enemy's body; fixing his claws in his hair and his thumbs on his eyes, gave them an instantaneous start from their sockets. The sufferer roared aloud, but uttered no complaint. The citizens again shouted with joy.

Ashe asked his landlord whether this habit spread down the Ohio.

I understood that it did, on the left-hand side, and that I would do well to land there as little as possible. . . . I again demanded how a stranger was to distinguish a good from a vicious house of entertainment. "By previous inquiry, or, if that was impracticable, a tolerable judgment could be formed from observing in the landlord a possession or an absence of ears."

The temper of the writer was at least as remarkable in this description as the scene he pretended to describe, for Ashe's *Travels* were believed to have been chiefly imaginary; but no one denied the roughness of the lower classes in the South and Southwest, nor was roughness wholly confined to them. No prominent man in Western society bore himself with more courtesy and dignity than Andrew Jackson of Tennessee, who in 1800 was candidate for the post of major-general of State militia, and had previously served as Judge on the Supreme Bench of his State; yet the fights in which he had been engaged exceeded belief.

Border society was not refined, but among its vices, as its virtues, few were permanent, and little idea could be drawn of the character that would at last emerge. The Mississippi boatman and the squatter on Indian lands were perhaps the most distinctly American type then existing, as far removed from the Old World as though Europe were a dream. Their language and imagination showed contact with Indians. A traveler on the levee at Natchez, in 1808, overheard a quarrel in a flatboat near by: —

"I am a man; I am a horse; I am a team," cried one voice; "I can whip any man in all Kentucky, by God!" "I am an alligator," cried the other; "half man, half horse; can whip any man on the Mississippi, by God!" "I am a man," shouted the first; "have the best horse, best dog, best gun, and handsomest wife in all Kentucky, by God!" "I am a Mississippi snapping-turtle," rejoined the second; "have bear's claws, alligator's teeth, and the devil's tail; can whip *any* man, by God!"

And on this usual formula of defiance the two fire-eaters began their fight, biting, gouging, and tearing. Foreigners were deeply impressed by barbarism such as this, and orderly emigrants from New England and Pennsylvania avoided contact with Southern drinkers and fighters; but even then they knew that with a new generation such traits must disappear, and that little could be judged of popular character from the habits of frontiersmen. Perhaps such vices deserved more attention when found in the older communities, but even there they were rather survivals of English low-life than products of a new soil, and they were given too much consequence in the tales of foreign travelers.

This was not the only instance where foreigners were struck by what they considered popular traits, which natives rarely noticed. Idle curiosity was commonly represented as universal, especially in the Southern settler who knew no other form of conversation: —

> Frequently have I been stopped by one of them, [said Weld] and without further preface asked where I was from, if I was acquainted with any news, where bound to, and finally my name. "Stop, Mister! why, I guess now you be coming from the new State?" "No, sir." "Why, then, I guess as how you be coming from Kentuck?" "No, sir." "Oh, why, then, pray now where might you be coming from?" "From the low country." "Why, you must have heard all the news, then; pray now, Mister, what might the price of bacon be in those parts?" "Upon my word, my friend, I can't inform you." "Ay, ay; I see, Mister, you be'ent one of us. Pray now, Mister, what might your name be?"

Almost every writer spoke with annoyance of the inquisitorial habits of New England and the impertinence of American curiosity. Complaints so common could hardly have lacked foundation, yet the Americans as a people were never loquacious, but inclined to be somewhat reserved, and they could not recognize the accuracy of the description. President Dwight repeatedly expressed astonishment at the charge, and asserted that in his large experience it had no foundation. Forty years later, Charles Dickens found complaint with Americans for taciturnity. Equally strange to modern experience were the continual complaints in books of travel that loungers and loafers, idlers of every description, infested the taverns, and annoyed respectable travelers both native and foreign. Idling seemed to be considered a popular vice, and was commonly associated with tippling. So completely did the practice disappear in the course of another generation that it could scarcely be recalled as offensive; but in truth less work was done by the average man in 1800 than in aftertimes, for there was actually less work to do. "Good country this for lazy fellows," wrote Wilson from Kentucky; "they plant corn, turn their pigs into the woods, and in the autumn feed upon corn and pork. They lounge about the rest of the year." The roar of the steam-engine had never been heard in the land, and the carrier's wagon was three weeks between Philadelphia and Pittsburgh. What need for haste when days counted for so little? Why not lounge about the tavern when life had no better amusement to offer? Why mind one's own business when one's business would take care of itself?

Yet however idle the American sometimes appeared, and however large the class of tavern loafers may have actually been, the true American was active and industrious. No immigrant came to America for ease or idleness. If an English farmer bought land near New York, Philadelphia, or Baltimore, and made the most of his small capital, he found that while he could earn more money than in Surrey or Devonshire, he worked harder and suffered greater discomforts. The climate was trying; fever was common; the crops ran new risks from strange insects, drought, and violent weather; the weeds were annoying; the flies and mosquitoes tormented him and his cattle; laborers were scarce and indifferent; the slow and magisterial ways of England, where everything was made easy, must be exchanged for quick and energetic action; the farmer's own eye must see to every detail, his own hand must hold the plow and the scythe. Life was more exacting, and every such man in America was required to do, and actually did, the work of two such men in Europe. Few English farmers of the conventional class took kindly to American ways, or succeeded in adapting themselves to the changed conditions. Germans were more successful and became rich; but the poorer and more adventurous class, who had no capital, and cared nothing for the comforts of civilization, went West, to find a harder lot. When, after toiling for weeks, they reached the neighborhood of Genesee or the banks of some stream in southern Ohio or Indiana, they put up a rough cabin of logs with an earthen floor, cleared an acre or two of land, and planted Indian corn between the tree stumps — lucky if, like the Kentuckian, they had a pig to turn into the woods. Between April and October, Albert Gallatin used to say, Indian corn made the penniless immigrant a capitalist. New settlers suffered many of the ills that would have afflcted an army marching and fighting in a country of dense forest and swamp, with one sore misery besides — that whatever trials the men endured, the burden bore most heavily upon the women and children. The chance of being shot or scalped by Indians was hardly worth considering when compared with the certainty of malarial fever, or the strange disease called milk sickness, or the still more depressing homesickness, or the misery of nervous prostration, which wore out generation after generation of women and children on the frontiers, and left a tragedy in every log cabin. Not for love of ease did men plunge into the wilderness. Few laborers of the Old World endured a harder lot, coarser fare, or anxieties and responsibilities greater than those of the Western emigrant. Not merely because he enjoyed the luxury of salt pork, whiskey, or even coffee three times a day did the American laborer claim superiority over the European.

A standard far higher than the average was common to the cities; but the city population was so small as to be trifling. Boston, New York, Philadelphia, and Baltimore together contained one hundred and eighty thousand inhabitants; and these were the only towns containing a white population of more than ten thousand persons. In a total population of more than five millions, this number of city people, as Jefferson and his friends rightly thought, was hardly American, for the true American was supposed to be essentially rural. Their comparative luxury was outweighed by the squalor of nine hundred thousand slaves alone.

From these slight notices of national habits no other safe inference could be drawn than that the people were still simple. The path their development might take was one of the many problems with which their future was perplexed. Such few habits as might prove to be fixed offered little clue to the habits that might be adopted in the process of growth, and speculation was useless where change alone could be considered certain.

If any prediction could be risked, an observer might have been warranted in suspecting that the popular character was likely to be conservative, for as yet this trait was most marked, at least in the older societies of New England, Pennsylvania, and Virginia. Great as were the material obstacles in the path of the United States, the greatest obstacle of all was in the human mind. Down to the close of the eighteenth century no change had occurred in the world which warranted practical men in assuming that great changes were to come. Afterward, as time passed, and as science developed man's capacity to control Nature's forces, old-fashioned conservatism vanished from society, reappearing occasionally, like the stripes on a mule, only to prove its former existence; but during the eighteenth century the progress of America, except in political paths, had been less rapid than ardent reformers wished, and the reaction which followed the French Revolution made it seem even slower than it was. In 1723 Benjamin Franklin landed at Philadelphia, and with his loaf of bread under his arm walked along Market Street toward an immortality such as no American had then conceived. He died in 1790, after witnessing great political revolutions; but the intellectual revolution was hardly as rapid as he must, in his youth, have hoped.

In 1732 Franklin induced some fifty persons to found a subscription library, and his example and energy set a fashion which was generally followed. In 1800 the library he founded was still in existence; numerous small subscription libraries on the same model, containing fifty or a hundred volumes, were scattered in country towns; but all the public libraries in the United States — collegiate, scientific, or popular, endowed or unendowed — could hardly show fifty thousand volumes, including duplicates, fully one third being still theological.

Half a century had passed since Franklin's active mind drew the lightning from heaven, and decided the nature of electricity. No one in America had yet carried further his experiments in the field which he had made American. This inactivity was commonly explained as a result of the long Revolutionary War; yet the war had not prevented population and wealth from increasing, until Philadelphia in 1800 was far in advance of the Philadelphia which had seen Franklin's kite flying among the clouds.

In the year 1753 Franklin organized the postal system of the

American colonies, making it self-supporting. No record was preserved of the number of letters then carried in proportion to the population, but in 1800 the gross receipts for postage were $320,000, toward which Pennsylvania contributed most largely — the sum of 55,000 dollars. From letters the Government received in gross 290,000 dollars. The lowest rate of letter postage was then eight cents. The smallest charge for letters carried more than a hundred miles was twelve and a half cents. If on an average ten letters were carried for a dollar, the whole number of letters was 2,900,000 — about one a year for every grown inhabitant.

Such a rate of progress could not be called rapid even by conservatives, and more than one stanch conservative thought it unreasonably slow. Even in New York, where foreign influence was active and the rewards of scientific skill were comparatively liberal, science hardly kept pace with wealth and population.

Noah Webster, who before beginning his famous dictionary edited the *New York Commercial Advertiser*, and wrote on all subjects with characteristic confidence, complained of the ignorance of his countrymen. He claimed for the New Englanders an acquaintance with theology, law, politics, and light English literature; "but as to classical learning, history (civil and ecclesiastical), mathematics, astronomy, chemistry, botany, and natural history, excepting here and there a rare instance of a man who is eminent in some one of these branches, we may be said to have no learning at all, or a mere smattering." Although defending his countrymen from the criticisms of Dr. Priestley, he admitted that "our learning is superficial in a shameful degree, . . . our colleges are disgracefully destitute of books and philosophical apparatus . . . and I am ashamed to own that scarcely a branch of science can be fully investigated in America for want of books, especially original works. This defect of our libraries I have experienced myself in searching for materials for the History of Epidemic Diseases. . . . As to libraries, we have no such things. There are not more than three or four tolerable libraries in America, and these are extremely imperfect. Great numbers of the most valuable authors have not found their way across the Atlantic."

This complaint was made in the year 1800, and was the more significant because it showed that Webster, a man equally at home in Philadelphia, New York, and Boston, thought his country's deficiencies greater than could be excused or explained by its circumstances. George Ticknor felt at least equal difficulty in explaining the reason why, as late as 1814, even good schoolbooks were rare in Boston, and a copy of Euripides in the original could not be bought at any bookseller's shop in New England. For some reason, the American mind, except in politics, seemed to these students of literature in a condition of unnatural sluggishness; and such complaints were not confined to literature or science. If Americans agreed in any opinion, they were united in wishing for roads; but even on that point whole communities showed an indifference, or hostility, that annoyed their contemporaries. President Dwight was a somewhat extreme conservative in politics and religion, while the State of Rhode Island was radical in both respects; but Dwight complained with bitterness unusual in his mouth that Rhode Island showed no spirit of progress. The subject of his criticism was an unfinished turnpike road across the State.

> The people of Providence expended upon this road, as we are informed, the whole sum permitted by the Legislature. This was sufficient to make only those parts which I have mentioned. The turnpike company then applied to the Legislature for leave to expend such an additional sum as would complete the work. The Legislature refused. The principal reason for the refusal, as alleged by one of the members, it is said, was the following: that turnpikes and the establishment of religious worship had their origin in Great Britain, the government of which was a monarchy and the inhabitants slaves; that the people of Massachusetts and Connecticut were obliged by law to support ministers and pay the fare of turnpikes, and were therefore slaves also; that if they chose to be slaves they undoubtedly had a right to their choice, but that free-born Rhode Islanders ought never to submit to be priest-ridden, nor to pay for the privilege of traveling on the highway. This demonstrative reasoning prevailed, and the road continued in the state which I have mentioned until the year 1805. It was then completed, and free-born Rhode Islanders bowed their necks to the slavery of traveling on a good road.

President Dwight seldom indulged in sarcasm or exaggeration such as he showed in this instance; but he repeated only matters of notoriety in charging some of the most democratic communities with unwillingness to pay for good roads. If roads were to exist, they must be the result of public or private enterprise; and if the public in certain States would neither construct roads nor permit corporations to construct them, the entire Union must suffer for want of communication. So strong was the popular prejudice against paying for the privilege of traveling on a highway that in certain States, like Rhode Island and Georgia, turnpikes were long unknown, while in Virginia and North Carolina the roads were little better than where the prejudice was universal.

In this instance the economy of a simple and somewhat rude society accounted in part for indifference; in other cases, popular prejudice took a form less easily understood. So general was the hostility to banks as to offer a serious obstacle to enterprise. The popularity of President Washington and the usefulness of his administration were impaired by his support of a national bank and a funding system. Jefferson's hostility to all the machinery of capital was shared by a great majority of the Southern people and a large minority in the North. For seven years the New York legislature refused to charter the first banking company in the State; and when in 1791 the charter was obtained, and the bank fell into Federalist hands, Aaron Burr succeeded in obtaining banking privileges for the Manhattan Company only by concealing them under the pretense of furnishing a supply of fresh water to the city of New York.

This conservative habit of mind was more harmful in America than in other communities, because Americans needed more than older societies the activity which could alone partly compensate for the relative feebleness of their means compared with the magnitude of their task. Some instances of sluggishness, common to Europe and America, were hardly credible. For more than ten years in England the steam engines of Watt had been working, in common and successful use, causing a revolution in industry that threatened to drain the world for England's advantage; yet Europe during a generation left England undisturbed to enjoy the monopoly of steam. France and Germany were England's rivals in commerce and manufactures, and required steam for self-defense; while the United States were commercial allies of England, and needed steam neither for mines nor manufactures, but their need was still extreme. Every American knew that if steam could be successfully applied to navigation, it must produce an immediate increase of wealth, besides an ultimate settlement of the most serious material and political difficulties of the Union. Had both the national and state governments devoted millions of money to this object, and had the citizens wasted, if necessary, every dollar in their slowly filling pockets to attain it, they would have done no more than the occasion warranted, even had they failed; but failure was not to be feared, for they had with their own eyes seen the experiment tried, and they did not dispute its success. For America this question had been settled as early as 1789, when John Fitch — a mechanic, without education or wealth, but with energy of genius — invented engine and paddles of his own, with so much success that during a whole summer Philadelphians watched his ferryboat plying daily against the river current. No one denied that his boat was rapidly, steadily, and regularly moved against wind and tide, with as much certainty and convenience as could be expected in a first experiment; yet Fitch's company failed. He could raise no more money; the public refused to use his boat or to help him build a better; they did not want it, would not believe in it, and broke his heart by their contempt. Fitch struggled against failure, and invented another boat moved by a screw. The Eastern public still proving indifferent, he wandered to Kentucky, to try his fortune on the Western waters. Disappointed there, as in Philadelphia and New York, he made a deliberate attempt to end his life by drink; but the process proving too slow, he saved twelve opium pills from the physician's prescription, and was found one morning dead.

Fitch's death took place in an obscure Kentucky inn, three years before Jefferson, the philosopher President, entered the White House. Had Fitch been the only inventor thus neglected, his peculiarities and the defects of his steamboat might account for his failure; but he did not stand alone. At the same moment Philadelphia contained another inventor, Oliver Evans, a man so ingenious as to be often called the American Watt. He, too, invented a locomotive steam engine which he longed to bring into common use. The great services actually rendered by this extraordinary man were not a tithe of those he would gladly have performed, had he found support and encouragement; but his success was not even so great as that of Fitch, and he stood aside while Livingston and Fulton, by their greater resources and influence, forced the steamboat on a skeptical public.

While the inventors were thus ready, and while state legislatures were offering mischievous monopolies for this invention, which required only some few thousand dollars of ready money, the Philosophical Society of Rotterdam wrote to the American Philosophical Society at Philadelphia, requesting to know what improvements had been made in the United States in the construction of steam engines. The subject was referred to Benjamin H. Latrobe, the most eminent engineer in America, and his Report, presented to the Society in May 1803, published in the Transactions, and transmitted abroad, showed the reasoning on which conservatism rested.

> During the general lassitude of mechanical exertion which succeeded the American Revolution [said Latrobe], "the utility of steam-engines appears to have been forgotten; but the subject afterward started into very general notice in a form in which it could not possibly be attended with much success. A sort of mania began to prevail, which indeed has not yet entirely subsided, for impelling boats by steam-engines. . . . For a short time a passage-boat, rowed by a steam-engine, was established between Bordentown and Philadelphia, but it was soon laid aside. . . . There are indeed general objections to the use of the steam-engine for impelling boats, from which no particular mode of application can be free. These are, first, the weight of the engine and of the fuel; second, the large space it occupies; third, the tendency of its action to rack the vessel and render it leaky; fourth, the expense of maintenance; fifth, the irregularity of its motion and the motion of the water in the boiler and cistern, and of the fuel-vessel in rough water; sixth, the difficulty arising from the liability of the paddles or oars to break if light, and from the weight, if made strong. Nor have I ever heard of an instance, verified by other testimony than that of the inventor, of a speedy and agreeable voyage having been performed in a steamboat of any construction. I am well aware that there are still many very respectable and ingenious men who consider the application of the steam-engine to the purpose of navigation as highly im-

portant and as very practicable, especially on the rapid waters of the Mississippi, and who would feel themselves almost offended at the expression of an opposite opinion. And perhaps some of the objections against it may be obviated. That founded on the expense and weight of the fuel may not for some years exist in the Mississippi, where there is a redundance of wood on the banks; but the cutting and loading will be almost as great an evil.

Within four years the steamboat was running, and Latrobe was its warmest friend. The dispute was a contest of temperaments, a divergence between minds, rather than a question of science; and a few visionaries such as those to whom Latrobe alluded — men like Chancellor Livingston, Joel Barlow, John Stevens, Samuel L. Mitchill, and Robert Fulton — dragged society forward. What but skepticism could be expected among a people thus asked to adopt the steamboat, when as yet the ordinary atmospheric steam engine such as had been in use in Europe for a hundred years was practically unknown to them, and the engines of Watt were a fable? Latrobe's Report further said that in the spring of 1803, when he wrote, five steam engines were at work in the United States — one lately set up by the Manhattan Water Company in New York to supply the city with water; another in New York for sawing timber; two in Philadelphia, belonging to the city, for supplying water and running a rolling and slitting mill; and one at Boston employed in some manufacture. All but one of these were probably constructed after 1800, and Latrobe neglected to say whether they belonged to the old Newcomen type, or to Watt's manufacture, or to American invention; but he added that the chief American improvement on the steam engine had been the construction of a wooden boiler, which developed sufficient power to work the Philadelphia pump at the rate of twelve strokes, or six feet, per minute. Twelve strokes a minute, or one stroke every five seconds, though not a surprising power, might have answered its purpose, had not the wooden boiler, as Latrobe admitted, quickly decomposed, and steam leaks appeared at every bolt-hole.

If so eminent and so intelligent a man as Latrobe, who had but recently emigrated in the prime of life from England, knew little about Watt, and nothing about Oliver Evans, whose experience would have been well worth communicating to any philosophical society in Europe, the more ignorant and unscientific public could not feel faith in a force of which they knew nothing at all. For nearly two centuries the Americans had struggled on foot or horseback over roads not much better than trails, or had floated down rushing streams in open boats momentarily in danger of sinking or upsetting. They had at length, in the Eastern and Middle States, reached the point of constructing turnpikes and canals. Into these undertakings they put sums of money relatively large, for the investment seemed safe and the profits certain. Steam as a locomotive power was still a visionary idea, beyond their experience, contrary to European precedent, and exposed to a thousand risks. They regarded it as a delusion.

About three years after Latrobe wrote his Report on the steam engine, Robert Fulton began to build the boat which settled forever the value of steam as a locomotive power. According to Fulton's well-known account of his own experience, he suffered almost as keenly as Fitch, twenty years before, under the want of popular sympathy: —

When I was building my first steamboat at New York [he said, according to Judge Story's report] the project was viewed by the public either with indifference or with contempt as a visionary scheme. My friends indeed were civil, but they were shy. They listened with patience to my explanations, but with a settled cast of incredulity upon their countenances. I felt the full force of the lamentation of the poet —

Truths would you teach, or save a sinking land,
All fear, none aid you, and few understand.

As I had occasion to pass daily to and from the building-yard while my boat was in progress, I have often loitered unknown near the idle groups of strangers gathering in little circles, and heard various inquiries as to the object of this new vehicle. The language was uniformly that of scorn, or sneer, or ridicule. The loud laugh often rose at my expense; the dry jest; the wise calculation of losses and expenditures; the dull but endless repetition of the Fulton Folly. Never did a single encouraging remark, a bright hope, or a warm wish cross my path.

Possibly Fulton and Fitch, like other inventors, may have exaggerated the public apathy and contempt; but whatever was the precise force of the innovating spirit, conservatism possessed the world by right. Experience forced on men's minds the conviction that what had ever been must ever be. At the close of the eighteenth century nothing had occurred which warranted the belief that even the material difficulties of America could be removed. Radicals as extreme as Thomas Jefferson and Albert Gallatin were contented with avowing no higher aim than that America should reproduce the simpler forms of European republican society without European vices; and even this their opponents thought visionary. The United States had thus far made a single great step in advance of the Old World — they had agreed to try the experiment of embracing half a continent in one republican system; but so little were they disposed to feel confidence in their success, that Jefferson himself did not look on this American idea as vital; he would not stake the future on so new an invention. "Whether we remain in one confederacy," he wrote in 1804, "or form into Atlantic and Mississippi confederations, I believe not very important to the happiness of either part." Even over his liberal mind history cast a spell so strong, that he thought the solitary American experiment of political confederation "not very important" beyond the Alleghenies.

The task of overcoming popular inertia in a democratic society was new, and seemed to offer peculiar difficulties. Without a scientific class to lead the way, and without a wealthy class to provide the means of experiment, the people of the United States were still required, by the nature of their problems, to become a speculating and scientific nation. They could do little without changing their old habit of mind, and without learning to love novelty for novelty's sake. Hitherto their timidity in using money had been proportioned to the scantiness of their means. Henceforward they were under every inducement to risk great stakes and frequent losses in order to win occasionally a thousandfold. In the colonial state they had naturally accepted old processes as the best, and European experience as final authority. As an independent people, with half a continent to civilize, they could not afford to waste time in following European examples, but must devise new processes of their own. A world which assumed that what had been must be, could not be scientific; yet in order to make the Americans a successful people, they must be roused to feel the necessity of scientific training. Until they were satisfied that knowledge was money, they would not insist upon high education; until they saw with their own eyes stones turned into gold, and vapor into cattle and corn, they would not learn the meaning of science.

II
Sectional Conflict and
Civil War

I Differences in East and West

East	West
1. Creditor section	1. Debtor section
2. urban and industrial	2. Rural, agricultural
3. Stressed rights of property	3. Stressed rights of man
4. Feared unchecked democracy	4. Rule of majority
5. Traditions, settled	5. moved a great deal
6. Feared cheap lands	6. Wanted cheap land
7. Looked on west as a source of power and wealth	7. Began to think of itself as an independent section

Pre-Civil War Sectionalism

by

FREDERICK JACKSON TURNER

["The Significance of the Section in American History," from *The Wisconsin Magazine of History*, VIII (March 1925), 255–265. Reprinted by permission.]

"The scientific study of American history in terms of the several sections," writes Fulmer Mood, a research scholar of great skill, "was well established at the University of Wisconsin before the year 1900." Here, Turner's undergraduate teacher, the remarkable William Francis Allen, was conscious of the importance of a sectional understanding of American history, even as his seminal mind anticipated Turner's frontier hypothesis.[1] But before the historians came to a real appreciation of sectional influences, the geographers were aware of their importance. For instance Jedediah Morse, "father of American geography," in 1793 made the concept of grouping by section explicit, by indicating the "Grand Divisions of the United States."[2]

During the nineteenth century, census statisticians began to make considerable use of the sectional idea in pointing up statistical differences between various parts of the country. Since 1900, there has been growing recognition of the usefulness of the sectional or regional concept in historiography and the social sciences, in business and government. However, many of those who employ the regional concept have been troubled by an inability to define it, there being no unanimity of lay or scholarly opinion concerning any one precise scheme of regional classification.[3] In 1939, when under the auspices of the Social Science Research Council a critical analysis was made of Walter P. Webb's The Great Plains, one of the points of contention was Webb's alleged failure to delimit properly the Great Plains region.[4]

Turner himself seemed to grasp this difficulty when he wrote of the many meanings of "sectionalism": "a geography of political habit, a geography of opinion, of material interests, of racial stocks, of physical fitness, of social traits, of literature, of the distribution of men of ability, even of religious differences." [5] *In the selection reprinted below, Turner used the term "section" as did Josiah Royce before him — "any one part of a national domain which is geographically and socially sufficiently unified to have a true consciousness of its own ideals and customs and to possess a sense of its distinction from other parts of the country."*

Sectionalism, thus understood, was probably stronger in the pre-Civil War period than since, in view of the later uniformities that industrialization and the spread of communications have imposed upon our society. And it is the part of Turner's essay devoted to the pre-Civil War era that is here reprinted.

Turner, before his death in 1933, taught at the University of Wisconsin and at Harvard.

A GENERATION ago I published in the *Proceedings* of this Society a paper, which I had read at the summer meeting of the American Historical Association, on "The Significance of the Frontier in American History." The Superintendent of the Census had just announced that a frontier line could no longer be traced, and had declared: "In the discussion of its extent, its westward movement, etc., it cannot therefore any longer have a place in the census reports."

The significance in American history of the advance of the frontier and of its disappearance is now generally recognized. This evening I wish to consider with you another fundamental factor in American history — namely, the Section. Arising from the facts of physical geography and the regional settlement of different peoples and types of society on the Atlantic Coast, there was a sectionalism from the beginning. But soon this became involved and modified by the fact that these societies were expanding into the interior, following the frontier, and that their sectionalism took special forms

in the presence of the growing West. Today we are substantially a
settled nation without the overwhelming influence that accompanied
the westward spread of population. Urban concentration, chiefly in
the East, has reversed the movement to a considerable extent. We
are more like Europe, and our sections are becoming more and more
the American version of the European nation.

First let us consider the influence of the frontier and the West
upon American sections. Until our own day, as I urged in that
paper, the United States was always beginning over on its outer
edge as it advanced into the wilderness. Therefore, the United
States was both a developed and a primitive society. The West was a
migrating region, a stage of society rather than a place. Each region
reached in the process of expansion from the coast had its frontier
experience, was for a time "the West," and when the frontier passed
on to new regions, it left behind, in the older areas, memories, traditions, an inherited attitude toward life, that persisted long after
the frontier had passed by. But while the influence of the frontier
permeated East as well as West, by survival of the pioneer psychology and by the reaction of the Western ideals and life upon the
East, it was in the newer regions, in the area called the West at
any given time, that frontier traits and conceptions were most in
evidence. This "West" was more than "the frontier" of popular
speech. It included also the more populous transitional zone ad-
jacent, which was still influenced by pioneer traditions and where
economic society had more in common with the newer than with
the older regions.

This "West," wherever found at different years, thought of itself
and of the nation in different ways from those of the East. It needed
capital; it was a debtor region, while the East had the capital and
was a creditor section. The West was rural, agricultural, while the
East was becoming more and more urban and industrial. Living
under conditions where the family was the self-sufficing economic
unit, where the complications of more densely settled society did
not exist, without accumulated inherited wealth, the frontier regions
stressed the rights of man, while the statesmen who voiced the interests of the East stressed the rights of property.

The West believed in the rule of the majority, in what John
Randolph, the representative of the Virginia Tidewater aristocracy,

called "King Numbers." The East feared an unchecked democracy, which might overturn minority rights, destroy established institutions, and attack vested interests. The buoyant, optimistic, and sometimes reckless and extravagant spirit of innovation was the very life of the West. In the East innovation was a term of reproach. It always "stalked" like an evil spirit. The East represented accumulated experience, the traditions of the family living generation after generation in a single location and under a similar environment, as President Thwing, of Western Reserve University, has aptly put it. But out in the newer West, through most of its history, men lived in at least two or three states in the course of their migrations. Of the hundred and twenty-four members of the first Wisconsin constitutional convention in 1846, the average was three states for each member. Four had moved eight times. Sixteen had lived in five or more different states, or foreign countries and states; six had lived in seven or more.

The West demanded cheap or free lands on which to base a democratic farming population. The ruling interests in the East feared that such a policy would decrease land values at home and diminish the value of lands which its capitalists had purchased for speculation in the interior. It feared that cheap lands in the West would draw Eastern farmers into the wilderness; would break down the bonds of regular society; would prevent effective control of the discontented; would drain the labor supply away from the growing industrial towns, and thus raise wages.

The West opened a refuge from the rule of established classes, from the subordination of youth to age, from the sway of established and revered institutions. Writing in 1694, when the frontier lay at the borders of Boston Bay, the Reverend Cotton Mather asked: "Do Old People any of them Go Out from the Institutions of God, swarming into New Settlements where they and their Untaught Families are like to Perish for Lack of Vision?" To their cost, he said, such men have "got unto the Wrong side of the Hedge" and "the angel of the Lord becomes their enemy."

No doubt all this makes too sharply contrasted a picture. But from the beginning East and West have shown a sectional attitude. The interior of the colonies on the Atlantic was disrespectful of the coast, and the coast looked down upon the upland folk. The "Men of the Western World" when they crossed the Alleghenies became self-conscious and even rebellious gainst the rule of the East. In the 1730's the Tidewater aristocracy was conquered by the Jacksonian democracy of the interior.

And so one could go on through the story of the antimonopolists, the Grangers, the Populists, the Insurgents, the Progressives, the Farmers' *Bloc,* and the La Follette movement, to illustrate the persistence of the sectionalism of the West, or of considerable parts of it, against the East.

Perhaps Eastern apprehension was never more clearly stated than by Gouverneur Morris, of Pennsylvania, in the Constitutional Convention of 1787. "The busy haunts of men, not the remote wilderness," said he, are "the proper school of political talents. If the Western people get the power into their hands they will ruin the Atlantic interests. The back members are always averse to the best measures." He would so fix the ratio of representation that the number of representatives from the Atlantic States should always be larger than the number from the Western States. This, he argued, would not be unjust "as the Western settlers would previously know the conditions on which they were to possess their lands." So influential was his argument that the convention struck out the provision in the draft which guaranteed equality with the old states to the states thereafter to be admitted to the Union. But on the motion that the representatives from new states should not exceed those from the Old Thirteen, the affirmative vote was cast by Massachusetts, Connecticut, Delaware, and Maryland; Pennsylvania was divided; and the motion was defeated by the votes of the Southern States plus New Jersey.

To the average American, to most American historians, and to most of the writers of our school textbooks (if one can trust the indexes to their books), the word *section* applies only to the struggle of South against North on the questions of slavery, state sovereignty, and, eventually, disunion.

But the Civil War was only the most drastic and most tragic of sectional manifestations, and in no small degree the form which it took depended upon the fact that rival societies, free and slave, were marching side by side into the unoccupied lands of the West, each attempting to dominate the back country, the hinterland, working out agreements from time to time, something like the diplomatic treaties of European nations, defining spheres of influence, and awarding mandates, such as in the Missouri Compromise, the Compromise of 1850, and the Kansas-Nebraska Act. Each Atlantic section was, in truth, engaged in a struggle for power; and power was to be gained by drawing upon the growing West. In the Virginia ratification convention of 1787 William Grayson, by no means the most radical of the members, said: "I look upon this as a contest for empire. . . . If the Mississippi be shut up emigrations will be stopped entirely. There will be no new states formed on the Western Waters. . . . This contest of the Mississippi involves the great national contest; that is whether one part of this continent shall govern the other. The Northern States have the majority and will endeavor to retain it." Similar conceptions abound in the utterances of North Atlantic statesmen. "It has been said," declared Morris in 1787, "that North Carolina, South Carolina and Georgia only, will in a little time have a majority of the people of America. They must in that case include the great interior country and everything is to be apprehended from their getting power into their hands."

If time permitted, it would be possible to illustrate by such utterances all through our history to very recent times how the Eastern sections regarded the West, with its advancing frontier, as the raw material for power.

To New England, until her own children began to occupy the prairies ("reserved by God," as her pioneers declared, "for a pious and industrious people"), this aspect of the West threatened to enable the South perpetually to rule the nation. The first great migration, the most extensive in the area covered, flowed into the interior from the Southern upland. Some of the extreme leaders of the New England Federalists did not so much desire to break away from the South as to deprive that section of the three-fifths representation for its slaves, and either to permit the Western States to leave the Union or to see them won by England. Then the Old Thirteen could be united under conditions which would check the expansion of the South and would leave New England in control.

Writing in 1786 Rufus King, of New York, later Senator and Minister to England, while admitting that it was impolitic at the time wholly to give up the Western settlers, declared that very few men who had examined the subject would refuse their assent "to the opinion that every Citizen of the Atlantic States, who emigrates to the westward of the Alleghany is a total loss to our confederacy."

Nature [he said] has severed the two countries by a vast and extensive chain of mountains, interest and convenience will keep them separate, and the feeble policy of our disjointed Government will not be able to unite them. For these reasons I have ever been opposed to encouragements of western emigrants. The States situated on the Atlantic are not sufficiently populous, and losing our men is losing our greatest source of wealth.

Of course the immediate complaint in New England and New York was against the South itself, its Jeffersonian principles (so obnoxious to New England puritanism), its slavery, its pro-French sympathies. But all these gained much of their force by the conviction that the West was a reservoir from which the South would continue to draw its power. Among the proposals of the Hartford Convention was that no new state should be admitted into the Union without the concurrence of two thirds of both houses of Congress. Had this proposed amendment been made, the New England States with two other states in the Senate could have blocked the West from future statehood. The report warned the old states against "an overwhelming Western influence" and predicted that "finally the Western States, multiplied in numbers and augmented in population will control the interests of the whole." Nathan Dane, after whom Dane County in this state [Wisconsin] is named, furnished the argument for this proposed amendment by his elaborate tabulations and schedules. He pointed out that in the commercial states capital was invested in commerce, and in the slaveholding states in Western lands. When "Kentucky, Ohio and Tennessee were raised up by this interest & admitted into the Union, then the balance was, materially, affected. The non-commerical states pressed the admission of Louisiana and turned the balance against the Northeast." "It clearly follows," he reasoned, "that if a bare majority in Congress can admit new States into the union (all interior ones as they must be) at pleasure, in these immense Western regions, the balance of

the union as once fairly contemplated, must soon be destroyed."
But Jackson defeated the British at New Orleans. The Mississippi
Valley remained within the Union, Louisiana's interests became
affiliated with the commercial states in many ways, and New England people poured so rapidly into the West that New England
found in the northern half of the Valley the basis for a new alliance
and new power as disturbing to the slaveholding South as the
Southern and Western connection had been to New England.

By the middle of the century the South was alarmed at the Western power much in the way that New England had been. "I have
very great fears," wrote Justice Campbell, later of the Federal
Supreme Court, from Mobile to Calhoun in 1847, "that the existing
territories of the Unites States will prove too much for our government. The wild and turbulent conduct of the members upon the
Oregon question and their rapacity and greediness in all matters
connected with the appropriation of the revenues induces great
doubt of the propriety of introducing new States in the Union so
fast as we do." Of the legislators from the Western States he said:
"Their notions are freer, their impulses stronger, their wills less restrained. I do not wish to increase the number till the New States
already admitted to the Union become civilized."

On the other hand, it must be clearly borne in mind that as the
West grew in power of population and in numbers of new senators,
it resented the conception that it was merely an emanation from a
rival North and South; that it was the dependency of one or another
of the Eastern sections; that it was to be so limited and controlled as
to maintain an equilibrium in the Senate between North and South.
It took the attitude of a section itself.

From the beginning the men who went West looked to the future
when the people beyond the Alleghenies should rule the nation.
Dr. Manasseh Cutler, the active promoter of the Ohio Company of
Associates, which made the first considerable permanent settlement
in the Old Northwest Territory, wrote in 1787 a *Description of
Ohio*. Though himself the minister at Ipswich, in the heart of that
stronghold of conservatism, the "Essex Junto," he declared that on
the Ohio would be "the seat of empire" for the whole Union. Within
twenty years, he predicted, there would be more people on the
western side of the Allegheny watershed than in the East, and he

congratulated these people that "in order to begin right there will be no wrong habits to combat and no inveterate systems to overturn — there will be no rubbish to remove before you lay the foundations." Evidently it did not take long to produce the Western point of view!

In the Senate in 1837 Benton, of Missouri, scorned the proposals of Calhoun regarding the disposition of the public domain, and boasted that after the census of 1840 had shown the weight of the West it would be so highly bid for that it would write its own bill. Perhaps the debate over the Compromise of 1850 brings out the self-assertive Western attitude in these years most clearly. Calhoun had argued that the equilibrium between North and South was being destroyed by the increase in free states made out of the Western territories. But Stephen A. Douglas, of Illinois, spoke for the West when he attacked the Southern statesman for the error of thinking of the West as property of the older sections. "What share had the South in the territories," he asked, "or the North, or any other geographical division unknown to the Constitution? I answer none — none at all." And Douglas calculated that if its right to self-determination were admitted, the West would form at least seventeen new free states, and that therefore the theory of equilibrium was a hopeless one.

It was not only the slavery struggle that revealed the Eastern conception of the West as merely the field of contest for power between the rival Atlantic sections, and the West's counter assertion of its own substantive rights. The same thing was shown in many different fields For example, rival Eastern cities and states, the centers of power in their respective sections, engaged in contests for the commercial control of the Mississippi Valley by transportation lines. The contests between rival European powers for the control of the Bagdad railway, the thrust of Germany toward the rich hinterlands made up of the Balkans and India, and the project of "Central Europe" in the history of the World War, have a resemblance to these American sectional contests for the still more valuable hinterland of the Mississippi Valley. American sections did not go to war over their trade and transportation interests. Nevertheless, they recognized that there were such interests. A Southern writer in DeBow's Review in 1847 declared:

"A contest has been going on between the North and South not limited to slavery or no slavery — to abolition or no abolition, nor to the politics of either whigs or democrats as such, but a contest for the wealth and commerce of the great valley of the Mississippi — a contest tendered by our Northern brethren, whether the growing commerce of the great West shall be thrown upon New Orleans or given to the Atlantic cities."

Shortly after this, in 1851, the *Western Journal* of St. Louis published articles lamenting that "the Western States are subjected to the relation of Provinces of the East" and that New Orleans was giving way to New York as their commercial city. Since (so the argument ran) exports can never build up a commercial city, the mouth of the Mississippi must be so improved that imports would enter the Valley by way of New Orleans. "Then," said the writer, "a line of cities will arise on the banks of the Mississippi that will far eclipse those on the Atlantic coast."

The middle of the century saw an extension of this sectional contest for economic power derived from the growing West; but it was the railroad trunk lines rather than the canals that occupied the foreground. The goal became the ports of the Pacific. The Memphis convention of 1845 and the Chicago convention of 1847 illustrate how interior cities were now repeating the rivalry for Western trade which had earlier been seen on the Atlantic Coast. The contests between New Orleans, Memphis, St. Louis, and Chicago influenced the Kansas-Nebraska Act, and the later strategy of the struggle for position between the Pacific railroads.

Throughout our history, then, there has been this sectionalism of West and East, and this Eastern conception of the West as recruiting ground merely for the rival Atlantic Coast sections. Nationwide parties have had their Eastern and Western wings, often differing radically, and yet able by party loyalty and by adjustments and sacrifices to hold together. Such a struggle as the slavery contest can only be understood by bearing in mind that it was not merely a contest of North against South, but that its form and its causes were fundamentally shaped by the dynamic factor of expanding Sections, of a West to be won.

[handwritten annotations across top margin:] urner - Jacksonian democracy was a frontier product
ernathy - Jackson not a liberal - chance + opportunism
iltse " " " - tried to consolidate his
personal and political power, used patronage
chlesinger - J. democracy as an Eastern working-
class movement - J. defender of common man
ammond - development of free enterprise system

William Leggett and Jacksonian Democracy

by

RICHARD HOFSTADTER

["William Leggett, Spokesman of Jacksonian Democracy," from Political Science Quarterly, LVIII (December 1943), 581–594. Reprinted by permission.]

Frederick Jackson Turner, interpreting American history through the medium of the frontier hypothesis, saw Jacksonian democracy as a frontier product.[1] Thomas Perkins Abernethy, however, who has studied Jackson's earlier career in Tennessee politics when that state was a frontier community, concludes that Jackson was anything but a liberal in his outlook and that he came to lead the democratic movement that bears his name through a combination of chance and opportunism.[2]

Charles M. Wiltse, biographer of Jackson's opponent, Calhoun, also denies Jackson the role of a liberal. Seeing Jackson through Calhoun's eyes, Wiltse reveals him as a President bent upon consolidating his personal and political power and making unscrupulous use of the Federal patronage to achieve this end.[3]

Arthur Schlesinger, Jr., sees Jacksonian democracy more as an Eastern working-class movement than as a derivative from the frontier. Schlesinger, who presents Jacksonian democracy as a forerunner of the New Deal and the Fair Deal, portrays Jackson as a defender of the common man on the frontier and in the city against a predatory business community.[4]

The Schlesinger understanding has been challenged on two counts: first, that worker support for Jackson was not nearly as strong as Schlesinger had believed;[5] second, that Schlesinger was incorrect in treating business response to Jacksonian democracy as

Dorfman - humanitarian + business elements
Hofstadter - jacksonian democracy was a
nationwide movement

a unit. According to Dr. Bray Hammond, Schlesinger errs in asso-
ciating the growth of Jacksonian democracy with labor alone, "and
not with business enterprise. There was no more important factor in
the Jacksonian movement than the democratization of business."
Hammond goes on to state that the age of Jackson was marked by
an accelerated development of the free enterprise system. In sup-
porting Jackson, business "had separated the corporate form of or-
ganizations from monopoly and put forth the promise that anyone
could be a capitalist, an investor or a speculator. . . . Business had
become rooted not so much in Wall Street as in the breasts of the
rural capitalists and village entrepreneurs — to the recurring em-
barrassment of liberal and radical causes ever since." [6]

Joseph Dorfman endorses Hammond's point of view, and ascribes
to business the driving force behind the Jacksonian democratic
movement. Jacksonian democracy, asserts Dorfman, "combined both
humanitarian and business elements; the humanitarian element
contributed a weak impress of reform, but it was decidedly thrown
into the shade by the business drive." [7]

It is the opinion of Professor Richard Hofstadter that Jacksonian
democracy "can best be understood as a nationwide movement,
supported by parts of the planting, farming, laboring and entrepre-
neurial classes." [8] *The following account of the career of William*
Leggett, representative of the "radical wing" of the Jacksonian Dem-
ocrats, illuminates some of the multiple aspects of the movement.
Richard Hofstadter is Professor of History at Columbia University.

WHEN William Leggett, one-time associate editor of the New
York *Evening Post,* died prematurely at his home in New Ro-
chelle in May 1839, he was all but unknown outside of New York.
But those who had followed his brief career set no small value on his
work. His friend and colleague, William Cullen Bryant, mourned
the passing of his "warm and mighty heart." * John Greenleaf

---

* In a poem, "William Leggett," *United States Magazine and Democratic
Review,* VI (November 1839), 430; see also the memoir by Bryant, "William
Leggett", *ibid.,* VI (July 1839), 17–28.

Whittier remembered him as one who had "labored more persever-
ingly, and in the end, more successfully," than any other man "to
bring the practice of American democracy into conformity with its
principles." * Walt Whitman coupled the doctrines of "the great
Jefferson and the glorious Leggett" and in his declining years spoke
of his great admiration for him.† A host of contemporary New York-
ers, who like Whitman had read Leggett's sharp editorials, continued to follow his principles and revere his name, and a recent historian of his times has described him as "one of the most sincere and
brilliant apostles of democracy that America has ever known."‡ No
less extravagant were the reactions of his political enemies during
his lifetime. William L. Marcy, a moderate leader of the New York
Democracy, thought of him as a "knave." § The aristocratic Daniel
Hone described his writings on various occasions as "infamous," "dis-
organizing," "slanderous," and "dastardly." || Rival editors, smarting
under his sallies, many times accused him of Jack Cade-ism, Fanny
Wrightism and "agrarianism," and confidently pronounced him insane.

With few exceptions historians have permitted Leggett's name to
suffer undeserved neglect. At a time when Jacksonian democracy
was sundered into radical and conservative factions, he was one of
the most prominent and forceful spokesmen of the radical wing.¶
He formulated the popular approach to currency, corporations,
monopolies and banks when these were paramount issues. As the
intellectual leader of the New York Locofoco movement, whose
principles had considerable effect on democratic practice,# Leggett

---

* *Old Portraits and Modern Sketches* (New York, n. d.), p. 197.
† See Allan Nevins, *The Evening Post: A Century of Journalism* (New York,
1922), p. 141.
‡ William Trimble, "The Social Philosophy of the Loco-Foco Democracy,"
American Journal of Sociology, XXVI (May 1921), 711.
§ Nevins, *op. cit.*, p. 152.
|| Allan Nevins, ed., *The Diary of Philip Hone* (New York, 1927), I, 163,
240–241, 399.
¶ William Trimble, "Diverging Tendencies in New York Democracy in the
Period of the Locofocos", *American Historical Review*, XXIX (April 1919), 398–
421; Dixon Ryan Fox, *The Decline of Aristocracy in the Politics of New York*
(New York, 1918), chap. xiii.
F. Byrdsall leaves no doubt of Leggett's intellectual leadership. *The History
of the Loco-Foco or Equal Rights Party* (New York, 1842), pp. 14–19, 22, 26–
27, 32, 33, 46, 98–99. For the nation-wide importance of the New York agita-

had a significance far out of proportion to his small direct influence. He was an articulate and popular writer, and his editorials expressed the social ideals and aspirations of a large segment of the Jacksonian following.

William Leggett was born in New York City in 1802.* After preliminary training there he was sent to Georgetown College, but his education was interrupted by the failure of his father's business. In 1819 the family moved to Illinois, where the youth remained long enough to gain a knowledge of frontier life which he later put to good use in his short stories. In 1822, he joined the United States Navy as a midshipman. During his four years of service he was assigned to an unusually cruel commander, and the harsh discipline doubtless had something to do with his lifelong hatred for authority. Finally, after undergoing court-martial for dueling with a fellow midshipman, Leggett resigned his commission. He had already contracted yellow fever in the West Indies, and his health was permanently impaired.

While at sea Leggett composed a set of poems which were published in 1825.† They were quite undistinguished, but some short stories on Western and maritime life subsequently brought him a small reputation.‡ In 1828 he married, settled in New York, and established a literary periodical entitled The Critic. For most of its issues, The Critic, which lasted eight months, was strictly a one-man production; Leggett wrote the reviews, drama notes, essays, stories and biographical sketches, set the type, and delivered the magazine to its subscribers. In 1829, at the death of William Coleman, senior editor of the New York Evening Post, Leggett was called to assist Bryant on the editorial staff.

Leggett joined the Post on the condition that he should not be asked to write about politics, "a subject which he did not understand

tion, see Trimble, "Diverging Tendencies," and F. J. Turner, The United States, 1830–1850 (New York, 1935), pp. 320–322; also Reginald C. McGrane, The Panic of 1837 (Chicago, 1924), chap. v.
* For biographical material see the sketch by Bryant, loc. cit., pp. 17–28; also Allan Westcott in Dictionary of American Biography, XI, 147–148; Nevins, The Evening Post, chap. vi.
† Leisure Hours at Sea (New York, 1825).
‡ Tales and Sketches by a Country Schoolmaster (New York, 1829); also Naval Stories (New York, 1834).

and for which he had no taste"; but in less than a year he had absorbed Bryant's free-trade principles and his Jacksonian democracy and was writing with assurance on tariffs, currency, abolitionism and constitutional law.* The opposition dubbed him and Bryant "the chanting cherubs of the *Evening Post*," but there was nothing cherubic about Leggett's spirit. He was free with epithets and often harsh in judging opponents. Bryant found that he "sometimes needs a curb." † But when the financial prosperity of the paper permitted Bryant to leave in the summer of 1834 for a journey to Europe, Leggett was left in charge, and he promptly assumed the role of agitator.

Leggett found it hard to make the compromises necessary to a large journalistic enterprise. Within a short time he had succeeded in alienating many local advertisers, and, worse still, had cut off the government patronage which the *Post*, as a party organ, had enjoyed. He criticized successively the Postmaster-General, the Secretary of the Treasury, the Secretary of the Navy, and the Collector of the Port of New York, and lost the advertising of all their agencies.‡ By January 1836, when Bryant was forced to leave France in haste because of Leggett's serious illness, the paper was in sad financial straits. Leggett himself had borrowed so much from Coleman's widow that she compelled him to surrender to her his share in the paper.§

For a year after fall 1835 Leggett was too ill to work. Then came a brief return to the staff of the *Post;* but in December 1836 he began the publication of his own organ, the *Plaindealer,* which ran for less than a year. Leggett's experiences had not changed his temper. "We establish this paper," he wrote in its first issue, "expecting to derive from it a livelihood. . . . But we cannot for the sake of a livelihood, trim our sails to suit the varying breeze of popular prejudice." || It has not been recorded whether the *Plaindealer* was

---

* Parke Godwin, *A Biography of William Cullen Bryant* (New York, 1883), I, 262.
† *Ibid.*, p. 319.
‡ James Melvin Lee, *History of American Journalism* (Garden City, 1917), pp. 223–224.
§ For Leggett's career on the *Post* see Nevins, *The Evening Post,* chap. vi.
|| Theodore Sedgwick, Jr., ed., *A Collection of the Political Writings of William Leggett* (New York, 1840), II, 112. Hereafter cited as *Political Writings.*

a financial success. At any rate, illness again forced Leggett to leave his journalistic labors. In the hope of regaining his health, he was preparing to go to Guatemala as American chargé d'affaires when death overtook him.

Leggett was so often accused of "agrarianism" — that standard nineteenth-century epithet for one who believed in a redistribution of property — that some of the tar was bound to stick to his reputation. A sympathetic historian has described the outlook of the Locofoco group, which Leggett inspired, as "nascent proletarianism." * But Leggett's own social philosophy, more traditional than this epithet implies, was compounded of a few well-hallowed elements: laissez-faire liberalism, the natural rights philosophy of the Declaration of Independence, and strict construction of the Constitution. That such a man should have been considered dangerously subversive is something of an anomaly in the history of a city that had known the agitations of Thomas Skidmore, Frances Wright, and George Henry Evans. It was not so much the substance of Leggett's thought as his exceedingly broad sympathies, his rhetorical excesses, and the severe logic with which he applied commonly accepted principles to political reality that made him seem profoundly revolutionary.

The period when Leggett's thought took shape was one of rapid economic change and great political ferment. For the first time in our history, the newly won political power of the unpropertied classes was being massed over an important issue. Andrew Jackson was waging his war upon the Bank of the United States, and agitations for democratic reform were rampant in the several states. Speculative activity was at a high pitch, corporate charters were multiplying, prices were rising, and real wages declining. Hard hit by the steeply rising cost of living, and resentful of increasing hardships in a time of great surface prosperity, labor was acting to defend its living standards. Organization took place with a rapidity that was not to be equaled again at any time in the nineteenth century. By 1836, it was estimated that 300,000 men were affiliated with

* Trimble, "The Social Philosophy of the Loco-Foco Democracy," p. 710.

the National Trades Union; and in New York City 11,500 workingmen, perhaps as much as two thirds of the city's gainfully employed
wage labor, were organized.*

Aroused and informed by the penny press and by Jackson's dram-
atization of the fight against "privilege," labor was also politically
conscious. While this was generally true of the larger Eastern cities,
in no place was it more evident than in New York. Traditionally
Tammany Hall had held the support of the city's politically active
lower class. But the Democratic machine was unable to face the
new issues. In particular, the radicals in the party resented its domination by a faction of local bankers. These men were benefiting by
Jackson's policy of removing Federal funds from the United States
Bank and placing them in state banks; and they remained loyal to
the Democratic Party until its leaders proposed to take government
money from all private banks. At the time when Leggett was left in
sole charge of the *Post,* the left wing split from the Tammany
machine and formed its own party, known to its enemies as the
"Locofocos." Always a minority, this group held the balance of power
between the major parties in the city; and its importance was increased by the fact that politicians throughout the country looked
anxiously to the New York City elections, in off years to determine
which way the winds were blowing.

The social attitudes of the workingmen can be understood only
with reference to the unsatisfactory banking practices of the time
and the peculiar limitations imposed by law upon the formation of
corporate businesses. To demand higher wages was the most feasible
course of action for the workingmen, but there is evidence that their
agitation was directed as much against the banking system as
against their immediate employers.† Particularly objectionable was
the fact that banks restricted competition and often prevented new
men from entering the avenues of enterprise. Bank credits were
beginning to play an essential part in business undertakings; the
extension of trade over rather large areas, with the resulting delay

* John R. Commons, *et al., History of Labour in the United States* (New
York, 1921), I, 348–349, 381, 396, 424, 478–484.
    † Commons, *op. cit.,* I, 218–219, 276–277, 278.

in collections, made business especially dependent upon credit facilities. The merchant capitalist was better able to secure the necessary credit than the more humble masters and journeymen. To the ambitious craftsmen who constituted such a large part of the union membership, the banks seemed part of a huge monopolistic conspiracy. Bank charters were issued by legislatures to special groups; the banking business was thus closed to the rest of the populace. The same was true of practically all other lines of enterprise requiring large amounts of capital. Except for manufacturing concerns capitalized for less than 10,000 dollars, which could be founded under a general incorporation law of 1811 in New York State, profit-making corporations were all created individually by special monopoly charters from the state legislature; and men whose capital or influence was too small to win charters from the lawmakers were barred from such profitable lines of corporate enterprise as bridges, railroads, turnpikes and ferries, as well as banks.

To set limits upon new enterprises either by restricting the flow of credit or by legislative ban seemed to the people a way of encouraging monopolistic price-making. "We cannot pass the bounds of the city," objected one of the Locofoco leaders, "without paying tribute to monopoly; our bread, our meat, our vegetables, our fuel, all, all pay tribute to monopolists." * And Leggett himself complained: "Not a road can be opened, not a bridge can be built, not a canal can be dug, but a charter of exclusive privileges must be granted for the purpose. . . . The bargaining and trucking away of chartered privileges is the whole business of our lawmakers." †

Workingmen had another grievance against the banks. They were often paid in notes of distant or suspected banks, which circulated below par value. Forced by employers to accept these notes at par, they were thus defrauded of a portion of their week's pay. It was a common practice for employers to go down to Wall Street on a Saturday morning and buy at a discount enough of these "uncurrent" notes to meet their payrolls.‡ The resulting dislike of banks

* *The Democrat*, March 18, 1836; see also March 26.
† *Political Writings*, I, 103.
‡ *Ibid.*, I, 226; see also pp. 41–43, 234–235; *cf.* Commons *op. cit.*, I, 218, 276–277, 349, 459; Horace Greeley, *Recollections of a Busy Life* (New York, 1873), p. 110.

among the working classes was quickly recognized by political leaders.*

Most of the agencies of wealth which the laborers held responsible for their declining fortunes were creatures of the state legislatures. Discontent soon found a political channel: workingmen saw corporations and banks not as natural economic growths, but as political creations based upon chicane, bribery and favoritism. They had no happy experience with government intervention in economic affairs. To them, government intervention meant corporate monopolies and banks; it meant exclusive privileges granted to men who had already dug deep into the pocket of national welfare. It was the very antithesis of the equal rights which they considered essential to their own advancement.

Freedom of enterprise, they believed, rather than government action, would redress the balance of affairs in favor of the poor and lowly. Legislatures need only refrain from weighting the scales in favor of the rich, and the people would rise through their own efforts. It was in this conviction that Leggett wrote.

The foundation stone of Leggett's political philosophy was the principle of equal rights, and it was this that the Locofocos — the "Equal Rights Party" — chose for their formal name. Leggett's political reasoning was distinguished by his insistence that this principle be applied not only to the formal aspects of democracy, such as suffrage and civil equality, but also to all legislation affecting economic life. Beyond doubt this philosophy was conceived by Leggett as a rationale for the working class, which had his full sympathy. During the bank struggle he stated that the present contest would "inevitably decide whether the rich or the laboring classes, the few or the many, are to rule this wide Confederation." † But he made it clear on a number of occasions that he proposed no class war or agrarian leveling. Indeed, one of his most urgent reasons for objecting to government interference in the private economic affairs of the people was that it would convert political strife into "deadly contests of the whole mass of the people whose pecuniary affairs are impli-

* Thurlow Weed, *Autobiography* (Boston, 1884), pp. 371, 424; *cf.* William H. Seward, *An Autobiography* (New York, 1891), I, 257–258, 299.
† *Political Writings*, I, 70.

cated in the event." * The fundamental purpose of government, he argued, is simply "to protect persons and property." This protection should be granted equally to all classes of the community. Government should not concern itself with regulating the profits of labor or the value of property. For the laboring classes, who constitute the great majority of the people, this amalgam of equal rights and laissez faire is the greatest bulwark of liberty.

> Their only safeguard against oppression is a system of legislation which leaves to all the free exercise of their talents and industry, within the limits of the GENERAL LAW, and which, on no pretence of public good, bestows on any particular class of industry, or any particular body of men, rights or privileges not equally enjoyed by the great aggregate of the body politic.†

Leggett denied any desire to "pull down the rich" or attack propertied institutions. His sole political aim was "that the property of the rich may be placed on the same footing with the labors of the poor." ‡ The poor, he explained, understood well the claims of property and had ample regard for property rights. In fact, the people who labor with their hands had a far greater proportion of the actual property of the country than the creatures of the inflated credit system.§ Leggett's opposition to the banking system was not the malcontent's hostility to all wealth, but the democrat's natural opposition to privileged monopolies instituted by law.‖ Every charter of incorporation, he pointed out, is a monopoly, because it confers upon a small group of people the right to carry on a particular branch of business not open to the community at large. In place of special acts of incorporation, Leggett proposed a general incorporation law which would permit men of small capital and no political influence to organize such concerns. "Such a law would be the very measure to enable poor men to compete with the rich." ¶ In this desire — that poor men should be enabled to compete with rich, in

---

* *Ibid.*, p. 164.
† *Ibid.*, I, 166; *cf.* p. 104; II, 135–142, 326.
‡ *Ibid.*, I, 78.
§ *Ibid.*, p. 107; *cf. Evening Post*, October 2, 1834.
‖ *Political Writings*, I, 97 *et seq.*
¶ *Ibid.*, p. 90; *cf.* p. 143.

the launching of business enterprises — was the core of Leggett's political motivation.

Leggett was careful to say that the democratizing of the laws should not interfere with established institutions. The legislature should not breach the public faith by recalling existing bank charters before their expiration.* Moreover, failure to renew the charters of expiring companies did not mean that the corporations must be broken up; if a general incorporation law were passed they could be continued under its provisions.† Even when outrageous monopolies had been granted, as in the case of the New York-Brooklyn ferry, the public pledge must not be violated.‡ Leggett's stand on property rights was made amply clear in October 1835, when the New York *American*, a paper which had frequently joined the chorus of those who called him an "agrarian," proposed that the ferry problem be settled by maintaining free ferries at municipal expense. Here, cried Leggett gleefully, was real agrarianism proposed by the very guardians of property and public order. He himself was firmly against free ferries as violations of private property. A free ferry at public expense would bestow a valuable gratuity on those who had occasion to use it, at the cost of other men who never stepped foot in a ferryboat. If the city were to provide free ferries, why not free houses, free markets, free everything? § Speaking of his own political doctrines, Leggett declared: "They rest . . . on the basis of inviolable respect for private right. We would not have even the legislature take private property, except for the public good, directly, not incidentally; and then only in the clearest cases, and by rendering the most equitable compensation." ‖ Such was the philosophy of this angel of destruction.

* *Ibid.*, pp. 41–42.
† *Ibid.*, pp. 142–143.
‡ *Ibid.*, p. 212.
§ *Ibid.*, II, 81–82. The reasoning in this editorial is identical with that used by William Graham Sumner forty years later in his assaults upon reformers.
‖ *Political Writings*, II, 81. Leggett was thoroughly consistent in his opposition to any expansion of state action. In an editorial strongly resembling some passages of Herbert Spencer's *Social Statics*, he even attacked a proposal to found a state-supported asylum for the insane poor. The care of the insane should be decentralized as much as possible, Leggett maintained. Not the state, but the county, the town, or, better still, their own kindred, should have the responsibility. (*Ibid.*, I, 79–82.) Like Spencer, Leggett pushed the laissez-faire

UNDERSTANDING THE AMERICAN PAST

Bolder and more original were Leggett's editorials in defense of labor unions, then commonly regarded as dangerous conspiratorial organizations. Leggett insisted that workingmen had as much right to act in concert as their opponents did. It was their "bounden duty," indeed, to organize in resistance to monopolies and the currency system. Only by combined effort could they prevent employers from paying them in depreciated notes, which unorganized workers could be forced to accept.* Leggett thought he could reconcile unionism with his cardinal principle of free trade. "Our notions of free trade . . . dispose us to leave men entirely at liberty to effect a proper object either by concerted or individual action. The character of combinations, in our view, depends entirely upon the intrinsic character of the end which is aimed at." Since fraudulent payment was unquestionably an evil, and since combination was beyond doubt the only remedy, it was fully justifiable.†

Leggett was not an uncritical supporter of the labor cause. When a union demonstration against high prices culminated in a flour riot, during the winter of 1837, Leggett joined other New York editors in condemning the trades unions. The unionists, he argued, had no moral ground for condemning the victimized merchants on the mere suspicion that they were withholding flour from the market. The laborers themselves were organized for the very purpose of withholding from the market an even more vital commodity than flour, in order to get their own price. The situation could not be improved by destroying part of the stock of a commodity already selling too dearly. There was only one cure for high prices. If flour dealers were monopolizing the commodity, they could be properly punished neither by civil law nor by mob law, but only by "the inevitable penalties of a violation of the laws of trade," — by which Leggett meant "natural" economic laws. But the same held true of the laborers, Leggett hastened to add. Society should take no action against them. The immutable principles of trade would infallibly teach them their error, if they would not graduate the price of labor according to the laws of supply and demand. "We are

---

principle to the extreme of proposing that the functions of the post office be left to private enterprise. (*Ibid.*, II, 190–196.)
  * *Ibid.*, I, 109, 228–229.
  † *Ibid.*, II, 125–126.

for leaving trade free," he concluded, "and the right to combine is an indispensable attribute of its freedom." The proper way to cheapen flour would be to abolish the paper-money system and destroy inflated values at the root.* When others proposed a measure to provide legislative indemnity to those who suffered property loss through mob action, Leggett was quick to condemn the idea as an improper extension of governmental functions.†

To defend labor unions was by no means an unheard-of thing for a Jacksonian Democrat, but to speak up for abolitionists was rank heresy. In upholding the civil rights of the antislavery agitators, and finally announcing his conversion to their cause, Leggett in effect read himself out of the Democratic Party. At first he had opposed emancipation on the ground that free Negroes would only compete with the labor of the North and lower its living standards.‡ But he became interested in the abolition movement when its circulars were barred from the mails and its speakers attacked by mobs. According to Whittier, he was converted by an American Anti-Slavery Society address sent to him in September 1835.§ Certainly, at that time, his editorials on the slavery question became sharper,|| and in an early issue of the *Plaindealer* Leggett avowed himself an abolitionist.¶ In 1838, when his friends were planning to nominate him for a Congressional office, he characteristically eliminated himself from the campaign by firmly restating his abolition sentiments.#

It would not be difficult for a severe critic to show that Leggett's economic ideas were in some respects as impractical as his editorial conduct of the *Post*. One may search in vain for some principle of consistency in the argument of a man who held that the banking system was already extended well beyond the business needs of the nation but who also urged that opening the banking business to all and sundry would be a prime remedy for economic ills. And Leg-

---

* *Political Writings*, II, 221–225. For this editorial Leggett was for the first time attacked by labor spokesmen.
† *Political Writings*, II, 244–250.
‡ *Ibid.*, I, 207–208.
§ *Old Portraits*, pp. 204–205.
|| *Political Writings*, II, 64–65, 76–80.
¶ *Plaindealer*, January 14, 1837. *Plaindealer*, February 25, March 4, 1837.
# *Political Writings*, II, 335–336.

gett's metaphysical faith in the all-sufficiency of the "laws of trade" was, to say the least, naïve. Perhaps the fatal weakness in his thinking was his failure to assign any of the hardships of his day to the inherent disorders of a growing economic system, his tendency to trace all difficulties to an evil conspiracy on the part of the rich and well-born.*

Leggett had no conception of history as an evolutionary process. To him, both political democracy and economic harmony were inherent in the natural equilibrium of society. "Democracy and political economy both assert the true dignity of man," he once wrote. "They are both the natural champions of freedom and the enemies of all restraints on the many for the benefit of the few." † Against this naturally beneficent state of affairs, the corporation and bank men were conspiring; and they would, if they were not checked by the people, subvert democratic laissez-faire institutions and establish an aristocracy based upon legislative privilege. This was not an unfamiliar point of view in the United States.‡ It had been the philosophy of Jefferson and John Taylor of Caroline.§ It was also the philosophy avowed by Jackson himself.

In spite of the simplicity of his outlook, there was much that was sound in Leggett's agitation; and it was not long before his labors, and those of more prominent leaders of the New York radical Democrats, began to bear fruit. While the Democratic Party came to grief over the attempt to abolish banknotes of the denominations in which workers were paid,‖ other proposals were written into law. In 1838 the New York legislature passed a Free Banking Act, which, although it did not fully satisfy the demands of the radicals, was a

---

* See for example *ibid.*, I, 110; II, 165.

† *Ibid.*, II, 109.

‡ Leggett was quite aware of this and of the tradition to which he belonged. See especially the *Evening Post*, October 3, 1834.

§ The continuity of early American democratic thought on laissez faire is discussed in Richard Hofstadter, "Parrington and the Jeffersonian Tradition," *Journal of the History of Ideas*, II (October 1941), 391–400; see also Edwin Mims, Jr., *The Majority of the People* (New York, 1941), pp. 244–246. Leggett's economics was shaped chiefly by "the invaluable work of Adam Smith." See *Evening Post*, September 18, 22, 1834. He was also fond of citing Sir Thomas More's *Utopia* on government as an agency of the rich. See especially *Political Writings*, II, 161, 165.

‖ See Seward, *op. cit.*, I, 359–360, 387, 392; Fox, *op. cit.*, p. 402.

long forward step in the development of banking law and an important move toward dissociating the corporation from monopoly.*

Finally, a general incorporation law was provided for in the state constitution of 1846. In national politics, the popular agitation for separation of bank and state bore fruit when Congress passed the Independent Treasury Act, which removed government deposits from state banks and authorized their safekeeping in Federal repositories.† This measure marked the victory of the radical Democrats in the party councils.

The agitation of men like Leggett probably did far more to develop the corporate institution in the United States than to destroy property rights.‡ This outcome is more understandable when it is realized that their aim was not to abolish, or even to limit, private property, but simply to democratize the country's economic life. Leggett proposed that the humble savings of the plain people should be given access to the great sources of profit and the great avenues of opportunity. He was willing to leave the distribution of wealth to the "natural" workings of ability and talent, if only the scales were not artificially weighted against the lower classes. Probably few men in America preached the bourgeois ideals of personal and property rights, freedom of contract, laissez faire, individualism, and private enterprise with as fine a sense for the needs and desires of the common man.

* On this measure, its importance, and its limitations, see Bray Hammond, "Free Banks and Corporations: The New York Free Banking Act of 1838," "Journal of Political Economy, XLIV (April 1936), 184–209. See also Leggett, Political Writings, II, 265–266.

† The Independent Treasury was created in 1840, abolished by the Whigs in 1841, and re-established in 1846.

‡ The spread of general incorporation laws throughout the states made the corporation form increasingly available to businessmen everywhere. Certainly these laws had much to do with the rapid growth of corporations in the two decades before the Civil War. See Thomas C. Cochran and William Miller, The Age of Enterprise (New York, 1942), p. 70.

The Impact of the Revolutions
of 1848 on American Thought

by

MERLE CURTI

[From *Proceedings of the American Philosophical Society,*
XCIII (June 1949), 209–215. Reprinted by permission.]

*Granted, said Carlton J. H. Hayes before the American Historical
Association in December 1945, "that the frontier has been a major
factor in the historical conditioning and development of what is
distinctive in the United States, a large and now, I believe, most
pertinent question remains about the American frontier. It is a frontier of what?"*

*To Professor Hayes, the advancing frontier in North America, like
similar frontiers in South America, Australasia, and South Africa, is
a frontier of Europe. Our historians, by concentrating too much upon
American themes, according to Hayes, have failed to give proper
recognition to this fact, and have contributed as well to what Hayes
characterized as a "growing intellectual isolationism in the United
States." [1]*

*As Professor Hayes suggests, the transit of civilization from
Europe to America, from the Eastern part of the United States to the
West* — and the reverse of this process — *are all of fundamental im-
portance to an understanding of American historical development.
It is true that this field has been little studied; but it has not been
entirely neglected either. Inevitably, the historians of European im-
migration to America like Marcus L. Hansen, G. W. Stephenson,
T. C. Blegen, Oscar Handlin, and Carl Wittke have touched upon*

certain aspects of civilization's transit. As early as 1901, Edward Eggleston pioneered in the study of the transit of ideas from Europe to America and, in 1926, in a paper read before the American Historical Association, Dixon Ryan Fox attempted to systematize the westward transit of civilization into four fairly well-defined stages.[2] A year later, Howard Mumford Jones's America and French Culture explored the problem of cultural impact.

In 1934, a symposium on Sources of Culture in the Middle West: Backgrounds versus Frontier *pointed up the inadequacy of the frontier explanation of American development by showing the persistence of Eastern and European influences in nineteenth-century America. In his volumes on the founding of American civilization,[3] Thomas J. Wertenbaker has stressed the continuing relationship between Europe and America while intellectual historians like R. H. Gabriel, the Beards, and Merle Curti reflect awareness of European influences upon the development of American thought. In 1944, the Princeton Program of Study in American Civilization produced a survey by many hands entitled* Foreign Influences in American Life *— the initial essay by Professor David Bowers being an analysis of the process of impact.*

In addition, during the 1940's, when there was growing recognition of the importance of an international viewpoint, Michael Kraus's Atlantic Civilization[4] *explored the historical roots of the Atlantic community and Ross J. Hoffman wrote of* The Great Republic *from a world perspective.[5] Finally, the reverse process — that is, the American impact on Europe — was discussed in a rather narrowly-defined study by R. H. Heindel,[6] and more broadly in Halvdan Kohn's* The American Spirit in Europe: A Survey of Transatlantic Influences.[7]

It is apparent, then, that even as Professor Hayes was complaining that the frontier interpretation bred isolationist sentiment in American historiography, American historians were not unaware of European influences. Indeed, Turner himself was conscious of interaction between Europe and America.[8] In the following selection, Merle Curti, Frederick Jackson Turner Professor of History at the University of Wisconsin, deals with the impact of the Revolution of 1848 upon the American scene.

THIS year [1948–1949] marks the hundredth anniversary of the seizure of power by Revolutionists over almost all of Western Europe. Some of the leaders in the upheavals of 1848 were bent on setting up republics; others put above all else national autonomy, with or without republican forms; and still others insisted on drastic social change. American reactions to the Revolutions of 1848 can be understood only by keeping in mind the distinct and sometimes contradictory aims of the revolutionists. In the second place, American responses are better understood by remembering the sequence of events in the great uprisings.

Broadly speaking, the first half of the year 1848 saw startling triumphs of the revolutionary upsurge: the overthrow of kings in Italy and France; the flight of Metternich and steps toward constitutionalism in Austria, Prussia, and other German states throughout the spring months; the meeting in Frankfort in May of the liberal assembly designed to unite the Germanies in a federal republic; and the June Days in Paris, which marked the height of the socialistic phase. Although the conservative swing of the pendulum was well under way in France by midsummer, the revolutionary fervor had not yet spent itself elsewhere. Pope Pius IX fled from Rome in November and a republic was proclaimed the following February. In the spring of 1849 the Hungarians, who had been fighting for autonomy, set up a republic.

But throughout the last half of 1848 many signs pointed to the weakness of liberalism and the strength of reaction. The Frankfort Parliament was petering out, and with it the hope of a united, liberal Germany. In October 1848 imperial troops dealt a severe blow to the rebel Hungarians. In France, the choice of Louis Napoleon as president foretold a retreat to the right. In June 1849 French and Austrian armies defeated Mazzini and Garibaldi, thus opening the way to the restoration of papal authority in Central Italy. On August 13, 1849, Austrian arms, strengthened by those of Czarist Russia, dealt a final blow to the Hungarian Republic. The last phase of the mid-century revolutions — the efforts of refugee leaders in England and America to seek help for a new outbreak — was by that time already well under way.

In every section of the United States, the early republican phase of these revolutions was generally greeted with sympathy and even enthusiasm. In Boston, New York, Philadelphia, Baltimore, Washington, Richmond, New Orleans, and Cincinnati monster mass meetings celebrated the happy events.* James Buchanan justly summed up matters in writing that "It was . . . with one universal burst of enthusiasm that the American people hailed the late glorious revolution in favor of liberty and republican government." † The American Minister in Paris on his own authority recognized the French Republic four days after it was proclaimed; and Congress, within less than three weeks on receiving the news, congratulated the French people on overturning the monarchy.‡ The enthusiasm for the prospective Federal republic in the Germanies was no less widespread.§ In condemning the Prussian king for imprisoning a poet who took the monarch to task, Henry Wadsworth Longfellow spoke for millions of his countrymen: "So long as a king is left upon his throne there will be no justice on the earth." || When the Hungarians declared a republic in April 1849, Americans in every section and in each of the major parties rejoiced.

The reasons for American sympathy with the efforts to launch republican institutions in Europe are not hard to find. Hatred of monarchies of any sort was deeply rooted in the American mind. To most Americans monarchy spelled tyranny. In an age of humanitarianism, moreover, warm-hearted impulses were quickened by

* Among the older historians to describe the enthusiasm for the Revolutions of 1848 were H. von Holst, *The Constitutional and Political History of the United States*, IV: 65 ff., Chicago, Callaghan, 1885; James Schouler, *History of the United States under the Constitution*, V, 226–234, Dodd, Mead, 1904; John Bach McMaster, *History of the People of the United States*, VIII: 143–157, N. Y., Appleton, 1913; and James Ford Rhodes, *History of the United States from the Compromise of 1850*, I: 231–242, N. Y., Macmillan, 1893.

† Moore, John Bassett, ed., *Works of James Buchanan* VIII: 33, Phila., Lippincott, 1909.

‡ Curtis, Eugene N., "American Opinion of French Nineteenth-Century Revolutions," *Amer. Hist. Rev.* 29: 255, 1924.

§ For American reactions to the revolutions in Central Europe see Gazley, John G., *American Opinion of German Unification 1848–1871*, N. Y., Columbia, 1926, and May, Arthur J., *Contemporary American Opinion of the Mid-Century Revolutions in Central Europe*, Phila., 1927.

|| Longfellow, Samuel, ed., *Life of Henry Wadsworth Longfellow, with extracts from his correspondence* II: 124, Boston, Ticknor, 1882.

tales of cruelty of Austrian despots toward captured Hungarian and Italian patriots, and of German kings toward high-minded republicans. Pride in the apparent imitation of American republican institutions further explained the enthusiasm in every part of the land. Republicanism was commonly believed to be not only a necessary ingredient of American civilization, but of civilization itself. It was easy to overlook the relation between prosperity and virgin resources, and to attribute the national success to political institutions alone. With a marked national self-consciousness and faith in republican ideas, destined it was felt to become universal, what was more natural than for Americans to sympathize with peoples trying to break the chains of despots and set up republics on the American model? Zeal for the spread of republican institutions was furthered by the requests of German and French leaders for copies of the Constitution, from which, it was thought, they might learn useful lessons.* The fact that the Germans were trying to work out a federal system likewise quickened national pride.†

It is true that in every section there was also, even in this first and chiefly republican phase of the revolutionary movement, a minority view. A study of the secular press has revealed that the *National Intelligencer*, the Whig organ at Washington, and the *North American Review* of Boston, spoke well of the Citizen King who had lost his French throne and made reservations about the new French Republic. To champions of legal authority, a revolution to bring about a republic was, after all, the work of a mob, the usurpation of power. With much prescience these journals foretold the triumph of a despotism in the wake of revolutionary chaos. Catholic opposition to revolution of any sort was, of course, expounded in ecclesiastical circles. But in Congress, John C. Calhoun was almost alone in fearing that the French were not yet ready for a republic and that the congratulations of the American Government were premature.

What was at first a decidedly minority view gained more and

* See Curtis, Eugene N., *The French Revolution of 1848 and American Constitutional Doctrine*, N. Y., Columbia, 1918, and the studies of Gazley and May, previously cited.

† Curti, Merle, "John C. Calhoun and the Unification of Germany," *Amer. Hist. Rev.* 40: 476–478, 1935.

more adherents as events pointed to the weakness of the infant republics. The election of Louis Napoleon as President of France aroused grave doubts in many American circles. These doubts were confirmed by the *coup d'état* of December 1851. Thus were only too fully realized the gloomy predictions that the French were after all too fickle, too inexperienced politically, and too used to central authority to steer a republican course. The collapse of the Italian republics and the restoration of Pius IX to temporal sovereignty was another blow to American enthusiasm. So, too, was the failure of the Frankfort Parliament to unite the Germanies in a federal republic.

The final defeat of the Hungarians, in the summer of 1849, vindicated the dark forebodings of those American conservatives who from the first had predicted the triumph of authoritarianism.

The Revolution of 1848 were not merely designed to achieve republican institutions. In some of the minor German states and above all in France the socialistic program was a crucial part of the movement. While the majority of American intellectuals viewed the European upheavals in political and moral terms, some from the start detected significant social and economic overtones. This was true of Albert Brisbane, the leading American Fourierist, who witnessed events in Paris in the spring and early summer of 1848. Brisbane grasped the plight of the workingmen and understood their aspirations.* His friend, Charles A. Dana, like him a correspondent of the New York *Tribune,* keenly diagnozed the dynamics of the French upsurge. The Revolution of 1789, he pointed out, had destroyed feudalism; the new revolution was "to destroy the moneyed feudalism and lay the foundations of social liberty." † Dana preferred social and economic change by evolution, rather than by revolution; only the refusal of the privileges to grant concessions led him to conclude that violence was inevitable. But the economic analysis of Brisbane and Dana made little dent on American thought, which for the most part looked on the upheavals as moral struggles for abstract political rights. Among leading American pa-

* Brisbane, Redelia, *Albert Brisbane, a Mental Biography,* p. 269, Boston, Arena Pub., 1893.
† New York *Tribune,* July 4, Aug. 3, 21, and 29, 1848.

pers only the New York *Tribune* and the New York *Globe* had a good word to say for the French left wing.*

Indeed, in every section of the land hostility to the socialistic aspects of the revolutions was marked. In New England, George Bancroft† and Henry Wadsworth Longfellow‡ testified to the fear of the conservative well-to-do. Charles Sumner was no less sure that "the rich and the commercial classes feel that property is rendered insecure, and with many of these the pocket is the chief sensorium." § Ralph Waldo Emerson, himself skeptical of the socialist experiments he had seen in Paris, nevertheless believed that much of the hostility in Boston to the revolutions rested on the devotion of the propertied classes to those Europeans already in possession.|| George Ticknor, a wealthy scholar who shared many of the views of State Street, doubted from the first whether the working classes in France were capable of governing either for the benefit of themselves or others.¶

Nor was opinion in the Middle States less hostile to the socialist phase of the revolutions. It is true that the New York *Herald* impishly poked fun at Wall Street's fear of socialism, but it had no more sympathy for the national workshops than other metropolitan journals. The liberal *Tribune* and the democratic *Post* upheld the "ferocious" suppression of those who led the June revolt. The New York *Journal of Commerce* expressed a general view in holding that "no sacrifice less dreadful could have secured the permanent triumph of order and law." #

Southern opinion was unanimous. George Kendall of the New Orleans *Picayune*, an eyewitness to the events in Paris, denounced the leaders as demagogues and their supporters as a rabble bent on

* Gazley, *op. cit.*, p. 248.
† Howe, M. A. De Wolfe, *The Life and Letters of George Bancroft* II: 91, N. Y., Charles Scribner's, 1908.
‡ Longfellow, *op. cit.* II: 111–112.
§ Pierce, Edward, *Memoir and Letters of Charles Sumner* II: 91, Boston, Robert Bros., 1893.
|| Emerson, Ralph Waldo, *Complete Works* XI: 362, Boston and N. Y., Houghton Mifflin, 1883. *Cf. Journals of Ralph Waldo Emerson* VII: 430–431, 454, Boston and N. Y., Houghton Mifflin, 1912.
¶ *Life, Letters, and Journals of George Ticknor* II: 230–232, Boston, James R. Osgood and Co., 1878.
# Gazley, *op. cit.*, pp. 246 ff.

avoiding honest toil and on paralyzing trade and industry.* The
Southern Quarterly Review printed an article, attributed to William
Gilmore Simms, highly critical of the national workshops and the
seizure of the railroads. All this, the writer argues, violated the
sacred principle of private property.† Maryland's novelist, John
Pendleton Kennedy, wrote from Paris of his unpleasant visions of
"that gentlest of sucking doves, the mob of Paris," sacking the
Tuileries while wages went up 100 per cent and rents came down
50 per cent.‡

Opinion about the socialist experiments was just as hostile in the
West, where the *Cincinnati Chronicle* laid the failure of the revolution at the door of "social geometry." Other Western journals were
no less scornful of attacks on property.§

American reactions to the Revolutions of 1848 were influenced by
the doctrine of national self-determination and national unity as well
as by republicanism and socialism. The struggle of Italians, Hungarians, and Bohemians to cast off the Hapsburgs and to win national
independence reminded Americans of the efforts of their own forefathers to break the chains of British rule. Nor could Americans
ignore the parallel between the transformation of the weak Confederation into the more perfect Union, and the endeavors of the
Germans to make a united nation. If space were at hand, it would
be easy to cite from the newspapers of every section and party
praise for the efforts of the revolutionists to win national freedom.

Deprecating sectional agitation over slavery, many stanch nationalists saw in American enthusiasm for European freedom a chance to
turn attention from cleavages at home and to strengthen the feeling
of national unity.|| Such an occasion came to Secretary of State
Daniel Webster when the Austrian chargé, the Chevalier Hülsemann, bitterly protested that the United States had violated its

---

* Copeland, Fayette, *Kendall of the Picayune*, pp. 246 ff., Norman, Okla.,
Univ. of Okla. Press, 1943.
† *Southern Quarterly Review* 14: 114–165, 1849; Trent, William Gilmore,
William Gilmore Simms, pp. 190, 340, Boston and N. Y., Houghton Mifflin, 1892.
‡ Tuckerman, Henry T., *The Life of John Pendleton Kennedy*, pp. 407–408,
N. Y., Putnam and Sons, 1871.
§ Gazley, *op. cit.*, p. 246.
|| Curti, Merle, Young America, *Amer. Hist. Rev.* 31: 34–55, 1926.

neutrality in sending A. Dudley Mann to recognize Hungarian independence if the situation warranted it. In his reply to Hülsemann, Webster, belittling "European despotism," declared that American sympathy would always be actively expressed in behalf of oppressed nationalities.* In boastfully predicting that the United States would yet see the downfall of absolutism in Europe as American influence spread over the world, Webster was, as he privately confessed, trying "to make a man feel *sheepish* and look *silly* who could speak of disunion." † Although some conservatives had no liking for the spreadeagleism of the letter to Hülsemann it was generally applauded as a fine expression of the solidarity of republican America in the great conflict between freedom and despotism.

The revolutions not only appealed to national pride and unity; they appealed hardly less to national self-interest. Many shared the view of well-placed officials that the triumph of a united Germany and Italy under republican leadership would pave the way to more favorable trade treaties than could possibly be wrung from fragmented states ruled by hostile tyrants. Freeman Hunt of the *Merchants' Magazine* saw, in the fall of the Metternich government which had taxed foreign tobacco, not only new markets for this product but for other American commodities as well. United under a single government, the German internal trade barriers, he thought, would break down and the free exchange between states could only be "productive of great results in a commercial point of view." ‡ Such ideas were echoed in many circles.

Pursuing the argument of national self-interest along a somewhat different line, William Henry Trescot, a young South Carolinian one day to become well known in American diplomacy, argued that the time had come for the United States in its own behalf to take a more positive role in world affairs. For American interests, he continued, were directly involved in Russian expansion in Asia; there-

* Curti, Merle, *Austria and the United States 1848–1852, Smith College Studies in History* II (3), 1926.
† *Writings and Speeches of Daniel Webster* XVI: 586, Boston, Little, Brown, 1903.
‡ *Merchants' Magazine and Commercial Review* 14: 85, 1848; *Grahams' Magazine* 23: 323–324, 1848.

fore any increase of Czarist power in Europe, such as that resulting from Russian intervention to put down the Hungarians, indirectly affected American interests. Having reached a position of world power, the United States might well, in union with England, insist on being heard at the council table whenever any issue of world importance was under debate.*

The impact of the Revolutions of 1848 on national thought became fully apparent only when refugees flocked to our shores to beg aid for renewed outbreaks. The French and Italian refugees, including Garibaldi, made little stir.† Gottfried Kinkel, a German revolutionist, was, however, favorably received, especially wherever his countrymen had settled.

But no refugee created such excitement as Louis Kossuth, who, after release from a Turkish prison, landed in New York on December 4, 1851. Huge demonstrations, with torchlight processions on banner-decorated streets, greeeted him. Delegations from far and near paid tribute. His portrait was hung in thousands of shops; the Kossuth mustache, beard, soft hat, and overcoat with flowing sleeves became the fashion of the day; Hungarian cakes, songs, and polkas were the new vogue. One youthful admirer, later to become a famous journalist, succumbed to Kossuth's romantic glamor and risked his life on a mission to Hungary, to ferret out the hiding place of the crown jewels which were needed as sinews for fresh revolt.‡ Emerson called Kossuth "the foremost soldier in this age" and Sumner hailed him as "grandly heroic, a living Wallace, a living Tell."

Despite their many expressions of sympathy with the Hungarians during and after their gallant revolt, Americans had given little thought to the means by which their sympathy might be implemented. Kossuth forced the issue on their attention. With flaming eloquence, he addressed a vast throng at Castle Garden: "I will conscientiously respect your laws, but within the limits of your

* Trescot, William Henry, A Few Thoughts on the Foreign Policy of the United States, Charleston, J. Russell, 1849.
† Garibaldi, Giuseppi, Autobiography I: 67, London, W. Smith and Innes, 1889.
‡ Stillman, William James, Autobiography of a Journalist, I, 142 ff., Boston and N. Y., Houghton Mifflin, 1901.

laws I will use every honest exertion to gain your operative sympathy and your financial, material, and political aid for my country's freedom and independence." *

A minority was ready to use both the diplomatic and the material resources of the country to aid the fallen revolutionists in the revolt they planned to stage. In New England, Dr. Samuel Gridley Howe, who had fought for the Greeks in their struggle against the Turks and tasted imprisonment for aiding the insurrectionary Poles, believed that Britain would yet be compelled to engage single-handed with the tyrants of the Continent, where the bourgeoisie had united for "the *peaceful* pursuit of *business* under the auspices of despotism." If so, he asked, "shall we merely *send* a 'godspeed' and not back it up by hearty blows at the enemies of the race? I say no, a thousand times no!" † In New York Horace Greeley wrote that Kossuth had come to "arouse us to a consciousness of the majesty of our national position and to the responsibilities it involves; to show us that we cannot safely sleep while despots are forging chains for the yet unfettered nations, as well as to bind more securely their present victims; and even if we have no regard for others' rights, we must assume an attitude of resistance to the expanding dominion of the autocrat if only to secure our own." ‡

In the West, many newcomers from Europe sympathized with the revolutionary movements. It was thus timely for political leaders in that section to open their ears to Kossuth's appeals. Stephen A. Douglas did not believe that national duty and interest would always warrant neutrality toward the conflicts between freedom and despotism in the Old World.§ Other spokesmen of the West in Congress, which heatedly debated the nature of the reception to be tendered Kossuth, took members of the legislative body to task for giving the great Hungarian a hand when they should have extended an arm. Senator I. P. Walker of Wisconsin declared in speaking for intervention that he would keep still if he had mere words to

* New York *Herald,* Dec. 13, 1851.
† Richards, Laura E., *Letters and Journals of Samuel Gridley Howe* II: 354, 358, Boston, D. Estes, 1909.
‡ Greeley, Horace, Introduction in Headley, P. C., *The Life of Louis Kossuth,* X, Auburn, N. Y., Derby and Miller, 1852.
§ *Cong. Globe,* 32d Cong., 1 sess., I: 34, 53.

offer Hungary.* Although a few in both houses, chiefly though not exclusively from the West, saw eye to eye with Walker in a readiness to draw the sword, there was at no time any real likelihood that the traditional policy of noninterference in the affairs of the Old World would be given up.

The opponents of Kossuth's appeal included, in the first place, the overwhelming majority of Southerners. The revolutions were largely middle class in character; and in the South the middle class was overshadowed by the great planters. Moreover, Southerners were sensitive to the rising tide of antislavery sentiment in Europe; the French revolutionary government had abolished Negro bondage in the colonies; and Britain was already clashing with Southern interests in using the Royal Navy to block the African slave trade. If the United States took a hand in the domestic affairs of the Old World, what was to keep a European power from meddling with slavery? †

The Roman Catholics, still few in numbers but growing in influence, also set themselves against the Kossuth mission. The revolutions everywhere, including Hungary, had been anticlerical in nature; and it was natural for the hierarchy to frown on sympathy for exiles. Catholic opposition had nipped in the bud plans for an official welcome to Garibaldi; and Archbishop Hughes of New York blasted the Kossuth excitement in no uncertain terms.‡ In New England the Catholic convert, Orestes A. Brownson, belittled the Hungarian and feared that the pressure of the interventionist "Young America" Democrats might inveigle the Pierce administration into aiding the revolutionary exiles.§

But opposition to Kossuth was not confined to conservative Southerners and Catholics. Far from looking on the Kossuth movement as a crusade for freedom, Francis Bowen, the scholarly editor of the *North American Review*, attacked the leaders of the Hungarian rebellion for their ruthless suppression of the Slav minorities.

* *Ibid.*, I: 111, 173, 177.
† *Ibid.*
‡ Hassard, John R. G., *Life of the Most Reverend John Hughes D.D.*, pp. 342–343, N. Y., D. Appleton, 1866.
§ Brownson, Orestes, *Works* X: 548; XVI: 187, 213, 229, 246, Detroit, T. Nourse, 1887.

Bowen was saying, as many in our own day have said: Beware of bids for sympathy and support from a revolutionary regime that masked despotism under banners of freedom. . . . His opposition to Kossuth spoiled his chances for an appointment to the McLean professorship of history at Harvard. But Bowen's stand opened many eyes that had seen nothing but good in the Hungarian leader.*

Kossuth was further crippled by his alienation of most abolitionists. Exhilarated by the early blows against despotism in Europe, the antislavery men had redoubled their own efforts against Negro bondage.† They hailed the decrees that freed the slaves in the French colonies; and they assumed that Kossuth, the great champion of freedom in Europe, would speak out against slavery in the United States. Aware that any statement on so burning an issue would cost him support, the Hungarian kept silent. William Lloyd Garrison and Wendell Phillips damned Kossuth, contrasting his position with that of well-known European friends of freedom who did not draw a line between the two hemispheres.

As the Kossuth excitement reached the fever point, the abolitionists insisted that the country was going out of its way to parade its love of freedom. Was it, they asked, trying to set itself right for the sin of selling the slave down the river of profit and expediency? ‡ The contention that American criticisms of tyranny abroad hardly squared with American indifference to evils at home was to be heard again and again in later conflicts between freedom and despotism.

But even more telling as opponents of interventionism than Catholics and abolitionists was the great body of Americans, who assumed that American concepts of freedom would someday triumph by the sheer force of example. This faith in the doctrine of inevitable progress provided a rationale for those who, like Webster, Clay, Longfellow, Irving, and others, shared the republican and nationalistic aims of the revolutionists, regretted the fall of European liberalism, and maintained that in due time the shining

* North American Review 70: 78–136, 1850.
† Pierce, Memoir and Letters of Charles Sumner II: 230; and Gardiner, O. C., The Great Issue, N. Y., Bryant, 1848.
‡ Phillips, Wendell, Speeches, Lectures, and Letters, pp. 66–67, second ser., Boston, Lee and Shepard, 1891; William Lloyd Garrison, the story of his life as told by his children III: 345, N. Y., Century, 1889.

example of the United States would act as the catalytic agent in bringing the triumph of freedom.*

The overwhelming weight of those who said "no" to Kossuth should not obscure the importance of his appeal in the history of American thought. With the repression that followed the Congress of Vienna in 1815 American leaders, giving up hope for liberalism in Europe, concentrated on the solidarity of the Western Hemisphere.

But now, in 1848 and the following years, the idea that Europe was to be given over to the despots was seriously challenged. In both official and unofficial circles many now insisted that freedom is indivisible, and that the United States must spring to the support of liberty lovers whenever they gave promise of seizing power. When this is added to the argument that the promotion of freedom abroad was advantageous from the standpoints of both economic advantage and power politics, it is clear that all the elements in the picture familiar in our own time were at hand.

The true significance of the Revolutions was their impact in formulating what were essentially new and lasting as well as competing concepts of national policy in relation to Old World conflicts between liberalism and reaction. If it is too much to hold that 1848 and its aftermath witnessed a dress rehearsal for future American entrances and exits to the stage of Old World conflicts, it is not too much to say that for the first time Americans read the lines in the drama. The constellation of parts, then crystallized, still trouble us and as never before now profoundly affect the whole world.

Alone among nations the United States had in 1848 the power to offer sanctuary to large numbers of refugees, to give them not only security in a hostile world but the means for living fully and freely. Although many scholars have studied the influence on the United States of hundreds of Frenchmen, Poles, Hungarians, Germans, and Italians who sought our shores in the mid-century years, there is much yet to be learned. We do know that many learned men who came to America at that time enriched our cultural life just as have refugees in our own time.† To such men and women,

* New York *Weekly Tribune*, Feb. 7, 1852, for Clay's speech.
† Wittke, Carl, "The German Forty-Eighters in America," *Amer. Hist. Rev.* 53: 711–715, 1948.

we owed the introduction of the kindergarten; improved techniques in lithographing; the development of musical taste; contributions to medicine, pharmacy, science, and scholarship. Many Forty-Eighters, including Siegel, Osterhaus, Willich, and Weydemeyer, possessed, too, knowledge of military art highly useful during the Civil War.

The influence of the refugees on the conflict between liberalism and conservatism, between isolationism and world-mindedness, is less easy to gauge. It is clear that by pen and mouth Reinhold Solger, Heinrich Bornstein, Frederick Hassaurek, Frederick Hecker, and Carl Schurz, to name only the best known, invigorated the antislavery movement. While some of the radical Forty-Eighters abandoned their early convictions as they succeeded in their new life, others, imbued with the psychology of opposition, clung to their anticlericalism, their skepticism, their anarchistic and socialistic ideas. * In much the same way the fanciful efforts of refugees to set up a radical, anticlerical German state within the country, to become the focal point of a world republic, re-enforced the rising opposition to immigrants. The nativists, or Know-Nothings, could thus argue that the newcomers were bent on entangling the country in wild, un-American schemes. As we know, the antiforeign sentiment not only influenced political patterns in the 1850's but likewise figured as a main eddy in American feeling. On the other hand, the growing conception of American destiny on the world stage may owe something to the sustained efforts of men like Carl Heinzen. In the words of his biographer, Carl Wittke, this refugee urged America "to crush the forces of reaction wherever they existed, to help make the world safe for democracy, and to build up an international organization based upon the reign of law and the rights of man." †

To the revolutionary upheaval in Europe, and the migration to America it set in play, may also be attributed the introduction of

* McCormick, Thomas J., ed., *Memoirs of Gustav Koerner* I: 518 ff., Cedar Rapids, Torch Press, 1908; *North American Review* 82: 260 ff., 1856.

† Wittke, Carl, *Against the Current: The Life of Carl Heinzen*, VI, Chicago, Univ. of Chicago Press, 1945.

Marxism.* Long before the *Communist Manifesto* of 1848 was finally published in America in 1871, associates of Marx and Engels laid the foundations of modern socialism in the United States. August Willich, a comrade of Marx and Engels in the London Communist League; Joseph Weydemeyer, a personal friend of the authors of the *Manifesto;* and Wilhelm Weitling, who had known Marx and Engels in Paris, all scattered socialist ideas in the German-language magazines and among workers, in the years following 1848. Marx's famous "Eighteenth Brumaire" first appeared in *Die Revolution,* edited by Weydemeyer in New York. All these men drifted away from socialism. But this was not the case with Frederick Sorge, who had also known the founders before reaching New York in 1852 as a refugee of reaction. For a time he kept body and soul together by giving music lessons, but within a few years he was vigorously organizing immigrant workers and propagating Marxist teachings. This is not the place to suggest, even in the broadest terms, the impact of Marxism on American thought. But among the impacts of the Revolutions of 1848 on America, Marxism, slight though it was at the time, was destined in the long run to be of great importance.

At the time, however, the aspects of 1848 chosen in this paper for emphasis seemed far more important to Americans, who thought about currents of doctrine and the grand events of the day. Closely related to the challenge of Marxism, however, was a profound comment on the revolutions and their aftermath which the historian, Richard Hildreth, made in 1853. This astute thinker posed a question that has troubled many intellectuals and that has not yet yielded a proximate solution. In commenting on the prevalence of the armed might of reactionary Europe, Hildreth asked just how this was to give way to freedom. For he assumed there could be no true freedom in an armed camp. These standing armies, he continued, from which America for the time was free and for which it had no immediate need, were a sort of substitute for poor relief, a useless sacrifice to the overstocked labor market too burdensome

---

* For Marx's and Engels's analyses of the Revolutions of 1848, which appeared in the New York *Tribune,* see Aveling, Eleanor Marx, ed., *Revolution and Counter-revolution; or Germany in 1848,* Chicago, Kerr, n.d.

for any community to endure without catastrophe. But the solution lay, not in barricades, not in the invocation of counterforce. It lay rather in "careful, comprehensive, and profound study of social relations, joined to intervals of peaceful co-operation in the production of great economic results."

There was no use, Hildreth concluded, in trying to blink socialism out of sight. Let the philosophers rather turn their attention to finding a solution; let the social engineers bridge the gulf of separation, for until this was done, "all the drumming and fifing and shouting in the world could not unite the divided column."*

* Hildreth, Richard, *Theory of Politics*, p. 274, N. Y., Harper and Bros., 1853.

The Reactionary Enlightenment

by

LOUIS HARTZ

[From *Western Political Quarterly* V (March 1952), 31–50. Reprinted by permission.]

The civilization of the pre-Civil War South is not without defense in contemporary American historiography. Much of this defense centers about the personality and political philosophy of John C. Calhoun. Opposing government by simple majority, Calhoun proposed instead the theory of the concurrent minority, guaranteeing to large economic interests and geographic units a veto on the majority determination. By giving the minority a "concurrent voice in making and executing the laws or a veto in their execution," Calhoun would protect the "different interests, orders, classes, or portions" of the community.[1]

Historians differ widely in their views of Calhoun's political doctrine. Biographers sympathetic to him, like Margaret Coit and Charles M. Wiltse, see Calhoun as both defending liberty and creating precedent for "all the shifting minorities of the future."[2] On the other hand, Richard Current[3] and Richard Hofstadter[4] see the principle of the concurrent minority as designed primarily for the protection of the interests of the slaveholders in the pre-Civil War South.

As for the civilization which Calhoun was striving to defend, Russell Kirk and Avery Craven peer beneath the blanket of slavery and find values in pre-Civil War society that they feel impelled to extol. In many respects their idealization of Southern agrarianism is reminiscent of the plea for tradition and provincialism represented in I'll Take My Stand,[5] in which, at the height of the industrial boom of the 1920's, a dozen Southerners, including the historian Frank Owsley, castigated industrialism and commercialism. Their position has even more remote sources in the novels of Thomas Nelson Page and in the Jeffersonian glorification of rural ways.

Today, with the Jeffersonian tradition being exploited by those opposed to the extension of the powers of government, Southern agrarianism asumes new significance. Witness the following passage and its current implication from Kirk's biography of John Randolph: "in the perspective of history, Northern abstract humanitarianism and Northern industrial selfishness are more guilty than these southerners of contempt for compromise and concession. With all the enduring evils it produced, the Civil War demonstrated at least one truth: that the power of government is not omnicompetent; that the alteration of social institutions is no mere automatic consequence of legislation; and that, when the government transcends certain bounds and threatens great interests and classes, it must be prepared to employ force, the negation of true government. Law has no right to tamper with the delicate social arrangements which only time can properly mend, Randolph and Calhoun declared. When government does usurp such powers, men will resist. The North never quite believed Randolph and Calhoun. The terror of the Civil War, the shameful years that followed — North and South — and much of the present sullen tone of American society are consequences." [6]

The following selection by Louis Hartz of Harvard University is an interpretation of the civilization of the pre-Civil War South in the pattern of liberal historiography.

"WE BEGIN a great conservative reaction," Virginia's George Fitzhugh proclaimed in 1863 on the eve of the battle of Gettysburg. "We attempt to roll back the Reformation in its political phases." The first American Revolution, Fitzhugh argued, had been a mere "reform." But the "Revolution of 1861," which raised the banner of Tories everywhere and resurrected even the dream of

Filmer, was a social upheaval that would ultimately shake the world.*

Here, surely, was a strange note to be coming out of America in the midst of its liberal tradition. What had happened? Had America suddenly produced, out of nowhere, a movement of reactionary feudalism? Was it beginning to experience, seventy-five years late and in an inverted way, a French Revolution that it had managed to escape before? Was its social thought, nourished for years in the easy atmosphere of liberal agreement, suddenly beginning to explode with all of the old historic tensions of Europe? If these things were true, the distinctive meaning of American history would have been canceled out at a single stroke. Tocqueville's statement that the Americans had been "born free" would have become a fond illusion, the silent unity of Hamilton and Jefferson would have led nowhere, and the "promise of American life," to borrow the words that Croly used in another connection, would have become one of the falsest promises of modern times. By 1863, when Fitzhugh raised the Tory standard in the South, the battle over the "political phases" of the Reformation had ended even in Europe. The Holy Alliance had been dead for a generation.

Certainly we cannot deny that the American Southerners, when they began to break with their Jeffersonian past around 1830, duplicated in every essential aspect the argument of Europe's feudal reaction. We do not find here the mere parroting of a few of Burke's phrases. We find a most fantastic array of theoretical schemes, some of them, to be sure, as Aristotelian as they are Burkean, some of them passionately Hebraic in their emphasis on the Bible, but all of them dominated in the end by the basic concepts of the Western reaction. There is a group of ardent traditionalists who cherish the "conservative principle": the novelist N. Beverly Tucker, Governor Hammond of South Carolina, Albert Bledsoe. There is a group of "feudal socialists" who lash out at Northern

---

* *Southern Literary Messenger* (Richmond: T. W. White), Vol. XXXVII (1863), 723; George Fitzhugh, *Sociology for the South* (Richmond: A. Morris, 1854), 209. Fitzhugh's acceptance of Filmer was qualified, but he did accept the notion of divinely appointed governors, which he held was the "doctrine of the South, and conservatives the world over." (*Messenger, op. cit.*, p. 720). Fitzhugh's view of the Reformation as a whole also oscillated, sometimes he even praised it, but he steadily denounced the right of "private judgment."

capitalism in the spirit of Disraeli and Carlyle: Fitzhugh, Chancellor Harper, George Sawyer, Edmund Ruffin.* There is even a group of sociologists determined after the fashion of Bonald and Comte to turn the law of nature upside down and prove that Locke is "metaphysical": Fitzhugh again, Professor George Frederick Holmes of the University of Virginia, and that Mississippi prodigy who published his system at the age of twenty-five, Henry Hughes. Nor is Holmes the only academic figure in the reactionary renaissance. College professors rush to the Tory standard from all sides, Dew of William and Mary giving it a Hegelian touch, Smith of Randolph-Macon showering it with an indiscriminate idealism, J. B. De Bow of Louisiana buttressing it with a solid array of statistics. We have here, indeed, one of the great and creative episodes in the history of American thought.

And yet it would be a mistake, even on the basis of this lush evidence, to jump to conclusions about the collapse of the American liberal tradition. When we penetrate beneath the feudal and reactionary surface of Southern thought, we do not find feudalism: we find slavery. The distinction is not unimportant. For it leads us to see at a glance that this massive revival of Burke, Comte, Disraeli, and Scott below the Mason-Dixon line was in large measure a simple fraud, and that instead of symbolizing the appearance of something new in American life, it symbolized the impending disappearance of something very old. Fraud, alas, was the inevitable fate of Southern social thought.

If the trouble with Southern slave society had merely been that it did not fit the American liberal formula, as historians have often noted, its ideologists might not have had so hard a time. But the real trouble with it was that it did not fit any formula, any basic categories of Western social theory. And so, when the Garrisons of the North arose to drive the Southerners out of their own Jeffersonian world, they were released from the anguish of one contradiction only to embrace the anguish of another even worse. They exchanged a fraudulent liberalism for an even more fraudulent feudalism: they stopped being imperfect Lockes and became grossly im-

* The "conservative principle" phrase is Fitzhugh's, and the "feudal socialism" label is the one applied by Marx to the Young England movement that influenced Southern thought before the Civil War.

perfect Maistres. This is the meaning of Fitzhugh's "great conservative reaction," and once we understand it, its appearance changes enormously.

The Civil War, in other words, if it seems on the surface like a French Revolution in reverse, is really nothing of the kind. The fact that it seems like one in reverse, that fact that the "reaction" of the South is also a "revolution," ought to suggest this to us at once. For a feudalism that has once been liberal can never be really feudal, and its impact on the history of a nation is bound to be unique. A false Maistre, a Maistre who only a few years ago was a Jeffersonian democrat, confronts a set of problems entirely his own. He slaughters himself with the traditionalist logic he tries to use; he cannot terrify the men he seeks to terrify; and once he is defeated in war, he is not only likely to be forgotten but he is likely to forget himself. We can call America's great internal struggle whatever we like, a revolution, a rebellion, or a war; but if we identify the South with the feudalism it sought to imitate, we miss the significance of its social incongruity, of the ties it had to the liberalism it sought to defy, and above all, of the swift disappearance of its Gothic dream. For the remarkable thing about the "great conservative reaction" of 1863, instead of being the way it scarred American political thought, was in fact the insignificance of the impact it had upon it. Even our historians have pretty much forgotten the Disraelis and the Bonalds of the ante-bellum South.

There is a book to be written in the psychiatric vein, or at the very least a heartrending romance, about the Southern search for a cultural code before the Civil War. In the time of Jefferson the agony of the South had been complex. Not only had John Taylor been embarrassed by slavery because of liberalism, but he had been embarrassed by liberalism because even then he had nourished a Disraelian streak. Now, in the age of Fitzhugh, when both of these problems would seem to have been solved, Taylor discovered that he could not be a real Disraeli even if given a chance to be one. He was a plantation capitalist, and in the Southwest, for all of its stratified social life, he was a very new, very raw, very fierce plantation capitalist. And so the sweat that had to go into making the South medieval was even greater than the sweat that had gone into making it modern. Henry Hughes had to twist slavery into a kind of feudal "warranteeism" when it was nothing of the sort. Fitzhugh had to link it up with European serfdom when there was a gulf between the two. A thousand Southern gentlemen had to call themselves "The Chivalry" when a Northerner like Frederick Olmsted would only call them "Cotton Snobs." It is easy to understand, perhaps, why some Southerners occasionally gave up the idea of becoming imperfect feudal lords and tried the experiment of becoming imperfect ancient Greeks or imperfect Hebrew Patriarchs. These roles, which just about exhausted the repertoire that Western culture offered, confused Fitzhugh's historical pattern by shifting it back to ancient times, but the first of them had the merit at any rate of seeming to retain half of the world of Locke in which the Southerners had been accustomed to move. Parrington, seizing upon the idea of "Greek democracy," has actually identified Southern thought with it.

There were good reasons, however, apart from the stratified nature of Southern white society, why the Greek idea did not become the master image of Southern political thought. Locke's scheme had been fashioned not in response to Pericles but in response to Filmer, and when the Southerners were forced to assail it, they found themselves, willy-nilly, drifting in Filmer's direction. There is a categorical logic to political arguments that Mannheim has brilliantly discussed. Since Garrison was using the doctrine of consent, Calhoun naturally replied with the doctrine of "Divine ordination." Since Garrison was using the concept of reason, Fitzhugh instinctively countered with the concept of human "prejudice." Since Garrison was using the idea of equality, Harper's course was clear: there was an "endless diversity in the condition of men."* Actually what we have here is a most remarkable twist coming out of America's odd relationship to modern political thought. A nation built in the liberal image and yet without the feudalism that liberalism destroyed, once it challenged the liberal formula it began to reproduce the philosophy of a feudal world that it had never seen.

* John Caldwell Calhoun, A Disquisition on Government, Richard K. Cralle, ed. (New York: P. Smith, 1943), p. 4; Sociology for the South, op. cit., p. 119; William Harper, "Harper on Slavery," in The Pro-Slavery Argument (Charleston: Walker, Richards & Co., 1852), p. 6.

This is why, even when the Southerners do not read the European conservatives, they write uncannily as if they did. Fitzhugh, who read the English conservatives but apparently not the French, resembles the French most. A ruthless and iconoclastic reasoner, he pursued the attack on Jefferson all the way back to a belief in absolute monarchy and a hatred of the Reformation.

But at this point a question arises, which brings us to the first of the various punishments that the American liberal world imposed on the feudal dreamers of the South. How can a man be an iconoclastic "conservative"? How can Maistre breathe the spirit of Voltaire? Surely if any movement in American thought resembles the French Enlightenment in its sheer passion to shock, to tear down ancient idols, to stick pins in the national complacency, it is this sudden Burkean outburst in the South. And yet the argument of Burke is straight traditionalism. Shouldn't the Southerners, by their own reasoning, be clinging to Jefferson rather than trying to destroy him? Shouldn't they in fact be denouncing themselves?

There is no exaggerating the philosophic pain the Southerners endured as a result of this contradiction. Not to be quite genuine while supporting the doctrine of Locke was one thing; not to be genuine while supporting the doctrine of Disraeli was another, but to have the second doctrine constantly reaffirming one's ancient allegiance to the first was as keen a torture as the devilish brain of history could devise. How under such circumstances could John Taylor ever forget his democratic past? How could he ever hide his liberal origins? Long before, in the seventeenth century, America had laid this trap for the Southern thinkers. By being "born free," by establishing liberalism without destroying feudalism, it had transformed the nationalist doctrine of Locke into the traditionalist reality of Burke, so that anyone who dared to use conservatism in order to refute liberalism would discover instead that he had merely refuted himself. I have said that the Southerners, simply by the logic of assailing Jefferson, were led to discover Bonald. But one thing has to be added to this: when they discovered him, they were no longer in America but in Europe. And when in triumph they tried to bring him back to America, he ceased to be Bonald and suddenly became Tom Paine. Surely Fitzhugh's attack on the Reformation, had he ever seriously extended it beyond its "political phases," would have caused a turmoil in his own Protestant South.

Under such conditions it is not surprising that Southern thought should try to cleave as much as possible to the European experience. After all, in a land where liberalism had destroyed nothing — unless it was the society of the Indians, which the Southerners were hardly trying to restore — it was very hard to denounce it in good conservative terms as being explosive, "metaphysical," and utopian. In order to use the arguments of Burke or Comte, one had deliberately to twist American liberalism into the millennial molds of Europe. One had to make the same mistake about it consciously that Condorcet, observing the American Revolution from Europe, had made about it accidentally. This was very distasteful. An American knew that Jefferson was really not Robespierre, that the idea of compact had been used by the soberest men in American history since the sailing of the *Mayflower*. The Southerners could scarcely wait until they could blend their discussion of Jefferson into a discussion of the French Revolution, though of course they always hid their eagerness behind straight faces. "The prophets of Utopia," Holmes soberly said, were to be found "on both sides of the Atlantic." * In the case of "feudal socialism" the situation was even worse, for if American liberalism had not been revolutionary, it had fulfilled itself to a remarkable degree in individual proprietorship. The Southern disciples of Carlyle and Disraeli were relieved of an awful burden when they managed to move from the miseries of the Northern worker to those of the English proletariat.

Locke, in other words, was too real, too empirical, too historical in America to attack. And the consequences of this are obvious. The God of the reactionaries was Himself on Locke's side, and the Southerners, when they assailed "metaphysicians," were committing a vigorous suicide. E. N. Elliott cherished the sociological relativism of Montesquieu, but the relative unfolding of America's culture has, alas, been liberal. Fitzhugh spoke of Burkean "prejuidces," but the prejudices of America were, alas, the prejudices of liberty and equality. Indeed, the "prejudice" argument was even more self-annihilating than the argument of cultural relativism. One might argue, in so far as slavery itself was concerned, that it was a

* *De Bow's Review* (New Orleans: James B. De Bow), XXII (1857), 137–138.

historic institution, despite its sudden expansion after 1830, and that Montesquieu's lesson for the American Negroes was therefore different from his lesson for the American whites. But on the plane of "prejudice," the problem was not so simple: in its Jeffersonian youth the South itself had considered slavery bad. How then could Burke be used to assail Locke when even below the Mason-Dixon line Burke actually equaled Locke?

Few political theorists, save possibly in a nightmare dream, have ever found themselves in a predicament quite as bad as this. Meaningful thought was difficult indeed. The more consistently a man advanced the antiliberal arguments of Burke, the farther away he got from the traditionalist substance they were designed to protect. The more consistently he cherished the traditionalist substance, the farther away he got from the antiliberal arguments. The only question was on which horn of the dilemma he wanted to impale himself. Most Southerners, unlike Fitzhugh whose logical passion led him to embrace only one of the horns, actually embraced both. Nor is this at all difficult to understand. It is not easy to work out a reactionary scheme of thought in twenty or thirty years, especially when it is far removed from reality. The Burkean power of America's liberal tradition manifested itself most clearly in the inability of the Southerners ever to get completely away from it. Down to the very end, to the Civil War, their theory was shot through and through with the Lockean principles they destroyed. In their glorification of "prejudice," they could not, alas, overcome the prejudices they had inherited.

Almost everywhere one turns one finds pathetic evidence of this. Calhoun repudiates the contractual rationalism of Locke, and yet when he assails the national tariff he advances a theory of minority rights and constitutional "compact" which carries it forward remarkably. Hammond poses as a defender of a feudal order, and yet he cannot help trying to preserve Jefferson in so far as the whites are concerned by building up a theory of race. Even Fitzhugh breaks down on one or two occasions. Denouncing Northern industrialism in the mood of the "English Tory Party," lamenting the emancipation of the serfs in Europe, he manages to smuggle into his theory a program for industrializing the South that would have delighted

Henry Clay. W. J. Cash, in his remarkable portrait of the Southern mind, tells the story of one of the new Cotton Gentlemen who could not help telling his guests how much the furniture in his mansion cost. This is exactly the pathos of Southern "feudal" thought: the old liberal and the old bourgeois preoccupations keep sticking out all over it, betraying it, contradicting it. Even if the South had never been thoroughly liberal and never thoroughly bourgeois, it had been liberal and bourgeois enough to vindicate the insight of Burke by being unable to embrace him completely.

A confusion as subtle as this, a scheme of thought pitched to begin with on a half-fantastic plane and then destroying itself even there, is not designed to win political controversies. The next punishment that America imposed on the Voltairean Maistres of the South follows logically enough. They were not taken seriously by the North.

We must remember that all of the agony of the South was good fortune for the North. If the South was neither decently revolutionary nor decently conservative, the North was decently both. The North had instigated the whole argument with its Garrisonian abolitionism, and hence was quite "jacobinical," but since it used the ancient arguments of the Declaration of Independence, and forced the Southerners to think up new arguments to refute them, it was quite traditionalistic as well. Having issued a violent attack, it could proceed to preserve ancient principles from the attack of others. This was the ironic replica in reverse of the whole Southern dilemma. Of course Garrison was forced to reject the Constitution, which recognized slavery, and in this sense could not play the part of a sober traditionalist. As a matter of fact he once exclaimed: "Thank God the Past is not the Present."* But to the extent that it recognized slavery the Constitution had itself been a historic anomaly, contradicting the larger liberal tradition in which it had been created. To reject it on this score was to purge, not to repudiate, America's political past.

Thus if Burke equaled Locke in America, the North had the moral force of both, and so why should it bother to reply to a set of philosophic actors who had the moral force of neither? Inherently,

* William L. Garrison, Selections from the Writings and Speeches of William L. Garrison (Boston: R. F. Wallcut, 1852), p. 259.

inevitably, the grandiose feudal discoveries of the South slid off the Northern mind with scarcely a trace of impact. Instead of reconstructing the Declaration of Independence in terms of the reactionary attack, as Mill for example reconstructed Bentham or Constant reconstructed Rousseau, the North simply affirmed its principles with a new and wilder fury. Instead of bothering to look at the great Gothic cathedrals that were suddenly arising in the South, the North simply stuck to the ancient liberal ground where they should have been built in the first place. Hence, ironically, the greatest moral crusade in American history produced practically no original political thought. Garrison is not a creator of political ideas, neither is Phillips. Even Channing is not. Conservatism is always unreflective, and since these men, by the fantastic upside-down logic that governed the slavery argument, are revolutionary conservatives, they unite with their very passion a strange and uncritical complacency. They will argue about the Bible, they will even say a few words in defense of the condition of the Northern worker, but in so far as the South's great "feudalist," "positivist," "corporatist" challenge to liberalism is concerned, it rarely occurs to them even to answer it. "Argument is demanded," Garrison once remarked — "to prove what?"*

This experience of being ignored, which every polemicist knows is the handwriting on the wall, produced a strange mixture of fury, gloom, and forced gaiety in the Southern literature. Chancellor Harper of South Carolina angrily assailed the North because it engaged in "denunciation disdaining argument," and then quietly, morosely, as if to himself, he said: "We can have no hearing before the civilized world." Fitzhugh, however, who pretended to believe in just the reverse idea, that the South was leading a world-wide revival of the principles of feudalism, would never let his anguish show. When the North paid no attention to his massive sociological proof that "free society" was a failure, he behaved happily as if he had won the argument: "The North is silent, and thus tacitly ad-

---

* William L. Garrison, *The Words of Garrison: A Centennial Selection (1805–1905) of Characteristic Sentiments from the Writings of William L. Garrison* (Boston and New York: Houghton, Mifflin & Co., 1905), p. 127. I do not mean here to deny that Northern politicians occasionally used the theory of the South to frighten free workingmen. I am concerned with the effort made to refute philosophically the Southern case.

mits the charge." * Fitzhugh was not naïve: he knew that silence can be a sign of intellectual security as well as of intellectual bankruptcy. But what else could he say? If the liberal formula was hopelessly entrenched in the mind of the nation, even in the mind of the South, he had nothing to gain by pointing that fact out.

As a world revolutionary, then, Fitzhugh was in an odd position: his message was ignored by half of the country in which he lived. He was a Calvin not taken seriously by half of Geneva, a Lenin not taken seriously by half of Russia. This was a harsh fate, but it was hardly more than he had a right to expect. Even in 1776 America had not issued an apocalyptic clarion call to the liberals of the world, largely because the "canon and feudal law" was not present here to inspire the inverted Christianity, the crusading secular visions of Rousseau and Condorcet. Was it reasonable to assume that America, nearly a hundred years later, would take a man seriously who issued such a call in defense of that law itself? The anguished fantasy of the Reactionary "Enlightenment," its incredible contradictions, and its failure to impress anyone, all come out most vividly in the claim that it is going to sweep the world.

When we examine more closely the inner tensions of Southern thought, the inability of the Southerners to emancipate themselves from the liberal ideas they were in the process of destroying, we find a record of turmoil as vivid as one might expect. It is not easy to live simultaneously in the dark world of Sir Walter Scott and the brightly lit world of John Locke. The contrasts are blinding, confusing, and in the end they drive a thinker mad. Calhoun, it seems to me, is our clearest proof of this.†

One makes such a remark about Calhoun with some trepidation, for he is the philosophic darling of students of American political thought, the thinker who is almost invariably advanced when someone of European stature is asked for in the American tradition. And yet despite the outward literary appearance of "rigor" and

* *Harper on Slavery, op. cit.*, p. 4; George Fitzhugh, *Cannibals All! or, Slaves Without Masters* (Richmond: A. Morris, 1857), p. xv.

† Some of the points presented in the next few pages on Calhoun I have developed at greater length in "South Carolina against the United States," an essay on the philosophy of nullification, included in *America in Crisis* (Daniel Aaron, ed.), to be published shortly by Knopf.

"consistency" in Calhoun's work, one is bound to affirm that the man is a profoundly disintegrated political theorist. What is "rigorous" about grounding the state in force and Providence after the fashion of Maistre and then creating a set of constitutional gadgets that would have staggered even Sieyès? What is "consistent" about destroying Locke's state of nature and then evolving a theory of minority rights that actually brings one back there for good? There are more impressive thinkers to whom the American historian can point. Fitzhugh, as I have suggested, must be ranked as one of these, for if on the surface he seems like a cracker-barrel commentator, at bottom he has a touch of the Hobbesian lucidity of mind. He, more than anyone else, sensed the awful way Calhoun betrayed the Reactionary Enlightenment when he based the sectional defense of the South on the ancient liberalism it tried to destroy. He fought continuously to substitute the concept of "organic nationality" for the concept of state "sovereignty," and there was the keenest logic to this substitution. By extracting a traditionalist type of Southern nationalism from the conservative theory of slavery itself, he was able to give up all of the compacts and all of the checks on which Calhoun relied.

We have to concede, however, that without this approach there was really no alternative to riding the two horses Calhoun tried to ride. For the theory of the reaction grounds itself on the divinity of existing coercions, and while this may serve a purpose for the defense of Negro slavery, it hardly serves a purpose for the liberation of the South from regional "slavery" to the North. The second type of slavery, if we take the Southerners at their word, was just as existent as the first, and if Calhoun's God ordained the one, how could He have failed to ordain the other? The irony of the conservative position, even in Europe, was that it became articulate at precisely the moment it became untenable, at the moment when God had introduced a new reality to challenge His old one, which meant that when Burke denounced the French Revolution he had to become something of a rationalist himself. Under these circumstances, lacking Fitzhugh's faith in the South's romantic nationalism, it is not hard to see why Calhoun in his battle against the North kept applying the ethos of the Kentucky-Virginia resolutions. After all an inconsistency is better than a logical surrender.

But let us make no mistake about the fact of inconsistency: It is not merely striking, it is doubly and triply striking. Had Calhoun merely maintained an ordinary faith in the mechanics of the American Constitution at the same moment that he grounded government in force and tradition, this would have been one thing. But his faith is not an ordinary one. There is a weird quality about Calhoun: he has a wild passion for the conclusions his premises nullify, as if a pang of guilt made him redouble his affection for the things that he destroyed. The idea of state "sovereignty" shatters a meaningful American union, and yet he insists with the most anguished repetition that this alone can serve as a national "preservative." The idea of a fixed Southern minority and a fixed Northern majority amounts to civil war, and yet the scheme of the "concurrent majority" which he builds upon it he describes in terms of compromise that are nothing short of idyllic.* The best example of this mounting love in the midst of murder is the one already mentioned: the attempt to ground both of these mechanical schemes on the organic naturalism that his social defense of slavery inspired.

For surely the idea that the Constitution is a "compact" among "sovereign" states, that states may therefore nullify Federal legislation, and that the proof of this is to be found in a diligent study of ratification procedures in 1787, is about as far away as one can get from the spirit of "Divine ordination." This not only makes the American system of government a rationalistic instrument of extreme delicacy but it pins its origin to a decisive moment in historical time just as Condorcet, misunderstanding American constitutionalism, pinned it in the eighteenth century. If the Southerners usually had to distort American liberalism in order to denounce it as "metaphysical," they would not, ironically enough, have had to distort Calhoun's version of its constitutional embodiment in order to denounce it in that way. That version met all of the "metaphysical" standards. It left nothing to tradition, nothing to force, and nothing to God. Nor is it the only thing that has to be considered. There is also Calhoun's theory of the "concurrent majority," which supple-

---

* *Note* the words in Calhoun, *op. cit.*, p. 49: "And hence, instead of faction, strife, and struggle for party ascendancy, there would be patriotism, nationality, harmony, and a struggle only for supremacy in promoting the common good of the whole."

mented state nullification with the nullification of individual "interests." When we pile the one on top of the other, we have a scheme of man-made political instruments which the French Enlightenment in its palmiest days never dared to develop.

It is here, in his passionate defense of the minority interest, that Calhoun goes back to Locke's state of nature after having destroyed it in a blaze of organic glory. For there are of course minorities within minorities — as Unionists like Hugh Swinton Legare did not fail to remind Calhoun in South Carolina in 1832 — and since Calhoun offers no reason why these should not be given a policy veto too, the idea of the "concurrent majority" quickly unravels itself out into separate individuals executing the law of nature for themselves. When Locke accepted majority rule, in other words, he accepted more force in politics than Calhoun, the great theorist of force and slavery, was ready to accept. When Locke accepted majority rule, he was more pessimistic than Calhoun, the great pessimist, would permit himself to be. What could be worse for the logic of the Southern position? Here are grim traditionalists denouncing Northern liberalism as a code of "anarchy," and Calhoun supplies them with a doctrine that even Daniel Webster can denounce as "anarchy." Here are ardent corporatists denying that a natural harmony of interests can ever exist — and Calhoun advances a logic of harmony that one would have to go to Godwin to duplicate.

Since Calhoun's mechanical suggestions were a failure, it is interesting that his new-found organic philosophy did not suggest the nature of their failure to him. One might say, as has often been said, that Calhoun was here merely extending the checking-and-balancing ethos of the Founding Fathers. If this is true, then his wild rationalism has a curious logic to it. Adams and Morris, instead of grounding their hope for America on a liberal unity that could support even their clumsy scheme of checks and balances, grounded it on the capacity of those checks and balances to contain and control frightful social conflicts that did not exist. In the only time in American history when such conflicts did appear, what was more reasonable than for a disciple of theirs to multiply passionately all of the checks and balances that were about to be exploded? But in his role as an antagonist of American liberalism, why didn't Calhoun see the futility of this reasoning? Why didn't his organic sense

for the importance of social solidarity make him realize that however much you compounded "interest" checks with other checks
none of them would work if the social fabric was actually torn
apart? There was at least this relevance of conservative traditionalism to the liberal cement of American life: that by concentrating on
the solidarity that comes from "prejudice" it might have exposed
the liberal prejudices that had held the country together to the view
of "realistic" thinkers who had managed not to see them. Some
Southern organic philosophers caught this point, but Calhoun himself did not: the lesson of Adams ran too deep for a sudden correction by Burke.

And yet it would be unfair, after all of this has been said, not to
notice that Calhoun was aware of the basic contradiction he faced.
In his famous *Disquisition* he drew a distinction between "government" and "constitution." Governments were rooted in force and
inspired by God even as Negro slavery was, but constitutions were a
different matter entirely. They controlled government, and being
the product of a later age, when "invention" replaced "superstition,"
they could be used to abolish the South's regional enslavement to the
North.* Here was a straightforward effort to deal with the problem
of Maistre Sieyès. But it reminds us, alas, of a man carefully
placing a match on top of a stick of dynamite. For clearly if "constitution" and "government" ever come together at any point, if it is
ever established that the one has any of the characteristics of the
other, an explosion is bound to occur which wipes the Southern
position off the face of the philosophic earth. Not only does the South
become validly enslaved to the North, but the whole structure of
"compact" and "concurrent majority" is swept away in a fierce tide
of irrationalism. What difference then does it make whether a genuinely "American people" did or did not exist in 1787? God could
have created one in the interval. What difference does it make
whether minorities are coerced? Coercion is a law of life. What
difference does it make whether the Southern "interest" is consulted?
Interests can never work together freely and harmoniously anyway. This was a great deal indeed to stake on a tenuous distinction
between "constitution" and "government." And to say that the dis-

* Calhoun, *op. cit.*, p. 62. Calhoun refers neither to slavery nor the sectional
struggle explicitly in the *Disquisition*, but the import of his remarks is obvious.

tinction was tenuous is putting the matter mildly. There are some who would argue that the control of government is actually the highest form of the governmental task.

Fitzhugh, then, was rightly terrified at the doctrines of the "Calhoun school." His theory of blood-and-soil nationalism, of "organic nationality," avoided all of the inner turmoil and the brink-of-destruction gyrations that the philosophy of Calhoun involved. Romantic, grounded in the claim of slave culture itself, it could never be assailed by the conservative theory that slavery produced. Nor should we assume that Fitzhugh was here a voice crying in the wilderness. Many Southerners, as the sense of their separateness was forced upon them and as the appeal of Scott and Disraeli grew, became attached to the principle of traditionalist nationalism with a deep and ardent feeling. Of course, few of them became attached to it enough to give up constitutional apologetics entirely, which meant that their original dualism of Burke and Locke was simply duplicated again on the plane of nationalism. But under the circumstances what is striking is not how little romantic nationalism there was in the political thought of the South but how little there was of it in the political thought of the "nationalistic" North. Daniel Webster remained as legalistic as Marshall, despite the fact that had he adopted some form of romantic nationalism (it would, of course, have to be a Rousseauian or a Mazzinian type in his case) — he would have been able to explode against Calhoun much of the dynamite with which he was dealing.

There was romanticism in the North, but with the exception of a few men like Barlow and Emerson, it spent itself in a Thoreauian individualism or a Garrisonian cosmopolitanism. Garrison denounced constitutional lawyers as fervently as Fitzhugh did, but he put on the masthead of the *Liberator*, "Our country is the world."

Thus, oddly, the South, the "sectionalist" South, became the real originator of romantic nationalism in American political theory. But an important thing has to be said about that nationalism: it radicalized the whole Southern position. For it is hard to control the claim of nationalism, and especially the claim of Scott's nationalism, with its love of chivalry, its faith in force, its ethos of blood and soil. Implicitly the solution that Fitzhugh offered called for independence and beat the drums of war.

And here the "Calhoun school," at least until 1860, might have offered a reply: it did not want independence and it did not want war. If it clung to contractualism because it wanted to defend the South against the North, it clung to contractualism also because it wanted them both to live together. Its inconsistency pointed in two directions. This is the larger secret of Calhoun's intellectual madness: he appears at a moment when the South's fear of the North and its love of the Union hold each other in perfect balance, so that starting with explosive premises like sovereignty and conflict and force, he drives himself somehow to avert the explosion with conclusions like nullification and the "concurrent majority." He was caught in the classic agony of the brink-of-war philosopher.

But the main point I want to emphasize is the coexistence in the Southern mind of its new Burkean traditionalism and its old Jeffersonian rationalism. Calhoun exemplifies it perfectly, a man whose thought is cut in two by the tug of the liberal past and the pull of the reactionary present. He slays Jefferson only to embrace him with passion in the end, he destroys the Founding Fathers only to carry their work forward. Under such circumstances why should Garrison bother to reply to the elaborate organic philosophy of the South? The South was doing a good enough job of replying to it itself. The point illustrates again the basic dilemma the Southerners faced: their liberalism was so traditional that even they could not get away from it. Garrison the "jacobin" had the power of their own historic irrationalism on his side, and they, the historic irrationalists, could not even be decent "jacobins." They were, in a sense, outside of time and space, carrying on a reactionary conversation with themselves in a kind of Alice-in-Wonderland world where nothing was what it seemed to be, nothing was what it ought to be, where liberalism was oddly conservatized and conservatism oddly liberalized. Or, if one prefers Stevenson to Carroll, they were a set of Dr. Jekylls constantly becoming Mr. Hydes — their own worst enemies and their own executioners.

The effort to save half of Locke by evolving a theory of Greek democracy presents us with the same problem. If it was hard to forget the Kentucky and Virginia resolutions, it was even harder to forget the simple prejudice in behalf of human freedom and human equality. There was a strange compulsion here. For in order to keep democracy for the whites, it was essential to develop a theory of separate race for the blacks, and so the retention of a part of liberalism grounded itself on one of the most vicious and antiliberal doctrines of modern times. This meant that when a stunted fragment of Locke reappeared to challenge the new Filmerians who had shattered him, what was actually at stake was a principle of racial inferiority that Filmer had never seen. Curiously enough, the battle between the South's old liberal image and its new feudal image was here fought out on a plane that was alien to liberalism and feudalism alike.

There was an important strategic reason behind the racialist challenge to the South's Burkean social dream. Unlike the Federal struggle which accounted for the persistence of Calhoun's contractual rationalism, that reason arose out of a tension in Southern society itself; but it was certainly no less real. The democratic age in which the "small proprietor" side of John Taylor's personality had dominated its "aristocratic" side could not quite be forgotten during the "feudal" age when the situation was reversed. Many of the poor whites who lived in the South, instead of feeling that the presence of slaves put them in the position of a privileged peasantry, actually had the audacity to feel that it put them on a kind of par with the "aristocrats" who led them. Burke himself, long before, had recognized that the effect of the "multitude of slaves" in Virginia and the Carolinas had been to give all the whites there a sense of common "rank and privilege."* Even Hinton Helper, who cried out against the unity of the "poor whites" with the Southern "lords of the lash," betrayed in the wild intensity of his own racial theories the sentiment of a common blood that had helped to produce it. Whatever the assailants of Locke might say, passionately as they might identify the stratified society of the South with the world of Sir Walter Scott, vigorously as they might insist on the principle of Tory socialism for all mankind, there was no avoiding the fact that one of the crucial elements in the solidarity of the South was a democratic spirit enhanced by the slavery on which it rested.

* Quoted from De Bow's Review, XXIII (1857), 349.

The religious issue played a two-sided role in this respect. Since a literal reading of Scripture supported the ownership of slaves, many Southerners began to think in terms of Hebrew Patriarchy, while the North became increasingly liberal as regards the Bible, with Garrison giving it up completely. But there was a problem here. Biblical slavery had not been confined to the Negro, and Genesis, moreover, asserted the common origin of man. This was the point at which Fitzhugh, determined to extend a feudalized concept of slavery to whites as well as to blacks, began to level his attack. Confusion necessarily reigned. Dr. George Armstrong could say that though in the first instance the Negro came from Adam, in the second instance he came from Ham; and Josiah Nott, departing from the Bible for a reason entirely different from the one that Garrison had, could develop an anthropology of different races. But these arguments tended to cancel each other, further confusing the issue with a Darwin-like struggle between science and religion before the arrival of Darwin. Fitzhugh, adopting a razor-edged fundamentalism, lashed out at the entire "argument about races" as an "infidel procedure" and insisted that since the Bible "expressly authorized" the enslavement of whites, the matter was closed.* Here was a case, in other words, where being a Hebrew Patriarch was a prerequisite to being a feudal lord. It was a strange situation, but it did not seem to bother Fitzhugh much. Even he, alas, could work within the madhouse of Southern thought before the Civil War.

The truth is, the racial theory was bound to pose difficulties so long as any human attribute was permitted to remain with the slave. And to take all humanity away from a human being was, even in pre-Christian Greece, more than the philosophic conscience could successfully accomplish. Aristotle, defining the slave as a "living tool" and nothing more, conceded at one point that the slave had a capacity for "friendship" — which was an intolerable admission, since the whole of the human community from which the slave was excluded was built around that capacity. In a Christian and a humanitarian age, the closest the Southerners could come to the Aristotelian definition was their legal concept of the slave as "property"; and this concept, as Channing shrewdly observed, they immediately reversed with restrictions on slaveholders which implicitly conceded

* *Ibid.*, p. 347.

that the slave was a human being. Outside of the law their admissions were vaster still. Not only did they make the Aristotelian concession, they embroidered it. The "affection" between slave and master was one of the finest things about Southern life. Not only did they agree that the slave had a soul, they were happy about it. They had saved his soul through giving him Christianity. Albert Bledsoe hastened to say that only the right to labor freely had been taken away from the slave. His "human character" had been impaired "in no part whatever."*

Thus if the racial theory tried to save the whites from the attack on Locke, an inescapable reality kept pulling them into its orbit, since their common humanity with the Negro could not easily be denied. Indeed the very compulsion they felt to attack Locke betrayed them on this score, since Locke had been concerned with men in general, not with Negroes in particular. If the Negro was not a "man," why bother to attack Locke? If the Negro was a parcel of property rather than a human being, why bother to attack Jefferson? Certainly Jefferson had believed in property rights. It is obvious that the Southerners could not remove the Negro from the human category, and that their logic of inequality was therefore bound to backfire upon them. Again we are confronted with that strange intellectual rationale whereby the South, assailing Locke, found itself going back to the hierarchical world that the theories of Locke had destroyed.

But of course this was, with half of its mind, exactly what the South wanted to do. Fitzhugh, who as always represented that half in a highly integrated form, assailed the other half with all the vigor at his command. He questioned the racialists about the "mulattoes, quadroons, and men with as white skins as any of us" who were in slavery everywhere. He asked them how they could reconcile the historic novelty of Negro slavery with their appeal to the "universal usages of civilized man." But it was when he came to the whole feudal scheme of Southern thought, its Tory socialist attack on the North, that his logical passion reached its peak. "We are all in the habit of maintaining that our slaves are far better off than the common laborers of Europe, and that those laborers were infinitely

* E. N. Elliott, ed., *Cotton Is King* (Augusta: Pritchard, Abbott, and Loomis, 1860), p. 318.

better situated as feudal serfs or slaves than as freemen. . . ." How then can the slavery argument be confined to the Negro? The racial argument, Fitzhugh cried, "has involved us in a thousand absurdities and contradictions."*

The theme by now is a familiar one: Fitzhugh trying to be a good reactionary, the South as a whole not quite having the courage to do so. Different as the issues seem, Fitzhugh's attack on the racial idea on which the halfway retention of Locke rested was cut from the same cloth as his attack on the "compact" theory of Calhoun. Fitzhugh wanted to see the Reactionary Enlightenment come to full bloom, but the South, wedded still to ancient liberal notions, was frightened of its appearance if it did. But if the South was frightened of the Reactionary Enlightenment, why should Wendell Phillips be frightened of the South? If Fitzhugh's "feudalism" was being slaughtered by his own comrades because of their love of Locke, why should Garrison take the trouble to slaughter it? Another theme appears, the basic theme: the Southerners were too conservative to be "conservative," which meant that the hotheads of the North could be as complacent as real conservatives. The whole story is fantastic of course, but it is fantasy we are dealing with. And the origin of that fantasy, the frantic search of an incongruous Southern culture for some sort of social identity, comes out as plainly as one might ask in the Southern discussion that we have just examined as to whether the South, instead of being feudal, or perhaps at the same time that it was feudal, might not be Biblical or Greek.

We are now prepared for the final punishment that the American liberal community imposed on the feudal dreamers of the South for daring to attempt an escape from its confines: after the Civil War they were soon forgotten and they all but forgot themselves.

Here the difference between the Civil War and a French Revolution becomes most apparent. For if the former had been the latter, military defeat would never have been able to annihilate the Tory philosophy it produced.† That philosophy would have clung to the

---

* *De Bow's Review, op. cit.*, p. 348. In 1861, however, Fitzhugh himself became a convert to racialism. See Harvey Wish, *George Fitzhugh, Propagandist of the Old South* (Baton Rouge: Louisiana State University Press, 1943), p. 298.

† I am reserving a more detailed analysis of Southern sociology and Tory socialism for another discussion.

conscience of the nation, providing a new dimension of its political thought, serving as a point of departure for a whole set of subsequent conservatives. But who in America would be reading Fitzhugh in twenty years? Who would be going back to Tucker, as Englishmen still go back to the Burke that he loved, for a lesson in political wisdom? The point is clear enough. The fact that the Southerners were false Burkes, halfway Burkes even in the time of their prime, insured a sorry fate for them after that prime was over. When the guns of the Civil War were stilled, the liberal self that the South could not sublimate even in the age of its great "reaction" would gradually come to the fore again, and as in the days of Jefferson, would unite it to the North. The logical agonies of Fitzhugh were the prelude to the emergence of Benjamin Hill.

The new age would not of course solve the philosophic problem of the South. Locke had been imperfect there to begin with, and the brute emancipation of the slaves was hardly enough to make him perfect when he came back to the scene again. The fact is, there was no solution to the philosophic problem of the South: its stark social incongruity was bound to remain, its search for a social identity bound to continue, inspiring as always a mixture of pain and strange hyperbole. But all of this would go on beneath the mainstream of American political thought, never resurrecting the Fitzhughs and the Holmeses of the ante-bellum era.

If we ask ourselves what we have remembered of the South's "feudal reaction," the answer we must give is ironic. We have remembered the very liberal rationalism its philosophers could not destroy in formulating it. It is Calhoun whom we are constantly rediscovering, and not because of the lush organic system that he shared with the philosophers of slavery. We rediscover him because of his defense of minorities, because of his Adamslike theory of the "concurrent majority," and so far are we from bothering to cherish his organic theories that we scarcely realize that they make a logical farce out of his whole Enlightenment structure. Indeed we do not find it incongruous for this great reactionary to be hailed as the chief philosopher of America's free-and-easy pressure-group system of politics, a system which, if it does anything, denies the principle of a divinely ordained "controlling power." What could be a more vivid commentary on the destiny of the Reactionary Enlightenment: that it should be remembered for its defects, for the traditional liberalism which it could not overcome?

The grim fate of the Southern reaction is reflected too in its treatment by historians. I do not refer now to the neglect into which its grandiose social theory fell when it began to be listed in textbooks as merely the "theory of slavery," a neglect which is happily being repaired by the excellent researches of men like Joseph Dorfman, Rollin Osterweiss, and Harvey Wish. I refer to something more devastating even than this: the fact that our familiar historical categories leave no room whatever for the feudalists of the ante-bellum South. Calling "conservative" men who are actually liberal, those categories shove out into the cold the only Western conservatives America has ever had. If John Winthrop is a "conservative," how should Fitzhugh be classified who denied the right of individual conscience altogether? If Daniel Webster is a "conservative," what are we to say about Hughes who wanted a system of authoritarian industry organized around seven different "sovereignties"? If William McKinley and Herbert Hoover are "conservatives," surely there is no place at all for a man like Holmes who cried over the death of feudalism.

But this is logical enough. Our current historical categories reflect but they do not analyze the American political tradition; and if America was destined to forget the Reactionary Enlightenment, those categories were destined to forget it too. Since after the Civil War Bryan and McKinley would pick up the classic battle between American democracy and American Whiggery where Jackson and Webster left it off, since Fitzhugh would look as his beloved Disraeli might look had he appeared for a moment in a tradition exhausted by the difference between Brougham and Cobbett, the fate of the Southerner was practically predetermined. The "conservative" label that he cherished more than anything else would be taken away from him; it would be given to William McKinley whom he would have hated with a violent passion, and he himself would be left nameless. History has been cruel to many thinkers after they have died, and historians have conspired in its cruelty, but there are few parallels for this.

But it might be asked, why should one be concerned with the fate of the Reactionary Enlightenment? Either when it slaughtered itself, or when Garrison ignored it, or when history forgot it, which of course are all parts of the same problem? If the episode was fantastic, why trouble about fantasy? If behind its elaborate feudal façade lay the vicious institution of slavery, why lament the fate of the façade?

The answer, it seems to me, is this: fantasy may serve a curious purpose for the American political mind, for it may well be the only technique whereby America can seize any perspective other than the liberal perspective which has governed it throughout its history. Even a good idea can be a little frightening when it is the only idea a man has ever had. A genuine feudal ideology could not by definition emerge in a world that had always been liberal, and there is some doubt as to whether a genuine socialist ideology can ever appear in such a world, for there is a relationship between the Bourbons and Babeuf that the work of Rousseau exemplifies and that America has missed. It is no defense of these ideas to say that a nation ought to know what they mean, and it is no disparagement of liberalism to say that a knowledge of it and nothing else can produce an absolute temper of mind that in the end is self-defeating. The Reactionary Enlightenment deserves evaluation in these terms. For this was the great imaginative moment in American political thought, the moment when America almost got out of itself, as it were, and looked with some objectivity on the liberal formula it has known since birth. Here was a time when a group of major thinkers, not men at the fringes of the American scene but men at its very center, dared to insist that life can be lived in an utterly different way from the way that Hamilton and Jefferson both agreed to live it. America's rejection of their philosophy was proper, but the way it rejected it was, I submit, not. For America rejected it in the purest mood of its liberal absolution, of the "opinion" that Sumner assailed in the colonial era, that Tocqueville noted in the Jacksonian era, and that has been a part of our national temper ever since: not through controversy, not after consideration, but by a vast and unbelieving neglect. Where in the whole history of American thought is the sublime assurance of that "opinion" better expressed than in the words of Garrison: "Argument is demanded — to prove what?" Reading these words on the part of a leading American philosopher in time of civil war, it it not hard to understand why America has not produced a great philosophic tradition in politics in time of peace. But these are words of a powerful perspective as well as of a limited one, and it may be asking too much that America have all the liberal virtues of a triumphant liberalism and all the liberal virtues, too, of one that is not so triumphant. The American experience remains, in this sense, forever paradoxical.

One thing in any case is clear. The political thought of the Civil War symbolizes not the weakness of the American liberal idea but its strength, its vitality, and its utter dominion over the American mind. The strange agonies the Southerners endured when they tried to break out of the grip of Locke and the way the nation greeted their effort stand as a permanent testimony to the power of that idea. It is not every day in Western history that a "great conservative reaction" dies without impact on the mind of a nation.

John Brown

by

ALLAN NEVINS

Although almost a century has elapsed since his execution, the personality of John Brown is evocative of the strongest emotions. Memorialized in song and story, John Brown did not become the subject of a full-length, scholarly biography until the appearance of James C. Malin's notable John Brown and the Legend of Fifty-Six.[1]

The historian, especially the biographical historian, cannot help speculate about the subconscious life of an individual he is writing about, since this factor is an undeniable force in history. To successfully convey to the reader an impression of subconscious motivation, without going overboard and guessing about what is to him unknowable, is part of the historian's art.

Inevitably, the figure of John Brown enters into Allan Nevins's narrative history of the Civil War period — a series of volumes which promises to be a historiographic landmark for this generation. In the following selection, Nevins synthesizes effective literary presentation and psychological insight to create a striking characterization.

Allan Nevins is DeWitt Clinton Professor of History at Columbia University.

JOHN BROWN was fifty-nine years old in May 1859. He was no ordinary man. All who saw him, whether friends or foes, were struck by his iron will, his consuming inner fire, and his intense though erratic devotion to causes outside himself. Great as were his faults, he united a certain elevation of character with the traits of a born leader. His intimates — members of his family, employees, his picked Kansas band, the Eastern conspirators soon to befriend him in a desperate venture — regarded him with deferential admiration. His business partners (who all rued the partnership) knew that it was hopeless to argue with his stubborn convictions. Proslavery settlers in Kansas, upon whom his murder of five men on the Pottawatomie had created a deep impression, breathed more easily when he left the Territory. He was the product partly of inheritance. He came of stern puritan stock, but of unhappy immediate antecedents. His father Owen, a man of strong religious and abolitionist convictions, was an industrious, respected citizen of his chosen Ohio community for more than fifty years, becoming a trustee of Oberlin and accumulating a substantial estate; but his mother, Ruth Mills Brown, like his maternal grandmother, died insane. John Brown was the product also of a peculiarly hard, failure-ridden life.*

A man of scanty schooling, speculative, of nomadic tastes and marked business incapacity, he made repeated migrations in a fruitless effort to better himself. From northeastern Ohio, where he made his start in life, he went for ten years to northwestern Pennsylvania; then back to Ohio again; then to Virginia, to look into the possibility of settlement; then to Springfield, Massachusetts, on wool business; and then to upper New York. He tried calling after calling; managing tanneries, land speculation, breeding racehorses, sur-

---

* Oswald Garrison Villard's *John Brown Fifty Years After* is exhaustive and judicious. Hill Peebles Wilson relentlessly states the adverse case in *John Brown, Soldier of Fortune: a Critique*, while Robert Penn Warren, in *John Brown, the Making of a Martyr*, attempts a balanced view. Of the older biographies Richard J. Hinton's *John Brown and His Men* is much the best. F. B. Sanborn's biography is not only inaccurate but suppresses vital particulars and mangles documents. James C. Malin's *John Brown and the Legend of '56* is indispensable. I have used collections of papers relating to John Brown in at least a dozen libraries from Boston to Topeka.

veying, selling cattle and sheep, wool factorage, and farming. Once he even contemplated wine-making. His large family — for his first wife bore him seven children, his second, thirteen — were reared in hand-to-mouth fashion. His character seemed full of contradictions. Usually rigidly honest, he sometimes showed a financial irresponsibility that approached dishonesty; a man of principle, he could be a provoking opportunist; kindly and philanthropic, he had a vein of harsh cruelty. All this, with his self-righteous stubbornness and utter intractability, pointed to some psychogenic malady.

All our evidence on his early years shows that he was an exemplary husband, father and citizen, public-spirited and industrious though incompetent in affairs. Of devout Congregational stock, he believed in predestination, foreordination, and providential interpositions, and prayed daily with family and apprentices. He had cherished in youth, he said later, a strong desire for death — doubtless a wish to be united with God. He showed a rigid probity. A journeyman who lived with him in Hudson, Ohio, for some years, testifies that he was stern in ferreting out dishonest employees, but with an eye to reformation rather than punishment. He took pride in good workmanship. A customer might come ten miles for five pounds of sole leather, yet if Brown detected the least particle of moisture in his stock, he sent the man home empty-handed. He was highly charitable. Once he learned that a neighboring family was destitute; he sought out the neighbor, struck a bargain with him for work the following summer, and made him take food and clothing as pay in advance. He studiously kept the Sabbath, but on other days he toiled hard. He abhorred fishing and hunting as a waste of time. His conversation was often jocose and mirthful, but never vulgar, and always studded with Biblical texts. He liked to argue stubbornly with others, and was eager to gain information from all comers. He despised any man who agreed with him at all points, respecting only those who had ideas of their own. On certain principles, however, he was unyielding. If a stranger entered the community, his first questions were whether the man observed Sunday, supported the gospel and common schools, and opposed slavery. If he failed on any point, Brown regarded him with suspicion.

His own early record on slavery was that of a moderate abolitionist. As a boy he had been shocked and grieved by a Northern innkeeper's maltreatment of a Negro lad his own age. In early manhood he had frequently concealed fugitive slaves. Indeed, a friend who knew him well in Ohio testifies that he repeatedly saw Brown come in at night with several blacks whom he had piloted all the way from the Ohio River; and a woman neighbor thought that he spent time and money on fugitives that might better have gone to the neglected education of his own children. In 1834, he proposed to his brother Frederick that the two enlist helpers and start a school for Negro children in Randolph, Pennsylvania, but the scheme came to nothing. While at first Brown seems to have been a nonresistant of the Garrisonian type, in 1850, helping some free and fugitive Negroes of western Massachusetts organize a League of Gileadites for mutual protection, he preached them a fighting doctrine.*

As he grew older, as the world gave him hard buffets, as his lack of business system and foresight plunged him into failure after failure; and as his skeptical temper weakened his religious dogmas, his character changed. One disaster was especially severe; the crash of the Franklin Land Company (1837), in connection with which he had made excessive realty purchases near Franklin Mills, Ohio. His affairs in 1837–1841 (which were gloomy depression years after the panic of 1837 anyhow) fell into utter confusion. Struggling in a morass of debt, he lost his reputation for probity. In 1839, he persuaded an agent of the New England Woolen Company of Connecticut to let him have twenty-eight hundred dollars for buying wool in Ohio. He converted the money to his own uses, and escaped punishment only because the corporation was lenient — perhaps also because he gave pledges of payment which he never wholly carried out. To reimburse some Ohio sureties who had put their names on one of his bonds or notes, he pledged them his rights to a certain piece of property; then, when this property was conveyed to him, he secretly recorded the deed and raised money on it by a mortgage. In 1840, he made an abortive effort to obtain a thousand acres in a tract of Virginia land belonging to Oberlin College. His busi-

---

* The *Ohio State Arch. and Hist. Quarterly* has printed valuable articles on Brown in Vol. XXX by C. B. Galbreath; in Vol. LXVII by Mary Land; and in Vol. LVIII by Louis Filler. Other aspects of his career are examined by Floyd C. Shoemaker in *Missouri Hist. Review*, XXVI, and by Ernest C. Miller in *Pennsylvania History*, XV.

ness misfortunes, combative temper, and failure to meet clear legal obligations had resulted in one controversy after another, so that between 1820 and 1845 he figured in twenty-one lawsuits in Portage County, Ohio. One case was specially embarrassing; the Bank of Wooster, suing him for a check which he had drawn on the Leather Manufacturers Bank of New York when he had no account there, recovered $917.65.

It was thus as a failure, a man who had lost part of his early integrity as well as his faith in organized Christianity, a soured, hardened reformer who took refuge from his own deficiencies in fighting the wrongs of others, that Brown in 1855 re-established his family on the farm at North Elba in the Adirondacks that he had obtained from Gerrit Smith, and saw his sons off to Kansas, himself soon to follow. His purpose was not to resist border ruffians, but to engage in farming and surveying. The Browns migrated to the frontier, like countless other families, to get a fresh start in life. It was only when the sons reported that many Missourians were hostile that John Brown collected arms and money for possible battle. That incisive Kansas historian, James C. Malin, tells us that Brown was not an idealist longing to liberate the prairies; that through years of toil, error, and frustration he had rather become a restless trader moving fom place to place in one business after another, constantly pursuing that will-o'-the-wisp, a spectacular stroke which would make his fortune. He tells us that Brown's murder of five men on Pottawatomie Creek in May 1856 probably had nothing to do with slavery, but was an act of political assassination.

This may be true, and yet not all the truth. Brown apparently remained a convinced hater of slavery, who had steeped himself in abolitionist literature and who regarded slaveholders as criminals. He remained, also, a man with a sense of mission — one on whom the finger of the Lord had been laid for some great object. Such a man was easily kindled by the heroic sturggle of the Free State men in Kansas.

The old veins of puritan idealism and reformative zeal were still to be found in his nature; but a vein of the ruthlessness peculiar to fanatics, and especially fanatics gnarled by failure, had asserted a dominant place. The cranky skepticism which now kept him from any formal church allegiance perhaps chiefly concerned the New

Testament. It is significant that in the many religious letters of his last year he makes but one reference to Christ, and none to Christian mercy. His belief in the harsh, implacable Jehovah of the Old Testament, however, remained unchanged. Charity and forgiveness had no place in his creed. When executed, he refused to let a Virginian minister go to the scaffold, for these ministers believed in slavery, and (said he), "my knees will not bend in prayer with them while their hands are stained with the blood of souls." He left a final injunction to his children to be good haters — to abhor that sum of all villainies, slavery. To him, the Missourians who mustered along the Kaw in 1856–1857 were as the Philistines who camped between Sokoh and Azekah; he was as Gideon against the Midianites; he was like the Samson who slew thirty citizens of Ascalon. The scarred, warped, self-tortured man who supervised the murders on the Pottawatomie told Mahala Doyle, whose husband and sons he killed, that if a man stood between him and what he thought right, he would take that man's life as coolly as he would eat breakfast.

"Always restless," wrote poor Mahala Doyle. "With an eye like a snake, he looks like a demon."

We are thus brought to the question of mental aberration, a subject on which much evidence is available. Most of it lies in affidavits in the papers of Governor Henry A. Wise of Virginia, sent him by people who knew Brown well. It can be summed up in a sentence written by Dr. W. W. Durbin of Canfield, Ohio, whose acquaintance was of long standing and who wrote emphatically: "I am fully satisfied he is and has been a crazy man for years." These affidavits are supplemented by other evidence. The word "monomania" is used with significant frequency. When Brown paid his last visit to Boston, in May 1859, that shrewd businessman John Murray Forbes noted "the little touch of insanity" about his glittering gray-blue eyes, an impression not lessened by Brown's loud insistence that only bayonets and bullets could settle the Kansas issue — though Kansas was then at peace. A correspondent of the Chicago *Tribune* declared in 1860 that many who knew Brown in Kansas believed that the slaying of his son Frederick had "made him a monomaniac on the subject of slavery"; and that, denying any motive of revenge, he labored under "a religious hallucination to the effect that he was the appointed instrument for putting an end to human slavery." *

In the parlance of the day, he had a tendency toward monomania. Endowed with a narrow, intense, dogmatic mind, he fastened it upon one subject with a fervor which shut out all other considerations. But how early did this tendency appear? Was it upon slavery alone that he was a monomaniac? If so, we might doubt the analysis, for by 1860 the country had a multitude of monomaniacs upon slavery. But evidence appears of inordinate preoccupation with one topic after another before he turned to slavery. He was subject to extravagant religious fixations. In 1852, worried because his son John did not exhibit piety, he spent an entire month writing a letter of pamphlet length to him, composed largely of Scriptural quotations. We might question the sanity of a nearly penniless man with a large family who devotes a month to such an exhortation — which proved futile. He seems in 1836–1837 to have shown a similar fixity of interest in land speculation. And while no final judgment is possible, his wool ventures may also point to psychogenic disorders amounting to mental disease.

That they did so was the belief of Aaron Erickson, a shrewd, well-educated wool dealer of western New York who saw much of Brown in the years when he engaged in sheep growing and wool selling. Brown in 1844 had gone into partnership with Simon Perkins, Jr., of Akron, in the sheep business. Two years later, Perkins & Brown had established an agency in Springfield, Massachusetts, for the sale of wool, with Brown in charge. In August 1846 a Springfield meeting issued a call for a wool-growers' convention in Steubenville, Ohio, the following year. It was duly held, with Alexander Campbell, founder of the Campbellite sect, as chairman. Brown was present, and delivered a shrewd, practical address on the preparation of wool for the market. He had gained a standing among farmers and stockmen by contributions to the *Ohio Cultivator* and other publications, and by a well-esteemed cure for bots in sheep. The Steuben-

* For testimony from many sources relating to Brown's sanity see material in the Villard Collection, Columbia University Library; John Brown Papers, LC; and State Executive Docs., Va. State Library. For a modern treatment of pertinent medical questions see Charles Berg's *Clinical Psychology;* E. H. Williams, *The Doctor in Court.* The author has been advised on this subject by Dr. Joseph Collins of New York and Dr. Bradford Murphey of Denver.

ville meeting adopted a report complaining that textile manufacturers and dealers generally did not properly grade wool, but
paid for fine and medium qualities on a low-grade basis; thus en-
dorsing a crusade long carried on by Brown.

Erickson had heard of this crusade; he had heard of local meetings
in Ohio at which Brown had declared with rhadamanthine unction
that his great mission in life was to right this wrong. Believing the
existing system fair, Erickson concluded that the man was some unscrupulous sharper imposing on the farmers' credulity. After Brown
had opened the Springfield agency, Erickson had taken pains to
meet him. He had been instantly disarmed of his suspicions. Instead
of a swindler, he found a man whose frank character, simple manners, and childlike ignorance of his great project stamped him a Dr.
Primrose, a deluded visionary. He had convinced himself, Erickson
writes, of a total fallacy.

Sometime later, Erickson called again at the Springfield headquarters, finding Brown in high elation. The Perkins & Brown
agency, designated as an Eastern depot by the Steubenville meeting
and supported by the *Prairie Farmer*, had received large consign-
ments of wool from its Western friends. Once more Brown showed
intense fervor in proclaiming his mission of doing justice to the
growers. Once more he praised his own grading system, which Erickson thought manifestly bad. The visitor seized an opportunity, when
Brown's back was turned, of transposing three fleeces; and when he
pointed to them, Brown emphatically maintained the accuracy of
his classification. The reformer, writes Erickson, had valued the finer
grades about 50 per cent above true market quotations, and the
coarser grades about 25 per cent below. He was deaf to warnings
that he had underestimated these lower grades, which would be
snapped up by buyers. When he persisted in his course, they were
quickly bought at ruinous prices, while the finer fleeces remained a
drug on the market. Some farmers interposed before the wool was
all sold, states Erickson, bringing a lawsuit which cost Perkins &
Brown heavy damages.

Talking of a manufacturers' conspiracy, Brown in 1849 decided
to ship his best grades to England. Fine British wools were then being imported despite the tariff; and Brown no sooner shipped two
hundred thousand pounds abroad than a Massachusetts manufac-

turer, who had unsuccessfully offered sixty cents a pound at home, brought a consignment back from London — at a cost, freight and duty included, of fifty-two cents. The loss on this venture may have reached forty thousand dollars, and Perkins & Brown went into liquidation. "These," Erickson writes, "were the acts of an insane man." This whole wool-agency business constitutes an intricate chapter. Much evidence on it has been lost, and Brown's supporters thought his general position sound. But that at least one astute judge believed him a monomaniac on wool grades and prices is certain.*

Medical science has long since discarded the term "monomania." It might now classify Brown's aberrations under the head of reasoning insanity, which is a branch of paranoia: that is, of mental disease marked by systematized delusions, but accompanied in many instances by great logical acumen. Such a man may mingle with others and most people will never suspect his disorder. One form of the disease is called litigious paranoia, the victim engaging in many lawsuits; another form is ambitious paranoia, in which the subject feels called to exalted missions. On all subjects but one the patient may appear eminently sane. It is perhaps significant in this connection that a son of one of Brown's partners states: "J.B. saw everything large; felt himself equal to anything . . . and would accept no suggestions, advice, or direction from anyone." If Brown was a paranoiac, he had moved by 1857 to a feverish absorption in the idea of guerrilla warfare upon slavery. As he did so, the sectional crisis reached a pitch which rendered the acts of such a cool, determined, fanatical leader potentially dangerous.

And Brown intervened in precisely the way that was calculated to do the gravest damage to sectional concord. The steps leading toward his intervention may be briefly exhibited in a series of scenes, all dramatic enough.

SCENE I: Concord, Massachusetts, on a February night in 1857. The Town House is ablaze with lights. A hundred citizens and more stamp in, taking off scarves and mittens in the grateful heat

* Brown's wool ventures deserve a separate monograph. While his business mismanagement was deplorable, much may be said for his effort to protect the wool growers. Many papers on the subject are in the Brown collections of the Boston Public Library, Columbia University Library, and Ohio Arch. and Hist. Society. Files of the *Prairie Farmer* are useful.

from the big stove. They glance curiously over their shoulders as tall, lanky Frank B. Sanborn, a young Harvard graduate whom Emerson had brought to the town as head of the academy, escorts down the aisle a worn but wiry man of medium height, with clean-shaven face, burning eyes, and grimly set mouth. Some townsfolk know that John Brown had come by the noon train, had lunched at Mrs. Thoreau's house with Henry and the boarders, and later had chatted with Emerson, who called on an errand. He begins to speak in a metallic, clipped voice, with positive gestures, about the Kansas troubles. He tells of the outrages committed by the border ruffians, of the murder of his son Frederick, and of the interference by Missourians in elections. Attacking the peace party in Kansas, he declares that the Territory needs men who will fight, and needs money too — for war is expensive where food, clothing, and arms must be carted for long distances. He shakes the chain that his son John wore when dragged for miles by Federal dragoons under a hot sun to prison. He also utters some telling epigrams. When he says that the proslavery marauders "had a perfect right to be hanged," Emerson and Thoreau exchange appreciative glances. His declaration that he and his five remaining sons will never stop battling against slavery brings a murmur of approval, and the townspeople march out into the chill night air manifestly impressed.*

This Concord address is one of many which Brown makes in his fund-raising tour of New York and New England in late winter and spring of 1857. Naturally, he says nothing of the coldblooded murders which he had instigated on the Pottawatomie the previous May; nothing of other homicides by Free State men; and nothing of the fact that the volunteer company he left in Kansas had (under his instructions) made a horse-stealing raid into Missouri.† It is only

* Authorities differ on details. Emerson's *Journals*, followed by Townsend Scudder in *Concord: American Town*, fixes the date of this meeting in February; F. B. Sanborn's *Recollections*, I, 108 ff., followed by Villard, places it in March. Edward Emerson's note to the *Journals* obviously confuses some parts of John Brown's two appearances in Concord. Scudder says Sanborn was on leave in Boston, while Sanborn says he was living in Concord. Such details are inconsequential. As evidence of the impression Brown made, see Thoreau's "Plea for Captain John Brown." Mr. Boyd B. Stutler, owner of valuable John Brown material, believes that the Concord meeting took place about February 18.
† Villard, *Brown*, p. 261.

the crimes of proslavery men that he lists. The time is well chosen for his appeal. The Dred Scott decision, the appointment of Walker as governor, the publication of Geary's attacks on the slavery party, have excited widespread Northern apprehension. Brown meets one important rebuff. He and Sanborn spend an afternoon with ex-Governor Reeder at Easton, Pennsylvania, trying to persuade him to go to Kansas as agent of the Massachusetts Kansas Committee, and to take the Kansas leadership away from moderate Charles Robinson. "I will serve as commander of field forces in guerrilla warfare," promises Brown. Reeder warily declines. Elsewhere, however, the fanatical leader has better success.*

Wherever he goes — Philadelphia, New York, Syracuse, Worcester, Boston — the gaunt, weather-beaten warrior pleads for money and arms; everywhere he denounces the Kansas peace party and predicts that war will again burst forth on the plains.† He induces the Massachusetts Kansas Committee (which includes the manufacturer George L. Stearns, the reformer Dr. Samuel Gridley Howe, and Sanborn) to give him custody of two hundred Sharps rifles at Tabor, Iowa, with four thousand ball cartridges and thirty-one thousand percussion caps, and to vote him five hundred dollars for their care. The same body grants another five hundred to him for the relief of Kansas. The National Kansas Committee in New York appropriates five thousand dollars to him in aid of defensive measures, but this results in an actual transfer of only a hundred and fifty to his pockets.‡ In Boston, various men, including Amos A. Lawrence and Wendell Phillips, give him one thousand dollars to complete the purchase of the farm at North Elba, New York, where his wife and some of the children reside. While the total of monetary donations falls far short of his goal of twenty-five thousand dollars, it is nevertheless considerable.§

* Brown had issued a well-printed circular, of which the Chicago Historical Society has a copy. It states that he intends to visit as many places as possible in his tour of the East "provided I am first informed of the disposition of the inhabitants *to aid me in my efforts. . . .*" He was so pressed for money that he wrote H. N. Rust offering to sell a captured saber, for "I am literally driven to beg: which is very humiliating." Brown Papers, Chicago Hist. Soc.

† Sanborn, *Recollections*, I, 117.

‡ Villard, 274–276; Sanborn, I, 118, 119.

§ R. J. Hinton, *John Brown and His Men*, 143–145.

SCENE II: A village drugstore in Collinsville, Connecticut, one February morning in 1857. A group are gathered about Brown, congratulating him on his Kansas lecture the night before, and asking for additional information. He launches into the story of his encounter at Black Jack with a little force led by Henry Clay Pate, captain of Missouri militia and deputy Federal marshal. Brown, boasting that with nine brave followers he had captured twenty-odd well-armed border ruffians, draws a vivid picture. "We came up at daylight to those black-jack oaks at the spring," he says. "It is on the Santa Fé trail. I ordered my men to get ready to attack. Pate and his crew were lurking in a ravine; plenty of bushes and trees for cover. I moved around to their flank, and drew in to close quarters. The sun was well up then and getting hot. The grass was dry; I remember thinking how it would look spattered with blood. Suddenly one of those border ruffians stood up with a white handkerchief on a long rod."

The listeners gape. Then they draw back as Brown whips from his bootleg a handsomely mounted bowie knife. "Look — this was Pate's. His Virginia friends gave it to him when he left for Kansas." Several men, including a blacksmith named Charles Blair, feel its keen edge. "If I had a lot of these blades fastened to poles about six feet long," says Brown, ruminatively, "they would make good weapons for our Free State settlers to keep in their cabins." The group choruses assent. With an air of sudden decision he turns to Blair. "You're a forge-master," he remarks. "You can make good edge tools. What would you charge to make five hundred or a thousand of these pikes?" Blair considers a moment. "Well," he ventures, "I could probably make you five hundred at a dollar and a quarter apiece, or a thousand at a dollar apiece." "I want them made," says Brown in his terse way; and a little later a contract is signed.*

Obviously, this order for pikes has curious aspects. With rifles and revolvers so abundant in Kansas, why an order for a thousand spears? They might be useful for men who could not handle fire· arms — say colored men — but not for hardy frontier folk. Why give the order to a Connecticut blacksmith, when an Iowan could fabri-

* *Mason Report* (36th Cong., 1st Sess., Senate Rept. No. 278), 121–199; Sanborn, I, 104. Brown made final payment for the pikes by a draft from Troy, N. Y., June 7, 1859; Brown Papers, Chicago Hist. Soc.

cate them just as well? Delivery is to be made July 1, 1857, but Brown is able to supply only five hundred dollars on the contract, and though Blair buys the materials, no weapons are shipped this summer.

It is also curious that Brown holds conferences this spring and summer with an Englishman now resident in New York, Hugh Forbes, who, at one time a silk merchant in Siena, had taken up arms with Garibaldi in the disastrous campaigns of 1848–1849. A middle-aged man of considerable ability as linguist, drillmaster, and military engineer, Forbes is a radical idealist of the Mazzini school, loves conspiracy, and is hungry for better employment than his odd jobs as fencing-master and translator and reporter for the *Tribune*. He and Brown talk eagerly of methods of guerrilla warfare. In fact, the two exchange ideas, and, if we may believe Forbes, hammer them together in what they call "The Well-Matured Plan." The Englishman agrees to serve at a hundred dollars a month instructing a volunteer company which Brown intends to raise, providing a handbook of tactics (*The Manual of the Patriotic Volunteer*, based on an earlier book), writing a tract to persuade American soldiers never to support wrong against right, and doing other work. When authorized to draw upon one of Brown's supporters for six hundred dollars, he does so within the month.* Partly as a result of his talks with Forbes, Brown is making some curious notes in his memorandum book. For example, he writes of the "valuable hints" for guerrilla warfare in a life of Wellington, adding: "*See also* same book Page 235 these words Deep and narrow defiles where 300 men would suffice to check an *army*." †

In truth, Brown's talk to certain Eastern supporters of defensive operations in Kansas is a blind. He is contemplating offensive activity, not merely in Kansas but in some part of the Southern Appalachians; perhaps the Shenandoah, perhaps farther south. He be-

---

* A Hartford gentleman, W. H. D. Callender, supplied this sum; Villard, 286.

† All statements by the adventurer Forbes require verification. He arrived in New York in 1850, and in 1851 delivered anti-Catholic lectures in the city. His tactical handbook was based on his *Manual of the Patriotic Volunteer* published in one volume in New York in 1854 and in two volumes in 1856. That with his military experience (treated in G. M. Trevelyan's volumes on Garibaldi), versatility, and dash he made an impression on Brown's thinking is indubitable. Hinton in *Brown and His Men*, 146–152, treats him rather favorably; Villard, 285, 317 ff., very unfavorably.

lieves that hundreds of slaves will rise at the first blow. He intends to place the thousand pikes in their hands, and to use the two hundred revolvers, which Stearns bought for him from the Massachusetts Arms Company, in hand-to-hand fighting.* Perhaps already he is scheming a dash at the Harper's Ferry arsenal, destroying what arms he cannot carry off.

How long he has revolved his plan for moving a well-armed force into the Appalachian country, making raids into slave areas, and destroying slavery by rendering it unsafe, we do not know. If we may credit the autobiography of Frederick Douglass, he had confided to that Negro leader in 1847 his belief that he could put a well-trained force into western Virginia, support them there, run off large numbers of slaves, keep the bravest while sending the weaker North by the "underground railroad," and thus so undermine the institution that it would topple in ruins.† Once seized with an idea, he is not the man to let it go. Early in August 1857 he reaches Tabor, Iowa, where two days later Forbes arrives. They agree that their volunteer company will need a school of instruction, Forbes presently goes back East to choose a place; Brown goes on to Kansas, to raise recruits and money.

SCENE III:A blazing campfire at night on the open prairie near Topeka in November 1857. Chill winds howl about, as Brown piles fuel on the embers. Four roughly dressed men sit near, their knapsacks and blankets affording partial shelter. These first recruits of

* Villard, Brown, p. 289.
† Frederick Douglass, Life and Times (London, 1882), 238–240. Brown knew how to dissemble his purposes. When the National Kansas Aid Committee, sitting in New York in January 1857, showed some inquisitiveness, he pretended to take offense. The secretary, H. B. Hurd, asked what he thought a pro forma question: "If you get the arms and money you desire will you invade Missouri or any slave territory?" Brown replied with asperity: "I do not expose my plans. No one knows them but myself, except perhaps one. I will not be interrogated; if you wish to give me anything, I want you to give it freely. I have no other purpose but to serve the cause of liberty." The committee, which had previously understood that Brown intended to arm some Kansas settlers who would not be called out except to protect the Free State population, became suspicious. He got his vote of five thousand dollars only for defensive purposes. At the same time, Brown was giving his abolitionist friends a fuller view. Gerrit Smith, Frank Sanborn, and T. W. Higginson knew that he intended violence, and that this violence might aid their disunionist schemes. (H. B. Hurd, March 19, 1860, to Stearns; Stearns Papers, Kansas State Hist. Soc.)

Brown's irregular company are fairly typical of the whole lot: a body of reckless, adventurous young drifters with a few true idealists. Physically the most striking is Aaron D. Stevens, a six-footer with magnificent chest and limbs and handsome face. He had run away from a Massachusetts home to fight in the Mexican War, had got into a drunken riot at Taos and struck an officer, and had been sentenced to three years in jail at Fort Leavenworth, whence he escaped to join the Free State men. The most talkative, an incessant chatterer, is John E. Cook, an impulsive Connecticut Yankee in his late twenties, one-time law clerk in Ogden Hoffman's office in New York. Fresh-faced and youthful-looking, he has never quite grown up. Intellectually the most distinguished is John Henry Kagi, an Ohioan of Swiss-English descent, whose speech gives evidence of a quick mind and superior education. Only twenty-two, this ardent young man, a devoted abolitionist, has been a schoolteacher, is proficient in Latin, French, and mathematics, has studied law, and has helped report the debates in the recent Kentucky constitutional convention. He talks with the skill of a trained debater.*

The four treat Brown with deep respect. They know that he has other recruits, but they wish to learn his plans; and they inquire where they are to serve.

Brown tells them that the whole company is to go back East, to drill. The Territory is quiet, and winter campaigning is impossible anyhow. His sons, with various other volunteers — Realf, Parsons, Tidd — will travel with them. He hands Cook a draft for $82.50. "Get this cashed in Lawrence tomorrow. We'll all meet again at Tabor in Iowa. Then I'll tell you just what we are going to do. If you want hard fighting you'll get plenty of it."

And at Tabor, as ten men gather about him, Brown's face wears a look of awakened resolution. "Our ultimate destination," he says, "is Virginia." †

SCENE IV: The town of Chatham in Upper Canada, not far from Detroit, on a Saturday in May 1858. It is a bustling city of six thousand, with one long shopping thoroughfare, King Street, wharves on

---

* Hinton knew these recruits and in *John Brown and His Men* gives excellent sketches; for fuller material see Villard, 678–687.
† See Cook's pamphlet "Confession" published in November 1859.

the Thames from which ships ply to all the Great Lakes ports, and prosperous industries — flour mills, woodworking establishments, iron foundries, wagon shops. It is also a center for refugee slaves, who constitute one third of the population. The streets are full of them; and, as even unskilled Negroes earn $1.25 a day, while many are artisans and farmers, they seem well dressed and happy. At least one colored man has a bachelor's degree from Oberlin.* On this May 8, a number of Negroes and whites are at a Negro school-house in Princess Street, where they say they are organizing a Masonic lodge.

Inside the schoolhouse, as ten o'clock strikes, the eyes of the eleven white and thirty-four colored men present are fixed on John Brown. He nods to a delegate named Jackson, who raps for order. The first business is the election of officers. A colored minister from Detroit, W. C. Munroe, is made president, and Kagi, an impressive figure with his long dark hair, large eyes, and fine forehead, is chosen secretary. A colored physician, Dr. Martin R. Delany — later to hold in the Civil War the highest rank, that of major, given to any colored man — moves that John Brown address them on the purpose of the meeting. Rising, the fiery-eyed leader begins to talk. He remarks that for more than twenty years the idea of giving freedom to the slaves has obsessed him. He describes how, when he visited Europe in 1851, including Waterloo, he inspected fortifications and especially earthworks.

"I have formed a plan of action," Brown asserts. All over the South, he explains, slaves are eager to escape from bondage. He wishes to strike a blow from some point in the mountain chain which thrusts diagonally down from Maryland and Virginia into Tennessee and north Alabama. He believes that slaves will rise all over the South and struggle to reach his standard; he will welcome them and put arms in their hands; they will entrench themselves, and make sudden descents into the plantation country on each side.

"But what if troops are brought against you?" asks one listener.

A small force will be sufficient to defend these Thermopylae ravines, responds Brown. We shall defeat the green State militia if they march against us. If United States troops come, we shall defeat them too. I hope, however, that little bloodshed will be neces-

* Chatham is fully described in the N. Y. *Weekly Tribune*, October 24, 1857.

sary. If the slaveholders resist us, we shall carry them back as hostages, holding them to guarantee proper treatment of any of our own men who may be taken prisoners. We shall soon be too strong to attack, for I expect the able-bodied free Negroes of the North to flock to my banner, and all the Southern slaves who can escape will do the same. Gradually we shall build up a powerful state. Our freed men will go to work tilling farms and running workshops; they will organize schools and churches. We shall not molest slaveholders who do not interfere with us, but of course we shall treat all enemies who attack us alike. I am confident that we can maintain ourselves, and can defy any enemy. John Brown draws himself more erect and gesticulates more emphatically. Thus, he concludes, the slave states will finally be compelled to emancipate the people they are holding in bondage, and we shall put an end to that accursed institution. That done, we shall reorganize our mountain state on a new basis, and elect a fresh set of officers.*

The next business is the adoption of a constitution for the proposed state, and the choice of a commander in chief, secretary of state, and secretary of war. Brown has his document ready, and after an oath of secrecy is taken by every member, it is read. "Whereas," its preamble began, "slavery throughout its entire existence in the United States is none other than a most barbarous, unprovoked, and unjustifiable war of one portion of its citizens upon another portion . . ." On motion of Kagi, the provisional constitution is adopted, and that afternoon, with congratulatory speeches, is signed. At an evening session Brown is elected commander in chief and Kagi secretary of war, while the next day a white recruit named Richard Realf is named secretary of state.

Monomania has reached its climax, for this Chatham gathering marks a full crystallization of Brown's plans. In every feature the scheme is preposterous: the idea that slaves are ready for wholesale revolt; the idea that State and national forces can be resisted; the idea that a temporary new commonwealth can be created. Yet there is method in Brown's madness. The preamble of his constitution is a declaration of war which justifies the killing of slaveholders, the liberation of slaves, the confiscation of other property, and the rav-

* See Realf's report of the speech, Villard, pp. 331, 332; *Mason Report*, pp. 96, 97.

aging of enemy lands. It does more than justify the fomenting of slave insurrections; it assumes that a universal and incessant slave insurrection is under way, and that only brute force is restraining it within bounds. Rejecting the American Constitution, Brown is establishing his own government and laws, under which he will be free to commit any act of belligerent violence. As he wages war against the slaveholders, the states, and the nation, his robberies will be called the confiscation of enemy property, his kidnapings will be termed the seizure of enemy hostages, and his murders will be denominated legitimate military operations. His knowledge of what had happened in Haiti when a war of races began does not daunt him, for he believes that without the shedding of blood there can be no remission of Southern sins, and that, as he has told Emerson, it is better that a whole generation of men, women, and children should pass away by violence than that slavery should endure.

Political Processes and Civil War

by

ROY F. NICHOLS

["American Democracy and the Civil War," from *Proceedings of the American Philosophical Society*, XCI (April 1947), 143–149. Reprinted by permission.]

Speculation concerning the causes of the American Civil War is very popular among professional historians. All sorts of explanations have evolved — moral, ideological, political, economic, social, psychological, and their combinations. Within each of these categories of explanation, the debate has been sharpened over whether the war was inevitable or avoidable.[1]

The political interpretation of the causes of the American Civil War, of the sort written by Dean Nichols in the article reprinted here, and in his book The Disruption of American Democracy,[2] *bears only slight resemblance to the older view of the political origins of the conflict. After the South was defeated, its apologists proved sensitive to the accusation that they had fought to preserve the slave system. Both Jefferson Davis[3] and Alexander H. Stephens,[4] President and Vice-president of the Confederacy respectively, wrote of the South as fighting for political principle — the right of secession — which they believed inherent in the Constitution as originally framed. Slavery, stated Davis, was "in no wise the cause of the conflict, but only an incident."[5]*

No such sensitivity to the slavery issue troubled Northern historians like von Holst, Rhodes, Schouler and Hart who did not hesitate to pronounce slavery the cause of the war.[6] However, emphasis upon political and constitutional history by the first generation of professional American historians led John W. Burgess[7] to oppose on political grounds the right of the South to secede.

Declining interest in political history during the twentieth century led the historian to seek other than political causes of the Civil War. In 1928, the Beards made a frontal attack upon the theory that the war came about because of differing political conceptions of the nature of the Union, and advanced their own thesis that the clash of opposing economic systems made the conflict inevitable.[8] *In the 1930's politics entered into the historiography of the American Civil War mainly in terms of the historian's interest in the leadership qualities of pre-Civil War politicians.*[9]

Dean Roy F. Nichols of the University of Pennsylvania has contributed to the revitalization of political history by integrating it with the broader social process. He avoids, on the one hand, the aridity of political history written by von Holst and Burgess (when hard pressed, Burgess once brought God into court as witness for the Unionist cause) and the opposite extreme of the studied avoidance of politics, characteristic of the History of American Life series. Carl Becker, himself one of the editors of the American Life series, once remarked that politics was as much an expression of the life of the American people as any other subject covered by these volumes, and poked sly fun at the veil which editors had drawn over the political scene. Now Dean Nichols writes of political history as "an important and often decisive factor in a cultural intepretation of history."

WHEN the Founding Fathers met, in Independence Hall, to create the United States of America, they were remarkably wise but at the same time much limited by the narrow bounds of contemporary social knowledge. Their political wisdom moved them to prescribe a Federal system, rather than to attempt to force the establishment of a centralized national government. They failed, however, to foresee how the processes of national growth were to affect their handiwork. They created a system without sufficient mechanism to operate it. Their successors, without their wisdom or purposefulness, had to create this machinery.

The crux of the problem of government, for which machinery was necessary, presented by the Federal system in operation, was the method of registering the popular will. All laws, all executive acts, all judicial determination were to be made by representatives of the people, or their appointees. How were these representatives to be chosen?

The makers of the Constitution were used to a state system of elections which was the product of colonial custom and experience rather than the result of comprehensive planning. In the main the drafters accepted these electoral customs and added but little to them. The two popularly elected groups, the members of the lower house of the Federal Congress, and that part of the Electoral College chosen by direct vote rather than by state legislatures, were to be selected at such times and by such voters as the states might prescribe. The only Federal requirement was that the Congressmen must be chosen in time to assemble on the first Monday in December of the odd years, and the Presidential electors so that they could meet in their respective state capitals in the December of every leap year. The result was that from the beginning each state determined its own times and seasons and as late as 1861 there had been little progress on the road to uniformity among the then thirty-four states. State and Congressional elections were held here and there in all months of every year, save January, February, June, and July. Election activity was never-ending.

A second mechanism for registering the popular will — the system of parties — was not envisioned by the gentlemen next door when they did their work in 1787, nor did it emerge quickly, as historians generally assume. Machine politics was of slow growth, and developed only after a phenomenal increase in the population. Political leaders in the 1820's and 1830's saw that elections could be carried most effectively by careful organization, and so a group of them created the Democratic Party between 1828 and 1836. They were clever and did their work so well that, barring accidents, they seemed destined to control permanently; they actually did rule this country, with the exception of two brief intervals, from 1829 to 1861 — thirty-two years.

This Democratic Party, and the various less successful organizations which attempted to oppose it, were in reality not national parties, as we understand such a term; in fact even our Republican and Democratic groups of today are not as national and centralized as people commonly assume. They are really federations of state machines, and these machines are generally very independent and often hard to handle, as any national chairman can testify. In the period just before the Civil War there was hardly any central organization at all, but some sixty-eight state parties acting with great individual independence.

Those chosen by the voters, in such a haphazard series of elections operated by parties so disorganized, must then direct the Federal system and must do so ostensibly as representatives of the states. As such they must apportion patronage and appropriations as well as answer legislative demands as Federal legislators and officials. They constantly employed diplomatic negotiating and bargaining. Legislation was more like treaty making than statute writing, and it often was done in an atmosphere of bad temper and antagonism, especially as the capital city, Washington, was so badly equipped and so unhealthful.

Their task was the more difficult because Federal relations among the states were so difficult. Few of the states were coherent or integrated units of opinion, and a large proportion of them were confused by various and conflicting internal interests and views. Such differences often crossed state lines. Even today, understanding of the true nature of the Federal system is hampered by the earlier emphasis on state rights and by the fact that certain states once seceded and formed a Southern republic. The North and the South, as the antagonists were then labeled, went to war. This eventual narrowing of the interest to two easily defined belligerents also gives a false impression of simplicity which is projected back into the antebellum years. The Federal system and its relation to the Civil War need a more penetrating analysis than can be had by concentrating on states and their rights and on the growing antagonism between two entities described as North and South.

Those chosen by the people to operate the Federal system were not only confused by the factors just mentioned but they were most handicapped because they failed to understand what sort of federalism they were representing. Before the Civil War the political leaders were deceived because they were thinking of federalism not in terms of the basic cultural situation; rather they were absorbed by an accidental political combination, a union of states. In fact the people of the new republic were not so much the citizens of the several states, or dwellers in two distinct sections growing continually more incompatible, as they were people activated by a series of attitudes. They were living within a cultural federalism, in which men and women of different attitudes were pooling their interests in the operation of a political Federal system. The basic fact is the cultural federation of attitudes rather than the political federation of states.

The men and women exhibiting these different attitudes were not isolated and separated by boundaries, they dwelt side by side and on occasion the same person might be moved by more than one attitude, or by different ones at different times. The emotional complex which was created by the variety of these attitudes and the tension which their antagonisms bred added such confusion to that already provided, by the chaotic electoral customs, and the poorly organized parties, that the total precipitated a resort to arms. The baffling problem was not how to maintain a balance among states but how to preserve a balance among a number of emotional units or attitudes. It was this that proved beyond the political capacity of the time.

Of the multitude of attitudes within this cultural federalism discernible during the ante-bellum days, there were five which were particularly dangerous in their conflict-breeding potentialities. Most prominent among them was a state of mind and emotion best called Southernism, which dominated not only many within the South but numerous migrants from that region as well as sympathizers with its situation who dwelt in the North. Its chief characteristic was its increasing defensiveness, its praise of slavery, its fear that Southern culture was in danger of destruction or degradation. A second divisive attitude was that dominating those eager to see the nation wax in wealth and power, who were anxious to exploit national resources, develop industry, provide transportation, and promote commerce and banking. These interests of the metropolis make it appropriate to speak of this attitude as Metropolitanism. It was characteristic of the era and was found everywhere, but it was less common in the South where the fear grew that such swift development might come at the South's expense. A third attitude, for convenience called Territorialism, was characterized by an intense interest in frontier development, in the organization of territories and the admission of new states. Here fortunes, financial and political, could be made — and interest was feverish. The urge for political growth vitally affected state and national politics during the ante-bellum years between 1815 and 1860, as sixteen new states were created. Most of them emerged from territorial status through political turbulence, in which men from various regions had fought furiously to control the pattern of development in the new communities.

The confusion was worse confounded by two other attitudes which injected a combination of hatred and moral indignation into the turmoil: by Antislaveryism and New Englandism. The existence of slavery in the Southern states troubled many people, as both anachronistic and sinful. Particularly in the Middle West many hated slavery and were moved by an intense desire to abolish it or at least to prevent its extension. Their hatred of slavery often was combined with antagonisms bred of struggles against persons dominated by Southern ways of thought and behavior, over the political and business problems of their states. Furthermore many people in New England were activated by a variation of Antislaveryism. That region had been losing ground politically and people of ambitions or pride felt thwarted. They found that the dominant Southern politicians stood most in their way and their bitterness at their inferiority easily could be translated into hatred of the sin of slavery and into attacks upon the slave power. This complex series of divisive attitudes — Southernism, Metropolitanism, Territorialism, Antislaveryism, and New Englandism — was underlined, emphasized, and exaggerated by two prevailing attitudes which had no suspicion of sectional location. They were found everywhere and their nature was such as to intensify the emotional stimulus which the divisive attitudes projected. These attitudes were the prevailing Protestantism and Romanticism so characteristic of the time. The first of these two emphasized morality and duty and caused many consciences to be concerned over sin in the community. Because of it there was in the free labor states therefore much hatred of slavery as a sin, and a very active and militant group of abolitionists. Sensitive conscience caused people to fight Southern political power in the name of a crusade against a national shame. In the South, on the other hand, the same Protestant attitude prevailed, but slavery was praised as a blessing because it enabled African heathen to secure Christian salvation. There, attacks upon the institution by abolitionists and opponents of slavery-extension were countered by denunciation of Northern materialism, wage slavery, general servitude to Mammon, and hypocrisy — all sins.

The intensity of these feelings was strengthened by the prevailing Romanticism of the period. A rosy optimism precluded a realistic view of perplexing problems. Virtues and vices stood unqualified. Few people would admit any dangers and most went on sublimely with the most naïve concepts of contemporary trends. This romantic state of mind placed a premium upon exaggeration; ideas and emotions that were attractive were embraced without critical appraisal of their validity. There was therefore a minimum of that commodity labeled "common sense." Too few could be convinced that concerted efforts should be made to encourage cohesive attitudes which would counteract the divisive tendencies.

The few who were endeavoring to encourage such cohesive attitudes sought to stimulate nationalism. They stressed the increasing strength of the nation, natural pride in the creation and maintenance of free institutions. The growing sense of the success of the United States gave some confidence that nationalism might counteract the divisive attitudes enough to overcome the disrupting tendencies. Others felt that the saving formula should be an appeal to fair play under the classic theory of democracy. Government should be by the rule of the majority. That majority which ruled in town meeting and county council, in state legislature and Congress, should rule everywhere. The people could be trusted; by and large the majority in the greatest number of cases was bound to be right. All vexing questions of dangerous import should be referred to the people and everyone should be bound to submit to the will of the majority. Yet neither nationalism nor democracy could satisfy the South. Both attitudes assumed that the Southern people as a minority must be subject to the will of others, an intolerable assumption. Yet, since some reconciling formula was necessary, their political philosophers must suggest an alternative. They began to encourage a concept of Regionalism, an autonomy designed to make the enactment of certain types of legislation dependent upon some form of regional consent.

The strength of those leaders endeavoring to encourage the cohesive attitudes was entirely inadequate for the task and they were further hampered by the general lack of understanding of the cultural federalism which was conditioning their problems. They thought they were dealing with a controversy which was primarily legal, involving merely a harmonization of rights, state and Federal. They sought — just as if they were settling a case at law — to achieve a legal formula which would reconcile states to Federal exercise of power and sovereignty. It was an era that throve on legal and political theory, on countless hours spent in oratory and in the writing and reading of those long, theoretical debates which we now think to have been so unrealistic. Unrecognized behind the oratory were the prevailing attitudes, giving direction to such dynamics as moral indignation (which some present-day blasé historians seem inclined to discount), thwarted ambition, fear of loss of face and power, and the countless confusions of a growing state.

The political leaders failed as they were bound to fail because they oversimplified their problem and tried to stop a flood with a sand pile. And this flood reached its crest because they themselves fed it by the constant agitation which rose out of the chaotic electoral system. Contests were waged not only continually but also on two levels, local and Federal. The same party organizations had to maintain themselves in power in the states and in Washington; and it was generally more important to maintain their local controls. They frequently brought national issues into state contests because of the greater potential interest. The people of one locality could easily be whipped into political fury about the sins of omission or commission of others in a distant region, and with little risk to the local agitators. This possibility bred irresponsibility about playing with emotional dynamite. Dangerous divisive attitudes were encouraged for local purposes by agitators of narrow vision, heedless of the consequences.

Thus the prime factor that made conflict irrepressible was political. The divisive and pervasive attitudes provided inexhaustible material for political controversy, and the will and the strength to carry it on vigorously whenever opportunity demanded. These controversies reached the bloodletting pitch because the chaotic election program called for contests somewhere nearly all the time. Issues were never allowed to rest. Political oratory, pamphleteering, inflammatory journalism, and, more important, corner store and tavern argument were going on all the time.

The swift growth of population brought a constant demand for the recognition of new political units to be fitted into the Federal government and the Federal party organizations. Controversy over these political re-alignments became more intense as the conflicting attitudes became stronger. The control of government was more sought-after as the growth of the country made Federal functioning more vital, particularly through subsidy, "protection," and the opening of new territory. The stakes of power were constantly growing higher, with many more men becoming politically ambitious and seeking office more intensively. So the contests were more vigorously waged. Popular interest in them could generally be captured more effectively by predictions of calamity and danger; so, quite heedlessly, literally hundreds of persons seeking public office stirred up increasing apprehension among the voters.

This rising tide of crisis agitation racked the political machinery operating the Federal system. The Democratic Party had been in power almost continuously through three decades. Its strength lay in its appeal as a people's party, in the heroic Jackson legend, in a swashbuckling, expansionist, foreign policy, in its effective political organization, but particularly in its laissez-faire phlosophy in domestic affairs. On questions of subsidy the party leaders, sensing some of the variety of interests and attitudes endangering the party's control, had avoided such issues by maintaining the Federal government as one of very limited powers. It attempted to encourage nationalism by its aggressive foreign policy. In domestic policy it was more and more sympathetic to regionalism.

But no party in this country has ever remained in power for much more than the life of a generation. As the 1860's approached, the ruling Democratic Party was more and more cursed by the resentments of those who had been thwarted by its laissez-faire policy, those disappointed in their ambitions for leadership and office, and of course by the rising generation inevitably at feud with its elders. The stage was set for schism and it came.

A new political group was ready to take advantage of these signs of discontent and rebellion. The old opposition party, the Whig, had never been very effective, in part because it took little advantage of the controversial issues of conflicting attitudes and merely tried to promote the cohesive idea of nationalism. It was now pushed aside by a new party, the Republican, which capitalized on division. They saw that the majority of the voters lived in regions where metropolitan, territorial, antislavery, and New England attitudes existed in profusion and confusion. Heedless of danger, they made a catch-all appeal. Combining moral indignation against slavery with promises to various promotional interests, and stressing the theoretical concept of the right of the majority to rule, they had an appeal strong enough to break the long-continued power of the South and of the Democratic Party.

The Democratic leadership saw this opposition swiftly rising but were incapable of coherent action to meet it. They were faced with a dilemma. The Free State Democrats saw the need of concessions to save their ranks from the onslaught of the Republicans, but their Southern associates refused these concessions — for they themselves were in danger. They had as their local opponents the Southern branch of the Whig Party, which had lost most of its Northern wing to the Republicans and therefore could go all-out for Southern interests. If the Southern Democrats agreed to concessions in the national platform to placate Free State opinion, they would be accused by their local opponents of betraying the South, and might well be driven from the state governments. Rather than lose local control, the Southern Democratic leaders sacrificed their national power — a phenomenon not unusual in American political history.

The result was the split of the Democratic Party at the national convention in 1860. The delegations from the Gulf States took a walk, probably expecting thereby to force a compromise which would restore unity. But then it appeared that the Northern state machines refused harmony because any concessions would destroy their slim chances of maintaining power. Indeed, the intricacies of a local feud in New York may have been the immediate cause of the failure of compromise. The system of federally organized parties had resulted in the exaltation of the local over the national, and had so hindered the growth of nationally minded leaders that there were none powerful enough to meet the crisis.

This schism made the election of 1860 unique in American political history. Hitherto there had never been more than two parties, or at most two major and one minor organization, at any one of the Presidential elections since 1824. Now, however, there were four substantial parties in contest: the Republicans, the Regular Democrats, the Bolting Democrats (largely though by no means exclusively from the South), and the Whig organization transformed by a new name into the Constitutional Union Party. In this four-cornered contest the Republicans won, though garnering only 40 per cent of the votes, because their minority of the popular votes was sufficient to gain a majority of the electoral ballots.

Then the constant agitation bore its fruit. There were enough Southerners so angered and fearful, after years of alarmist campaigning in their own and in the free-labor communities, that they demanded and secured secession by eleven states in the interest of preserving their freedom. In the Free States indignation at this attempt to break up the great democratic experiment led to a resort to arms, to preserve the Union against these secessionists.

Thus war came when the American people for the first time refused to abide by a national election. The parties which had been promoting the cohesive attitudes had broken down, and their disorganization had permitted the new Republican organization to win through direct appeal to the divisive attitudes. The constant heat generated in the frequent elections brought an explosion. The social, economic, and cultural differences had been so used by the political operators as to produce secession and civil war.

The war came because no means had been devised to curb the extravagant use of the divisive forces. Statesmanship seemed poverty-stricken. The work of the nationalists, who sought to find the formula with which to overcome the divisive attitudes, was vain. Too few even saw the need for the formula; they ran heedlessly down the path to disruption.

In the last analysis, the war was the product of the chaotic lack of system in ascertaining the public will, a chaos exploited by irresponsible and blind operators of local political machinery without adequate central organization.

The Civil War fortunately did not spell destruction to the Republic. It left its lessons behind it. Growing social coherence, the nationalism accelerated by the war, at length produced more orderly democratic procedures. Elections were now concentrated in the autumn of the even years; there were long breathing spells between campaigns. Parties were better organized with more centralized management. Isolated, irresponsible action became somewhat less frequent. The two-party system was resumed. Although there have been a score of small parties, and upon occasion three large enough to become major, the disintegration of 1860 has never been repeated.

Lincoln and the
Governance of Men

by

JAMES G. RANDALL

[From *The Abraham Lincoln Quarterly*, VI (June 1951), 327–352. Reprinted by permission of the Abraham Lincoln Association, Springfield, Illinois.]

There are tendencies in the writing of biography, perhaps more than any other form of history, for the biographical historian to want (or not want) to establish rapport with the central figure; to go out of his way to defend or condemn. This is true of Lincoln biographers although such tendencies have been brought under increasing control with the entrance of the professional historian into the field of Lincoln studies.

Lincoln's first biographer, Josiah G. Holland, made him into a model youth and an almost perfect man. Holland wrote of a religiously-orthodox Lincoln "developed by the providence of God." [1] *Very different in tone was Ward Hill Lamon's* The Life of Abraham Lincoln, *a departure from the highly moral Lincoln portrayed by Holland. Based in considerable measure upon information furnished by Lincoln's law partner, William H. Herndon, it presented Lincoln's mother as illegitimate and suggested that Lincoln was too; Thomas Lincoln as an improvident good-for-nothing; Lincoln, himself, as a sometimes unethical politico, with a liking for off-color anecdotes; Mary Lincoln as a shrew, and the married life of the Lincolns as anything but a desirable relationship. The Lamon biography first developed the legend that Ann Rutledge of New Salem was the only woman Lincoln ever loved and that Lincoln left Mary waiting at the church the first time they planned to marry. Lamon found Lincoln wanting in religious orthodoxy, and — Lamon be-*

ing *a Democrat like his ghost writer, Chauncey F. Black — he disagreed with Lincoln's politics.*[2]

These stories were repeated in Herndon's Lincoln: The True Story of A Great Life[3] *which was written in collaboration with Jesse W. Weik. The latter, like Lamon, drew heavily upon the materials and reminiscences of William H. Herndon — the improvident, erratic, but invariably interesting law partner of Abraham Lincoln — who was a fountainhead of fact and myth about Lincoln.*[4]

Then, in 1890, there appeared the gigantic and adulatory work of John G. Nicolay and John Hay, entitled Abraham Lincoln: A History, *in ten volumes. Nicolay and Hay based their narrative largely on Lincoln's personal papers lent the authors by Robert Todd Lincoln, and used by them under the watchfulness of the latter's censorious eye. These papers were then sealed until 1947.*[5] *It was Lincoln the partisan leader that Nicolay and Hay presented; and so impressed was Theodore Roosevelt with the work that he wrote Hay: "I do congratulate myself that my father was a Republican and that I am a Republican."* [6]

Ida Tarbell's Lincoln (1896) *exploded many of the legends contributed by Herndon and others. A realist and no idolator, Miss Tarbell nevertheless nurtured the hope that Lincoln's love affair with Ann Rutledge would not be proved untrue. "I have always been a believer in this romance," wrote the lady who later did a man's job in the muckraking of Standard Oil, "and have believed it was the only time romance touched Abraham Lincoln. . . ."*[7] *By 1928, when Albert J. Beveridge's nonprofessional but scholarly Lincoln biography appeared, the author wrote of the courtship of Ann by Lincoln as "misty" with neither of the parties displaying "any of the precipitancy of passion." Resolved to present facts and not legends in his life of Lincoln, Beveridge nevertheless still repeated the story of Lincoln's not putting in an appearance the first time he was to marry Mary.*[8]

Until the mid-1930's there can be no doubt that the figure of Lincoln was more attractive to the journalist and the amateur than to the professional historian. In 1934, Professor James G. Randall's "Has the Lincoln Theme Been Exhausted?" [9] *sought to awaken professional historians to the rich potentialities of the Lincoln theme. Since that time, the situation has reversed itself, with the professional scholar taking over almost entirely (a conspicuous exception is, of course, Carl Sandburg's Lincoln biography,[10] an invariably interesting but rambling and not always reliable account).*

Activation of the Abraham Lincoln Association of Springfield, establishment of the Abraham Lincoln Quarterly, and the opening of the Robert Todd Lincoln collection of Abraham Lincoln's personal papers in 1947 have all contributed to stimulating the interest of professional historians in "the Lincoln theme." In fact, so many nooks and crannies of Lincoln's life had been subjected to microscopic examination by the professional scholar that in 1952 Benjamin Platt Thomas was quite justified in stating that sufficient new Lincoln material had become available to justify his publication of a one-volume Lincoln biography[11] in the tradition of Lord Charnwood's treatment thirty-five years earlier.[12]

The dean of professional Lincoln scholars was the late Professor Randall, for many years Professor of History at the University of Illinois, whose three-volume Lincoln the President is testament of both his own careful researches and the scrupulously acknowledged findings of other scholars. In the following selection, Professor Randall examines Lincoln's technique in the governance of men from the perspective of the recently developed concept of human relations.

TODAY we consider Lincoln and the governance of men. This is not a theme that we can adequately cover. We can only introduce it. When we say *governance* we have in mind not so much the end result of subjecting a people to ruling power, but rather the manner of a leader toward his people, the mode of aproach, the choice of procedures, the conduct and deportment that characterize an administration, or the behavior of him who has been clothed with authority and invested with office.

With Lincoln, the technique of public relations was closely bound up with the art of human relations.* In personal dealings Lincoln

* Lincoln's human relations have been treated by the author in *Elks Magazine,* February 1950.

put a new meaning into the word "tact." He could maintain poise, avoid awkward "show-down," and steer the conversation. In his presence embarrassment disappeared, courtesy was raised to an exquisite level, and a touch of human interest was added to the passing moment or the everyday routine. In the personal and also the public technique Lincoln gave attention to both theory and practice. He did not rely upon whim or untrained intuition. To speak of Lincoln's greatness, as is often done, in terms of his being untrained, as if that were the significant thing, is quite the wrong emphasis. Lincoln's merit was not that of an unsophisticated Horatio Alger hero who suddenly shot up from prairie obscurity to the White House. His success did not come by chance, nor by blundering into the right approach, nor by any game of hit or miss. What he did in public appeal was a matter of deliberate thought, preparation, and self-training. His address of February 22, 1842, at the age of thirty-three, showed how he had deliberately pondered the best mode and conduct in influencing the heads and hearts of men.

Lincoln thought of both the head and the heart. He considered the heart the "highroad to reason." What he meant by this was that rational methods should prevail in public thinking, but that this was best achieved by the friendly approach. It was not to be produced by ignoring the heart, by forcing or dictating a man's judgment, or by setting him down as one to be despised. He was writing this passage as if, to him, the public appeal was virtually identical with the personal human appeal.

In Lincoln's eloquent face and in his manner of meeting people there was the appeal of a friendly and magnetic personality. One visitor wrote: "His presence is commanding — his manner winning to a marked degree. . . . You recognize in him a high-toned, unassuming, chivalrous-minded gentleman, fully posted in all the essential amenities of social life and sustained by the infallible monitor of common sense." *

We have this description from life by the antislavery journalist, Jane Swisshelm, reporting a levee at the White House: "I watched

---

* Utica *Morning Herald*, June 27, 1860, reprinted in Sacramento *Daily Union*, Aug. 15, 1860. The writer has been identified as Ellis Henry Roberts, editor of the Utica *Morning Herald*. Rufus Rockwell Wilson, *Intimate Memories of Lincoln*, p. 299.

the President and Mrs. Lincoln receive. His sad, earnest, honest face was irresistible in its plea for confidence, and Mrs. Lincoln's manner was so simple and motherly . . . that I doubted the tales I had heard." *

To say that a man is tactful is to say that he is personally skillful and understandingly human. Lincoln was not merely tactful in the abstract. He was considerate toward Seward, who calmly planned to conduct his administration for him; toward Weed, whose grasping for Warwick-like power in 1861 was a major embarrassment; toward Chase, the center of intrigue to displace the President; and toward Stanton, who was described as "discourteous," "dictatorial," "disrespectful," and almost impossible to deal with. These are but examples. The list could be vastly multiplied.

Some of Lincoln's priceless utterances were by way of adjusting personal feuds and quarrels, for which he had no earthly use. In his oral reprimand to Captain J. Madison Cutts, a classic whose significance has been newly brought to light, Lincoln said: "Quarrel not at all. No man resolved to make the most of himself, can spare time for personal contention. Still less can he afford to take all the consequences, including the vitiating of his temper, and the loss of self-control." †

The Cutts reprimand was in 1863, but nearly a quarter-century earlier Lincoln had given some of his keenest advice on the subject of quarreling. We are speaking now of Lincoln letters that have newly come to light in Chicago. In early 1839, when Lincoln was in Vandalia, he took a hand in adjusting a sharp quarrel between two valued friends, Edward D. Baker and William Butler, both of Springfield. It is not our present concern to inquire into the first

* Jane Grey Swisshelm, *Half a Century*, p. 236.

† Lincoln's autograph memorandum of the reprimand to Captain Cutts is in the R. T. Lincoln Collection, nos. 27496–98. Until the summer of 1947 (so far as the author's knowledge goes) this Lincolnian gem had been neglected. It had never been given out in such a way as to show what the document was, with identification as to the name of Cutts and with even a suggestion of attendant circumstances. Yet it had been quoted in fragments without such identification in Nicolay and Hay, *Complete Works* (12 vol. ed.), I, 151–152 footnote; Sandburg, *Prairie Years*, II, 277; and *Abr. Lincoln Quar.* (article by Logan Hay), I, 91 (1940). The common source was obviously Nicolay and Hay. By a search in the National Archives the author has obtained considerable light on this incident. Sometimes the document is erroneously designated as a letter. Instead, it is a memorandum of an oral reprimand.

causes or initial war aims of this personal dispute, but we cannot omit quoting some of Lincoln's statements written to Butler: "Your first letter to him [to Baker] was written while you were in a state of high excitement, and therefore ought not to have been construed as an emination [*sic*] of deliberate malice. Unfortunately however it reached Baker while he was writhing under a severe toothache, and therefore he at that time was incapable of exercising that patience and reflection which the case required. The note he sent you was written while in that state of feeling, and for that reason I think that you ought not to pay any serious attention to it." To all the well-known crises that Lincoln sought to adjust, let us add this one: the crisis of personal bad feeling, on the one hand, coming up against a raging toothache on the other.

Lincoln's next statement to Butler, in this new-found letter, deserves to be preserved in copybooks and anthologies. He wrote: "It is always magnanimous to recant whatever may have been said in passion, and when you and Butler have done this, I am sure there will be no difficulty left between you." * The main importance of such a situation as the Cutts reprimand, or the Butler-Baker adjustment, is that instances of this nature were typical. This was Lincoln's habit, his code, his philosophy, his custom in dealing with fellow men.

Lincoln's leadership was intellectual, but at the same time stirring; restrained, but with the rallying power of a bugle. His approach was along the avenue of reason. It was from the "solid quarry of sober reason," he said, that he would hew the pillars of the temple.† Though pre-eminently a rational man, he was also sentimental. "I love the sentiments of those old-time men," ‡ he once said, referring to the Revolutionary fathers. In the matter of inward sentiment he cherished a piece of paper that contained not a violet, but the stain of a violet which Joshua Speed's Fanny had sent him.§ Reason and sentiment with Lincoln were in balance. Both, he knew, were requisite to a wholesome personality. He could touch the

* These newly found letters, among the papers of George M. Pullman, have been donated to the Chicago Historical Society.
† Roy P. Basler, ed., *Abraham Lincoln: His Speeches and Writings*, p. 84.
‡ *Ibid.*, p. 305.
§ *Ibid.*, p. 146. Lincoln to Speed, Springfield, Mar. 27, 1842, photostat in Abraham Lincoln Assoc., original in Barrett Collection.

chords of human feeling but never with the tearful appeal. There was no play-acting in his emotional passages.

Part of our problem is to inquire into the manner of Lincoln in controversy. Such a test goes far in the appraisal of any leader. Lincoln's methods seemed always to be natural; yet if you study them you find that they were adroit rather than naïve; they showed *savoir faire* rather than amateurish inexperience. When Lincoln took part in a controversial discussion he was, to begin with, informed. He did not lack ammunition; he had his facts, his documents, his references to volume and page, his understanding of intricate or complicated subjects, such as the bank question in Illinois in 1837, or the Federal subtreasury in 1839, or the question of treaties, boundaries, and settlements as between the Mexicans and the Americans in the late Forties. He was careful to keep the record straight, and often he would bring the documents right in with him for use as he spoke. It was characteristic of Lincoln that his arguments went to the heart of a subject. He had, as was said of another, an instinct "for the hinge or turning point of a debate." *

He showed no resemblance to an American political speaker described by the British writer Graham Wallas in his excellent book *Human Nature in Politics*. This gentlemen had his technique. He would place a heavy board on the platform. Then, as he made each point, he would take a hammer and drive a nail into the plank. We are told that this theatrical performance went over well with his audiences.†

Seriously, what we have in mind is irrational inference in politics. We see the tendency in those who would gain votes by wearing red galluses, wearing no socks, or passing the biscuits. We like to believe that our political judgments are well based, but at times they are not judgments at all, but thoughtless reactions. A politician may, if he wishes, count on unreason and exploit it, and some do little else, but all praise should be due to the leader who, like Lincoln, makes his appeal to intelligence and not to unthinking prejudice.

Lincoln avoided catchwords and tricks. He had no wish to split

---

* Stewart Mitchell, *Horatio Seymour of New York*, p. 95.
† Graham Wallas, *Human Nature in Politics*, pp. 106–107; Gilbert K. Chesterton, *Heretics*, p. 122.

hairs. He realized that inflammatory words could be a nuisance or a menace. In a passage that ought to be read by every man in public life he said: ". . . When men wrangle by the mouth with no certainty that they mean the same thing while using the same word, it perhaps were as well if they would keep silence." He had in mind the inexact use of the word " 'coercion' . . . often with some temper and hot blood." * In insisting that words be chosen carefully for their meanings he was well aware of that rather modern science that we call "semantics." Being aware of it, he was disturbed by the senseless wranglings that could have been avoided by simply remembering that words are sometimes dynamite, and that their irresponsible use may be as tragic as the fumbling discharge of a gun by a child that does not know it is loaded. Of course that matter of the potency of words can work both ways and there is comfort in the fact that the effect of words may be favorable. A humorous suggestion along that line was given in the comment of the Boston *Courier* on the Emancipation Proclamation. "The Proclamation may lose us Kentucky, but it has given us Mr. Wendell Phillips. He will now doubtless take the field with a formidable army of twenty-five thousand adjectives." †

Lincoln preferred to keep controversy on a high level, free as he said from "vulgarity and blackguardism." ‡ He wanted debate but not ill feeling. Of Douglas he said: "He and I are about the best friends in the world." § When arguing a hotly contested law case, he said "he did not purpose to assail anybody . . . he expected to grow earnest as he proceeded but not ill-natured." || And on Douglas' side we must not forget his unstinted and patriotic support of Lincoln and of the Union cause in the secession crisis.

What we are dealing with here is the matter of self-control in verbal conflict. Let two men be engaged in discussion, be it a forum, committee room, or the floor of Congress. One of these men is short

* Basler, p. 571.
† Quoted in Ralph Korngold, *Two Friends of Man*, p. 312.
‡ Nicolay and Hay, ed., *Complete Works of Abraham Lincoln* (1905), III, 335 (herein cited as *Complete Works*). Reference is to the twelve-volume edition, which "bears the names of Nicolay and Hay . . . who had put out a two-volume edition in 1894, but the actual editor appears to have been Francis D. Tandy." Paul M. Angle, *A Shelf of Lincoln Books*, p. 7.
§ Allan Nevins, *Emergence of Lincoln*, I, 376.
|| *Complete Works*, II, 340.

on self-control. He raises his voice. He spurts and sputters. He reaches wildly for excessive and extravagant words. He may call his antagonist a traitor or a liar. It may be that he grasps recklessly for headlines or descends to discreditable character assassination. He loses the thread of his discourse, repeats words of hate, fumbles, and with each new fumbling gets redder in the face.

Now we will put opposite him a man of a different type. His voice is free from nervousness. His manner is deliberate. We see that he is steering, watching the road. His driving is not a combination of gas and alcohol. His steadier tones command attention by reason of contrast with the impulsive shouts of his opponent. The deliberateness of his words calls attention to their content. His appeal is to the mind of his audience; or, if the appeal is to sentiment, it is as if he knows that, being patriotic and rightly disposed, his hearers cannot fail to respond where the cause is pitched on so high a level and the challenge is so convincing. His case is the stronger because it is not necessary for him to use tricks, or threaten, or whip up the laggard spirit.

It is clear that Lincoln belonged to the second type of speaker. It can be admitted that he sometimes did get excited. Of the Ottawa debate he said: "Douglas and I . . . crossed swords here yesterday; the fire flew some, and I am glad to know I am yet alive." * Yet, having "better self-control" than Douglas, as Allan Nevins writes, he added also "a patent sincerity and common-sense logic." Douglas looked like a man in an intense rage. "Lincoln never lost his simple, self-possessed blend of honesty and good humor, which lent persuasiveness to his clear, compact arguments." † Not that he was always gentle. He could make his antagonist squirm. His sarcasm sometimes cut like a Damascus blade. We know that he *could* use powerful invective, as in the legislature in answer to Linder in January 1837. If, therefore, he refrained from scorching sarcasm, as he usually did, it was not for want of ability or lack of vocabulary.

An example of Lincoln's restraint in controversy was his last speech in the senatorial campaign of 1858, a speech at Springfield on October 30, which is omitted in the Nicolay-Hay edition of the so-called "Complete Works." Lincoln and Douglas had argued up

* *Ibid.*, III, 270.
† Nevins, *Emergence*, I, 378.

and down the state of Illinois in seven formal joint debates and many more interim speeches. The strenuous campaign was over. Election day was at hand. The speakers had shot their bolts.

The issue rested with the people. In that taut suspense, that torturing eagerness for victory, Lincoln made a short, but a very special address. His first thought was that he was among friends; his next, that he had not gone off the track, had shown no undue severity or bad temper. "My friends," he said, "today closes the discussions of this canvass. The planting and the culture are over; and there remains but the preparation, and the harvest. I stand here surrounded by friends — some *political, all personal* friends I trust. May I be indulged, in this closing scene, to say a few words of myself. I have borne a laborious, and, in some respects to myself, a painful part in the contest. . . . To the best of my judgment I have labored *for,* and not *against* the Union. As I have not felt, so I have not expressed any harsh sentiment toward our Southern brethren. . . . I have meant to assail the motives of no party, or individual; and if I have, in any instance (of which I am not conscious) departed from my purpose, I regret it." He did not disclaim ambition; but, if slavery extension could be allayed, he said, "I would, in consideration, gladly agree, that Judge Douglas should never be *out,* and I never *in,* an office, so long as we both or either, live." *

Lincoln's self-control in debate probably disappointed some of his admirers — as, for instance, one of them who wrote telling him how he should handle Douglas: ". . . You [are] *too mild . . .* on the fellow . . . *give him fits.*" † Perhaps we need not inquire whether "give him fits" is the alpha and omega of enlightened debating. What we should remember is that Lincoln was severe against Douglas, but his tactic was not to reach wildly for any unfair weapon just because it came easiest and cheapest.

Much could be written on Lincoln's technique of public relations while President. There was in those days no such thing as organized presidential publicity. There was a kind of publicity, but it was casual; certainly it did not involve such things as the regular press conferences or news releases of today. And column writers were

* Oliver R. Barrett, *Lincoln's Last Speech in Springfield in the Campaign of 1858* (Univ. of Chicago Press, 1925).
† R. T. Lincoln Collec., Libr. of Cong., no. 1282.

scarce in Lincoln's time, though there were a few, such as George William Curtis of *Harper's* "Easy Chair," or George A. Townsend, known as "Gath." There was no Drew Pearson, though perhaps Townsend if he were alive today would give us a pretty good "Merry-Go-Round." An unfortunate gap in Lincoln's publicity was that the President did not then deliver his messages to Congress in person. It was Wilson, who, with his distinguished eloquence and with vital content in what he said, restored that useful practice to life after more than a century of disuse. It is interesting to reread Lincoln's excellent messages to Congress — notably that of July 4, 1861 — with a thought as to how much more it would have meant if he could have delivered those words in person in public joint session of Senate and House. Lincoln did not have a "presidential spokesman," though on one occasion, as reported by John Hay, Seward said to a deputy marshal: " 'The President instructs you that the habeas corpus is suspended in this city' " — i.e., in Washington. (Seward then turned to John Hay.' " 'That is what the Pres^t says, is it not, Mr. Hay?' 'Precisely his words,' I replied and the thing was done." *

Lincoln, however, did give attention to statements for the public mind. Sometimes he would use a letter to an editor. His famous declaration that Union was his paramount object was put forth in an open letter to Greeley.† On an important matter of policy he found in March 1862 that the New York *Times* had referred to compensated emancipation as too expensive. He then wrote to Raymond of the *Times* refuting this idea, and added: "Please . . . consider whether there should not be another article in the 'Times.' " ‡ Similarly, he wrote a letter to Crosby and Nichols of the *North American Review*, calling attention to a point on which his views had been misinterpreted.§

Some of Lincoln's most famous letters as instruments of presidential publicity were issued during 1863. That was the year of the Emancipation Proclamation, of the draft, of draft riots, of Missouri troubles, of Copperhead turbulence, of hard military cam-

---

* Tyler Dennett, ed., *Lincoln and the Civil War in the Diaries and Letters of John Hay*, p. 30.
† Basler, pp. 651–652.
‡ *Complete Works*, VII, 119.
§ *Ibid.*, IX, 284–285.

paigns in which fate was wavering. It was a year in which regular constitutional government broke down in Indiana and Illinois. It was to an intense degree and to a high pitch a year of "politics." People seem to have forgotten how much 1863 was an election year. There were state elections all over the map, including one in New York that would have been minor except that it involved the prestige of Governor Seymour, and one in Ohio that was certainly not minor because Vallandigham was a candidate for governor. It can simply be said that under Lincoln every year was an election year. Some of the states chose congressmen in 1861 and 1863. It was a curious and somewhat disturbing feature of the 1863 election in Maryland that Henry Winter Davis, one of Lincoln's relentless opponents in the Republican party, was elected without any rival candidate in a Baltimore district in which only 6200 votes were cast for him. This seems remarkable when it is remembered that, in the apportionment formula for that day (according to the 1860 census), there was to be one congressman for a population of about 120,000. Baltimore had not done so well by Lincoln at the time of the journey as President Elect in February 1861, and Baltimore did little good to Lincoln in the congressional election of 1863.

Among Lincoln's carefully written political appeals of 1863, the letters to Corning in New York, Birchard in Ohio, and Conkling in Illinois were especially significant. In his eloquent letter to James C. Conkling of Springfield, Illinois, he sounded the keynote for a great Union rally on September 3. He cared a good deal about the reception of this letter, asking Conkling to read it slowly, and expressing disappointment when it was garbled in the press. In this letter he patiently reasoned with those who doubted his policy as to Negroes. Then he turned from self-defense to strike the uplifting note, and as he did so there came a change of tone as when a composer changes the movement of a symphony. "The signs look better," he wrote. "The Father of Waters again goes unvexed to the sea. . . . Thanks to all. For the great republic — for the principle it lives by, and keeps alive — for man's vast future — thanks to all."*

The Corning letter (June 16, 1863), in answer to a meeting in Albany, was like a great state paper, though the President was on an

* Basler, pp. 720–724.

unpleasant theme as he defended his policy touching summary arrests and took a pot shot at Vallandigham.* So also his letter to an Ohio group headed by Mr. Birchard. This was addressed in reality to the whole nation, with particular reference to Ohio, where the coming issue as to Vallandigham's candidacy was vital to the Lincoln cause. It was a suave and dignified answer to Ohio gentlemen who were quite ready to cause the President all the embarrassment they could.† The result, or sequel, was seen in Vallandigham's defeat.

John Hay wrote in 1863: "The old man sits here and wields like a backwoods Jupiter the bolts of war and the machinery of government. . . . His last letter is a great thing. Some hideously bad rhetoric — some indecorums that are infamous — [all of which implied that John Hay knew more about rhetoric and decorum than Lincoln] — yet the whole letter takes its solid place in history, as a great utterance of a great man. The whole Cabinet could not have tinkered up a letter which could have been compared with it. [Perhaps only John Hay could have done better.] He [Lincoln] can snake a sophism out of its hole, better than all the trained logicians of all schools." ‡ Hay does not indicate what document of Lincoln he was grading. It may have been the aforementioned letter to Conkling dated August 26, 1863. Perhaps the young secretary did not like the expression "Uncle Sam's web-feet," or the statement "they have been and left their tracks."

Lincoln was not a spokesman of the war mind, with its snarling clamor, its forgeries, its atrocious war poetry, its vulgarity, its whispering campaigns, and its songs of hate. He utterly detested the profiteering and ignoble phases of that war period, when, as he said: "Every foul bird comes abroad and every dirty reptile rises up." § He had respect for Lee and was willing that Jefferson Davis should depart "unbeknown" from the country. (That was one flight into oblivion that did not occur.) He strongly disapproved of the vindictive program of the Republican radicals. There was not a trace of hatred in his Gettysburg address, not a syllable of it in ei-

* *Complete Works*, VIII, 298–314.
† *Ibid.*, IX, 1–10.
‡ Hay to Nicolay, Sep. 11, 1863, Dennett, p. 91.
§ Lincoln to Charles D. Drake and Others, *Complete Works*, IX, 157.

ther of his inaugurals. The grandeur of the second inaugural was
that it rose above the hatreds of the hour. That North and South
should be locked in an unnatural and devastating war was to him
something utterly illogical, something he could not explain. Both
read the same Bible and prayed to the same God. It was beyond
comprehension, inscrutable; but the triumph of the Union was
within understanding because that triumph, if promoted in Lincolnian terms, would mean an end of sectional ill will. His second inaugural meant getting back to the very things he stressed in his first
inaugural. In the midst of the clamor and the tumult he appealed
from madness to normality. It was as if he were looking his people
squarely in the eye and asking them to remember that they, including those on the other side, were human beings, asking them
to snap out of it, to avoid that malignity of hate which is most
destructive to the man who harbors it.

Lincoln was a party man, which may be said somewhat as a matter
of course because doing things by parties was, as it remains, the
custom; but his greatness and statesmanship are not to be expressed
in partisan terms. He objected to a situation in which the "immutable principles of justice . . . make way for party interests," *
and during the war he declared: "In this time of national peril I
would have preferred to meet you upon a level one step higher than
any party platform because I am sure that from such more elevated
position we could do better battle for the country we all love than we
possibly can from those lower ones where, from the force of habit,
the prejudices of the past, and selfish hopes of the future, we are
sure to expend much of our ingenuity and strength in finding fault
with and aiming blows at each other." † That is what Lincoln
thought of the party spirit.

Men of Lincoln's party often did not agree with him. Early in
1861 congressmen of that party passed territorial laws as to Colo-
rado, Nevada, and Dakota which followed the Douglas pattern, not
the Lincoln pattern, concerning slavery in the territories.‡ The
Congress of his day did not put into effect Lincoln's scheme of
compensated emancipation, much less his program of reconstruc-

* Complete Works, I, 164–165.
† Basler, p. 706.
‡ Randall, Lincoln the President, I, 228–231.

tion. They did pass the confiscation act of 1862, of which he strongly disapproved.*

Lincoln's court of appeal, his source of strength, was the people. . . . The nation's destiny, he said at Indianapolis as President Elect in 1861, rested with the people, "not with politicians." † That was at least the way he wanted it. He believed that the majority should be in the driver's seat, but without oppression to the minority. Confidence in the people was his keynote.

We find one of the paradoxes of the whole confused period when we see how this man was unmercifully and incredibly abused during his and the nation's ordeal. At times, as in August 1864, to hear the disgruntled politicians you would have thought that Lincoln had no friends. But much of the value of the Lincoln Papers is that you catch in them something more than the utterings of politicians, though such utterings are not absent. You get the groundswell of popular feeling in the words of undistinguished men and women — words in which there runs the refrain: *Mr. Lincoln, the people are with you.* And so it turned out in the election of 1864.

People would ask for a lock of Lincoln's hair. In one appeal it was specified: "send us by mail as large a lock as you can well spare." ‡ The gifts he received were bountiful, miscellaneous, and amusing: a pair of moccasins "gorgeously quilled" (the "Tycoon . . . put them on and grinned"); a beautifully finished cushion; honorary membership in the "New York Workingmen's Democratic-Republican Association" which he genuinely appreciated and graciously acknowledged; a piece of the "Charter Oak" from Hartford, Connecticut, carved in the shape of a small Bible and finished in gold; an honorary degree from Columbia College, New York, presented by Francis Lieber; and a like degree from Knox College. In March 1865 he was informed that an institution at Lincoln, Illinois, has been started with the name "Lincoln College." Gifts came in by the bushel or the tub; a quill of the great Bald Eagle of the Rocky Mountains (he could use it in signing some historic document); "a pair of American eagles . . . captured on the banks of

* *Ibid.*, II, 227–229; *Constitutional Problems Under Lincoln*, pp. 279–280.
† *Complete Works*, VI, 112.
‡ R. T. Lincoln Collec., no. 29402.

the Neuse River in North Carolina" (lest it remain a mystery it was pointed out in the case of this pair that one was male and the other female); skeleton leaves from the battlefield of Gettysburg; a very patriotic scarf; a tub of butter; a pocket knife; a "smoking pipe made expressly for you"; a "Box of Pineapples"; and a "Jug of Shaker Maple Syrup." *

One of the many letters read: "Thousands and tens of thousands of Christian men and women are praying for you. . . . May God bless you and through you all of us." † The fact that so many of these letters were preserved, while few letters of hate were saved, was probably due to the fact that Lincoln cared for these letters of sincere but humble appreciation, or his secretaries knew he cared for them, while much of the crank or vicious mail was relegated to the presidential wastebasket. A humanly touching gift came from a soldier after the election of 1864, sending his re-enlistment stripes to the President who had re-enlisted for a second term.

There were different levels and dimensions to this principle that the people were with Lincoln. For instance, there came in to him a letter from a colored refugee freedman on the Island of St. Helena off the coast of South Carolina. His name was signed "don carlous Butler" to a letter written for him by a lady teacher of freedmen. Years before he had been a confidential servant in the aristocratic Alston family, and had waited on Theodosia Burr Alston. Now he asked Lincoln to tell him what to do about his little bit of land. Would it be taken from him, he wondered, and should he put up any buildings? He was fixing up his house and wanted the President to know he was lathing it and filling in with moss so it would be comfortable in winter. He said: "What ever *you* say I am willing to do, and I will attend to whatever you tell me." The lady who wrote the letter for this ex-slave added: "He, with others of the Freedmen, often expresses a wish to be able to speak to Massa Linkum feeling sure that *he* will listen to their plea for land & do

---

* For this array of gifts the references are too numerous to be supplied here. The main sources are the *Complete Works* and the R. T. Lincoln Collection. See also Dennett, ed., . . . *Diaries* . . . *of John Hay*, p. 43; Washington *Daily Chronicle*, Mar. 5, 1864, p. 2; Frank Friedel, *Francis Lieber: Nineteenth-Century Liberal*, p. 307.

† Joel Manning to Lincoln. Joliet, Ill., Feb. 4, 1861, R. T. Lincoln Collec., nos. 7105–7105.

what is best for them." Don Carlos was well on in years, just emerging from slavery into untried freedom. How should he plan and with whom should he advise? He instinctively felt that he could turn to "Massa Linkum." Lincoln would know. He would care. He could give the answer, if he could only talk with him. How many Presidents could have inspired that kind of untutored faith? Of all the orders that Lincoln could not possibly fill, these naïvely confident appeals of lowly people turning to the Man in the White House were among the most touching.*

Lincoln's understanding of the people and theirs of him was not easily definable nor readily traceable. It existed as something in the air; it traveled in the manner of the grapevine telegraph. It was a thing that you sensed though you could not always locate it. One factor was simply that Lincoln believed in the people and they in him. Part of it was his appearance. No other President had looked so much like a man of the people. He was approachable. A correspondent of Anna E. Dickinson wrote in October 1864: "Our best men often made mistakes, as you have seen in the case of Mr. Lincoln. . . . He is full of stories . . . , but they are always apt, and . . . adapted to illustrate the point in issue. I would rather see a man in the White House of his stamp than a distant and morose fellow, whom no one ever felt like approaching." †

On the day of his second inaugural there was written one of the most exquisite letters of them all. In a CBS broadcast in September 1947 this letter was used, with others of the humanly appealing sort; at the suggestion of Carl Sandburg the program opened with the sound of rippling bells. It did not start as a conventional congratulation — this letter from Mary A. Dodge of Hamilton, Massachusetts — though it was dated March 4, 1865. She wrote:

MR. LINCOLN
DEAR SIR
I only wish to thank you for being so good — and to say how sorry we all are that you must have four years more of this ter-

---

* Letter signed "don carlous Butler" to Lincoln, St. Helena Is., S. C., "Frogmoor" [Frogmore], May 29, 1864; dictated to and transmitted by Laura Towne, "Teacher of Freedmen on St. Helena Is." R. T. Lincoln Collec., nos. 33391–33393.
† Anna E. Dickinson MSS., Libr. of Cong., Oct. 2, 1864.

rible toil. But remember what a triumph it is for the right, what a blessing to the country — and then your rest shall be glorious when it does come!

You cant tell anything about it in Washington where they make a noise on the slightest provocation. But if you had been in this little speck of a village this morning and heard the soft, sweet music of unseen bells rippling through the morning silence from every quarter of the far off horizon, you would have better known what your name is to this nation.

May God help you in the future as he has helped you in the past . . .*

Lincoln thought of the continuing nation, not only of a country at war. He thought it ethically right that any appeal to bullets and slaughter should fail of its purpose. Evidence does not support the contention that he deliberately maneuvered the South into "firing the first shot" — in other words, that his conduct was intentionally provocative and productive of war. "If I had had my way," he said, "this war would never have been commenced." That was in his statement to the Quaker, Mrs. Gurney.† He made similar statements at other times. He did not hold to the theory, or notion, that war is "inevitable." Nor did he believe that eradication of slavery required war. This did not mean that he failed in his consciousness of the evil of slavery. It did mean that a man of his broad views could be intensely aware of the need to abolish a great social abuse, and yet could also realize that, in such abolition, war is not the civilized answer.

While the war was on he tried to mitigate its severity, to avoid brutal retaliation (as in the Fort Pillow affair), to keep military measures within bounds, and at all times to remember that the military power is subordinate to the civil.‡ As President, he was Commander in Chief of the Army and Navy. This did not mean that he commanded in the field or gave orders from a flagship. It meant what George Mason meant in that great document, the Virginia

* R. T. Lincoln Collec., nos. 41055–41056.

† Lincoln's reply, interview with Mrs. Gurney, Complete Works, VIII, 50–51. The interview occurred on October 27, 1862, but is incorrectly dated September [28?] by Nicolay and Hay.

‡ On retaliation, and on civil and military power, see Randall, Constitutional Problems Under Lincoln, revised ed. (1951), xvi–xx.

Declaration of Rights of 1776 — "the military should be under strict subordination to . . . the civil power." This was another way of saying that military revolutions should not take the place of elections, that a *coup d'état* of a man on horseback is not the American way, and that political control should not be seized by generals with armies at their backs. At various times the Civil War President made it clear that political functions were not to be taken over by generals.

Lincoln had deep thoughts of human governance. His writings and speeches belong to the fundamental literature of political and social philosophy. He was, by genuine definition of the term, a liberal. He wanted liberal causes to succeed. His basic views of government and society, as he himself testified, were those of Thomas Jefferson.* He believed in tolerance. He was the opposite of the fanatic and the fire-eater. His opposition to the nativist or antiforeign movements of his day (in which he stood apart from many fellow Whigs) was an unbroken part of his record. His feeling for the Negro, his solid contribution to the elevation of the colored race, was and remains a factor indelibly connected with his very name. His revulsion toward war was another unmistakable token of his enlightened liberalism. His friendliness to labor, taking into view the harmony among workingmen of this and other nations, was frequently and vigorously expressed.

Part of his broad appeal to the people arose from the fact that laboring men looked upon him as one of them. Harriet Beecher Stowe expressed this idea in February 1864. She argued that the struggle in America was "a war for a principle which concerns all mankind." It was, she wrote, "THE war for the rights of the working classes of mankind, as against the usurpation of the privileged aristocracies." Then she added: "Abraham Lincoln is in the strictest sense *a man of the working classes.*" Pointing out that Lincoln grew up as a laborer himself, she declared, with religious emphasis, that Al-

* Lincoln said at Peoria, Oct. 16, 1854: "Mr. Jefferson . . . is, and perhaps will continue to be, the most distinguished politician of our history. . . ." Basler, p. 284. See also Dumas Malone, "Jefferson and Lincoln," *Abr. Lincoln Quar.*, V, 327–347 (June 1949). In this context Lincoln used the word "politician" to designate a man concerned with "politics" in the original (Greek) sense — *i.e.*, with affairs of state. See also Randall, *Lincoln the President*, I, 23–25.

mighty God chose Lincoln "with a visible reference to the rights and interests of the great majority of mankind, for which he stands." *

Lowell called Lincoln the "first American," but in the measure of his Americanism there is more to be said. He was the primal American — the rugged type — but also the nature-minded American. He was one with his time, but he was also ahead of his generation. We do not usually think of him as part of the Victorian Age. Still less does his "unparlorable" figure (as Gamaliel Bradford called it) harmonize with that of his foreign contemporaries. Indeed it comes with a startling sense of contrast to recall that Lincoln was part of an age that included an oriental tycoon, a Hohenzollern, a militaristic Bismarck, a flamboyant Napoleon III, and a phantom-crowned Maximilian. It included also that Siamese potentate whose fearsome story appears in *Anna and the King of Siam*.

Lincoln's Americanism was too basic to be self-advertised. His patriotism was tempered with humility. To him the thought of America's tremendous advantages produced not boasting, but soul searching. Lincoln was more concerned with public conscience than with publicized ballyhoo. He prized eternal vigilance more than eternal *clichés* of nationalism. He was never the superficial patrioteer. His patriotism was never jingoistic or antiforeign.

Lincoln was no dictator. In his administration the Constitution was stretched but not subverted. There were arbitrary arrests but their purpose was preventive rather than punitive. Even Vallandigham, after a short period of banishment, was allowed to go free. Strictly political arrests were few, and extended political imprisonments still fewer. Elections continued in wartime. There was no all-pervading secret police as in totalitarian dictatorships. The people were free to vote Lincoln down in 1864, if that was their wish. Subversive activity was dealt with, but not by any irresponsible witch hunt. Conditions were legally abnormal, but the Lincoln administration, in its difficult dilemma between two opposite tendencies, did not forget the American principle that government, while strong, must also be democratically just.

There was no contradiction in Lincoln's combination of liberalism with realism. It was as a liberal that he was tough-minded; for

* *Littell's Living Age*, vol. 80, 282–284 (Feb. 6, 1864).

it is our liberals who have had the insight and vision to see reality, while the misreading and wrong calculation of events and trends has been a well-known failing of reactionaries who have worn the false label of "realists."

If there was one principle above others that Lincoln deemed fundamental and eternally vital, it was the importance of maintaining democracy at home and extending it by example and friendly cooperation abroad. That theme — the significance of the American experiment as a force to promote world democracy — comes to us today with greater intensity, though also with more bitter disappointment, than ever before. It comes in the midst of fearful world crisis and at a time of confusion and disunity. Yet this theme was the *motif* of the Gettysburg Address and it reappears in other distinguished utterances of Lincoln. With its corollaries and applications, that principle may be taken to explain Lincoln's philosophy. He did not think of American influence for democracy in the world as easy, nor as a foregone conclusion. It was a continuing challenge, and in his response to that challenge we have the measure of Lincoln's personality and statesmanship.

III
Forces in America to the First World War

Tom Watson and the Negro

by

C. VANN WOODWARD

["Tom Watson and the Negro in Agrarian Politics," from *Journal of Southern History*, IV (February 1938), 14–33. Reprinted by permission.]

In the 1930's the manifest attractiveness of the forensic displays of Hitler and Mussolini to the German and Italian masses, plus the fact that the European dictators were finding American imitators, brought historians to a growing awareness of the role of demagoguery in American history. A number of studies of individual demagogues were made, and in 1951 Reinhard H. Luthin attempted a "historical summing-up of some of America's more influential mob-masters," one that attempted to "clarify the meaning of demagoguery and its significance in United States history."

Dr. Luthin reveals the demagogue as exploiting the gullibility of the masses in an era of increasing democratization of the franchise. Without attempting much in the way of a psychological analysis of the demagogue's appeal, Luthin sees the typical "mob-master" as long on gasconade and bluster, and short of public service and constructive thinking. Issues of national importance are ignored or lost in a bedlam of sound and fury. The 'gentleman' is eliminated from politics. . . . Ethics and morality count for little, and causes are but means to an end, to be dropped or reversed when they lose their vote-catching value. But, conversely, the demagogue owes his rise and continued presence to the people he courts, who delight in his entertaining showmanship, his noisy, rabble-rousing techniques, and his fiery tirades in which emotion substitutes for thought."

"American demagogues," Luthin's analysis continues, "have been confined neither to a single party nor to a particular social viewpoint nor to one section of the country." We have had demagogues

who were anti-Federalist, anti-Mason, Jacksonian Democrats, anti-Jackson Whigs, antislavery Republicans, proslavery Democrats, Tammany Democrats, Anglophobe Republicans, "bloody shirt" Republicans, and Southern Populist-Democrats.[1]

While it would be a mistake to regard demagoguery as a uniquely Southern institution, it is true that the South, since the Reconstruction Period in its history, has provided a fertile field for demagoguery. This is caused in part by the fact that the tradition of aristocratic government has been strong in the South, and that the aristocracy was unmindful of Jefferson's advice to develop an education system that would prepare for public responsibilities that "natural aristocracy" which, he said, existed among the masses. Consequently, when the governing class went down to defeat in the Civil War, the tensions engendered by Reconstruction made a relatively uneducated population prey to demogogic appeals.

In the following selection, C. Vann Woodward, Professor of History at Johns Hopkins University, deals with the demagogue's exploitation of the racial issue. He also touches upon the interesting problem of the relationship of liberal and radical movements to racial and religious intolerance. Traditionally, minorities have been held to be rather safe with the left of center and correspondingly unsafe with the politically right of center. However, Oscar Handlin believes that American anti-Semitism has grass-roots sources in the free-silver and Populist agitation of the 1890's; in the stereotyped view, presented by demagogues of the left, of a Jewish "moneyed interest." It is also true that in 1940, under the auspices of the America First movement, anti-Semitism was exploited demagogically by many former Progressives including Senators Wheeler and Nye.[2]

"CONSIDER the advantage of position that Bryan had over me," once wrote Thomas E. Watson, with the vehemence that characterized his later utterances. "His field of work was the plastic, restless, and growing West: mine was the hide-bound, rock-ribbed

Bourbon South. Besides, *Bryan had no everlasting and overshad-owing Negro Question to hamper and handicap his progress: I HAD.*" * There is no doubt that Watson thought of the Negro prob-lem as the nemesis of his career. He wrestled with it mightily all his days. At the outset he came to grips with it boldly and courageously, and in the end he took refuge in every retreat and subterfuge known to Southern politicians.

Born of a slaveholding family of planters in the upper part of the Georgia black belt in 1856, Watson spent an impoverished child-hood growing up among the most violent scenes of Reconstruction in the state. The Negroes were in the majority in his county and the adjoining ones, and the Ku Klux Klan did its work in that sec-tion with remarkable thoroughness.†

The class that seized power in Georgia after the overthrow of the Reconstruction regime was neither the old planter oligarchy nor the small farmer. It was the rising class of industrial capitalists, aggres-sively led by the so-called "Bourbon Triumvirate": the millionaire industrialist, Joseph E. Brown, extensively interested in coal, iron, and railroads; General John B. Gordon, promoter of an astonishing multiplicity of railroad, mining, publishing, insurance, and land schemes; and Alfred H. Colquitt, a representative of the large planter class who was heavily interested in railroads and a partici-pant in several of Gordon's schemes. These three men bandied the highest offices of the state back and forth among themselves from 1872 to 1890. Strict submission was demanded from all classes in the name of "White Supremacy."

In 1880 the small farmer democracy of the rural counties revolted from the "ring-rule" of the industrial capitalists. A major cause of resentment was the sudden resignation from the Senate of Gordon, Colquitt's appointment of Brown to the vacant seat, and Colquitt's candidacy to succeed himself as governor. At the Democratic con-vention before which Colquitt sought renomination, Tom Watson, then a redheaded youth of twenty-three, made his political debut in

---

* *Jeffersonian*, January 20, 1910. This weekly paper underwent several changes in title and place of publication. For a while it was called *Watson's Weekly Jef-fersonian;* then *"Watson's"* and later *"Weekly"* were dropped from the title. It was published at Atlanta, Thomson, and Augusta.

† C. Mildred Thompson, *Reconstruction in Georgia, Economic, Social, Politi-cal, 1865–1872* (New York, 1915), p. 366.

UNDERSTANDING THE AMERICAN PAST

the role he played for the next thirty years. In a stirring speech he called for a revolt from the rule of the industrial clique even if it meant splitting the white man's party.* The ensuing contest was said to have been "such a tornado of violence as to make all previous disturbances mere child's play." † In its effort to employ the Negro vote, the party of white supremacy revived the corrupt methods of the Carpetbaggers as well as its own development, the Ku Klux Klan. "Those of us who were in the thick of that fight," recalled Watson, "will never forget the wild enthusiasm, the whoop and hurrah, with which the Negro, roused from his sleep of more than twelve years, rushed back into political activity." ‡ Although the agrarian insurgents seem to have polled a majority of the white vote, they were overwhelmed by the Negro vote brought out by their opponents.§ From this first experiment in revolt the discontented whites learned that any serious opposition against the businessman's domination would be met by the same methods that were used to overthrow the Reconstruction regime, plus some of the methods of the Carpetbaggers themselves.

The career of agrarian rebellion that Watson opened brilliantly in 1880 was virtually closed to him throughout the next decade. The businessman and the industrial capitalist were in the saddle, and behind these leaders Georgia plunged forward into the adventure of industrial revolution with a rush of eager enthusiasm that swept aside all restraints. The farmer's troubles were forgotten and his leaders were ignored. Many of the farmers, indeed, were persuaded by the eloquence of Henry W. Grady, the most articulate spokesman of the industrialists, to support the businessman's regime. Grady believed that the self-made businessman had "sunk the cornerstone of the only aristocracy that Americans should know";‖ yet he always had a sympathetic word for the farmer. Toward the end of the eighties the farmers, ripe for renewed revolt, began to join

---

* Atlanta *Daily Constitution,* August 7, 1880.
† Isaac W. Avery, *History of Georgia, 1850–1881* (New York, 1881), p. 555.
‡ Quoted by William H. Skaggs, *The Southern Oligarchy* (New York, 1924), p. 141.
§ Rebecca L. Felton, *Memoirs of Georgia Politics* (Atlanta, 1911), pp. 273–274; Avery, *History of Georgia,* p. 591; Atlanta *Daily Constitution,* September 29, October 9, 1880.
‖ Atlanta *Daily Constitution,* August 15, 1880.

the National Farmers' Alliance by the thousands. Grady bent every effort to mollify their discontent and pledge their loyalty to the industrialist regime. Addressing a great convention of the Alliance in Atlanta in 1889, he told the farmers, "There is no room for divided hearts in the South." Because of the threat of Negro domination all white men were morally obliged to vote together "without regard to class." * Grady's program meant strict subordination of class conflict in the South in the interest of the *status quo* of a businessman's regime identified in the popular mind with White Supremacy. There were those, he admitted, who believed that "the South should divide, the color line be beaten down, and the Southern States ranged on economic or moral questions as interest or belief demands." This, he asserted, was "the worst in my opinion that could happen." The only "hope and assurance of the South" was "the clear and unmistakable domination of the white race." "What God hath separated let no man join together. . . . Let not man tinker with the work of the Almighty." †

Impressed by such solemn admonitions, the farmer, for the time being, agreed to subordinate his interests to the demands of racial solidarity. Grady's death in December 1889, however, marked the passing of an era. The following year there occurred a party revolution that filled the offices with men pledged to the Farmers' Alliance platform. The heir to Grady's editorial chair took comfort in the reflection that, "After all, business is the biggest thing in this country. When the princes of commerce and industry say to the politicians that they must let dangerous experiments alone they will be heard and obeyed." Furthermore, "There are some things more important than reforms that merely affect the pocket" — namely, White Supremacy.‡ The farmer, on the other hand, soon began to despair of gaining his reforms through the old party and to show signs of leaving it to found a party of his own.

Tom Watson, the most outspoken champion of the Alliance platform in the state, was overwhelmingly elected to Congress from the tenth district in 1890. Chosen as a nominee of the Democratic Party,

---

* *Ibid.*, October 25, 1889.
† Joel Chandler Harris (ed.), *Henry W. Grady: His Life, Writings and Speeches* (New York, 1890), pp. 99–101.
‡ Atlanta *Constitution*, January 8, 13, 1890.

he nevertheless felt that his first obligation was to Alliance principles. He therefore refused to enter the Democratic congressional
caucus and pledge himself to support a candidate for the speaker-
ship who was known to be an enemy of those principles. After can-
vassing his district he openly broke with the old party and threw in
his lot with the Alliance-elected Western Congressmen to organize
the People's Party. As its official leader in the House, and its first
member from the South in Congress, Watson was the logical man to
formulate the Populist policy toward the Negro. The Farmers' Alliance had already laid the groundwork for the agrarian experiment in interracial co-operation by organizing a million and a
quarter Negroes in the Colored Farmers' Alliance.* On this foundation Watson sought to construct a political alliance between the
races in the South.

According to Watson's plan, the third party was to recruit its
ranks from the farmers of all classes and both races and from the
working class of both races in the cities. He framed his appeal in
this way: "Now the People's Party says to these two men, "You are
kept apart that you may be separately fleeced of your earnings. You
are made to hate each other because upon that hatred is rested the
keystone of the arch of financial despotism which enslaves you both.
You are deceived and blinded that you may not see how this race
antagonism perpetuates a monetary system which beggars both.'" †

Watson believed that interracial co-operation for economic and
political reform was impossible in either of the old parties. "The
Republican Party represented everything which was hateful to the
whites," he declared; "The Democratic Party, everything which was
hateful to the blacks." A new party was therefore an absolute necessity. This appeal for united action was framed in terms of economic
realism rather than in the language of idealism. "Gratitude may
fail; so may sympathy and friendship and generosity and patriotism;
but in the long run, self-interest *always* controls. Let it once appear
plainly that it is to the interest of a colored man to vote with the
white man, and he will do it." The same rule applied to the white
man's attitude toward the black. "The People's Party will settle the

* John D. Hicks, *The Populist Revolt* (Minneapolis, 1931), pp. 114–115.
† Thomas E. Watson, "The Negro Question in the South," in *Arena* (Boston,
1889–1909), VI (1892), 548.

race question," he announced. "First, by enacting the Australian ballot system. Second, by offering to white and black a rallying point which is free from the odium of former discords and strifes. Third, by presenting a platform immensely beneficial to both races and injurious to neither. Fourth, by making it to the *interest* of both races to act together for the success of the platform." *

This bold program called for a reversal of many of the articles of Grady's racial creed, as well as the altering of race prejudices and traditions deeply ingrained in Southerners. In place of race hatred, political proscription, lynch law, and terrorism, it was necessary to foster tolerance, friendly co-operation, justice, and political rights for the Negro.

Georgia's lynching record in those years stood highest among the states. It should be the object of the Populist Party, said Watson, to "make lynch law odious to the people." † The state platform of the People's Party in 1896 carried a plank denouncing lynch law, Ku Kluxism, and terrorism, and demanding justice for the Negro. Another plank called for the abolition of the iniquitous convict lease system, which fell heaviest upon the blacks.‡ Negroes became prominent as organizers of the new party and several found high office in the party organization. At the state convention of the party in 1894 Watson seconded the nomination of a Negro "as a man worthy to be on the executive committee of this or any other party from the State at large." "Tell me the use of educating these people as citizens," he demanded, "if they are never to exercise the rights of citizens. [*Applause.*] Tell me the sense of saying to them, 'You have rights only so long as you live under the benign guardianship of the Democratic party.' [*Laughter and Applause.*]" § In the same spirit of racial amity Watson frequently mentioned praiseworthy accomplishments of the Negro race at home and abroad. There was the "manly" conduct of the king of a South African tribe who courageously resisted the encroachments of Cecil Rhodes and British imperialists. Again there was the "good work" of a Negro member of the legislature who was exposing the brutalities practiced

* *Ibid.*, p. 544–547.
† Atlanta *People's Party Paper*, November 3, 1893.
‡ Atlanta *Constitution*, August 7, 1896.
§ Atlanta *People's Party Paper*, May 25, 1894.

upon the convicts leased to Senator Joseph E. Brown's coal mines.*

In 1890 the Conservative party in the Lower South began the process of constitutional amendment with the avowed purpose of disfranchising the Negro — thus driving another wedge between the races in the lower classes of society. Discontented whites protested that the amendments might be turned with equal success to the work of disfranchising poor and illiterate members of their own race, and they offered convincing evidence that this was being done.† In 1895 Ben Tillman led the movement for a disfranchising amendment in South Carolina. Tom Watson wrote an indignant denunciation of the proposal:

All this re-actionary legislation is wrong.

There can be no sound principle, consistent with our democratic theory of government, which says that a negro worth $300 is a better citizen than one worth $200.

Nor is there any satisfactory reasoning to support the claim that a negro who can read is better fitted to vote than some who cannot read.

The whole scheme of the democrats of South Carolina is to perpetuate the rule of their party. . . .

Old fashioned democracy taught that a man who fought the battles of his country, and paid the taxes of his government, should have a vote in the choosing of rulers and the making of laws.‡

No one was more keenly aware of the overwhelming odds against the racial aspect of his social program than Tom Watson himself. On the very outset of the Populist movement he wrote despairingly in an article in the *Arena*:

You might beseech a Southern white tenant to listen to you upon questions of finance, taxation, and transportation; you might demonstrate with mathematical precision that herein lay his way out of poverty into comfort; you might have him "almost persuaded" to the truth, but if the merchant who furnished his farm supplies (at tremendous usury) or the town

* *Ibid.*, December 2, 1892; December 29, 1893.
† Joseph C. Manning, *The Fadeout of Populism* (New York, 1928), p. 59; Skaggs, *The Southern Oligarchy*, pp. 142–145.
‡ Atlanta *People's Party Paper*, November 8, 1895.

politician (who never spoke to him excepting at election times) came along and cried "Negro rule!" the entire fabric of reason and common sense which you had patiently constructed would fall, and the poor tenant would joyously hug the chains of an actual wretchedness rather than do any experimenting on a question of mere sentiment. . . . The Negro has been as valuable a portion of the stock in trade of a Democrat as he was of a Republican.*

Again and again Watson was called upon to meet the Democrats' charge that he was advocating "social equality," encouraging "Negro domination," and promoting disloyalty to White Supremacy. He ridiculed these charges as the stale tricks of demagogues and denied their implications. "The question of social equality does not enter into the calculation at all," he declared. "This is a thing each citizen decides for himself." He repeatedly told blacks and whites that he did not advocate social mixing of the races, that he thought it better for both to stay apart. "But when it comes to matters of law and justice," he emphasized, "I despise the Anglo-Saxon who is such an infernal coward as to deny legal rights to any man on account of his color for fear of 'negro domination.' 'Dominate' what? 'Dominate' how? 'Dominate' whom?" It was from his "very pride of race" that there sprang his "intense scorn of that phantasm manufactured by the political bosses and called 'negro domination.'" "Away with such contemptible timidity counsel," he cried. Nor could he see what threat to white supremacy lay in teaching the Negro tenant that he was "in the same boat as the white tenant; the colored laborer with the white laborer." "Why cannot the cause of one be made the cause of both?" he asked. "Why would this be dangerous? I can see very well where it is dangerous to Ring Rule, to Bossism, the iron rule of the Money Power." †

The Negroes responded to Watson's message with great enthusiasm. They thronged to his rallies by the thousands and stood side by side with white farmers listening to him speak from the same platform with speakers of their own race. A favorite device of Watson was to pledge the white listeners to defend the Negroes' constitu-

* Watson, "The Negro Question in the South," loc. cit., p. 541.

† Thomas E. Watson, The Life and Speeches of Thomas E. Watson (2nd ed., Thomson, Ga., 1911), pp. 128–129; id., "Address to My Fellow Citizens of Georgia," in Atlanta People's Party Paper, March 17, 1892.

UNDERSTANDING THE AMERICAN PAST

tional rights, making them hold up their hands and promise. Never before or since have the two races in the South come so close together politically. The Negroes, it should be emphasized, continued their support of Populism in the face of as much or more intimidation and violence than they encountered from the Democrats during Reconstruction. Negro speakers who campaigned for Watson or other Populist candidates did so at the risk of their lives.

"Political campaigns in the North," wrote a veteran of Alabama Populism, "even at their highest pitch of contention and strife, were as placid as pink teas in comparison with those years of political combat in the South." * The pattern of violence, always characteristic of the South, took its shape mainly from the intensification of economic strife by the complexity of race.

One of the most effective workers for Watson's cause was H. S. Doyle, a young Negro preacher of intelligence and courage. In the face of repeated threats upon his life, Doyle made sixty-three speeches in behalf of Watson's candidacy for Congress during the campaign of 1892. Toward the close of that campaign he was threatened with lynching at Thomson and fled to Watson for protection. Watson installed him on his private grounds and sent out riders on horseback for assistance. All night armed farmers poured into Thomson. The next morning the streets were "lined with buggies and horses foaming and tired with travel." All that day and the next night farmers continued to assemble until "fully two thousand" Populists crowded the village — arms stacked on Watson's veranda. Prominent among them was the Populist sheriff of McDuffie County. They marched to the courthouse under arms, where they were addressed by Doyle and Watson. "We are determined," said the latter, "in this free country that the humblest white or black man that wants to talk our doctrine shall do it, and the man doesn't live who shall touch a hair of his head, without fighting every man in the People's Party." The farmers remained on guard for two nights.†

* Manning, *Fadeout of Populism*, pp. 5, 142–144.
† *Contested Election Case of Thomas E. Watson vs. J. C. C. Black from the Tenth Congressional District of Georgia* (Washington, 1897), pp. 669, 683, 717, 793–794; Atlanta *Constitution*, October 25, 26, 1892; Augusta *Chronicle*, October 26, 1892.

The spectacle of white farmers riding all night to save a Negro from lynchers was rare in Georgia. So shocking was the incident to the Democratic press that one paper was sure that "Watson has gone mad," and another declared that "the whole South, and especially the tenth district [of Georgia], is threatened with anarchy and communism" because of the "direful teachings of Thomas E. Watson." * While Doyle was speaking at Louisville, Georgia, a week later, a shot intended for him struck a white man in the back and killed him. Two days later when Watson and Doyle spoke at Davisboro they were accompanied by a guard of forty men carrying Winchester rifles. In the county where the previous murder occurred a Negro was killed the following week by white Democrats. At Dalton a Negro man who had spoken for the Populists was called out of his home and murdered by unknown men, and at Rukersville five Negro Populists were shot down at the polls by men to whom they were said to have belonged in slavery days. The verdict of "justifiable homicide" in such cases was rarely contested, and then futilely. One estimate had it that fifteen Negro Populists were killed in Georgia during the state election in 1892.†

"After that," testified Doyle in regard to the Thomson incident, "Mr. Watson was held almost as a savior by the Negroes. The poor ignorant men and women, who so long had been oppressed, were anxious even to touch Mr. Watson's hand, and were often a source of inconvenience to him in their anxiety to see him and shake hands with him, and even to touch him." ‡

The sincerity of Watson's appeal to the Negro has been called into question — as has the sincerity of any appeal to the Negro vote. Whatever his motives, nothing that Watson did in this period reflects upon his fidelity. It is interesting to note in passing that W. E. B. Du Bois, a Negro leader not given to uncritical enthusiasm for Southern politicians, was sufficiently convinced of the sincerity of

* Augusta *Chronicle*, October 25, November 6, 1892; Atlanta *Constitution*, October 28, 1892.

† Harlem (Georgia) *Farmer's Light*, October 20, 1892; Atlanta *People's Party Paper*, October 14, 28, 1892; *Contested Election Case of Thomas E. Watson* vs. *J. C. C. Black*, p. 781; Augusta *Chronicle*, November 4, 8, 10, 1892.

‡ *Contested Election Case of Thomas E. Watson* vs. *J. C. C. Black*, p. 782.

Watson to regard the failure of his movement as a calamity for the Negro race.*

The question of what substantial benefit the Negroes derived, or might have reasonably expected to derive, from their loyal and hazardous support of Tom Watson presents some difficulties. In the first place, although Watson waged his fight for Populism with astounding courage and perseverance, and although a majority of the voters seem to have been with him, Populism never achieved power in Georgia, and its program was therefore never put to test. Moreover, in his battle against industrial capitalism Watson sought to align within his ranks all agrarian forces, whether landowners, tenants, or laborers. The Populist ideology was that of the landowner, and at that time the landowning farmers about equaled the landless farmers. On the other hand, the great majority of Negro farmers owned no land. That class contradictions were not magically resolved in the Populist-agrarian potpourri is indicated by various signs. Once the Colored Farmers' Alliance proposed to call a general strike of Negro cotton pickers. Colonel L. L. Polk, president of the National Farmers' Alliance (white), did "not hesitate to advise our farmers to leave their cotton in the fields rather than pay more than 50 cents per hundred to have it picked." The Negroes were attempting "to better their condition at the expense of their white brethren. Reforms should not be in the interest of one portion of our farmers at the expense of another." †

It was fairly plain that what material benefit the landless Negro might expect from Populism must perforce accrue to him from the general improvement to which agrarian interests might aspire through the Populist program of checking the greed of industrial capitalism by government ownership and monetary legislation. The benefits, however substantial, would come indirectly.

More immediate, however, were the political and social profits that the Negro derived from his Populist experience. Tom Watson was perhaps the first native white Southern leader of importance to

* W. E. B. Du Bois, "Georgia: Invisible Empire State," in Ernest Gruening (ed.), *These United States* (2nd Ser., New York, 1926), pp. 339–340.
† Editorial in Raleigh *Progressive Farmer*, September 15, 1891. See, also, Washington *National Economist*, September 26, 1891.

treat the Negro's aspirations with the seriousness that human strivings merit. For the first time in his political history, the Negro was regarded neither as the incompetent ward of white supremacy, nor as the ward of military intervention, but as an integral part of Southern society with a place in its economy. Grady's assertion in 1889 that "the Negro as a political force has dropped out of serious consideration" was absurd in 1892. Moreover, it was now possible for the Negro to escape the dilemma of selling his vote to the Democrats or pledging it blindly to the Republican bosses. Under the tutelage of Watson and the Populists, also, a part of the Southern white people were learning to regard the Negro as a political ally bound to them by economic ties and a common destiny, rather than as a slender prop to injured self-esteem in the shape of White Supremacy. Here was a foundation of political realism upon which some more enduring structure of economic democracy might have been constructed. The destruction of that foundation constitutes a tragic chapter in Southern history.

The story of how Tom Watson abandoned his dream of uniting the Southern masses of both races against industrial capitalism, and came to be regarded as the leading exponent of racial bigotry, and of how the Southern white masses followed the same course, is a part of the story of how Southern Populism went to seed. It is a small part of the larger story, but a significant part.

"Politically I was ruined," wrote Watson of his predicament after the debacle of Populism in 1896. "Financially I was flat on my back. How near I came to loss of mind only God who made me knows — but I was as near distraction, perhaps, as any mortal could safely be. If ever a poor devil had been outlawed and vilified and persecuted and misrepresented and howled down and mobbed and hooted and threatened until he was well nigh mad, I was he." [*] Time after time since the election of 1892 he had been defeated by the old Reconstruction practices of terror, fraud, chicanery, and intimidation. A part — but only a part — of the methods used to defraud

---

[*] Editorial in *Watson's Jeffersonian Magazine* (Atlanta, Thomson, 1907–1917), X (1910), 818. *"Jeffersonian"* was deleted from the title of this magazine in March 1912.

the Populists had been the corruption of the Negro vote, especially in the cities.

Embittered by frustration and by what he considered a betrayal within his own ranks in 1896, Watson retired from public life for a period of eight years. His silence reflected the discouragement of the Populist masses. Twice during this period Watson emerged to denounce the Spanish–American War and to speak for a child-labor amendment, but otherwise he confined his activity to historical writing and law practice. Aroused by the triumph of the reactionary element of the Democratic Party that resulted in the nomination of Alton B. Parker, Watson accepted the Populist nomination for President in 1904. His nation-wide campaign reawakened Populist hopes and provided the only diverting element in a dull election, but he was bitterly disappointed in the small vote he received in the South. His next move was to found *Tom Watson's Magazine* in New York and plunge into the muckraking and reform movement with the hope of mobilizing reformers and progressives for Populism.

More and more Watson was coming to regard the Negro as the perennial stumbling block in his path. In 1892 he declared that "The argument against the independent political movement in the South may be boiled down into one word — NIGGER." * He scoffed at the argument then. Now in the reform movement he met the same argument. To the plea for government ownership John Sharp Williams and other conservatives replied, as Watson interpreted them: "The North, the East, and the West may adopt Government Ownership of railways, but the South never will — because of the negro." With any other reform, industrial or political, the reply was the same, according to Watson. "No matter what direction Progress would like to take in the South she is held back by the never-failing cry of 'Nigger!'

"It sickens me to the very soul to witness the unscrupulous skill, on the one hand, and childlike ignorance and prejudice, on the other, which make the negro question the invincible weapon of Bourbon Democracy in the South." †

---

* Atlanta *People's Party Paper*, August 26, 1892.
† Editorial in *Tom Watson's Magazine* (New York, 1905–1906), II (1905), 19.

About this time Watson shifted his position on the Negro and put forth his second answer to the political-racial dilemma that Grady propounded in the 1880's. He might be said to have "backed into" the reactionary position, for while still clinging to his older views, he embraced the very doctrine he professed most to despise.

In his campaign for the Presidency in 1904 Watson had been met from one end of the South to the other by a revival of the Democratic dialectic of the 1890's: "the ominous shadow of Negro domination." Elsewhere he ridiculed the cry, but in Georgia he met it with a challenge and a promise to his Democratic enemies. He was "not at all afraid of any negro domination," and never had been. Furthermore, he believed that "the cry that we are in danger from 'the nigger' is the most hypocritical that unscrupulous leadership could invent." What could the Negro do? He had been disfranchised in nearly every state in the South except Georgia. There he had been "white-primaried." If the Democrats were honest in their fears, why did they not write the principle of the white primary into the state constitution, as other states had done? He would tell them: "In Georgia they do not dare to disfranchise him [the Negro] because the men who control the Democratic machine in Georgia know that a majority of the whites are against them. They need the negro to beat us with." The white primary, being nothing but a party rule, could be shelved at any time the machine needed to vote the Negro. He therefore pledged his support, and the support of the Populists, to any antimachine Democratic candidate running upon a suitable platform that included a pledge to "a change in our Constitution which will perpetuate white supremacy in Georgia." *

Watson's offer did not long go begging. Early the following year a serious rift opened in the Democratic Party between the conservative machine, led by Clark Howell, and the opposing wing, led by Hoke Smith. Both men sought Watson's assistance in their race for governor in 1906.† Smith outbid his opponent, however, by writing what Herbert Quick pronounced "the most radical platform ever

* Speeches of the 1904 campaign, Watson MSS., University of North Carolina Library, Chapel Hill; Atlanta *Constitution*, September 2, 1904.
† Clark Howell to Watson, August 4, 1905; Hoke Smith to Watson, September 16, 1905, Watson MSS.

adopted, with perhaps one exception, by a state convention of either of the two great parties of these times." * Containing demands for several reforms aimed at direct popular government together with demands for stringent control and regulation of railroads and corporations, Smith's platform might have been written by a Populist. In curious juxtaposition with these reforms, the following pledge appeared permanently in Smith's paper: THE ELIMINATION OF THE NEGRO FROM POLITICS . . . BY LEGAL AND CONSTITUTIONAL METHODS . . . WITHOUT DISFRANCHISING A SINGLE WHITE MAN.

With some difficulty Watson was finally persuaded to join hands with his former enemy. "Hoke Smith is trying to do what we want done and cannot do ourselves," he announced to the Populists. With his assistance Smith defeated Howell in the most bitterly fought race since the 1890's. Race hatred was keyed to an unprecedented pitch, and lynching flourished. An unforeseen sequel to the campaign was the Atlanta race riot of 1906, the most hideous the state ever experienced. However remote Watson's connection with it, that tragedy was a milepost in the road he now traveled, and others not unlike it lay before him.

In rationalizing his desertion of his Negro allies Watson had argued that only by such a sacrifice could Populism triumph in the South. "The white people dare not revolt so long as they can be intimidated by the fear of the negro vote," he explained. Once the "bugaboo of negro domination" was removed, however, "every white man would act according to his own conscience and judgment in deciding how he should vote." † There was another consideration that he did not mention. With the Negro vote eliminated, Watson and the white Populists stood in much the same relation toward the two factions of the Democratic Party as the Negro had previously occupied toward Populists and Democrats: they held the balance of power.

Somehow the white Populist revolt, for which Negro disfranchisement was to prepare the way, never did occur. True, Watson made

---

* Herbert Quick, "Hoke Smith and the Revolution in Georgia," in The Reader (New York, 1902–1908), X (1907), 241.

† Atlanta Journal, July 27, 1906.

some pretense of running for President in 1908, but the main exception he took to the candidacy by Bryan was the liberal Democratic attitude toward the Negro. He stressed the Japanese problem of the West Coast as the chief bond of union between his old agrarian allies of the West and his own section — which had its Negro problem. Western Populists could not understand his position on the Negro and fell away from him, as did also his progressive friends (for example, Upton Sinclair) in the East. He changed the name of his magazine, which was becoming narrowly sectional in interest, to *Watson's Jeffersonian Magazine* and moved its headquarters from New York to Hickory Hill, his home.

Likewise on the local front the Populist revolt failed to materialize. Although Smith accomplished wonders in fulfilling his reform pledges, frequently consulting the wishes of his Populist ally, Watson became convinced that Smith was attempting to undermine his power by destroying the "county-unit system," which gave rural counties an advantage out of proportion to their population. *"The evil of pure democracy,"* proclaimed Watson, recalling Calhoun, *"is that the minority have no protection from the majority."* * In 1908 he shifted his support to Joseph M. Brown, son of his old enemy Joseph E. Brown, and defeated Smith. That Brown, besides being a defender of the county-unit system, was also an outspoken champion of railroads and corporate interests, as well as a bitter critic of organized labor and reformers, did not seem to trouble Watson. Instead, he took pleasure in reflecting that "we hold the balance of power in the country counties and the country counties rule the state." † Thenceforth he succeeded in establishing himself as a virtual boss of state politics by shifting this balance of power from one faction of the Democrats to the other.

The next stage in the development of Watson's policy toward the Negro followed from his conclusion that he had been wrong in supporting Smith's disfranchisement program. The opponents of the measure had been correct, he decided, in holding that it would eliminate illiterate whites and encourage literate Negroes. The idea developed into an issue in one of his campaigns against Smith and took on exaggerated proportions in his mind: "it gives the negro

* *Jeffersonian,* April 2, May 3, 1908.
† *Ibid.,* November 12, 1908.

the balance of power," he maintained. "It brings back the danger of negro domination. It imperils white supremacy. . . . It is a stimulant to them to learn to read and write." Therefore all such half-measures were inadequate and more drastic action was demanded in face of the menace. "The hour has struck for the South to say that the Fifteenth Amendment is not law, and will no longer be respected." The Republican Party was split against itself and the South and West "find that their interests coincide on the race question." "This is a white man's civilization, and the white man must maintain it." *

At this point in the development of his ideology Watson had arrived somewhere near the position that Mr. Justice Taney announced in 1857: that the Negro had "no rights or privileges but such as those who held the power and the government might choose to grant them." This was as reactionary a policy as any serious leader of the South dared advance in Watson's period. Yet he was destined to carry his position even further toward reactionism.

At the seat of Watson's confusion was the fact that he was still thinking in the capitalist-agrarian conflict pattern of the 1890's in an era where that dichotomy no longer applied. He still thought of the farmers as solidly aligned against the industrialists, and ignored or sought to explain away the rift in the agrarian ranks clearly implied by the great increase in tenancy between 1890 and 1910. The fact that he now estimated his wealth at $258,000, counted himself one of the largest planters in the state, and had twice as many tenants on his roll books as his father owned slaves did not prevent his thinking of himself as a "farmer." As for a certain agitator who was "demanding that land ownership be restricted to his own narrow notions" and seeking to "sow discord and strife between landlord and tenant," Watson put him down as "A Contemptible little Demagogue." † It was nonsense to say that any industrious tenant could not acquire land: some farmers simply "prefer to rent." Privately he confessed the fear that socialism would "sweep the rural districts like a prairie fire if not opposed in time," ‡ and publicly he did his bit in opposing the doctrine by a voluminous series of articles and

* Ibid., September 8, 1910.
† Ibid., February 17, 1910.
‡ Watson to Dr. John N. Taylor, April 23, 1910, Watson MSS.

pamphlets attacking socialism and defending rent, interest, and land ownership as "not only just but sacred." Daniel De Leon, answering the attack in a series of articles, remarked that "Mr. Watson and his 'Niggers' have their hands in each others' wool." "Hit the Junker," he said, "and the capitalist will yell — we are seeing the spectacle in Great Britain in the matter of the House of Lords; hit the capitalist, and the Junker will shriek — we are seeing the spectacle in Mr. Watson's deportment." *

One way of concealing the cleavage in the agrarian ranks was to identify tenancy, landlessness, and dependency with the Negro — who was by this time politically incapacitated, friendless, and generally accepted as an incompetent ward of White Supremacy. Calling attention to the alleged increase of impertinence, rape, and social ambitiousness on the part of Negroes, Watson now advocated a policy of repression so severe and so firm that "the great mass of the negroes would gradually reconcile themselves to the condition of a recognized peasantry — a laboring class." † It is clear from the context that Watson employed the word "peasantry" in the sense of the word "peonage." Shortly after he was chosen vice-president of the Confederacy, Alexandar H. Stephens said of the new nation: "Its corner-stone rests upon the great truth that the negro is not equal to the white man; that slavery — subordination to the superior race — is his natural and normal condition." Tom Watson, who occupied Stephens's old chair in Congress for a term in the 1890's, held much the same idea in 1910 that his predecessor had held in 1861.

In the course of Watson's gyrations as political boss of the state, his traditional battle against plutocracy, corporate interests, and industrial capitalism underwent a gradual transformation. As his interests narrowed to sectional issues the enemies became exclusively "Yankee" corporations and "Northern" capitalists. Then little or nothing was heard of them at all. In their place was substituted "The Roman Catholic Hierarchy: The Deadliest Menace to Our Liberties and Our Civilization"; socialism, which would reduce all

---

* Daniel De Leon, *Watson on the Gridiron* (New York, 1911), pp. 20, 31, 39.
† Thomas E. Watson, "The Negro Question," in *Watson's Jeffersonian Magazine*, I (1907), 1032–1040.

women "to the same level of sexual depravity"; and the Northern Jew, Leo Frank, who had violated Southern womanhood, whose rich Jewish friends on Wall Street had corrupted Georgia courts, who, in fact deserved to be lynched — and was.

Perennially defeated in their ancient feud with industrial capitalism, the Southern agrarian masses joined in Watson's later crusades with great enthusiasm. They were more exciting, the victories more immediate, and the enemy more vulnerable. Socialists could be jailed, priests booed, and Jews lynched.

For his attacks upon the Negro, Watson reserved a peculiar venom lacking in his other crusades. Perhaps the explanation lay in the fact that of all his later victims the Negro was the only one that he had once befriended — and later betrayed. Few if any Southern politicians rivaled Watson in his insistence upon "*the superiority of the Aryan*" and the "HIDEOUS, OMINOUS, NATIONAL MENACE" of Negro domination. These onslaughts were sometimes prefaced by the conventional tribute to a Negro mammy,* and the familiar claim — "if there is any human creature that I do understand it is the Southern negro." The attacks usually involved a sex theme and necessitate only a few examples to make clear their trend:

> They will ravish girls who have hardly passed babyhood; they will go in squads, surprise some white man, and take turns lying with his wife, in his presence: they will grab a white girl at her door, gag her, drag her away to the negro section, violate her repeatedly all night long, then brutally kill her, and throw her lacerated body into the street. They will rape an old woman who is so bent and enfeebled by age that she can hardly walk with the aid of a stick. The very animals in the stables are not safe from their bestiality.†

One of the few Southern politicians who chose to ignore the outcry created by the Roosevelt-Booker Washington luncheon (Watson was one of the President's luncheon guests himself a few years after), he later pursued the Negro leader relentlessly. Washington, said Watson, was as "imitative as an ape; was as bestial as a gorilla"; and

* Thomas E. Watson, *Bethany: A Story of the Old South* (New York, 1904), p. 15.
† Same author, *Sketches* (Thomson, Ga., 1912), p. 40.

was once "chased out of a white woman's sleeping apartment, in New York, *and beaten as he ran from street to street.*" * In his publications Watson frequently condoned the lynching of a Negro, and in fact openly advocated the practice. *"Lynch law is a good sign,"* he wrote; *"it shows that a sense of justice yet lives among the people."* He himself would no more hesitate to help lynch a Negro rapist than he would to "shoot a mad dog, a wolf, or a rattlesnake." "In the South," he explained, "we have to lynch him [the Negro] occasionally, and flog him, now and then, to keep him from blaspheming the Almighty, by his conduct, on account of his smell and his color." † Georgia had managed to retain pre-eminence in lynchings over her sister states by a safe margin ever since the 1890's, but in this period, the second decade of the century, that pre-eminence was annually written in two figures, while her closest rivals trailed with one.

It was a far cry from the Jeffersonian equalitarianism and humanitarianism of the 1890's to the Watson of 1920. His changing attitude toward the Negro was symptomatic of the changing racial views and policies of agrarian politics in the South.

* Harlem (Georgia) *Columbia Sentinel,* November 7, 1919.
† *Jeffersonian,* January 2, May 15, 1913; January 4, 1917.

Henry Villard: Entrepreneur

by

THOMAS COCHRAN

["The Legend of the Robber Barons," from *The Pennsylvania Magazine of History and Biography*, LXXIV (July 1950), 307–321. Reprinted by permission.]

Much of the recent research in American business history has centered in the role of the entrepreneur, particularly during the post-Civil War period of industrial capitalism. At Harvard, under the direction of Arthur H. Cole, there has been established a Research Center for Entrepreneurial History, the purpose of which in the cryptic language of Business Week *is "to find out what makes the businessman tick and how his ticking has influenced the course of American history."* [1]

As part of the program of the Research Center, Thomas Cochran has made a study of railroad entrepreneurship, mainly in the latter part of the nineteenth century. To this study the selection reprinted below is related.

Cochran and Cole, like Allan Nevins, do not hold with the Veblenesque view of the businessman as motivated solely by greed and the desire for profit. Influenced not a little by the work of Joseph Schumpeter, Cole sees the entrepreneur as making a "creative response" to the problems that confront him. And it is the sum-total of creative responses, in all fields of human endeavor, including the field of business enterprise — Cole argues, as did Schumpeter — that makes for human progress.

Cochran, who is Professor of History at the University of Pennsylvania, like the Harvard group generally, subscribes neither

*to the recent tendency to eulogize the businessman, characteristic of
Stewart Holbrook's Age of the Moguls, nor to the earlier description
of the businessman as a "robber baron."* [2] *Instead, he strives for
"real understanding of the social processes which have channeled the
economic life of the nation" and of "the business process in society."* [3]

BETWEEN business history, which has concentrated attention
upon the administration of the firm, and general social or economic history, which has frequently omitted business processes altogether, there is a broad, vacant area. In this twilight zone lie the
relations of business leaders with similar men in other firms, the in-
teractions of businessmen with society as a whole, and the economic
effects of business decisions. Scholars viewing this area have seen
such a host of related problems that a group composed of representatives from some of the East Coast universities has given the study
a special name: entrepreneurial history.* In defining this field, the
term "entrepreneur" has not been restricted to the conventional
American textbook meaning of one who risks capital in enterprise.
Rather, the older French definitions of Cantillon and Say have been
re-expressed in broader language, to make entrepreneur roughly
equivalent to business executive. In the research of the group, the
function of entrepreneurship, or business leadership, is conceived as
operating in a broad socio-economic setting.

The systematic pursuit of a new interest of this kind requires a
series of assumptions as to what should be examined, some tenta-
tive hypotheses about relationships and dynamics, and then historical facts against which to test and expand the original concepts.†
The major assumption of entrepreneurial history is that it requires
the exploration of the economic and social roles played by the entrepreneur: how he did his job, and what doing his particular job
meant from the standpoint of his personality, his interests, and his

---

* The Research Center for Entrepreneurial History at Harvard, organized by
Arthur H. Cole, is one result of the deliberations of the East Coast group.

† It is worth noting that although data may vary in age from six months to
five hundred years, any that can be collected are necessarily historical.

other social roles. To gain adequate perspective, these explorations should take place in various historical settings.

What is such study likely to mean for history of the social sciences? For one thing, it will correct the elimination of man from most current economic theorizing. The necessity for including the human factor in economic equations is very obvious when we take a look at the history of a country like Venezuela. Venezuela has all of the factors usually assumed to be necessary for rapid industrial development. It has oil and iron ore, both readily available to water transportation; it has been populated for many years by people who have known of European technology; and one finds it hard in studying its history to discover any conventional economic reason for the failure of these people to develop their resources. Yet Venezuela remained a backward farming country until American oil companies began to develop it following the concessions granted in 1921, and its iron resources remained unexploited until the United States Steel Company entered the picture at a somewhat later date. The answer obviously is that the general culture of Venezuela was not such as to encourage entrepreneurship; or to carry this a step further, economic growth does not depend simply upon a population and a given body of resources and transportation facilities; it depends upon the whole cultural complex that may or may not lead to enterprise, savings, reinvestment of capital, and further development.

The economists, of course, have recognized the importance of entrepreneurship abstractly; but they have failed to make any satisfactory use of this factor in setting up their equations or developing their theories. The inclusion of this factor in economic history, for example, will unquestionably reorient it in the direction of anthropological and sociological knowledge. It will not necessarily make the businessman a hero, but it will affirm the necessity of seeing economic growth in cultural terms.

For the general historian, it will mean a re-evaluation of the roles and importance of business leaders, particularly in countries such as the United States. Our present history generally has seen business leaders as parasites on a deterministic process. Historians who are in no other way determinists nevertheless seem to assume that our economic development would have gone along in good and productive paths if left to itself, whereas grasping and unscrupulous business leaders deflected this natural progress into antisocial lines for their own advantage. The corrective needed is not a eulogy of business, but real understanding of the social processes which have channeled the economic life of the nation.

An analysis of the period in which many American historians have discussed the businessman, the age of the "robber barons," will illustrate the reinterpretation that may come from entrepreneurial history. The "robber barons" are usually selected from among the railroad, industrial, and financial leaders of the period, from about 1865 to 1900, and more often than not are the only businessmen who appear in college textbooks covering this period. According to the present historical mythology, they are seen as "bad" or unusually grasping and unscrupulous types in our culture, against the background of a "good" public. The interest in discussing them has been to illustrate business malpractices, and, presumably, to convey moralistic warnings against such activities, rather than to understand the business process in society.

In distinction to this pathological approach, the entrepreneurial historian is interested in the culture patterns and social structures which have produced these assumed types, and in whether or not the types have been correctly delineated. In pursuing such a study, the first thing is to decide what some of the major cultural themes were that guided or sanctioned the roles of these men. I think we can pick out three about which there will be little controversy: the concept of the autonomous economy that was self-adjusting; the idea that progress came through competition and the survival of the fittest; and the belief that profit or material gain was the only reliable incentive for action. These themes operated throughout the society as a whole. The truckman delivering dirt for railroad construction was as much motivated by profit and as firm a believer in these themes as was the "robber baron" who was building the road. The dissident element in the society, those who denied the value of these major themes, seem during these years to have been a relatively small, or at least uninfluential, portion of the population. Therefore, if value judgments are to be formed, they should be applied to this type of society or culture. It is rather futile to assert that the culture would have been all right if it were not for the kind of people and activities that resulted directly from its major themes.

If one accepts the additional and continuing American theme that material growth is a reliable index of progress, and its usual corollary that rapid progress is desirable, one question that may be asked of the culture as a whole is whether such progress could have taken place faster if other beliefs had prevailed. Since it is impossible to conceive deductively what the United States would have been like if built up on some other system, such a decision requires the establishment of a comparative standard. But if recourse is had to the history of another nation in order to observe the application of different cultural patterns to economic development, none seems like the United States and so none offers satisfying parallels. It is interesting, however, to note that in one of the somewhat similar economic situations, that of Australia, where railroads and frontier development went on through more state enterprise, about the same things were complained of that commentators here in the United States blamed upon private enterprise. In other words, a number of the difficulties seem to have been inherent in the rapid development of a pioneer area, rather than in the particular means by which the development went on.

Avoiding, therefore, such unanswerable questions, and concentrating on a better understanding of the operation of American culture, let us examine the historical legend of the "robber baron" by analyzing the "case history" of Henry Villard. Villard is an interesting "robber baron" because he was brought up outside the American culture in a German bureaucratic or official family. His father was a German lawyer and judge, who ultimately became a member of the Supreme Court of the Kingdom of Bavaria. Villard, after attendance at three European universities, decided to come to the United States to try his fortune. Supported to some extent by family money, he entered journalism and built himself a successful career as a correspondent for European and American newspapers. The Civil War, particularly, gave prestige to young Villard. He was able to interview Lincoln and to offer many interesting and penetrating views of contemporary events. In the early 1870's he went back to

Germany, and through his family connections came to know the chief financial men of Frankfort and Munich. These contacts led to his being sent over as a representative of German bondholders in the Oregon railroad and steamship enterprises that had fallen into difficulties during the depression following the panic of 1873.

It is interesting that when Villard was placed in the position of having to make judgments regarding what should be done on the unfinished Oregon and California Railroad, and in regard to the river nagivation projects, he readily assumed the entrepreneurial role in just about the same form as men who had been brought up in business. In other words, the entrepreneurial role seems to have been so much a part of the cultural pattern of America, and possibly of middle-class Germany, at this time, that there was no great gulf between the attitude of the professional intellectual or journalist and that of the businessman. Villard identified himself quickly with the development of the Oregon area, and, instead of advising liquidation and withdrawal for his German clients, he counseled rather the investment of still more capital in order to complete the enterprises. In this way his essential role was that of attracting foreign capital to a frontier development. It is not clear that he was ever deeply interested in problems of technology and management — that is, in just how the capital was applied for productive purposes; rather, he became a public relations man for the area, and an over-all or general entrepreneurial supervisor of where the capital should be allocated.

One factor of great importance in the Villard story is that he started new activities at just about the bottom of the deep depression that lasted from 1873 to 1879, and his ventures from then on, or at least from 1877 on, were first on a gradually rising market, and finally, from 1879 to 1882, on a market that boomed.

Villard saw quickly that the Northern Pacific Railroad, which was being built across the country from Duluth and St. Paul, would have to make, or at least should make, an agreement to connect with whatever road occupied the Columbia River valley. With this long-range plan in mind, he secured foreign and domestic help for the building of the Oregon Railroad and Navigation Company up the Columbia, at a time when Northern Pacific construction was moving very slowly into eastern Montana.

It is from this point on that the most interesting differences occur between the dramatic "robber baron" explanation of Villard's activities and the more sober and socially complex explanation offered by entrepreneurial history. The "robber baron" story is that, as Villard found the Northern Pacific management nearing the Columbia Valley but unwilling to agree to make use of his facilities — that is, threatening to build either a parallel line, or to cross the Cascade Mountains to Tacoma and Seattle — he decided that he must get control of the Northern Pacific. So great was his prestige for successful operation by this time that he had the boldness to ask a group of his friends in Wall Street to put up eight million dollars for some project that he would not reveal to them. And, as the story went, he had no difficulty in more than raising the first payment requested for this "blind pool," money which he used secretly to buy control of the Northern Pacific Railroad. The "robber baron" analogy is, of course, obvious and exciting. The "robber baron," Villard, seizes control of a strategic pass and then exacts tribute from the railroad that represents a great, nationally subsidized enterprise.* Villard's blind pool has all of the trappings of high drama and shady financial dealings. The "robber baron" story then goes on to assert that Villard robbed the Northern Pacific and his other properties in the course of construction in such a way that by 1883 they were bankrupt, while he himself had become very rich.

As usual, the actual story is not so dramatic. What appears to have happened is that, when the Northern Pacific secured Drexel Morgan financing in the latter part of the year 1880, and the Drexel Morgan-Winslow Lanier syndicate learned that Frederick Billings, the president of Northern Pacific, was planning to build duplicate facilities to the coast without regard to the already existing Oregon Railroad and Navigation Company, they became worried over the economic loss involved in constructing nearly parallel lines. The bankers, not sharing in the loyalties to individual companies that presidents and other officers almost inevitably develop, could see no reason why Northern Pacific and O.R. & N. could not get together in one co-operating line. But some of the officers of Northern Pacific, particularly Billings, regarded the railroad as their greatest

* The Northern Pacific had the largest land grant of any in the Western railroads.

lifework; they felt that to compromise and make the final road a joint venture between the "upstart" Villard and the great Northern Pacific enterprise was a personal defeat. Whereupon Morgan, at least, decided that the only way of bringing about a compromise and preventing unnecessary construction was to establish a common control for the two companies. Since Villard, who had, from the financial standpoint, acquitted himself well as receiver for Kansas Pacific, was now anxious to get this joint control, and assured Morgan that he independently had the resources to do so, the syndicate gave him their blessings, and even offered him their help. The "blind pool" was, therefore, chiefly a product of Villard's love of drama, of doing things in a spectacular fashion. Had he been willing to forgo these dramatic frills, control could quietly have been bought through the syndicate over about the same period. Of course, it cannot be overlooked that successfully doing the job himself gave Villard great personal prestige in Wall Street.

The difficulties from 1881 on to the completion of the road in 1883 seem to have been to some extent inevitable, and to some extent to have resulted from the usual overoptimism of American promoters. Villard formed a holding company, called the Oregon and Transcontinental Company, which was to own stocks in his various enterprises, make the construction contracts, and generally conduct the building which would weld Northern Pacific and O.R. & N. into one system. Undoubtedly, the Oregon and Transcontinental Company stock was a source of large profit for Villard; in fact, it seems probable that all the money Villard made in connection with these enterprises came from floating, buying, and selling the securities in Wall Street. It may be that Villard profited from the construction contracts, but there is no clear evidence of this; and it is quite possible, by analogy to similar situations, that the profits of construction went largely to local contractors in the West. At all events, the major difficulty was a lack of sufficient traffic to warrant the high construction cost of building railroads through the Rockies and the Oregon coastal regions. The completion of the through-line in August of 1883 was almost simultaneous with the beginning of a steady recession in general business that ended in a crisis the following March. As a result, the difficulties that the system would have experienced in paying returns under any circumstances were accentuated.

When the companies were not able to pay dividends and their securities declined, Villard, temporarily losing the confidence of the banking syndicate, was forced to retire from the control of the various enterprises.

One way, therefore, of looking at this whole story is that Villard, a relatively inexperienced entrepreneur, took hold of a series of frontier developments at the bottom of the business cycle, carried them along through his connections and personal enthusiasm during the rise of the cycle, completed them just at the peak of the boom, and was then unable to steer them through the ensuing depression. Viewed from this angle, the whole development was a normal and repetitive one in both big and small business. The general history of even a small retail store or factory enterprise was often just about the same; if the enterprise started at a favorable time in the business cycle, it could last until a major depression. Then, unless it has had farsighted and unusually able management, or had been lucky in making more profit than was possible for most young enterprises, it lapsed into bankruptcy and had to be reorganized with the injection of new capital. The roles that Villard played extremely well were those of a mobilizer of capital resources for pioneer investments, and effective public relations for the development of an area. The roles that he played poorly were those of an expert railroad builder and conservative business forecaster.

What do entrepreneurial historians expect to gain from such a study? In the first place, the study of outstanding examples such as that of Villard may be instructive for the study of the normal practices and operations of business. A detailed study of the Villard enterprises will show more exactly the nature of such practices as the strategic type of entrepreneurship that went into railroad building. The seizing of the transportation route down the Columbia River is merely a dramatic example of the general type of planning done by all Western railroad builders. The strategic occupation of territory was like a great game of chess. Each leading entrepreneur had to guess where his rivals were likely to build next, how he could forestall their entrance into an area by throwing a line of track through some valley or across some river, often planning these moves a decade or more ahead. Little is known of the local economic and social results of this process beyond the fact that it extended railroad transportation at an extremely rapid rate.

Trying to assess the larger economic and social effects of Villard's activities, we might note that he mobilized about sixty million dollars in capital, and applied it to Western development at a social cost of perhaps one or two million dollars. That is, he may have made more money than that, but the one or two million dollars represent an estimate of what he actually spent on living and personal durable goods during these years. His other money came and went in stock-market operations, and presumably represented a transfer of capital from one set of holders to another. The question remains: granting that this was not a high rate of commission to pay for the mobilization of so much money, was the long-run effect of the development for which the money was spent economically and socially desirable? Undoubtedly, this particular development of transportation was premature, and it was carried on at the cost of some other types of goods or services that could have been produced with the same expenditure. But this in turn raises another question from a purely nationalistic standpoint: could the foreign capital have been attracted for more prosaic and routine operations? To the extent that foreign money was invested unprofitably in Western development, it was an economic loss to Germany and the other investing nations, but a net gain to the United States. As to the loss of domestic resources in these developments, it can be noted that, at least, this is what the men of the culture apparently wanted to do with their economic energy. Villard noted in his promotion activities that the word "Oregon" had a kind of popular magic to it in the 1870's, and early 1880's. Then it was the promised land of the American West, and it stimulated the imagination of Americans along entrepreneurial lines. The historian should try to assess the extent to which the dramatic development of natural resources may actually raise the rate of saving in the community, and may increase output of energy in the population as a whole. These are, of course, very difficult and intangible problems, but yet they are just as much a part of the picture of economic development as the old stand-by of assessing the value of natural resources and the cost of getting them to market.

There is a cultural paradox involved in all of this that makes it difficult for the unwary investigator. At the same time that Americans were saving at a high rate for development purposes and investing in railroad securities, they had a distrust of the railroad operator and were inclined to make the railroads a scapegoat for many of their ills. In other words, there was a kind of national Manichaean heresy, whereby people were willing to sell themselves to the devil, to worship evil, as it were, but at the same time were not ready to forget the fact that it was really the devil and not good that they were supporting. This whole problem of ambiguity of attitude toward business leaders, and the reactions it led to on the part of the executives themselves, is one of the most fruitful fields of American cultural history.

This leads directly to the problem of social sanctions: what codes of conduct, ethics, mores, and folkways were recognized by the railroad entrepreneur? The "robber baron" approach has implied that there were few sanctions recognized, that these men operated on the basis of nearly complete expediency. To anyone familiar with the study of cultures, this is obviously a very questionable assertion. Actually, there were many but varying sanctions operative upon the business leaders of the period. They varied with types of activity — horse trading, for instance, having one set of ethics, banking quite another; with the conditioning of the entrepreneur — whereby a man brought up in the strict and staid business community of Philadelphia would have different ethics from one brought up in a less rigidly structured society; and with the geographical region — the frontier, in general, being an area of greater opportunity and larger adherence to the "end-justifies-the-means" philosophy than more settled areas — the mining town of Virginia City and Boston, perhaps, illustrating extreme poles.

Let us take a particular type of social sanction and see how it operated on the basis of these differing situations. One of the most important ones was the feeling of a fiduciary obligation toward stockholders and bondholders — the recognition of the fact that managers were trustees for the real owners of the property. From this standpoint, the distinction between men and regions may be brought out by analyzing the promotion of an extension up the

Mississippi River by the directors of the Chicago, Burlington & Quincy Railroad.

But before proceeding to the details of these operations, it is necessary to understand some of the culture patterns of pioneer development and railroad building. The ultimate growth and welfare of the community was a rationalization that to the Westerner justified almost any means that he might employ — particularly in the handling of Easterners' capital. Added to this was the fact that railroad companies were not fitted to do their own construction work and had to let local contractors do the building. That the construction work was not done by contract simply to rob the stockholders is abundantly illustrated by the facts that the most mature and best-managed companies continued to build through contractors, even though they might readily have undertaken the work themselves, and that railroad contractors sometimes bankrupted themselves by bidding too low. The difficulties were that building was a specialized enterprise for which the railroad had no regular staff, that it was occasional rather than continuous and, therefore, did not justify the maintenance of a specialized staff, and that often the work was remote from the railroad offices and could not readily be supervised by the chief executives. In order to facilitate such large-scale work by local interests, it would often be necessary for the road itself, or the directors or large stockholders of the road, to put up cash to assist the local contractor. This would be done by buying stock in a construction company of which the operating executive would usually be a local builder. The construction company took its pay in railroad stocks or bonds, which might in the case of an old road be almost as good as cash, but in the case of many young roads might be of very speculative and dubious value. The par value of securities taken for construction work, therefore, is not a safe guide to the amount of profit actually realized by construction companies. But there is little question that a great deal of Eastern stockholders' money went West into construction companies and stayed there as profit to local entrepreneurs, including subcontractors all the way down the line, and even to the owners of local sandbanks and hardware stores. Sometimes the Eastern directors and stockholders who had advanced money for construction company stock made hand-

some profits; at other times, as in the case to be discussed, they lost what they had put in; but in any case, the local people were likely to make a profit. As John Murray Forbes, Boston railroad promoter and conservative financier, put it, "My feeling is . . . that the Landowners and R. Road contractors are the ones who too often get the whole benefit of the money that Capitalists put into the West." *
Charles E. Perkins, long-time president of the C. B. & Q., went even further: "Iowa people make more money in farms and other industries including contracting and building than in railroads . . . and it is only the Eastern capitalist who cannot use his money to advantage at home who is willing to risk it in Western railroads and take the low average return which he gets, a return very much lower than the average of other investments in this state [of Iowa]." †

This background is necessary to an understanding of the contracts for the so-called River Roads that were to go up the Mississippi from Clinton, Iowa, ultimately to Minneapolis and St. Paul. The central Western city involved in this development was Dubuque, Iowa, and the local entrepreneur who undertook to do the construction was J. K. Graves. He was a small-scale, general entrepreneur interested in banking, building, and all the wide range of local enterprises usual to the small-city capitalist. In order to undertake construction on these roads, he persuaded a group of the C. B. & Q. directors, headed by ex-president James F. Joy, to put up about half a million dollars cash in return for securities of the construction company. They then entered into a contract with the two railroad companies that were to own and operate the lines after they had been built, whereby the construction company took pay partly in stocks and bonds. The rest of the bonds of these companies were to be marketed to the holders of C. B. & Q. bonds and stock, who would buy them readily because of the endorsement of their own directors; this would in turn provide additional capital that could be used to pay for the construction.

Some of the members of the C. B. & Q. board, particularly John Murray Forbes and J. N. A. Griswold, were not told at the time

* John Murray Forbes to Charles S. Tuckerman, Apr. 14, 1880. President's Letters, Chicago, Burlington & Quincy Archives, Newberry Library, Chicago, Illinois.
† Charles E. Perkins to James W. McDill, Jan. 26, 1885. President's Letters, Chicago, Burlington & Quincy Archives, Newberry Library.

they endorsed the sale of the bonds that their fellow directors were actually interested in the stock of the construction company. It seems probable that this knowledge was withheld because Joy and the directors who did buy such stock recognized that Forbes would not approve of their being involved in this kind of relationship. In other words, there appears to have been a difference in the business morality or sanctions recognized by James F. Joy, a Western businessman, and those recognized by old, conservative, upper-class Easterners like Forbes and Griswold.

The working out of the pattern has much in common with the Villard story; Graves may or may not have been a good railroad builder. Examination of hundreds of letters to and from Graves, and letters discussing the situation among C. B. & Q. directors, has failed to provide conclusive information on this point. At least, he held the confidence of Joy and the other interested directors right up to the final failure of the enterprise. The contracts were let in the boom of 1871, and, when the depression hit after the panic of 1873, the roads had not been completed. With revenues of all kinds falling off, Graves started borrowing from the funds of the unfinished River Roads to support his other local enterprises. The result was a slowing down of construction, a default on the bonds of the River Roads, and a financial situation that would not bear close scrutiny by accountants. In all this it is very hard to pass moral judgments. Graves had undoubtedly thought that he was doing the best thing possible for Dubuque and the surrounding country by trying to build up many enterprises at once. He had made no plans for a break in the boom and the coming of depression. As a result, he found himself hopelessly involved in ventures that could not all be kept going; yet the abandonment of any one of them then meant a postponing of all or most of the benefit that was expected to accrue from it. In this situation he tried to borrow from Peter to pay Paul, hoping that Peter would raise additional funds. The same kind of situation has turned pillars of society into scoundrels time and time again in American business history.

In the case of the River Roads, when the default occurred, Forbes and Griswold became interested in investigating the situation and soon found out the identity of the construction company's stockholders and the nature of the contracts. Forbes denounced Joy, and when the latter refused to assume personal responsibility to the C. B. & Q. investors for the interest in the River Road bonds — a procedure which would have been highly unusual — Forbes decided that Joy and certain other directors involved must be put off the C. B. & Q. board. Forbes succeeded in doing this in a proxy battle at the next stockholders' meeting and the River Roads passed ultimately into the hands of the Chicago, Milwaukee and St. Paul. This, in the long run, turned out to be a great mistake, as a decade later C. B. & Q. had to build a parallel line under less advantageous circumstances.

The quarrel was due to a conflict in sanctions based upon differences in situation. As one of Joy's followers in the matter, J. W. Brooks, a C. B. & Q. director who had had much experience in the West, put it, "Loosely as these things were done [branch-line contracts and construction in general] they as a whole have proved the salvation of the C. B. & Q. . . . we do not claim to be immaculate beyond expediency, but are content with right intentions and the good results obtained on the whole. . . ." *

Perhaps the above examples have demonstrated the difficulty in regarding any particular group of business leaders as "robber barons" without careful analysis of the situation involved, the popular and local codes of ethics, and the general pressure for "justification by profit" that ran all through American culture.

These illustrations have shown only limited aspects of entrepreneurial history. They have touched on, but not elaborated, the political science of the business corporation and the analysis of power within the corporation, showing only in the latter case that it is not easy to put one's finger on the exact location of control in any given instance. Real control over a situation may rest with some contractor or underling in the West, despite the façade of power in the Eastern executive officers. Many other relations have not been brought out at all in these two accounts — for example, the relation of business roles to other social roles, which carries with it the discussion of the role of the business elite in relation to cultural leadership. Many railroad men, for example, were active leaders in na-

---

* John W. Brooks to James F. Joy, Mar. 11, 1875. Joy Collection, Michigan Historical Collections, Ann Arbor, Michigan.

tional or state politics; others were patrons of the arts, or supporters of education. To what extent were these attitudes outgrowths of general social mores, to what extent did business sanctions indicate that these supplementary roles should be played, and to what extent were they peculiarities of the individuals?

Comparative studies need to be made of the place of entrepreneurship in varying national cultures. There seems little doubt that such studies will go further toward explaining the economic progress of different regions than will any assessment of potential natural resources. It is these cultural elements, to a very large extent, that determine who will become entrepreneurs (the quantity and quality of the supply of entrepreneurship), and also the likelihood of entrepreneurial success in various types of endeavor. A culture with feudal standards of lavish living or the support of elaborate ceremonial organizations of church and state will obviously not have the capital to invest in economic development that will be available in a culture where frugal living, saving, and work are the custom.

The resources in theory and scope of interest of all the social sciences may be applied more readily to historical problems in the study of special roles and functions, such as entrepreneurship, than in the general study of the enormous conventional fields of economic, social, political or intellectual history. To learn more about how human beings behave and have behaved in history, it is wise to start with a manageable and definable group of human beings performing certain functions, rather than with the activities of the society as a whole.

Karl Marx and Samuel Gompers

by

JOHN R. COMMONS

[From *Political Science Quarterly*, XLI (June 1926), 281–286.
Reprinted by permission.]

It was not until 1918 that a comprehensive history of the American labor movement began to appear. In that year, Professor John R. Commons of the University of Wisconsin and his associates (David J. Saposs, E. B. Mittleman, H. E. Hoagland, and Selig Perlman, together with Helen L. Sumner and John B. Andrews) published the first two volumes of the History of Labour in the United States from colonial beginnings to 1896. A third volume by Don D. Lescohier and Elizabeth Brandeis, and a fourth by Selig Perlman and Philip Taft, bringing the story of the American labor movement to the advent of the New Deal, were published in 1935.

Even as Turner stressed the uniqueness of American political institutions as a consequence of the impact of the frontier, so Commons, who was Turner's colleague at the University of Wisconsin, wrote of the American labor movement as distinct from its European counterpart — the result of the impact of uniquely American conditions. Among the factors shaping the distinctive character of the American labor movement, Commons included the existence of the frontier and free land, political democracy, the vast market available for capitalist exploitation, and the resultant high social and economic mobility that prevented the growth of class-consciousness among American workers. While European labor, continued Commons, was class-conscious, American labor was job-conscious, and job-consciousness rather than class-consciousness was the key to a proper undertanding of American labor history.[1]

While this thesis has been amplified by Commons's disciples,[2] *it has been challenged sharply by the Marxist analysis of Philip S. Foner.[3] However, what seems to be most needed is a history of the labor movement integrating the spadework of Commons with more recent findings.[4]*

Commons saw in the program of the American Federation of Labor — its job-consciousness, which he equated with individuality, craft-unionism, and avoidance of political panaceas and even of political participation — the materialization of his theoretical conception of the American labor movement. In the following selection, he offers an appreciative account of the ideology of Samuel Gompers, one of the founders of the American Federation of Labor.

IT IS interesting to compare the theories of the two great Jewish leaders of labor movements, Karl Marx and Samuel Gompers. Gompers's *Autobiography** stands for American trade-unionism where Marx's *Communist Manifesto* and *Das Kapital* stand for international Socialism. Each is an economic interpretation of history and each is a program of action based on that interpretation.

Marx got his education in the German universities and did his investigating in the British Museum. Gompers left the public schools of London at the age of ten and got his education in Cooper Union, but did his investigating in the cigar shops of New York. Marx converted the dominant philosophy of his time from Hegel's idealism of a future German Empire into the economic materialism of a future World Communism. Gompers learned the *Communist Manifesto* and Marx's theories from the Socialist exiles from Europe, and it was "this insight into a world of hidden thought," he says, "that aroused me to master the German language in order that I might read for myself." (I, p. 74.) What he learned from Marx was this: "Economic organization and control over economic power were the fulcrum which made possible influence and power over other fields. Control over the basic things of life gives power that

* Samuel Gompers, *Seventy Years of Life and Labor*, 2 vols. (New York, E. P. Dutton and Company, 1925).

may be used for good in every relationship of life." This, he says, was the "fundamental concept on which the A. F. of L. was later developed." (I, p. 223.)

Gompers recites that Marx was primarily a trade-unionist, and that he opposed both the political and anarchistic elements in the labor movement. But it was, as he says, "the Lassallean program of political action that won over the militant economic program of Marx both in Germany and France" — and it was the Anarchists, led by Bakunin, who succeeded in splitting, in 1872, the International Workingmen's Association, which Marx and the British trade-unions had formed in 1864. This split and the reaction in Europe drove to America, in the early 1870's, the Marxian Socialists, but apparently without the Lassallean Socialists or Anarchists. The latter did not come in numbers until after the German anti-Socialist law of 1878, although there was a "large sprinkling" of French Communists in New York after the downfall of the Paris Commune. (I, p. 91.)

Gompers's intimate associates were the Marxian Socialists, from about 1873 to 1878. There was F. A. Sorge, Marx's friend and successor as executive of the International Workingmen's Association when the headquarters were moved from London to New York to escape the Anarchists, where Sorge "was in charge of the disintegration that followed." (I, p. 84.) There was J. P. McDonnell, who "had spent several years in London in the office of Karl Marx." (I, p. 88.) There was David Kronburg, "easily the master mind," a member of the International. There was P. J. McGuire, a member of the I. W. A., "a fiery young orator with a big heart, and as yet immature judgment." (I, p. 88.) Especially was there Ferdinand Laurrell, to whose memory Gompers dedicated this autobiography as "a workman all his life who was my mental guide through many of my early struggles." Laurrell "had been in the inner circles of Marx's International and knew more of its connections with European revolutions than was generally known." (I, p. 85.) He was a Swede and had been secretary of the International for the three Scandinavian countries, and "knew from experience the revolutionists, the socialists, the anarchists, and the trade-unionists. . . . Strong and vigorous mentally and physically, he forged to the head of both the revolutionary and labor movements." (I, p. 71.)

Gompers makes it quite plain that Laurrell was his teacher, who carried him through an investigation of all the philosophies and tactics of all schools of the various labor movements, besides critically examining Gompers's own theories.

I remember going to him one day and enthusiastically telling him some wild plans I had for human betterment. When I had finished, convinced that I had talked well, I sat back with manifest satisfaction to let Laurrell reply. He had been working silently, but had not missed a point, and I began to feel physically smaller as Laurrell systematically and ruthlessly demolished my every statement. By the time he had finished I vowed to myself "Never again will I talk that stuff — but I will find principles that will stand the test." (I, p. 73.)

Again, "in those days I was full of fire and dreams and burning with sentiment, and I might have followed any course or associated myself with any movement that seemed to promise freedom for my pals and fellow workers. It was the wise counsel of my friend Laurrell that saved me: 'Never permit sentiment to lead you, but let intellect dominate action.'" (I, p. 162.) Also Laurrell advised him to attend the Socialist meetings, "listen to what they have to say and understand them, but do not join the party." Gompers never joined, but it was his habit to attend their Saturday evening meetings. (I, p. 74.)

Indeed, Ferdinand Laurrell conducted a remarkable research seminar in economics in the only union cigar shop in New York, owned by David Hirsch, one of the German exiles, and an employer of fifty or sixty exiles and others. Gompers entered this shop in 1873, at the age of twenty-three, having been working at his trade in New York since 1863, and he remained there five years, and afterwards worked in other shops until 1887, altogether twenty-four years in a cigar shop.

In Hirsch's shop the workers subscribed to labor and other papers, read aloud to each other while they worked and conducted a "labor forum." (I, p. 68 *et seq.*) Piecework, handwork, skilled work, quiet work, no rules against talking, and Ferdinand Laurrell made Gompers an "intellectual."

Gompers joined also, during the Seventies, a group of labor investigators, "*die zehn Philosophen*," who were, in fact, "an inner circle" of the International Workingmen's Association. At least three of these philosophers, including Gompers, afterwards became well-known leaders in the American Federation of Labor.

We dreamed together and then thrashed out our dreams to see what might be of practical value. From this little group came the purpose and initiative that finally resulted in the present American labor movement — the most effective economic organization in the world. We did not create the American trade union — that is the product of forces and conditions. But we did create the technique that guided trade unions to constructive policies and achievements. [I, p. 87.]

Then, in 1877, came "the great strike" of New York cigar makers against the tenement-house system. The strike was partly compromised but mainly lost. Gompers's job at Hirsch's was filled. He had pawned everything but his wife's wedding ring. Eventually he found another job, but he moved to cheaper quarters in a distant part of Brooklyn, so that, on account of the distance and the needs of his family, he imagined himself separated from active work in the labor movement.

But his union made him chairman of a committee on administration. He moved back to New York. "That, in my opinion, was the turning point of my life." (I, p. 163.)

Following this disastrous strike, Gompers and his associates began to reorganize the cigar makers, basing their plans on the experience of their own weakness, on the trade-union philosophy of the ten philosophers, and on a Marxism revised to fit American conditions.

I mention these five years of Gompers's life because occasionally scholastic critics speak of him as having no theories, no philosophies, no understanding of the "intellectuals," no science, no ultimate goal, but as merely a man of cunning, pugnacity, intuition, expediency and honesty. Yet, as I see such things, he was the greatest "intellectual" of them all and the most scientific of the theorists. Here was a true experimenter in the science of economics, trying out his theories on one of the most experienced teachers of the subject and on the ten philosophers, in what would now be called a set of research seminars, and all the while trying them out on the world of industry where he worked. Here was a continual revision of theories until one was found that would work — and the American Federation of Labor was the way it worked. This, I suspect, is the truly scientific method, and those who pride themselves on being the intellectuals, whom Gompers learned to reject, would scarcely nowadays, in sciences other than economics, be permitted to have respectful, much less than patient, attention. Gompers says of himself, "at no time in my life have I worked out definitely articulated economic theory," but have reached conclusions gradually, "after discarding proposals to which I temporarily subscribed." (I, pp. 17, 24.) Which is the *greater* intellect, I do not know — the brilliant scholar who propounds anything or everything and leads nowhere, or the slow-minded Gompers or Darwin who works patiently for decades, theorizing and experimenting? Which is the more *scientific* intellect there seems to be no doubt.

The Marxian philosophy has, it is true, been described by its followers as "scientific" Socialism. What Marx did was to take Ricardo's economics and Hegel's philosophy, and to find in the one the secret of "control over the basic things of life" and in the other the clue that would trace that control through all history from primitive communism to world-communism. He did, as Gompers did not, build an "articulated economic theory" and provided not only a string to carry his mass of facts, but also a visibly articulated goal where the string ended. Gompers's experimental method had neither a fixed mechanism for reaching the goal nor even a visible goal. While Marx's mechanism and goal were government, Gompers's mechanism and goal were liberty. With Marx the individual was subordinate, in every respect and at all times, to a government of some kind that controls the economic foundations. With Gompers the individual was supreme but coerced, and was to acquire liberty by collectively imposing shop rules for control of the economic foundations. This difference appears in their theories regarding trade unions.

Gompers maintains that "whatever modifications Marx may have taught in his philosophical writings, as a practical policy he urged the formation of trade-unions and the use of them to deal with the problems of the labor movement." (I, p. 85.) He cites Marx's letters, and, of course, he knew this fact from Marx's intimate followers. Marx was, indeed, closely affiliated with the British trade-union leaders in the decade of the 1860's, during a part of his long residence in London. But the trade-unions of the Sixties and Seventies, as Gompers frequently makes note, had no very clear distinctions in philosophy or tactics that might keep them separate from those who were not wage-earners, and hence they had no rules that held the unions to the actual economic problems of the shop as against the general reforms of anarchism, socialism, politics, in which non-wage-earners were adepts. Here it was Laurrell, again, who gave him the cue, fashioned on his own wide experience: " 'Study your union card, Sam, and if the idea doesn't square with that, it ain't true.' My trade-union card came to be my standard in all new problems." (I, p. 75.)

In this way, eventually, Gompers became even more class-conscious than Marx himself, for Marx's International Working-men's Association admitted all classes of labor reformers to membership and it was this that eventually caused the British unions to withdraw and the Association itself to split on the rocks of Anarchism and Socialism. But the significant thing was not merely that the "intellectuals" were admitted to the labor unions, but that the unions were thereby diverted from attention to the shop rules which, in American and British unions since that time, have been imposed in such abundance for the protection of the individual worker on the job. The intellectuals looked upon labor as a mass, and it was the "solidarity" of labor to which Marx looked for the conquest of capitalism *en masse*. The individual worker did not count for much. But for Gompers and his teacher, Laurrell, who were workers themselves, it was the individuality of the laborer that counted, and economic power for them meant power of the union to protect the individual in his job. Previously it had been wages and hours for all, as a class — now it became, also, how to prevent the employer from using his economic power arbitrarily against the individual. Henceforward "recognition of the union," "grievance committees," "business agents," union cards, arbitration, hiring, firing, restrictions on speeding up, promotions, transfers, even such small items as priority in having the better place to work in the shop (I, p. 65) —

these became the economic foundations of individual liberty for the wage-earners, and for Gompers as one of them.

Needless to say, these small matters could not attract the attention of Karl Marx or the intellectuals or the revolutionaries — they were interested in large things such as the world production of wealth, but these shop rules restricted output. They were interested in who should get the whole product of the whole social-labor power, but these rules turned on the petty sorrows, oppressions and envies of individuals hidden away under the mass. Somewhere even Marx decries these restrictive policies of trade-unions which stood in the way of raising labor as a class, and the German trade-unions did not resort to them until after the Great War. They had previously relied on politics and ultimate Socialism, rather than on what Gompers would call self-help in the shop. Yet these shop rules are all-important for the individual worker, for they are his liberty.

Finally, when Gompers and the others built up the American Federation of Labor, they did not have a centralized big union where Gompers would be a dictator and have control of the funds and discipline, but a loose federation, with shop autonomy, union autonomy, craft autonomy — "autonomy" everywhere, and only two rules — union card and no dual unions. There was no ultimate goal about such an arrangement, and little that could satisfy an intellectual who idealizes order and logic, but it was liberty through control of economic power.

There is scarcely space to summarize further how Gompers "learned the weakness of radical tactics," the weaknesses of legislation, the injury done to labor orgaization by "intellectuals," his account of the "fight to the finish" with the Knights of Labor, who included intellectuals and represented the idea of centralized labor government, his account of "socialists as I know them," of the injunction, and of the part he played in the Great War. All of these have as their central theme LIBERTY THROUGH ECONOMIC POWER.

Kansas

by

CARL BECKER

[Reprinted from *Essays in American History Dedicated to Frederick Jackson Turner* (copyright 1910), pp. 84–111. By permission of Henry Holt and Company, Inc.]

The problem confronting the editor as to what to include on the subject of the frontier and the West in the period between the Civil and World Wars would seem to find easy resolution in Turner's essay on "The Significance of the Frontier." Without denying the enormous influence of Turner on American historiography, however, his 1893 statement has been so riddled by critical shot and shell as to cause us to omit it, particularly in a volume whose main emphasis is upon contemporary American historiography.

In defending Turner against his critics, Avery Craven argues that Turner has been taken too literally by his opponents; that Turner was interested in "general effects" rather than in specific applications. Turner, in speaking of "democracy and nationalism" on the frontier, according to Avery Craven, "had reference not to sharp, well-defined, all-inclusive qualities but rather to general tendencies which stood out amid contradictions and variation but which were, nevertheless, easily distinguished and universally recognized." [1]

In the following selection, Carl Becker has employed Turnerian concepts much in the spirit that Craven believes Turner had intended them to be used — more as points of departure than as precise directives to be followed implicitly. True, we are bound to quarrel with statements by Becker, following Turner, to the effect that "individualism is everywhere characteristic of the frontier" and "on the frontier . . . everything is done by the individual and noth-

ing by organized society." But the fact remains that Becker's analysis of Kansas neither stands nor falls with these generalizations. One feels that if Turner had not written quite as he did, Becker's understanding of the Kansas spirit would be by that much diminished. At the same time, it is only proper to point out that Becker's view of Kansas is both optimistic and democratic, following Turner's roseate presentation of the impact of the frontier. There are darker aspects of life on the frontier and in Kansas which Turner and Becker overlooked.

SOME years ago, in a New England college town, when I informed one of my New England friends that I was preparing to go to Kansas, he replied rather blankly, "Kansas?! Oh." The amenites of casual intercourse demanded a reply, certainly, but from the point of view of my New England friend I suppose there was really nothing more to say; and, in fact, standing there under the peaceful New England elms, Kansas did seem tolerably remote. Some months later I rode out of Kansas City and entered for the first time what I had always pictured as the land of grasshoppers, of arid drought, and barren social experimentation. In the seat just ahead were two young women, girls rather, whom I afterwards saw at the university. As we left the dreary yards behind, and entered the half-open country along the Kansas River, one of the pair, breaking abruptly away from the ceaseless chatter that had hitherto engrossed them both, began looking out of the car window. Her attention seemed fixed, for perhaps a quarter of an hour, upon something in the scene outside — the fields of corn, or it may have been the sunflowers that lined the tract; but at last, turning to her companion with the contented sigh of a returning exile, she said, "*Dear old Kansas!*" The expression somehow recalled my New England friend. I wondered vaguely, as I was sure he would have done, why anyone should feel moved to say "Dear old Kansas!" I had supposed that Kansas, even more than Italy, was only a geographical expression. But not so. Not infrequently, since then, I have heard the same expression — not always from emotional young girls. To understand why people say "Dear old Kansas!" is to understand that Kansas is no mere geographical expression, but a "state of mind," a religion and a philosophy in one.

The difference between the expression of my staid New England friend and that of the enthusiastic young Kansan is perhaps symbolical, in certain respects, of the difference between those who remain at home and those who, in successive generations, venture into the unknown "West" — New England or Kansas — wherever it may be. In the seventeenth century there was doubtless no lack of Englishmen — prelates for example, in lawn sleeves, comfortably buttressed about by tithes and the Thirty-nine Articles — who might have indicated their point of view quite fully by remarking, "New England?! Oh." Whether any New Englander of that day ever went so far as to say "Dear old New England," I do not know. But that the sentiment was there, furnishing fuel for the inner light, is past question. Nowadays the superiority of New England is taken for granted, I believe, by the people who live there; but in the seventeenth century, when its inhabitants were mere frontiersmen, they were given, much as Kansans are said to be now, to boasting — alas! even of the climate. In 1629, Mr. Higginson, a reverend gentleman, informed his friends back in England that "The temper of the aire of New England is one special thing that commends this place. Experience doth manifest that there is hardly a more healthful place to be found in the world that agreeth better with our English bodyes. Many that have been weake and sickly in old England, by coming hither have been thoroughly healed and growne healthfull strong. For here is a most extraordinarie cleere and dry aire that is of a most healing nature to all such as are of a cold, melancholy, flegmatick, rheumatick temper of body. . . . And therefore I think it a wise course for all cold complections to come to take physic in New England; for a sup of New England aire is better than a whole draft of Old England's ale." Now, we who live in Kansas know well that its climate is superior to any other in the world, and that it enables one, more readily than any other, to dispense with the use of ale.

There are those who will tell us, and have indeed often told us, with a formidable array of statistics, that Kansas is inhabited only in small part by New Englanders, and that it is therefore fanciful in the extreme to think of it as representing puritanism transplanted.

It is true, the people of Kansas came mainly from "the Middle West" — from Illinois, Indiana, Ohio, Iowa, Kentucky, and Missouri. But for our purpose the fact is of little importance, for it is the ideals of a people rather than the geography they have outgrown that determine their destiny; and in Kansas, as has been well said, "it is the ideas of the Pilgrims, not their descendants, that have had dominion in the young commonwealth." Ideas, sometimes, as well as the star of empire, move westward, and so it happens that Kansas is more puritan than New England of today. It is akin to New England of early days. It is what New England, old England itself, once was — the frontier, an ever-changing spot where dwell the courageous who defy fate and conquer circumstance.

For the frontier is more than a matter of location, and puritanism is itself a kind of frontier. There is an intellectual "West" as well as a territorial "West." Both are heresies, the one as much subject to the scorn of the judicious as the other. Broad classifications of people are easily made and are usually inaccurate; but they are convenient for taking a large view, and it may be worth while to think, for the moment, of two kinds of people — those who like the sheltered life, and those who cannot endure it; those who think the world as they know it is well enough, and those who dream of something better, or, at any rate, something different. From age to age society builds its shelters of various sorts — accumulated traditions, religious creeds, political institutions, and intellectual conceptions, cultivated and well kept farms, well built and orderly cities — providing a monotonous and comfortable life that tends always to harden into conventional forms resisting change. With all this the home-keeping and timid are well content. They sit in accustomed corners, disturbed by no fortuitous circumstance. But there are those others who are forever tugging at the leashes of ordered life, eager to venture into the unknown. Forsaking beaten paths, they plunge into the wilderness. They must be always on the frontier of human endeavor, submitting what is old and accepted to conditions that are new and untried. The frontier is thus the seed plot where new forms of life, whether of institutions or types of thought, are germinated, the condition of all progress being in a sense a return to the primitive.

Now, generally speaking, the men who make the world's frontiers, whether in religion or politics, science, or geographical exploration and territorial settlement, have certain essential and distinguishing qualities. They are primarily men of faith. Having faith in themselves, they are individualists. They are idealists because they have faith in the universe, being confident that somehow everything is right at the center of things; they give hostages to the future, are ever inventing God anew, and must be always transforming the world into their ideal of it. They have faith in humanity and in the perfectibility of man, are likely, therefore, to be believers in equality, reformers, intolerant, aiming always to level others up to their own high vantage. These qualities are not only puritan, they are American; and Kansas is not only puritanism transplanted, but Americanism transplanted. In the individualism, the idealism, the belief in equality that prevail in Kansas, we shall therefore see nothing strangely new, but simply a new graft of familiar American traits. But as Kansas is a community with a peculiar and distinctive experience, there is something peculiar and distinctive about the individualism, the idealism, and the belief in equality of its people. If we can get at this something peculiar and distinctive, it will be possible to understand why the sight of sunflowers growing beside a railroad track may call forth the fervid expression, "Dear old Kansas."

Individualism is everywhere characteristic of the frontier, and in America, where the geographical frontier has hitherto played so predominant a part, a peculiarly marked type of individualism is one of the most obvious traits of the people. "To the frontier," Professor Turner has said, "the American intellect owes its striking characteristics. That coarseness and strength combined with acuteness and inquisitiveness; that practical, inventive turn of mind, quick to find expedients; that masterful grasp of material things, lacking in the artistic but powerful to effect great ends; that restless nervous energy; that dominant individualism, working for good and for evil, and withal that buoyancy and exuberance that comes from freedom." On the frontier, where everything is done by the individual and nothing by organized society, initiative, resourcefulness, quick, confident, and sure judgment are the essential qualities for success. But as the problems of the frontier are rather restricted and definite, those who succeed there have necessarily much the same kind of initiative and resourcefulness, and their judgment will be sure only in respect to the problems that are familiar to all. It thus happens that the type of individualism produced on the frontier and predominant in America, has this peculiarity, that while the sense of freedom is strong, there is nevertheless a certain uniformity in respect to ability, habit, and point of view. The frontier develops strong individuals, but it develops individuals of a particular type, all being after much the same pattern. The individualism of the frontier is one achievement, not of eccentricity, an individualism of fact arising from a sense of power to overcome obstacles, rather than one of theory growing out of weakness in the face of oppression. It is not because he fears governmental activity, but because he has so often had to dispense with it, that the American is an individualist. Altogether averse from hesitancy, doubt, speculative or introspective tendencies, the frontiersman is a man of faith: of faith, not so much in some external power, as in himself, in his luck, his destiny; faith in the possibility of achieving whatever is necessary or he desires. It is this marked self-reliance that gives to Americans their tremendous power of initiative; but the absence of deep-seated differences gives to them an equally tremendous power of concerted social action.

The confident individualism of those who achieve through endurance is a striking trait of the people of Kansas. There, indeed, the trait has in it an element of exaggeration, arising from the fact that whatever has been achieved in Kansas has been achieved under great difficulties. Kansans have been subjected, not only to the ordinary hardships of the frontier, but to a succession of reverses and disasters that could be survived only by those for whom defeat is worse than death, who cannot fail because they cannot surrender. To the border wars succeeded hot winds, droughts, grasshoppers; and to the disasters of nature succeeded in turn the scourge of man, in the form of "mortgage fiends" and a contracting currency. Until 1895 the whole history of the state was a series of disasters, and always something new, extreme, bizarre, until the name Kansas became a byword, a synonym for the impossible and the ridiculous, inviting laughter, furnishing occasion for jest and hilarity. "In God we trusted, in Kansas we busted," became a favorite motto of emigrants, worn out with the struggle, returning to more hospitable climes; and for many years it expressed well enough the popular opinion of that fated land.

Yet there were some who never gave up. They stuck it out. They endured all that even Kansas could inflict. They kept the faith, and they are to be pardoned perhaps if they therefore feel that henceforth there is laid up for them a crown of glory. Those who remained in Kansas from 1875 to 1895 must have originally possessed staying qualities of no ordinary sort, qualities which the experience of those years could only accentuate. And as success has at last rewarded their efforts, there has come, too, a certain pride, an exuberance, a feeling of superiority that accompany a victory long delayed and hardly won. The result has been to give a peculiar flavor to the Kansas spirit of individualism. With Kansas history back of him, the true Kansan feels that nothing is too much for him. How shall he be afraid of any danger, or hesitate at any obstacle, having succeeded where failure was not only human, but almost honorable? Having conquered Kansas, he knows well that there are no worse worlds to conquer. The Kansas spirit is therefore one that finds something exhilarating in the challenge of an extreme difficulty. "No one," says St. Augustine, "loves what he endures, though he may love to endure." With Kansans, it is particularly a point of pride to suffer easily the stings of fortune, and if they find no pleasure in the stings themselves, the ready endurance of them gives a consciousness of merit that is its own reward. Yet it is with no solemn martyr's air that the true Kansan endures the worst that can happen. His instinct is rather to pass it off as a minor annoyance, furnishing occasion for a pleasantry, for it is the mark of a Kansan to take a reverse as a joke rather than too seriously. Indeed, the endurance of extreme adversity has developed a keen appreciation for that type of humor, everywhere prevalent in the West, which consists in ignoring a difficulty, or transforming it into a difficulty of precisely the opposite kind. There is a tradition surviving from the grasshopper time that illustrates the point. It is said that in the midst of that overwhelming disaster, when the pests were six inches deep in the streets, the editor of a certain local paper fined his comment on the situation down to a single line, which appeared among the trivial happenings of the week: "A grasshopper was seen on the courthouse steps this morning." This type of humor, appreciated anywhere west of the Alleghenies is the type *par excellence* in Kansas. Perhaps it has rained for six weeks in the spring. The wheat is seemingly ruined; no corn has been planted. A farmer, who sees his profits for the year wiped out, looks at the murky sky, sniffs the damp air, and remarks seriously, "Well, it looks like rain. We may save that crop yet." "Yes," his neighbor replies with equal seriousness, "but it will have to come soon, or it won't do any good." When misfortunes beat down upon one in rapid succession, there comes a time when it is useless to strive against them, and in the end they engender a certain detached curiosity in the victim, who finds a mournful pleasure in observing with philosophical resignation the ultimate caprices of fate. Thus Kansans, "coiners of novel phrases to express their defiance of destiny," have employed humor itself as a refuge against misfortune. They have learned not only to endure adversity, but in a very literal sense to laugh at it as well.

I have already said that the type of individualism that is characteristic of America is one of achievement, not of eccentricity. The statement will bear repeating in this connection, for it is truer of Kansas than of most communities, notwithstanding there is a notion abroad that the state is peopled by freaks and eccentrics. It was once popularly supposed in Europe, and perhaps is so yet, that Americans are all eccentric. Now, Kansans are eccentric in the same sense that Americans are: they differ somewhat from other Americans, just as Americans are distinguishable from Europeans. But a fundamental characteristic of Kansas individualism is the tendency to conform; it is an individualism of conformity, not of revolt. Having learned to endure to the end, they have learned to conform, for endurance is itself a kind of conformity. It has not infrequently been the subject of wondering comment by foreigners that in America, where everyone is supposed to do as he pleases, there should nevertheless be so little danger from violence and insurrection. Certainly one reason is that while the conditions of frontier life release the individual from many of the formal restraints of ordered society, they exact a most rigid adherence to lines of conduct inevitably fixed by the stern necessities of life in a primitive community. On the frontier men soon learn to conform to what is regarded as essential, for the penalty of resistance or neglect is extinction: there the law of survival works surely and swiftly. However eccentric frontiersmen may appear to the tenderfoot, among themselves there is little variation from type in any essential matter. In the new community, individualism means the ability of the individual to succeed, not by submitting to some external formal authority, still less by following the bent of an unschooled will, but by recognizing and voluntarily adapting himself to necessary conitions. Kansas, it is true, has produced its eccentrics, but there is a saying here that freaks are raised for export only. In one sense the saying is true enough, for what strikes one particularly is that, on the whole, native Kansans are all so much alike. It is a community of great solidarity, and to the native it is "the Easterner" who appears eccentric.

The conquest of the wilderness in Kansas has thus developed qualities of patience, of calm, stoical, good-humored endurance in the face of natural difficulties, of conformity to what is regarded as necessary. Yet the patience, the calmness, the disposition to conform, is strictly confined to what is regarded as in the natural course. If the Kansan appears stolid, it is only on the surface that he is so. The peculiar conditions of origin and history have infused into the character of the people a certain romantic and sentimental element. Beneath the placid surface there is something fermenting which is best left alone — a latent energy which trivial events or a resounding phrase may unexpectedly release. In a recent commencement address, Mr. Henry King said that conditions in early Kansas were "*Hair-triggered.*" Well, Kansans are themselves hair-triggered; slight pressure, if it be of the right sort, sets them off. "Every one is on the *qui vive*, alert, vigilant, like a sentinel at an outpost." This trait finds expression in the romantic devotion of the people to the state, in a certain alert sensitiveness to criticism from outside, above all in the contagious enthusiasm with which they will without warning espouse a cause, especially when symbolized by a striking phrase, and carry it to an issue. Insurgency is native in Kansas, and the political history of the state, like its climate, is replete with surprises that have made it "alternately the reproach and the marvel of mankind." But this apparent instability is only the natural complement of the extreme and confident in-

dividualism of the people: having succeeded in overcoming so
many obstacles that were unavoidable, they do not doubt their
ability to destroy quickly those that seem artificially constructed.
It thus happens that while no people endure the reverses of nature
with greater fortitude and good humor than the people of Kansas,
misfortunes seemingly of man's making arouse in them a veritable
passion of resistance; the mere suspicion of injustice, real or fancied
exploitation by those who fare sumptuously, the pressure of laws
not self-imposed, touch something explosive in their nature that
transforms a calm and practical people into excited revolutionists.
Grasshoppers elicited only a witticism, but the "mortgage fiends"
produced the Populist régime, a kind of religious crusade against
the infidel Money Power. The same spirit was recently exhibited in
the "Boss Busters" movement, which in one summer spread over the
state like a prairie fire and overthrew an established machine supposed to be in control of the railroads. The "Higher Law" is still
a force in Kansas. The spirit which refused to obey "bogus laws"
is still easily stirred. A people which has endured the worst of
nature's tyrannies, and cheerfully submits to tyrannies self-imposed,
is in no mood to suffer hardships that seem remediable.

Idealism must always prevail on the frontier, for the frontier,
whether geographical or intellectual, offers little hope to those who
see things as they are. To venture into the wilderness, one must
see it, not as it is, but as it will be. The frontier, being the possession
of those only who see its future, is the promised land which cannot
be entered save by those who have faith. America, having been
such a promised land, is therefore inhabited by men of faith: idealism is ingrained in the character of its people. But as the frontier in
America has hitherto been geographical and material, American
idealism has necessarily a material basis, and Americans have often
been mistakenly called materialists. True, they seem mainly interested in material things. Too often they represent values in terms of
money: a man is "worth" so much money; a university is a great
university, having the largest endowment of any; a fine building is
a building that cost a million dollars, better still, ten millions. Value
it extensive rather than intensive or intrinsic. America is the best
country because it is the biggest, the wealthiest, the most power-

ful; its people are the best because they are the freest, the most energetic, the *most* educated. But to see a materialistic temper in all this is to mistake the form for the spirit. The American cares for material things because they represent the substance of things hoped for. He cares less for money than for making money: a fortune is valued, not because it represents ease, but because it represents struggle, achievement, progress. The first skyscraper in any town is nothing in itself, but much as an evidence of growth; it is a white stone on the road to the ultimate goal.

Idealism of this sort is an essential ingredient of the Kansas spirit. In few communities is the word "progress" more frequently used, or its meaning less frequently detached from a material basis. It symbolizes the *summum bonum,* having become a kind of dogma. Mistakes are forgiven a man if he is progressive, but to be unprogressive is to be suspect; like Aristotle's nonpolitical animal, the unprogressive is extra-human. This may explain why every Kansan wishes first of all to tell you that he comes from the town of X ——— , and then that it is the finest town in the state. He does not mean that it is strictly the finest town in the state, as will appear if you take the trouble to inquire a little about the country, its soil, its climate, its rainfall, and about the town itself. For it may chance that he is free to admit that it is hot there, that the soil is inclined to bake when there is no rain, that there is rarely any rain — all of which, however, is nothing to the point, because they are soon to have water by irrigation, which is, after all, much better than rainfall. And then he describes the town, which you have no difficulty in picturing vividly: a single street flanked by nondescript wooden shops; at one end a railroad station, at the other a post office; side streets lined with frame houses, painted or not, as the case may be; a schoolhouse somewhere, and a church with a steeple. It is such a town, to all appearances, as you may see by the hundred anywhere in the West — a dreary place which, you think, the world would willingly let die. But your man is enthusiastic; he can talk of nothing but the town of X ——— . The secret of his enthusiasm you at last discover in the inevitable "but it will be a great country some day," and it dawns upon you that, after all, the man does not live in the dreary town of X ——— , but in the great country of *some day.* Such are Kansans. Like St. Augustine, they have their City of

God, the idealized Kansas of some day: it is only necessary to have faith in order to possess it.

I cannot illustrate this aspect of Kansas idealism better than by quoting from Mrs. McCormick's little book of personal experience and observation. Having related the long years of struggle of a typical farmer, she imagines the Goddess of Justice revealing to him a picture of "the land as it shall be" when justice prevails.

John beheld a great plain four hundred miles long and two hundred miles wide — a great agricultural state covered with farmers tilling the soil and with here and there a city or village. On every farm stood a beautiful house handsomely painted outside and elegantly furnished inside, and equipped with all modern conveniences helpful to housekeeping. Brussels carpets covered the floors, upholstered furniture and pianos ornamented the parlors, and the cheerful dining-room had elegant table linen, cut glass, and silverware. Reservoirs carried the water into the houses in the country the same as in the cities. The farmers' wives and daughters, instead of working like slaves without proper utensils or house furnishings, now had everything necessary to lighten work and make home attractive. They had the summer-kitchen, the wash-house, houses for drying clothes, arbors, etc. The door-yards consisted of nicely fenced green lawns, wherein not a pig rooted nor mule browsed on the shrubbery nor hen wallowed in the flower-beds. Shade trees, hammocks, and rustic chairs were scattered about, and everything bespoke comfort. Great barns sheltered the stock. The farms were fenced and subdivided into fields of waving grain and pastures green.

This is what John is supposed to have seen on a summer's day when, at the close of a life of toil, he had just been sold up for debt. What John really saw had perhaps a less feminine coloring; but the picture represents the ideal, if not of an actual Kansas farmer, at least of an actual Kansas woman.

This aspect of American idealism is, however, not peculiar to Kansas: it is more or less characteristic of all Western communities. But there is an element in Kansas idealism that marks it off as a state apart. The origin of Kansas must ever be associated with the struggle against slavery. Of this fact, Kansans are well aware. Kansas is not a community of which it can be said, "Happy is the people without annals." It is a state with a past. It has a history of which its people are proud, and which they insist, as a matter of course, upon having taught in the public schools. There are Old Families in Kansas who know their place and keep it — sacred bearers of the traditions of the Kansas Struggle. The Kansas Struggle is for Kansas what the American Revolution is for New England; and while there is as yet no "Society of the Daughters of the Kansas Struggle," there doubtless will be someday. For the Kansas Struggle is regarded as the crucial point in the achievement of human liberty, very much as Macaulay is said to have regarded the Reform Bill as the end for which all history was only a preparation. For all true Kansans, the border wars of the early years have a perennial interest: they mark the spot where Jones shot Smith, direct the attention of the traveler to the little village of Lecompton, or point with pride to some venerable tree bearing honorable scars dating from the Quantrill raid. Whether John Brown was an assassin or a martyr is a question which only a native can safely venture to answer with confidence. Recently, in a list of questions prepared for the examination of teachers in the schools, there appeared the following: "*What was the Andover Band?*" It seems that very few teachers knew what the Andover Band was; some thought it was an iron band, and some a band of Indians. The newspapers took it up, and it was found that, aside from some of the old families, ignorance of the Andover Band was quite general. When it transpired that the Andover Band had to do with the Kansas Struggle, the humiliation of the people was profound.

The belief that Kansas was founded for a cause distinguishes it, in the eyes of its inhabitants, as pre-eminently the home of freedom. It lifts the history of the state out of the commonplace of ordinary westward migration, and gives to the temper of the people a certain elevated and martial quality. The people of Iowa or Nebraska are well enough, but their history has never brought them in touch with cosmic processes. The Pilgrims themselves are felt to have been actuated by less noble and altruistic motives. The Pilgrims, says Thayer, "fled from oppression, and sought in the new world 'freedom to worship God.'" But the Kansas emigrants migrated "to meet, to resist, and to destroy oppression, in vindication of their principles. These were self-sacrificing emigrants, the others were self-seeking. Justice, though tardy in its work, will yet load with the highest honors the memory of the Kansas pioneers who gave themselves and all they had to the sacred cause of human rights."

This may smack of prejudice, but it is no heresy in Kansas. The trained and disinterested physiocratic historian will tell us that such statements are unsupported by the documents. The documents show, he will say, that the Kansas emigrants, like other emigrants, came for cheap land and in the hope of bettering their condition; the real motive was economic, as all historic motives are; the Kansas emigrant may have thought he was going to Kansas to resist oppression, but in reality he went to take up a farm. At least, that many emigrants thought they came to resist oppression is indisputable. Their descendants still think so. And, after all, perhaps it is important to distinguish those who seek better farms and know they seek nothing else, from those who seek better farms and imagine they are fighting a holy war. When the people of Newtown wished to remove to Connecticut we are told that they advanced three reasons: first, "their want of accommodation for their cattle"; second, "the fruitfulness and commodiousness of Connecticut"; and finally, *"The strong bent of their spirits to remove thither."* In explaining human history perhaps something should be conceded to "the strong bent of their spirits." Unquestionably cattle must be accommodated, but a belief, even if founded on error, is a fact that may sometimes change the current of history. At all events, the people of Kansas believe that their ancestors were engaged in a struggle for noble ends, and the belief, whether true or false, has left its impress upon their character. In Kansas the idealism of the geographical frontier has been strongly flavored with the notion that liberty is something more than a by-product of economic processes.

If Kansas idealism is colored by the humanitarian liberalism of the first half of the last century, it has nevertheless been but slightly influenced by the vague, emotional, Jean Paul romanticism of that time. Of all despondent and mystic elements, the Kansas spirit is singularly free. There are few Byrons in Kansas, and no Don Juans. There is plenty of light there, but little of the "light that never was on land or sea." Kansas idealism is not a force that expends itself in academic contemplation of the unattainable. It is an idealism that is immensely concrete and practical, requiring always some definite object upon which to expend itself, but, once having such an object, expending itself with a restless, nervous energy that is appalling: whatever the object, it is pursued with the enthusiasm, the profound conviction given only to those who have communed with the Absolute. It would seem that preoccupation with the concrete and the practical should develop a keen appreciation of relative values; but in new countries problems of material transformation are so insistent that immediate means acquire the value of ultimate ends. Kansas is a new state, and its inhabitants are so preoccupied with the present, so resolutely detached from the experience of the centuries, that they can compare themselves of today only with themselves of yesterday. The idea embodied in the phrase, "*Weltgeschichte ist das Weltgericht*," has slight significance in a community in which twenty years of rapid material improvement has engendered an unquestioning faith in indefinite progress towards perfectibility. In such a community, past and future appear foreshortened, and the latest new mechanical device brings us an appreciable step nearer the millennium, which seems always to be just over the next hill. By some odd mental alchemy it thus happens that the concrete and the practical have taken on the dignity of the absolute, and the pursuit of a convenience assumes the character of a crusade. Whether it be religion or paving, education or the disposal of garbage that occupies for the moment the focus of attention, the same stirring activity, the same zeal and emotional glow are enlisted: all alike are legitimate objects of conquest, to be measured in terms of their visual and transferable assets, and won by concerted and organized attack. I recall reading in a local Kansas newspaper some time ago a brief comment on the neighboring village of X —— (in which was located a small college mistakenly called a university), which ran somewhat as follows: "The University of X —— has established a music festival on the same plan as the one at the State University, and with most gratifying results. The first festival was altogether a success. X —— is a fine town, one of the best in the state. It has a fine university, and a fine class of people, who have made it a center of culture.

X —— lacks only one thing; it has no sewers." Perhaps there are people who would find the juxtaposition of culture and sewers somewhat bizarre. But to us in Kansas it does not seem so. Culture and sewers are admittedly good things to possess. Well, then, let us pursue them actively and with absolute conviction. Thus may an idealized sewer become an object worthy to stir the moral depths of any right-minded community.

An insistent, practical idealism of his sort, always busily occupied with concrete problems, is likely to prefer ideas cast in formal mold, will be a little at a loss in the midst of flexible play of mind, and look with suspicion upon the emancipated, the critical, and the speculative spirit. It is too sure of itself to be at home with ideas of uncertain pressure. Knowing that it is right, it wishes only to go ahead. Satisfied with certain conventional premises, it hastens on to the obvious conclusion. It thus happens that Americans, for the most part, are complaisantly satisfied with a purely formal interpretation of those resounding words that symbolize for them the ideas upon which their institutions are supposed to rest. In this respect Kansas is truly American. Nowhere is there more loyal devotion to such words as liberty, democracy, equality, education. But preoccupation with the concrete fixes the attention upon the word itself, and upon what is traditionally associated with it. Democracy, for example, is traditionally associated with elections, and many of them. Should you maintain that democracy is not necessarily bound up with any particular institution, that it is in the way of being smothered by the complicated blanket ballot, you will not be understood, or, rather, you will be understood only too well as advocating something aristocratic. Democracy is somehow bound up with a concrete thing, and the move for the shorter ballot is therefore undemocratic and un-American. Or, take the word socialism. Your avowed socialist is received politely, and allowed to depart silently and without regret. But if you tell us of the movement for the governmental control of corporate wealth, we grow enthusiastic. The word socialism has a bad odor in Kansas, but the thing itself, by some other name, smells sweet enough.

If one is interested in getting the essential features of socialism adopted in Kansas, or in America itself, the name to conjure with is indeed not socialism, but equality.

In a country like America, where there is such confident faith in the individual, one might naturally expect to find the completest toleration, and no disposition to use the government for the purpose of enforcing uniform conditions: logically, it would seem, so much emphasis on liberty should be incompatible with much emphasis on equality. Yet it is precisely in America, and nowhere in America more than in the West, that liberty and equality always go coupled and inseparable in popular speech; where the sense of liberty is especially strong, there also the devotion to equality is a cardinal doctrine. Throughout our history, the West has been a dominant factor in urging the extension of the powers of the national government, and Western states have taken the lead in radical legislation of an equalizing character. This apparent inconsistency strikes one as especially pronounced in Kansas. The doctrine of equality is unquestioned there, and that governments exist for the purpose of securing it is the common belief. "A law against it" is the specific for every malady. The welfare of society is thought to be always superior to that of the individual, and yet no one doubts that perfect liberty is the birthright of every man.

Perhaps the truth is that real toleration is a sentiment foreign to the American temper. Toleration is for the skeptical, being the product of much thought or of great indifference, sometimes, to be sure, a mere *modus vivendi* forced upon a heterogeneous society. In America we imagine ourselves liberal-minded because we tolerate what we have ceased to regard as important. We tolerate religions but not irreligion, and diverse political opinion, but not unpolitical opinion, customs but not the negation of custom. The puritans fought for toleration — for themselves. But having won it for themselves, straightway denied it to others. No small part of American history has been a repetition of the puritan struggle; it has been a fight, not for toleration as a general principle, but for recognition of a civilization resting upon particular principles: in exterior relations, a struggle for recognition of America by Europe; in interior relations, a struggle for recognition of "the West" by "the East." The principle of toleration is written in our constitutions, but not in our minds, for the motive back of the famous guarantees of individual liberty has been recognition of particular opinion rather than toleration of every opinion. And in the nature of the case it must be so. Those who create frontiers and establish new civilizations have too much faith to be tolerant, and are too thoroughgoing idealists to be indifferent. On the frontier conditions are too hazardous for the speculative and the academic to flourish readily: only those who are right and are sure of it can succeed. Certainly it is characteristic of Americans to know that they are right. Certainly they are conscious of having a mission in the world and of having been faithful to it. They have solved great problems hitherto unsolved, have realized utopias dreamed of but never realized by Europe. They are therefore in the van of civilization, quite sure of the direction, triumphantly leading the march towards the ultimate goal. That everyone should do as he likes is part of the American creed only in a very limited sense. That it is possible to know what is right, and that what is right should be recognized and adhered to is the more vital belief.

That liberty and equality are compatible terms is, at all events, an unquestioned faith in Kansas. The belief in equality, however, is not so much the belief that all men are equal as the conviction that it is the business of society to establish conditions that will make them so. And this notion, so far from being inconsistent with the pronounced individualism that prevails there, is the natural result of it. In Kansas at least, no one holds to the right of the individual to do as he likes, irrespective of what it is that he likes. Faith in the individual is faith in the particular individual, the true Kansan, who has learned through adversity voluntarily to conform to what is necessary. Human nature, or, at all events, Kansas nature, is essentially good, and if the environment is right all men can measure up to that high level. That the right environment can be created is not doubted. It is not possible for men so aggressive and self-reliant, who have overcome so many obstacles, to doubt their ability to accomplish this also. Having conquered nature, they cheerfully confront the task of transforming human nature. It is precisely because Kansans are such thoroughgoing individualists, so resourceful, so profoundly confident in their own judgments, so emancipated from the past, so accustomed to devising expedients for every new difficulty, that they are unimpressed by the record of the world's failures. They have always thrived on the impossible, and the field of many failures offers a challenge not to be resisted.

To effect these beneficent ends, the people of Kansas turn naturally to the government because they have a very simple and practical idea of what the government is and what it is for. The government, in Kansas, is no abstract concept. It is nothing German, nothing metaphysical. In this frontier community no one has yet thought of the government as of a power not ourselves that makes for evil. Kansans think of the government, as they think of everything else, in terms of the concrete. And why, indeed, should they not? Within the memory of man there was no government in Kansas. They, Kansans, made the government themselves for their own purposes. The government is therefore simply certain men employed by themselves to do certain things; it is the sum of the energy, the good judgment, the resourcefulness of the individuals who originally created it, and who periodically renew it. The government is the individual writ large; in it every Kansan sees himself drawn to larger scale. The passion for controlling all things by law is thus not the turning of the hopeless and discouraged individual to some power other and higher than himself for protection; it is only the instinct to use effectively one of the many resources always at his command for achieving desired ends. Of a government hostile to the individual, they cannot conceive; such a government is a bogus government, and its laws are bogus laws; to resist and overthrow such a government, all the initiative and resourcefulness is enlisted that is devoted to supporting one regarded as legitimate. There is a higher law than the statute book; the law of the state is no law if it does not represent the will of the individual.

To identify the will of the individual with the will of society in this easy fashion presupposes a certain solidarity in the community: an identity of race, custom, habits, needs; a consensus of opinion in respect to morals and politics. Kansas is such a community. Its people are principally American-born, descended from settlers who came mainly from the Middle West. It is an agricultural state, and the conditions of life are, or have been until recently, much the same for all. "Within these pastoral boundaries," says ex-Senator Ingalls, in his best Kansas manner, "there are no millionaires nor any paupers, except such as have been deprived by age, disease, and calamity of the ability to labor. No great fortunes have been brought to the state and none have been accumulated by commerce, manufactures or speculation. No sumptuous mansions nor glittering equipages nor ostentatious display exasperates or allures." And the feeling of solidarity resulting from identity of race and uniformity of custom has been accentuated by the peculiar history of the state. Kansans love each other for the dangers they have passed; a unique experience has created a strong *esprit de corps* — a feeling that while Kansans are different from others, one Kansan is not only as good as any other, but very like any other. The philosophy of numbers, the doctrine of the majority, is therefore ingrained, and little sympathy is wasted on minorities. Rousseau's notion that minorities are only mistaken finds ready acceptance, and the will of the individual is easily identified with the will of society.

And in a sense the doctrine is true enough, for there is little difference of opinion of fundamental questions. In religion there are many creeds and many churches, but the difference between them is regarded as unimportant. There is, however, a quite absolute dogmatism of morality. Baptism is for those who enjoy it, but the moral life is for all. And what constitutes the moral life is well understood: to be honest and pay your debts; to be friendly and charitable, good-humored but not cynical, slow to take offense, but regarding life as profoundly serious; to respect sentiments and harmless prejudices; to revere the conventional great ideas and traditions; to live a sober life and a chaste one — to these they lay hold without questioning. Likewise in politics. One may be Democrat or Republican, stalwart or square-dealer, insurgent or stand-patter: it is no vital matter. But no one dreams of denying democracy, the will of the people, the greatest good to the greatest number, equal justice and equal opportunity to all. Whether in respect to politics or economics, education or morals, the consensus is very nearly perfect: it is an opinion that unites in the deification of the average, that centers in the dogmatism of the general level.

It goes without saying that the general level in Kansas is thought to be exceptionally high. Kansans do not regard themselves as mere Westerners, like Iowans or Nebraskans. Having passed through a superior heat, they are Westerners seven times refined. "It is the quality of piety in Kansas," says Mr. E. H. Abbott, "to thank God that you are not as other men are, beer-drinkers, shiftless, habitual lynchers, or even as these Missourians." The pride is natural enough, perhaps, in men whose judgment has been vindicated at last in the face of general skepticism. Having for many years contributed to the gaiety of nations, Kansas has ceased to be the pariah of the states. Kansans have endured Job's comforters too long not to feel a little complacent when their solemn predictions come to naught. "While envious rivals were jeering . . . pointing with scorn's slow unmoving finger at the droughts, grasshoppers, hot winds, crop failures, and other calamities of Kansas, the world was suddenly startled and dazzled by her collective display of . . . products at the Centennial at Philadelphia, which received the highest awards." It is inevitable that those who think they have fashioned a cornerstone out of the stone rejected by the builders should regard themselves as superior workmen.

To test others by this high standard is an instinctive procedure. There is an alert attention to the quality of those who enter the state from outside. The crucial question is, are they "our kind of men?" Do they speak "the Kansas language?" Yet the Kansas language is less a form of speech, or the expression of particular ideas, than a certain personal quality. Some time since, a distinguished visitor from the East came to the state to deliver a public address. He was most hospitably received, as all visitors are, whether distinguished or otherwise, and his address — permeated with the idealistic liberalism of a half century ago — was attentively listened to and highly praised. But to no purpose all these fine ideas. The great man was found wanting, for there was discovered, among his other impedimenta, a valet. It was a fatal mischance. The poor valet was more commented upon than the address, more observed than his master. The circumstance stamped the misguided man as clearly not our kind of man. Obviously, no man who carries a valet can speak the Kansas language. Needless to say, there are no valets in Kansas.

The feeling of superiority, naturally attaching to a chosen people, equally inclines Kansans to dispense readily with the advice or experience of others. They feel that those who have worn the hair shirt cannot be instructed in asceticism by those who wear silk. In discussing the university and its problems with a member of the state legislature, I once hazarded some comparative statistics showing that a number of other states made rather more liberal appropriations for their universities than the state of Kansas did for hers. I thought the comparison might be enlightening, that the man's pride of state might be touched. Not at all. "I know all about that," he replied. "That argument is used by every man who is interested in larger appropriations for any of the state institutions. But it doesn't go with a Kansas legislature. In Kansas, we don't care much what other states are doing. Kansas always leads, but never follows." And, in fact, the disregard of precedent is almost an article of faith; that a thing has been done before is an indication that it is time to improve upon it. History may teaching that men cannot be legislated into the kingdom of heaven. Kansans are not ignorant of the fact, but it is no concern of theirs. The experience of history is not for men with a mission and faith to perform it. Let the uncertain and the timid profit by history; those who have at all times the courage of their emotions will make history, not repeat it. Kansans set their own standards, and the state becomes, as it were, an experiment station in the field of social science.

The passion for equality in Kansas is thus the complement of the individualism and the idealism of its people. It has as its basis an altruistic motive, aiming not so much to level all men down as to level all men up. The Kansan's sense of individual worth enables him to believe that no one can be better than he is, while his confident idealism encourages him to hope that none need be worse.

The Kansas spirit is the American spirit double-distilled. It is a new grafted product of American individualism, American idealism, American intolerance. Kansas is America in microcosm: as America conceives itself in respect to Europe, so Kansas conceives itself in respect to America. Within its borders, Americanism, pure and undefiled, has a new lease of life. It is the mission of this self-selected people to see to it that it does not perish from off the earth. The light on the altar, however neglected elsewhere, must ever be replenished in Kansas. If this is provincialism, it is the provincialism of faith rather than of the province. The devotion to the state is devotion to an ideal, not to a territory, and men can say "Dear old Kansas!" because the name symbolizes for them what the motto of the state so well expresses, *ad astra per aspera.*

The Business Attitude toward the Spanish–American War

by

JULIUS W. PRATT

[Reprinted by permission from *Expansionists of 1898*, The Johns Hopkins Press (Baltimore, 1936), pp. 232–252.]

In describing aspects of public opinion in the past, the historian, except for our most recent history, is limited to the written record. His method, therefore, differs from that of the analyst of contemporary opinion who has recourse to polls, questionnaires and punch cards processed through IBM machines. These are relatively recent innovations, and although historians have made use of polling data in order to analyze public reactions to such a recent event as World War II,[1] it is impossible for them to go, questionnaire in hand, back into the remote past.

Despite the absence of quantitative data throughout most of our history, a number of historical monographs have been written about aspects of American public opinion. For historians interested in this aspect of research, the ebullient spirit of the American people at the time of the Spanish–American War has provided an attractive field for analysis. Joseph E. Wisan's The Cuban Crisis is a detailed and meticulously-documented account of how events in Cuba between 1895 and 1898 were treated in six New York newspapers. Published in 1934, Wisan's study antedates most of the experimental work in the field of propaganda analysis which was done in the middle and late 1930's. A different kind of approach to the problem of the climate of opinion is Walter Millis's The Martial Spirit, in which the author, drawing upon a variety of sources, gives an impressionistic account of public sentiment preliminary to American entrance into the war. G. W. Auxier has described the propaganda activities of a specific agency, the Cuban Junta, in causing American involvement.[2]

Thus, the historian, relying solely on the written record, can explore the agencies and the machinery of propaganda and (if he has a mind to) the techniques of propagandists. According to Richard Hofstadter, the historian can then push his analysis a step further by venturing into the field of social psychology. "Historians state," declares Hofstadter, "that the war was brought on by sensational newspapers. The press, spurred by the rivalry of Pulitzer and Hearst, aroused sympathy with the Cubans and hatred of Spain and catered to the bellicosity of the public. No one seems to have asked: Why was the public so fatally receptive to war propaganda?" It is Hofstadter's impression that the events of the 1890's brought "frustration and anxiety to civically conscious Americans. . . . I suspect that the readiness of the public to over-react to the Cuban situation can be understood in part through the displacement of feelings of sympathy or social protest generated in domestic affairs; these impulses found a safe and satisfactory discharge in foreign conflict."[3]

As Hofstadter himself admits, it is difficult to develop this conclusion from the evidence. And it is further apparent that while the historian might be able to analyze propaganda and explore its sources, he can only guess or at best estimate roughly its impact. Similarly, it is difficult for Wisan and Auxier to demonstrate convincingly the over-all influence of the specific propaganda media they have explored upon the popular mind and upon national policy. But in pointing to this limitation of the historical method, it should be recognized that the polls are not too helpful in providing this kind of information concerning the current scene even as, from the evidence of the last two presidential elections, they have been shown to be fallible in gauging public feeling.

In the selection reprinted below, Dean Julius W. Pratt, of the University of Buffalo, outstanding authority on American expansionism, explores a relatively narrow but very significant segment of public opinion concerning the Spanish–American War.

SO RELIABLE a scholar as Professor H. U. Faulkner has asserted that "the great cause for the war" with Spain is to be found in the fact that by 1898 the United States was "sufficiently advanced for financial imperialism," implying that the war was fought for markets and fields for investment.* This interpretation was directly contradicted by the late James Ford Rhodes, who declared quite as categorically that "the financial and business interests of the country were opposed to the war." † We may well inquire, therefore, what was, in reality, the attitude of American business both to the war (or to the intervention in Cuba, which brought on the war) and to the question of territorial expansion.‡

We may begin with a generalization. . . . American business, in general, had strongly opposed action that would lead to war with Spain. American business had been either opposed or indifferent to the expansionist philosophy which had arisen since 1890. But almost at the moment when the war began, a large section of American business had, for reasons that will become apparent, been converted to the belief that a program of territorial expansion would serve its purposes. Hence business, in the end, welcomed the "large policy" and exerted its share of pressure for the retention of the Spanish islands and such related policies as the annexation of Hawaii and the construction of an isthmian canal.

One public man to whom the welfare of American business was of so much concern that he may almost be considered its spokesman in the Senate was McKinley's friend, Mark Hanna. No one was more unwilling than he to see the United States drift into war with Spain. To Hanna, in the words of his biographer, "the outbreak of war seemed to imperil the whole policy of domestic economic amelioration which he placed before every other object of political action." § Hanna's attitude appears to have been identical with that of leading businessmen. This conclusion is based not only upon

---

* H. U. Faulkner, *American Economic History*, pp. 624–625.

† J. F. Rhodes, *The McKinley and Roosevelt Administrations*, p. 55.

‡ The discussion which follows is adapted, with slight changes, from the writer's article, "American Business and the Spanish-American War," *Hispanic American Historical Review*, XIV, 163–201.

§ Croly, *Marcus Alonzo Hanna*, p. 278.

the few published biographies of such men,* but also upon the study of a large number of financial and trade periodicals, of the proceedings of chambers of commerce and boards of trade, and of material in the *Miscellaneous Files* of the Department of State, containing numerous letters and petitions from businessmen and organizations.

That business sentiment, especially in the East, was strongly antiwar at the close of 1897, and in the opening months of 1898, is hardly open to doubt. Wall Street stocks turned downward whenever the day's news seemed to presage war and climbed again with information favorable to peace.† Bulls and bears on the market were those who anticipated, respectively, a peaceable and a warlike solution of the Cuban question.‡ The "jingo," in Congress or the press, was an object of intense dislike to the editors of business and financial journals,§ who sought to counteract his influence by antiwar editorials in their columns.‖ Boards of trade and chambers of commerce added their pleas for the maintenance of peace to those

* *Cf.* A. Carnegie, *Autobiography of Andrew Carnegie*, chap. xxviii; B. Alderson, *Andrew Carnegie: The Man and His Work*, pp. 101–102; C. Adler, *Jacob H. Schiff, His Life and Letters*, I, 308–309; J. G. Pyle, *Life of James J. Hill*, II, 77; G. Kennan, *E. H. Harriman*, I, 170; II, 1; H. A. Gibbons, *John Wanamaker*, I, 371–376. Carnegie, Schiff, and Hill were strongly antiwar and anti-imperialist. John Wanamaker supported the war and raised a regiment (which never saw service); there is no evidence in his biography that he was interested in annexations. Harriman's Union Pacific Railroad profited from American operations in the Philippines. It is not hinted that he foresaw this or worked for it. His business relations with the Far East did not begin till 1905. Biographies of Morgan, Rockefeller, Frick, Robert Bacon do not discuss the attitude of those men to the war or imperialism. An apparently contradictory opinion of the attitude of businessmen was expressed by Thomas Beer in *Hanna*, pp. 199–200.

† *Cf. Wall Street Journal*, December 3, 31, 1897; January 25, April 21, 1898; *Railway World*, XLII, 105, 217 (January 29, February 26, 1898).

‡ *Wall Street Journal*, December 31, 1897; February 17, 1898.

§ *Ibid.*, November 18, December 3, 1897; *Railway World*, *loc. cit.*; *Banker and Tradesman*, XXVI (February 23, 1898), 78; *American Banker*, LXIII (March 30, 1898), 528; *Journal of Commerce and Commercial Bulletin*, November 27, 1897; *Commercial and Financial Chronicle*, LXV (October 2, 1897), 597.

‖ *Journal of Commerce and Commercial Bulletin*, February 28, 1898; *Commercial and Financial Chronicle*, April 2, 1898; *Boston Journal of Commerce*, LII (April 16, 1898), 40; *Drugs, Oils and Paints*, XIII (April 1898), 401; *Railway World*, XLII (March 5, 1898), 241–242; *Banker and Tradesman*, *loc. cit.*; *Daily Commercial News and Shipping List*, March 25, 1898.

of the business newspapers and magazines.* So marked, indeed, was the antiwar solidarity of the financial interests,and their spokesmen that the jingoes fell to charging Wall Street with want of patriotism. Wall Street, declared the Sacramento *Evening Bee* (March 11, 1898), was "the colossal and aggregate Benedict Arnold of the Union, and the syndicated Judas Iscariot of humanity." Senator Thurston, of Nebraska, charged that opposition to war was found only among the "money-changers," bringing from the editor of *The American Banker* the reply that "there is not an intelligent, self-respecting and civilized American citizen anywhere who would not prefer to have the existing crisis culminate in peaceful negotiations." †

This antiwar attitude on the part of several leading financial journals continued up to the very beginning of hostilities. The New York *Journal of Commerce and Commercial Bulletin* declared on February 28 that the only possible excuses for war would be (1) a finding by the naval board investigating the "Maine" disaster that the ship had been destroyed by an official act of the Spanish Government; or (2) a refusal by Spain to make reparation if the board should hold that she had failed to exercise due diligence in safeguarding the vessel. Either of these events it held to be almost inconceivable. The *Commercial and Financial Chronicle* expressed the belief on March 12 that the opposition of the financial interests would yet prevent war; and on April 2 the same journal branded as "monstrous" the proposition to settle the Cuban and "Maine" questions by war while the slightest chance remained for a peaceful solution. On April 16, after the House of Representatives had passed the Cuban resolutions, the Boston *Journal of Commerce* declared: "Sober second thought had but little to do with the deliberations. . . . The members were carried off their feet by the war

* Chamber of Commerce of the State of New York, *Fortieth Annual Report, 1897–1898*, p. 127; Boston Chamber of Commerce, *Thirteenth Annual Report, 1898*, pp. 115–116; Baltimore Board of Trade, *Report of President and Directors for Year Ending September 30, 1898*, p. 67; Philadelphia Board of Trade, *Sixty-Sixth Annual Report*, pp. 50–51; Cleveland Chamber of Commerce, *Fiftieth Year*, p. 66; Indianapolis Board of Trade, *Annual Report for Year Ending June 1, 1898*, p. 20. Of the resolutions printed in these reports, some spoke out strongly against war; others merely commended President McKinley's conservative course in seeking a peaceful solution of the Cuban question.

† *American Banker, loc. cit.*

fever that had been so persistently worked up since the Maine explosion. . . ." *

The reasons for this attitude on the part of business are not far to seek. Since the panic of 1893 American business had been in the doldrums. Tendencies toward industrial revival had been checked, first by the Venezuela war scare in December 1895, and again by the free silver menace in 1896.† But in 1897 began a real revival, and before the end of the year signs of prosperity appeared on all sides. The New York *Commercial* conducted a survey of business conditions in a wide variety of trades and industries, from which it concluded that, "after three years of waiting and of false starts, the groundswell of demand has at last begun to rise with a steadiness which leaves little doubt that an era of prosperity has appeared." January 1898, said the same article, is "a supreme moment in the period of transition from depression to comparative prosperity." ‡ This note of optimism one meets at every turn, even in such a careful and conservative sheet as the *Commercial and Financial Chronicle*. As early as July 1897 this paper remarked: "We appear to be on the eve of a revival in business"; and in December after remarking upon the healthy condition of the railroads and the iron industry, it concluded: "In brief, no one can study the industrial conditions of today in America without a feeling of elation. . . ." § The *Wall Street Journal* found only two "blue spots" in the entire country: Boston, which suffered from the depressed demand for cotton goods, and New York, where senseless rate cutting by certain railroads caused uneasiness. "Throughout the west, southwest and on the Pacific coast business has never been better, nor the people more hopeful." ‖ A potent cause for optimism was found in the striking expansion of the American export trade. A volume of exports far in excess of those of any recent year, a favorable balance of trade of $286,-

* *Com. & Fin. Chron.*, LXVI, 641; Boston *Jour. of Com.*, LII, 40.
† G. H. Hull, *Industrial Depressions* . . . *or Iron the Barometer of Trade*, pp. 161–173.
‡ New York *Commercial*, January 3, 1898. The only flaw in the picture was continued depression in the cotton goods industry.
§ *Com. & Fin. Chron.*, LXV (July 24, December 4, 1897), 134, 1046.
‖ *Wall Street Journal*, December 23, 1897.

000,000, and an especially notable increase in exports of manufactures of iron, steel, and copper, convinced practically every business expert that the United States was on the point of capturing the markets of the world. "There is no question," said one journal, "that the world, generally, is looking more and more to the United States as the source of its supply for very many of the staple commodities of life."* Especially elated were spokesmen of the iron and steel industry. Cheaper materials and improved methods were enabling the American producer to undersell his British competitor in Europe and in the British possessions,† and Andrew Carnegie was talking of a great shipbuilding yard near New York to take advantage of these low costs.‡ The *Iron Age*, in an editorial on "The Future of Business," foretold the abolition of the business cycle by means of a better planned economy, consolidation of railroads and industries, reduction of margins of profit, higher wages, and lower prices to consumers.§

To this fair prospect of a great business revival the threat of war was like a specter at the feast. A foreign complication, thought the *Commercial and Financial Chronicle* in October 1897, would quickly mar "the trade prosperity which all are enjoying." Six months later (April 2, 1898), after a discussion of the effect of war rumors on the stock exchange, it declared: ". . . Every influence has been, and even now is, tending strongly towards a term of decided prosperity, and that the Cuban disturbance, and it alone, has arrested the movement and checked enterprise." || The *Banker and Tradesman* saw in the Cuban complication the threat of a "material setback to the prosperous conditions which had just set in after five years of panic and depression." The same journal summarized a calculation made by the Boston *Transcript* showing that in February 1898, the wave of prosperity had carried the average

---

* *Banker and Tradesman*, XXVI (April 20, 1898), 297. Cf. *American Banker*, LXIII (February 2, 1898), 178; *Age of Steel*, LXXXIII (January 1, 1898), No. 1, p. 57; *Rand-McNally Bankers' Monthly*, XV (January 1, 1898), 19; *Statistical Abstract of the U. S.*, 1931, p. 488.

† *Iron Age*, December 9, 1897, p. 22; *Banker and Tradesman, loc. cit.; Railway World*, XLI (August 21, 1897), 837.

‡ *Daily Commercial News and Shipping List*, March 7, 1898.

§ *Iron Age*, December 23, 1897, pp. 19–20.

|| *Com. & Fin. Chron.*, LXV, 597–599; LXVI, 636.

price of twenty-five leading stocks within 5½ points of the high for the preceding ten years and 30 points above the low of 1896, and that the Cuban trouble had, in a little over two months, caused a loss of over ten points, or more than one third of the recent gain.*
"War would impede the march of prosperity and put the country back many years," said the *New Jersey Trade Review*.† The *Railway Age* was of the opinion that the country was coming out of a depression and needed peace to complete its recovery. "From a commercial and mercenary standpoint," it remarked, "it seems peculiarly bitter that this war should have come when the country had already suffered so much and so needed rest and peace."‡

The idea that war could bring any substantial benefits to business was generally scouted. It would endanger our currency stablility, interrupt our trade, and threaten our coasts and our commerce, thought the *Commercial and Financial Chronicle*. It would "incalculably increase the loss to business interests," said the *Banker's Magazine*; while the *United States Investor* held that war was "never beneficial from a material standpoint, that is, in the long run." § The *Railroad Gazette* predicted that war would result in "interruption of business enterprise of every kind, stopping new projects and diminution of the output of existing businesses and contraction of trade everywhere." Railroads would lose more than they would gain. Even arms manufacturers were not all agreed that war would be desirable.‖ Journals speaking for the iron and steel industry also argued that war would injure business. It "would injure the iron and steel makers ten times as much as they would be benefited by the prevailing spurt in the manufacture of small arms, projectiles

* *Banker and Tradesman*, XXVI (April 27, 1898), 326. *Cf. ibid.*, XXVI (March 9, 1898), 130.
† *New Jersey Trade Review*, March 1, 1898.
‡ *Railway Age*, XXV (April 1, 15, 1898), 215, 253.
§ *Com. & Fin. Chron.*, LXVI, (February 12, 1898), 308; *Banker's Magazine*, LVI (March 1898), 358; *U. S. Investor*, IX (April 9, 1898), 529.
‖ *Railroad Gazette*, XXX (April 1, 1898), 236. As to the position of arms and ammunition manufacturers, it is interesting to find a representative of a New York firm engaged in that trade writing to the Secretary of the Interior in March 1898, in behalf of a peaceful settlement in Cuba. M. Hartley to C. N. Bliss, March 16, 17, 1898. *Miscellaneous Letters* (Dept. of State), March 1898, II. Hartley represented Hartley and Graham, of New York, associated with the Union Metallic Cartridge Co. and Remington Arms Co.

and steel plates for war ships," in the opinion of one of these.* The *American Wool and Cotton Reporter* of New York and the *Northwestern Miller* of Minneapolis agreed that war was never materially beneficial in the long run, while trade journals in Atlanta, Chattanooga, and Portland, Oregon, saw as fruits of the approaching conflict only destruction, debt, and depressed industry.†

Many conservative interests feared war for the specific reason that it might derange the currency and even revive the free-silver agitation, which had seemed happily dead. The subsidence of that agitation and the prospect of currency reform were among the hopeful factors at the close of 1897.‡ It was not uncommonly charged that the jingoes were animated in part by the expectation that war would lead to inflation in paper or silver. The New York *Journal of Commerce,* in an editorial on "The Breeding Grounds of Jingoism," had called attention to the fact that the jingoes were generally silverites, including in their number "the financiers who desire to force bankruptcy on the country as a means of breaking down the gold standard," and had quoted with approval an editorial from another paper charging that Senator Morgan's championship of the Cuban insurgents was part of "his wild scheming in the interest of the silver standard." § The *Commercial and Financial Chronicle* endorsed this view, declaring that many of the Cuban agitators "are only interested in the establishment of a free-silver standard, a plan which they think war would advance." || Similar views were expressed by the *American Banker* of New York, the

* *Iron and Steel,* LXXII, No. 15 (April 9, 1898), p. 10. *Cf. Iron Age,* March 17, 1898, p. 21; *Age of Steel,* LXXXIII, No. 10 (March 5, 1898).

† *American Wool and Cotton Reporter,* XII (April 7, 1898), 439; *Weekly Northwestern Miller,* XL (April 29, 1898), 667; *"Dixie,"* A Monthly Journal Devoted to Southern Industrial Interests, XIV, No. 5, (May 1898), pp. 21–23; *Tradesman,* XXXIX (May 1, 1898), 60; Portland (Ore.) *Board of Trade Journal,* XI (May 1898), p. 6.

‡ *Wall Street Journal,* November 18, December 31, 1897.

§ New York *Journal of Commerce and Commercial Bulletin,* May 21, June 5, 1897. A. W. Dunn relates that Senator Pettigrew, of South Dakota, said to him: "... I want a war with Spain, because I believe it will put us on a silver basis." (A. W. Dunn, *From Harrison to Harding,* I, 232.)

|| *Com. & Fin. Chron.,* LXIV, 974; LXVI (May 22, 1897; February 12, 1898), 308. *Cf.* John D. Hicks, *The Populist Revolts,* p. 390: "The voting of bond issues to aid in financing the war drew fire from the Populists, who would have preferred issues of treasury notes, ..."

BUSINESS ATTITUDE TOWARD THE SPANISH-AMERICAN WAR   415

United States Investor of Boston, and the *Rand-McNally Bankers'*
Monthly of Chicago. The last-named, quoted from a speech of Secretary of the Treasury Gage, delivered in Chicago in February
1898, in which he had declared that "it would be scarcely possible
for this nation to engage in war in its present condition . . . without a suspension of specie payments and a resort to further issues of
Government notes." A war of any duration, in the opinion of the
United States Investor, would certainly derange the currency and
reduce business to a gambling basis.*

Something of a freak among New York financial journals was
the *Financial Record*, which, in November 1897, denounced "the
cowardice of our Administration in refusing the phenomenally
brave Cubans the commonest rights of belligerency" as "a disgrace
to the United States," and argued that war with Spain, far from
depressing securities or injuring business, "would vastly increase the
net earning power of every security sold on our market today." †
The mystery of this jingo attitude is explained when we discover
that this journal had been a warm advocate of the free coinage of
silver.

Business opinion in the West, especially in the Mississippi Valley,
appears to have been less opposed to war and less aprehensive of
if results than that of the Atlantic Coast. The Kansas City Board of
Trade, at the beginning of 1897, had urged recognition of Cuban
independence.‡

The Cincinnati Chamber of Commerce, at a meeting on March
29, 1898, adopted "amidst much enthusiasm" resolutions condemning Spain for cruelties to the Cubans and the destruction of the
Maine, and calling for a "firm and vigorous policy which will have
for its purpose — peacefully if we can, but with force if we must —

* *American Banker*, LXII, 912–913; LXIII (May 26, 1897; March 9, 1898),
394; *United States Investor*, IX (March 12, 1898), 368; *Rand-McNally Bank-*
ers' Monthly, XV (April 1898), 294; T. S. Woolsey, in his *America's Foreign*
Policy, pp. 13–14, remarked that currency reform would be impeded by any
unusual complication, such as a war, and added: "This, perhaps, will suggest a
certain subtle connection between Jingoism and the fiat money advocates."
† *The Financial Record, An Investors' Manual*, November 4, 17, 1897.
‡ The proposal of the Kansas City Board of Trade was forwarded with a request for endorsement to the Philadelphia Board of Trade, which rejected it.
(Philadelphia Board of Trade, *Sixty-Fourth Annual Report*, p. 15.)

the redress of past wrongs, and the complete and unqualified independence of Cuba." * The Chicago *Economist* denied that war would seriously hurt business or endanger the gold standard and asserted that the liberation of Cuba, by peace or war, would mean another star of glory for the United States and would produce "results of the highest value to mankind." † The *Rand-McNally Bankers' Monthly*, of the same city, while opposing war, called attention to the fact that while the war scare had demoralized the stock market, "general business activity apparently received an impetus." ‡ Similarly the *Age of Steel* (St. Louis), while much preferring peace, "when not secured at the price of national honor," comforted its readers with the thought that although foreign trade might suffer, home trade and industries would be stimulated by war.§ A St. Louis bank president, Mr. Lackland, believed that war would "cause a boom in many lines of business in this country . . . and give employment to a large number of persons who are now out of work." ‖ The Chattanooga *Tradesman* stated on March 1, 1898, that a "small prospect" of war had already stimulated the iron trade in certain lines and had benefited the railroads by hurrying forward shipments of grain and other commodities in anticipation of war prices.¶ The *Mining and Scientific Press*, of San Francisco, while holding that, in general, war "lets loose havoc and waste, and entails destructive expense," conceded that "to nearly everything related to the mining industry the war will be a stimulus." #

Even in New York, businessmen saw some rays of light piercing the war clouds. Stock-market operators, according to the *Wall Street Journal*, just after the *Maine* explosion, "did not look for any great break in the market, because actual war with Spain

* *Fiftieth Annual Report* of the Cincinnati Chamber of Commerce and Merchant's Exchange, p. 49.

† The *Economist, A Weekly Financial, Commercial and Real-Estate Newspaper*, XIX, 233, 322 (February 26, March 19, 1898).

‡ *Rand-McNally Bankers' Monthly*, XV (March 1898), 199–201.

§ *Age of Steel*, LXXXIII, Nos. 10, 11 (March 5, 12, 1898).

‖ St. Louis *Republic*, March 3, 1898.

¶ The *Tradesman*, XXXIX (March 1, 1898), 58. The same paper, however, in its May issues, denied that any permanent good to business could result from war. *Supra*, p. 241.

Mining and Scientific Press, LXXVI (April 9, 1898), 390. In the issue of April 23, it remarked that war between the two chief copper-producing countries would occasion a boom in that metal. *Ibid.*, p. 438.

would be a very small affair compared with the Venezuela complication with Great Britain." Their expectation was for a drop in stocks at the beginning of hostilities, followed by a resumption of the recent advance. In fact, the first shock might well be followed by a boom.* "The nation looks for peace," declared *Dun's Review*, March 5, "but knows that its sources of prosperity are quite beyond the reach of any attack that is possible." *Bradstreet's* contrasted the jumpiness of Wall Street over war news with "the calm way in which general business interests have regarded the current foreign complications," and *Dun's Review* of March 12 stated that no industry or branch of business showed any restriction, while some had been rapidly gaining, that railroads were increasing their profits while speculators sold their stocks, and that there was a growing demand for the products of all the great industries.†

Despite such expressions as these, there seems little reason to question the belief that an overwhelming preponderance of the vocal business interests of the country strongly desired peace. By the middle of March, however, many organs of business opinion were admitting that a war with Spain might bring no serious disaster, and there was a growing conviction that such a war was inevitable. In the Senate on March 17, Senator Redfield Proctor, of Vermont, described, from his own observation, the terrible sufferings of the Cuban *reconcentrados*. Proctor was supposedly no sensationalist, and his speech carried great weight. The *Wall Street Journal* described its effect among the denizens of the Street. "Senator Proctor's speech," it said, "converted a great many people in Wall Street, who have heretofore taken the ground that the United States had no business to interfere in a revolution on Spanish soil. These men had been among the most prominent in deploring the whole Cuban matter, but there was no question about the accuracy of Senator Proctor's statements and as many of them expressed it, they made the blood boil." ‡ The *American Banker*, hitherto a firm

* *Wall Street Journal*, February 17, 24, 1898.
† *Dun's Review*, March 5, 12, 1898. *Bradstreet's*, XXVI (March 12, 1898), 161. Similar views were expressed by the *Dry Goods Economist*, April 9, 1898.
‡ *Wall Street Journal*, March 19, 1898. It was at this time that W. C. Beer, attempting to estimate the strength of war sentiment for the life insurance companies, noted (in the words of Thomas Beer) "that the solidarity of Wall Street was imperfect. John Jacob Astor wore a buttonhole of red, white, and blue

opponent of intervention, remarked on March 23 that Proctor's speech showed an intolerable state of things, in view of which it could not understand "how any one with a grain of human sympathy within him can dispute the propriety of a policy of intervention, so only that this outraged people might be set free!" It still hoped, however, for a peaceful solution, declaring that the United States ought to urge the Cubans to accept the Spanish offer of autonomy.* That this growing conviction that something must be done about Cuba was by no means equivalent to a desire for war was clearly revealed a few days later. Rumors circulated to the effect that Spain was willing to sell Cuba and that J. P. Morgan's return from a trip abroad was connected with plans to finance the purchase. "There is much satisfaction expressed in Wall Street," said the *Wall Street Journal*, "at the prospects of having Cuba free, because it is believed that this will take one of the most disturbing factors out of the situation. . . . Even if $200,000,000 is the indemnity demanded it is a sum which the United States could well afford to pay to get rid of the trouble." Even $250,000,000, it was thought, would be insignificant in comparison with the probable cost of a war.†

It remains to examine the attitude of certain American businessmen and corporations having an immediate stake in Cuba, or otherwise liable to be directly affected by American intervention. Much American capital, as is well known, was invested in the Cuban sugar industry. Upon this industry the civil war fell with peculiarly devastating effect, not only cutting off profits on capital so invested, but also crippling a valuable carrying trade between Cuba and the United States. Naturally enough, some firms suffering under these conditions desired to see the United States intervene to end the war, though such intervention might lead to war between the United States and Spain. In May 1897, a memorial on the subject bearing over three hundred signatures was presented to John Sherman, Secretary of State. The signers described themselves as "citizens of the United States, doing business as bankers, merchants, manu-

---

flowers. John Gates, Thomas Fortune Ryan, Wm. Rockefeller and Stuyvesant Fish all were sounded before March 24, and were found to be feeling militant." Beer thought the only steady opponents of war were the life insurance people and the small bankers. Thomas Beer, *Hanna*, pp. 199–200.

* *American Banker*, LXIII, 489.

† *Wall Street Journal*, March 31, April 1, 1898.

facturers, steamship owners and agents in the cities of Boston, New York, Philadelphia, Baltimore, Savannah, Charleston, Jacksonville, New Orleans, and other places and also other citizens of the United States, who have been for many years engaged in the export and import trade with the Island of Cuba." They called attention to the serious losses to which their businesses had been subjected by the hostilities in Cuba and expressed the hope that, in order to prevent further loss, to re-establish American commerce, and also to secure "the blessings of peace for one and a half millions of residents of the Island of Cuba now enduring unspeakable distress and suffering," the United States Government might take steps to bring about an honorable reconciliation between the parties to the conflict.*

Another memorial, signed by many of the same subscribers, was presented to President McKinley on February 9, 1898, by a committee of New York businessmen. It asserted that the Cuba war, which had now continued for three entire years, had caused an average loss of $100,000,000 a year, or a total loss of $300,000,00 in the import and export trade between Cuba and the United States, to which were to be added "heavy sums irretrievably lost by the destruction of American properties, or properties supported by American capital in the Island itself, such as sugar factories, railways, tobacco plantations, mines and other industrial enterprises; the loss of the United States in trade and capital by means of this war being probably far greater and more serious than that of all the other parties concerned, not excepting Spain herself."

The sugar crop of 1897–1898, continued the memorial, appeared for the most part lost like its two predecessors, and unless peace could be established before May or June of the current year, the crop of 1898–1899, with all the business dependent upon it, would likewise be lost, since the rainy season of summer and fall would be required "to prepare for next winter's crop, by repairing damaged fields, machinery, lines of railways, &c." In view of the the importance to the United States of the Cuban trade and of American participation "in the ownership or management of Cuban sugar

* *Miscellaneous Letters* (Dept. of State), May, 1897, II. The memorial is covered by a letter from Geo. R. Mosle (of Mosle Bros., 16 Exchange Place, New York) to Hon. John Sherman, May 17, 1897. The list of signers is headed by Lawrence Turnure & Co.; August Belmont & Co. appear near the top.

factories, railways and other enterprises," the petitioners hoped that the President would deem the situation "of sufficient importance as to warrant prompt and efficient measures by our Government, with the sole object of restoring peace . . . and with it restoring to us a most valuable commercial field." *

How much weight such pressure from special interests had with the administration there is no way of knowing. But it is to be noted that the pressure from parties directly interested was not all on one side. Mr. E. F. Atkins, an American citizen who divided his time between Boston and his sugar plantation of Soledad near Cienfuegos, Cuba, which he had developed at a cost of $1,400,000, had been able, through protection received from the Spanish Government and through a corps of guards organized and paid by himself, to continue operations throughout the period of the insurrection. He was frequently in Washington, where he had influential friends, during both the Cleveland and McKinley administrations and worked consistently against the adoption of any measures likely to provoke war.†

Unlike some of the sugar plantations, American-owned iron mines in Cuba continued to do active business despite the insurrection. Three American iron and manganese enterprises in the single province of Santiago claimed to have an investment of some $6,-000,000 of purely American capital, a large proportion of which was in property which could easily be destroyed. "We are fully advised as to our status in case of war," wrote the representative of one company to the Assistant Secretary of State, "and that this property might be subject to confiscation or destruction by the Spanish Government." War between Spain and the United States, wrote the president of another company, "will very likely mean the destruction of our valuable plant and in any event untold loss to our

---

* *Ibid.*, February 1898, I. The memorial was signed by seventy persons or firms from New York and nearby cities; forty from Philadelphia; and sixty-four from Mobile. It was presented to the President on the morning of February 9, 1898, by George R. Mosle, Wm. Moore Carson, and George Turnure, and thereafter, at the President's suggestion, sent to Assistant Secretary Wm. R. Day. See accompanying letter from the committee to Mr. Day.

† E. F. Atkins, *Sixty Years in Cuba*, pp. 209, 212, 274, *et passim.* Atkins's attitude is illustrated by his query (p. 209) "whether the sentimental feeling of sympathy with the Cubans should outweigh the property interests amounting to some $30,000,000 of United States citizens in Cuba."

Company and its American stockholders."* An American cork company with large interests in Spain; a New York merchant with trade in the Mediterranean and Black Sea; a Mobile firm which had chartered a Spanish ship to carry a cargo of timber — these are samples of American business interests which saw in war the threat of direct damage to themselves.† They are hardly offset by the high hopes of an enterprising gentleman of Norfolk, "representing a party of capitalists who are enthusiastic suporters of the Government," who applied to the State Department for a letter of marque "to enable us to lawfully capture Spanish merchant vessels and torpedo boats," adding: "We have secured option on a fine steam vessel, and on receipt of proper documents will put to sea forthwith." ‡

It seems safe to conclude, from the evidence available, that the only important business interests (other than the business of sensational journalism) which clamored for intervention in Cuba were those directly or indirectly concerned in the Cuban sugar industry; that opposed to intervention were the influence of other parties (including at least one prominent sugar planter) whose business would suffer direct injury from war and also the overwhelming preponderance of general business opinion. After the middle of March 1898, some conservative editors came to think intervention inevitable on humanitarian grounds, but many of the most influential business journals opposed it to the end.

* Juragua Iron Co., Ltd. (per Josiah Monroe, Secy. and Treas.) to Day, Philadelphia, April 14, 1898. *Miscellaneous Letters* (Dept. of State), April 1898, II. Spanish-American Iron Co. (per C. F. Rand, Pres.) to Day, New York, April 8, 1898. (*Ibid.*, April, 1898, I.)

† Armstrong Cork Co. to Secretary Sherman, March 8, 1898. *Ibid.*, March 1898, I. John Duer to Department of State (telegram), March 28, 1898; R. H. Clarke (Mobile) to Hon. J. Wheeler, March 26, 1898. *Ibid.*, March 1898, III.

‡ C. R. Fowles to Secretary Alger, April 23, 1898. (*Ibid.*, April, 1898, III.)

The California Progressive

by

GEORGE E. MOWRY

["The California Progressive and His Rationale: A Study in Middle-Class Politics," from the *Mississippi Valley Historical Review*, XXXVI (September 1949), 239–250. Reprinted by permission.]

Charles A. Beard, in An Economic Interpretation of the Constitution *made use of, according to Hofstadter, "the technique of illuminating a historical movement or event through a composite, quantitative account of the economic and social backgrounds of the personnel involved in it." In his celebrated chapter devoted to the economic biographies of the members of the Constitutional Convention, Beard fixed the status of the Founding Fathers and related the adoption of the Constitution to the class structure of early American society. Beard used, in 1913, adds Hofstadter, "a somewhat rudimentary form of the systematic career-line study, which political scientists and sociologists have begun to use only recently and which American historians have hardly used at all."* [1]

The following selection by Professor George E. Mowry, of the University of California, employs this form of presentation in analyzing the California progressive against the background of the structure of California society. Other recent examples of this method include C. Wright Mills, "The American Business Elite: A Collective Portrait"; [2] *David Donald, "Toward a Reconsideration of Abolitionists," in which Donald presented a composite picture of the typical antislavery radical by classifying 106 principal abolitionists according to age, sex, race, place of birth, occupation of parents, education, religion, and political affiliation;* [3] *and Thomas Cochran,* Railroad Leaders 1945–1890. [4]

CONSIDERING the fact that the origins of early twentieth-century progressivism lay in the agrarian Middle West, California in 1905 did not seem to be the logical place for the projection of the doctrines first associated with the names of William J. Bryan, Robert M. La Follette, George W. Norris, and Albert B. Cummins. For in almost every important particular, the state offered more contrasts to the land of William Allen White than it did similarities. As opposed to the relatively homogeneous population of the corn and wheat belt states, there existed in California a veritable welter of first- and second-generation immigrants.* Contrasted with the Middle Western one-farm, one-family type of staple agriculture, the California countryside was characterized by the tremendous holdings of corporations and cattle and lumber men on the one hand, and by the smaller but intensively cultivated fruit and vegetable plats on the other. Irrigation on the latter was but one factor in producing extremely high cost land as well as a high rate of absentee ownership and an itinerant labor force. By 1905 factories in the fields had already made their appearance south of the Tehachapi and in the San Joaquin and lesser valleys of the state.†

By 1910, 60 per cent of California's population was urban, and to make the comparison with the progressive Middle West a little sharper, almost one half of the state's population in the same year lived in the three metropolitan counties of San Francisco, Los Angeles, and Alameda. Moreover, throughout these urban districts organized labor was on the move as it was in few other places in the nation. After the general strike of 1901, San Francisco was often called "the most closed shop city in the country." And while Harrison Gray Otis and the Los Angeles Merchants and Manufacturers Association had managed to preserve an open-shop town, organized labor never gave up its fight to break through this anti-union domination. In fact, one of the two basic state-wide conflicts in California from 1905 to 1916 was the continuous and often bloody struggle between organized capital and organized labor.

---

* *Thirteenth Census of the United States,* 11 vols. and abstracts (Washington, 1913), *Population,* II, 157–158.

† California Commission of Immigration and Housing, *Annual Report* (Sacramento, 1916), 325–326. See also California State Tax Commission, *Annual Report* (Sacramento, 1917), 278.

The second great state-wide clash of interests in California during these years was the one between the Southern Pacific Railroad and the state's farmers, shippers, merchants, and the ratepaying public. Until Hiram Johnson's victory in 1910, the one constant and almost omnipotent factor in California politics was the railroad. So deep were the tentacles of the "Octopus" sunk into the commonwealth that its agents even selected the receiving surgeons of city hospitals to insure favorable medical evidence whenever accidents occurred on the company's property. * During the years before 1910, numerous economic and political groups had fought the railroad. But through its own powerful political machine, through extensive nonpartisan corruption, and through careful nurture of the state's widespread gambling, liquor, and vice interests, the Southern Pacific weathered every popular storm. Until 1910 its rule was disputed only in a few local communities and in San Francisco.

In the Paris of the West, as San Francisco proudly styled itself, the Union Labor party ruled from 1901 to 1911. But far from contributing to honest, efficient, and responsible government, the Union Labor machine, under the able but cancerously corrupt Abraham Ruef, turned out to be a partner in pelf with the railroad. Often for a cash consideration Ruef's "pack of hounds" supplied the votes for the continuing control of the Southern Pacific. The only other force in the state, with the exception of the rising progressives, capable of voicing much protest was the Socialist Party. At the crest of their power in 1911, the California Socialists elected a mayor of Berkeley and came within an eyelash of winning control of the city of Los Angeles.† But for one reason or another the Socialists were never able to summon up the strength to win a major victory, and it remained for the progressives alone to challenge the Southern Pacific machine.

Just what was a California progressive before he took office in 1910 and before power and the exigencies of politics altered his beliefs? What were his springs of action, his personal aspirations, and his concepts of what constituted the good society? The rest of

* Frederick L. Bird and Francis M. Ryan, *The Recall of Public Officers* (New York, 1930), p. 23.
† See the Los Angeles *Express*, November 1 – December 6, 1911, for details of the Socialist campaign in Los Angeles.

this paper is devoted to an attempt to answer these questions in the hope that it may shed some light on the origins of progressivism, not only in California but in the rest of the nation as well, and perhaps even direct a few faint rays on the class structuring of American politics before 1917.

Fortunately, the men who first organized the California progressive movement were both literate and historically minded. The nine solid collections of personal manuscripts they so considerately left behind them, * the diaries, documents, and innumerable published articles, afford the historian perhaps an unrivaled opportunity in recent American history to inquire into the origins of a grass-roots movement. Moreover, this group was small. Fewer than a hundred men attended the two state-wide Progressive Conferences† in 1907 and 1909 before victory swelled the number of the organization's would-be leaders. Of this number, the author has been able to discover biographical data on forty-seven men, which produces in total a striking picture of similarity in background, economic base, and social attitudes. Compositely, the California progressive was a young man often less than forty years old.‡ A majority of them was

* Perhaps the most significant collection of manuscripts for the study of California progressivism are the Meyer Lissner Papers in the Borel Collection, Stanford University. Less rewarding, but still important, are the papers of John D. Works, John C. Needham, and Rufus L. Green, also in the Borel Collection. A more significant collection of the John D. Works manuscripts is to be found in the Bancroft Library, University of California, Berkeley. There also are the letters of Dr. George C. Pardee, William R. Davis, and a small but important collection of the letters of Lincoln Steffens, most of which were written to Francis J. Heney. Of major importance are the letters of Chester H. Rowell, a portion of which are now deposited in the Bancroft Library at Berkeley, and the William Kent Papers in the Yale University Library, New Haven. The voluminous Franklin Hichborn manuscripts and those of Dr. John Randolph Haynes are preserved in the John Randolph and Dora Haynes Foundation, Los Angeles, California. Edward A. Dickson and Marshall Stimson, both of Los Angeles, have preserved many of their own letters of the period, and both are more than generous in aiding the historian in his quest. The Hiram Johnson manuscripts are not yet open for inspection.

† The two meetings of the Lincoln Roosevelt Republican League were held in Oakland.

‡ In 1910 the average age of ten of the most prominent progressives was thirty-eight. These and the following figures were taken from biographical data found in the standard reference works, including Who's Who in California (San Francisco, 1929), in county histories, and in newspapers.

born in the Middle West, principally in Indiana, Illinois, Wisconsin, and Iowa. A good minority was native to the state.* Almost all carried North European names and many of them, with two notable exceptions, were of old American stock.

The long religious hand of New England rested heavily upon California progressivism as it has on so many American movements. Of the twenty-two progressives indicating a religious affiliation in their biographies, seven were Congregationalists, two were Unitarians, and four were Christian Scientists.† Three of every four had a college education, and three of the group had studied in European universities. Occupationally, the California progressive held a significant niche in the American economic structure. In the sample obtained, there were seventeen attorneys, fourteen journalists, eleven independent businessmen and real-estate operators, three doctors, and three bankers. At least one half of the journalists owned their own papers or worked for a family enterprise, and the lawyers, with two exceptions, were not practicing politicians.‡ In the entire group apparently only two had any connection with a large industrial or financial corporation save for the ownership of shares. Obviously this was a group of traditional small independent free enterprisers and professional men.

While not wealthy, the average California progressive was, in the jargon of his day, "well fixed." He was more often than not a Mason, and almost invariably a member of his town's chamber of commerce. Finally, by all available evidence he usually had been, at least until 1900, a conservative Republican, satisfied with William McKinley and his Republican predecessors.§

Naturally, some fundamental questions arise about these fortunate sons of the upper middle class. Inheriting a secure place in society, earning a reasonably good living and certainly not radical by temperament, what prompted their political revolt and what

---

* Of the forty-six available places of birth, twenty-four were in the Middle West and seventeen in California.

† Five Catholics, three Methodists, and one Lutheran made up the total twenty-two.

‡ The total is more than the original forty-seven because some men listed two occupations. Many of the others, of course, speculated in real estate.

§ Like William McKinley, many conservative California Republicans had been for free silver until Marcus A. Hanna spoke.

THE CALIFORNIA PROGRESSIVE 427

did they want? The answer to the first of these questions, of course,
is clear. The California progressive reacted politically when he felt
himself and his group being hemmed in and his place in society
threatened by the monopolistic corporation on one side and organized labor and socialism on the other. Proof for this general conclusion is not hard to find. The earliest manifestation of what later
became progressivism in California is apparent in two local movements starting in 1906, one aimed against the Southern Pacific political machine in Los Angeles and the other against the control of the
Union Labor party in San Francisco. From that time until victory
in 1910, the progressive literature was full of criticism for both politically organized capital and politically organized labor.*

The adverb "politically" in the last paragraph is important, for the
progressive revolt was not alone a matter of economics. It might be
pointed out that progressivism arose in an extremely prosperous period in California, and that the men who really organized the movement were not employers of any significance. In addition, far from
beggaring these lawyers, journalists, and real-estate operators, a
good case can be made out that the Southern Pacific Railroad actually befriended many of them economically. Moreover, the
California progressives never attacked the corporate form of business organization or the labor union as such. And although they
believed that the closed shop was "antisocial, dangerous and intrinsi-
cally wrong," many of them repeatedly went to the union's defense
when industry organized to break the unions and create open shops.†

"Modern politics," Henry Adams wrote in his *Education*, "is a
struggle not of men but of forces. The men become every year more
and more creatures of force massed about central power houses."
With the struggle for power between capital and labor penetrating
to almost every level of California life in the period, and with the
individual more and more ignored, the California progressive was
increasingly sensitive to that drift and increasingly determined to

---

* See, for example, the speech of Marshall Stimson which launched the pro-
gressive campaign in Los Angeles in the spring of 1906. Preserved in Dr. John R.
Haynes, Personal Clippings, John Randolph and Dora Haynes Foundation, Los
Angeles.

† Fresno *Morning Republican*, August 23, 1911; San Francisco *Labor Clarion*,
April 25, 1905; Commission on Industrial Relations, *Report*, Senate Document
No. 415, 64 Cong., 1 Sess., V, 4868.

stop it if possible. This was obvious in the progressive obsession with the nightmare of class-consciousness and class-rule. "Class government is always bad government," the progressive Los Angeles *Express* vehemently declared as it exclaimed that "unions had no more right to usurp the management of public affairs than had the public service corporations." * Chester Rowell, probably the most intelligent of the California progressives, went on to gloss that statement. "Class prejudice among the business men," he wrote, "excuses bribery and sanctifies lawlessness and disorder among labor. When the specter of class rule is raised, then all questions of truth, right, and policy disappear, and the contest is no longer over what shall be the government but wholly who shall be it." This class spirit on both sides, the editor of the Fresno *Republican* lamented, "is destroying American liberty." When it became predominant he predicted American institutions would have to be changed. "For upon that evil day reform ends and nothing but revolution is possible." †

Clearly what troubled these independent progressives about both organized capital and labor was not alone a matter of economics but included questions of high politics, as well as group prestige, group morality, and group power. Involved also was the rising threat to an old American way of life which they represented and which they enthusiastically considered good.

The progressives were members of an old group in American. Whether businessmen, successful farmers, professional people, or politicians, they had engaged in extremely individualistic pursuits and had since the decline of the colonial aristocracy supplied most of the nation's intellectual, moral, and political leadership. Still confident that they possessed most of society's virtues, the California progressives were acutely aware in 1905 that many of society's rewards and badges of merit were going elsewhere. Although finely educated, they were all but excluded from politics unless they accepted either corporate or labor domination, a thing they were exceedingly loath to do. Their church, their personal morality, and their concept of law, they felt, were demeaned by the crude power struggle between capital and labor. Before the days of the Rotarians and kindred organizations, they were excluded from, or did not care

* Los Angeles *Express*, July 31, 1907.
† Fresno *Republican*, March 10, 1907.

to participate in, either the Union League Club or the union labor hall.

On the defensive for the first time since the disappearance of the old aristocracy, this class of supreme individualists rationally enough developed a group-consciousness themselves. Although generally overlooked by the historian, this consciousness had already evolved among some farming elements in the Populist period. Nothing else can be concluded from the words of the official organ of the Michigan State Farmers' Alliance. "It has been truly said," remarked that paper, "that the People's Party is the logical and only nucleus for every element of the American population that stands for social stability and constitutional rights. It is the bulwark against anarchy of the upper and lower scum of society." * Now in the twentieth century, flanked by organized labor on the one side and organized capital on the other, the urban California progressives took up that song. Their letters, journals, and speeches are full of the phrases, "Our crowd," "the better element," and "the good people of the state." Even their political enemies recognized their separateness as indicated by the names they conferred upon them. The phrases "Googoo" and "Our Set" dripped with ridicule. But they also indicated an awareness of the progressives' claim to ethical and political superiority. Finally, no clearer expression of the progressives' self-confidence in their own moral elevation and their contempt for the classes above and below them can be found than that in an editorial of their state-wide organ, the *California Weekly*. "Nearly all the problems which vex society," this illuminating item ran, "have their sources above or below the middle-class man. From above come the problems of predatory wealth. . . . From below come the problems of poverty and of pigheaded and brutish criminality." † Despite the fact that it was made up of extremely individualistic elements, this was unmistakably an expression of a social group on the march.

The California progressive, then, was militantly opposed to class control and class-consciousness when it emanated from either be-

* Jackson (Mich.) *Industrial News*, March 8, 1894, cited in Seymour Lutzky, "Survey of the Conflict of Labor, Progressive and Radical Newspapers, 1890–1896" (M.A. Thesis, State University of Iowa, 1948), p. 90.
† *California Weekly* (San Francisco), I (December 18, 1908), p. 51.

low or above him. This was his point of opposition. What was his positive creed? In the first place this "rank individualist," as he gladly styled himself, was in most cases an extremely religious man. His mind was freighted with problems of morality, his talk shot full of Biblical allusions. He often thought of the political movement he had started as a part of the "Religion Forward Movement." * As early as 1903 Arthur J. Pillsbury, who was later to become a leading progressive, praised Theodore Roosevelt for coming nearer "to exemplifying the New England conscience in government than any other President in recent times." †

But if the religion of the California progressive was old American in its form, much of its content was a product of his recent past. Gone was the stern God of the puritan, the abiding sense of tragedy, and the inherent evilness of man. As William Allen White later wrote, the cult of the hour was "to believe in the essential nobility of man and the wisdom of God." ‡ With an Emersonian optimism, the California progressive believed that evil perished and good would triumph. Under the influence of Darwinism, the rising social sciences, and a seemingly benign world, the progressive had traded some of his old mystical religion for a new social faith. He was aware that evil still existed, but it was a man-made thing and upon earth. And what man created he could also destroy. For the then present sinful condition of man was the result of his conditioning. As Fremont Older's San Francisco *Bulletin* editorialized, "the basic idea behind this age of liberalism is the simple one that all men, prisoners and free, rich and poor are basically alike in spirit. The difference usually lies in what happens to them." § And from that, one could conclude that when all men were given justice most of them would return justice to society. The progressive, then, not only wanted to abolish a supernatural hell; he was intent upon secularizing heaven.

There were, of course, individual variations from these generalizations. Chester Rowell, for one, while agreeing that men should not be treated as free moral agents, protested against considering them as "mere creatures of environment." "If we try to cure the trouble by

* San Francisco *Bulletin*, March 2, 1912.
† Oakland *Herald*, August 21, 1903.
‡ Introduction to Fremont Older, *My Own Story* (New York, 1926), 9.
§ San Francisco *Bulletin*, May 11, 1914.

curing the environment," Rowell argued, "we shall never go far enough, for however much we protect men from temptation there will be some left and men will fall to that. . . . Dealing with society the task is to amend the system. But dealing with the individual man the task is to reiterate forever, 'thou shall not steal' and tolerate no exceptions." * But Rowell was more of a child of his age than even he himself realized. Despite his strictures on the sinfulness of man, one found him writing later that William H. Taft's peace treaties made international war impossible because "the moral influence on nations (for peace) would be tantamount to compulsion." †

"The way to have a golden age," one progressive novelist wrote, "is to elect it by an Australian ballot." This was an extreme affirmation of democracy, but it followed logically from the progressive belief in the fundamental goodness of the individual. For according to progressive thought, behind every political question was a moral question whose answer "could safely be sought in the moral law." ‡ Since all men were moral agents, then public opinion was the final distillate of moral law. "It was a jury that can not be fixed," according to Lincoln Steffens, and indeed to some progressives, "God moving among men." § Thus Charles D. Willard objected to Theodore Roosevelt's characterization of democracy as just a means to an end. To Willard democracy was a positive moral force in operation, a good in itself. "It is," he wrote, "a soul-satisfying thing." ||

Back in the 1890's Senator John J. Ingalls of Kansas had remarked that "the purification of politics is an iridescent dream." Dream or not, that was one of the major goals of the California progressive a decade later. There was but one law for him — that of the church-going middle class — and he was convinced that it should be applied equally to the home, to government, and occasionally even to business. It was in this spirit that Hiram Johnson admonished his followers to forget how to make men richer and concentrate on how to make them better.¶ This attitude helps to explain much of the

* Chester Rowell to Lincoln Steffens, August 1, 1908, Lincoln Steffens Papers.
† Fresno *Republican*, May 18, 1911.
‡ *Ibid.*, May 21, 1909.
§ Steffens to Francis J. Heney, June 1, 1908, Steffens Papers.
|| Charles D. Willard to Theodore Roosevelt, [?], 1911, Theodore Roosevelt Manuscripts (Division of Manuscripts, Library of Congress).
¶ San Francisco *Bulletin*, August 12, 1912.

progressive interest in sumptuary legislation. Individualism was a sacred thing as long as it was moral individualism; otherwise it needed to be corrected. Thus the progressive proposals for the abolition of prize fighting, "a form of social debauchery," gambling, slang, "since it is a coverup for profanity," prostitution, and the liquor traffic. And thus their demands for the censorship of literature, the drama, and social dancing.

In protest against these "holier than thou people" among his fellow progressives, Charles J. McClatchey, owner of the Sacramento *Bee*, wrote that he was his "brother's keeper only in so far as I should set him a good example." * And though most progressives vehemently denied the full import of this statement when applied to morality, the majority of them was not in complete disagreement with McClatchey's views when they were applied to economics. Good Christian as he was, and on the whole benevolent, the California progressive did not quarrel with the doctrine of wardship provided it was not pushed too far. Thus he stood ready in 1910 to protect obviously handicapped individuals. And he was ready and even eager to eradicate what he called "special privilege," which to his mind was the fundamental factor in limiting opportunity for the man on the bottom to make his way economically upward. A few individuals on the left of the movement, like Congressman William Kent, felt that soon "property rights were going to tumble about the heads of the men who had built themselves pyramids of money in a desert of want and suffering." † And Older raised the disturbing question of why men should be paid fortunes who had been lucky enough to be born with brains or in fortunate environments. One might as well go back to the feudal system, Older answered himself, because there was no more personal merit "in having talent than in having a noble lineage." ‡ But for the most part, the progressive majority was content with the basic concepts of the economic system under which 1910 American capitalism awarded its profits and pains.

What the progressive did object to in the year of his triumph was

* Charles J. McClatchey to Franklin Hichborn, December 25, 1915, Franklin Hichborn Papers.
† San Francisco *Bulletin*, September 8, 1911.
‡ *Ibid.*, April 17, 1909.

not 1910 capitalism as such but rather the ideological, moral, and political manifestations arising from that system. He was confident, at least in 1910, that there was not an inevitable causal relation between them. And he felt confident that he could cure these ills of society through the political method and through preaching and legislating morality.

The California progressive, then, wanted to preserve the fundamental pattern of twentieth-century industrial society at the same time he sought to blot out the rising clash of economic groups, and for that matter, the groups themselves as conscious economic and political entities. But he sought to do all this, at least before he had actually taken power, without profound economic reform. "The people," Rowell wrote sometime after the sweeping progressive victory in 1910, "elected Governor Johnson to get moral and political reform." The word "economic" was significantly absent from the statement.*

From today's dark vantage point, the progressive aim of a capitalist commonwealth —

Where none were for a class and all were for the state,
Where the rich man helped the poor and the poor man loved the great,

— may seem incredibly naïve. His stress on individualism in a maturing industrial economy was perhaps basically archaic. His refusal or inability to see the connection between the economic institutions and the rising class-consciousness indicated a severe case of social myopia. His hopes to avert class strife by political and moral reform alone were scarcely realistic. And paradoxical in extreme was his antipathy to the class-consciousness of organized capital and labor without his being aware of his own intense group loyalties.

When the California progressives confidently took control of the state in 1910, the road ahead was uncertain indeed. What, for example, would happen to the fundamental beliefs of this group if they found their ends could not be achieved without substantial economic reform, or, if in spite of their efforts, labor through one program or another threatened their economic and political estate, or if many of them became economically and psychologically ab-

* Fresno *Republican*, August 14, 1911.

sorbed by the advancing corporate system, or again in a less prosperous age than 1910, if the clash between economic groups for a livelihood created an intense social friction? Would their moral calculus, their spirit of benevolence, their faith in men, and their reverence for democracy still persist? The answers to these questions, of course, lay beyond 1910 and belong to another story, another chapter.

But the composite California progressive in 1910 was perhaps the best his economic and social group produced. He was educated, intelligent, able. A man of unquestioned sincerity and public integrity, he was also benevolently aware of the underprivileged groups around him. Devoted to the extension of political democracy and civil rights, he stood as a worthy representative of that long historical lineage of Americans who had dreamed and worked for a better commonwealth. If such a small group is ever able to amend or to alter a little the drift of society, the California progressive's chances seemed better than an even bet.

How We Got into World War I

by

WALTER MILLIS

["How We Entered the Last One," from *The New Republic*,
July 31, 1935. Reprinted by permission.]

To John Bach McMaster, writing in 1918, the explanation of
American intervention in the First World War was relatively simple.
A follower of Wilson, McMaster believed our entrance into the war
was both motivated and justified in the light of Germany's waging
unrestricted submarine warfare, which the historian considered to
be both inhumane and illegal.[1]

By the mid-1920's, however, this point of view which reflected
faithfully Wilsonian idealism, was engulfed in a wave of post-war
disillusionment. Harry Elmer Barnes's Genesis of the World War
(1926) contrasted our tolerant attitude towards illegal seizures by
the British of American shipping with our intolerance of German
submarine warfare. He concluded that our condoning of the actions
of the British was indicative of over-all sympathy with the allied
cause. Three years later, C. Hartley Gratton, who had been a student of Barnes's, attributed American involvement to our economic
ties to the entente cause, propaganda, and inept statesmanship.
Under the circumstances, argued Grattan, the Germans had no
alternative but to resort to the submarine.[2]

Charles Seymour, in 1934, affirmed the thesis that Germany's use
of the submarine was the reason for our intervening, documenting
this point of view from some of the unpublished papers of Wilson's
adviser, Colonel House, and from what survivors of the intervention
crisis told him. The following year, Walter Millis's The Road to War
was less analytical of why we fought than the selection reprinted,
here, but as a background account the book is very valuable.

Shortly before The Road to War *was published, a congressional committee headed by Gerald Nye began a sensational inquiry into the economic pressures which, allegedly, had involved us in war.*[3] *In the depression, bankers and businessmen were none too popular and the Nye comittee, encouraged by liberal and radical opionion, had a ready-made scapegoat in banker, businessman, and munition-maker who were portrayed as maneuvering insidiously behind the scenes in order to bring about our intervention.*

This kind of thinking was assailed by Charles A. Beard in The Devil Theory of War.[4] *Beard attacked the single cause theory of our involvement, advanced by Nye on the economic level and by Seymour in terms of submarine warfare. And yet, a careful reading of Beard's book reveals him as less an advocate of multiple causation than the author pretends. The book has a kind of backstairs argument which places heavy stress upon the Wilson loan policy as bringing about our involvement.*

Mainly as a consequence of the Nye committee findings, Congress enacted neutrality legislation to prevent a recurrence of a pattern of events that, the legislators felt, had brought the nation into World War I. Coincidentally, Edwin Borchard and W. P. Lage argued that American intervention was the consequence of Wilson's failure to adhere steadfastly to the laws of neutrality. Borchard and Lage placed great stress upon the "blundering" of Wilson and his aides, reflecting in their work not only the impact of newspaper headlines but also the growing recognition by historians of leadership influences in history.[5] *Similarly, such books as James D. Squires's* British Propaganda at Home and in the United States (1935) *was expressive of the historian's interest in propagandist influences.*

By 1938 with the publication of Charles Tansill's America Goes to War, *it is apparent that the American historian in dealing with our entrance into World War I had come full-cycle. Two decades earlier, McMaster, in the spirit of Wilsonian idealism, had written of our participation in World War I as brought about mainly by German inhumanity finding expression in unrestricted submarine warfare. Tansill saw no single cause but rather a multiplicity of causes leading to our involvement — a thesis which found expression in a volume that reflected so little of the spirit of Wilsonian idealism as to conclude that American involvement in World War II was a greater evil than the German victory that might have eventuated had we not gone in.*

Thus, the round of interpretation from McMaster to Tansill was complete as Hitler's armies marched into Poland and World War II began. And, as we shall see further on, historians were no more agreed in their view of the reasons for, or the wisdom of, our going into World War II than they were of our relationship to the earlier conflict. At least two historians, Harry Elmer Barnes and Charles Tansill, are in the thick of the revisionist movement in American historiography having to do with World War II, even as they were in the vanguard of World War I revisionism.[6]

Walter Millis is military commentator of the Herald Tribune.

THE CURRENT debate upon the question of how the United States is to avoid entanglement in the next war should naturally begin with the problem of how, in fact, we got into the last one. In confronting the future, the first guide is the experience of the past. As such, the experience of 1914–1917 has the defects of most historical experience. It is confused and baffling in the extreme. The deceptive simplicity of the facts conceals a matted jungle of motives, of conflicting economic and psychological influences, of unstated assumptions as to the proper bases of national action or the nature of the social process. Even to traverse this jungle to any purpose it is necessary first to agree upon certain fixed-datum points, concerning which there is today no agreement; to establish the "cause" of the American declaration of war in April 1917, one must solve an equation in innumerable variables, although there is as yet no consensus as to the values that should properly be attached to any of them.

It is not difficult to describe what happened. When the European complex exploded in August 1914, the shock to the American economy was almost as violent as that to the American emotions. The situation was in both respects something with which American opinion and American statesmanship were utterly unprepared to deal. The government issued its formal proclamation of neutrality and consigned the problems of our practical relationship with the warring powers to the uncertain and contradictory principles of international law. The more influential and more vocal elements of public opinion took refuge in an attitude of hostility towards the Central Powers — as reactionary, autocratic governments that had willed the war in the hope of achieving world hegemony — and of sympathy for the Entente as the defenders of ideals and political institutions similar to our own against a brutal and unwarranted aggression. If the government, however, was willing to leave the future to international law, this majority opinion was no less willing to leave it to the Allies. There were very few, in or out of the government, who either grasped the possibility that the United States might be involuntarily entangled or saw any reasons of national interest that might compel us to become a participant. The United States proposed to take up the role of interested spectator.

Immediately, however, as one writer has recently put it, "the truism that the world is economically interdependent became grimly apparent." It did not appear, it is important to note, in the form of a question as to whether the United States should retreat into a prudent isolation until the storm had passed. We found ourselves isolated with a devastating abruptness. European selling forced the New York Stock Exchange to close on July 31, 1914, and it dared not reopen until December. Practically the whole of our trans-Atlantic commerce came to a standstill; and if the two belligerents had been equally able to interfere with each other's trade, we might have found ourselves cut off for an indefinite time from all our more important foreign markets. Germany's geographical disadvantage and the overwhelming superiority of the British navy combined to prevent this; the seas were soon reopened, but not to commerce with the Central Powers. Cotton, one of our two great export crops, of which Germany was a heavy taker, could not be sold, and the South was brought to the verge of ruin. At the same time, the normal trade with the Entente countries was, of course, seriously dislocated; and the late summer and fall of 1914 saw our already somewhat depressed economy sinking towards prostration.

The first economic problem presented by the war, consequently, was not one of eschewing the excess profits of death; it was one of regaining some of the ordinary profits of peace. The unemployed, who were filling the streets in the latter part of 1914, had to be provided for no less than the stockholders. Two methods presented themselves. The State Department devoted itself to reopening, so far as possible, the normal channels of trade with the civil population of the Central Powers. The businessmen, and subsequently the bankers, turned with a greater realism to develop from the war needs of the Entente a substitute for the markets of which they had been deprived in Germany and Austria.

The State Department's attempt to obtain the adoption of the Declaration of London was essentially an attempt to confine the savage violence of the European War within the gentlemanly limits which the Great Powers had in the past been able to impose upon such private quarrels as that between Russia and Japan in 1904. While the armies fought, the normal business of the world would be conducted as usual. The attempt promptly failed, partly because our diplomatists had no conception of the pressures they would have had to apply if it was to succeed; but the department continued to work to the same end by insisting upon strict construction of the elaborate precedents concerning blockade and contraband, which are supposed to establish the rights of neutrals in time of war. It was continuously baffled, both by the elusive and frequently inapplicable nature of the precedents and by the practical fact that the British navy possessed the physical power to enforce its own interpretation of them.

Upon this solid basis of sea power, the Allies had, by the beginning of 1915, erected an intricate structure of controls over American foreign commerce. It amounted to a practically complete blockade of our direct trade to and from the Central Powers and a hardly less complete interdiction upon trade by way of the European neutrals. Many of these controls were indirect, maintained by threats and promises rather than by official action, and policed by the "voluntary" undertakings of American businessmen themselves. It is difficult to say that any of the main features of this system were flatly "illegal," although the British were hard put to it to defend a number of important details from the bitter protests launched against them by the State Department. Whether the controls were legal or illegal, however, it is possible that the United States could have compelled their relaxation had it applied economic pressure or the threat of war; it is certain that, given the preponderant naval power of the Entente, it could have kept the seas more or less open in no other way.

Such pressures, however, were never seriously applied. Here was the first important consequence of the fact that the majority sentiment of the country had not actually been neutral from the outbreak of the war. The President, his more influential advisers, all the important people in the foreign service (except Secretary Bryan), shared the hostility toward Germany and the sympathy for the Entente that filled every leading newspaper and the after-dinner speeches of most public figures. These sentiments were now being powerfully reinforced by the Entente propaganda; they were likewise being reinforced in another way. American business had turned to solve the problems of war depression by seeking war markets in the Entente. By the end of 1914 it was beginning to find them. The United States started out to supply the Entente because the Entente markets alone were open and because the United States badly needed business. But as the war demand rapidly developed (after the end of the 1914 campaign had revealed to the belligerents the colossal material requirements of the new warfare), it began to be realized that the United States had stumbled upon a gold mine. The Allies' power to offer or withhold these stupendous contracts became one of their most useful instruments in organizing American enterprise to enforce the boycott of Germany while serving the needs of the Entente. The contracts themselves, needless to say, intensified the emotional fervor of all the leading elements of the community for the Entente cause; just as the original sympathy for the Entente had facilitated the development of the war-supply business.

For the State Department to exert any serious pressure upon the Allies in order to keep open some trade with Germany early became a political, a psychological and an economic impossibility; while the unexpected, seemingly miraculous, appearance of the huge war-supply business removed the original economic motive for such an attempt. Many different and intricately interrelated factors (not all of which need by any means operate in the same way in the event of another foreign war) had combined to produce this result, almost accidentally. Not because of any conscious policy — rather indeed because of the lack of any sufficiently conscious policy — the United States had become a chief source of supply for one side in a life-and-death struggle, at the same time acquiescing in the complete exclusion of the other side from her markets.

The other side inevitably sought for some means of reacting against this situation; and in the spring of 1915 a means was discovered. Here again there is an accidental element in the sequence of events. Had the Germans earlier developed the submarine as a commerce destroyer, it is possible that our economic alliance with the Entente would not have become established as it did; if, on the other hand, they had waited to perfect the weapon before resorting to it, American policy might more clearly have recognized its importance and adjusted itself to the new factor. From the American point of view, the German declaration of the submarine war zone in February 1915 came at just the wrong time. It was too late then to revert to the original policy of forcing open the seas for commerce with the civil populations of the belligerents; it was too early to realize the immense strategic value of the new weapon. President Wilson summarily ordered the Germans not to use their submarines as they proposed to do against the American traffic with the Allies. Only later was he to perceive the difficulty of enforcing such an order.

This refusal to accept, or at the least to discuss, the German theory of a maritime war zone must be ascribed in part to the personal temperament of Mr. Wilson, a strong moralist who was at bottom emotionally enlisted on the side of the Allies; in part to the similar temper of the public; in part to the resultant political considerations that made it difficult for any official to seem to favor Germany; in part to Allied propaganda, which discounted the submarines as strategically ridiculous. Though the Germans had a legal case for this use of the submarine, it was, at any rate on the surface, a much weaker one than the Allies' case for their blockade measures; it challenged the conventional ideas of national right in a much more dramatic way, while the whole issue was of course profoundly obscured in the fogs of passion that had accumulated. Had the proposed war zone ever been seriously discussed, economic considerations must likewise have come into play, for it would have been obvious that the United States could not appear to sanction a free war upon a trade that promised the one means of excape from a serious depression. Actually, few seem to have supposed that the submarines could materially affect our exports, and the issue was met upon a more emotional plane. The President did not attempt to defend the great bulk of the war-supply business that was carried under foreign flags. He did commit himself irrevocably to the demand that the Germans desist from the destruction either of American-flag ships or the lives of American citizens on the high seas.

A war situation had thus been prepared, for ultimately there was no peaceful issue from this demand except acquiescence by Germany or its withdrawal by the United States. A war situation does not, of course, inevitably produce a war; accident, however, was again to play a part in intensifying the crisis. The submarine campaign might have developed gradually, in a slow crescendo of incidents, permitting both statesmanship and opinion to work out some peaceful adjustment to the problem. Instead, from February until May the campaign proceeded almost unnoticed, confirming the view that the whole matter was of small consequence, only to explode on May 7, with the torpedoing of the *Lusitania*, in an incident so shocking and so unexpected as to render any dispassionate treatment of the broad question very nearly impossible. The *Lusitania* did not bring the United States into the War; it did not even convince any decisive majority of the American people that war was desirable. It did have the important psychological effect of surrounding the President's position on the submarine campaign with an intense emotional field which added to the natural difficulties of retreat and constantly impeded any attempt to remove the war danger that had been created.

The war propaganda continued to operate to bring the public mind to a point at which it would support, if not clamor for, participation in the conflict. The preparedness agitation — in which patriotism seems so inextricably interwoven with less attractive motives that it is now useless even to try to disentangle them — undoubtedly contributed to the same end. The original sympathy with the Entente had been refined and deepened, through the operation of many factors, into an influential belief that permanent world peace might be erected upon an Entente victory; and this supplied a high and impressive reason for bringing the United States into the struggle to assure the victory and participate in the peace system. The growing dependence of our domestic prosperity upon the Entente war orders exerted its far-reaching, if perhaps somewhat subtle, influence. The more closely we became a partner of the Entente, the more genuine a menace, both politically and economically, did the prospect of German victory become. If at any time the Entente had actually seemed to be on the verge of defeat, the economic factor might have appeared more plainly as a positive force driving us into the war; as it was, its influence was rather the negative one of hindering any attempt to restore the country to a position of more genuine neutrality. The actual declaration was precipitated in another way; and in spite of all these forces working in the direction of our entanglement, it is still not inconceivable that the United States might have remained technically at peace.

It is fair to say that in one sense the United States had entered the European War by the middle of 1915. We were an intimate part of the war complex. Our economic power was wholly enlisted upon one side, and we were no longer neutral either in sentiment or in policy. Even so, a military participation, though likely, was hardly inevitable. In considering a future war there is the question of whether the development of this kind of one-sided relationship to the struggle can be avoided; but there is also the narrower question of whether, once it was established, an astute statesmanship might not still manage to retain a legal neutrality.

What actually effected the transition from legal neutrality to practical belligerence in 1917 was the war situation, prepared by Mr. Wilson with his first stand on the submarine and set, as it were, by the emotional shock of the *Lusitania*. The President was able to postpone the crisis for some two years by forcing upon the Germans a long series of compromises and partial surrenders. Although the submarines managed to torpedo many vessels and kill a considerable number of American citizens in the course of this correspondence, the Germans never forced the President to abandon his fundamental position. From the *Lusitania* crisis until the declaration of unrestricted submarine warfare on February 1, 1917, Mr. Wilson emerged substantially successful from each incident that arose. It was in this way that he avoided war. But each success only made a subsequent retreat more difficult for him; as time went on he became more and more the prisoner of his own victories.

The final victory came in May 1916, when to surmount the *Sussex* crisis he compelled the Germans to agree formally to use their submarines only in accordance with the rules of visit and search. In doing so, however, he posed an issue of American rights upon the high seas in such a form that there was no possible future escape from it. This would have been a satisfactory method of keeping us out of war had Mr. Wilson possessed any threat powerful enough to compel the Germans to live up to the engagement. Unfortunately, he did not; for it requires a very powerful threat indeed to compel a power fighting for its life to leave untouched a weapon it believes to be the key to victory. In January 1917, the Germans took it up again. They had done what the President had declared would be a *casus belli*, and what every shade of influential opinion, including his political opponents as well as many of his supporters, had agreed with him would be a *casus belli*. President Wilson found himself almost automatically at war.

This, in brief, is more or less what actually happened. Yet to recount it leaves one with a sense of dissatisfaction. Even at the time, the specific issue of the right of certain American citizens to travel through a war zone seemed inadequate to explain why the people of the United States should be going down into the most frightful and most exhausting war in history. Many of those who urged us on at the time (including the President) were careful to explain that it was not really because of the ship question that we should take up the sword — but in the interests of peace and civilization, or the Monroe Doctrine or international law. Since then, many quite different reasons have been advanced to resolve the conundrum that unquestionably remains. Why did not the United States modify its position on the submarine when the issue was presented with the Gore-McLemore resolutions in February 1916. We might have warned Americans not to travel in the war zone, left the question of ship sinkings to post-war adjudication (as we left the questions of Entente interference with our cargoes) and allowed the belligerents to decide the issue of the sea war themselves. Why did Mr. Wilson in February 1917, at once break off diplomatic relations instead of accepting the German action and making the best of it? Why did Congress pass the war resolution, when there was no passionate demand for war in the country and when many of the members themselves probably preferred not to?

For the answer it is necessary to seek among the factors that have already been mentioned — the propaganda, the economic relationships, the personalities of statesmen, the exigencies of domestic politics, the fears and hatreds (whether well founded or not) of German imperialism, the altruistic dreams of world peace. These, however, are all elusive and insubstantial quantities, one shading into another in a baffling fashion and each presenting, when the attempt is made to isolate it as the primarily significant factor, certain difficulties. The influence of "Allied propaganda" for instance is today very generally misconceived. The effective propaganda for the Entente cause was that generated in the United States and by the Americans; undoubtedly it was powerfully reinforced by the spontaneous outpourings from all sources of Entente opinion, but the conscious use of censorship and official propaganda bureaus hardly did more than give precision and effect to forces that could never have been created in that way.

"The bankers" present a similar difficulty. J. P. Morgan and Company, and the other houses that participated in the Entente financing, appear to have been much more the channels than the generators of the forces they are supposed to have wielded. In the early days they assisted greatly in setting up the machinery that connected the American need for markets with the Entente need for supplies, but they could never themselves have established the tremendous potential they thus helped to discharge. Their machinery at first ran almost entirely upon cash. It was not until the late summer of 1916 that it was necessary to resort to credit upon a significant scale, and by that time domestic prosperity had become so intimately dependent upon the war-supply business that credit must almost certainly have been forthcoming even had the bankers been less eager to supply the facilities. Finally, the private loans floated from that time onward were in general fully secured. The financial crisis that appeared with the beginning of 1917 arose from the fact that the Allies' security was beginning to run out. The point of Mr. Page's famous telegram of March 5, 1917, urging the President to enter the war to save the war-supply business was not that the government should bail out the bankers, but that it should replace them. Here again one must set down the role of the specifically banking interest as at most an indirect one.

One may broaden the charge to cover the whole complex of profit-making business of which the bankers were an essential part. No doubt the "profit motive," as a generalized concept, may be held responsible for almost anything in a profit-making society. More narrowly, there were quite probably many individual businessmen who perceived that their bread was buttered on the side of belligerency. It is difficult to detect any specific intrigue, however, in which such men selfishly applied pressure to influence the critical decisions of the President or the Congress in regard to the submarine. The profit motive may have helped to get us into a war situation and hindered our attempts to get out, but it did not directly control the transition from formal neutrality to formal belligerence.

There is a similar elusiveness about each of the many other factors that have been cited by one or another commentator as the decisive one. Those who pin the major responsibility upon the vanity and irascibility of President Wilson seldom attempt to explain how another statesman might, in fact, have met the situation as it was abruptly presented to him in February 1917. Those who cling to the wartime view that the United States actually entered the struggle in order to preserve democratic institutions and the freedom of peoples from a German aggression must still meet many metaphysical difficulties in showing why there was so long a delay in taking up the issue, why so many in 1917 refused to accept this as the true issue and why the mass of the population was still hoping that war would be avoided at the moment it was finally declared upon a point that even at the time seemed to be of relatively minor importance.

The facts of the period from 1914 to 1917 are complex enough to support almost any theory of historical causation that one may apply to them, at the same time that they are obstinate enough to resist almost any theory of how the ultimate entanglement could have been prevented. An examination of the facts must remain as an essential foundation of any policy designed to control a similar situation in the future. Yet it is to be suspected that before the facts can be of much use there will have first to be agreement upon many profound issues as to the ends which the control should serve, the proper philosophy of international relations, the real character and objects of the state in the international and domestic complex — issues the very existence of which seems to be scarcely realized as yet by most of those participating in the current debate. They have so far confined themselves to the problem of how the nation is to avoid entanglement in another foreign war. The far more important question of whether the nation (whatever they may conceive that to mean) will want to avoid entanglement has hardly even been raised.

I V
Our Times

Middle Western Isolationism

by

RAY ALLEN BILLINGTON

["The Origins of Middle Western Isolationism," from *Political Science Quarterly*, LX (March 1945), 44–64. Reprinted by permission.]

The Middle West, thanks to the writings of Frederick Jackson Turner, has come to be regarded as a melting pot par excellence. Here, according to Turner, shortly before the mid-nineteenth century, native and diverse foreign-born elements engaged in a process of mutual education "in which all gave and all received and no element remained isolated." In the Midwest the world was taught a "lesson of national cross-fertilization instead of national enmities, the possibility of a newer and richer civilization, not by preserving unmodified or isolated the old component elements, but by merging the individual life in the common product — a new product which held the promise of world brotherhood."[1]

Apparently, we are not to take Turner's generalization at its face value. He himself realized that all was not smooth in the melting-pot process in a series of articles he wrote on immigration in 1901.[2] And, as the following selection by Professor Ray Allen Billington of Northwestern University suggests, isolationist sentiment in the Midwest derives in no small measure from inherited customs and allegiances of first-, second-, and even third-generation Americans.

Samuel Lubell's provocative book, The Future of American Politics, argues more strongly than does Billington that the "hard core" of isolationism in the United States is "ethnic and emotional," and that the center of such sentiment is the Midwest. Lubell also believes that since Russia and the United States are today's major military powers, the ethnic basis of isolationism has been destroyed, since the argument for isolationism against Russian aggression cannot *enlist the support of the ethnic elements that have been most ardently isolationist in the past. Lubell predicts the emergence of a new isolationism, deriving less from ethnic factors than from general disillusionment and weariness with the cold war.*[3]

THROUGH the nineteenth century the Middle West shared with the rest of the United States a lively interest in the world-wide struggle against tyranny.* Its people, living in what they liked to think was the cradle of democracy and invigorated by the influence of the frontier, regarded themselves as the patrons of the liberal uprisings that periodically rocked Europe; and they reacted accordingly. The Greek Revolt of the 1820's, the French Revolutions of 1830 and 1848, the Hungarian struggle for independence in the late 1840's, all aroused the Westerners to violent demonstrations of approval; fiery resolutions were adopted by mass meetings and legislatures, funds were collected to aid the revolutionists, and Congressmen were goaded into such violent speeches that they frequently embarrassed their neutral government.† Only a few of the more rabid Midwesterners advocated American intervention in these European quarrels, but all paid enthusiastic lip service to each new blow struck at established authority.

In the first years of the twentieth century the Western attitude shifted. The people of that section, above all others, insisted that

---

* The Middle West today comprises the areas defined by the Census Bureau as the East North Central and West North Central States: Ohio, Indiana, Illinois, Michigan, Wisconsin, Minnesota, Iowa, Missouri, North Dakota, South Dakota, Nebraska and Kansas. Missouri has remained predominantly Southern in its social attitudes, but is included in the Middle West in this paper. See Howard W. Odum and Harry E. Moore, *American Regionalism* (New York, 1938), pp. 462 *et seq.*

† These activities are described in Myrtle A. Cline, *American Attitude toward the Greek War of Independence, 1821–1828* (Atlanta, 1930), pp. 62, 99–100; E. N. Curtis, "American Opinion of the Nineteenth Century French Revolutions," *American Historical Review*, XXIX (January 1924), 249–270; Arthur J. May, *Contemporary American Opinion of the Mid-Century Revolutions in Central Europe* (Philadelphia, 1927), pp. 49 *et seq.*; and in John W. Oliver, "Louis Kossuth's Appeal to the Middle West," *Mississippi Valley Historical Review*, XIV (March 1928), 481–495.

Europe's fate was no concern of theirs; the United States, they said, should seek peace and security by isolating itself from the rest of the globe. This about-face was partly due to the changed relationships between the Old and New Worlds; for the shrinking Atlantic had brought the Americans uncomfortably close to an imperialistic, war-bound continent, and meddling now might mean actual involvement. Yet more than this was needed to explain the shift in Midwestern ideology, for national security was not the only issue. The Eastern and Southern "militarists" of 1916, "internationalists" of 1919, and "interventionists" of 1940 were not concerned alone with preserving American nationalism through collective action; they believed that the eradiction of Kaiserism, power politics and fascism was necessary to rid the world of antidemocratic institutions and ideals. The Middle Western "isolationists," although just as devoted to democracy, thought the rest of the world beyond redemption. These same people who in the nineteenth century had vigorously upheld universal self-government were in the twentieth content to protect their own treasures on their own soil.

This attitude became apparent during the chain of events leading to the Spanish–American War. The West's first reaction to the Cuban struggle for independence was true to the section's humanitarian traditions; Westerners viewed the conflict as one between autocracy and self-rule which deserved their unwavering support. These sentiments were freely voiced in a number of mass meetings held during the fall of 1895 in Middle Western cities, where resolutions were passed favoring the immediate recognition of Cuban independence, government aid to Cuba, and even the American seizure of the island.* Those whose enthusiasm was not satisfied by these outspoken demands collected funds to aid the revolutionists, a cause sponsored by the Chicago *Tribune* and imitated by other Midwestern papers.† Others joined the filibustering expeditions which were regularly launched against the Spanish rulers of Cuba.

---

* Chicago *Inter-Ocean*, October 1, 1895; Cincinnati *Tribune*, October 1, 1895; Marcus M. Wilkerson, *Public Opinion and the Spanish-American War* (Baton Rouge, 1932), pp. 56–60. At least eight of the twelve Midwestern states participated in these meetings. Wilkerson, *op. cit.*, p. 57; Chicago *Tribune*, October 1, 1895; Cincinnati *Tribune*, October 8, 1895; *Congressional Record*, 54th Cong., 1st Sess., pp. 32, 140, 482, *ibid.*, 2nd Sess., p. 230.

† The campaign was started by the Chicago *Tribune*, April 14, 1896.

Chicago trade-unions began contributing their men to this effort in the fall of 1895, and a year later a recruiting agent in Cincinnati reported that he had sent three hundred men from that city while a thousand had left from St. Louis and the entire Columbus, Ohio, contingent of the National Guard had offered its services.* No other section contributed so generously to the cause of Cuban independence.

Equally indicative of the region's humanitarianism was the attitude of its press, although here a significant division occurred which was of great importance in explaining the West's shift to isolationism. While editors stood in a solid phalanx to support the Cuban cause, their belligerency varied with their political beliefs. At first Republican editors were markedly more aggressive than their Democratic rivals. Most outspoken of all was the Chicago *Tribune*. As early as September 1895 it was saying: "Why do we wait longer? . . . Is it not time to say to Spain, 'Take your flag out of Cuba and give the people their liberty.'" A year later this paper urged the use of American battleships against the Spanish fleet and referred to war as something inevitable and desirable. By November 1896, the *Tribune* favored immediate recognition of Cuban independence, "and if Spain wants to go to war about it, the war will be a welcome one and she will get all the fighting she wants." † This violent prowar attitude was matched by other Republican papers, nine of which favored the recognition of Cuban belligerency during 1895 and 1896, while seven advocated forceful annexation of the islands.‡

The election of McKinley in 1896 led to an immediate change of front. Although a few Republican papers, notably the Chicago *Tribune*, continued to demand war, the majority adopted a less belligerent tone. At the same time the Democratic press, although sympathetic to Cuba in the past, now grew more bellicose. Thus the Cincinnati *Enquirer* saw "no reason why Cuba should not be

* Chicago *Inter-Ocean*, October 7, 1895; Cincinnati *Times-Star*, December 15, 1896; Wilkerson, *op cit.*, pp. 59–60.

† Chicago *Tribune*, September 24, 1895, August 15, 1896, November 28, 1896. The quotations are from Wilkerson, *op. cit.*, pp. 47–50.

‡ This is the conclusion of a careful student after a thorough study of the Midwestern press during this period. George W. Auxier, *The Cuban Question as Reflected in the Editorial Columns of Middle Western Newspapers (1895–1898)* (Ann Arbor, University Microfilm, 1941), p. 244. This excellent work has been relied on for most of the material concerning the Western press at this time.

part of the United States within the next thirty days," the Cleveland *Plain Dealer* urged the use of the navy to protect our interests on the island, and the Omaha *World-Herald* branded as criminal McKinley's "dilly-dallying" attitude.* These editors were willing to advocate intervention partly to embarrass the governing faction. Yet there was no doubt that the Middle West favored the war; six of the eight important independent papers there constantly advocated intervention, while even the business leaders showed less fear of war than industrialists in other sections.†

This pro-war sentiment was made clear to Western Congressmen by a flood of petitions from legislatures, boards of trade, mass meetings and organizations. Of seventy-nine received by Midwestern Senators, seventy-four favored the Cuban cause. Ten of these merely expressed sympathy, but twenty-eight demanded the recognition of the island's independence, and three urged the United States to enter the war at once.‡ Little wonder that the section's Congressmen played a leading rôle in the war party at Washington. Of the twenty-four Senators from the Middle West, all but four voted or spoke consistently for intervention.§ Some of the most warlike demands were voiced by Westerners, who urged everything from "sending the most powerful battleship of the United States to Cuban waters," to "giving Cuba what Lafayette gave to Washington at Valley Forge." ‖ When the vote on war was taken, eighteen of these twenty-four Senators sided with the majority who favored military intervention. In the House of Representatives, where the war resolution was adopted by a vote of 173 to 121, only twenty-five Westerners opposed the war.¶

* *Ibid.*, pp. 53, 57, 151–152, 233. Dr. Auxier examined more than a dozen Democratic papers and found the shift in policy clearly marked in all but two.

† *Ibid.*, p. 233; Julius W. Pratt, *Expansionists of 1898* (Baltimore, 1936), pp. 234–244.

‡ Compiled from petitions printed in the *Congressional Record* during this period.

§ This figure has been arrived at by a study of the Senate speeches made during the first two sessions of the 55th Congress, and by an analysis of the vote on resolutions authorizing the recognition of Cuban belligerence, Cuban independence, and actual intervention. *Ibid.*, 55th Cong., 1st Sess., p. 1394, 2nd Sess., pp. 3993, 4040–4041, 4079–4090.

‖ *Ibid.*, 1st Sess., pp. 1132, 1170.

¶ The war resolution passed the Senate by a vote of 67 to 21. *Ibid.*, 55th Cong., 2nd Sess., pp. 4063, 4079–4080.

Western interest in expansion did not decline when the nation, with the war won, debated the disposition of the conquered Spanish territory. President McKinley sought an answer to this problem by sounding public opinion on a speaking tour through the Midwest. Wherever he went his oratorical question, "Who will haul down the flag?" in the Philippines, was answered with shouts of "It will stay there." "I know what this means," he told a cheering crowd at Terre Haute. "It means, my fellow citizens, that the people of the United States want the victories of the army and navy to be recognized in the treaty of peace." *

McKinley, in this judgment, failed to note two significant variations in the section's opinion. One followed economic lines, for, although the business interests solidly supported expansion, the workers and farmers were less sure that this was desirable. The farmer-labor point of view was expressed by the president of the Ohio Federation of Labor, who argued that, as civilization could not be transplanted, low wages would continue in the Philippines and the United States would be flooded with cheap tariff-free goods to the detriment of the American worker. Moreover, the 20,000,000 dollars due Spain and the cost of developing colonial possessions promised higher taxes without immediate gain for the laborer or farmer.† Western businessmen, on the other hand, caught a vision of vast Oriental markets for their goods lying beyond the Philippine gateway. They stood solidly in support of McKinley's imperialistic inclinations and urged the retention of every inch of territory taken from Spain.‡

A second and more important division in Middle Western opinion

---

* Columbus *Dispatch,* October 15 and 20, 1898. McKinley later declared that he based his decision to keep the Philippines partly on the enthusiastic response of Western audiences to this suggestion. Quoted in Pratt, *op. cit.,* pp. 336–337.

† *United Mine Workers' Journal,* December 8, 1898; Ashland (Ohio) *Press,* November 9, 1898; Clermont (Ohio) *Sun,* November 9, 1898; Harrison County (Ohio) *Democrat,* December 1, 1898; Chicago *Inter-Ocean,* quoted in *Literary Digest,* November 12, 1899. Western Congressmen received from farmers numerous petitions opposing expansion. *Congressional Record,* 55th Cong., 3rd Sess., pp. 1066–1067, 1157.

‡ Pratt, *op. cit.,* pp. 246–278, describes the conversion of this group. See also Bellaire (Ohio) *Herald,* August 11, 1898; Canton (Ohio) *Repository,* December 1, 1898; Clermont (Ohio) *Sun,* November 30, 1898; Columbus *Dispatch,* January 23, 1899.

followed political lines. In the debate over expansion Republicans were wholeheartedly in favor of colonial possessions, Democrats unalterably opposed. Only Republican domination of the West accounted for that section's imperialism.

This division was reflected in the editorial opinion which filled Western newspapers between 1898 and 1902. Republican editors saw colonial possessions as the panacea for all the nation's ills; from them would stem eternal prosperity, the prestige fitting a great nation, and enlightenment for downtrodden natives of tyranny-ridden lands. They supported the Treaty of Paris with its provisions for annexation, and urged a vigorous war upon Aguinaldo and his rebellious followers.* The Democratic press, true to the section's established humanitarianism, saw expansion as a wicked conspiracy to steal possessions in the name of humanity, a sure prelude to participation in a world war, and the first step in the downfall of the Republic. Editors urged the defeat of the Treaty of Paris and looked upon Aguinaldo as a second Washington struggling for his people's liberty.†

These strict party lines influenced Congressmen more than did sectional attitudes. Democrats from the Middle West introduced resolutions against annexation, and heatedly declared that we should forsake McKinley imperialism and return to the principles of our Revolutionary forefathers who had fought to make a subject people free.‡ Their pleas went unheeded. Republicans controlled the Middle West and assured that section's support of expansion. When the final vote on the Philippine act was taken, sixty-four Midwestern Representatives favored American control of the islands and only twenty-three were against.§ The Middle West remained

---

* Columbus *Dispatch*, October 3 and 5, December 14, 1898; Bellefontaine (Ohio) *Republican*, November 1, 1898; Ashland (Ohio) *Times*, November 2, 1898; Dayton *Daily Journal*, February 7, 1899; *Literary Digest*, November 18, 1898, Febuary 4, 1899.

† Bellaire (Ohio) *Herald*, July 28, 1898, August 25, 1898; Caldwell (Ohio) *Press*, November 10, 1898, December 8 and 22, 1898; Ashland (Ohio) *Press*, December 7, 1898; Cleveland *Plain Dealer*, January 5, 1899; Delaware (Ohio) *Democratic Herald*, January 5, 1899; Coshocton (Ohio) *Democrat*, January 9, 1899; Hocking (Ohio) *Sentinel*, October 19, 1899; Milwaukee *Journal*, Chicago *Chronicle* and St. Louis *Republic*, quoted in *Literary Digest*, October 28, 1899.

‡ *Congressional Record*, 55th Cong., 3rd Sess., pp. 93, 1261, 1265, 1486, 1678.

§ *Ibid.*, 57th Cong., 1st Sess., pp. 6231, 7487.

true to expansionism, but now its loyalties to the Republican Party transcended any idealistic beliefs.

Behind this shift in opinion, which was to hold the key to later Western isolationism, lay both changing economic and social conditions in the West and the turbulent domestic situation of the 1890's. The latter was particularly important, for the ramifications of the free-silver crusade split the Middle West into two antagonistic camps and prepared both to adopt an insular attitude toward their nation's foreign policy. One of these groups was composed of the industrial-urban element, which by 1900 was on the verge of wresting economic supremacy from the traditional agrarian rulers of the West. The other was made up of the farmers and workers, who had seized on free silver as a panacea for the depression in which they had been bogged for a quarter-century.

The rabid enthusiasm of these agrarians profoundly shocked the members of the first group, the Western businessmen and city dwellers. Bryan, to them, was the archetype of all that was bad; his path led to inflation, destruction of private property, and anarchy. McKinley, by contrast, was looked upon as the custodian of all that was good; a vote for him in 1896 or 1900 was not only a vote for sound business but also for civilization. The frantic efforts of these conservatives prevented Bryan from carrying the Middle West in either election, but the danger was too great to be forgotten. Any division within the party's ranks might open the door to Bryan and chaos; blind adherence to Republicanism on every issue would alone assure salvation. Hence when McKinley embraced the imperialistic cause, he swung a majority of Midwestern Republicans with him. From that time on they shaped their views on foreign policy to that of their party's leaders. Any Democratic President who favored interventionism was certain to meet determined resistance from Middle Western Republicans.

The free-silver crusade also moved the powerful agrarian groups in the West along the path to isolationism. To them the defeat of inflation, which doomed them to a continuing struggle with poverty and debt, could be laid at the door of Eastern and British capitalists. From this belief stemmed several prejudices which became entrenched in Western thought. One was a dislike for England. Another was an intensified sectional antagonism which inclined farmers there to look with disfavor on anything sanctioned by Easterners. Thus, if the East favored intervention in world affairs, they would automatically swing in the opposite direction. The third and most important prejudice was directed against Eastern bankers and industrialists. This "money power" had been hated by the frontier since the days of Andrew Jackson, and now these hatreds seemed confirmed. Its wealth not only had defeated inflation but had engineered imperialism, after the Spanish–American War, for its own selfish ends. These antagonisms were strengthened by the violent antitrust agitation of the Progressive era, and by the unfolding Caribbean policy which seemed to increase the poor man's taxes for the benefit of a few wealthy corporations. Thousands of Westerners came to believe that intervention was only another tool of the trusts in their battle against the people.

The rapidly maturing industrial society of the Middle West also accounted for the section's changing opinion. Between 1880 and the turn of the century its manufactures increased threefold, until by 1900 the output of its 182,467 factories was valued at nearly four and a half billion dollars. Its agricultural products in the same year were worth nearly two and a half billion dollars.* This happy combination of farm and factory created an economic self-sufficiency unrivaled by any other section. Its farmers were no longer dependent on foreign or Eastern markets, and its manufacturers were less concerned with international trade, for they could sell most of their produce in the rural regions at their door. The West, enjoying the prosperity of rapid expansion as it developed into a self-contained economic unit, could close its eyes to the rest of the world as could no other section.

As important as these material factors in explaining the growing isolationism of the Middle West was the rise to political power of the section's immigrant population. For half a century its fertile lands had lured Europe's refugees, until by 1900 more than half the male voters of every Western state but Ohio, Kansas, and Indiana were either foreign-born or the children of parents born

* Abstract of the Twelfth Census of the United States, 1900 (Washington, 1904), pp. 250, 331.

abroad; in Wisconsin, Minnesota, and North Dakota they numbered almost 80 per cent of the population, in South Dakota nearly
70 per cent, and in Michigan and Illinois 60 per cent. The nationality
of these immigrants helped shape their attitude toward world
affairs. Of the four million foreign-born living in the section at the
turn of the century, half came from Germany or neighboring states
in Central Europe, while another six hundred thousand were from
the Scandinavian countries.*

The great mass of these first- and second-generation Americans
favored isolation. Many retained a half-hearted loyalty to their
Central European homelands; for, although they were but lightly
touched by the upper-class nationalism of that day, they still disapproved of American entry into wars directed against the Central
Powers. Others feared that participation in world politics would re-
awaken Old World hatreds and retard the process of Americanization which was bringing them peace and prosperity. Still more,
particularly among the foreign-born, made the maintenance of their
adopted country's democracy without essential change their principal political objective; and they shied with inherent conservatism
from any deviation from the established courses. Finally, the second
and third generations of newcomers developed an exaggerated
Americanism as they hurried to slough off all Old World taints, and
this too inclined them to look askance at entanglements which
would revive influences they were anxious to leave behind. In
general the immigrants were thoroughly conservative, particularly
in the upper Mississippi Valley, and this fitted well with the pattern
of isolationism.†

Less important than these economic and racial factors, but still of
some influence, were the large number of evangelical religious sects
that were rooted in the Middle West. Many of these were avowedly
pacifistic; others were European in origin and spread their cynical
Old World doctrines among their worshipers. Thus, many of the
Lutheran pastors were immigrants who brought to the United
States both a hatred of war and a belief that Europe's conflicts were

* *Twelfth Census of the United States, Statistical Atlas* (Washington, 1903),
Plate No. 46; *Abstract of the Twelfth Census,* pp. 58–63.
† Marcus L. Hansen, *The Immigrant in American History* (Cambridge, 1940),
pp. 77–96.

imperialistic struggles engineered by a few greedy capitalists.* Listening to these messages from the pulpit, the Scandinavians and Americans who followed this faith were influenced against any participation in the quarrels of the Continent.

These prejudices of alarmed businessmen, discontented farmers, immigrant voters, and pacifistic churchgoers were openly expressed between 1914 and 1917 when the nation debated its rôle in the First World War. The West's first reaction was one of thankfulness for its geographic isolation from a war that was considered "wicked, unnecessary and altogether horrible," and a fervent prayer of thanks that "we have gone no farther than we have in becoming a world power." † This complacency was easily translated into an indifference which was typified by the reply of a small-town policeman when asked, shortly after the *Sussex* sinking, what the people were saying about Germany: "Germany? Well, lessee. I reck'lect I *did* hear some of 'em talking some about Germany along five or six months ago, maybe, but I don't think there's been no talk about Germans for a good while lately. No sir, not around *our* community." ‡ That this attitude was common was shown by a poll of newspaper editors in the fall of 1914. In the Middle West 122 were either indifferent to the outcome of the war or pro-German, while only 13 favored the Allies. This contrasted with the East, where 44 were neutral or pro-German and 34 pro-Ally, and the South with 56 neutral and pro-German editors against 47 supporting the Allies.§

During the next two years this sectional attitude was clearly demonstrated in each issue that arose. Western opinion most violently opposed any increase in the army and navy, taking refuge in the belief that "preparedness brought on the war," and insisting that "our splendid isolation" made defense unnecessary.|| This

---

* George M. Stephenson, "The Attitude of Swedish Americans towards the World War," Mississippi Valley Historical Association, *Proceedings*, X (July 1920), 79–94; idem, *The Religious Aspects of Swedish Immigration* (Minneapolis, 1932), pp. 451–452.

† Dayton *Daily News*, August 8, 1914; Springfield (Ohio) *Daily News*, July 31, 1914.

‡ Booth Tarkington, "Middle Western Apathy," *American Magazine*, LXXXIII (June 1917), 31–32. See also Cedric Cummins, "Indiana Looks at the War," *Indiana Magazine of History*, XXXVII (December 1941), 343.

§ *Literary Digest*, November 14, 1914.

|| *Ohio State Journal*, November 21, 1914, February 3, 1915.

opposition was centered in the states west of the Mississippi where Populism had attracted most support* and was motivated partially by hatred of the Eastern "money trust." One Nebraska editor summed up the sentiment of his state when he charged the "preparedness-propagandists" with being in "the pay of the munitions-factory magnates and steel trust," and another insisted: "The terror which has seized Maxim and the manufacturers of war materials is not felt by the people of this section. There is no fear of invasion here." †

This sentiment helped shape Western opinion on the sale of military supplies to the warring Powers. Petitions favoring an arms embargo were showered on Congress from the beginning of the war, many of them from Middle Western communities with large German populations. "Better to have an embargo covering the entire coast," one editor wrote, "than to get into the war." ‡ Senator Kenyon of Iowa expressed the views of many of his constituents when, in presenting Congress with an embargo petition bearing a million signatures, he declared: "The jingle of the dollar can not drown the cry of suffering from the battlefields of Europe. It may be all right to sell these things according to international law, but it is against the moral law." §

The Western press did not react as violently to the German submarine campaign as did the editors of other sections. The only two papers to defend the sinking of the *Lusitania* were the Milwaukee *Free Press* and the St. Louis *Times*, both located in areas with a large German population. Others, unwilling to go this far, insisted that Americans should hold themselves aloof by refraining from travel on belligerent ships, and that U-boats had as much

* This was revealed by a poll of newspaper editors published in the *Literary Digest*, March 11, 1916, which showed that sixty-six living west of the Mississippi saw militarism as a real danger while sixty-four did not. This was in marked contrast with other sections, such as the East, where eleven feared militarism while eighty-five did not, or the Middle Western states east of the Mississippi whose editors voted twenty-three to sixty that such dangers were remote. This was also made clear by a large number of Western petitions to Congress against increasing the size of the army and navy. *Congressional Record*, 64th Cong., 1st Sess., pp. 935, 1185, 1733, 2251, 2491.
† *Literary Digest*, March 11, 1916.
‡ *Ohio State Journal*, February 7, 1915.
§ *Literary Digest*, February 12, 1916.

right in American waters as British warships.* When Congress in 1916 acted on a resolution forbidding citizens to travel in vessels of warring Powers, twelve of the fourteen favorable Senate votes came from Middle Westerners, while that section's Representatives alone cast a majority of votes in its favor.† Probably a Kansas farmer mirrored the views of many of his fellows when he told an interviewer:

We will — every man of us — fight in a minute if the country is invaded, but we won't go a step farther. We'd keep every American off belligerent ships. We'd keep every American out of Mexico. We'd let the Japs take the Philippines and be damned, if they wanted 'em. We'd defend our homes, but when any American goes where he has no right to go, if he gets into trouble, it's his own fault. The honor of the country doesn't get outside our boundaries that we can see.‡

By the spring of 1917 the Middle West was no longer isolationist, for the opening of unrestricted submarine warfare and the Zimmerman Note solidified national opinion in favor of war. Yet in that section, as in no other, there remained a group of die-hards who resisted the popular clamor. When President Wilson asked Congress for authority to arm merchant vessels the resulting measure was talked to death by twelve Senators, eight of whom were from the West. Three of the five votes cast against the declaration of war in the Senate, the thirty-six of the fifty in the House, were from Representatives of that section.§ Hatred of the Eastern money power, a large German population, and distrust of a Democratic President combined to center isolationism in the upper Mississippi Valley.

The important rôle of partisan politics in this attitude was again demonstrated when peace brought the League of Nations before the American public. The West's first reaction to Wilson's proposal was mildly favorable; even the Chicago *Tribune* admitted that "the

* *Ibid.*, May 22, 1915. An excellent summary of Western attitude concerning the submarine question is in H. J. Haskell, "The U-53 and the Middle West," *Outlook*, October 1916, pp. 414–415.

† In the House the delegations from Iowa, Nebraska, Minnesota, and Wisconsin were unanimous in their approval. *Congressional Record*, 64th Cong., 1st Sess., p. 3720.

‡ *Literary Digest*, February 12, 1916.

§ *Congressional Record*, 65th Cong., 1st Sess., pp. 412–413.

UNDERSTANDING THE AMERICAN PAST

scheme is not one which need be feared," and the equally isolationist Cincinnati *Times-Star* grudgingly conceded that the League "held promise to at least make wars less frequent."* A poll of newspaper editors in the spring of 1919 showed that 250 of the section's papers were favorable, 200 conditionally favorable, and only 70 absolutely opposed.† Yet only four months later these Western editors were vying in heaping calumny on the League, and Western Senators were preparing to cast a virtually solid vote against it. This abrupt change of front was caused by the decision of Henry Cabot Lodge and his Republican followers to fight the League as a means of discrediting Wilson and the Democrats.

The predominantly Republican West fell readily into line with this partisan campaign to obscure the Covenant by amendments and reservations, while delaying the final decision until popular interest waned. For two months the treaty languished in the hands of the Senate Foreign Relations Committee while its friends pleaded with Wilson to accept reservations and the President retaliated by carrying the case to the people. When debate began, the cause was already lost, but Republican obstructionists were still cautious. Their attack, mild at first, mounted in intensity as passing months lessened League support. By mid-September even such a vacillating politician as Warren G. Harding felt sure enough of his constituents' isolationism to take a firm anti-League stand, while other Western Senators were warning that internationalism meant rule by the dark-skinned peoples of the world, or by the Pope.‡ By this time, too, many moderate Republicans saw that Wilson would not compromise and reluctantly swung to complete opposition.

This increased bitterness in the Senate was reflected in the Middle Western press. As the summer progressed editors who had first favored the League turned gradually from cautious support to bitter attack. Some of the more outspoken, such as the Chicago *Tribune,* kept up a constant barrage of editorial invective and flagrant misrepresentation; others reflected a growing popular antipathy by

* Chicago *Tribune,* February 17, 1919; Cincinnati *Times-Star,* April 29, 1919. See also *Literary Digest,* April 5, 1919.

† *Literary Digest,* April 5, 1919.

‡ *Congressional Record,* 66th Cong., 1st Sess., pp. 235–237, 1436, 4453–4455, 5219–5225.

refusing to print details of the wearisome Senate debate. Senator Lodge sensed this slump in public morale and in November agreed to a roll call on the fifteen reservations. In rapid succession they were taken up and passed, with the vote following rigid party lines.* With these reservations added, the treaty came before the Senate for final decision. Thirty-five Republicans and four Democrats recorded themselves as in favor, while forty-two Democrats and thirteen irreconcilable Republicans combined their votes to defeat the measure. Five of the thirteen irreconcilable votes were cast by Midwestern Senators. A call for unconditional ratification of the treaty without reservations resulted in thirty-eight votes in favor and fifty-three opposed. Only one Middle Western Republican favored the League in this form, only one Democrat was opposed.† Partisan politics, centered in the Republican Middle West, had struck a death blow at Wilson's idealistic internationalism.

The President, however, was unwilling to admit defeat. In January 1920 he referred to the coming election as a "great and solemn referendum" on the League of Nations and appealed to the people to repudiate Republican opposition at the polls. This challenge the Republicans refused to accept openly but their candidate, Warren G. Harding, was known for his anti-League stand, and most people understood that a vote for him was a vote against internationalism. The result was decisive. Harding was carried into office by a landslide vote that was particularly pronounced in the Middle West. Republican Senators from that section now outnumbered their Democratic rivals by 21 to 3, while the Democrats could salvage only 5 seats in the House to 138 for their rivals. Domestic issues were more important than foreign in this one-sided victory, but most of Harding's Middle West applauded when he declared in his victory speech: "You just didn't want a surrender of the United States of America; you wanted America to go under American ideals. That's why you didn't care for the League, which is now deceased." ‡

With this pronouncement friends of internationalism turned to

---

* Only one Western Republican, Senator Porter McCumber of North Dakota, voted against two of the reservations; only Senator James Reed of Missouri deserted his Democratic colleagues to vote for them.

† *Congressional Record,* 66th Cong., 1st Sess., pp. 8767, 8803. McCumber voted for the League without reservations; Reed was opposed.

‡ New York *Times,* November 5, 1920.

the Permanent Court of International Justice in their attempt to salvage at least something from Wilson's peace program. In theory, at least, adherence to the World Court was not a partisan issue, for both Harding and Coolidge were favorable, so long as they could attach reservations divorcing the Court from any League connections. Thus safeguarded, the protocols were presented to the Senate in March 1924. A few Midwestern papers, headed by the Chicago *Tribune* and the Kansas City *Star*, leaped to the attack with all the avidity that had marked their campaign against the League,* but the more usual reaction was one of indifference or ignorance. Most papers ignored the important Senate debate in both their news and editorial columns, for the average Western editor shared with the average Western citizen the belief that such impracticable matters deserved little attention amid the booming prosperity of the 1920's. When the amended protocol was accepted by the Senate in January 1926 by a vote of seventy-six to seventeen, ten of the small opposition group were from the Middle West, a disproportionate number which indicated the continued isolationism of the section.†

When the reservations insisted on by the Senate proved unacceptable to the League Council, Western editors shed no tears. "The reds, pinks and yellows may rave and try to change the situation," one declared, "but they will find . . . that the color combination loved by the citizenship of America is red, white and blue." ‡ Statesmen, however, refused to give up hope of a formula that would be acceptable to both the League Assembly and the United States; they helped develop the Root Plan which was accepted by the League and submitted to the American Government in 1929. Traditionally isolationist papers in the West looked upon this compromise with jaundiced eye, but President Hoover was sufficiently impressed to sound the state of public opinion on the thorny issue. A careful survey showed that 66 per cent of the people favored the World Court, while 26 per cent were opposed. Of the opposition

---

* Chicago *Tribune*, January 21, 23, 25, 27, 1926; Kansas City *Star*, April 29, 1925, January 9, 1926; Cincinnati *Enquirer*, January 2, 1926.

† In a proportional distribution these twelve states should have cast only five votes against the Court. *Congressional Record*, 69th Cong., 1st Sess., p. 2820.

‡ Cincinnati *Enquirer*, February 11, 1927. For similar comments see Chicago *Tribune*, February 11, 1927, and Kansas City *Star*, February 10, 1927.

vote 41 per cent came from the Middle West — another indication of that section's isolationism. Yet two out of every three people favored adherence, and in December 1929 Hoover transmitted the protocols with the Root amendments to the Senate with a request for favorable action. They were referred to the Foreign Relations Committee, where they remained until January 1935.

When at that time President Roosevelt urged their adoption, a storm of protest arose from the Middle West. Congressmen and editorial writers hurled again the anti-Court barbs a decade old, and added others even more telling. Why, they asked, should the United States meddle in European affairs when so much economic reconstruction was needed at home? Why should the nation bother with a world drifting anew toward war when our reward for saving civilization in 1917 had been unpaid debts? Why should a depression-ridden country enmesh itself in the debased standards of the poverty-stricken Old World when millions of Americans were out of work?* As the time for a Senate vote neared, the isolationist fervor steadily mounted. Thousands listened to the Reverend Father Charles E. Coughlin, the rabble-rousing Michigan priest, whose pleas to radio listeners to wire their Congressmen swamped one Ohio newspaper with calls from persons asking the names of their Senators.†

The final vote showed fifty-two of the Senate in favor, thirty-six opposed. This was seven votes less than the necessary two thirds, and the World Court was again, and finally, defeated. Thirteen of the thirty-six negative votes were cast by Middle Western Senators. Thus the resolution failed to secure even a majority vote from this section, while every other section was favorable by more than a two-thirds majority.‡ Partisan politics doubtless played some part

---

* A number of Western editorials against the Court are in *Congressional Record*, 74th Cong., 1st Sess., pp. 686–687. The same point of view is expressed by a petition from the Wisconsin legislature in *ibid.*, pp. 1296–1297.

† Cleveland *Plain Dealer*, January 28, 1935.

‡ The sectional division was more important than the political. Twenty Democrats deserted the administration to vote with fourteen Republicans and two Independents against the Court; forty-four Democrats and eight Republicans voted for adherence. A bloc of four Western states, North Dakota, South Dakota, Minnesota, and Iowa, cast no votes in favor, while every other state in the section supplied at least one negative vote, excepting Michigan, Indiana, and Missouri. *Congressional Record*, 74th Cong., 1st Sess., p. 1147.

468   UNDERSTANDING THE AMERICAN PAST

in explaining the West's isolationism, for the Democratic origins of the Court and its endorsement by Roosevelt rankled some Western Republicans. Ignorance and indifference, combined with postwar disillusionment and preoccupation with depression problems, were more important in shaping the opinion of the Middle West.

It was in this state of mind that Westerners listened approvingly to the findings of the Nye Committee, solidly supported by the so-called neutrality legislation of the mid-1930's, and then smugly watched Europe drift toward war, certain that this struggle was no concern of theirs. Nor did the Munich settlement jar their complacency; for, while most agreed that war was now inevitable, they clung to the belief that the United States would surely remain aloof. A majority firmly opposed the attempted repeal of the arms embargo during the summer of 1939,* and applauded their congressional representatives who urged the people to "refrain from making the job of halting the drifting border sands of Europe a W.P.A. project for the relief of the unemployed millions of our American homes." † Only in this section, according to an Institute of Public Opinion poll in the fall of 1939, did a majority favor retention of the embargo on the shipment of arms abroad.‡

Hitler's invasion of Poland and the outbreak of war did not materially change Western opinion. When President Roosevelt called a special session of Congress to repeal the neutrality legislation he was opposed by a solid bloc of isolationist Congressmen from the Midwest. Some maintained that England and France were the aggressors and did not deserve aid; others that we would certainly be drawn into the war, or that repeal was favored only by munitions makers and international bankers "to sell guns to make a profit even

* Chicago *Tribune*, August 24 and 25, 1939.
† *Congressional Record*, 76th Cong., 1st Sess., Appendix, p. 3377. For other expressions of this sentiment by Western Congressmen see *ibid.*, pp. 1144, 1573, 2025, 2687. Western petitions against repeal of the arms embargo are in *ibid.*, pp. 1144, 1573, 4516.
‡ Repeal was favored by 51 per cent of the people of the East, sixty per cent of the Southerners, 51 per cent of the Pacific Coast residents, and only forty-seven per cent of the Westerners. *Public Opinion Quarterly*, IV (March 1940).

if those guns bathe the earth in mothers' tears."* When the final vote was taken in November 1939, the Middle West was the only section to cast a majority of its House votes against repeal. In only two Western states, Illinois and Missouri, did a majority favor revision; in the four states of Wisconsin, Nebraska, North Dakota, and South Dakota the entire delegation voted for retention. While a slim majority of Midwestern Senators opposed the embargo, in no other section was the vote so close. The important rôle of partisan politics was indicated by the fact that only two of the West's thirty-five Representatives who voted for repeal were Republicans.†

The next months witnessed a rapid shift of American opinion as the fall of Norway, the Low Countries and France brought home the dangerous position of the United States. Some Westerners concluded that this demonstration of Axis strength showed the futility of opposition and increased their demands for complete neutrality, but a larger number decided that American preservation depended on greater aid for the democracies and the increase of our own defenses.‡ Yet even now the West lagged significantly behind other sections. In June 1940 a poll of its people showed that, while 57 per cent of them favored peacetime conscription, 68 per cent of the rest of the nation thought this step necessary.§ When this issue was presented to Congress in the Burke-Wadsworth Selective Service Act, the Middle Westerners in both House and Senate cast a majority of their votes in opposition, while every other section was favorable. Michigan, Wisconsin, North Dakota, and South Dakota gave the measure no support, and only one Representative each from Nebraska, Kansas, Iowa, Minnesota and Indiana voted

* *Congressional Record,* 76th Cong., 2nd Sess., p. 1306. For a convenient summary of isolationist argument during this debate see *New Republic,* May 18, 1942.

† Only nine Democrats deserted their party to join the solid Republican bloc for the embargo. In the House the Eastern states voted 53 to 37 for revision, the Southern 102 to 5, the Pacific states 23 to 9, and the Middle Western 35 to 73. In the Senate the East voted 12 to 6 for revision, the South 27 to 4, and the Middle West 13 to 11. *Congressional Record,* 76th Cong., 2nd Sess., pp. 1024, 1389.

‡ For a convenient summary of Western editorial opinion on this subject see *What America Thinks* (Chicago, 1941).

§ *Public Opinion Quarterly, IV* (September 1940).

in favor. Again the rôle played by partisan politics was shown when only one Midwestern Republican in the House and one in the Senate backed the administration bill.*

These sectional lines did not waver during the critical spring of 1941 when Congress debated the Lend-Lease Bill. Although national opinion was now almost solidly behind the President, a few die-hards fought to the bitter end. In the vanguard were a number of Western Congressmen and the Chicago *Tribune* — which hailed the passage of the act in March 1941 with banner headlines proclaiming "Senate Passes Dictator Bill." "Sinister and suspicious demands for dictatorship powers," "the complete abdication of Congress," "a war bill, a dictatorship bill, a bankruptcy bill" — these were phrases used by Midwesterners in their attack. Nor did the final vote show any change in sectional alignment. Again the West, alone among the sections, cast a majority of its votes against Lend-Lease in both House and Senate.† On this last important issue, before the bombs that fell on Pearl Harbor substituted action for debate, the Middle West remained true to its isolationist tradition.

From this survey certain conclusions seem obvious. The Western swing to isolationism coincided with the free-silver excitement, which solidified political divisions and intensified sectional jealousies. From that date the Middle West viewed with suspicion the the extension of American interests beyond the seas, partly because Democratic presidents were largely responsible and partly because interventionism was favored by Eastern bankers and corporations. Important, too, in shaping that attitude were the large numbers of first- and second-generation Americans who lived in the upper Mississippi Valley: Germans who disliked to make war on the Father-

---

* The Middle West cast 84 votes against and 23 in favor. In the East conscription was favored by a vote of 70 to 21, in the South 103 to 3, and in the Far West 20 to 12. In the Senate the West voted against compulsory service 14 to 7, while the East was in favor 14 to 3 and the South 28 to 2. *Congressional Record*, 76th Cong., 3rd Sess., p. 11142.

† The debate is summarized in the *New Republic*, May 18, 1942. In the House the Middle West voted against Lend-Lease 94 to 41. The East favored the measure 71 to 40, the South 120 to 5, and the Far West 21 to 20. Middle Western Senators voted 14 to 8 against the bill. In the East the vote was favorable by 11 to 6, in the South 29 to 1, and in the Far West 12 to 10. *Congressional Record*, 77th Cong., 1st Sess., pp. 2097, 2229.

land and Scandinavians who brought from the Old World a strong tradition of isolationism. These national attitudes were bolstered by the religious concepts of the many evangelical sects which flourished in the West. Humanitarianism and missionary zeal enlisted their support for the Spanish–American War, but their pacifism inclined them against participation in the wars of Europe.

These prejudices and attitudes, bolstered by the sense of security which stemmed from the section's geographic position and economic self-sufficiency, help to explain Middle Western isolationism. More conservative than the rest of the nation, the West clung to nineteenth-century traditions after other regions had recognized the inevitability of a new world rôle for the twentieth-century United States.

The Third-Generation American

by

MARCUS L. HANSEN

["The Problem of the Third-Generation Immigrant," from Augustana Historical Society Publications (1938). Reprinted by permission.]

The continuous stream of immigrants to this country's shores from all parts of the world has been a unique feature of American history. For a long time, however, the historiography of immigration was largely in the hands of the amateur historian and the filiopietist who, while serving as trail blazers for latecoming professional historians, frequently did so in the spirit of attempting to prove that the peoples they were writing about were as good as, nay better than, other ethnic groups in the American population. John Fiske, no innocent himself when it came to singing the praises of the Anglo-Saxon, nevertheless was quite justified in wondering in connection with extravagant claims of achievement made by the ethnic historians, "whether the people about whom we are reading . . . ever left anything for other people to do. . . ." [1]

In the 1920's the field of immigration found an outstanding advocate among professional historians in the person of Marcus L. Hansen. His essay "The History of American Immigration as a Field for Research" pointed out a great many avenues of historical investigation connected with the impact of immigration on American development, and he invited scholars to explore this rich field. [2]

American historians, however, did not respond to Hansen as they did to the Turner thesis. Nevertheless, with the growing emphasis upon minority problems in the 1930's and 1940's — among the mass of good, bad, and indifferent literature ground out in this area — some notable work in the history of immigration was done by

Hansen himself, who died prematurely in 1939, and by Carl Wittke, Theodore C. Blegen, Oscar Handlin, and George M. Stephenson. These scholars have evolved two rather distinct approaches to the history of immigration. The first stresses the contribution of the immigrant group to the over-all culture pattern; the second centers in the immigrant community, its internal evolution and external relationships. Carl Wittke's We Who Built America *is an outstanding example of the first approach and Oscar Handlin's* Boston's Immigrants *well typifies the second. However, what George M. Stephenson said in 1929 still holds true today: that there has not yet appeared "the man with the magic touch, who by a process known only to the master" could produce a "masterpiece of historical synthesis" in the field of immigration.*[3]

Hansen seemed to be on his way toward this goal and, if he had lived, might have achieved it. He was a master historian and every scholar working in the field of immigration is indebted to him.

In the selection below, Hansen is concerned with an aspect of immigration which has been of particular significance since the enactment of the restrictive immigration measures of the 1920's and the still more restrictive requirements of the Immigration Act of 1952. Because the flow of immigrants has been halted, we no longer have in America what publicists and scholars throughout most of our history used to call an "immigration problem." Instead, an ethnic problem of the present and very likely of the future is the relationship of groupings in the American population to ancestral cultures, which are not likely to be re-enforced by a steady stream of immigrants from European homelands.

The following is the text of an address by Hansen delivered before the Augustana Historical Society.

B Y LONG-ESTABLISHED custom whoever speaks of immigration must refer to it as a "problem." It was a problem to the first English pioneers in the New World scattered up and down the Atlantic coast. Whenever a vessel anchored in the James River and a few score weary and emaciated gentlemen, worn out by three months upon the Atlantic, stumbled up the bank, the veterans who had survived nature's rigorous "seasoning" looked at one another in despair and asked: "Who is to feed them? Who is to teach them to fight the Indians, or grow tobacco, or clear the marshy lands and build a home in the malaria-infested swamps? These immigrants certainly are a problem." And three hundred years later, when in the course of a summer more than a million Europeans walked down the gangplanks of the ocean greyhounds into the large reception halls built to receive them, government officials, social workers, journalists, said: "How are these people from the peasant farms of the Mediterranean going to adjust themselves to the routine of mines and industries, and how are they going to live in a country where the language is strange, and how are they, former subjects of monarchs and lords, going to partake in the business of governing themselves? These immigrants certainly are a problem."

They certainly were. The adventurers (call them colonists or immigrants) who transferred civilization across the Atlantic numbered more than forty million souls. Every one of them was a problem to his family and himself, to the officials and landlords from whom he parted, to the officials and landlords whom he joined. On every mile of the journey, on land and on sea, they caused concern to someone. The public authorities at the ports of embarkation sighed the traditional sigh of relief when the emigrant vessel was warped away from the dock and stood out to the open sea carrying the bewildered persons who for a week or more had wandered about the streets; the captain of that vessel was happy when the last of his passengers who had complained of everything from food to weather said good-bye — often with a clenched fist; and the officers of New York and Baltimore were no less happy when the newly arrived American set out for the West. How much of a problem the forty million actually were will not be known until their history is written with realism as well as sympathy.

The problem of the immigrant was not solved; it disappeared. Foreign-born to the number of almost fifteen million are still part of the American population, but they are no longer immigrants. By one adjustment after the other they have accommodated themselves and reconciled themselves to the surrounding world of society, and when they became what the natives called "Americanized" (which was often nothing but a treaty of peace with society) they ceased to be a problem. This was the normal evolution of an individual, but as long as the group classified as immigrants was being constantly recruited by the continual influx of Europeans the problem remained. The quota law of 1924 erected the first dam against the current and the depression of 1929 cut off the stream entirely. Statistics reveal what has happened. During the year ended June 30, 1936, there were admitted as immigrants only 36,329 aliens. During the same period 35,817 aliens left the United States for permanent residence abroad — a net gain of only 512. But this was the first year since 1931 that there had been any gain at all. The great historic westward tide of Europeans has come to an end and there is nothing in American conditions or sentiment that it will ever be revived.

Thus there has been removed from the pages of magazines, from the debates in Congress, and from the thoughts of social workers the well-known expression: "the problem of the immigrant." Its going has foreshadowed the disappearance of a related matter of concern which was almost as troublesome as the first, a rather uncertain worry which was called "the problem of the second generation."

The sons and the daughters of the immigrants were really in a most uncomfortable position. They were subjected to the criticism and taunts of the native Americans and to the criticism and taunts of their elders as well. All who exercised any authority over them found fault with the response. Too often in the schoolroom the Yankee schoolmistress regarded them as mere dullards hardly worthy of her valuable attention. Thus neglected they strayed about the streets where the truant officer picked them up and reported them as incorrigible. The delinquency of the second generation was talked about so incessantly that finally little Fritz and little Hans became convinced that they were not like the children from the other side of the tracks. They were not slow in comprehending the source of all their woes: it lay in the strange dualism into which they had been born.

Life at home was hardly more pleasant. Whereas in the schoolroom they were too foreign, at home they were too American. Even the immigrant father who compromised most willingly in adjusting his outside affairs to the realities that surrounded him insisted that family life, at least, should retain the pattern that he had known as a boy. Language, religion, customs and parental authority were not to be modified simply because the home had been moved four or five thousand miles to the westward. When the son and the daughter refused to conform, their action was considered a rebellion of ungrateful children for whom so many advantages had been provided. The gap between the two generations was widened and family spirit embittered by repeated misunderstanding. How to inhabit two worlds at the same time was the problem of the second generation.

That problem was solved by escape. As soon as he was free economically, an independence that usually came several years before he was free legally, the son struck out for himself. He wanted to forget everything: the foreign language that left an unmistakable trace in his English speech, the religion that continually recalled childhood struggles, the family customs that should have been the happiest of all memories. He wanted to be away from all physical reminders of early days, in an environment so different, so American, that all associates naturally assumed that he was as American as they.

This picture has been deliberately overdrawn, but who will deny that the second generation wanted to forget, and even when the ties of family affection were strong, wanted to lose as many of the evidences of foreign origin as they could shuffle off?

Most easy to lose was that which, if retained, might have meant the most to the civilization of the American republic. The immigrant brought with him European culture. This does not mean that the man who wielded the pickax was really a Michelangelo or that the one who took to house painting was in fact an unrecognized Rembrandt. They brought a popular though uncritical appreciation of art and music; they felt at home in an environment where such aspects of culture were taken for granted and (what is not to be overlooked in any consideration of the development of American life) they did not subscribe to the prevailing American sentiment that it was not quite moral for a strong, able-bodied man to earn his living by playing a fiddle. If they did not come in loaded down with culture, at least they were plentifully supplied with the seeds of culture that, scattered in a fertile soil, could flourish mightily.

The soil was not fertile. Americans of the nineteenth century were not entirely unfriendly to a little art now and then if it were limited to the front parlor and restricted to the women. . . . The second generation was entirely aware of the contempt in which [any other artistic] activities were held and they hastened to prove that they knew nothing about casts, symphonies or canvas. Nothing was more Yankee than a Yankeeized person of foreign descent.

The leaders among the natives proclaimed loudly: "It is wonderful how these young people catch the spirit of American institutions!" The leaders among the foreign-born sighed and said to themselves:

This apostasy means nothing good. It is not good for the sons and daughters who give up a heritage richer than farm acres and city lots; it is not good for this uncouth pioneer nation which has spent its time chopping down trees and rolling stones and has never learned how the genius of one might brighten the life of many and satisfy some human longings that corn bread and apple pie can never appease. Blind, stupid America . . . they said . . . the one nation of the globe which has had offered to it the rich gifts that every people of Europe brought and laid at its feet — and it has spurned them all! The immigrants, perhaps, may be excused. Their thoughts and efforts were taken up with material cares and they were naturally under some suspicion. But nothing can absolve the traitors of the second generation, who deliberately threw away what had been preserved in the home. When they are gone, all hope will be lost and the immigration of the nineteenth century will have contributed nothing to the development of America but what came out of the strong muscles of a few million patient plodders. . . .

These pessimists were wrong. All has not been lost. After the second generation comes the third; and with the third appears a new force and a new opportunity which, if recognized in time, can not only do a good job of salvaging but probably can accomplish more than either the first or the second could ever have achieved.

Anyone who has the courage to codify the laws of history must include what can be designated "the principle of third-generation interest." The principle is applicable in all fields of historical study. It explains the recurrence of movements that seemingly are dead; it is a factor that should be kept in mind, particularly in literary or cultural history; it makes it possible for the present to know something about the future.

The theory is derived from the almost universal phenomenon that what the son wishes to forget the grandson wishes to remember. The tendency might be illustrated by a hundred examples. The case of the Civil War may be cited. The Southerners who survived the four years of that struggle never forgot. In politics and in conversation the "lost cause" was an endless theme. Those who listened became weary and the sons of the Confederate veterans were among them. *That* second generation made little effort to justify the action of their fathers. Their expressed opinion was that, after all, the result was inevitable and undoubtedly for the best. These sons went North and won success in every field of business and in every branch of learning. But now the grandsons of the Confederates rule in the place of the sons and there is no apologizing for the events of 1861; instead there is a belligerency that asserts the moral and constitutional justice of their grandfathers' policy. The South has been revived. Its history is taught with a fervid patriotism in the universities and schools. Recently there has been formed the Southern Historical Association as an evidence of the growing interest. The great novel of the Civil War and Reconstruction era was not written by one who had participated in the events or witnessed the scenes. It did not come from the pen of one who had listened to a father's reminiscences. *Gone with the Wind* was written by a granddaughter of the Confederacy, in the year 1936, approximately sixty years after the period with which it dealt had come to an end.

Immigration not only has its history, it has its historiography. The writing of descriptions of that great epic movement began almost as early as the movement itself. Every immigrant letter written from new shores was history, very personal and very uncritical. Every sheaf of reminiscences written by one of the participants in his later years was also history, a little more uncritical. There was much to be recounted, and since sons would not listen the gray-headed participants got together and, organized as pioneer societies, they told one another of the glorious deeds that they had seen and sometimes performed and listened to the reading of the obituaries of the giants that had fallen. When the last of them had joined his ancestors, the pioneer society automatically disbanded — leaving behind as the first chapter of immigrant historiography a conglomerate mass of literature, much and often most of it useless. All of it seemed useless to the son who cleared out his father's desk and he resolved not to waste any of his time on such pointless pursuits.

As a broad generalization it may be said that the second generation is not interested in and does not write any history. That is just another aspect of their policy of forgetting. Then, however, appears the "third generation." They have no reason to feel any inferiority when they look about them. They are American-born. Their speech is the same as that of those with whom they associate. Their material wealth is the average possession of the typical citizen. When anyone speaks to such a generation about immigrants, he always makes it clear that he has in mind the more recent hordes that have been pouring through the gates and any suggestion that the onrush should be stemmed is usually prefaced with the remark that recent immigrants are not so desirable as the pioneers that arrived in earlier times. It is in an attitude of pride that the substantial land owner or merchant looks about him and says: "This prosperity is our achievement, that of myself and of my fathers; it is a sign of the hardy stock from which we have sprung; who were they and why did they come?" And so their curiosity is projected back into the family beginnings. Those who are acquainted with the universities of the Middle West, where a large proportion of the students are grandchildren and great-grandchildren of the nineteenth century immigrants can sense this attitude of inquiry and cannot escape the feeling of pride in which they study the history and culture of the nations from which their ancestors came.

To show how universal this spirit has been we can retrace some periodic resurgences of national spirit and relate them to the time of immigration. There were Irishmen in America before the Revolution but there is no reason to question the generalization that until 1840 two-thirds of the emigrants from Ireland were the so-called

Scotch-Irish. In the 1830's their influx was particularly large; in fact, the great proportion of Ulstermen who came to America arrived in the course of the decade. Sixty years later (at the time of the third generation) a renaissance of Scotch-Irish sentiment in the United States was strikingly apparent. Local societies were formed that met in monthly or quarterly conclave to sing the praises of their forebears and to glory in the achievements of the Presbyterian Church. Beginning in 1889 and continuing for more than a decade representatives of these societies met in an annual national meeting called a "Scotch-Irish Congress." Then the movement lost its impetus. Leaders died or took up other activities; members refrained from paying dues; attendance at sessions dwindled. After 1903 no more Scotch-Irish congresses were held.

We can pass to another example. The large German immigration reached its crest in the late 1840's and early 1850's. A little over half a century later, in the first decade of the twentieth century, a breeze of historical interest stirred the German-American community. One of the number was moved to offer a prize for the best historical discussion of the contribution of the German element to American life. Not only the prize-winning work (the well-known volume by A. B. Faust) but many of the manuscripts that had been submitted in the competition were published, forming a library of German-American activity in many fields. Several local and state historical societies were formed and the study of German literature in universities and schools enjoyed an amazing popularity that later observers could ascribe only to the propaganda of an intriguing nation. The Theodore Roosevelt Professorship established at the University of Berlin in 1907 was an expression of the same revival. The war naturally put an end to this activity and obscured much of the valuable work that the investigators had performed.

The auspices under which we have met this evening suggest the next example to be cited. The large Scandinavian immigration began in the 1850's and after the interruption of the Civil War reached its culmination in the 1880's. True to expectations we find that at present the most lively interest in history of this nature is exhibited in Sandinavian circles in America. Among Scandinavians, Norwegians were pioneers and in historical research they are also a step in advance. The Swedes came a little later and an intelligent prophet of that period looking forward to the cultural development of the nationality in their new home would have said: "About 1930 a historical society will be formed." It was. In June 1930 the Augustana Historical Society was organized among the members of the Augustana Synod which so faithfully represents the more than a million people of Swedish descent who are citizens of the American republic. And now . . . I come to the topic of the evening, a subject which will be interpreted in the light of the foregoing remarks. It reads: The problem of the third-generation immigrant.

As problems go it is not one to cause worry or to be shunned. It has none of the bitterness or heart-breaking features of its predecessors. It is welcome. In summary form it may be stated as follows: Whenever any immigrant group reaches the third-generation stage in its development a spontaneous and almost irresistible impulse arises which forces the thoughts of many people of different professions, different positions in life, and different points of view to interest themselves in that one factor which they have in common: heritage — the heritage of blood. The problem is: How can this impulse be organized and directed so that the results growing therefrom will be worthy of the high instincts from which it has sprung, and a dignified tribute to the pioneers, and at the same time be a contribution to the history of the United States which has received all Europeans on a basis of equality and which should record their achievements in the same spirit of impartiality. . . ?

The Swedish stock in America is fast approaching the third-generation stage. During the decade of the 1880's their coming reached its height in numbers. The census of 1930 records that, of the persons born in Sweden giving the date of their arrival in the country, 52 per cent landed before 1900 — and this in spite of the great mortality that the newcomers of that period have suffered. The children that crowd the Sunday School rooms of the churches of this Synod, it is well known, are the grandsons and granddaughters of the pioneers that built the churches; grandsons and granddaughters, I am also sure, are present in increasing numbers in the student body of this college which those same pioneers, at the cost of many sacrifices, built for the sake of those who were to come after them. Among the leaders of this society are men of the first generation and of the second generation but they are the proverbial exception, or it may be better to say they are third generation in spirit. No matter how active they are in leadership the organization can succeed only if the grandchildren of the pioneers will follow.

We will assume that this will be the case; that the membership the Augustana Historical Society will continue to increase in numbers, that the members will continue to pay their dues, that a few patrons will arise to sponsor special enterprises in research and publication. It is not my object to enlighten you on how to bring about this happy condition. . . . My suggestions will be of a different nature and will center about another set of questions: What fields shall be investigated? Where shall the emphasis be put in research and publication? What should be the attitude in which the past, which belongs not only to the Swedes but also to the Americans, should be approached? In attempting an answer I speak with no authority except that which comes from several years of delving into the records of pioneer and historical societies of America.

Everyone accepts the premise that self-laudation is not the end in view. Nevertheless it will be hard to keep out because of the human characteristic of speaking nothing but good of the men who labored hard and have now disappeared from the earthly stage. At the first meeting of the Scotch-Irish Congress the speakers presented one paper after the other which dealt with the achievements of the Ulsterman at home and abroad, during all ages and in all spheres of human effort. Finally one of the delegates arose and made a cutting remark that only a Scotch-Irishman would dare to make. While listening to the programs, he said, he had been asking himself the question: "What on earth have the rest of creation been doing for the last eighteen hundred years?" That question should be in the mind of every writer who is tempted to generalize on the contribution of ethnic groups to the development of American life.

If not to the laudation of great men, to what activities should the efforts of the society be directed? Let that question first be approached by a calm realization of the fact that the society will not live forever. The time will come when membership will dwindle, when promising subjects for research will be few in number and of little popular interest. That has been the life-course of every organization of this nature. The constituency becomes gradually thinned out as the third generation merges into the fourth and the fourth shades off into the fifth. Even societies with substantial endowments have in their later years found it difficult to continue to produce work of high scholarly quality. The final judgment rendered regarding the success or failure of this society as of others will rest upon the answer given to two pertinent inquiries: Did they, when the time was appropriate, write the history of the special group with whom they were concerned on broad impartial lines? Did they make a permanent contribution to the meaning of American history at large? A few proposals by the following of which a satisfactory reply can be given to both of those questions are now in order.

First of all, let it be remembered that the history of any immigrant stock in America is far broader than the history of the particular religious organization that was predominant in the number of communicants that it could claim. The neglect of that fact was the first error made by historical writers in America. When they set out to write the story of the settlement of Englishmen in New England they centered it all about the migration of the puritan church and neglected a hundred other factors that surrounded the coming and establishment of the colonies on that coast. In recent years some correction has been made but the traditional emphasis has been so great that in spite of the labors of many scholars and the resources of a dozen secular institutions, the history of New England is still less satisfactory than that of any other section of the older part of the country. From such a false start may the Augustana Historical Society be preserved!

Religion must certainly be a leading theme in the program. The church was the first, the most important and the most significant institution that the immigrants established. Its policies reacted upon every other phase of their existence; but in turn, and, in fact, first, those other phases of their existence established the conditions under which the church was planted and grew. If one should study the agriculture, the system of land purchase, the distribution of population, the state of the roads, the circulation of books and newspapers, the development of amusements, he would be in a better position to appraise the situation that the church did occupy in the life of every community. In Mr. Rölvaag's stirring novel *Giants in the Earth* no episode is presented with more effect than that which recounts the coming of the clergyman, and the effect is produced not by the description of the man and his mission. It is the background of dull, material routine that has preceded that gives to the brief chapter its epic quality. History had been made before the clergyman and the church appeared, and to be understood they must be placed in their proper order in the sequence of events.

Moreover, for an understanding of religious development, to the formation of those churches that broke with the faith of the old country, relatively more attention should be given than the number of their communicants would warrant. In no other experience was the psychology of the immigrant more clearly reflected. When they said that they passed from the old world to the new, many of them meant that the world should be new in all respects. When they gave up allegiance to a government it was easy to give up allegiance to a church. The secessions from the Lutheran faith can be dealt with conveniently, quickly, and without embarrassment by ascribing them to the successful methods of proselyting that the well-financed American home missionary societies employed. But the immigrant met the proselyter halfway — perhaps more than halfway — and when one knows what was going on in the mind of the person who did break away from his mother church it will be easier to understand the actions of some of those who did not break away but certainly caused frictions within the church to which they remained true, and created situations that could not have arisen in the old Swedish parish from which they had recently come.

Even the study of politics is not entirely foreign to an organization which has chosen as its mission the history of the Augustana Synod. The clergymen of that Synod, like the clergymen of any other religious body in the Republic, had no intention of destroying the fundamental separation of church and state which the fathers of the Constitution had ordained; but how they itched to go into politics! How they lived to find in every Sunday's text some idea that could be applied to the decision of that burning political issue that the men in the audience had been discussing before the services had begun, and which they would surely begin to discuss again as soon as the benediction had been pronounced! There is much evidence to suggest that the immigrant church had a great influence in determining the way in which the naturalized citizen would cast his vote. But not a single study has been made of church influence in any election and the results of such a study would throw as much light upon the status of the church as it would upon the political history of that election.

The church had some competitors in the matter of interest, affection, and usefulness. Whatever the difficulties that attended the founding of the pioneer congregation, that of inducing the immigrant to join was hardly existent. The immigrant was an inveterate joiner — a habit which was, without question, the result of his feeling of lonesomeness. In Europe the individual was born into many groups that he had to join in America and he entered into them rather lightheartedly hoping that from all he would derive the satisfaction that no single one could yield. When some energetic spirit said to him "Come and join this fraternal organization," he went; when the suggestion of a singing society was broached, he fell in with the plan; when someone undertook to line up a shooting corps he took down his gun and practiced marksmanship. All of these pursuits weakened somewhat the hold of the church, and the minister was led to adopt an uncompromising attitude toward amusements that otherwise would have been held both innocent and useful. Therefore, it can be said that without a knowledge of the social environment the policy of the church can not be understood.

If these suggestions should be followed, the product would be a history of the Swedes in America that no one could accuse of being tainted with partiality. Perhaps not all the passages would be read with a glow of pride, but there would be no humiliation, and the pride in the achievement of what no other ethnic group in America has been willing to do would soon overcome regrets that arose out of what truth made it necessary to say. In such an accomplishment the Augustana Historical Society would achieve all that its founders had hoped for it in the field of religious history, and the incidental products would give to the world a true and inspiring picture of what the Swedish pioneers had done in the task of subduing the primitive American wilderness.

Although a historical society has justified its existence when it has faithfully recorded the experiences and achievements of the particular element in the population or the particular region in the country that it was created to serve, still, unless the story that is written from these records can be made to fit in as one chapter in the larger volume that is called American histroy, the charge of antiquarianism can hardly be escaped. Men of insight who understand that it is the ultimate fate of any national group to be amalgamated into the composite American race will be reconciled to the thought that their historical activities will in time be merged with the activities of other societies of the same nature and finally with the main line of American historiography itself. How such a merging may profoundly influence the course of all national historical writing is illustrated by reference to that one group which is the most mature among the population minorities.

The Scotch-Irish Congress during the fourteen years of its existence published ten volumes of *Proceedings.* A study of the contents of these volumes reveals the widening nature of the interests growing out of the researches. The laudatory character of the contributions to the first publication has been mentioned. Such papers are not entirely absent from the last volume but there also appear titles such as these. "Paths and Roads of our Forefathers," "The Colonial Defenses of Franklin County," "German Life and Thought in a Scotch-Irish Settlement" — substantial contributions to the pioneer history of the environment in which the group developed.

It is well known that during the decade of the 1890's the character of American historical writing changed. A new emphasis appeared. Scholars looked beyond the older settlements ranged along the seaboard into the communities in the back country. A word that every schoolboy can now explain crept into the textbooks. This word and this theory now almost dominate every page in the volume. The word is "frontier" and the theory is the "frontier interpretation of American history." . . .

This new emphasis is universally credited to Professor Frederick J. Turner. However, Turner or no Turner, the frontier hypothesis was bound to come and to appear in the very decade during which he wrote his famous essay. In fact, the hypothesis may be distilled from the conglomerate mass of information and theory jumbled together in the ten volumes of Scotch-Irish *Proceedings*. It is doubtful whether the pronouncement of one man, no matter how brilliant, could have turned the course of historical writing unless it were already veering in that direction. It is quite possible that Turner, who wrote in 1893, drew upon the frontier interest that the Scotch-Irish were arousing by their studies of the part that the Ulstermen took in the movement of settlement into the West. The interest that they awakened united with the scholars that Professor Turner trained to give to American history its new and significant social interpretation.

The frontier doctrine in its original narrow statement has been overdone. We are beginning to see that the Mississippi Valley was for fifty years the frontier of Europe as well as of the Eastern states, and that it reacted upon England, Germany, and Scandinavia with a force comparable to that which it exerted upon Atlantic America. Some historians with the orthodox professional training have recognized this fact, and they are attempting, in a rather clumsy way, to analyze the operation of these influences. There is, however, one omission in their training. They know nothing about the hundreds of immigrant communities in America that formed the human connecting link between the Old World and the New, nothing about the millions of personal contacts that brought humble public opinion on both sides of the Atlantic so close together.

The next stage in American historical writing will concern itself with this widened outlook. Herein lies not only the great opportunity but also the great obligation of the third-generation historical activity. It alone can provide the atmosphere; it alone can uncover the sources; it alone can interpret the mentality of the millions of persons who had not entirely ceased to be Europeans and had not yet become accepted Americans. The problem of the third-generation immigrant is to undertake the job that has been assigned and to perform it well.

The close of this discourse may very properly be a warning. It can be assumed too readily that the history of migration cannot be anything but a desirable influence. That is not necessarily the case. Prejudice and super-nationalism may be the product. Societies organized with the laudable intention of commemorating the deeds of which any people should be proud may fall into the hands of those who will use them for instruments of propaganda. Instead of a world covered with a network of associations which will foster an appreciation of the best that each nation has produced, we may find international societies for the promotion of hatred and intolerance. Historians must recognize an obligation to guide the national curiosity to know the past along those lines which will serve the good of all.

If told as it transpired, the epic of migration can add an ideal to take the place of one of the many that recent decades have shattered. For it is a simple story of how troubled men, by courage and action, overcame their difficulties, and how people of different tongues and varied culture have managed to live together in peace.

Franklin D. Roosevelt
and the New Deal

by
ERIC F. GOLDMAN

[This chapter, originally entitled "Second Honeymoon," is reprinted from RENDEZVOUS WITH DESTINY by Eric F.
Goldman, by permission of Alfred A. Knopf, Inc. Copyright
1952 by Alfred A. Knopf, Inc.]

*Franklin Delano Roosevelt is perhaps the most fully-documented
individual in American history. There are, estimates Frank Freidel,
who is in the midst of a planned six-volume biography of Roosevelt,
approximately forty tons of Roosevelt papers in the library at Hyde
Park, New York. Roosevelt, in 1939, explained this enormous ac-
cumulation by recalling that while he was serving as librarian of
the Hasty Pudding Club at Harvard, an elderly book dealer advised him to save everything. That advice, Roosevelt continued,
"has been thrown in my teeth by all the members of my family
almost every week that has passed since that time. I have destroyed practically nothing. As a result, we have a mine for which
future historians will curse as well as praise me."* [1]

*In addition to the vast collection of Roosevelt papers, almost
everyone who came into contact with him as President, from cabinet officers to White House guards, has rushed into print with their
impressions. Contrast this situation with that which followed Lincoln's death, when twenty-three years elasped before a member of
Lincoln's cabinet, Hugh McCullogh, published his memoirs; while
Lincoln's own papers were not released until 1948. There is, too,
a great deal more material available about Roosevelt than others of
our Presidents because words and deeds that in earlier periods in
our history would have passed unnoticed have been recorded,
thanks to technological advance and the kind of news coverage
given presidential doings and public affairs generally. Conse-*

quently, Mr. Freidel can now undertake, so soon after Roosevelt's death, the kind of detailed biographical treatment that Dumas Malone, Irving Brant, and Arthur Link are at this late date attempting for Jefferson, Madison, and Wilson respectively.

The presence in overwhelming quantities of materials bearing upon Roosevelt does not make easier the evaluation of the controversial character of his administration. Nor, for that matter, does it cast too much light on Roosevelt as a personality, who, for all that his family, associates, and friends — including Mrs. Roosevelt, the children, and Harry Hopkins — have told us, still remains obscure.[2]

One of the more controversial aspects of the Roosevelt administration is the New Deal, concerning the wisdom and achievement of which historians are as divided as is the country as a whole. On the one hand, Louis Hacker sees in the New Deal "the real danger of a bureaucracy: that it tended to associate its own well-being with the general welfare. This was one of the vexing problems the New Deal had created. It was not possible to dismiss it lightly or seek to disguise its perils by referring to the new state as the 'social service state.'"[3] On the other hand, Hacker's colleague at Columbia University, Professor Henry Steele Commager, disputed the former's contention that the New Deal had wrought a "third American Revolution" by introducing the principle of the "interventionist state." According to Commager, "The 'Roosevelt revolution' was no revolution, but rather the culmination of half a century of historical development. . . . Indeed, the two major issues of the Roosevelt administration — the domestic issue of the extension of government control for democratic purposes, and the international issue of the role of America as a world power — emerged in the 1890's, and a sound perspective will see the half-century from the 1890's to the present as an historical unit. The roots of the New Deal, the origins of our participation in this war [World War II] go deep into our past, and neither development is comprehensible except in terms of that past."[4]

In the following selection, Princeton's Professor Eric F. Goldman presents the New Deal's first "hundred days" against the background of American liberalism and Roosevelt's personal development.

IT STARTED like 1873. On October 29, 1929, scrambling, yelling traders dumped 16,410,000 shares of stock on the New York Stock Exchange, and the United States refused to believe what it was watching. A nation returned to the cult of captains of industry did not expect its gods to fail it. "Wall Street may sell stocks," thousands chorused with the *Saturday Evening Post,* "but Main Street is buying goods." After a period of collapsing businesses, people still grinned with the billboards: "Wasn't the Depression Terrible?" Then, as unemployment mounted at the rate of four thousand a week, confidence gave way to worry, worry to bitterness. By 1931 Amos was asking Andy: "Did you hear about the fellow who registered at the hotel and the clerk said, 'For sleeping or jumping, sir?' " * The 1930's, like the 1870's, had finally admitted that the captains of industry did not have the situation in hand.

But having started so much like '73, the new depression soon took on far grimmer lines. All the things that had shocked the country in the Seventies reappeared in doubly disturbing form. Small businesses were going down at a rate never before approached, and the number of farmers losing their lands was nearing the three-quarters-of-a-million mark. Henry George in '73 may have been horrified by so much poverty amid so much technological advance. He did not live during a decade when, on the one hand, the New York World's Fair unveiled television, the Rust brothers devised a mechanical cotton-picker, and Clarence Birdseye's frozen foods entered mass production, while, on the other hand, as soon as the truck pulled away from the Chicago garbage dump, "men, women and children . . . started digging with sticks, some with their hands, grabbing bits of food and vegetables." † The pillaging and bloodshed of the strike of 1877 had been disquieting, but in the early Thirties, food riots were becoming common, 15,000 angry veterans milled around the national Capitol, and in the Midwest, where the Seventies had produced nothing more violent than Greenback speeches, farmers dragged from his bench a judge who tried to foreclose mortgages, beat him, then strung him up until he fainted.

* Quoted in Dixon Wecter: *The Age of the Great Depression* (Macmillan, 1948), p. 13, and Don Ross: "Blue Anniversary," New York *Herald Tribune,* October 30, 1949.
† Quoted in Wecter, p. 13.

As the depression ground past its third year, an unprecedented fear seeped through the nation. Would the old America, the America of bountiful opportunity, ever reappear? Men had asked the question before; this time the questioning was much more widespread, much more persistent. Didn't all the violence and talk of violence mean that the United States had reached the iron class lines of Europe? Hadn't the onrush of laborsaving inventions made large-scale unemployment permanent under any system approximating free enterprise? How could the country ever escape the consequences of the final settlement of the West?* Perhaps an eighty-year-old Californian had hit it right when he told his story to the State Unemployment Commission. The depression of 1873 had cost him his job as a machinist, the old man said, but "at that time the whole West was open to Homesteaders. At that time the mountains were honeycombed with . . . new mines. . . . Railroads had been building all over the country. . . . New towns were being opened." A railroad hired him as a section hand, then he went on to the grocery business, until by the Nineties he was prospering. The hard times of 1893 ruined him again, and once more, by homesteading, he climbed back. But now, he was sure in his old bones, there was no way back for him or for millions of younger men. "There isn't an acre of decent land to be had for homesteading," he told the Commission. "There isn't a railroad to be built anywhere. There isn't a chance for a new factory. . . . Years ago Horace Greeley made a statement, 'Young man, go West and grow up with the country.' Were he living today, he would make the statement, 'Go West, young man, and drown yourself in the Pacific Ocean.' " †

Gloomy and restive, the nation watched its President finding rea-

* In an interesting passage Franklin Roosevelt later remarked that when he took office, "millions of people, gripped by . . . fear, had begun to feel that the machinery of modern American economics and Government had broken down so completely under the strain of the new demands placed upon it by modern civilization, that an entirely new type of mechanics for existence would have to be invented. They were not clear in their own minds as to what type they should seek; but their confidence and morale were so shaken that many of them would have been willing to accept any form of specious glittering guarantee of a chance to earn a livelihood." (Samuel I. Rosenman, ed.: The Public Papers and Addresses of Franklin D. Roosevelt (Random House, 1938), II, 3.)

† Quoted in California State Unemployment Commission: Report and Recommendations (San Francisco, 1932), pp. 94–95.

sons for hesitating, mincing ahead to small measures, mumbling promises of recovery. Few were sure what should be done; millions were sure that, whatever should be done, this administration was not likely to do it. As unemployment crossed the thirteen-million mark and corn sank below thirty cents for the first time since the Civil War, the voters swept into office the man who was running against Herbert Hoover.*

The voters were reaching desperately into the dark. They knew little about Franklin Roosevelt beyond the luster of his family name, the fact that he had made a good if unspectacular record as Governor of New York, his obvious pleasantness and energy. Roosevelt's campaign speeches hardly filled out the picture. He spoke kindly of "the forgotten man at the bottom of the economic pyramid" and made clear that he proposed a "New Deal" for the nation. But some of the campaign sounded as if he intended to use the old cards of government economy, sound currency, and antitrust action, while other speeches suggested a crisp new pack.† He was sure Roosevelt was against Prohibition, Elmer Davis wrote after listening to the candidate define the New Deal. "For the rest, you could not quarrel with a single one of his generalities; you seldom can. But what they mean (if anything) is known only to Franklin D. Roosevelt and his God." Then Davis contributed his vote against Hoover and kept on wondering, with the rest of the country, what kind of man he was backing for the White House.‡

Promptly, on Inauguration Day itself, the country decided one thing about its new President. Early on that bleak morning the creeping paralysis of bank closings touched the nerve center of

---

* Estimates of unemployment varied widely. Frances Perkins, Roosevelt's Secretary of Labor, stated that the estimates at the time Roosevelt took office ranged from 13,300,000 to 17,900,000. *The Roosevelt I Knew* (Viking, 1946), p. 182.

† Rosenman, I, 625, 659. In one address — the Commonwealth Club speech — Roosevelt did clearly anticipate a sweeping progressive program (Rosenman, I, 742–756), but the purport of this speech was blurred by other utterances.

‡ Quoted in Frederick L. Allen: *Since Yesterday* (Harper, 1940), pp. 81–82. Mr. Davis has added: "I had hopes after Roosevelt's Commonwealth Club speech in September, but he said so many other things during the campaign that I didn't know till Inauguration Day whether he meant it or not." (Letter to me, October 31, 1951, quoted by permission of Mr. Davis.)

New York; by eleven A.M., the nation's financial system had come to a dead stop. Hoover, half-sick from worry, began the day with a despairing "We are at the end of our string."* Roosevelt, hatless and coatless in the chill March air, his voice strong and clear, his jaw jutted out, told the United States: "This great Nation will endure as it has endured, will revive and will prosper. So, first of all, let me assert my firm belief that the only thing we have to fear is fear itself — nameless, unreasoning, unjustified terror which paralyzes needed efforts to convert retreat into advance." Heartfelt cheers, the first real cheers Washington had heard since 1929, roared up from the crowd. Roosevelt paused, calmly brushed a speck from his manuscript. "We do not distrust the future. . . . The people of the United States have not failed. In their need they have . . . asked for discipline and direction under leadership. They have made me the present instrument of their wishes. In the spirit of the gift I take it." † As the new President drove away, he responded to applause by shaking his hands over his head like a cocky prizefighter. It was all wonderful theater; it could have been little more. But in that yearning hour most Americans were sure they had stumbled upon a leader who was totally devoid of fear that closed frontiers, laborsaving devices, or anything else need alter the fundamental way of American life.

Almost as soon, and beyond anyone's questioning, the new President revealed another characteristic. Franklin Roosevelt was the most complete devotee of playing by ear the White House had ever known. Restless and mercurial in his thinking, a connoisseur of theories but impatient with people who took theories seriously, he trusted no system except the system of endless experimentation. "I have no expectation of making a hit every time I come to bat," the President flipped in an early Fireside Chat. Or more seriously, in an address at Oglethorpe University: "The country needs . . . bold, persistent experimentation. It is common sense to take a me-

* Quoted by Arthur M. Schlesinger, Jr.: "The First Hundred Days of the New Deal," in Claire Leighton, ed.: *The Aspirin Age* (Simon & Schuster, 1949), p. 275.

† Rosenman, II, 11, 15–16. The astounding number of 460,000 citizens wrote to the President as a result of the speech. Rexford G. Tugwell: "The New Deal in Retrospect," *Western Political Quarterly* (December 1948), I, 378.

thod and try it: If it fails, admit it frankly and try another. But above all, try something."*

Yet even the most casual doctrinaire has his ideological guide-posts, and Roosevelt's thinking acquired its direction in one of the tiny number of families that fit precisely the definition of the American patrician. There were the ancestral acres at Hyde Park, the income connected with business America largely by coupons han-dled in a distant broker's office, the tutors, Harvard, the trips to Europe, and presiding over it all, Sara Delano Roosevelt, serenely sure that she and her kind were the natural custodians of the nation's destiny. At Harvard, Roosevelt showed an upper-dog concern for the underdog, avoided the doubtful taste of either flunking or get-ting too near the top of the class. When marrying time came, no one was surprised that the bride was a female counterpart of Frank-lin, or even, considering the exclusiveness of the circle in which the Roosevelt family moved, that she was a distant relative.

At the wedding the bride and the bridegroom did not receive anywhere near their due. Among their common relatives was the President of the United States, and "Uncle Ted" so completely stole the show that another relative growled: "When he goes to a wed-ding, he wants to be the bride, and when he goes to a funeral, he wants to be the corpse." † The shadow of Uncle Ted stretched far across the earlier years of Franklin Roosevelt. The older man had a considerable affection for his handsome, high-spirited fifth cousin

---

* Rosenman, I, 646, and II, 165. Tugwell has suggested that Roosevelt's ap-parent casualness about programs was, at least in part, a desire to avoid tele-graphing his punches — to his supporters as well as his enemies. Roosevelt, ac-cording to Tugwell, was wary of letting his progressive support know too much of his plans because, disliking some feature or other, they would be likely to denounce them. Roosevelt liked to repeat some remarks made to him by Wilson: "Roosevelt, we progressives never beat the conservatives because they, wanting to disturb nothing, and maintaining a purely defensive position, have the co-hesiveness and resistance of a closed fist; but we, being determined to make progress and each knowing best how it should be done and being therefore utterly unable, any of us, to support any others of us, have about as much striking power as you'd expect from the fingers of an open hand, each pointing in a slightly different direction." "The New Deal: the Progressive Tradition," *Western Political Quarterly* (September 1950), III, 395–396.

† Quoted in Gerald W. Johnson: *Roosevelt: Dictator or Democrat* (Harper, 1941), p. 69.

and nephew-in-law. The youth, in turn, respected and admired Uncle Ted, and the relationship brought Franklin Roosevelt a continuous suggestion that politics was a permissible career for a patrician, that a patrician's politics should be reform, and that reform meant broad Federal powers wielded by executive leadership in the pattern of the New Nationalism.*

Until the time of Theodore's father, all the Roosevelts had cansidered themselves as much Democrats by birth as they were Dutchmen or Episcopalians by birth. Under the extreme provocation of the Civil War, Theodore Roosevelt's branch of the family turned Republican, but the Dutchess County wing stuck to the traditional allegiance. Having a family like the Roosevelts in the Democratic Party of that day had its amusing aspects (when Franklin ran for office the first time, politicians had to caution him not to campaign in a riding habit), but it soon brought significant consequences. Young Roosevelt was the first New York Democratic politician of importance to support Wilson's Presidential candidacy, and shortly after Wilson entered the White House, Roosevelt was offered his reward. Passing by assistant secretaryships in the State and War Departments, he chose Uncle Ted's old office of Assistant Secretary of the Navy, and in a few months Washington veterans were chuckling at the reincarnation they were watching, even to the frequent use of "Bully!" But the Assistant Secretary was also soaking up the New Freedom of the man he called "the Chief," in genuine if somewhat distant admiration. Given the Democratic Vice-president nomination in 1920, Roosevelt's campaigning on domestic issues often sounded unmistakably like the Wilson of 1912.

The election of 1920 over, and the Democratic candidates unemployed, Roosevelt was ready for new jobs and new ideas. He was much more ready than many other patrician reformers for the

---

* But F. D. R. could disagree with his senior relative, and one such disagreement has its amusing aspect in view of F. D. R.'s own actions as President. In 1902, when he was at Harvard, he wrote of T. R.'s intervention in the coal strike: "In spite of his success in settling the trouble, I think that the President made a serious mistake in interfering — politically, at least. His tendency to make the executive power stronger than the House of Congress is bound to be a bad thing, especially when a man of weaker personality succeeds him in office." Elliott Roosevelt, ed.: *F. D. R.: His Personal Letters* (Duell, Sloan & Pearce, 1947–1950), I, 481.

idea of Associational Activities that the new business thinkers were developing. The New Nationalism he had imbibed from Uncle Ted contained its own acceptance of big business. Moreover, Roosevelt's wartime Navy work had brought him into contact with a good many of the advocates of Associational Activities, including a man named Herbert Hoover, who, with his wife, frequently dined with their good friends the Roosevelts. Part New Nationalist when the war began, increasingly sympathetic to Associational Activities during the war, entering a decade when the New Freedom seemed almost irrelevant, Roosevelt in 1921 accepted a position that made him, for a brief period, a key figure in the new business ideology.

The position grew out of a legislative investigation of the New York building industry. Construction work in New York, the investigation revealed, was a sorry mess of outmoded techniques, corrupt relations with the unions, and ravenous competitive tactics that hurt both the companies and the public. Worried into a new approach, the principal firms set up the American Construction Council in 1922, with the declared purposes of giving the industry a code of ethics, modernizing its practices, and providing "a unification of effort" — to use the Council's phrase for industry-wide understandings that could easily turn into by-passes around the antitrust laws.*

The American Construction Council was one of the first major trade associations of the 1920's, and its founding provoked a great deal of excitement among men interested in luring business away from its old tooth-and-fang ideas. "The tremendous possibilities of such an organization," the Council preened itself in a brochure, "induced Mr. Herbert Hoover to consent to preside at the formal organization meeting and Mr. Franklin D. Roosevelt to accept the presidency of the organization." The Council, Hoover told the organizational meeting, "is a step I have long looked for. . . . You are taking one of the most important steps ever taken in the history of this nation." Roosevelt, enthusiastically agreeing with Hoover, added: "The tendency lately has been toward regulation of industry. . . . But government regulation is not feasible. It is unwieldy; it is expensive. It means employment of men to carry on this phase

* *The American Construction Council* (American Construction Council, Washington, 1922), p. 11.

of the work; it means higher taxes. The public doesn't want it; the industry doesn't want it. . . . There has been no system, no co-operation, no intensive national planning. The time was ripe for an organization such as that being formed."* How much the Council intended to "co-operate" with government in working out its program, the record does not reveal, but it is clear that the Roosevelt of the early Twenties had little of the traditional reformer's feeling against the drawing together of industries into larger organizations and even less of the nineteenth-century businessman's apotheosis of competition.

Roosevelt had been president of the council only a short while when infantile paralysis struck. He did not return to full-time work for seven years, and then it was to the kind of position most likely to submerge any interest in Associational Activities. Roosevelt's election to the governorship of New York in 1928 not only directed his attention toward state problems and away from concern over nationally organized business. It also meant that he had to function in the shadow of Al Smith, who was out of the State House only because he left to run for the Presidency, and whose New Freedom administrations had won him enormous popularity in the state. The Wilsonianism in Franklin Roosevelt came to the fore again, and he swung easily into the Smith tradition.

A Wilsonian — that was the impression Roosevelt gave most people who were willing to venture a classification as he entered the White House. But beneath surface appearances he was something far less predictable — a patrician reformer whose mind was a pot-pourri of the three major programs that had emerged in the previous half-century: the New Freedom associated with Wilson, the New Nationalism of Theodore Roosevelt, and the Associational Activities of the Twenties.

The day after the Inaugural the new President proclaimed a four-day bank holiday, summoned Congress into special session, and started day-and-night White House conferences on emergency banking legislation. The bill was ready seventy-two hours later. The House of Representatives debated it thirty-eight minutes. The Senate debated it three hours. That night the President signed it. The

* *Ibid.*, Title page and p. 6; New York *Times*, June 4, 1922.

Hundred Days were under way, the most controlled, directed, over-powered period in all the history of Congress.

Many of the bills whisked through Congress bespoke the central idea common to both principal reform traditions, the New Freedom and the New Nationalism — the belief that the best solution for economic and social ills was action by the Federal government under strong executive leadership. The powerful leadership of Franklin Roosevelt set up Federal protections for bank depositors and for all investors in stocks. Federal credit eased the burden of debt on farmers and householders, and Federal guidance reorganized the railroads. A variety of Federal devices made phony bankruptcy proceedings more difficult, imposed excess-profit and dividend taxes, created the Civilian Conservation Corps for the youthful unemployed and raised prices by taking the country off the haloed gold standard. "Liberal" measures, the country called them, and quite clearly liberalism had come to mean not the Mencken-type emphasis of the Twenties but a full-blown revival of economic and social reformism. Talk of liberty in reform circles now was likely to produce a yawn, if not a scowl; opportunity, at least opportunity for the millions to have jobs, was the point.

The New Deal handling of the desperate unemployment problem produced the most sweeping reaffirmation of general progressive doctrine. For three years Herbert Hoover and the conservative press had been arguing against the outright gift of large-scale Federal funds for unemployment relief. Such a practice, they contended, would bring about a dangerous political centralization, tear down the character of the recipients, and violate the economic law that the national debt cannot go beyond a fixed point without bankrupting the government. To these arguments, liberals of a dozen schools of thought made substantially one set of replies. Unemployment on its 1933 scale was too big a problem for the states and cities, and handling it required tremendous Federal funds and centralized administration; environment-shaped human character, and Federal relief funds, by helping to remove squalor, would build character rather than injure it. The conservative appeal to "economic laws" was met by a barrage of Reform Darwinism, even by a fresh Reform Darwinian formulation of economics.

Well before the depression began, a number of economists had

500   UNDERSTANDING THE AMERICAN PAST

been developing theories which brushed aside the alleged "economic law" standing in the way of large-scale public spending. During the Thirties the long-time leader in world reform thinking, John Maynard Keynes, was rapidly developing these ideas into a persuasive system. The supposed economic law, Keynes argued in the authentic manner of Reform Darwinism, was simply the rationalization of upper-income groups who did not want to pay heavy taxes. There was nothing dangerous about running up a government debt. On the contrary, when private expenditures of money fell off, a sensible government would start compensatory spending. "A dollar spent on relief by the government," Keynes summarized his theory to an American friend, "was a dollar given to the grocer, by the grocer to the wholesaler, and by the wholesaler to the farmer, in payment of supplies. With one dollar paid out for relief or public works or anything else, you have created four dollars' worth of national income."*

Franklin Roosevelt, together with a large segment of the liberal movement, distrusted the Keynes argument in the early New Deal days. At heart they hankered for a balanced budget. Yet the idea of large-scale Federal spending on relief, with its implied contempt for rigid economics, its assignment of a key role to the national government, and its promise of quick alleviation of human distress, was a natural for the President and his following. Amid the roar of the Hundred Days, Congress passed a half-billion-dollar relief bill, and the President gave the administration of the money to a *de facto* Keynesian whose economics consisted largely of an urge "to feed the hungry, and Goddam fast." †

Harry Hopkins had always been in a hurry. He was already in

* Paraphrased by Frances Perkins, p. 226.
† Quoted by the late Harold Ickes, in an interview. There is considerable dispute as to when, and to what extent, Keynesianism influenced the New Deal. Certainly his ideas were not the only ones pushing New Deal thinking in the direction of deficit spending, and all varieties of the idea were more influential in the later stages of the New Deal. A good deal of what has been called Keynesianism was simply the result of an attempt to solve a practical problem. For example, Marriner Eccles, one of the leading advocates of deficit spending in the New Deal, later commented: "The concepts I formulated, which have been called Keynesian, were not abstracted from books. . . . My conceptions were based on naked-eye observation and experience. . . . Moreover, I have never read Keynes's writings except in small abstracts up to this day." *Beckoning Frontiers* (Alfred A. Knopf, 1951), p. 132.

a hurry when his father, a convivial jack-of-all-trades, finally settled
the family in Grinnell, Iowa, and the homely youngster hustled his
way to the title of "Big Man of the Class" at Grinnell College. On
graduation, Hopkins almost took a job on a Montana newspaper;
he almost did a dozen things; and somewhere in the midst of it all,
a professor urged him to sign up as counselor in a boys' camp in
New Jersey. A charitable boys' camp sat well with the son of a pious
Methodist mother, who had bundled her five children off to church
every Sunday and made them repeat the minister's points afterward.
A boys' camp sponsored by influential people and near New York
City had special attractions for the ne'er-do-well's son, who was
determined to find a place for himself in the exciting world of
power. The professor did not have to urge long.

Nor did Hopkins remain long in the camp organization. Quickly
he was off to a series of successes in the social-work profession. By
1933 Hopkins had attained the number-one social worker's position
in the nation, director of emergency relief in New York State, and a
striking if somewhat mixed reputation. Associates knew him as a
man who thought more swiftly than anyone working for, with, or
against him, a first-class administrator with a habit of cutting through
red tape like so much confetti, a wraith of quick cigarettes, frayed
suits, curt sarcasms, and a highly developed ability to confuse advancing mankind with advancing Harry Hopkins.

Transferred to Washington to direct the New Deal relief program, Hopkins sat down at his desk before the workmen had
moved it out of the hallway and in two hours spent more than
five million dollars. During the ensuing months Hopkins's shabby
little office in the old Walker-Johnson Building, with the faded
paint and the water pipes running up and down the walls, became
the most swift-acting agency in all frenzied Washington. When
somebody brought in a plan that "will work out in the long run,"
Hopkins snapped: "People don't eat in the long run — they eat
every day." When inspectors from the Budget Bureau came around
to see the "organizational chart," they heard that Hopkins had
ordered: "I don't want anybody around here to waste any time
drawing boxes. You'll always find that the person who drew the
chart has his own name in the middle box."* Out of the fury came

* Robert E. Sherwood: *Roosevelt and Hopkins* (Harper, 1948), pp. 49, 52.

striking new practices of unemployment relief, a devil for conservatives to flay, and an application of liberal doctrine so personal that its effects sank deep into the national mind.

Roosevelt's close friend, the level-headed businessman Frank Walker, discovered just how personal the application was when the President sent him on a tour to inspect the workings of the relief program. In his home state of Montana, Walker found former businessmen digging ditches and laying sewer pipes in their old business clothes because they had no money to buy overalls and rubber boots. And one of the ditch-diggers spoke for millions when he said to Walker: "I hate to think what would have happened if this work hadn't come along. The last of my savings had run out. I'd sold or hocked everything I could. And my kids were hungry. I stood in front of the window of the bake-shop down the street and wondered just how long it would be before I got desperate enough to pick up a rock and heave it through that window and grab some bread to take home."*

In the White House the lights burned late six or seven nights a week. Wearing out assistants by his energies, amazing intimates by his ability to toss off worries, Roosevelt kept prodding, brain-picking, quipping, politicking the Hundred Days ahead. Federal relief would alleviate distress; it could hardly cure a depression.

There was no lack of advice on the cure. The president of the Chamber of Commerce, a charwoman from Butte, the head of the A. F. of L., Harvard classmates of Roosevelt, the third vice-president of Kiwanis, and some five thousand other people all brought or sent the President sure-fire remedies. Immediately around the President was the group of brilliant and contentious minds that the country had been calling the Brain Trust since the early phases of the campaign of 1932. Yet amid all the babble the proposals from informed and responsible people revealed a striking fact: many business leaders and labor officials, Farm Bureau men and liberals, Brain-trusters and Kiwanians, agreed on certain fundamentals of a recovery program.

Some agreement from supposed ideological opposites was not surprising. During the Twenties the New Nationalist type of think-

* Quoted in *ibid.*, p. 54.

ing had not entirely lost its influence and, while the New National-ism and the Associational Activities outlook had important differ-ences, they agreed on encouraging the formation of large economic units and on an important role for government economic life. The depression of 1929, by presenting free enterprise in its most cha-otic and inhumane form and by raising serious doubts about its ability to get back on its feet, brought an onrush of converts to the general idea of national planning of national economic units. New Freedomite reformers, who had so long battled any pro-gram that accepted the concentration of industry, now forgot their old battle in their concern with getting government controls over the existing situation. Businessmen who had railed at any system re-stricting their independence besought the government to tell them what to do to avoid bankruptcy. (According to Herbert Hoover, during the campaign of 1932 a "leading industrialist" brought him a plan for over-all Federal controls of industry, and when Hoover rejected the plan as "fascism," the industrialist and many of his friends gave campaign contributions to the Democrats.*) As the banks closed and the abyss seemed near in March 1933, free enter-prise virtually abdicated. "There was hardly an industrial, eco-nomic, financial, commercial, reform, or agricultural leader who did not advance some idea of governmental intervention," one Wash-ington insider has recalled. "A snowfall of paper plans drifted about the Capitol, and there was not one of them that would not, in some measure, have modified the Antitrust Acts." †

The merger of Associational Activities ideas and New Nation-alist thinking in a demand for national planning of large-scale eco-nomic units was plain in the Brain Trust. Raymond Moley, chief of the group, perfectly represented the coalescence in his own ami-able, hardheaded self. As a boy in Berea, Ohio, Moley wept at the 1896 defeat of William Jennings Bryan, and as a young man he made a hero of Tom Johnson. Then, while the trust-busters kept on thundering and the trusts kept on growing, Moley began to wonder whether traditional, anti-Big-Business reform was not trying to change the tides of economic development. He turned down an

* Interview with Mr. Herbert Hoover.
† Hugh S. Johnson: *The Blue Eagle from Egg to Earth* (Doubleday, 1935), p. 189.

offer to plunge into the progressive politics of the New Freedom era; he decided he was not a "professional reformer"; and, as a professor of political science, first in the Midwest and then at Columbia, Moley sought solutions of the nation's ills that assumed the necessity of a battle against "ignorance" rather than against "sin." The nature of the proper enlightenment was not always clear. But the Professor Moley who became important in the Roosevelt circle was a man who talked easily with people of an Associational Activities persuasion and whose own doctrine, if it was contained in any one place, was found in the Crolyite book that Theodore Roosevelt had quoted to the Bull Moose convention, Van Hise's *Concentration and Control*. The Moley of 1933, eschewing trust-busting, had sidled toward national economic planning, by self-governing action if possible, by planning under Federal compulsion if necessary. The essential was to end "the thoughtlessness and aimlessness" of free competition.*

The merger of the New Nationalism and Associational Activities was no less striking in the relations of two of the important figures who gathered around Moley in the Brain Trust. No human beings could have seemed more different than Hugh Johnson and Rexford Tugwell. Johnson learned to spell to the whinnying of cavalry horses and the bawling of top sergeants at Fort Scott, Kansas, yelling to anyone who would listen to him: "Everybody in the world is a rink-stink but Hughie Johnson and he's all right!" Tugwell, the son of a prosperous farmer and cannery-owner in Sinclairville, New York, was raised to a genteel tradition of concern with community problems, almost to a Rooseveltian *noblesse oblige*. West Point remembered Johnson as the most talented hazer and the possessor of the biggest nose in the history of the school. The University of Pennsylvania recalled Tugwell as a handsome, smartly dressed ideologue, a gourmet with a special pride in his elaborate salads, who was given to practicing his sharp wit on bourgeois America and was more than likely to steer his date to a reform soiree. While Johnson was doing a hell-roaring border patrol along the Rio Grande, Tugwell was showing intimates a poem that included the lines:

* Raymond Moley: *After Seven Years* (Harper, 1939), pp. 4–5.

I am sick of a Nation's stenches;
I am sick of propertied Czars;
I have dreamt my great dream of their passing.
I have gathered my tools and my charts;
My plans are fashioned and practical:
I shall roll up my sleeves — make America over! *

The mature careers of the two men showed no more similarities. Johnson swashbuckled his way to a brigadier general's stars, interrupting his military life only for tossing off children's books that were chock-full of carnage and last-minute touchdowns. Somewhere along the line, the Army discovered that its leathery-faced cavalryman, a perfect Captain Flagg in his rough talk and his sentimentality, also had a mind, a quick, perceptive instrument that expressed itself in curiously effective off-beat phrases. The Army sent Johnson to law school, then made him its principal representative on the War Industries Board of World War I. Excited by his contact with industry, Johnson resigned from the Army after the Armistice and entered business, first as an officer of the Moline Plow Company, later as one of the men who helped Baruch manage his web of interests. Still clattering across any room in a roar of Army attitudes, deeply involved with large-scale industry and finance, Johnson in 1933 seemed a caricature of the traditional reform type. Tugwell was close to being a type-case of the liberal professor. Settled at Columbia, he was entrancing classes by his iconoclasm, making a national reputation as a heretical agricultural economist, visiting the Soviet Union and coming back with the declaration that Russian rural life was entering a "renaissance" even if Bolshevik totalitarianism was objectionable.† It was hardly surprising that at early Brain Trust sessions the relations between Tugwell and Johnson were a study in hostility, Tugwell holding Johnson off with witticisms, Johnson snapping and snarling at his debonair torturer.

Yet with the passage of a few months, Tugwell and Johnson were

---

* Quoted in *Current Biography 1940* (H. W. Wilson), p. 431, and *1941*, p. 874.

† Tugwell: "Russian Agriculture," in Stuart Chase *et al.*, eds.: *Soviet Russia in the Second Decade* (John Day, 1928), p. 101.

soon bending happily over the same charts and memoranda. Johnson had emerged from his service with the War Industries Board and his work with Baruch an ardent advocate of Associational Activities, though he added to Hoover's reliance on co-operation between government and economic units the belief that some degree of governmental compulsion should be used. Tugwell had emerged from his books and his indignation a highly involved economic thinker but fundamentally a New Nationalist. The line between Johnson's planning by partial co-operation and Tugwell's planning by over-all compulsion was a wavering one, much too wavering not to be pushed aside by the impact of depression. The common denominator of their thinking in 1933, and of Moley's own, was described by Moley when he wrote of the Brain Trust's "rejection of the traditional Wilson-Brandeis philosophy that America . . . could once more become a nation of small proprietors, of corner grocers and smithies under spreading chestnut trees. . . . We believed that any attempt to atomize big business must destroy America's greatest contribution to a higher standard of living for the body of its citizenry — the development of mass production. . . . We recognized that competition, as such, was not inherently virtuous; that competition . . . created as many abuses as it prevented." So the Brain-trusters, Moley summarized, turned "from the nostalgic philosophy of the 'trust busters,'" turned to national economic planning.[*]

This was the kind of thinking swirling around the President during the Hundred Days, and it did not disturb him. In the period immediately preceding his election Roosevelt had begun to submerge the New Freedom element in his own thinking; he too could find little in trust-busting liberalism that seemed to apply to the emergency at hand. The real question for him, the real quarrel among his advisers, was not national planning versus free competition. The issue was: should the planning hew closer to the Associational Activities pattern, with its emphasis on noncompulsory relations between the government and economic life, or should it follow more the New Nationalist pattern of powerful Federal controls?

[*] Moley, p. 24.

Next to feeding the hungry, the most urgent problem was agriculture. Another good crop was on its way and, with farm prices already perilously low, another good crop could mean disaster. Even during the campaign of 1932, while most of his program was still a cloud of generalities, Roosevelt edged toward a specific program of national planning for agriculture. Shortly before the nominating convention, Tugwell began urging on Moley a plan that was the product of many minds but had been most actively propagandized by Professor Milburn L. Wilson, of the Montana State College. Wilson's proposal assumed that the American farmer could no longer depend on the foreign market. Instead of calling on the Federal government to arrange dumping abroad, as the McNary-Haugen bill had done, Wilson argued that the government should plan crop-control at home by an elaborate procedure known as the "Domestic Allotment Plan." The Wilson program appealed to the planner in Moley; when Moley arranged a conference between Roosevelt and Tugwell, the plan appealed no less to the planner in Roosevelt. Roosevelt wanted to know more, and just as the convention was about to vote on the nomination, Tugwell wired Wilson to meet him in Chicago. The two men talked for a day in a hotel room; then Tugwell reported to Hyde Park on the long-distance phone. Roosevelt was sufficiently impressed to slip into his acceptance speech an endorsement of the basic Wilson principle that the Federal government should make itself responsible for ridding the farmer of the curse of surpluses without resorting to attempts at dumping abroad.

But just how was the responsibility to be fulfilled? Advocates of an Associational Activities tendency — most notably Hugh Johnson's crony George Peek — urged as little compulsion as possible. Peek argued long and ably that the chief mechanism for raising farm income should be a payment to the farmer for whatever money he lost by having to sell at a low price in foreign markets; only in years of superabundant yield should the actual size of his crop be curtailed, and then not until the crop was actually in growth. Professor Wilson, backed by a group including Tugwell, proposed crop curtailment, even in normal years and before planting, by offering attractive rentals to farmers on acreage taken out of production. The final legislation, the bill establishing the Agricultural Adjustment Administration, made the execution of either or both plans possible. But the Triple-A plainly contained ample provisions to make it the boldest use of national agricultural controls in the modern history of Western civilization.

The next week or so, the already famous Roosevelt smile was especially radiant. The President was busy with the final stages of a bill which, of all the New Deal legislation, was his labor of love. The idea of a Tennessee Valley Authority lit fires in a dozen cubicles of Roosevelt's mind. A TVA would provide a yardstick for power costs; it would mean a giant stride in conservation, an enthusiasm of Franklin no less than of Theodore Roosevelt; it would chain a capricious, destructive river to the development of one of the most depressed areas of the country.

Shortly before the bill went to Congress, its chief sponsor, Senator George Norris, came to dinner at the White House, and the two men, the Dutchess County patrician and the son of a Nebraska dirt farmer, sat talking enthusiastically over TVA's possibilities.

"What are you going to say when they ask you the political philosophy behind TVA?" Senator Norris laughed.

"I'll tell them it's neither fish nor fowl," Roosevelt laughed back, "but, whatever it is, it will taste awfully good to the people of the Tennessee Valley."

Until midnight that evening the President squeezed dry his interlude, talking of forests and schoolhouses and the future, far away from the nagging present of hungry men and warring policies.[*]

Congress was just beginning debate on TVA when the present returned with the jarring report that the Senate had passed the Black bill. In the bleak months of 1932 Senator Hugo Black, like so many other Americans, had become convinced that a return to the 1929 level of prosperity was impossible. Sure that technology had reached the point where there would never be enough jobs to go around unless everybody worked less, he had introduced a bill decreeing a thirty-hour week.

To Roosevelt the bill seemed a menace. It assumed a closed economy, with no room for expanding production and opportunity. It contained no minimum-wage provisions and would almost certainly

[*] Interview with the late George W. Norris.

result in a wholesale slashing of take-home pay. It was completely rigid, allowing for no seasonal variations or the special hours required by some occupations. How could you order farmers up in his country to work their hired hands thirty hours, the President asked. "There have to be hours adapted to the rhythm of the cow." * But there it was, a piece of legislation already approved by the Senate of the United States and, because of its patness and its appeal to the fears of the day, a bill that was soon likely to end up on the President's desk.

Quite clearly, the practical alternative to the Black bill was different legislation that also promised escape from industrial unemployment. Roosevelt had not wanted to rush industrial-recovery legislation. He felt that, though there was general agreement on the need for national planning, too much disagreement over key points still existed among important economic leaders. One school believed that industrial reorganization alone would bring recovery; another school, reflecting the growing influence of the ideas of Keynes and similar thinkers, insisted that industrial reorganization had to be accompanied by a pump-priming public-works program. There were also serious differences over the degree of governmental compulsion that should be involved. The President was reluctant to force the decisions. But now, with the Black bill close to final Congressional approval, Roosevelt could no longer wait. Soon after the legislation passed the Senate, Roosevelt summoned the proponents of the more important plans to his office, listened to them wrangle, then told them to go lock themselves in a room until they could agree on one bill.

The order quickly produced a draft. After two days the conferees emerged with a bill, and the President accepted it with only minor modifications. With respect to the pump-priming issue, the National Industrial Recovery Act compromise, providing for public works as part of the general program but appropriating for them a sum much smaller than the ardent pump-primers wanted. The heart of the bill, the machinery for industrial planning, was less of a compromise. The codes were to be originally drafted by representatives of industry, which meant the trade associations in most cases; the antitrust laws were suspended; and no prohibition was placed on price fixing. All of these provisions had been major goals of business-minded

* Quoted in Frances Perkins, p. 194.

planners since George Perkins's day. But the codes of hours, wages, and conditions of competition were to be written under the supervision of a Federal administrator: they had to be approved by the President as the representative of the national welfare, and, once given White House approval, they carried the force of Federal law. Herbert Hoover, speaking up from the deepest oblivion any living ex-President has ever known, was horrified. "Fascism, pure fascism," the advocate of Associational Activities called the enormous governmental powers granted to the National Recovery Administration.*

Raymond Moley was jubilant. His Brain-trusters, representing quite different approaches, had joined in giving the nation blueprints for both industry and agriculture which brushed aside the Wilsonian hostility to large-scale economic units and brought all enterprises, large and small, into a government-sponsored national planning. To the program of Associational Activities had been added the idea of Federal compulsion, which men like Croly and Van Hise had long been advocating. The appointments of the top personnel of the Triple-A and the NRA emphasized the way in which the New Deal was sweeping Associational Activities into a bolder pattern. None other than Bernard Baruch's World War I assistant, George Peek, accepted the post as head of the Triple-A. Another Baruch protégé, Hugh Johnson, not only moved into the top position of the NRA; he promptly began talking Federal power in a way that made businessmen feel like so many captured peasants herded before the Czar.

Happily Moley worked away on the draft of the Fireside Chat in which Roosevelt was to present the Triple-A and the NRA to the public, working into the speech a huzza to the coming era of national planning. The President seemed to like the passage, and Moley pressed his advantage. Having spent two years in almost daily conversation with Roosevelt, Moley was keenly aware of the President's many minds, his zest in playing by ear.

Did the President, Moley asked, realize to its fullest significance the "enormous step" he was taking? Did he realize that the Triple-A and the NRA were committing him to a sharp break not only with the conservative adulation of free enterprise but with the appeal for

* Hoover interview.

a return to the free enterprise of New Freedom liberalism? Did he really approve, in its deepest meaning, this passage extolling national planning?

Roosevelt was quiet for a few minutes, then he replied solemnly: "I never felt surer of anything in my life than I do of the soundness of this passage." *

Uncle Ted, thrashing out his last years in impotent fury at Woodrow Wilson, had died too soon. For in the clear import of basic legislation, and in the mind of the President of the United States, the nation was close to the repudiation of trust-busting and the dependence on compulsory Federal planning which Theodore Roosevelt had appealed for under the name of the New Nationalism.

For once, Franklin Roosevelt admitted he was tired. Hastily signing the National Recovery Act, he climbed aboard the little *Amberjack II*, put on his oilskins, and went sailing up the New England coast to Campobello.

He left behind an enormously relieved nation. Across the country, the doubts of 1932 were disappearing with the swiftness of a summer shower. Businessmen, coming out of their storm cellars, drove up the idex of manufacturing production from 56 in March, when the Hundred Days began, to 65 in April, then up to 77 in May and 93 in June. Labor, losing the wildness of despair, hurried into unions and turned the frantic violence of 1932 into businesslike strikes. With the flood of Triple-A checks starting out of Washington, the farm areas were regaining hope in the old America, even to the extent of a few furtive elections of Republicans once again. The technological wonders of a World's Fair no longer seemed entirely ironical, and as families roamed around the exhibits, planning when they could buy a Mixmaster or a car with free wheeling, those who were up on the latest movies were whistling, "Who's afraid of the Big Bad Wolf?"

Hard times were still grimly present, but a liberalism that had been able to conquer fear seemed the obvious program to conquer a mere depression. In the years immediately after 1933, New Deal liberalism gained a hold on the American mind such as no previous

* Quoted in Moley, p. 189. The similarity in over-all conception of the NRA and the Triple-A is underlined by the fact that one important part of the Triple-A, the marketing agreements, was the direct forerunner of the NRA codes.

reform movement had known. Among the educated, the shame of the Babbitts was being forgotten in the horror of poverty. Writings in economic and social reform shoved Mencken and Fitzgerald into the farthest stacks of libraries, and Sinclair Lewis kept a toehold on the front shelves only by *Ann Vickers*, portraying a social worker, and *It Can't Happen Here*, a fictionalized warning that unemployment was the seedbed of fascism. During the Hundred Days, Prohibition was repealed with only a few hiccups of excitement, and the next year the Catholic Legion of Decency began its censorship of the movies amid the merest scattering of protest. The news about sex, *Fortune* reported after surveying the colleges, was that sex was no longer news. "I am now definitely ready to announce," the postgraduate Robert Benchley added in his dramatic column, "that Sex, as a theatrical property, is as tiresome as the Old Mortgage. . . . I am sick of little Southern girls who want 'to live.' . . . I am sick of rebellious Youth and I am sick of Victorian parents, and I don't care if all the little girls in all sections of the United States get ruined or want to get ruined or keep from getting ruined." *

Among educated and uneducated alike, millions were rejecting conservatism with the vehemence of men trying to forget their pasts. New Deal critics stormed and threatened. But when the Congressional elections of 1934 came, and the only discernible issue was the New Deal, the overwhelming Democratic majority of 1932 became still more overwhelming (an especially emphatic endorsement, because it is phenomenal in American politics when the party in power increases its strength in an off-year election). In the cities and states, public pressure was bringing an avalanche of social legislation — more in the first two years of the New Deal than in the administrations of Theodore Roosevelt and Woodrow Wilson combined. Symbolically, the nation's metropolis chose for its Mayor none other than Fiorello La Guardia, chunkier and more reform-minded than ever. "They didn't elect me for my looks," said La Guardia. "They wanted things done and they knew damn well I'd do them." †

And above it all, rapidly approaching a popularity unexceeded in American history, was the President of the United States, who be-

---

* "Youth in College," *Fortune* (June 1936), XIII, 155–156; Benchley: "Hail to the King," the *New Yorker* (November 29, 1930), VI, 36.
† Interview with the late Fiorello La Guardia.

lieved that his party's function was to be "the party of militant liberalism."* The voters may have sent Franklin Roosevelt to the White House as a pleasant man who could hardly be worse than Hoover. Now they were cheering him as the most effective of American reform leaders. A good part of the nation had respected Wilson, as they respected their ministers, and delighted in Teddy Roosevelt, as they delighted in a dashing Sunday-dinner uncle. They found Franklin Roosevelt delightful too, and far removed from ordinary politicians in the respect he called up, but there was also something else — an intangible mass feeling that converted attacks on him into intensified support. A man who remained so jaunty under heavy strain would not fail to pull things through somehow; a reformer so skillful at political deals would know how to get reforms effected; a President who had suffered so much himself would understand and care about all the nagging todays and worrisome tomorrows of ordinary men and women. In North Carolina a reporter from an anti-Roosevelt paper approached a millworker and grilled him about his enthusiasm for the President. Did he realize, the reporter asked, that the New Deal was based on crackpot theories and was certain to bankrupt the country? The millworker squirmed and reddened. Then, finally, he managed to get out his answer. "Mr. Roosevelt," the millworker said, "is the only man we ever had in the White House who would understand that my boss is a sonofabitch." †

In Washington, paunching old Harold Ickes, who had known all the delights of reform achievements in the early 1900's, delivered himself of a historical judgment from his new post as a member of the President's Cabinet. "By God," Ickes declared, "I never thought I'd live to see this. Why this is a second honeymoon." ‡

* Rosenman, VII, xxxi.
† Interview with the late Stephen T. Early, who was told the story by the North Carolina worker.
‡ Ickes interview.

Roosevelt and His Detractors

by

ARTHUR SCHLESINGER, JR.

[Reprinted by permission from *Harper's Magazine* CC (June 1950), 62–68. Copyright 1950 by Harper & Bros.]

Like World War I, the Second World War has bred among historians the seeds of disillusionment. This can be credited in part to a survival of prewar isolationist sentiment arguing, in effect, "I told you so," and to the feeling that our contribution to the destruction of fascism served merely to strengthen the Communist adversary that now confronts us. Finally, there flows through certain of the revisionist tracts a conviction of the diabolism of the late President Roosevelt, seeing him as consciously plotting, frequently with the worst possible motives in mind, to involve us in war.[1]

Harry Elmer Barnes, who, it will be remembered, was a leading spokesman for the post-World-War-I disillusionment, has recently charged the existence of a "historical blackout" concerning American intervention in the Second World War by historians, publishers, and government authorities — most of whom he accuses of being committed to the interventionist point of view and of deliberately obscuring the true situation. In a pamphlet entitled The Struggle against the Historical Blackout, *Barnes has attacked a number of historians whom he accuses of being pro-Roosevelt.[2]*

The late Charles A. Beard, prominent in the campaign to keep the United States out of World War II, in the last two books he wrote, charged President Roosevelt with maneuvering the country into war while appearing to want peace.[3] Beard did not examine too closely the motives which led Roosevelt to act as he did. But Frederick C. Sanborn,[4] Harry Elmer Barnes, and John T. Flynn[5] do not hesitate to accuse Roosevelt of plotting war in order to insure his re-election and to cover the failure of his domestic program. The enormous gains made by Russia as a consequence of World War II and our own worsened relations with the Communist world have caused the edge of the debate concerning the wisdom of our involvement in World War II to be sharpened. Publication in 1952 of Chester Wilmot's The Struggle for Europe *gave comfort to the revisionist cause in its attempt to show that Churchill was right in distrusting Russia in the war and immediate postwar period, and that the reason for our present predicament is that a contrary policy, advanced by Roosevelt, had been followed.*[6]

The revisionists, of course, are not without opposition.

With regard to their contention that Roosevelt led the American people into war, while professing that he had no desire to do so, even relatively objective scholars are divided. Some, like Thomas A. Bailey, do not deny this, saying that "the masses are notoriously short-sighted" and that a creative and far-sighted statesman like Roosevelt was "forced to deceive them into an awareness of their own long-run interests." [7] *On the other hand, Dexter Perkins uses evidence from public-opinion polls to show that the measures taken by Roosevelt were not in advance of the opinion of the country.*[8] *The study of William L. Langer and S. Everett Gleason not only denies that Roosevelt consciously plotted our involvement, but sees the Roosevelt and Hull policy as calculated to avoid bringing this about.*[9]

Samuel Eliot Morison has sharply assailed the revisionist position, particularly the point of view expressed by Beard.[10] *R. E. Osgood contends that American participation in World War II marked the congruence of the lines of national idealism and self-interest.*[11]

An attempt to strike a mean between the two historical positions was made by Dr. Louis Morton before the December 1953 meeting of the American Historical Association. Morton, while agreeing with the revisionist contention that the Fascist powers were not an immediate military menace to the United States, nevertheless does not deny the wisdom of intervention.[12] *However, the revisionist debate was fueled again in April 1954 with the publication of Rear Admiral R. A. Theobald's* The Final Secret of Pearl Harbor. *Theobald alleges that President Franklin Delano Roosevelt encouraged the Japanese attack upon the Pacific Fleet by purposefully weakening it; that*

Roosevelt deliberately withheld information about the Japanese plans to attack Pearl Harbor from Admiral Kimmel and General Short; and that the President did this purposefully, making scapegoats of Kimmel and Short, so that he might lead the nation into war. Aspects of this thesis are affirmed by Admirals Kimmel and Halsey, even as they are denied by General George C. Marshall and Admiral Harold C. Stark.[13]

In the following selection, Arthur Schlesinger, Jr., who is Professor of History at Harvard University, states his objection to the revisionist position as it had developed to mid-1950.

THE STORM of controversy around the foreign policy of Franklin D. Roosevelt is already as furious and looks to be as enduring as that which has raged around the foreign policy of Woodrow Wilson since 1919. War brings an almost inevitable aftermath of disillusion; and the failure of this last war to produce even an approximation of peace has charged our contemporary disillusion with a bitter sense of betrayal. As the revisionists of the Twenties turned on Wilson, so the revisionists of the Forties are today turning on Roosevelt.

The Wilson policies had only to face the relatively uncomplicated attacks of the outright isolationists — men like Harry Elmer Barnes and the early Walter Millis, who had a naïve conviction that the United States could live safely apart from the world. Such naïve isolationism is not, of course, wholly absent from revisionism today. Charles A. Beard, the intellectual leader of the isolationist wing of the revisionists, dedicated two volumes to a trenchant attack on the very foundations of Roosevelt's prewar policy — a scorching indictment which a number of isolationist journalists, such as John T. Flynn and George Morgenstern, have lived off ever since, and which, one understands, Professor C. C. Tansill of Fordham is planning to extend into the war years. Even an intimate member of the Roosevelt circle like Admiral Leahy could believe in 1945, *after* World War II, that "involvement in European politics would inevitably bring us into another European war," and that "there still remained a hope that we might succeed in avoiding entangling ourselves in European political difficulties."

But contemporary revisionism is on the whole a far more complex phenomenon. In its more serious aspects, it entirely accepts the necessity of American intervention into world affairs. It attacks Roosevelt, not for having intervened at all, but for having intervened unwisely, inadequately, or ineffectively. A whole series of critics — William C. Bullitt, Edgar Ansel Mowrer, Richard H. S. Crossman, Henry Luce, Raymond Moley, and most recently, Hanson Baldwin in his book *Great Mistakes of the War* — have argued that Roosevelt's foreign policies, particularly his insistence on subordinating politics to strategy during the war, have made the postwar problems even more exasperating and hopeless than they would have been anyway.

Into this embattled atmosphere Judge Samuel Rosenman has now released the last four volumes of his invaluable collection, *The Public Papers and Addresses of Franklin D. Roosevelt.* To these Judge Rosenman has contributed introductions and notes containing a crisp and informed defense of Roosevelt's wartime policies. The series is a model of editing and bookmaking; and the last four volumes in particular are essential for anyone concerned with the politics of the Second World War.

Judge Rosenman's volumes make available much material which is essential for a judgment of Roosevelt's foreign policy. At the same time, Basil Rauch, whose *History of the New Deal* is the best short volume on the legislative and administrative record of Roosevelt's first few years in office, has now completed *Roosevelt: from Munich to Pearl Harbor,* a survey of Roosevelt's prewar policies. And our knowledge of the war policies, and in particular of the Yalta conference, has been increased by the publication of Walter Johnson's book for Edward R. Stettinius, Jr., *Roosevelt and the Russians,* and by Admiral William Leahy's *I Was There.*

How does Roosevelt's foreign policy stand up in the barrage of defense and attack? The first clear point is that much of the crossfire obscures what may go down as Roosevelt's grand contribution to the strengthening of democracy: his insight into the military conditions of democratic survival. In the dark and bloody world of the mid-century, we forget the fact that a generation ago peace was accounted the normal and natural state of man. The liberal and democratic movements of the West, forgetting that they had themselves come to power through violence, had been lulled by the placid nineteenth century into thinking that wars could be localized and, in the not too distant future, eliminated entirely. The First World War was considered to be an unfortunate accident, the exception that proved the rule; and no drastic conclusions were drawn from it. An atmosphere of pacificism and proto-pacificism settled over the democratic left.

This atmosphere left Roosevelt singularly untouched. His seagoing background, his admiration for his jingo cousin Theodore Roosevelt, his own exciting tour of duty as Assistant Secretary of the Navy in the First World War — all these immunized him against the malaise which overtook the George Lansburys and the Oswald Garrison Villards. He recognized that free society could not endure on good will alone — that it must be prepared to face up to the military requirements of survival. At an early stage he disappointed the pacifist wing of his liberal admirers by slipping rearmament into the recovery program, blandly initiating the program of naval construction in 1933 "as a means of furthering national recovery."

This was the period when the fatuity of the Kellogg Pact was still the complacent expression of altogether too much liberal purpose. Stuart Chase had terrified the left in 1929 with his picture of "the two-hour war" in which a surprise air attack would blot out civilization by gas bombs: "not even a rat, not even an ant, not even a roach, can survive . . . There is no defense." The reflex was the Oxford Oath: young men in Britain swearing never to take up arms for king or country, and young men in the United States avidly following their dubious example. Even the rise of Nazism could not dent the pacifist fantasies. Somehow the fascist challenge to civilization would be met in any way except on the field of battle.

We have forgotten too quickly the tenacity of pacifism in the left at this time. In March 1935 Clement Attlee, leading the Labor Party in its fight against the mild rearmament proposals recommended by the National Government as insurance against Hitler, could lecture the House of Commons, with sublime irrelevance: "We are told in the White Paper that there is danger against which we have to guard ourselves. We do not think you can do it by national defense. We think you can only do it by moving forward to a new world — a world of law, the abolition of national armaments with a world force and a world economic system." An honorable member rudely interrupted: "Tell that to Hitler."

By whatever fortune, Roosevelt knew about Hitler; he was spared this particular form of the great illusion of pacifism. The liberals who admired the TVA but disliked the construction of the aircraft carriers *Enterprise* and *Yorktown* accordingly denounced Roosevelt or made preposterous excuses for him: the Navy, they said, was a kind of hobby, and the President must be indulged in it. Six years later the whole world could only regret that Roosevelt had not indulged himself with far less deference to pacifist opinion. The Navy, instead of being too large for democratic survival, was too small. The odious *Enterprise* turned out, in the words of Bernard Brodie, to be "the undisputed champion of all American warships in terms of combat record." Young men who had signed the Oxford Oath now fought in Normandy or in the South Pacific. There seemed to be a more direct connection between democracy and national defense than it had been fashionable for liberals to admit a decade before.

The United States was lucky in having as President a liberal who, in this respect at least, was unfashionable. Roosevelt's basic insight into the military conditions of democratic survival was, it is true, often overlaid in the Thirties by concessions, vain hopes, and bad inconsistencies. He retreated before the pressures incited by the Nye investigation and signed neutrality legislation designed to secure what he must have known, in other moods, was beyond the possibility of securing. He remained detached before the challenge of the civil war in Spain. Doubtless a fear of alienating Catholic support explained Roosevelt's Spanish policy in part; but more important, one feels, was the fact that he never really grasped the moral or even the strategic issues in Spain.

Professor Beard, marshaling his evidence with the skill and the selectivity of a master prosecutor, has made the most of the ebb and flow of Roosevelt's prewar policies. Yet there can be no serious doubt that Roosevelt had a basic and steady purpose, revealed first in the "quarantine" speech in Chicago in 1937. The rise of fascism had revived Roosevelt's insight into the fact that the United States would not long survive as a free nation in a totalitarian world. With the means at his disposal, he began the long labor of educating the people to the dimensions of the fascist threat to America.

Basil Rauch's *Roosevelt: from Munich to Pearl Harbor* provides an extremely able, clear, and fascinating account of this process of education. Rauch's cogent narrative has as only an incidental purpose the correction of Beard's manifold distortions and omissions; but rarely in the process of incidental commentary has one historian more effectively destroyed the work of another. Professor Rauch's revision of the revisionists brings much needed sense and proportion into the discussion of the period from Munich to Pearl Harbor. His book accentuates the personal tragedy which led one of the great American historians into succumbing in his last days to the "devil theory of war" which he had once himself so effectively exposed.

War itself brought new perplexities. Roosevelt was always a pragmatist, playing by ear, as he liked to say, his improvisations controlled, not by logical analysis nor by an explicit moral code so much as by a consistency of emotion and instinct. In domestic affairs this was fine: the crisis was less inexorable, the margin of error greater. But war lined his pragmatism up against the wall. "It is common sense to take a method and try it," he had said in ushering in the New Deal. "If it fails, admit it frankly and try another." This may indeed have been common sense in peace. It certainly was not in war, where the price of failure was defeat. Roosevelt simply could not shuffle his strategic plans the way he had shuffled programs for domestic recovery.

No one knew this better than Roosevelt himself. The insouciant cigarette holder and the press conference flippancies served only as an easy means of distracting attention from the eyes ever more shadowed, the cheeks ever more hollow, the expression ever more careworn and somber. And, in this dilemma, his pragmatism — even a pragmatism so superbly grounded in a brilliance of instinct and a generosity of emotion — tended to betray him. Had he been a man committed to abstract and explicit principles, like Wilson, he might have developed a specific political strategy for the war. But as a pragmatist, reluctant to sacrifice American lives to a political strategy of whose value he temperamentally could have no doctrinaire certitude, he had no choice but opportunism and expediency.

The four new volumes of *The Public Papers and Addresses* give a full if oblique reflection of Roosevelt's political dilemma. He did not direct the war in a political vacuum, of course. He set forth what he hoped would be the framework of the peace in such extremely general statements as the Atlantic Charter and the Four Freedoms. But these were essentially moral rather than political expressions: they were statements of hope rather than of decision. His world political strategy, as a consequence, was compounded of sentiments rather than of ideas.

Some of the sentiments which tempered the basic pragmatism were wise and commendable: Roosevelt's deep faith in the "massed, angered forces of common humanity"; his hatred of colonial imperialism; his genuine and capacious internationalism. Other sentiments were more ambiguous, such as the profound detestation of Germany which committed him to German policies of an impractical harshness, or his delight in what Isaiah Berlin has called the "royal cousin" approach to international diplomacy. At its best, Roosevelt's exultant sense of himself as the embodiment of a nation dealing with other archetypal heads of state could lead to a rich working relationship with men like Churchill and Mackenzie King. At its worst, it involved him in an entirely unworthy and cheapening preoccupation with crowned heads and royal families, so that the Archduke Ottos and the King Peters and the other bargain-basement remains of European monarchies could command a disproportionate amount of his time and his interest.

But his essential approach to the politics of war remained negative. And, as one main result, when he came to particular decisions, he often had little definite to insist on against the very clear, specific, and intelligible criterion of the military: the belief that any political decision was good which would shorten the war. Now this is not a bad criterion; it is certainly one not to be lightly overridden except where the political advantages of the longer way around are indisputable and conclusive. Hanson Baldwin has recently argued that Churchill was right in advocating the invasion of Europe through the Balkans rather than through France; but this is surely an instance where we would have paid a much higher military cost without gaining very clear or certain political advantages — indeed, with the possible result of producing a third world war before the second was over.

Yet, with a political strategy, so general and undefined, the criterion of military expediency became increasingly important. The day-to-day politics of the war grew increasingly to be a function, not of the State Department, but of the theater commanders. In his press conference after the Darlan deal in North Africa, Roosevelt quoted what he said was a Balkan proverb: "My children, you are permitted in time of great danger to walk with the Devil until you have crossed the bridge." But often in the smoke of war no one knew where the bridge was, or it constantly receded, while the Devil remained close and familiar. It was ironical that General Marshall, when he became Secretary of State, found himself the impatient prisoner of a system of military initiative in foreign policy which he himself had exacted from Roosevelt five years before.

The two areas of Roosevelt's wartime policy which have received special criticism are the policy of "unconditional surrender" and the policy toward the U.S.S.R. Both were in a peculiar sense personal policies; and both proceeded directly from the lack of specific content in his political objectives. The first, oddly enough, was opposed by the military and constituted one of the few cases of Roosevelt's overruling the military on political questions; the other was supported by the military and, indeed, in the Yalta phase was pushed to extreme lengths by the Army's passionate desire to insure Soviet participation in the war against Japan.

Hanson Baldwin recently called the unconditional surrender policy "the biggest political mistake of the war." Mr. Churchill evidently agrees, judging by his efforts to get out from under responsibility for it; contemporary records, however, give him a larger role in its formulation than his present memory will concede. But it remains clear that "unconditional surrender" was exclusively a Roosevelt inspiration; and that he alone continued to insist on it, after the Russians, the British, and the U. S. State Department and Army had done their separate bests to get him to forget it. It has become evident, in addition, that Roosevelt's infatuation with "unconditional surrender" derived in part from an entirely garbled recollection of American history. Roosevelt had an *idée fixe* that Grant had called for "unconditional surrender" at Appomattox and then had responded to such a surrender by acts of generosity to the defeated foe. "Lee surrendered unconditionally to Grant," Roosevelt actually wrote to Hull at one point, "but immediately Grant told him that his officers should take their horses home for spring plowing. That is the spirit I want to see abroad." Thus "unconditional surrender" had for Roosevelt the connotation of magnanimity to a helpless enemy. Yet the facts are that Grant talked of "unconditional surrender" at Fort Donelson and at Vicksburg; he said nothing about it at Appomattox. If the term had any historical connotation for most people, it was certainly not the amiable connotation which it incorrectly had for Roosevelt.

Still there was more to "unconditional surrender" than a foolish slip of memory on Roosevelt's part. He was looking hard in 1943 for a formula which would achieve two objectives: on the one hand, reassure the Russians against their fear that the West might seek a separate peace; and, on the other, make absolutely certain this time that the Germans would not escape the full consciousness and stigma of defeat. At the same time he wanted to keep the question of the terms of peace open, because, with his basic pragmatism, he could not know what the exact terms should be until the moment of peace had arrived. The principle of "unconditional surrender" seemed a perfect answer to the triple dilemma. And, while it is clear that Roosevelt tended to push the principle too far, particularly in regard to the satellite states, it is not at all clear to me that the principle itself, as Mr. Baldwin has argued, "discouraged opposition to Hitler, probably lengthened the war [and] . . . cost us dearly in lives and time."

Mr. Baldwin's assumption evidently is that "unconditional surrender" deterred the German people from an anti-Hitler revolution. Yet such a theory is surely based on a musket-over-the-fireplace conception of revolution, altogether irrelevant to a totalitarian state where police controls were reasonably intact. And there is no reason to believe in any case that the failure to gain terms from the Allies deterred any serious anti-Hitler movement; it certainly did not discourage the heroes of the 1944 *Putsch* from making their courageous attempt on Hitler's life. What "unconditional surrender" may have deterred is the attempt on the part of someone like Goering to win special terms for himself. While the defection to the Allies of Goering and part of the *Luftwaffe* might conceivably have shortened the war, it is not clear that it would have simplified the peace. It was a correct desire to guard against some such contingency as this which led Roosevelt to favor "unconditional surrender" in the first place. On the point of the effect of "unconditional surrender" the arguments of Wallace Carroll (in *Persuade or Perish*) and H. R. Trevor-Roper (in *The Last Days of Hitler*) seem far more convincing to me than the more modish views of Hanson Baldwin.

The question of the U.S.S.R. puts Roosevelt's pragmatism to the most severe of tests. As a pragmatist, Roosevelt reacted to the Soviet Union in terms of specific situations. When the U.S.S.R. was invading Finland, it seemed to him "a dictatorship as absolute as any other dictatorship in the world." But when the Red Army was beating back the Nazis at Stalingrad, the U.S.S.R. took on for him a more genial aspect — as it did for most of the free world. It was in this mood that he told Sumner Welles that both the U.S.A. and the U.S.S.R. were modifying their systems and that, though American democracy and Soviet Communism could never meet, they would become enough alike to keep the peace.

Thus the pragmatism which prevented Roosevelt from assessing the theoretical implications of a totalitarian system was one factor in his Russian policy, as another was his instinctive generosity in the face of Russian courage and sacrifice. His pragmatism — his refusal to anticipate the terms of peace — affected his Russian policy in another way. "People all over the world are shell-shocked," he wrote to George Norris in 1943 — "and they will require a period of recuperation before final terms are laid down in regard to boundaries, transfers of population, free intercourse, the lowering of economic barriers, planning for mutual reconstruction, etc." But what was to happen in the interim? "I have been visualizing," Roosevelt told Norris, "a superimposed — or if you like it, superassumed — obligation by Russia, China, Britain, and ourselves that we will act as sheriffs for the maintenance of order during the transition period. . . . It will be so much easier to enter into lasting agreements after the transition period." Thus the conception of the big-power partnership — the Big Three, as it soon became — emerged as an easy substitute in Roosevelt's mind for more specific political objectives. And another factor encouraging this conception was surely his affable relations with his "royal cousin" Stalin.

Some revisionists, following the lead of William C. Bullitt, have criticized Roosevelt for not conditioning lend-lease aid to Russia in 1941 upon the acceptance of postwar political commitments. This argument overlooks the fact that it was almost as essential to us as to the Russians — and fully as essential to Mr. Churchill and the British — that the Red Army continue to kill Germans. It overlooks the even more crucial fact — which these same people, still following the lead of Bullitt, are always the first to assert in other contexts — that the U.S.S.R. would certainly not have kept such agreements, particularly when exacted under duress. Roosevelt, indeed, had very little choice but to postpone political discussions until the military crisis began to recede.

The test of his Russian policy thus came at Yalta; and Yalta, in the minds of many revisionists, has become the pat and comfortable explanation for everything that has gone wrong since the end of the war. There can be no question that Yalta represented the downfall of Rooseveltian pragmatism. For such pragmatism in international relations could succeed only among nations and leaders sharing the same or similar moral and social values; it was useless in dealings with men of opposed and hostile values. Thus pragmatism was a means of working out problems with Churchill, but it was an exposure of weakness to Stalin; and this Roosevelt did not know till after Yalta. Richard Crossman has argued persuasively that Roosevelt's foreign policy was obsessed by a desire to avoid the "mistakes" of Wilson; yet that herein Roosevelt was wrong, and that Wilson's narrow and zealous faith in abstract principle, rather than Roosevelt's limitless flexibility, was what was needed to counter Communism. "There can be little doubt," writes Crossman, "that Woodrow Wilson would have been a far more formidable adversary for Stalin than Franklin D. Roosevelt."

In general, this is a just criticism. But in detail, and as applied to Yalta, it can be much exaggerated. The actual import of that conference, indeed, has been recklessly distorted, including the really vicious attempt to blow up Alger Hiss into having been a major

Presidential adviser. Edward R. Stettinius, Jr., and Walter Johnson in *Roosevelt and the Russians,* and Judge Rosenman in his cogent and admirable brief note on the Yalta conference (pages 537–548 in the last volume of *The Public Papers and Addresses*), dispose conclusively of the central misunderstandings and misrepresentations of the Yalta transactions.

It seems fairly clear that the so-called Yalta "concessions" were both justified in terms of the information available to Roosevelt and Churchill and without decisive practical effect on subsequent developments. The Yalta agreement on Eastern Europe, far from being a concession at all, represented an extension of democratic principles so far in advance of democratic power that there was no possibility of enforcing it once the U.S.S.R. decided to ignore them. The agreements on the UN were, on the whole, minor and inconsequential; who cares today how many votes the U.S.S.R. commands in the General Assembly?

As for the concessions in the Far East, these were made with the specific purpose of assuring Soviet entrance into the Japanese war by a designated date. The Army, not knowing at the time whether the Manhattan Project would ever produce anything and determined to reduce the hundreds of thousands of casualties anticipated in the invasion and subjection of Japan, pressed upon Roosevelt the absolute necessity of getting a firm commitment from Stalin. Even to someone like Admiral Leahy, who disagreed with the military estimate of the Far Eastern situation, the final arrangements seemed "very reasonable." "No one was more surprised than I," Leahy writes in *I Was There,* "to see these conditions agreed to at Yalta labeled as some horrendous concessions made by President Roosevelt to an enemy." Nor is it easy to argue convincingly that the situation in the Far East is any different as a result of the concessions. It is hard to see that anything short of the commitment of American troops to China could have averted the Communist triumph over Chiang Kai-shek.

Stalin probably negotiated in good faith at Yalta — in good faith, that is, within terms of the Soviet wartime policy of collaboration. That policy was not to be abandoned until military developments in the weeks after Yalta showed conclusively that the military crisis in Europe was over, and that collaboration was no longer necessary.

At this point, Soviet policy rapidly switched to its postwar objective of the political conquest of Europe — a switch manifested in March 1945 by the tough Soviet interventions in Eastern Europe by the instructions through Jacques Duclos to the Communist Parties of the West to cease their "Browderite" tactics of collaboration, and by Stalin's own fantastic charges against Roosevelt. Ever the pragmatist, Roosevelt reacted swiftly to the new direction of Soviet policy. It is a misfortune that his death came in April before he had had occasion to embody his rapidly growing misgivings over Soviet policy in anything but secret cables to Stalin and to Churchill and in private conversations.

But, even if the consequences of Yalta have been rashly overstated, it still can be argued that Roosevelt's basic pragmatism throughout the war betrayed the democratic cause and lost the peace. This judgment seems to me, however, essentially mistaken. The fact is that the ambiguities in Roosevelt's attitude toward the Soviet Union corresponded precisely to the ambiguities in the whole Western attitude toward the U.S.S.R.; and this is a fact the historian cannot ignore, whatever subsequent wisdom hindsight may have given to the commentators.

The central reason for Wilson's failure had been that he incarnated convictions which the American people did not share; and that as a consequence Presidential policy outran the possibilities of national support. This error Roosevelt took great care to avoid. I happen to have been one of those myself who mistrusted Russia even in the glowing days of Stalingrad, but my argument for mistrust was essentially an intellectual one; and no one in control of democratic foreign policy could have assumed the responsibility for initiating an anti-Soviet policy in advance of demonstrated Soviet purposes of systematic hostility toward the West. Such purposes were not demonstrated during the war till March 1945.

Roosevelt described his policy toward the U.S.S.R. as a "great gamble." But it was a gamble which the American people were prepared to make. How much greater the gamble would have been, and how much less the chances of popular support, had U.S. policy based itself on the opposite hunch — the theory of Soviet noncollaboration — before the evidence was in to convince the people of the correctness of that theory! André Malraux, no friend of the Soviet Union or of Communism, has stated the problem with precision. Roosevelt went to Yalta, Malraux writes, "for reasons which, even today [1948], do not seem so bad to me. Our attempt to reach an agreement with the Russians entailed a liability which was, for France, very heavy. But would it not have been still heavier if we had refused even the attempt? I do not think that anyone could have remained in power in France, or even in the United States, if he had brought about a break with Russia, which at that time would have seemed to have no justification."

Given the pragmatic genius of the American people, Roosevelt's policy toward Russia was the only possible policy. The problem of whether the West had a community of values with the Soviet Union could only be solved pragmatically. And it was not solved pragmatically till the period after Yalta.

The defects in Roosevelt's wartime policy thus seem to be reflections of the defects in the American climate of opinion. With his superb political instincts, Roosevelt knew, as Wilson did not know, that the American people learned by experience, not by logic. And, because he learned by experience himself, he could not anticipate what had not happened. He rallied a nation broken and dispirited by depression; he led it successfully through the greatest war of our history; he left it morally strong and materially prosperous. He was not a worker of miracles. To demonstrate that he was not a deity is hardly to build up a case against his greatness as a democratic leader.

The "Sitting Ducks" of Clark Field

by

LOUIS MORTON

["The First Days of War," reprinted by permission from *The Fall of the Philippines* (Washington, D. C., 1953), pp. 77–90.]

"Few military disasters of modern times," writes Dr. Louis Morton (chief of the Pacific Section, Office of the Chief of Military History, Department of the Army), "are as sparsely documented or inadequately recorded as the defeat of America's forces in the Philippines in the first six months of World War II." Two of the more important gaps in the historical record are caused by the disappearance of essential papers sent out from the Philippines by Generals Douglas MacArthur and Jonathan Wainwright, in February and April 1942.[1]

There appears to be some question as to whether these papers are lost or merely not available. Morton writes of indisputable evidence that Wainwright's records "were received in Melbourne and placed in a vault in General [Richard K.] Sutherland's office." However, both Sutherland and Wainwright have denied knowledge of the whereabouts of these data. Although Morton has traced a foot-locker containing MacArthur's papers from the Philippines to a bank in Washington, and from there "by officer courier to General MacArthur," the latter insists that he has no knowledge of the missing records.[2]

The loss of key records is a recurrent phenomenon in historical writing, as old as Clio herself. And the ability of the historian to unfold a balanced narrative based upon incomplete evidence is a vital phase of his art. The selection below is an admirable demonstration of this aspect of historical reconstruction, even though the author because of the mass of conflicting testimony, hazy memories, and lost or missing records is unable to fix blame for the cause of the disaster at Clark Field.

Evidence that has come to light since publication of The Fall of the Philippines *does not change by very much the picture presented in this volume. General MacArthur, one of the few leading figures in the American army command in the Philippines to resist being interviewed by Dr. Morton, nevertheless did reply in writing to questions submitted to him by the author. The replies were received too late to be included in the book.*

One of these questions focused upon the question of why the American air force at Clark Field was not ordered to attack the Japanese base on Formosa in an attempt to beat the Japanese to the punch. MacArthur's reply follows: "My orders were explicit not to initiate hostilities against the Japanese. . . . While I personally had not the slightest doubt we would be attacked, great local hope [in Manila] existed that this would not be the case. Instructions from Washington were very definite to wait until the Japanese made the first overt move. Even without such a directive, practical limitations made it unfeasible to take the offensive. . . ." [3] *This, as is apparent from the selection reprinted below, is consistent with the MacArthur press release of September 27, 1946, but not in keeping with MacArthur's expressed determination to attack Formosa by air on the morning of December 9.*

Investigation of the cause or causes of what happened at Clark Field is part of the historian's attempt to understand a past which can never be totally recovered. The phenomenon of causation is linked intimately to historical understanding and even as historians disagree as to the nature of such understanding, there is further conflict among them concerning their conception of cause. Probably a majority of the historical guild would agree that the term "cause" should be regarded as "a convenient figure of speech, describing motives, influences, forces and other antecedent interrelations, not fully understood." They would use "cause" only with the *greatest circumspection, and as operating as part of a complex or series rather than as a single phenomenon. They would also admit that to get at the causes of a particular incident in the past, is a great deal more difficult than it would seem to be.*[4]

At the same time, very few historians would go along with Charles A. Beard and Alfred Vagts in the contention that the terms "cause" and "causality" should never be used in written history. Cause, argue Beard and Vagts, "is unnecessary to the making of true statements concerning history-as-actuality and owing to the ambiguity and connotations of its meanings, is more likely to be misleading than correctly informing to the reader. . . . Where historians are concerned, as they should be, with consequential and co-existing relations between events and personalities and interests, which are intimate in nature and have the appearance of necessity, they can describe such relations in terms more precise than those of causality. . . ."[5]

Most historians, in their quest for understanding, continue to think and write in terms of causes. It is true, moreover, that "the concept of causality has entered into narrative to such an extent that the writing of history might become mere cataloguing or chronology without it."[6] *The testing and refining of causal relationships, in the light of evidence, is vital to the furtherance of historical understanding. Should new sources of information become available concerning the early days of the Pacific War, the historian may be able to delineate more sharply causal sequences and advance understanding of the events preliminary to the Clark Field disaster.*

The following selection is an outstanding example of the newer military history.

F OR THOSE on the west side of the international date line, the "date which will live in infamy" came on 8 December 1941. Few responsible military or naval men had believed that the Japanese would be able to strike in more than one place. The number and diversity of their attack took the Allies completely by surprise. During the early morning hours of the eighth, Japanese naval and air forces struck almost simultaneously at Kota Bharu in British Malaya (0140), Singora, just across the border in Thailand (0305), Singapore (0610), Guam (0805), Hong Kong (0900), Wake, and the Philippines.*

Landing operations began almost immediately. By dawn, Japanese forces were in possession of Shanghai. Even as the first bombs were dropping on Hong Kong, Japanese troops were on their way into the leased territory. By the end of that day they were only a few miles from Kowloon, which they took on the thirteenth. Hong Kong fell on Christmas Day.

Within an hour after the first bombardment of Kota Bharu, Japanese troops from Indochina began to land on the beaches against bitter opposition. The same day, when the main force of the 25th Army arrived, the beachhead was secured. The landings at Singora were unopposed. There, the troops marched down the east coast of the Kra Isthmus, while one division crossed the Thailand-British Malay border and moved down the west coast. Thus began a two-month campaign which ended with the fall of Singapore on 15 February.

On Guam the air attacks continued for two days. Finally, at dawn on 10 December, the South Seas Detachment and supporting naval units landed on the island. A few hours later, the garrison there surrendered. This was the first American possession to fall into Japanese hands. At Wake Island, the Marine detachment under Maj. James P. S. Devereux was better prepared for the enemy and offered heroic resistance. The first attempt to land was beaten off and the Japanese returned to Kwajalein to lick their wounds and collect more troops for the next attempt. They were back at Wake on the twenty-second and the next morning landed in force. That same day the garrison surrendered.†

The fall of Wake and Guam cut the line of communications between Hawaii and the Philippines and left the United States with no Central Pacific base west of Midway, 4500 miles from Manila. But even before this, on the first day of war, the Japanese attack on Pearl

---

* All times are Tokyo time.

† Lt. Col. Robert D. Heinl, Jr., *The Defense of Wake* (USMC Hist Sec, 1947);*Opns of South Seas Detachment, 1941–1942*, Japanese Studies in World War II, No. 36, p. 3. For operations at Hong Kong and in Malaya, see *Japanese Landing Operations, December 8, 1941–June 8, 1942*, Military Intelligence Service (MIS) Campaign Study 3.

Harbor had destroyed the Battle Force of the Pacific Fleet and nullified all plans to come to the aid of the Philippines.

East of the date line, Vice Adm. C. Nagumo's *Pearl Harbor Striking Force* of six carriers reached its launching position 200 miles north of Oahu exactly on schedule, at 0600 on the morning of 7 December (0100 of 8 December, Tokyo time). Two Jakes (Zerotype reconnaissance planes), which had taken off at 0530 to reconnoiter, returned with the report that, except for the richest prize, the three carriers, the entire Pacific Fleet was in port. Pilots of the Japanese First Air Fleet, amidst shouts of "banzai" from their comrades, took off from the flight decks and climbed above the overcast into a magnificent sunrise. At 0750, while "Pearl Harbor was still asleep in the morning mist," * the Japanese planes came in over the island. Five minutes later, just an hour before Nomura presented his government's reply to Mr. Hull, they dropped their first bombs.†

The next two hours of that Sabbath morning in Hawaii were a nightmare. Bombs and torpedoes dropped everywhere, on the ships in the harbor, on Army installations, on depots, and other targets. Dive bombers machine-gunned planes on the ground and men on the ships. Within a half hour every battleship at Pearl Harbor had been badly damaged.

Hickam and Wheeler Fields were struck in the first attacks. The Army planes, parked in close order, wing tip to wing tip, made perfect targets. By ten o'clock the raid was over and the last Japanese planes had returned to their carriers, leaving behind them death and destruction. Tactical surprise had been as complete as strategical surprise.‡

The Japanese pilots knew exactly what to go after. Though there

* The quotation is from an account by a Japanese naval officer and is quoted in Morison, *Rising Sun in the Pacific*, p. 94.

† At 0800, Admiral Kimmel broadcast the message: "Air Raid on Pearl Harbor. This is no drill." Secretary Knox, when he read the message in Washington, exclaimed, "My God! This can't be true, this must mean the Philippines." *Pearl Harbor Attack Report*, p. 439.

‡ The best account of the attack on Pearl Harbor has been written by Morison, *Rising Sun in the Pacific*, Ch. V. For the Air Forces' story, see Craven and Cate, *The Army Air Forces in World War II*, I, 194–201. Much personal testimony and firsthand accounts of the attack can be found scattered through the Congressional hearings on the Pearl Harbor attack. A summary of the action can be found in *Pearl Harbor Attack Report*, pp. 53–72.

were ninety-four naval vessels in the harbor they concentrated on the Battle Force, sinking 3 battleships, capsizing 1, and damaging 4 more. In addition to the battleships, 3 light cruisers, 3 destroyers, and miscellaneous vessels were badly damaged. Ninety-two naval planes were lost and 31 damaged. The Army lost a total of 96 planes, including those destroyed in depots and those later stripped for parts. Army and Navy installations were badly hit. Fortunately, the Japanese failed to destroy the repair shops at Pearl Harbor or the oil tanks, filled to capacity. The carriers, then at sea, escaped the attack altogether. American casualties for the day were 2280 men killed and 1109 wounded. The Japanese lost only 29 aircraft and 5 midget submarines. "The astoundingly disproportionate extent of losses," concluded the Joint Committee which investigated the attack, "marks the greatest military and naval disaster in our Nation's history." *

With this smashing blow, the Japanese made obsolete the carefully prepared plans of defense in the event of war in the Pacific.† The RAINBOW plan called for the progressive movement of the Pacific Fleet across the Central Pacific by the capture of the Caroline and Marshall Islands and the establishment of an advanced base at Truk. The fleet would thus open the line of communications, establish superiority in the western Pacific, and come to the relief of the Philippine Islands. Along this protected line of communications would flow the supplies and men that would enable the Philippine garrison to beat back any Japanese effort to seize the Islands. By 1000 on the morning of 7 December, the force required to put RAINBOW into effect, the Battle Force of the Pacific Fleet, lay in ruins in Pearl Harbor. The Philippines were isolated, cut off from the nearest base 5000 miles away, even before they had felt the first

* *Pearl Harbor Attack Report*, p. 65. The breakdown of casualties is as follows:

	Killed	Wounded
Navy and Marines	2,086	749
Army	194	360
Total	2,280	1,109

In an earlier volume of this series, Watson, *Chief of Staff*, p. 517, the number of dead is placed at 2,403, including civilians. Mr. Watson's figures are from Morison, *Rising Sun in the Pacific*, first ed., p. 126, and are based on 1947 estimates.

† Min, JB Mtg, 8 Dec. 41, OPD Reg. Doc.

blow of the war. Their only hope now lay with the Far East Air Force and the Asiatic Fleet.

THE ATTACK ON CLARK FIELD

The duty officer at Asiatic Fleet headquarters in the Marsman Building in Manila on the night of 7–8 December (Philippine time) was Lt. Col. William T. Clement, USMC. At 0230 of 8 December (0800, 7 December, Pearl Harbor time), the operator at the Navy station intercepted the startling message, "Air Raid on Pearl Harbor. This is no drill." Recognizing the technique of the sender, an old friend stationed at Pearl Harbor, the operator brought the message to Colonel Clement. Within a half hour, it was in Admiral Hart's hands. He broadcast the news to the fleet immediately, and then, with his chief of staff, hurried to his office.*

Shortly after 0330 General Sutherland received the news of the Pearl Harbor attack, not from the Navy but from commercial broadcasts. He passed the news on to MacArthur over the private wire to the general's penthouse apartment in the Manila Hotel, then notified all commanders that a state of war existed with Japan. Troops were ordered to battle position immediately.†

At Clark Field the news flash about Pearl Harbor was also picked up from commercial broadcasts. The operator immediately notified headquarters at the field and all units were alerted. "I knew," Brereton later wrote, "we could expect an attack from the Japs any time after daylight." Before leaving for MacArthur's headquarters, he ordered Colonel Eubank, the bomber commander at Clark Field, to come down to Manila at once. At about 0500 in the morning Brereton was waiting outside MacArthur's office for orders.‡

* Hart, Narrative of Events, Asiatic Fleet, pp. 36–37; Morison, *Rising Sun in the Pacific*, pp. 168–169. Captain Morison secured additional information from Admiral Hart by interview after the war.

† Hunt, *MacArthur and the War Against Japan*, p. 27; Wainwright, *General Wainwright's Story*, p. 18; interviews, author with Col. Diller, 24 Aug. 49; Gens. Sutherland and Marshall, 12 Nov. 46 and 7 Apr. 48, OCMH. Admiral Hart states that Colonel Clement, unable to "get response from USAFFE Headquarters," passed the news "to one of the staff duty officers at his home." Ltr. Hart to Maj. Gen. Orlando Ward, 19 Dec. 51, OCMH.

‡ Brereton, *Diaries*, pp. 38–39. It is evident from internal evidence that the diary for this period was put in its present form at a later date and cannot therefore be considered always a contemporaneous record.

By breakfast, the news of the attack on Pearl Harbor had reached all ranks. The men had for so long accepted the fact that war with Japan might come that the event itself was an anticlimax. There was no cheering and no demonstration, but "a grim, thoughtful silence." * War with Japan was not, for the American and Philippine troops, a remote war across a wide ocean. It was close and immediate.

PROLOGUE TO ATTACK

On Formosa airfields, 500 miles away, Japanese Army and Navy pilots were standing by, their planes gassed and ready to take off for Luzon, when the first news of Pearl Harbor reached Manila. Around midnight of the seventh dense clouds of heavy fog had closed in on the island, blanketing airfields and preventing the scheduled take-offs at dawn.

This unforeseen development filled the Japanese commanders with nervous apprehension. The timetable for the attack was extremely close and left little leeway. As the early morning hours rolled by, anxiety increased. By this time, the Japanese believed, the American high command in the Philippines would have received news of Pearl Harbor and either sent the Far East Air Force southward or set up an effective defense against the impending raid. All hope of surprise would be lost.

Even more frightening was the possibility that this delay would enable the heavy bombers of the Far East Air Force to attack the planes lined up on Formosa fields. Indeed, at 0800, the Japanese intercepted an American radio message which they interpreted as meaning that such an attack would come off in two hours. At 1010 a Japanese plane mistakenly reported B-17's approaching Formosa and the frightened Japanese began passing out gas masks.†

* Mallonée, Bataan Diary, I, 34.
† Interrog. of Capt. Takahashi Chihaya, Imperial Japanese Navy (IJN), 20 Oct. 45, and of Comdr. Ryosuke Nomura, Opns Officer, 23d Air Flotilla, 11th Air Fleet, 28 Nov. 45, in USSBS, *Interrogations of Japanese Officials*, 2 vols. (Washington 1946) I, 74–76; II, 531; *14th Army Opns*, I, 41.
It is difficult to understand the origin of the 0800 message. While there was discussion of such a raid at USAFFE, there was no need to send radios on the subject. It is possible that orders sending B-17's at Clark aloft to avoid being

Japanese fears of an American attack against Formosa were not without foundation. Such plans had already been made and target data had been prepared. The objective folders were far from complete, however, and lacked calibrated bomb-target maps and bomb release lines for given speeds and altitudes. "But we had something complete enough," thought Capt. Allison Ind, a Far East Air Force intelligence officer, "to make this bombing mission a very far cry from the blind stab it would have had to be otherwise." *

On his first visit to USAFFE headquarters about 0500, General Brereton had been unable to see MacArthur and had talked with Sutherland. At that time he had requested permission to carry out a daylight attack against Formosa. MacArthur's chief of staff had told him to go ahead with the necessary preparations, but to wait for MacArthur's authorization before starting the attack. Brereton returned to his headquarters at Nielson Field, where he talked with Colonel Eubank, who had just flown down from Clark Field. Orders

---

caught on the ground were in some way intercepted and misunderstood by the apprehensive Japanese. *14th Army Opns*, I, 41, refers to the report as "intelligence reports," but does not indicate its origin any further. *5th Air Gp Opns, Japanese Studies in World War II*, No. 3, p. 6.

* Lt. Col. Allison Ind, *Bataan, The Judgment Seat* (New York, 1944), p. 92. Material used with the permission of The Macmillan Company, publishers.

The official air force account of the attack on Clark Field is contained in Craven and Cate, *The Army Air Forces in World War II*, I, 201–214. General Brereton has a full account in his *Diaries*, pages 38–44, which must be considered as the evidence of an interested party in the dispute later arising over responsibility for the disaster. Army Air Action in Phil and NEI, Chapter III, covers the Clark Field attack and is substantially the same as that given in the air force history.

Official records of the events surrounding the attack are practically nonexistent. An effort has been made by the author to supplement the existing accounts with interviews with those participants not interviewed by the air force historians. Persons interviewed were Generals Sutherland and R. J. Marshall, Colonels Diller, Collier, and Campbell, the last of whom was aircraft warning officer of USAFFE.

Mr. Walter D. Edmonds, who was commissioned by the air force to write the account of air operations in the Philippines, interviewed General Sutherland in Manila in June 1945, as well as a large number of air force officers. A copy of his notes taken on the Sutherland interview is included in Army Air Action in Phil and NEI, Appendix 9, and a portion is printed in Craven and Cate, *The Army Air Forces in World War II*, I, 205. The information Edmonds secured is directly at variance with information the present author secured in two interviews with General Sutherland. Edmond's findings are embodied in an article entitled "What Happened at Clark Field," *Atlantic* (July 1951), pp. 20–33.

were issued to get the B–17's ready. At about 0715 Brereton apparently went to MacArthur's headquarters again to request permission to attack Formosa. Again he was told by Sutherland to stand by for orders.*

About this time the Far East Air Force commander received a transoceanic telephone call from his air force chief, General Arnold. Brereton explained what he was trying to do, and Arnold told him what had happened at Pearl Harbor, so that, as he later explained, Brereton would not be caught in the same way and have his "entire air force destroyed." †

By this time, reports of enemy flights were being received at air force headquarters and planes of the Interceptor Command were sent up. Around 0800 the heavy bombers at Clark Field were ordered aloft on patrol, without bombs, to avoid being caught on the ground.

At 1000 Brereton renewed his request to take offensive action. "I personally called General Sutherland," he says, "and informed him . . . that if Clark Field was attacked successfully we would be unable to operate offensively with the bombers." ‡ Again the request was denied. Ten minutes later, Colonel Eubank started back to Clark Field with instructions to dispatch a photographic reconnaissance mission immediately to southern Formosa.

No sooner had those orders been issued than Brereton received a telephone call from General MacArthur. He told MacArthur that since Clark Field had not yet been attacked, he would hold the

* Summary of Activities, Far East Air Force, entry of 8 Dec. 41, in Air University Hist. Off. This document is evidently a transcription from notes hastily made during December 1941. Errors in dating the year of entry are explained as the result of "harried field conditions." Despite the imperfections of this document it remains one of the few written contemporary sources for the events of 8 December 1941. Ltr. Col. Wilfred J. Paul, Air University Hist. Off., to Gen. Ward, 7 Dec. 51, OCMH. The official air force account in Craven and Cate, *The Army Air Forces in World War II,* I, 206 note, takes cognizance of the mistakes in dating in this document. Edmonds, "What Happened at Clark Field," pages 24–26, contains an excellent account of the discussions at air force headquarters that morning.

† Gen. Henry H. Arnold, *Global Mission* (New York: Harper & Brothers, 1949), p. 272.

‡ Brereton, *Diaries,* p. 40. The author has also used a letter written by Brereton to the AAF Hist. Off. expanding the diary entries. 1st Ind., Brereton to Paul, 30 Jan. 43, Air University Hist. Off. See also Edmonds, "What Happened at Clark Field," p. 25.

bombers in readiness until he received reports from the reconnaissance mission already authorized. They agreed that if no reports were received, the bombers would attack Formosa late that afternoon. MacArthur left to Brereton "the decision for offensive action." *

Brereton called in his staff and told them of his conversation with MacArthur. Orders were then dispatched to Clark Field to call in the heavy bombers. Three were to be readied for the photo reconnaissance mission; the others were to be briefed for offensive missions. At 1120 Field Order No. 1 of the Far East Air Force was sent by teletype to Clark Field. It confirmed Brereton's instructions to Eubank, given at 1045, to attack southern Formosa with two heavy bombardment squadrons "at the latest daylight hour today that visibility will permit." By 1130 the bombers were back on the field, being loaded with 100- and 300-pound bombs; the fighters had also return to base for refueling. At 1156 Brereton gave Sutherland a full report of the situation over the telephone, and informed him that he planned to attack Formosa fields late that afternoon.†

General Sutherland's account of the proposed raid on Formosa differs from the air force story. On one occasion, Sutherland recollected that there had been some plan to bomb Formosa on 8 December but that "Brereton said he had to have the photos first." On another occasion Sutherland took the opposite and more consistent position that when Brereton asked for permission to attack Formosa, he, Sutherland, had ordered a reconnaissance first.‡

* Summary of Activities, Far East Air Force, entry of 8 Dec. 41. General Brereton omits entirely any mention of his conversation with General MacArthur, and states that he received the authorization to attack Formosa at 1100 from General Sutherland. In an interview with the present author in June 1951, Sutherland declared that he does not recall that Brereton spoke with MacArthur that morning. Brereton, *Diaries*, p. 41.

† Summary of Activities, Far East Air Force, entry of 8 Dec. 41.

‡ The first version was given in his interview with Walter D. Edmonds in Manila in June 1945. The second version was given in an interview with the present author in November 1946. This author interviewed Sutherland a second time in June 1951 and on being presented with both versions, Sutherland was most emphatic in asserting that it was he who had ordered the reconnaissance because Brereton did not have sufficient information to warrant an attack against Formosa. USAFFE and air force records do not contain any material relating to this incident.

General MacArthur's statements do not throw any light on this question. He had received word from Washington early that morning (at 0530) that hostilities with Japan had begun, and that he was to carry out the tasks assigned in RAINBOW.* Brereton's surmise, therefore, that he was not permitted to attack Formosa because MacArthur was under orders not to attack unless attacked first and that the Pearl Harbor attack "might not have been construed as an overt act against the Philippines" must be dismissed.† MacArthur had authority to act, and RAINBOW specifically assigned as one of his missions "air raids against Japanese forces and installations within tactical operating radius of available bases." ‡

General Brereton's surmise, however, was not entirely without foundation. It was evidently based on the 27 November warning from the War Department. That warning had stated that "if hostilities cannot be avoided the United States desires that Japan commit the first overt act." § The War Department had been careful, however, not to restrict MacArthur's freedom of action, and had authorized him in the same message to "undertake such reconnaissance and other measures as you deem necessary" prior to hostile Japanese action. In the event of war he was to execute the tasks assigned in RAINBOW.

In the period between the receipt of this message and the outbreak of hostilities, the B-17's had flown reconnaissance missions nort of Luzon in the direction of Formosa. Their search sectors, according to General Sutherland, reached to "the southern edge of Formosa with one segment of the pie running up the east coast of the island a little way." || But General Brereton declares that he was instructed by MacArthur to limit reconnaissance to "two-thirds of the distance between North Luzon and Southern Formosa." ¶ Later, he says, he secured permission to extend the northern limit of the search sector to the international· treaty boundary between the Phil-

* Rad, Marshall to MacArthur, No. 736, 7 Dec. 41, WPD 4544-20.
† Brereton, *Diaries*, p. 39n; ltr, Brereton to Paul, Air University Hist. Off.
‡ Ltr, CofS to CG USAFFE, 21 Nov. 41, sub: U.S.–British Co-operation, including War Plan RAINBOW 5, WPD 4402-4112.
§ Rad, Marshall to MacArthur, 27 Nov. 41, No. 624, WPD 4544-13; see above, IV, 71.
|| Interview, Edmonds with Sutherland, Jun 45, and confirmed in interv., Morton with Sutherland, 12 Nov. 46.
¶ Brereton, *Diaries*, pp. 34-35.

ippines and Formosa.* On the bases of Sutherland's statement, then, it was possible to conduct a partial reconnaissance of Formosa before the war; according to Brereton there was no prewar reconnaissance on MacArthur's orders.

On Brereton's proposal to bomb Formosa, General MacArthur expressed himself most clearly. When Brereton's diaries were published in 1946, MacArthur released a statement to the press recounting in full his recollection of the events of 8 December 1941. The press release, issued on 27 September 1946, read:

> General Brereton never recommended an attack on Formosa to me and I know nothing of such a recommendation having been made. . . . That it must have been of a most nebulous and superficial character, as no official record exists of it at headquarters. That such a proposal, if intended seriously, should have been made to me in person by him; that he never has spoken of the matter to me either before or after the Clark Field Attack. That an attack on Formosa with its heavy concentrations by his small bomber force without fighter support, which because of the great distance involved, was impossible, would have had no chance of success.†

On 8 December, in summarizing the results of the Japanese attack, MacArthur had told the War Department: "I am launching a heavy bombardment counterattack tomorrow morning on enemy airdromes in southern Formosa." ‡ It is evident, then, that MacArthur himself planned, by the afternoon or evening of the 8th, to execute an attack against Formosa with the remaining B–17's.

Faced with these conflicting accounts, the historian can be sure only of five facts: (1) That an attack against Formosa was proposed; (2) that such an attack was deferred in favor of a photo reconnaissance mission requested either by Brereton or Sutherland; (3) that about 1100 on 8 December a strike against Formosa, to take place that day, was finally authorized; (4) that the heavy bombers were back on Clark Field after 1130 on the morning of 8 December; and

* Ibid.

† New York Times, September 28, 1946, p. 6.

‡ Rad, MacArthur to AGWAR, No. 1133, 8 Dec. 41. The raid was canceled the next day. Rad, MacArthur to AGWAR, No. 1135, 9 Dec. 41. Both in AG 381 (11–27–41 Gen) Far East.

542 UNDERSTANDING THE AMERICAN PAST

(5) that MacArthur planned an attack against Formosa for the morning of 9 December.

THE ATTACK

The Japanese, fearing an air attack against Formosa, had meanwhile made haste to get their planes off the ground. The fog, which had grounded the 11th Air Fleet, had lifted to the east at dawn, permitting twenty-five twin-engine Army bombers to take off for Luzon.*

Shortly before 0900 the Japanese Army bombers were reported by the aircraft warning service on Luzon to be heading south over Lingayen Gulf in the direction of Manila. It was probably this report that sent the B–17's at Clark Field aloft without bombs. The 20th Pursuit Squadron at Clark took off to intercept the strike and the 17th Pursuit Squadron rose from Nichols Field to cover Clark. But the Japanese Army planes, liimted to targets north of the 16th latitude, turned east as they approached Lingayen Gulf. One group struck Tuguegarao at about 0930 while another concentrated on barracks and other installations at Baguio, the summer capital of the Commonwealth, where Quezon was staying at this time. The Japanese bombers returned to base without having sighted any American aircraft. Far East Air Force reports between 1000 and 1030 of a flight of enemy bombers, first in the Cagayan valley, and then "turned around and proceeding north," apparently referred to these Japanese Army planes.†

By the time the false report of approaching B–17's had been received on Formosa, the fog had lifted sufficiently to permit the naval planes of the Japanese 11th Air Fleet to take off. At 1015, a force of 108 twin-engine bombers escorted by eighty-four Zeros set out for Clark and Iba. Only the very best and most experienced pilots had been assigned to this important mission.‡

* 5th Air Gp Opns, p. 16.
† Summary of Activities, Far East Air Force, 8 Dec. 41; Craven and Cate, *The Army Air Forces in World War II*, I, 207–08; Edmonds, "What Happened at Clark Field," p. 24; 5th Air Gp Opns, p. 16; USSBS, *Japanese Air Power* (Washington, 1946), p. 7.
‡ Japanese Naval Opns in Phil Invasion, pp. 6–7; interrog of Capt Takahashi and Comdr Nomura, USSBS, *Interrogations of Japanese Officials*, I, 75; II, 531.

As the Japanese planes approached northern Luzon, the airborne American aircraft received the all-clear signal and were instructed to land. By 1130 nearly all the planes were back at their bases. The two squadrons of B–17's were on Clark Field, loading with gas and bombs for the raid against Formosa. The 20th Pursuit Squadron was also at Clark after its vain attempt to intercept the last Japanese flight. At Nichols, the 17th Pursuit Squadron, which had been covering Clark, was landing to refuel. The 3d and 34th Pursuit Squadrons were standing by at Iba and Del Carmen.*

Shortly before 1130, reports of an approaching enemy formation began coming in to the plotting board at Nielson. In addition to radar reports, almost every postmaster along the northwest coast of Luzon reported the high-flying enemy bombers to the air warning center by telephone or telegraph.† Colonel George, chief of staff of the Interceptor Command, was in the plotting room when the reports were coming in, and predicted "that the objective of this formidable formation was Clark Field." ‡

At about 1145, according to Col. Alexander H. Campbell, the aircraft warning officer, a warning message went out to Clark Field by teletype. If the message did not get through, as is frequently asserted, this fact was not known to the officers in the plotting room at Nielson. It is asserted also that an attempt to warn the field by radio over the Far East Air Force net was made, but with no success. The reason for this failure can only be guessed. Col. James V. Collier, a G–3 officer in USAFFE headquarters, later stated, "The radio operator had left his station to go to lunch," and another source states, "Radio reception was drowned by static which the Japanese probably caused by systematic jamming of the frequencies." § Apparently other available means of communication, such as the long distance telephone lines, telegraph, and the command radio net to Fort Stotsenburg, were not used or thought of. Colonel Campbell

---

* The account of the attack is based, except where otherwise noted, on Craven and Cate, *The Army Air Forces in World War II*, I, 207–213; Brereton, *Diaries*, pp. 38–44; History of the Fifth Air Force (and its Predecessors); Edmonds, "What Happened at Clark Field," pp. 28–31; *Japanese Naval Opns in the Phil Invasion*, p. 6; *5th Air Gp Opns*, p. 12.
† Collier, Notebooks, I, 49.
‡ *Ibid.*
§ *Ibid.*, 50; Army Air Action in Phil and NEI, p. 55.

did get a telephone message through to Clark Field and talked with an unknown junior officer there. This officer intended, said Campbell, to give the base commander or the operations officer the message at the earliest opportunity.*

Meanwhile, Colonel George at Nielson had dispersed his fighters to meet the attack. The 34th Squadron was ordered to cover Clark Field; the 17th, the Bataan peninsula; and the 21st, the Manila area. The 3d Squadron at Iba was dispatched to intercept a reported enemy formation over the South China Sea.† At Clark Field, two squadrons of B–17's and the 20th Pursuit Squadron were still on the ground. Sometime shortly before 1145 the fighters were ordered aloft as soon as refueling was completed to cover their own base.‡

The 3d Pursuit Squadron took off from Iba to intercept the enemy flight over the South China Sea. A thick haze of dust prevented the 34th at Del Carmen from taking off, and at 1215 the 20th Pursuit Squadron at Clark, whose planes had just completed refueling, made ready to take off.§

At that moment the first formation of Japanese bombers appeared over Clark Field.‖ All but one of the B–17's was lined up on the

* Interv, author with Col Campbell, Sept. 46; Collier, Notebooks, I, 50. Colonel Campbell's notebook contains the following entry: Sgt. Alfred H. Eckles, Hopkinsville, Ky., was on duty with Maj. Sam Lamb's communication detail Hqrs. F. E. A. F. 8 Dec. and carried message to Teletype operator re flight of planes heading toward Clark Field, saw it sent and acknowledged as received by them. This at about 11:45 (?) A.M., about 30–45 min. before arrival of bombers and bombing of Clark Field. I, together with Coyle, George and Sprague watched this particular flight for considerable length of time. I kept urging them to do something about it, but they insisted on waiting until they reached a certain distance from field. Sprague typed wrote out message showed it to George and myself. I asked what "Kickapoo" meant in message. Was told it meant, "Go get 'em." Sprague then took message into Teletype Room for transmission, about 15 minutes before bombing.

† Craven and Cate, *The Army Air Forces in World War II*, I, 209.

‡ Hist of Fifth Air Force, p. 16. This statement would imply that Colonel George was in communication with the pursuit squadron at Clark Field after 1145, although the Bomber Command could not be reached at this time.

§ Hist of Fifth Air Force, p. 16.

‖ It is not possible to state the exact time of this attack. Like so many other matters, this question, too, is controversial. The author has selected this time, about 1220, since it is supported by the weight of evidence. Walter D. Edmonds gives the time as 1240 in his account of the attack. *They Fought with What They Had*, pp. 100, 102n.

field and the fighters were just getting ready to take off. After the warning of the Pearl Harbor attack, and after the loss of several valuable hours because of bad weather, the Japanese pilots did not expect to find so rich a harvest waiting for them. But they did not question their good fortune. The first flight of Japanese planes consisted of twenty-seven twin-engine bombers. They came over the unprotected field in a V-formation at a height estimated at 22,000–25,000 feet, dropping their bombs on the aircraft and buildings below, just as the air raid warning sounded. As at Pearl Harbor, the Japanese achieved complete tactical surprise.

The first flight was followed immediately by a similar formation which remained over the field for fifteen minutes. The planes in this formation, as in the first, accomplished their mission almost entirely without molestation. American antiaircraft shells exploded from 2000 to 4000 feet short of the targets. After the second formation of bombers, came thirty-four Zeros — which the Americans believed were carrier based — to deliver the final blow with their low-level strafing attacks on the grounded B–17's, and on the P–40's with their full gasoline tanks. This attack lasted for more than an hour.

With the first high wail of the siren, the men on the field below streamed from the mess halls. As the bombers passed over, the Americans could see the falling bombs glistening in the sunlight. Then came the explosions, hundreds of them, so violent that they seemed to pierce the eardrums and shake the ground. Throwing aside momentary disbelief and stupefaction, the men rushed to their battle stations. The scene was one of destruction and horror, unbelievable to the men who only a few minutes before had been eating lunch or servicing the planes. Flash fires sprang up and spread rapidly to the trees with long cogon grass around the field "roaring and crackling like an evil beast." * Dense smoke and a heavy cloud of dust rose over the field.

Against such odds, the Americans could offer little opposition. The 200th Coast Artillery (AA) experienced considerable difficulty with its 3-inch gun ammunition, the most recent of which was manufactured in 1932. The percentage of duds was abnormally high and "most of the fuses were badly corroded." Only one

* Miller, *Bataan Uncensored*, p. 67.

UNDERSTANDING THE AMERICAN PAST

of every six shells fired, says one observer, actually exploded.* Acts of personal heroism were commonplace. Ground and combat crews manned the guns of the grounded planes, and men dashed into flaming buildings to rescue their comrades as well as supplies and equipment. Others braved the strafing gunfire to aid the wounded. One private appropriated an abandoned truck and made seven trips with wounded men to the station hospital.

During the attack, 3 P–40's of the 20th Pursuit Squadron managed to get into the air, but 5 more were blasted by bombs as they taxied for the take-off.† A similar number was caught in the strafing attack. The 3 airborne fighters shot down 3 or 4 Japanese fighters.

The 34th Pursuit Squadron, still at Del Carmen, could see the great clouds of smoke rising from Clark. The old P–35's of the squadron finally managed to take off and were soon in action against the superior Zeroes over Clark. Though outclassed and outnumbered, the squadron knocked down three enemy fighters without loss to itself. But few of its planes were without serious damage. The 17th and 21st Pursuit Squadrons, on patrol over Bataan and Manila, made no effort to attack the Japanese aircraft, presumably because the communications center at Clark had been bombed out and news of the raid did not reach the Interceptor Command in time to dispatch aid.‡

The 11th Air Fleet's attack against Clark was even more successful than the worried Japanese had expected. The operation had been well planned and executed. The first flights of bombers had concentrated on the hangars, barracks, and warehouses, and left them a burning ruin. Some of the grounded planes had been damaged in these bombings but the greatest casualties were inflicted by the low-level attacks of the Zeros which followed. Casualties in men were fifty-five killed and more than one hundred wounded.

* *Ibid.;* Prov CA Brig (AA) Rpt of Opns, p. 3, Annex IX, USAFFE–USFIP Rpt of Opns; interview, author with Gen Sage, 28 Feb. 51.

† This account of the operations of the 20th Pursuit Squadron is based on an interview with the squadron commander, Col. Joseph H. Moore, 12 August 1949. It varies slightly from the official air force account which places four planes in the air before the attack.

‡ It is strange that the pilots over Bataan and Manila did not see the heavy columns of smoke and dust rising from Clark, only fifty miles away.

Simultaneously with the raid against Clark, other 11th Air Fleet planes were attacking the fighter base at Iba. The 12 planes of the 3d Pursuit Squadron, which had been patrolling over the China Sea, low on gas, returned to base. As they were circling to land, Iba was struck by 54 Japanese twin-motored naval bombers escorted by 50 Zeros. Effective action by the P-40's resulted in the loss of 2 Japanese fighters (probables) and kept the Zeros from carrying out the low-level attacks which were so successful at Clark. But the losses at Iba were almost as great as at Clark. Barracks, warehouses, equipment, and the radar station were destroyed. Ground crews suffered heavy casualties and all but 2 of the 3d Squadron's P-40's were lost.

The reaction from Washington headquarters of the Air Forces was delayed but explosive, despite a radio from MacArthur stating that the losses had been "due to overwhelming superiority of enemy forces." * General Arnold, when he received the news of the losses in the Philippines, "could not help thinking that there must have been some mistake made somewhere in my Air Force command," and he decided "to tell Brereton so." † Brereton had just returned from an inspection of Clark Field when he received a transociatic telephone call from an irate General Arnold asking "how in the hell" an experienced airman like himself could have been caught with his planes down. Apparently Brereton felt his explanation had not satisfied General Arnold, for he immediately reported the conversation to MacArthur and asked his help in presenting the situation to the Army Air Forces chief. According to Brereton, MacArthur was furious. "He told me to go back and fight the war and not to worry," Brereton recorded in his diary. "As I walked out of his office he asked Sutherland to get General Marshall on the phone." ‡ Unfortunately, there is no record of the telephone conversation that followed.

Thus, after one day of war, with its strength cut in half, the Far East Air Force had been eliminated as an effective fighting force. Of the modern combat aircraft, only 17 of the original 35 B-17's re-

---

* Rad, MacArthur to Arnold, 10 Dec 41, AG 381 (11–27–41 Gen) Far East.
† Arnold, *Global Mission*, p. 272.
‡ *Ibid.*; Brereton, *Diaries*, p. 50. General Sutherland has no recollection of such a telephone call. Interview, author with Sutherland, 12 Jun 51.

mained. Fifty-three P–40's and 3 P–35's had been destroyed, and an additional 25 or 30 miscellaneous aircraft (B–10's, B–18's, and observation planes) were gone. In addition, many of the planes listed as operational were heavily damaged. Installations at Clark and Iba were either burned out or badly hit. Total casualties for the day were 80 killed and 150 wounded. The total cost to the Japanese was 7 fighters.* The conclusion of the Joint Congressional Committee which investigated the Pearl Harbor attack, that it was the greatest military disaster in American history, is equally applicable to the Philippines.

POST-MORTEM

The catastrophe of Pearl Harbor overshadowed at the time and still obscures the extent of the ignominious defeat inflicted on American air forces in the Philippines on the same day. The Far East Air Force had been designed as a striking force to hit the enemy before he could reach Philippine shores. The heavy bombers were an offensive weapon, thought capable of striking the enemy's bases and cutting his lines of communication. Hopes for the active defense of the Islands rested on these aircraft. At the end of the first day of war, such hopes were dead.

The tragedy of Clark Field, where the heavy bombers were caught like so many sitting ducks, becomes even more tragic when one considers the strange sequence of events that preceded it. Even before the war, the danger of basing the B–17's on Clark Field had been recognized. General MacArthur had written to General Marshall on 29 November, "The location of potential enemy fields and types of aircraft indicate that heavy bombers should be located south of Luzon where they would be reasonably safe from attack." He intended at the time to base the bombers in the Visayas.† Time did not permit the construction of fields there, but before the out-

---

* Japanese Naval Opns in Phil Invasion, p. 7. An additional Japanese fighter of the 4th Carrier Squadron was lost at Davao. Craven and Cate, *The Army Air Forces in World War II*, I, 213. There is some disagreement on the number of P–40's lost, some sources placing the figure as low as 42. USSBS, *Japanese Air Power*, p. 7.

† Ltr, MacArthur to Marshall, 29 Nov. 41, WPD 3489–21.

break of hostilities he did order General Brereton to move the heavy bombers from Clark Field to Mindanao.*

During the first week in December, Brereton had sent two squadrons of B–17's to the recently constructed field at Del Monte in Mindanao. The decision to move only two squadrons, Brereton states, was based on the expected arrival from the United States of the 7th Bombardment Group which was to be stationed at Del Monte. Had all the heavy bombers on Clark been transferred to Mindanao, there would have been no room for the 7th when it arrived.†

General Sutherland's version of the same incident differs considerably from that of the air force commander. It was at his insistence, he recollected, that even the two squadrons were sent south. "General Brereton," he says, "did not want them to go." Sutherland says he had ordered all the B–17's moved to Del Monte. On checking, he had found that only half of the planes had been sent and that General MacArthur's orders had not been obeyed.‡

Wherever the responsibility lies for failing to move all the B–17's south, there still remains the question of why the remaining bombers were caught on the ground. Brereton argues that had he been permitted to attack Formosa when he wished, the planes would not have been on the field. Implicit is the assumption that if the raid had been successful, the Japanese could not have made their own attack. MacArthur denied knowledge of such a proposal in 1946, but in a radio sent on 8 December 1941 he stated that he intended to attack Formosa the next morning. General Sutherland, in one interview, claimed that Brereton was responsible for deferring the attack, and in another interview, that he himself deferred the attack because the Far East Air Force did not have sufficient target data for such an attack. It is clear that this project was discussed by Brereton and Sutherland, that MacArthur mentioned it in a radio that day, and that authorization to execute the attack was delayed until 1100 that morning.

Whether such an attack would have had a serious chance of suc-

* *New York Times*, September 28, 1946, p. 6; interv, author with Sutherland, 12 Nov. 46.
†Brereton, *Diaries*, pp. 35–36.
‡ Interviews, author and Edmonds with Sutherland. General Kenney was also told this story by Sutherland. *General Kenney Reports*, p. 27.

cess is not argued by either Sutherland or Brereton. Knowing now what the Japanese had at Formosa, the possibility of a successful raid by the B–17's seems extremely remote. The Far East Air Force admittedly had sketchy information on the strength and disposition of the Japanese forces on Formosa. Had it been known that there were over five hundred Japanese planes waiting on Formosa, ready to take off, it is doubtful that anyone would have considered the project seriously. Moreover, the B–17's would have had to fly to Formosa, out of fighter range, unescorted. Once there, they would have been greeted by swarms of Zeros. "An attack on Formosa, with its heavy air concentrations," MacArthur later wrote, ". . . was impossible, would have had no chance of success." * Sutherland's request for a photo reconnaissance mission prior to an attack would appear, therefore, to have been entirely justified. The heavy bombers were indeed far too valuable to risk in so hazardous a mission.

Another unresolved question is why the warning of approaching Japanese aircraft did not reach the bomber commander at Clark Field in time to meet the attack. All forces in the Philippines had knowledge of the attack on Pearl Harbor hours before the first Japanese bombers appeared over Luzon. A dawn raid at Davao had given notice that the Japanese had no intention of bypassing the archipelago. The early morning bombings on Luzon gave even more pointed warning that an attack against the major air base in the Islands could be expected. Colonel Campbell testifies that Clark Field had received word of the approaching Japanese aircraft before the attack. Colonel Eubank states that no such warning was ever received. Other officers speak of the breakdown of communications at this critical juncture. There is no way of resolving this conflicting testimony.

Assuming that Colonel Eubank did not receive the warning from Nielson Field, there still remains one final question. Were the aircraft on the field adequately dispersed for wartime condition? It is not possible to state definitely how the aircraft were dispersed when they came in at 1130. There surely must have been some recognition

* *New York Times*, September 28, 1946, p. 6.

of the danger of an enemy air attack at any moment. The Japanese state that they were "surprised to find the American aircraft lined up on the field." * And at least one flight of four B–17's was lined neatly on the field when the Japanese came over. Captain Ind tells of finding photographs, one of which was taken by an American pilot flying over the field, showing the planes inadequately dispersed for any but high-level bombing attacks. "This entire set of photographs," he says, "was removed from my desk a few nights later. No one seemed to know what had happened to them." † This question, like the others, remains unanswered.

The full story of the events which preceded the Japanese air attacks against the Far East Air Force on the first day of the war will probably never be known. There was no time for reports, and if any records ever existed they have since been lost. The historian must rely on the memories of participants whose stories conflict at numerous points. General Arnold, eight years after the event, wrote that he was never able "to get the real story of what happened in the Philippines." Brereton's diary, in his opinion, did not provide "a complete and accurate account," and General Sutherland's story "does not completely clear it up, by any means." ‡

Whatever the answers to the questions one may ask about the events of 8–9 December 1941 on Luzon, the significance of these events is clear. As at Pearl Harbor, the Japanese had removed in one stroke the greatest single obstacle to their advance southward. The Philippine garrison could expect little help in the near future. It was now almost entirely surrounded. The only path open lay to the south, and that, too, soon would be closed.

* Interrog of Comdr Nomura, 28 Nov 45, USSBS, *Interrogations of Japanese Officials*, II, 531; Japanese Naval Opns in Phil Invasion, p. 6.

† Ind, *Bataan, The Judgment Seat*, p. 101.

‡ Arnold, *Global Mission*, p. 272.

American Character

by

HENRY S. COMMAGER

[From *The Nineteenth Century*, April 1949]

The key to national character is a perennial quest among American historians. The nineteenth-century American historian sought the clue to national behavior in the essentially Anglo-Saxon and Protestant composition of the American people. With the vogue of the Teutonic hypothesis, to these factors were added the elements of Teutonism and Aryanism. Turner broke sharply with the belief that the American was a transplanted Teuton, and found the determining American traits on the frontier and in the wilderness.[1]

World War I and its aftermath induced considerable speculation as to how Americans differed from Europeans. It is to the credit of the historical profession that no reputable American historian, in the 1920's, joined the attempts by Lothrop Stoddard,[2] Clinton Stoddard Burr,[3] and Madison Grant[4] to fashion a Nordic interpretation of American nationality. During the 1930's, with the popularity of the economic interpretation of history, the historian was not too much interested in speculation about the American type. As a consequence of World War II there was renewed interest in our own national character as well as in that of our allies and enemies.

In the pattern of the earlier effort by Henry Adams to describe American character in the year 1800 and again in 1817,[5] Professor Commager here characterizes the twentieth-century American.

This type of historical writing is, perhaps, the most difficult of all. Essentially impressionistic, it requires a broad synthetic viewpoint and an effective writing style, so that the reader is touched both intellectually and emotionally. At the same time, the author ventures upon dangerous ground in attempting to generalize about so elusive a concept as national character.

One could quarrel with certain of Commager's generalizations; just as one could dispute the findings of other historians bold enough to attempt to come to grips with this problem. At the same time, what is the historian to do when confronted by the problem of national characterization? To strike his professional banner and abandon the field to the sociologists and anthropologists does not appear to be the solution. The sociologists, it is clear, despite some interesting work in this area, have not done much to advance our understanding of the central problem.[6] The same might be said of the highly controversial theories of the American psyche advanced by Margaret Mead[7] and Geoffrey Gorer,[8] who write from the psycho-anthropological point of view.

Henry S. Commager is Professor of History at Columbia University.

IF LAWS of history were ever to be formulated, Henry Adams said half a century ago, they must of necessity be based largely on American experience. After the lapse of two generations whose wars and disasters gave some support to Adams's theory of the collapse of civilization itself, it is clear that the American experience is even more relevant to the formulation of laws of history than Adams realized. The peoples of the Old World and of the New now acknowledge that America will direct, if she does not indeed control, the course of world history in the second half of the twentieth century. Outside Russia and her satellites few look upon this prospect with misgivings. There are some, to be sure, who have reservations about the Marshall Plan, and more who look askance at the Truman Doctrine; there are some who are suspicious and many who are envious. Yet no one can fairly argue that the Western World regards the rise of America to world leadership as more of a misfortune than good fortune. For if a future directed by America is not wholly clear, neither is it a blank, and those who know this nation best are ready to admit that its values are sound, its intentions good, and its will strong.

The America that will so largely shape the unknown future is an America whose character has been formed, whose standards have been set, in the known past. The lineaments of that character are familiar, the nature of those standards recognized and acceptable. That the future is precarious no one will deny; that it is an enigma is untrue. It confronts us with a series of questions, but the very phrasing of those questions, their grammar and vocabulary as it were, are dictated by the American past and the American character.

For in the end the important questions about any nation, as the important questions about any individual, come back to character. "What kind of people do they think we are? " cried Churchill at a momentous crisis in history, and it was because Hitler and Mussolini had failed to appreciate what kind of people the British — and the Americans — were that their audacious and wicked plans were frustrated. It is because we know — and have long known — what kind of people the British are that we have been able to maintain an American foreign policy. That foreign policy has, in fact, been largely an Anglo-American one. Though the Monroe Doctrine was not originally announced as a bilateral policy, it has actually been that in large measure: if — thanks to John Quincy Adams — Britain did not join the United States in the original announcement of the freedom of Latin America from European dominion she has sustained that policy for a century. The Open Door policy, too — for whatever it is worth — was in origin partly British, and its invocation — maintenance is too strong a term — has rested upon implicit and sometimes explicit British support. Even more important has been Britain's role as keystone in the arch of the Atlantic Community. Americans customarily say that twice, in the twentieth century, the United States had to come to the aid of Britain; the English can, with equal truth, say that twice Britain has held the line until the United States was prepared to come in and fight for her own security. However the argument is phrased, the underlying truth is that British and American interests and values have been substantially the same. It is because we can confidently make certain assumptions about the English character, that we are now able to plan for the future with some degree of assurance that our plans will not miscarry. Does the American character offer a comparable reassurance to the peoples of the Western World?

What is that character? It was formed out of an amalgam of inheritance, environment and experience. The inheritance is chiefly British, but it is, too, the whole of Western Christendom. The environment has been at once a challenge and a reward — a succession of wildernesses that demanded the utmost of men, and natural resources that rewarded industry and ingenuity richly. The experience has been a long education in self-government and tolerance, and a swift growth of responsibility in domestic, hemispheric and world affairs. Out of this combination has come an American character which, for all its diversity, is distinctive and recognizable, and which appears to have permanence.

The American is optimistic, takes for granted that his is the best of all countries, the happiest and most virtuous of all societies, and that the best is yet to be. He lives, therefore, much in the future, makes ambitious plans, thinks nothing beyond his powers, has boundless faith in each new generation. It is commonly said that America is a young country. That is only partially true, but it is certainly true that it is, above all others, a country made for young people, a paradise for children — at least for children who have the good fortune to be Nordic.

The American has always known good fortune — material and spiritual; he has been victorious over nature, and over all enemies. He takes good fortune for granted, and regards any interference with it — any setback, depression, defeat — as an outrage against nature. He is, in many ways, singularly innocent. He is unfamiliar with evil, as the Germans, for example, or the Russians have known it, and of all his philosophers only Josiah Royce — largely neglected — has attempted to solve the problem of evil. Even two world wars, even Dachau and Buchenwald, have not brought home to him a sense of evil, and he is therefore, in some degree, incapable of understanding the fear and despair that affect so large a part of the world.

This optimism, and what we must call innocence, has its drawbacks. The corollary of the feeling that America is superior is the assumption that other nations and peoples are inferior. This assumption goes back to the early days of the Republic, when it was almost an article of faith among Jeffersonians. In our own time it has found support in the high standard of material prosperity which Americans enjoy and in our fortunate freedom from what we call "power politics." We tend to ascribe to our own genius much that is in fact ascribable to the bounty of nature and the accident of geography. Lowell's famous complaint that the nineteenth-century English displayed a "certain condescension toward foreigners" might be echoed now by most European people when thinking of Americans. It cannot be denied that there is a tendency among Americans to equate plumbing and kitchen fixtures with civilization.

This is natural enough, for American culture is predominantly material, its thinking quantitative, its genius inventive, experimental and practical. The American tends to compute almost everything in numbers — even qualitative things. He takes pride in statistics of population growth, of college enrollment, of magazine circulation. He wants the highest office buildings, the largest number of telephones, the most books in his libraries.

This faith in numbers is often looked upon as naïve, sometimes as vulgar, by Europeans. It has its advantages. For the American wants the highest standard of living; he rejoices when another million children are at school. He can fight when outnumbered — as the history of the Confederacy testifies — but prefers to fight with the largest numbers and the best equipment, and those who lament American materialism will do well to remember the tens of thousands of planes and tanks, the millions of tons of shipping, that turned the tide in the last war. Faith in numbers has something to do, too, with the cheerfulness with which Americans accept political defeat, for most Americans believe that the majority cannot be wrong.

The American is ingenious and experimental. This is in part an inheritance from the frontier, in part a consequence of democracy. He likes to do old things in a new way, and the fact that something has never been done before seems to him a challenge rather than an obstacle. Wonderfully inventive in all merely mechanical matters, he is almost equally inventive in the realm of politics, social relationships, and war. There were antecedents, of course, but he largely invented the federal system, the written constitution, the constitutional convention, and the modern colonial system, and there are some who would insist that he took out the original patent on democracy. His willingness to experiment augurs well for international relations. No one person or people can claim authorship of international organization, but none will deny that Woodrow Wilson was chiefly responsible for the League of Nations and Franklin Roosevelt for the United Nations.

The American is, too, intensely practical. He is the born enemy of all abstractions, all theories and doctrines. Benjamin Franklin is his favorite philosopher and, after him, William James, who asserted that it was only minds debauched by learning that ever suspected common sense of not being true. He requires that everything serve a practical purpose — religion, education, culture, science, philosophy. He has produced great speculative sciences, but he admires Edison rather than Willard Gibbs; he has produced speculative philosophers, but he cherishes William James above Santayana or Royce. His education is practical, and only in America do you find graduate schools of journalism, of business administration, of architecture and of law.

This trait, also, is regarded by many Europeans as deplorable, but it has its points. It means that philosophy has been used for practical purposes. Pragmatism, the most characteristic of American philosophies, is the obvious example. Even more interesting, however, is the Americanization of Idealism or Transcendentalism. That philosophy, which in Germany, and even in England, lent itself to the cultivation of individual salvation and to conservatism and even reaction, became in America a powerful instrument for social reform. It means that education has broken away from its classical mold and been required to serve the needs of society. It means that religious leaders have abandoned theology for humanitarianism. It means that in the realm of politics the American will not waste his vote on third parties; will not follow the will-o'-the-wisp of speculative theories.

Every foreigner laments that there are no discernible differences between the Democratic and the Republican Parties, but Americans know instinctively that parties are organizations to run the government, not to advance theoretical principles, and the American party system is, along with the British, the most efficient in the world. American practicality extends into the fields of international relations. Americans want an international organization that can function efficiently, regardless of abstract questions of sovereignty. They are interested in its practical activities — in relief, in science and education, in the suppression of civil war and disorder, and they judge any organization by its immediate effectiveness.

Yet the American record here is not wholly encouraging, and some of the difficulties of present-day international relations — to say nothing of the fiasco of the League of Nations — are traceable to qualities in the American character. The American is accustomed not only to success, but to speedy success. He is something of a perfectionist, and he is not patient. As he has solved his own problems of Federal relation, he is inclined to think that the problems of international relations are equally simple, and to ascribe the failure of international organizations, whether imperial or world, to a natural depravity in foreigners.

He is always ready with advice to other nations — ready to tell the British how to manage India, for example, or to advise the French what to do about their Far Eastern Empire. He thinks a federation of Europe should be as easy as a federation of American states. He has little patience with that long agony of trial and error that makes up so much of European history, and if he cannot have some assurance of speedy success he is likely to lose interest.

The American is politically mature — a statement which will seem palpably mistaken to outsiders who are accustomed to regard American politics as childish. Superficially — and sometimes more than superficially — American politics are childish: the conventions, the campaigns, the antics of Congressmen, of State Legislatures and Governors. Yet it is simply a historical fact that the American people have had longer experience in self-government than any other people. The American is the oldest Constitution, the oldest federal system and the oldest democracy in the world. While people like the French, the Germans, the Italians, who pride themselves on their political wisdom, have gone through revolution after revolution, the Americans have never known a revolution, unless the Civil War be regarded as one, and American political history has been singularly peaceful and even placid.

In America, as in Britain, change has come through evolution, rather than through revolution, and on the whole it has kept pace with the will of the people. The American Congresses can hold their own with any other legislative body in the world; American Presidents have been as able, on the average, as the Presidents or Prime Ministers of any other nation. In every crisis Americans have chosen courageous and bold leaders. There is no reason to suppose that this capacity for political maturity is on the wane.

American political maturity is something to be read from the long term rather than the short term of history. There was nothing politically mature about the Congress that defeated the League of Nations, or about the Congress that enacted the Smoot-Hawley tariff of 1929, or about the Congress that took refuge in the neutrality legislation of the mid-Thirties. Foreigners may be forgiven if they are bewildered by American vacillation on the Palestine issue, or the recent curious reservations on expenditures under the Marshall Plan. They may be forgiven too, if they find themselves bewildered by the political immaturity that finds short-term dividends in appeal to racial and national prejudices — by the appeals to the Irish vote, the Jewish vote, the Italian vote.

Americans customarily regard politics as a game, and bring to it some of the standards of sportsmanship that they bring to their games. These standards are not as high as they were a generation ago, but they are still high. The American has tried to conduct his wars, too, in accordance with the rules of the game, and has never been able to understand opponents who disregarded the rules. He has made peace in a spirit of sportsmanship and fairness, and Churchill's famous phrase, "magnanimous in victory," applies to the United States as well as to Britain. Historians were long inclined to regard Reconstruction as a ruthless affair, but by comparison with what happened after civil wars in France, in Spain and in Russia, American Reconstruction was a love-feast. Spain was overwhelmingly defeated in 1898, but the treaty was a fair one, and to the astonishment of most Europeans the United States actually gave up Cuba — though not the Monroe Doctrine which seemed to justify hegemony over the Caribbean. Nor did the United States ask — or expect — anything of a material character for herself after either World War I or World War II. There is no reason to suppose that the American character has changed in this respect. Many Europeans are inclined to regard the Marshall Plan as a sinister device to get control of the European economy for American profit, but to the average American it is simply a new form of lend-lease.

For the American — it seems almost immodest to say it — is good-natured and generous. That generosity springs, to be sure, from abundance, and therefore comes easy. In no other country has philanthropy been so extravagant. The individual American is kindly, amiable, gregarious and friendly, and these qualities characterize Americans in the mass, as well. As the G.I., overseas, was ready to make friends — even with the enemy — so the nation has been ready to make friends, perhaps a bit too ready — witness our Latin-American policy. This generosity has been casual rather than calculated, and it has not always extended to things of the mind and spirit. Yet, on its purely material side, it is something that can be counted on, confidently enough, in the future.

The American is democratic and equalitarian, by conviction, if not in practice. He takes for granted the superiority of democracy to any other form of government or society, and he proclaims, with utmost sincerity, his faith in equality. The sense of equality — as Tocqueville pointed out over a century ago — permeates his conduct, his language and literature, and religion. Democracy has deep philosophical foundations, but it is not so much the conclusion of philosophy as the common sense of the matter, and so, too, with equality. Southerners, who defiantly "keep the Negro in his place," repeat the phrases of the great Declaration with no consciousness of insincerity; Northerners, who tremble at the prospect of being inundated by southern Europeans and Jews, regard themselves, without conscious hypocrisy, as real democrats. What seem to outsiders palpable insincerity are to most Americans merely embarrassing exception to the rule. The exceptions are outrageous, but it is significant that no one suggests changing the rule.

Yet here, too, there are important qualifications to be made. As the American tends to take both democracy and equality for granted, he does not inquire too closely into palpable violations of both. He assumes, for example, that his political system is the most democratic in the world, whereas in fact it is less democratic than that of several other nations — Britain, for example, or Norway.

He is less prepared to correct economic inequalities than are most other peoples, and excuses the most extreme variations in wealth and poverty on the easy theory of rugged individualism. Thus he tolerates conditions of poverty, slums, ill-health and inadequate educational facilities that would not be tolerated in any other democratic nation of comparable wealth and are not in fact tolerated in Scandinavia or in Australia or New Zealand or Switzerland.

Long convinced that there are no "classes" in America in the Old World sense, he seems unaware of the rapid growth of class-consciousness and the potential danger of class conflict in the twentieth century. He is ready to preach to all other peoples the gospel of democracy and equality, but deeply resents the suggestion that he set his own house in order first. He exposes himself to suspicion and resentment by the extent to which he indulges in anti-Semitism, condemns Negroes to the status of second-class citizens, and accepts the Nazi doctrines of racism.

The American as an individualist is inclined to distrust any public or official bodies. He is, by nature, anti-authoritarian. His own experience has given him little reason to fear or distrust government, but that distrust is deeply ingrained. On the whole he prefers private charity to public, prefers even private international organizations to official ones. He believes that almost anything can be achieved if people will only sit down and talk things over, and Franklin Roosevelt's tendency to circumvent the State Department and rely upon personal relations was entirely characteristic.

This individualism, so sharp in the nineteenth century, is on the wane. Americans who were, in the past, fierce nonconformists, are coming increasingly to demand conformity. In a hundred ways — in speech, dress, manners, food, furnishing — America is becoming more and more uniform and standardized. The demand for conformity is extending even to things of the mind — witness the interest in loyalty oaths, in patriotic clichés, in agreement on political and even economic fundamentals. All this is in part the result of recent pressures, which always tend to squeeze out the eccentric, and in part, the result of growing stability in society and economy.

Along with individualism, and related to it, goes carelessness and lawlessness. The American is careless about speech, dress and manners, about tradition, precedent and law, about the rights of others. He is careless, too, about larger things — about natural resources, for example, or about honesty in politics or in business. This carelessness is, doubtless, a trait of youth; it may be doubted whether a United States that has achieved world leadership can continue to indulge itself in it.

Can the American, who is too careless even to vote in Presidential elections, be trusted with democracy? Can the Congress, which cannot even reform its own procedure, which yields so readily to lobbies and pressure groups, which shows so little appreciation of its dignity and responsibility, be trusted to conduct foreign affairs? Can a people who pay so little attention to the history, traditions and character of other nations be trusted with world leadership? These are awkward questions.

Most of the traits which we have distinguished as American are positive; most of them, too, might be called favorable. There are, of course, traits that are less flattering. On the whole Europeans can be relied upon to call these to our attention.

There is an undeniable strain of vulgarity in the American character — vulgarity which can be seen at its worst in advertisements, in the movies, and on the radio and television. There is a strain of lawlessness which can be traced in the statistics of police courts or can be noted by anyone who cares to check on traffic violations. With the passing of orthodox religion and of puritanism, and with growing urbanization, moral standards have grown lax. Divorces and juvenile delinquency are on the increase; the soldier of World War II was far laxer in morals than the soldier of World War I, and neither compared favorably with the soldiers of the Union and Confederate Armies. There has been a gradual decline in the standards of sportsmanship; there has been a gradual growth in class-consciousness and snobbery; there has been an alarming increase in intolerance.

What does all this add up to, so far as the role of America in world affairs is concerned? What emerges most impressively are the positive traits. The American is optimistic, experimental, practical, intelligent, mature, generous, democratic and individualistic. He has heretofore fulfilled his responsibilities and can be expected to do so in the future. He has, in the last analysis, little confidence in other countries — except Britain — little confidence in their ability, their intelligence, or their good will. He is therefore inclined to think that the rest of the world will have to follow American leadership — not primarily because America is so rich and powerful, but because the American way is the sensible, practical and right way.

NOTES

HISTORICAL UNDERSTANDING IN DEMOCRATIC AMERICA

1. *Yale Review,* XXXIII (March 1944), 385–404.
2. "Report of the Executive Secretary and Managing Editor," *Annual Report of the American Historical Association* (Washington, 1950), p. 12. For a discouraging report on the sale of certain titles in American history see W. Stull Holt, "Who Reads the Best Histories?" *Mississippi Valley Historical Review* XL (March 1954), 613–619.

JEFFERSON-JACKSON AND FEDERALIST-WHIG

1. Russell B. Nye, *George Bancroft: Brahmin Rebel* (New York, 1944), p. 104.
2. *Ibid.,* p. 96; G. P. Gooch, *History and Historians in the Nineteenth Century* (New York, 1949), p. 404.
3. *The History of Historical Writing in America* (Boston, 1891), p. 104.
4. M. A. DeWolfe Howe, *Life and Letters of George Bancroft* (2 vols., New York, 1908), II, 183.
5. "The Problem of Richard Hildreth," *New England Quarterly,* XIII (June 1940), 241–251.
6. "The Democratic Theme in American Historical Literature," *Mississippi Valley Historical Review,* XXXIX (June 1952), 4–5.
7. Alfred Goldberg, "School Histories of the Middle Period," Eric F. Goldman, ed., *Historiography and Urbanization* (Baltimore, 1941).
8. *Constitutional and Political History,* I, x; IV, 244.
9. Eric F. Goldman, "Hermann Eduard Von Holst: Plumed Knight of American Historiography," *Mississippi Valley Historical Review,* XXIII (March 1937); Edward N. Saveth, *American Historians and European Immigrants, 1875–1925* (New York, 1948), 150–157.
10. 9 vols., New York, 1893–1922.
11. *Historical Essays* (New York, 1909), p. 54.
12. *History,* VIII, 52–87.
13. 8 vols., New York, 1938.
14. *Ibid.,* I, 1–2.
15. Eric F. Goldman, *John Bach McMaster, American Historian* (Philadelphia, 1943), p. 143.
16. *Ibid.,* 79–101.

THE PROFESSION OF HISTORIAN AND THE SCIENCE OF HISTORY

1. W. Stull Holt, "The Idea of Scientific History in America," *Journal of the History of Ideas*, I (June 1940), 356.
2. *Annual Report of the American Historical Association* (Washington, 1951), p. 14.
3. Edward Eggleston, "The New History," *Annual Report of the American Historical Association*, I (Washington, 1901), 37–47; Charles Hirschfeld, "Edward Eggleston: Pioneer in Social History," in Eric F. Goldman, ed., *Historiography and Urbanization*, pp. 189–210. On the authenticity of an early nonprofessional historian, see M. M. Hutcheson, "Mercy Warren, 1728–1814," *William and Mary Quarterly*, X (July 1953), 396–400. On the authenticity of George Bancroft, see W. H. Dawes and F. T. Nichols, "Revaluing George Bancroft," *New England Quarterly* VI (June 1933), 278–79.
4. Holt, *op. cit.*, pp. 356–357.
5. Samuel Eliot Morison, "Jared Sparks" in *Dictionary of American Biography* (20 vols., 1930–1936), XVII, 430–434.
6. 6 vols., New York, 1925. I, preface.
7. 4 vols., New York, 1950; 8 vols., New York, 1936–54.
8. J. S. Bassett, *The Middle Group of American Historians* (New York, 1917), p. 315.
9. W. C. Ford, ed., *The Letters of Henry Adams, 1858–1918* (2 vols., Boston, 1930–1938), I, 219; W. H. Jordy, *Henry Adams, Scientific Historian* (New Haven, 1952), pp. 73–120; "The Tendency of History," *Annual Report of the American Historical Association* (1894), pp. 17–18.

THE COMPARATIVE METHOD AND THE TEUTONIC HYPOTHESIS

1. Saveth, *op. cit.*, pp. 13–64.
2. "The Germanic Origin of New England Towns," *Johns Hopkins University Studies in Historical and Political Science* (Baltimore, 1883), first series, no. II, *passim*.
3. Moses C. Tyler, *The Literary History of the American Revolution, 1763–1783* (2 vols., New York, 1897), I, viii–ix.
4. "Historical Instruction in the Course of History and Political Science at Cornell University," in G. S. Hall, ed., *Methods of Teaching History* (Boston, 1883), p. 3.
5. *Political Science and Comparative Constitutional Law* (2 vols., Boston, 1891), I, 33.
6. "Methods of Teaching History," in Hall, *op. cit.*, p. 3.
7. See, for example, *American Political Ideas Viewed from the Standpoint of Universal History* (New York, 1911), pp. 17–18, and Saveth, *op. cit.*, pp. 32–42.

8. *Excursions of an Evolutionist* (Boston, 1893), pp. 175–202, 240–241, 286–288; *A Century of Science and Other Essays* (Boston, 1899), p. 135.
9. *American Political Ideas*, pp. 20, 42, 44; *The Beginnings of New England; or, The Puritan Theocracy in Its Relation to Civil and Religious Liberty* (Boston, 1889), p. 25.
10. For the conservatism of John Fiske see his *Essays, Historical and Literary*. (2 vols., New York, 1902), I, 130, 174, 179, 310–311, 324; II, 158–159, 164, 173, 195; *The Critical Period of American History, 1783–1789* (New York, 1916), pp. 101, 106. See, too, H. B. Adams, "Leopold Von Ranke," *American Academy of Arts and Sciences*, XXII, pt. 2, p. 550. For Burgess, "The Ideal of the American Commonwealth," *Political Science Quarterly*, X (September 1895), 413.
11. "Letters of Sanford B. Dole and John W. Burgess," *Pacific Historical Review*, V (1936), 74. E. F. Fisk, ed., *The Letters of John Fiske* (New York, 1940), p. 706.
12. "Written History as an Art of Faith," *American Historical Review*, XXXIX (January 1934), 276–277.

THE FRONTIER HYPOTHESIS

1. Charles McLean Andrews, writing of the status of the "Theory of the Village Community" in 1891, observed that "so wide has been its acceptance, and so strongly instilled is it in the minds both of students and readers, that it may seem more bold than discreet to raise the question regarding the soundness of the theory." *Papers of the American Historical Association*, V (New York, 1891), 47.
2. Andrews was joined by Channing in dissenting from the Teutonic hypothesis. Remarks on "The Genesis of the Massachusetts Town and the Origin of Town-Meeting Government," *Proceedings of the Massachusetts Historical Society*, VII (January 1892), 244, 250. A. C. McLaughlin also expressed his misgivings in a review of Freeman's "Introduction to American Institutional History," in J. N. Larned, ed., *The Literature of American History* (Boston, 1902), p. 295. As late as 1918, however, James Truslow Adams fully accepted the Teutonic hypothesis. *History of the Town of Southampton (East of Canoe Place)* (Bridgehampton, Long Island, 1918), pp. 94–96.
3. "The Significance of the Frontier in American History," in Frederick Jackson Turner, *The Frontier in American History* (New York, 1920).
4. C. S. Skinner, ed., "Turner's Autobiographic Letter," *The Wisconsin Magazine of History*, XIX (September 1935), 101–102.
5. Review of Theodore Roosevelt, *The Winning of the West*, *Dial* (Chicago), August 1889.
6. Fulmer Mood, "The Development of Frederick Jackson Turner as a Historical Thinker," *Publications of the Colonial Society of Massachusetts*, XXXIV (December 1939), *passim*.

7. Turner, *Frontier*, pp. 1, 2. "Social Forces in American History," *American Historical Review*, XVI (January 1911), 225.

8. In his Commonwealth Club Address (1932), Roosevelt said: "Our last frontier has long since been reached, and there is practically no more free land. . . . There is no safety valve in the form of a Western Prairie to which those thrown out of work by the Eastern machines can go for a new start." See also, Curtis Nettels, "Frederick Jackson Turner and the New Deal," *Wisconsin Magazine of History*, XVII (1934), 257–265.

9. Henry Nash Smith, *Virgin Land; The American West as Symbol and Myth* (Cambridge, 1950), pp. 250–260.

10. Richard Hofstadter, "Turner and the Frontier Myth," *American Scholar* (Autumn 1949), 435. There are, however, indications of Turner's influence upon the Socialist historian Algie M. Simons, *Class Struggles in America* (Chicago, 1903); *Social Forces in American History* (New York, 1911).

11. *The American Spirit* (New York, 1942), p. 363.

HISTORY AND SOCIETY

1. "Social Forces in American History," p. 226.

2. William M. Sloane, President of the American Historical Association in 1911, asserted that "history must have no thesis nor be used to maintain one." "The Substance and Vision of History," *American Historical Review*, XVII (1912), 235–251.

3. "History and the Philosophy of History," *American Historical Review*, XIV (1909), 236.

4. *Ibid.*, p. 237.

5. *Abraham Lincoln* (2 vols., Boston, 1928), I, v.

6. M. A. DeWolfe Howe, *James Ford Rhodes, American Historian* (New York, 1929), pp. 149–150, 277.

7. James H. Robinson, *The New History; Essays Illustrating the Modern Historical Outlook* (New York, 1911), pp. 21–24; Luther Virgil Hendricks, *James Harvey Robinson, Teacher of History* (New York, 1946), pp. 35–38. For criticism of Robinson's approach to history, see Henry Johnson, *Teaching of History in Elementary and Secondary Schools* (New York, 1940), pp. 19–24; Robert L. Schuyler, "Some Historical Idols," *Political Science Quarterly* XLVII (March 1932),18.

8. See footnote 10 in section on "The Comparative Method and the Teutonic Hypothesis."

BEARD'S *Economic Interpretation of the Constitution*

1. This account was written before publication of the collection of essays about Beard edited by Howard K. Beale. Merle Curti, "A Great Teacher's Teacher," *Social Education*, XIII (1949), 263–266.

2. Eric F. Goldman, "The Origins of Beard's *Economic Interpretation of the Constitution*," *Journal of the History of Ideas*, XIII (April 1952), 235.
3. Richard Hofstadter, "Beard and the Constitution: The History of an Idea," *American Quarterly*, II (Fall 1950), 6.
4. Arthur F. Bentley, *The Process of Government* (Chicago, 1908), pp. 152, 244, 272, 295.
5. *An Economic Interpretation of the Constitution of the United States* (New York, 1913), pp. 14 ff.
6. New York, 1902.
7. New York, 1911.
8. New York, 1907.
9. *Ibid.*, pp. 400–401.
10. *Economic Interpretation of the Constitution*, p. 5.
11. *Ibid.*, vi, 73–151.
12. *Ibid.*, pp. 16–17.
13. C. C. Regier, *The Era of the Muckrakers* (Chapel Hill, 1932), 194–195.
14. "Muckraking the Fathers," *Nation* C (January 31, 1915).
15. Henry F. Pringle, *Life and Times of William Howard Taft* (2 vols., New York, 1939) II, 860; Maurice Blinkoff, *The Influence of Charles A. Beard Upon American Historiography* (Buffalo, 1936), pp. 17–19.
16. Beard, *Economic Interpretation*, introduction to the 1935 edition, vi.
17. Eric F. Goldman, "Origins of Beard's *Economic Interpretation*," p. 249.
18. There is an analysis of this book in Morton G. White, *Social Thought in America, The Revolt Against Formalism* (New York, 1949), pp. 32–46.

THE BROADENING FRAMEWORK OF HISTORY —
TO WORLD WAR I

1. Edward Eggleston, "The New History," American Historical Association, *Annual Report*, 1900, I, 37–47; *The Transit of Civilization from England to America* (New York, 1901), Preface, vii; Charles Hirschfeld, *op. cit.*
2. Carl Becker, "Some Aspects of the Influence of Social Problems and Ideas Upon the Study and Writing of History," *The American Journal of Sociology*, XVIII (March 1913).
3. Jameson, *op. cit.*, pp. 137–138.
4. "American Colonial History, 1690–1750," *Annual Report of the American Historical Association* (Washington, 1898), p. 49.
5. H. L. Osgood, "England and the Colonies," *Political Science Quarterly*, II (September 1887), 441.
6. *Ibid.*, 467

7. *American Historical Review* (October 1935), p. 81.
8. Quoted in Michael Kraus, *A History of American History* (New York, 1937), p. 425.
9. *The Mississippi Valley in British Politics* (2 vols., Cleveland, 1917), II, 250
10. B. L. Pierce, *Public Opinion and the Teaching of History* (New York, 1926).
11. *North American Review*, XXIII, 276–292.
12. L. W. Dunlap, *American Historical Societies 1790–1860* (Madison, 1944), vii, 129.
13. H. Hale Bellot, *American History and American Historians* (Norman, Oklahoma, 1952), pp. 25–35; E. D. Ross, "A Generation of Prairie Historiography," *Mississippi Valley Historical Review*, XXXIII (December 1946), 391–410. There were by 1904 between 400 and 500 local historical societies, according to Henry E. Bourne, "The Work of American Historical Societies," *Annual Report of the American Historical Association* (1904), p. 119.
14. William B. Hesseltine and Larry Gara, eds. "Postwar Problems of a Virginia Historian," *The Virginia Magazine of History and Biography*, LXI (April 1953), 193–195. In the last twenty years there has been great progress in the history of the South, manifest particularly in the *Journal of Southern History* and the ten-volume *A History of the South*, now in progress.
15. W. H. Stephenson, "A Half-century of Southern Historical Scholarship," *The Journal of Southern History*, XI (February 1945), 3–32.
16. J. W. Caughey, "The Mosaic of Western History," *Mississippi Valley Historical Review*, XXXIII (March 1947), 604.

THE CONTINUING "RENAISSANCE"

1. "Introduction," vii.
2. "The Postwar Generation in Arts and Letters," *Saturday Review of Literature* (March 14, 1953), p. 11.
3. "An Editor's Second Thoughts," in W. E. Lingelbach, ed., *Approaches to American Social History* (New York, 1937).
4. J. G. Palfrey, *History of New England* (5 vols., 1858–1890) is an outstanding example of filiopietism in American historiography. For an early critique by a prominent New England historian of the trend typified by Palfrey, see Charles Francis Adams, *Massachusetts: Its Historians and History* (Boston, 1893).
5. *Infra*, p. 67.
6. Joseph Zeitlin, *The Life and Letters of Stuart Pratt Sherman* (2 vols., New York, 1929), II, 482–489.
7. *Infra*, p. 217.
8. H. E. Bolton and Thomas M. Marshall, *The Colonization of North America* (New York, 1920). See also Bolton's earlier *Athanase de*

NOTES 573

Mezières and the Louisiana–Texas Frontier, 1768–1780 (2 vols., Cleveland, 1914).
9. Marcus L. Hansen, "The History of American Immigration as a Field for Research," *American Historical Review*, XXXII (April 1927), 500–518.
10. "Letters of Richard D. Arnold, M.D., 1808–1876," *Trinity College Historical Society* (Durham, 1929).
11. *Wisconsin Domesday Book. Town Studies*, vol. I (Madison, Wisc., 1924). *Wisconsin Magazine of History* IV (1921), 61–74; "The Microscopic Method Applied to History," *Minnesota History Bulletin* IV (1922), 3–20.
12. *The Rise of American Civilization* (New York, 1927), I, 124.
13. *Main Currents in American Thought* (New York, 1930), Foreword, p. 1.
14. David F. Bowers, "American Socialism and the Socialist Philosophy of History," in Donald Drew Egbert and Stow Persons, eds., *Socialism and American Life* (2 vols., Princeton, 1952), I, 419.

DEPRESSION TRENDS

1. Howard K. Beale, "On Rewriting Reconstruction History," *American Historical Review*, XLV (July 1940), 807–827; A. A. Taylor, "Historians of Reconstruction," *Journal of Negro History*, XXIII (January 1938), 16–34; T. Harry Williams, "An Analysis of Some Reconstruction Attitudes," *Journal of Southern History* XII (November 1946), 469–486; Louis Ruchames, "Charles Sumner and American Historiography," *The Journal of Negro History*, XXXVIII (April 1953), 139–160; John Hope Franklin, "Whither Reconstruction Historiography," *The Journal of Negro Education*, XVII (1948), 446–461.
2. Ulrich B. Phillips, "The Central Theme of Southern History," *American Historical Review*, XXXIV (October 1928), 43.
3. A. M. Arnett, *The Populist Movement in Georgia: A View of the "Agrarian Crusade" in the Light of Solid-South Politics* (New York, 1922).
4. F. B. Simkins, *The Tillman Movement in South Carolina* (Durham, 1926).
5. James W. Garner, *Reconstruction in Mississippi* (New York, 1901); C. Mildred Thompson, *Reconstruction in Georgia, Economic and Political, 1864–1872* (New York, 1915).
6. C. Vann Woodward, *Tom Watson, Agrarian Rebel* (New York, 1938).
7. Horace Mann Bond, "Social and Economic Forces in Alabama Reconstruction," *Journal of Negro History*, XXIII (July 1938), 290–348; *Negro Education in Alabama: A Study in Cotton and Steel* (Washington, 1939).

574   UNDERSTANDING THE AMERICAN PAST

8. V. L. Wharton, *The Negro in Mississippi, 1865–1890* (Chapel Hill, 1947).
9. Roger W. Shugg, *Origins of Class Struggle in Louisiana: A Social History of White Farmers and Laborers During Slavery and After, 1840–1875* (University, La., 1939).
10. *The Critical Year* (New York, 1930).
11. Quoted by John D. Hicks in the *Saturday Review of Literature*, March 14, 1953, p. 14.
12. "American Urban History Today," *American Historical Review*, LVII (July 1952), 919.
13. "The City in American History," *Mississippi Valley Historical Review*, XXVII (June 1940), 66. The urban interpretation of history is attacked by William Diamond, "On the Dangers of an Urban Interpretation of History," in *History and Urbanization*, and defended by W. Stull Holt, "Some Consequences of the Urban Movement in American History," *Pacific Historical Review*, XXII (November 1953), 337–51.
14. "Culture and Agriculture," *Saturday Review of Literature* V (October 1928).
15. *Nation*, CXXXVII (July 26, 1933), 108–110.
16. "Frederick Jackson Turner," *Marcus W. Jernegan Essays in American Historiography* (Chicago, 1937).
17. "The Wage-Earner in the Westward Movement I," *Political Science Quarterly*, L (June 1935), 161–185; "The Wage Earner in the Westward Movement II," *Political Science Quarterly*, LI (March 1936), 61–116.
18. "Some Considerations on the Safety Valve Doctrine," *Mississippi Valley Historical Review*, XXIII (September 1936), 169–188.
19. "The Homestead Act and the Labor Surplus," *American Historical Review*, XLI (July, 1936), 637–652.
20. "A Post Mortem on the Labor-Safety-Valve Theory," *Agricultural History*, XIX (January 1945), 31–37.
21. "Political Institutions and the Frontier," *Sources of Culture in the Middle West*, Dixon Ryan Fox, ed. (New York, 1934).
22. *The Civil War and Reconstruction* (New York, 1937).

BUSINESS HISTORY

1. Quoted in G. W. Pierson, "The Frontier and American Institutions," *New England Quarterly*, XV (June 1942), 224. For a somewhat different view and an affirmation of the opportunities offered by the frontier, see W. P. Webb, *The Great Frontier* (Boston, 1952). According to Webb, the "new frontiers" of science or economics will not halt the drift toward socialism or absolutism; future generations can only make available what is now present by changing its form or position, not by adding anything new as did the "Great Frontier."

2. John D. Rockefeller, II, 707–714.
3. John F. Gerstung, "Louis M. Hacker's Reappraisal of Recent American History," *The Historian*, XII (Spring, 1950), 161.
4. "The Social History of the Corporation in the United States," *The Cultural Approach to History* (New York, 1940), pp. 168–181.
5. Archibald MacLeish, *The Irresponsibles: A Declaration* (New York, 1940).
6. Lewis Mumford, *Faith for Living* (New York, 1940).
7. *Yale Review* (March 1944), 385–404.
8. For a fuller account of this trend as it affected foreign policy see R. E. Osgood, *Ideals and Self Interest in America's Foreign Relations* (Chicago, 1953), p. 369.
9. "The Businessman in Fiction," *Fortune* (November 1948); John Lydenberg, "Mobilizing Our Novelists," *American Quarterly* (Spring 1952), pp. 35–48.
10. Henry S. Commager, *The American Mind* (New Haven, 1950), p. 274.
11. N. S. B. Gras, "Are You Writing a Business History?", *Bulletin of the Business Historical Society* XVIII (October 1944), pp. 73–110.
12. Cambridge, 1952.
13. Studies in economic history prepared under the direction of the Committee on Research in Economic History, Social Science Research Council. See especially the volumes by Oscar and Mary Handlin and Louis Hartz.
14. New York, 1942.
15. Madison, 1952.
16. Merle Curti, *The Growth of American Thought* (New York, 1952), pp. 507–527.

THE CONSERVATIVE AND LIBERAL TRADITIONS

1. *American Historical Review*, LVII (April 1952), 803.
2. "Faith of a Historian," *ibid.*, LVI (January 1951), 272–273.
3. T. Harry Williams, "Abraham Lincoln: Principle and Pragmatism in Politics," *Mississippi Valley Historical Review*, XL (June 1953), 96, 101.
4. See the report of Malin's paper "The Problem of Conservative and Liberal Traditions in the Historiography of the United States," *American Historical Review*, LVII (April 1952), 802–803.
5. *Rendezvous with Destiny*, pp. 1–3.
6. *Seedtime of the Republic* (New York, 1953).
7. *Ibid.*, pp. 415–416; Review by Jensen in *Pennsylvania Magazine of History and Biography*, LXXVII (October 1953), 487.
8. *History*, III, 44, 45.
9. Howe, *Bancroft*, II, 225–226.
10. Schlesinger, "Hildreth," *passim*.

11. *Supra*, p. 18.
12. F. L. Owsley, "The Fundamental Cause of the Civil War. . . ." *The Journal of Southern History* VII (February 1941), 4–6.
13. *The Age of Jackson*, pp. 520–521.
14. "Wealth Against Commonwealth, 1894 and 1944," *American Historical Review*, L (October 1944), 49–69.
15. Bray Hammond, "Public Policy and National Banks," *The Journal of Economic History*, VI (May 1946), 79–84; Joseph Dorfman, "The Jackson Wage-Earner Thesis," *American Historical Review*, LIV (January 1949), 306.
16. *Age of Enterprise*, 356.
17. *Triumph of American Capitalism*, 409.
18. New York, 1946.
19. Margaret L. Coit, *John C. Calhoun, American Portrait* (Boston, 1950); Charles M. Wiltse, *John C. Calhoun* (3 vols., Indianapolis, 1944–1951).
20. Russell Kirk, *Randolph of Roanoke; A Study in Conservative Thought* (Chicago, 1951).
21. Avery Craven, *The Coming of the Civil War* (New York, 1942), p. 37.
22. *The Selected Writings of John and John Quincy Adams* (New York, 1946).
23. New York, 1948.
24. L. W. Labaree, *Conservatism in Early American History* (New York, 1946).
25. Thornton Anderson, *Brooks Adams, Constructive Conservative* (Ithaca, 1951).
26. John A. Garraty, *Henry Cabot Lodge* (New York, 1953).
27. (Cambridge, 1954). Goldman's review appeared in the *New York Times Book Review*, April 11, 1954.
28. Other books which set out to explore aspects of the conservative tradition, but rather unsympathetically, include: R. G. McCloskey, *American Conservatism in the Age of Enterprise* (Cambridge, 1951), and Bernard Brown, *American Conservative: The Political Thought of Francis Lieber and John W. Burgess* (New York, 1951).
29. "Faith of a Historian," p. 273.
30. *The Vital Center* (Boston, 1949), p. 25.

THE CHALLENGE TO ECONOMIC DETERMINISM

1. See Beard's Preface to the 1935 edition of *An Economic Interpretation of the Constitution*.
2. John Higham, "The Rise of American Intellectual History," *American Historical Review*, LVI (April 1951), 461.
3. *Reunion and Reaction* (Boston, 1951), ix.

4. Michael Kraus, *A History of American History* (New York, 1937), 252.
5. Eric F. Goldman, *Rendezvous With Destiny* (New York, 1952), 235–236.
6. *Ibid.*, 383–384.
7. "The Causes of the Civil War: A Note on Historical Sentimentalism," *Partisan Review*, XVI (1949), 969–981.
8. Louis M. Hacker, "Politics and Economics in History," *Pennsylvania Magazine of History and Biography*, LXXII (January 1948), 161–162.
9. "The Need for a Cultural Comprehension of Political Behavior," *The Pennsylvania Magazine of History and Biography*, LXXII (Philadelphia, 1948), 181–184.
10. Howard K. Beale, "What Historians Have Said about the Causes of the Civil War," in *Theory and Practice in Historical Study* (New York, 1946), 83–84; T. J. Pressly, *Americans Interpret Their Civil War* (Princeton, 1954), pp. 280–281.

POLITICAL HISTORY, MILITARY HISTORY, AND THE INDIVIDUAL'S ROLE

1. Roy Nichols, "Unfinished Business," *Pennsylvania Magazine of History and Biography*, LXXII (April 1948), 109–115.
2. Pendleton Herring, "A Political Scientist Considers the Question," *ibid.*, 118–184.
3. "The Significance of the Constitution of the United States in the Teaching of American History," *Historian*, XIII (Autumn, 1950), 12. Other historians who recognized the increased importance of political history were John D. Hicks, *The American Nation, A History of the United States from 1865 to the Present* (Boston, 1941), v; and F. L. Paxson in his trilogy, *American Democracy and the World War* (1936–1938).
4. *The Republic* (New York, 1943).
5. T. Harry Williams, *Lincoln and His Generals* (New York, 1952); Kenneth P. Williams, *Lincoln Finds a General* (3 vols., New York, 1949–1952). Note particularly the Appendix to vol. II, pp. 777–810.
6. Princeton University has created an Editorial Board of the Princeton University Marine Corps History Project. Its initial publication is Jeter A. Iseley and Phil A. Crowl, *The U.S. Marines and Amphibious War* (Princeton, 1951). See also Paul J. Scheips, "The Historian and the Nature of History: Some Reflections for Air Force Historians," *Military Affairs*, XVI (Fall 1952), 123–131.
7. Edward Eggleston, "The New History," pp. 37–47. Herman Ausubel, *Historians and Their Craft* (New York, 1950), pp. 309–314.
8. Introduction to *Lincoln and His Generals*.

578 UNDERSTANDING THE AMERICAN PAST

9. Sidney Hook, *The Hero in History: A Study in Limitation and Possibility* (New York, 1943), p. 3.
10. Alvord to A. J. Beveridge, Nov. 4, 1922. Cited in Marion Dargen, Jr. "Clarence Walworth Alvord," in *The Marcus W. Jernegan Essays*, p. 331.
11. Introduction, ix.
12. *Journal of the History of Ideas*, II (January 1941), 95–109.
13. Rudolph Von Abele, *Alexander H. Stephens* (New York, 1946).
14. James G. Randall, "Historianship," *American Historical Review*, LVII (January 1953), 255.
15. "Need for a Cultural Comprehension of Political Behavior," pp. 181–84.

INTELLECTUAL HISTORY

1. There is a discussion by John Higham of "The Rise of American Intellectual History," *The American Historical Review*, LVI (April 1951), 453–471.
2. *Ibid.*, pp. 456–457; Jessica T. Austen, ed., *Moses Coit Tyler, 1835–1900: Selections from His Letters and Diaries* (New York, 1911), pp. 42–44; Howard M. Jones and T. E. Casady, *The Life of Moses Coit Tyler* (Ann Arbor, Mich., 1933), pp. 141, 149–150.
3. *Puritanism and Democracy* (New York, 1944).
4. *The Course of American Democratic Thought: An Intellectual History Since 1815* (New York, 1940).
5. New Haven, 1950; Preface, p. viii.

SYNTHESIS AND *Kulturgeschichte*

1. Kenneth B. Murdock's *Literature and Theology in Colonial New England* (Cambridge, 1949) has a brilliant and altogether delightful discussion of the puritan historians, pp. 67–97.
2. George Bancroft, *A History of the United States*, Preface to vol. I, (1834). See also, Murdock, *op. cit.*, p. 187.
3. *The Problem of Asia, and Its Effect upon International Policies* (Boston, 1900), p. 168. See also J. W. Pratt, "Alfred Thayer Mahan," in *Jernegan Essays*, pp. 223–255.
4. "On Self-government," *Papers* of the American Historical Association, II (New York, 1888), 7–13.
5. See particularly Fiske's *American Political Ideas*, passim.
6. Roy Nichols, "The Dynamic Interpretation of History," *New England Quarterly*, VIII (June 1935), 163–178; William Jordy, *Henry Adams: Scientific Historian* (New Haven, 1952), passim. The "Letter to American Teachers of History" is in Brooks Adams, ed., *The Degradation of the Democratic Dogma* (New York, 1919). See also Brooks Adams's fascinating Introduction to this volume.

7. In 1908 J. Franklin Jameson recommended to his colleagues that they build their syntheses about the subject of religion. Said Jameson: "He who would understand the American past and present time, and to that end would provide himself with data representing all classes, all periods, all religions, may find in the history of American religion the closest approach to the continuous record he desires." "The American Acta Sanctorum," *American Historical Review*, XIII (January 1908), 286–302. William Warren Sweet's work in the field of American religious history is in the spirit of Jameson's argument. *Religion in the Development of American Culture 1765–1840* (New York, 1952), vii. Perry Miller's *Orthodoxy in Massachusetts, 1630–1650* (Cambridge, 1933), endeavored to demonstrate that "the narrative of the Bay Colony's early history can be strung upon the thread of an idea [religion]."

8. "What Then Is the American, This New Man," *American Historical Review*, XLVIII (1942–1943), p. 225.

9. See also, Ralph Barton Perry, *Characteristically American* (New York, 1949) and the penetrating study by the English historian, D. W. Brogan, entitled *The American Character* (New York, 1944).

10. "The New Crusade," *American Historical Review* XXXIV (1929), p. 232; T. C. Cochran, "A New Era in United States History," *Revista de Historia de América* XXXIII (June 1952), 72–73.

11. Gooch, *op. cit.*, pp. 573 ff.

12. For a discussion of Lamprecht see Gooch, *op. cit.*, 588–593, and *Encyclopedia of the Social Sciences*, IX, 27.

13. Preface to the second edition of *The Law of Civilization and Decay* (New York, 1896), p. ix.

14. Saveth, *op. cit.*, p. 87. See also Henry Adams's criticism of Brooks Adams's manuscript, quoted in C. A. Beard's Introduction to the 1943 edition of *The Law of Civilization and Decay*, p. 23.

15. Preface, v.

16. Foreword, vii–viii.

17. Roy F. Nichols, "Postwar Reorientation of Historical Thinking," *American Historical Review*, LIV (October 1948), 82.

18. M. L. Hansen, *The Immigrant in American History* (Cambridge, 1942) and *The Atlantic Migration 1607–1860: A History of the Continuing Settlement of the United States* (Cambridge, 1941); T. C. Blegen, *Norwegian Migration to America: The American Transition* (Northfield, 1940); Oscar Handlin, *Boston's Immigrants 1790–1865: A Study in Acculturation* (Cambridge, 1941); George M. Stephenson, *The Religious Aspects of Swedish Immigration: A Study of Immigrant Churches* (Minneapolis, 1942); Carl Wittke, *We Who Built America* (New York, 1939).

19. Minneapolis, 1947.

20. Published by the American Association for State and Local History beginning in 1949.

21. There was an increase in the number of historical societies in the United States from approximately 545 in 1936 to approximately 833 in 1944. C. Crittenden, ed., *Historical Societies in the United States and Canada: A Handbook* (Washington, 1944), pp. vi–vii.
22. Donald D. Parker, *Local History How to Gather It, Write It, and Publish It* (New York, 1944). Edited by Bertha E. Josephson for the Committee on Guide for Study of Local History of the Social Science Research Council.
23. Most significant in this respect is the *Wisconsin Magazine of History*. A number of more or less popular books have been written about American regions and localities, including the following series: *American Folkways, Rivers of America, American Lakes, American Scene*.
24. Dixon Ryan Fox, *Ideas in Motion* (New York, 1935), p. 88. As early as 1921, Joseph Schafer commented upon "the absence of a feeling for general historical results on the part of workers in the local field." "Documenting Local History," *Wisconsin Magazine of History*, V (1921), 3. However, an important regional study, R. H. Buley, *The Old Northwest* (2 vols., Indianapolis, 1950), lists as the second most important source upon which the book was based, "the accumulated publications of the historical societies of the Old Northwest." I, preface, vii.

RELATIVISM AND OBJECTIVISM

1. *A Charter for the Social Sciences* (New York, 1932); *Conclusions and Recommendations* (New York, 1934), p. 9. For a point of view opposed to these reports see James C. Malin, *Essays on Historiography* (Lawrence, Kansas, 1946), pp. 116 ff.
2. "Written History an Act of Faith," *American Historical Review*, XXXIX (January 1934), 276–277.
3. *Theory and Practice in Historical Study*, p. 135. Proposition VI.
4. "Some Observations on Contemporary Historical Theory," *American Historical Review*, LV (April 1950), 503–529.
5. *Op. cit.*, pp. 116 ff.
6. "Faith of a Historian," *American Historical Review*, LVI (January 1951), 268.
7. *Pennsylvania Magazine of History and Biography*, LXXIII (April 1949), 173.
8. Cochran, "A Decade of American Histories," *ibid.*, 161–166; Curti, "The Democratic Theme," p. 26.
9. See, for example, B. J. Lowenberg, "Some Problems Raised by Historical Relativism," *Journal of Modern History*, XXI (March 1949).
10. Kirkland, *op. cit.*, p. 173.
11. "The Need for a Cultural Comprehension of Political Behavior," p. 186.

HISTORICAL UNDERSTANDING AND THE PRESENT CRISIS

1. Conyers Read, "The Social Responsibilities of the Historian," *American Historical Review*, LV (January 1950), 283.
2. "Faith of a Historian," p. 270.
3. "The Democratic Theme," p. 26.
4. "Report of the Committee on Historians and the Federal Government," *Annual Report of the American Historical Association, 1949*, pp. 54–59. W. G. Leland, "The Historian and the Public in the United States," *Revista de Historia de América* XXXIII (June 1952); W. Stull Holt, "Historical Scholarship," *American Scholarship in the Twentieth Century* (Cambridge, 1953), p. 87.
5. A. S. Link, "A Decade of Biographical Contributions to Recent American History," *Mississippi Valley Historical Review*, XXXIV (March 1947), 652. Note how high Parrington rates in a recent study of historians' reading preferences. John W. Caughey, "Historians' Choice: Results of a Poll on Recently Published American History and Biography," *ibid.*, XXXIX (September 1952), 289–302. Hofstadter, although a liberal historian, speaks of "the theoretical impotence of the agrarian opposition" to capitalism. "Parrington and the Jefferson Tradition," *Journal of the History of Ideas* II (October 1941), 400.
6. Anxious to crystallize an American conservative creed, Peter Viereck is perhaps overenthusiastic in his reception of Russell Kirk's *Randolph. Shame and Glory of the Intellectuals* (Boston, 1953), p. 203.
7. "Manifest Destiny and the Philippines," in *America in Crisis* (New York, 1953), p. 180.
8. Chester M. Destler attacks Nevins's conception of Rockefeller's contribution in "Wealth against Commonwealth," *American Historical Review* L (October 1944), 49–69. Nevins replies, *ibid.* (April 1945), 676–689.
9. Review by Frank L. Owsley of Dwight L. Dumond, ed., *Letters of James Gillespie Birney, Journal of Southern History*, V (May 1939), 263.
10. Peter Geyl, "American Civil War and the Problem of Inevitability," *New England Quarterly*, XXIV (June 1951), 147–168.
11. *American Historical Review*, LIV (January 1949).
12. New York, 1952, p. 82.
13. *A Study of History* (6 vols., London, 1940–1946), IV, 256–58.
14. *History and Human Relations* (New York, 1952), pp. 137–40.
15. *Theory and Practice in Historical Study*, p. 128.
16. H. A. Washington, ed., *The Writings of Thomas Jefferson* (Washington, 1853–4), VII, p. 82.

I. THE AMERICAN MOLD

THE PURITAN TRADITION

1. "Faith of a Historian," p. 272.
2. *Three Episodes of Massachusetts History* (2 vols., Boston, 1892), II, 561, 802.
3. *The Emancipation of Massachusetts* (Boston, 1887).
4. *History of the Town of Southampton*, p. 85.
5. *The Declaration of Independence*, p. xiii.

THE VIRGINIANS

1. 2 vols., New York; II, 246.
2. 2 vols., Boston, 1897; II, 16. T. J. Wertenbaker, *Patrician and Plebeian in Virginia* (Charlottesville, Virginia, 1910), claims that Fiske's estimate of the Cavalier element in the Virginia population is exaggerated (pp. 28, 233).
3. *Ibid., passim*. However, in the opinion of Louis B. Wright, the reaction against the belief that "the aristocratic families were without exception dispossessed Cavaliers, or adventurous younger sons of the nobility . . . has been so strong that we are likely to forget that a considerable number of the seventeenth-century settlers did come from families of the gentry — enough, perhaps, to serve as leaven for the developing aristocracy, enough to set an example of the manners and behavior of the English country gentlemen." (*The First Gentlemen of Virginia* [San Marino, 1940], p. 40.)
4. *Provincial Society* (New York, 1927), p. 216.

THE DECLARATION OF INDEPENDENCE

1. *Constitutional and Political History*, I, 32.
2. *History of the United States of America*, V, 29–30, 220.
3. J. H. Hazelton, *The Declaration of Independence* (New York, 1906).
4. Preface to the 1942 edition of *The Declaration of Independence*, p. xiii.

MERCANTILISM AND THE AMERICAN REVOLUTION

1. Nye, *op. cit.*, pp. 165–166, 177–180. *History of the United States* (Boston, 1834–1874), II, 43–47, 122, 157–158, 198–199; V, 159; VI, 72, 290.
2. "The Revolution Impending" in Justin Winsor, *Narrative and Critical History of America*, VI, 63–64.
3. *British Colonial Policy, 1754–1765* (New York, 1907), p. 3.
4. "The First American Revolution," *Columbia University Quarterly*, XXVIII (September 1935), 293.
5. *The Colonial Period of American History* (4 vols., New Haven, 1938), IV, 425.
6. O. M. Dickerson, *The Navigation Acts and the American Revolution* (Philadelphia, 1951), pp. 299–300.
7. "The American Revolution as an Aftermath of the Great War for the Empire, 1754–1763," *Political Science Quarterly*, LXV (March 1950), 104.

RADICALS AND CONSERVATIVES AFTER INDEPENDENCE

1. Merrill Jensen, *The Articles of Confederation* (Madison, 1940); *The New Nation* (New York, 1950). John Fiske, *The Critical Period*, pp. 101, 106.
2. *Articles of Confederation*, p. 7.
3. "The Virginia Convention of 1788: A Criticism of Beard's *An Economic Interpretation of the Constitution*," *The Journal of Southern History*, XIX (February 1953), 63–72.

THE SPIRIT OF THE CONSTITUTION

1. White, *op. cit.*, p. 147.
2. Beard, *Supreme Court*, pp. 3–8, 126.

GEORGE WASHINGTON: ADMINISTRATOR

1. Mason L. Weems, *The Life of Washington* (Philadelphia, 1834), pp. 168, 170–171. There is an admirable treatment of "The Washington Theme in American History" by Curtis P. Nettels, *Publications of the Massachusetts Historical Society*, LXVIII (Boston, 1952), pp. 171–198. Early biographies of Washington are discussed in W. A. Bryan, *George Washington in American Literature, 1775–1865* (New York, 1952), pp. 86–120.
2. *The Life of George Washington* (2 vols., Philadelphia, 1832).
3. *The Life of George Washington* (Boston, 1839).
4. *Life of George Washington* (5 vols., New York, 1855–1859).

5. *Op. cit.*, II, 447.
6. *George Washington* (2 vols., Boston, 1889), I, 12.
7. Lodge, *op. cit.*, 349.
8. Boston, 1922; p. 258. Nettels, *op. cit.*, p. 181.
9. A. K. Weinberg, "Washington's Great Rule," in *Historiography and Urbanization*, p. 133.
10. Nettels, *op. cit.*, 183–185.
11. *George Washington and American Independence* (Boston, 1951),
12. *George Washington and the West* (Chapel Hill, 1936), 186–187.
13. *George Washington, A Biography* (4 vols., New York, 1948).
14. *Op. cit.*, pp. 14–20, 105–106.

ALEXANDER HAMILTON: NATION MAKER

1. R. G. Tugwell and Joseph Dorfman, "Alexander Hamilton: Nation-Maker," *Columbia University Quarterly* XXX (March, 1938), 70–71.
2. *Jefferson and Hamilton* (New York, 1925), pp. 483–485.
3. *Economic Origins of Jeffersonian Democracy* (New York, 1914), p. 464.
4. *The Shaping of the American Tradition*, I, 239.
5. *Enduring Federalist* (New York, 1948), p. 10.
6. *Dictionary of American Biography*, IV, 177.

THOMAS JEFFERSON AND THE CONSTITUTION

1. Schachner, *Hamilton*, p. 473.
2. Julian P. Boyd, ed. *Papers* [of Thomas Jefferson] (7 vols., Princeton University Press, 1950–1953).

THE AMERICAN PEOPLE IN 1800

1. *History of the United States* I, 1–184.
2. Jordy, *op. cit.*, p. 81.
3. *History of the United States*, I, 73.
4. *Ibid.*, IX, 241.
5. *Ibid.*, IX, 241–242.
6. *The Degradation of the Democratic Dogma*, pp. 267–311.

II. SECTIONAL CONFLICT AND CIVIL WAR

PRE-CIVIL WAR SECTIONALISM

1. "The Origin, Evolution and Application of the Sectional Concept, 1750–1900," in *Regionalism in America*, Merrill Jensen, ed., (Wisconsin, 1951), p. 85.
2. Jedidiah Morse, *The American Universal Geography* (2 vols., Boston, 1793), I, 309–310.
3. Vernon Carstensen, "The Development and Application of Regional-Sectional Concepts, 1900–1950," Jensen, *Regionalism*, pp. 108–115.
4. *An Appraisal of Walter Prescott Webb's The Great Plains: A Study in Institutions and Environment* (New York, 1940), p. 73.
5. *The Significance of Sections in American History* (New York, 1932), p. 45.

WILLIAM LEGGETT AND JACKSONIAN DEMOCRACY

1. *Frontier in American History*, pp. 302, 342–343.
2. *From Frontier to Plantation in Tennessee* (Chapel Hill, 1932); "Andrew and the Rise of Southwestern Democracy," *American Historical Review*, XXXIII (October 1927), 64–77.
3. "Calhoun: An Interpretation," *Proceedings of the South Carolina Historical Association* (1949), 26–37.
4. *The Age of Jackson* (Boston, 1948), p. 521.
5. William A. Sullivan, "Did Labor Support Andrew Jackson?" *Political Science Quarterly*, LXII (December 1947), 569–580; Edward Pessen, "Did Labor Support Jackson?: The Boston Story," LXIV (June 1949), 262–274.
6. Hammond's review of *The Age of Jackson* in the *Journal of Economic History*, VI (May 1946), 79–84.
7. "The Jackson Wage-Earner Thesis," *American Historical Review*, LIV (January 1949), 305.
8. "Turner and the Frontier Myth" in *American Scholar* (Autumn 1949), 439.

UNDERSTANDING THE AMERICAN PAST

THE IMPACT OF THE REVOLUTIONS OF 1848 ON AMERICAN THOUGHT

1. "The American Frontier — Frontier of What," *American Historical Review*, LI (January 1946), 200.
2. "Civilization in Transit," *American Historical Review*, XXXII (July 1927), 753–768. This was later incorporated in the book *Ideas in Motion* (New York, 1935).
3. *The Old South: the Founding of American Civilization* (New York, 1942); *The Puritan Oligarchy: the Founding of American Civilization* (New York, 1947); *The Founding of American Civilization: the Middle Colonies* (New York, 1949).
4. Ithaca, 1949.
5. *The Great Republic: A Historical View of the International Community and the Organization of Peace* (New York, 1942).
6. *American Impact on Great Britain* (Philadelphia, 1940).
7. Philadelphia, 1949.
8. Saveth, *op. cit.*, pp. 136–137.

THE REACTIONARY ENLIGHTENMENT

1. Charles M. Wiltse, "Calhoun: An Interpretation," pp. 26–38.
2. Coit, *op. cit.*, p. 190; Wiltse, *op. cit.*, I, pp. 11, 388.
3. "John C. Calhoun, Philosopher of Reaction," *Antioch Review* (Summer 1943), 223–234.
4. See Hofstadter's essay on Calhoun in *The American Political Tradition and the Men Who Made It* (New York, 1948), pp. 67–92.
5. New York, 1930. Owsley's article is entitled "The Irrepressible Conflict."
6. *Op. cit.*, p. 162.

JOHN BROWN

1. Philadelphia, 1942. Malin, who is amply qualified by temperament and training to deal with the legendary element in history, found a suitable subject in John Brown. According to C. Vann Woodward, of the fourteen biographies of Brown published since 1859, not one has been written by a professional historian. "John Brown's Private War" in Daniel Aaron, ed. *America in Crisis*, p. 110.

POLITICAL PROCESSES AND CIVIL WAR

1. Howard K. Beale, "What Historians Have Said about the Causes of the Civil War," *Theory and Practice in Historical Study*, pp. 55–92.
2. New York, 1948.

NOTES 587

3. *The Rise and Fall of the Confederate Government* (2 vols., New York, 1881).
4. *A Constitutional View of the Late War between the States* (2 vols., Chicago, 1868–1870).
5. *Op. cit.* I, 3.
6. Beale, "What Historians Have Said . . . ," pp. 62–63.
7. *The Civil War and the Constitution, 1859–1865* (2 vols., New York, 1901).
8. *Rise of American Civilization,* II, 52–54.
9. The idea of a "needless" Civil War induced by a poverty of statesmanship found expression in 1934 in George Fort Milton, *The Age of Hate.* See too, Mary Scrugham, *The Peaceable Americans* (New York, 1921), pp. 101–105.

LINCOLN AND THE GOVERNANCE OF MAN

1. *The Life of Abraham Lincoln* (Springfield, Mass., 1866).
2. *The Life of Abraham Lincoln* (Boston, 1872).
3. 3 vols., New York, 1889.
4. There is an admirable appraisal of this volume in David Donald, *Lincoln's Herndon* (New York, 1942), pp. 343–373.
5. Benjamin Thomas, *Portrait for Posterity: Lincoln and His Biographers* (New Brunswick, 1947), pp. 110–119.
6. Tyler Dennett, *John Hay* (New York, 1933).
7. Thomas, *op. cit.,* pp. 195–196.
8. *Ibid.,* p. 257. On the Rutledge romance and other Lincoln "myths," see James G. Randall, "Moot Points in the Lincoln Story" in *Lincoln the Liberal Statesman* (New York, 1947), pp. 5–6; appendix to Randall's *Lincoln the President: Springfield to Gettysburg* (2 vols., New York, 1945); R. P. Randall, *Mary Lincoln: Biography of a Marriage* (Boston, 1953).
9. Speech before a joint meeting of the Mississippi Valley Historical Association and the American Historical Association, December, 1934.
10. Carl Sandburg, *Abraham Lincoln: The Prairie Years* (2 vols., New York, 1926); *Abraham Lincoln: The War Years* (4 vols., New York, 1939).
11. Sandburg, *Abraham Lincoln,* Preface.
12. G. R. B. Charnwood, *Abraham Lincoln* (New York, 1917).

III. FORCES IN AMERICA TO THE
FIRST WORLD WAR

TOM WATSON AND THE NEGRO

1. "Some Demagogues in American History" *American Historical Review*, LVII (October 1951), 22–46.
2. "American Views of the Jew at the Opening of the Twentieth Century," *Publications of the American Jewish Historical Society*, XL (June 1951), 323–344. See, too, my review of Russell B. Nye, *Midwestern Progressive Politics, Commentary* (October 1951).

HENRY VILLARD: ENTREPRENEUR

1. *Business Week*, April 12, 1952, p. 86.
2. Cochran's review of *Age of the Moguls* in *Saturday Review of Literature*, October 10, 1953.
3. In adopting this approach, Cochran (along with N.S.B. Gras and Henrietta M. Larsen) has been accused by Chester M. Destler of a tendency toward shutting their eyes toward ethical considerations and writing the history of American business from the point of view of the sympathetic administrative insider. (Vaughn D. Bornet, "Those 'Robber Barons'," *Western Political Quarterly*, VI [June 1953], 343.) The difference between Cochran's view of the entrepreneur and Destler's is apparent if a comparison is made between "Henry Villard: Entrepreneur" and C. M. Destler, "Entrepreneurial Leadership: The 'Robber Barons': A Trial Balance," *The Tasks of Economic History* (September 1946), 28–49.

KARL MARX AND SAMUEL GOMPERS

1. Introduction to the *History of Labour*, I, 3–7 ff.
2. John T. Dunlop, "The Development of Labor Organization: A Theoretical Framework," in Richard A. Lester and Joseph Shister, eds., *Insights Into Labor Issues* (New York, 1949), p. 164 fn. 1.

3. Philip S. Foner, *History of the Labor Movement in the United States* (New York, 1947), pp. 10–11.
4. Howard K. Beale, "The Professional Historian His Theory and His Practice," *Pacific Historical Review* XXII (August 1953), 245.

KANSAS

1. "Frederick Jackson Turner," in *Jernegan Essays*, pp. 256, 267–269.

THE BUSINESS ATTITUDE TOWARD THE SPANISH AMERICAN WAR

1. Thomas A. Bailey, *The Man in the Street* (New York, 1948); William L. Langer and S. Everett Gleason, *The Challenge to Isolation, 1937–1940* (New York, 1952).
2. "The Propaganda Activities of the Cuban *Junta* in Precipitating the Spanish-American War, 1895–1898," *The Hispanic American Historical Review*, XIX (August 1939), 286–306.
3. "Manifest Destiny and the Philippines," in Aaron, ed., *America in Crisis*, p. 180.

THE CALIFORNIA PROGRESSIVE

1. Richard Hofstadter, "Beard and the Constitution," p. 9.
2. Supplement V to *Journal of Economic History* (December 1945), pp. 20–44; William Miller, "American Historians and the Business Elite," *Journal of Economic History*, IX (November 1949), 184–208.
3. Summary in the *American Historical Review*, LVII (April 1952), pp. 818–819.
4. (Cambridge, 1953).

HOW WE GOT INTO WORLD WAR I

1. There is an excellent discussion of the historical literature dealing with American intervention, in R. W. Leopold, "The Problem of American Intervention, 1917," *World Politics*, II (April 1950). *The United States in the World War* (2 vols., New York, 1920).
2. *Why We Fought* (New York, 1929).
3. *American Neutrality, 1914–1917.*
4. New York, 1936, pp. 14, 19, 89 et. seq.
5. New Haven, 1937, pp. 57–58, 79–82.
6. *Infra*, pp. 514–515.

IV. OUR TIMES

MIDDLE WESTERN ISOLATIONISM

1. *The Frontier in American History*, pp. 2–4, 23, 29, 190, 206, 249–251, 264, 281–282, 350.
2. "Studies of American Immigration," *Chicago Record-Herald*, August 28, September 4, 11, 18, 25, October 16, 1901. See my analysis of the Turner melting-pot concept in *American Historians and European Immigrants*, pp. 130–36.
3. New York, 1951, p. 157.

THE THIRD-GENERATION AMERICAN

1. *The Dutch and Quaker Colonies in America* (2 vols., Boston, 1900), I, 27–28.
2. *American Historical Review*, XXXII (1927), 500–518.
3. "When America was the Land of Canaan," *Minnesota History*, X (September 1929), 237.
4. It should be noted in passing that Margaret Mead, using a psycho-anthropological approach to the American scene, is not as convinced as was Hansen of the interest of the third generation in the ethnic culture pattern. According to Miss Mead, "When the third-generation boy grows up, he finds the task of leaving his father a comparatively simple one. . . . The grandchild is told in school, in the press, over the radio, about the founding fathers; they are in ninety-nine cases out of a hundred, somebody else's ancestors. Anytime one's own father . . . tries to get in one's way, one can invoke the founding fathers — those ancestors of the real American; the American who got here earlier. . . . Washington does not represent to the third-generation American the past to which one belongs by birth, but the past to which one tries to belong by effort. Washington represents the thing for which grandfather left Europe at the risk of his life, and for which father rejected grandfather at the risk of his integrity. Washington is not that to which Americans passionately cling but that to which they want to belong, and fear, in the bottom of their hearts, that they cannot and do not.

"This odd blending of the future and the past, in which another man's great-grandfather becomes the symbol of one's grandson's future, is an essential part of American culture." *And Keep Your Powder Dry: An Anthropologist Looks at America* (New York, 1943).

FRANKLIN D. ROOSEVELT AND THE NEW DEAL

1. *Franklin D. Roosevelt: The Apprenticeship* (Boston, 1952), p. 373.
2. D. M. Potter, "Sketches for the Roosevelt Portrait," *Yale Review* (September 1949), 39–53.
3. *Shaping of the American Tradition*, II.
4. "Twelve Years of Roosevelt," *American Mercury*, LX (April 1945), 391–401.

ROOSEVELT AND HIS DETRACTORS

1. *Infra.*
2. N. d., Eighth revised and enlarged edition. See also, Barnes's *Perpetual War for Perpetual Peace* (Caldwell, Idaho, 1953).
3. *American Foreign Policy in the Making, 1932–1940* (New Haven, 1946); *President Roosevelt and the Coming of the War, 1941* (New Haven, 1948).
4. *Design for War* (New York, 1951).
5. *The Truth about Pearl Harbor* (New York, 1944).
6. See A. M. Schlesinger, Jr.'s review in the *New Statesman and Nation* and Wilmot's reply *ibid.*, May 31, 1952.
7. *The Man in the Street* (New York, 1948), p. 13.
8. Report of a paper read before the 1950 meeting of the American Historical Association, *American Historical Review*, LVI (April 1951), 717.
9. *The Challenge to Isolation, 1937–1940.*
10. "Did Roosevelt Start the War — History through a Beard," *Atlantic Monthly* (August 1948).
11. *Op. cit.*
12. Dr. Morton has made available to me the text of his presentation, "Japanese Military Plans."
13. *New York Times*, April 18, 1954. Note how the Theobald thesis is anticipated in C. C. Tansill *Back Door to War* (Chicago, 1952), p. 647.

THE "SITTING DUCKS" OF CLARK FIELD

1. *Fall of the Philippines*, p. 585.
2. *Ibid.*, pp. 585–586.

3. MacArthur's replies to Morton's questionnaire were made available to Hanson W. Baldwin, from whose review of Morton's book in the *New York Times Book Review* of December 27, 1953, the quoted portion is taken. In the same review, Baldwin quotes a letter from Morton indicating that the latter made numerous "official" and "unofficial" efforts to interview MacArthur, all of which were unsuccessful.
4. *Theory and Practice in Historical Study*, p. 137.
5. *Ibid.*, p. 136 fn.
6. *Ibid.*, p. 136.

AMERICAN CHARACTER

1. Conceptions of the American character, manifest particularly in the attitudes of historians toward immigrant groups, are to be found in Saveth, *American Historians and European Immigrants*.
2. T. Lothrop Stoddard, *Re-forging America* (New York, 1927).
3. *America's Race Heritage* (New York, 1922).
4. *The Conquest of a Continent* (New York, 1923).
5. *Supra*, p. 140.
6. Morroe Berger, "Understanding National Character — And War," in *Commentary* (April 1951), pp. 375–385.
7. *Op. cit.*
8. *The American People* (New York, 1948).

INDEX

Index

ABBOTT, E. H., 403
Abolitionism, 268. *See also* John
    Brown
Abolitionists, 254
Abstinence, 70
Adams, Brooks, 43, 54, 67, 145
Adams, Charles Francis, 67
Adams, George B., 19
Adams, Henry, 11, 43, 52, 54, 552,
    553; on American people, 190-213;
    on politics, 427
Adams, Herbert Baxter, 12, 13, 15, 16,
    18, 28
Adams, James Truslow, 40, 53, 67, 81
Adams, John, 21, 43, 96, 98, 99, 112,
    118, 119, 121, 122; inaugurated, 146
Adams, John Quincy, 43, 554
Adams, Samuel, 49, 96, 98, 118, 119,
    121, 131, 136
Age of Enterprise, 39
Age of Jackson, 42
Agrarian rebellion, 342
Agricultural Adjustment Administra-
    tion, 507
Agriculture, in Virginia, 82
Aguinaldo, 457
Aliens. *See* Immigrants
Allen, Frederick Lewis, 9
Allen, William Francis, 16, 217
Alvord, Clarence W., 26, 49
Ambler, Charles, 145
American, 53
American Colonies . . . (Osgood), 25
American Constitutional Council, 497-
    498
American Federation of Labor, 377,
    380, 383
American folkways, 190-213
American Heritage, 55
American Historical Association, 4, 9,

15, 24, 29, 38, 40, 47, 52, 56, 57, 62,
    218, 242, 243, 515
American Historical Review, 9
American life, series, 31; way of, 192;
    on farm, 202; conservatism in, 204;
    industry in, 207; inertia in, 212
American Mind, 51, 53
American Nation Series, 9
American Negro Slavery, 25
American Quarterly, 51
American Revolution, 116; writing of,
    25-26; and Navigation Acts, 101;
    mercantilism and, 101-114; taxes
    and, 111; government during, 132;
    factors detrimental to, 169; financ-
    ing of, 170; and tariffs, 171; peace
    of 1783, 174
American Revolution . . . (Jameson),
    26
American Spirit, 54
Ames, William, 70
Anarchists, 378
Andrews, Charles McLean, 25, 26, 102
Andrews, John, 119
Andros, Governor, 113
Anglo-Saxons, 12, 14
Annapolis convention (1786), 134,
    135
Antimonopolists, 221
Anti-slavery, 256, 308
Aptheker, Herbert, 32
Aristocracy, in Virginia, 87, 89
Armstrong, Dr. George, 278
Arnett, A. M., 33
Arnold, General, 538, 547
Articles of Confederation, 115, 131,
    133, 136; weaknesses of, 131; in-
    adequate, 134; revised, 135
Aryans, 12; historical evolution, 14
Ashe, on Kentucky, 193

Ashley, Sir William, 103
Asia, Russian expansion in, 250
Atkins, E. F., 420
Atlanta race riot (1906), 354
Atlantic Charter, 521
Attlee, Clement, 518
Augustana Historical Society, Hansen on, 481-485
Augustana Synod, 484
Austin, J., 119
Authority and the Individual, 180
A·ixier, G. W., 407

Babbitt, 39, 42
Bacon's rebellion, 82
Bailey, Thomas A., 515
Baker, Edward D., and Abraham Lincoln, 319
Bakunin, 378
Baldwin, Hanson, 517, 522, 523
Bancroft, George, 4, 5, 10, 25, 41, 56, 59, 60, 63, 101, 248
Bancroft, Hubert Howe, 28, 30
Banking, 207
Banks, closing of (1933), 493, 499
Barbados, 74
Barlow, Joel, 210
Barnes, Harry Elmer, 435, 437, 514
Baruch, Bernard, 510
Bassett, John Spencer, 11
Baxter, Richard, 78
Beard, Charles A. and Mary, 15, 31, 32, 34, 37, 40, 43, 44, 45, 46, 50, 51, 53, 54, 56, 62, 115, 116, 159, 243, 422, 436, 514, 516, 531; *Economic Interpretation of the Constitution*, 20-24; on Turner, 21-22; importance of work, 31; on Civil War, 41; on the spirit of the Constitution, 128-143
Beard, William, 21
Beale, Howard K., 33
Becker, Carl, 3, 19, 25, 29, 38, 50, 68, 94, 117; on Kansas, 384-405
Beer, George Louis, 26, 101, 102, 103
Behavior studies, 39
Benchley, Robert, 512
Bentley, Arthur F., 21
Benton, Senator, on sectionalism, 225
Berlin, Isaiah, 521

Bermuda, 74
Bernard, Governor, 119, 120
Beveridge, Albert J., 316
Bidwell, Percy, 29
Big Three, 524
Bill of Rights, 180-184, 185
Billington, Ray Allen, on Middle Western isolationism, 451-471
Billings, Frederick, 366
Biographical writings, 41
Biography, 39
Black Bill, 308
Black, Chauncey F., 316
Black, Hugo, 508
Blackstone, on Constitution, 130
Bland, Richard, 90, 98
Bledsoe, Albert, 261, 279
Blegen, Theodore C., 55, 242, 473
Blum, John, 43
Bluntschli, Johann, 12
Bolting Democrats, 313
Bolton, Herbert E., 29
Bond, H. M., 33
Borchard, Edwin, 436
Border society, 200
Bornstein, Heinrich, 256
Boston, 79, 96; port closed, 124
Boston Tea Party, 164
Bourbon restoration, 34
Bourbon triumvirate, 341
Bowen, Francis, 253
Bowers, Claude, 33, 145, 158
Bowers, David S., 32, 243
Bowdoin, 118, 119, 121, 123, 124, 129, 134
Brain Trust, 502
Brandeis, Elizabeth, 378
Brant, Irving, 48, 490
Breasted, Prof. J. H., 53
Brereton, Gen. L. H., 537, 538, 539, 540, 541, 550
Brodie, Bernard, 519
Brown, John, 285-302; education, 286; early years, 287; on slavery, 287; and finances, 288; at Oberlin College, 288; migration to frontier, 289; and Free Statism, 289; death of, 290; in Boston, 290; "monomaniac," 291, 293, 301; religion of, 291; and sectionalism, 293; at Concord, Mass., 293; on Kansas, 293; at Col-

linsville, Conn., 296; and slave uprisings, 298, 300; at Topeka, 298; in Canada, 299
Brown, Joseph E., 341, 346, 355
Brown, Joseph M., 355
Brownson, Orestes A., 253
Brisbane, Albert, 247
Bridenbaugh, Carl, on the Virginians, 80-93
British Empire, The . . . (Gipson), 11
Bruce, Philip, 80
Bryan, William Jennings, 20, 355, 423, 458, 503
Buchanan, James, 245
Buckle, 50
Bulletin of the Business Historical Society, 29, 38
Bullitt, William C., 517, 525
Bülow, H. W., 196
Burgess, 53
Burgess, John W., 16, 20
Burgesses, House of, 91
Burke-Wadsworth Selective Service Act, 469
Burr, Aaron, 170, 207
Burr, Clinton Stoddard, 552
Business history, 37-39, 361
Business, and Spanish American War, 406-421; and Cuban independence, 415; and bankruptcy (1929), 503
Bush, Vannevar, 180
Butler, Nicholas Murray, 23
Butler, William, and Lincoln, 319
Butterfield, Hubert, 62

CABOT, GEORGE, 125
Calhoun, John C., 21, 42, 246, 259, 264, 273, 275; on sectionalism, 225
California, progressives in, 422-434; population, 423; in 1705, 423; labor in, 423; effect of New England on, 426; vice in, 432
Calvinism, 71, 77
Canada, and French, 112
Canals, 211
Candidates, The, 91
Cambridge University, 76
Campbell, Alexander, 291
Campbell, Justice, 224
Campbellites, 291

Capitalism, 212
Carnegie, Andrew, 412
Carnegie Corporation, 24, 29
Carnegie Foundation, 47
Caroline Islands, 534
Carpetbaggers, 342
Carroll, Wallace, 524
Carter, Robert Wormeley, 83, 91, 93
Cartwright, 77
Cash, W. J., 268
Catholic League of Decency, 512
Catholics, in Maryland, 74. *See also* Roman Catholics
Censorship, of movies, 512
"Central Theme in Southern History, The," 33
Chainbearer, 193
Chamberlain, John, 39
Chamberlain, Mellen, 101
Channing, Edward, 10
Character, American, 552-563
Charles I, 72
Chase, Salmon P., and Lincoln, 319
Chase, Samuel, attacked by Hamilton, 169
Chase, Stuart, 518
Chiang Kai-shek, 526
Chicago, Burlington & Quincy railroad, 371-374
Chicago Convention (1847), 226
"Christian Understanding of History," 62
Christianity, in New England, 69
Christmas, forbidden by puritans, 78
Church of England, 88
Church-state rule, in New England, 76; in Virginia, 88
Churchill, Sir Winston S., K.G., 521, 522, 525, 526, 554, 559
Cigar makers' strike, 380
Civil War, 7, 62, 260; as guidepost in history, 27; destructive force, 28; "second American revolution," 41; reconstruction, 43; sectionalism prior to, 217-226; compared with French Revolution, 263; and cultural code, 263; and slavery issue, 303; political processes and, 303-314; effect of, 314
Civilian Conservation Corps, 499
Clergy, puritan, 70

Clark, L. P., 49
Clark, Victor S., 29
Clark Field, attack on, 529-551
Class forces, 32
Class rule, 91
Classicism, 75
Clay, Henry, 268
Cleveland, Grover, 40
Clossy, Samuel, 162
Cobbett, 195
Cochran, Thomas, 37, 38, 39, 42, 422; on Henry Villard, 360-375
Coit, Margaret, 42, 259
Cole, Arthur H., 360
Colonial Merchants . . . (Schlesinger), 26
Colonies, smuggling in, 110; social reform in, 112-113
Colored Farmers' Alliance, 344, 350
Colquith, Alfred H., 341
Columbia Studies in American Culture, 51
Commager, Henry Steele, 39, 51, 53, 60, 490; on American character, 552-563
Commerce, and World War I, 438; controls over, 439
Commission on Social Studies, 56
Committee on Historiography, 56
Committee on Civil Rights, 188
Committee on Higher Education, 188
Common Sense, 122
Commons, John R., 24; on Karl Marx and Samuel Gompers, 378-383
Communism, 59
Communist Manifesto, 257, 377
Compendium of the Eleventh Census, 16
Compromise of 1850, 222
Conkling, James O., 326
Cook, John E., 299
Coolidge, Calvin, 466
Cooper, Myles, 162, 163, 164, 193
Conant, James Bryant, 180, 187
Congregationalism, 69
Congress of the Confederation, 133; advocates Constitution, 133; Washington's relations with, 153
Congress of Vienna, 255
Connecticut, and puritans, 69
Constitution, 121-143, 272; Beard on,

20-24; framing of, 129; men who drafted, 130; and principle of judicial control, 130; and Articles of Confederation, 131; advocated by Congress, 133; goes into effect, 139; checks and balances, 140; enforcing, 141; adopting of, 142; ratification of, 143; Hamilton and, 173, 176; and Bill of Rights, 180-184; and elections, 305; Lincoln and, 334; 15th Amendment, 356
Constitution of 1778 (Mass.), 123
Constitution of 1780 (Mass.), 123
Constitutional Convention of 1787, 115, 135-137, 151; and sectionalism, 221
Constitutional and Political History . . . (von Holst), 7
Constitutional Union Party, 313
Constitutions, state, during American Revolution, 132
"Contributions to American Economic History," 24, 29
Conservatism, 39-43, 115-117; 204
Conservative principle, and Civil War, 261
Continence, 70
Continental Congress, 119
Copperheads, 325
Corning letter, 326
Corporate studies, 39
Cotton, The Reverend John, 70, 71
Coughlin, Father Charles E., 70, 467
Cowley, Abraham, 77
Crane, Stephen, 28
Craven, Avery, 35, 42, 45, 259, 384
Cresswell, Nicholas, 90
Cromwell, Oliver, 73
Crossman, Richard H. S., 517, 525
Cuba, and Spanish-American War, 409; American interest in, 418
Cuban independence, 415, 453-455
Cultural history, 55
Culture, 556; and race, 13; under Puritanism, 73; and Civil War, 263; in South, 264, 307; in Kansas, 398; European, 476
Cummins, Albert B., 423
Currency, revolutionary, 132
Currency Act of 1764, 102, 113
Current, Richard, 259

Curti, Merle, 7, 39, 51, 56, 58; on Revolutions of 1848 and American thought, 242-256
Curtis, George William, 325
Customs, American, 192
Cutler, Dr. Manasseh, 224
Cutts, Capt. J. Madison, 319

DANA, CHARLES A., 247
Dane, Nathan, 223
Darlan, Adm. Jean, 522
Darwinism, 14
Davis, Elmer, 493
Davis, Henry Winter, 326
Davis, Jefferson, on slavery, 303; Lincoln on, 327
Davison, Sol, 35, 36
DeBow, J. B., 262
de Conscientia, 70
de Rochefoucauld-Liancourt, 85, 192
de Vattel, Emerick, 99
De Voto, Bernard, 9, 60
Declaration of Independence, 131, 136, 179; Beckeron, 29
Declaration of London, 439
Declaration of Rights of 1774, 96
Degradation of the Democratic Dogma, 145
Delany, Dr. Martin R., 300
Demagoguery, 339
Democracy, 191
Democratic Party, 305, 344; laissez-faire philosophy, 311; split in, 312-313; 1905 rift, 353
Depression, of 1929, 31, 35, 491-493; trends, 33-37; and frontier theory, 35-36
Destler, Chester M., 42, 56
Deutsche Geschichte, 54
Dewey, John, 21, 31, 45, 51
Dexter, Timothy, 125
Dickerson, Oliver M., 102, 119
Disfranchisement of Negro, 355
Divorce, 71
Documentary History of American Society, 24
Dodsworth, 39
Domestic Allotment Plan, 507
Donald, David, 422
Donne, John, 77, 87

Dorfman, Joseph, 42, 282; on Alexander Hamilton, 158-177
Douglas, Stephen A., 225, 252; Lincoln on, 322, 323-325
Douglass, Frederick, 298
Doyle, H. S., 348
Draft riots, 325
Draper, Lyman C., 27
Dred Scott decision, 295
Dreiser, Theodore, 39
Drexel Morgan-Winslow Lanier syndicate, 366
Dryden, John, 77
DuBois, W. E. B., 349
Duclos, Jacques, 527
Duer, William, 170
Dumond, D. L., 62
Dunning, William A., 28, 33, 34, 37
Durbin, Dr. W. W., 290
Durkheim, Emile, 55
Dwight, Timothy, 192, 197

Early American Conservatism, 43
Eastman, Max, 32
Economic determinism, 43-45
Economic History of the United States, 53; of Virginia, 80
Economic Interpretation of the Constitution, 20-24
Economic Interpretation of History, 21
Economics, 44; and history, 32; and sectionalism, 226; and World War I, 436, 437
Economy, in Colonial America, 103; and taxes, 113; trends in, 187; late Colonial, 207
Edison, Thomas Alva, 557
Education, and puritanism, 75; plantation, 85; Jefferson on, 184; of immigrants, 475
Education in a Divided World, 180
Eggleston, Edward, 9, 24, 47, 243
Electoral system, 310
Electricity, 204
Elizabeth I, 69
Elliot, Jonathan, 27
Elliott, E. N., 266
Emancipation, of Negro, 345
Emancipation Proclamation, 322, 325
Emerson, Ralph Waldo, 248, 294

Employment, 186
England, Puritanism in, 69, 77; and colonial trade, 107, 108, 109; and removal of French from Canada, 112; treatment of colonies, 112; and New England struggle, 116; taxing of colonies, 164; midwest dislike for, 459; and Oxford Oath, 518
English Bill of Rights, 180
Entente, sympathy toward, 438, 440
Entrepreneurial history, 361-364; and case histories, 368-370, 374
Equality, 401
Erickson, Aaron, 291, 292
Essex junto, 224
Estates-General, 137
Europe, influence on American life, 12-13; and westward migration, 242; republics in, 245-246; liberalism in, 254; influence of, on Midwest, 460
Evans, Oliver, 208, 210

Falconer, John, 29
Farm life, 202
Farmers' Alliance, 344
Farmers' Bloc, 221
Farmers' Home Administration, 183
Fascism, 520
Faulkner, Prof. H. U., 408
Federal government, and relations with states, 306; and population growth, 311
Federalist, 43, 140, 143; No. 10, 139; No. 22, 141
Federalist-Whig tradition, 5-8
Feudal socialism, 266
Feudal socialists, 261
Feudalism, in South, 265
Financier, 39
Finl..nd, Russia invades, 534
Fireside Chats, 494, 570
First Continental Congress, 92
Fiske, John, 13, 14, 20, 52, 80, 472
Fitch, John, 208, 209
Fitzhugh, George, 260, 275, 276, 281
Flynn, John T., 37, 514, 516
Folk history, 55
Folkways, 190-213; diet, 192-194; curiosity, 201
Foner, Philip S., 32, 377

Food habits, American, 192-194
Forbes, Hugh, 297
Forbes, John Murray, 290, 372
Force, Peter, 27
Ford, Guy Stanton, 3
Foreign policy and World War II, 517
Formosa, 536, 541
Forty-eighters, 256
Four Freedoms, 521
Founding of New England, 67
Fourierists, 247
Fox, Dixon Ryan, 29, 55, 243
France, blitzed, 38; aid to U.S., 166; proclamation of Republic in, 245; political upheaval in, 247-249
Frankfort Parliament, 244, 247
Franklin, Benjamin, 193, 204; and Declaration of Independence, 95
Free silver, 459
Free State Democrats, 312
Freeman, Douglas A., 48, 145
Freeman, Edward Augustus, 12
Freidel, Frank, 48
French and Indian Wars, 102, 150
French Revolution, 452
Friends of Liberty and Trade, 120
Frontier, idealism, 393-396
Frontier theory, 15-18, 22, 27, 35, 37, 41, 53, 218, 384, 388, 486. See also Turner, Frederick Jackson
Fulton, Robert, 209, 210, 212
Fur trade, 109

Gabriel, Ralph H., 51, 243
Gage, Secretary of the Treasury, 415
Gage, Colonel Thomas, 147
Gallatin, Albert, 203, 212
Galloway, Joseph, 119
Garibaldi, 244, 251
Garner, James W., 33
Garraty, John, 43
Garrison, William Lloyd, 254, 264
Geismar, Maxwell, 28
George III, 97, 102, 112
Georgia, lynching in, 345
Germany, invades France, 38; uniting of, 244, 247; trade unions, 383; and World War I, 435; trade during World War I, 440; Wilson compromise with, 443; diplomatic rela-

tions severed, 445; invades Poland, 468; immigration, 480
Gerry, Elbridge, 118, 121, 126, 137
Gettysburg, 260
Gettysburg Address, 327
Gibbs, Willard, 557
Gilmer, Francis Walker, 85
Gipson, Lawrence H., 11, 102
Gleason, S. Everett, 515
God, 52; role of, in determining history, 14; Puritan concept of, 72
God's Gold, 37
Goering, Hermann, 524
Goldman, Eric F., 8, 23, 40, 64; on Franklin D. Roosevelt and New Deal, 489-513
Gompers, Samuel, 378-383
Goodrich, Carter, 35, 36
Gordon, General John B., 341
Gore, Christopher, 125
Gore-McLemore resolutions, 444
Gorham, Nathaniel, 125
Gorer, Geoffrey, 553
Grady, Henry W., 342, 343, 351
Grangers, 221
Grant, Madison, 552
Grants-in-aid policy, 188
Gras, N. S. B., 29, 39
Grass Roots History, 55
Grattan, C. Hartley, 435
Graves, J. K., 372
Gray, William, 125
Grayson, William, 222
Great Plains, 217
Greek revolution, 452
Greeley, Horace, 325, 492
Greenfield, Kent Roberts, 47
Griswold, A. Whitney, on Thomas Jefferson, 178-189
Griswold, J. N. A., 372
Growth of American Thought, 51
Guam, 532

HACKER, LOUIS M., 32, 35, 37, 38, 42, 44, 101, 102, 159, 490
Hall, John, 98
Halsey, Admiral, 516
Hammond, Bray, 42
Hammond, Governor, 261
Hamilton, Alexander, 42, 49, 98, 106, 118, 127, 134, 137, 139, 141, 143, 153, 154, 155, 157, 158-177, 180;

and adoption of Constitution, 134, 173, 176; on presidential veto, 140; boyhood, 160; at Kings College, 160, 162-165; an aristocrat, 161, 170; compared with Jefferson, 161; as officer in Revolution, 165; and French aid to U.S., 166; married, 166; and Continental Congress, 166; as cabinet officer, 167; writings of, 167-169; attacks Samuel Chase, 169; and financing Revolution, 170; on tariffs, 171; at Mt. Vernon, 172; and Edmund Randolph, 173; and establishing a government, 174; on liberty, 175
Hancock, John, 118, 119, 121, 126, 153
Handlin, Oscar and Mary, 54, 55, 60, 242, 473; on radicals and conservatives, 115-127
Hanna, Mark, 408
Hansen, Marcus L., 30, 242; on third-generation American, 472-488
Hapsburg regime, 249
Harding, Warren G., 464, 465, 466
Harper, Lawrence A., on mercantilism and the American Revolution, 101-114
Harper's Ferry, 298
Harrison, Benjamin, 92
Hart, Admiral, 534
Hart, Albert Bushnell, 9, 13
Hartford Convention, 223
Hartz, Louis, on the "Reactionary Enlightenment," 259-284
Harvard University, establishes chair of business history, 29; research center for entrepreneurial history, 260, 361
Hassaurek, Frederick, 256
Hay, John, 316, 325; on Lincoln, 327
Hayes, Carlton J. H., 242
Hazard of New Fortunes, 39
Hearst, William Randolph, 407
Hecker, Frederick, 256
Heindel, R. H., 243
Heinzen, Carl, 256
Helper, Hinton, 277
Henry, Patrick, 80, 90, 136, 137
Herbert, George, 27
Herndon, William H., 315, 316
Herring, Pendleton, 46

Hickam Field, 533
Hildreth, Richard, 6, 10, 21, 41, 44, 257
Hill, Benjamin, 281
Hirsch, David, 379
Hiss, Alger, 525
Historian, role of, in American society, 3-5; 19th-century, 8-10; profession of, 8-11; European, 12; scientific, 13, 14; and factual foundations, 19; objectivity of, 19; influences on, 45; professional, 59; as psychologist, 61; moral conviction of, 62
Historical series, 53
Historical societies, formation of, 27
Historical teleology, 6
Historical understanding, 57-64
Historical writing, 60
Historiography, 4; scientific, 10; narrative, 10; scientific method in, 15; provincialism in, 30; Stalinist, 32; traditions, 41; and Civil War, 45; politics and, 46; and *Kulturgeschichte*, 52; and regimentation, 58; Soviet, 58; American, 59; and immigration, 472, 478
History, popular, 7; science of, 8-11; and politics, 8; and science, 9; scientific, 10; 19th-century, 10; comparative method, 11-15; Teutonic hypothesis, 11-15; an interrelated pattern, 12; and religion, 14; and society, 18-24; broadening framework of, 24-28; "continuing renaissance," 28-37; class forces in, 32; economic forces in, 32; economic interpretation of, 34; business, 37-39; conservative and liberal traditions, 39-43; and novelist, 39; and economic emphasis, 44; and social sciences, 45; military, 45-51; political, 45-51; and biography, 48; and psychology, 49; intellectual, 50-51; and synthesis, 52-55; folk, 55; relativism and objectivity, 55-57; economic interpretation of, 61; business, 361; conservatism in, 261; entrepreneurial, 361-364
History of Agriculture (Falconer), 29; *of American Life,* 29, 53; *of Civilization in England,* 50; *of*

Labour, 24; *of Manufactures* (Clark), 29; *of the People* (McMaster), 8; *of the Standard Oil Company* (Tarbell), 37; *of the United States* (Adams), 52; (Bancroft), 4, 5; (Channing), 10; (Hildreth), 6; (Rhodes), 7; (Schouler), 6
Hitler, Adolf, 38, 44, 468, 519, 554; attempt on life of, 523
Hobbes, Thomas, 97, 98
Hoagland, H. E., 378
Hoffman, Ross J., 243
Hofstadter, Richard, 41, 60, 61, 64, 259, 407, 422
Holland, Josiah G., 314
Holmes, Prof. George Frederick, 262
Holmes, Henry, 266
Holmes, Oliver Wendell, 21
Holy Alliance, 261
Homestead Act, 36, 183
Hong Kong, 532
Hook, Sidney, 32, 47
Hopkins, Harry, 500-502
Hoover, Herbert C., 467, 493, 499, 503, 510
Horse racing, 197; breeding, 198
House of Burgesses, 92; Washington and, 151
Howard, John, 71
Howe, Dr. Samuel Gridley, 295
Howell, Clark, 353
Howells, William Dean, 39
Hughes, Archbishop, 253
Hughes, Henry, 262, 264
Hülsemann, Chevalier, 249-250
Hundred Days (1953), 499, 500, 506; and manufacturing, 511
Hungarian revolution, 251-255, 452
Hungary, republic in, 244; republic declared, 245, 246, 247; independence reorganized, 250; revolution in, 251-255, 452
Hunt, Freeman, 250
Hurlburt, Archer B., 24
Hutchinson, William T., 46

ICKES, HAROLD, 513
Idealism, and frontier, 393-396; and liberalism, 297

Immigration, 472-488; fr m Europe, 242; in 1848, 251, 255; to Kansas, 396 and Midwest, 459; in Virginia, 473; education of, 475; historiography of, 477, 478; and Americanism, 477; and South, 478; Irish, 479; Scotch-Irish, 480; German, 480; Scandinavian, 480, 481; imports culture, 476; 2d generation immigrants, 479; religion of, 483
Individualism, in Kansas, 387-393
Ingalls, John J., 402, 431
Industrial Revolution (1848), 242-258
Industry, late colonial, 207; in Midwest, 459
Inns, colonial, 195
Insurgents, 221
Intellectual history, 50-51
Intellectualism, in Massachusetts, 74; effect of Oxford and Cambridge on, 76
Intemperance, 196
International Workingmen's Association, 378, 380
International socialism, 377
Internationalism, in Midwest, 465
Irish, immigration of, 479
Iron curtain, 59
Irving, Washington, 144
Isolationism, 516; Middle Western, 451-471

Jackson, Andrew, 6, 200, 224, 459
Jackson, Jonathan, 124
James I, 77
James, William, 557
Jameson, Prof. James F., 25, 26
Japan, and World War II, 522, 532; policy on invading, 526
Jay, James F., 372
Jay, John, 19, 143, 154
Jefferson, Thomas, 48, 80, 93, 98, 99, 100, 118, 127, 131, 136, 145, 150, 154, 155, 157, 158, 173, 178-189, 203, 207, 208, 212; Summary View, 87; and Declaration of Independence, 95, 179; compared with Hamilton, 161; and Bill of Rights, 180-184; hostile to Supreme Court, 181; agrarianism, 183; and property, 83; and laws of primogeniture, 183; and

equal opportunity, 184; and social security legislation, 184; and education, 184; and "republic," 186; on voting, 186-187; effects of, on modern government, 186-187
Jensen, Merrill, 41, 115
Jews, leaders among, 377
Jingoism, 409, 414
Johns Hopkins Graduate School, 423
Johnson, Hiram, 423, 431, 433
Johnson, Hugh, 504-506, 510
Johnson, Tom, 503
Johnson, Walter, 60, 517, 526
Jones, Howard Mumford, 243
Josephson, Matthew, 37
Journal of Economic and Business History, 29
Judaism, 70
Judicial control, principle of, 130
Justice of the peace, 89

Kagi, John Henry, 299
Kane, Murray, 35
Kansas, 384-405; John Brown and, 289; and Free State issue, 293-302; individualism in, 389-393; immigration to, 396; culture in, 398; liberality and equality in, 401; government in, 402; and Cuban independence, 415
Kansas-Nebraska Act, 222, 226
Kapital, Das, 377
Keayne, Robert, 70
Kellogg Pact, 518
Kentucky, Ashe on, 193; and sectionalism, 223
Kelvin, Lord, 191
Kelvin's law, 52
Kendall, George, 248
Kennedy, John Pendleton, 249
Kent, William, 432
Keynes, John Maynard, 500
Kimball, Mary, 178
Kimmel, Admiral, 516
King, Henry, on Kansas individualism, 392
King's College, 162-165
Kinkel, Gottfried, 251
Kirk, Russell, 42, 259
Kirkland, Edward C., 39, 56
Knights of Labor, 383

Know-Nothing Party, 256
Knox, 155
Koch, Adrienne, 43
Kohn, Halvdan, 243
Kossuth, Louis, 251-255
Kota Bharu, 532
Kraus, Michael, 243
Kronburg, David, 378
Ku Klux Klan, 341, 342, 345
Kulturgeschichte, 52-55

LABAREE, LEONARD, 43
Labor, Party (British), 21; movement, 378; in California, 423; and Hundred Days, 511
Lafayette, 166
La Follette, Robert M., 423
La Follette movement, 221
La Guardia, Fiorello, 512
Lamon, Ward Hill, 315
Lamprecht, Karl, 54
Langer, William L., 515
Langdon, Woodbury, 153
Lage, W. P., 436
Laissez-faire principle, 17
Lassallean Socialists, 378
Latourette, Kenneth Scott, 62
Latrobe, Benjamin H., 209, 210
Laud, Bishop, 72
Laurrell, Ferdinand, 378, 382
Law of Civilization and Decay, The, 54
Law of Nations, 99
Lawrence, Amos A., 295
League of Decency, 512
League of Gileadites, 288
League of Nations, 463-464, 557, 558, 559; opposition to, 464
Leahy, Admiral William, 517
Legare, Hugh Swinton, 273
L'Enfant, Pierre, 155
Lee, Richard Henry, 90, 96
Lee, Robert E., 48; Lincoln on, 327
Lee, Colonel Thomas, 81
Leibnitz's theory, 99
Lend-lease, 44, 470
Lenin, N., 32
Lescohier, Don D., 378
Letters to American Teachers . . . (Adams), 52
Leviathan, 97

Lewis, Sinclair, 39
Lewisohn, Ludwig, 30
Liberalism, 39-43, 44, 61; in Europe, 254; and slavery, 262; in South, 265; and idealism, 397; and New Deal, 511
Liberty, 401, conception of, 175
Library of Congress, 60
Library of Congress Series, 53
Libraries, 204
Life of Washington, 144
Lilienthal, David, 180
Lincoln, Abraham, 40, 48, 49, 315-335; tact of, 318-320; and cabinet, 319; leadership of, 320; on controversies, 321; and semantics, 322; on Douglass, 322, 323-325; suspends *habeas corpus,* 325; as votegetter, 326; and Conkling letter, 326; Hay on, 327; on Davis and Lee, 327; Gettysburg address, 327; relations with Congress, 328; second inaugural address, 328, 331; a party man, 328; and people, 329-332; and civil and military power, 332; social and political philosophy, 333; and Constitution, 334; Lowell on, 334
Lincoln: A Psycho-Biography, 49
Lincoln, Mary, 315
Lincoln, Robert Todd, 316
Lincoln, Thomas, 315
Lincoln-Douglas debates, 323-325
Link, Arthur, 490
Liquor traffic, 78
Literature, 206; late Colonial, 192
Livingston, Chancellor, 209, 210
Locke, John, 96, 97
Locomotive, 208, 211
Lodge, Henry Cabot, 43, 144, 159; on League of Nations, 464
London, Jack, 28
Longfellow, Henry Wadsworth, 245, 248
Longstreet, Judge A. B., 199
Los Angeles Merchants and Manufacturers Association, 423
Louis Napoleon, 244, 247
Louisiana, and sectionalism, 223, 224
Lowell, James Russell, on Lincoln, 334
Loyalists, 120

Lubell, Samuel, 451
Luce, Henry, 517
Ludwell, Philip, 99
Lusitania, 442, 462
Lutherans, 484
Luthin, Reinhard H., 339
Lynching, in Georgia, 345, 348; Thomson incident, 349; Watson on, 359

MACARTHUR, GENERAL DOUGLAS, 529, 530, 538, 540, 541, 548, 549
McClatchey, Charles J., 432
McCollum vs. *Board of Education* (1948), 189
MacDonald, J. Ramsay, 21
McDonnell, J. P., 278
McGuire, P. J., 378
Mackay, Mungo, 125
Mackenzie King, 521
McKelvey, Blake, 34
McKinley, William, 456, 458; election of, 454; imperialism, 457; and Spanish-American War, 419
MacLeish, Archibald, 38, 44
Machtpolitik, 49
McMaster, John Bach, 8, 9, 24, 435
McNary-Haugen bill, 507
Madison, James, 21, 23, 48, 80, 92, 129, 137, 138, 139, 143, 154, 167, 180
Mahan, Alfred Thayer, 52
Main Currents in American Thought, 31, 98
Maine, sinking of, 410, 416
Majority rule, 309
Malaya, 532
Malraux, André, 528
Malin, James C., 40, 56, 285; on John Brown, 289
Malenkov, G., 59
Malone, Dumas, 48, 178, 490
Manhattan project, 426
Mann, A. Dudley, 250
Manners, American, 196
Manufacturing, 207; colonial, 106; iron, 109; Spanish-American War and, 412; and Hundred Days, 511
Marlowe, 72
Marprelate, Martin, 78

Marshall, General George C., 516, 522
Marshall, John, 80, 144, 181
Marshall Islands, 534
Marshall Plan, 188, 553, 559, 560
Marx, Karl, 32, 45, 378-383
Marxism, 53, 257
Marxist Quarterly, 32
Maryland, 74, 79
Massachusetts, voting in, 91; radicals and conservatives in, 115-117, 119; and American Revolution, 118; Loyalists, 120; state constitutions of, 121, 123; racing in, 198
Massachusetts Bay Colony, 69, 76; intellectual life in, 74. *See also* Puritans
Massachusetts Kansas Committee, 295
Mason, George, 80, 90; and Declaration of Independence, 95
Mather, Cotton, 77, 220
Mazzini, 244
Mead, Margaret, 553
Metternich, 244, 250
Mellon, Andrew, 159
Melting pot, 451
Memphis Convention of 1845, 226
Men in Business, 39
Mercantilism, 169; defined, 103; and American Revolution, 101-114
Metropolitanism, 307, 308
Mexico, 74
Middle Ages, 54
Middle West, forges ahead of South, 28; and Spanish-American War, 454; economics, 456; social conditions, 456; dislike for England, 459; industry in, 459; and immigrants, 459; and religious sects, 460; and European influences, 460; and pacifism, 461; and World War I, 461; and League of Nations, 463-464; Republicans in, 464; and internationalism, 465; and World War II, 468; and Selective Service Act, 469; and Lend-Lease, 470
Military history, 45-51
Miller, William, 39, 42
Millis, Walter, 406, 516; on U.S. entry into World War I, 435-447
Mills, C. Wright, 422

Milton, John, 77
Mining, 207
Mississippi Valley, 225, 226
Mississippi Valley Historical Association, 58
Mississippi Valley Historical Review, 27
Mississippi Valley Historical Society, 27
Missouri Compromise, 222
Mitchell, Samuel L., 210
Mittelman, E. B., 378
Modern Arms and Free Men, 180
Moderne Geschichtswissenschaft, 54
Molasses, 110; taxes, 111
Molasses Act of 1733, 107
Moley, Raymond, 503-504, 507, 510, 517
Monroe Doctrine, 529
Mood, Fulmer, 217
Moore, Thomas, 196
Morals, American, 196
Moravians, 73
Morison, Samuel Eliot, 30, 40, 43, 47, 56, 58, 60, 515; on the puritan tradition, 67-79
Morris, Gouverneur, 138, 221, 222
Morris, Robert, 170, 172
Morgan, J. Picrpont, 418, 445
Morgan-Drexel, 366
Morgenstern, George, 516
Morse, Jedediah, 217
Morton, Louis, on "sitting ducks" of Clark Field, 529-551
Motley, John Lothrop, 8
Mount Vernon, 149
Movies, censorship of, 512
Mowrer, Edgar Ansel, 517
Mowry, George E., *The California Progressive,* 422-434
Muckraking, 37
Mumford, Lewis, 38
Munford, Col. Robert, 91
Munich, 519
Murdock, Kenneth, 30
Mussolini, 554
Music, puritanism and, 73

Nagumo, Admiral, 533
Narragansett pacer, 198
Narrative and Critical History, 9

Narrative historiography, 10
National Archives, 60
National Farmers' Alliance, 343, 350
National Industrial Recovery Act, 509
National Intelligencer, 246
National Kansas Committee, 295
N.R.A., 510, 511
Native Races of the Pacific States . . . , 28
Nature and Man in America, 24
Navigation Acts, 101, 102, 104, 105, 111, 163
Nazis, growth of, 44
Negro, history, 32; and white supremacy, 33, 347; and reconstruction, 34; vote of, 342, 346, 354; emancipation of, 345; Populist Party and, 347, 349; Tom Watson benefits to, 350; and election of 1904, 353; role of, in politics, 354; disfranchisement, 355; and election of 1908, 355; Justice Taney on, 356; repression of, 357; Watson's attack on, 358
Nettels, Curtis, 145
Neutrality, 559; and World War I, 436; legislation, 468
Nevins, Allan, 11, 37, 38, 39, 60, 62, 64, 160, 323, 360; on John Brown, 285-302
New Deal, 40, 489-513
New England, puritans in, 13; provincialism, 30; non-English elements, 30; and puritan tradition, 67-69; intellectualism in, 74, 76; church-state rule in, 76; effect of Oxford and Cambridge on, 76; 17th-century theology, 76; puritan migration to, 77; population (1640), 79; resistance to England, 112-113; struggle with Britain, 116; manners and morals, 196; and sectionalism, 222; and Republican Party, 312; and West, 385-386; effect of, on California, 426
New England Quarterly, 51
New Englandism, 308
New Hampshire, ratifies Constitution, 143
New Haven, 76; Puritanism in, 69

"New History," 19, 23, 24-25, 29, 40, 45, 46, 50-51, 54
New Orleans, battle of, 224
New Viewpoints in American History, 28, 49
Newspapers, late Colonial, 192
New York, ratifies Constitution, 143; inns in, 195; and sectionalism, 223
New York Commercial Advertiser, 225
New York Stock Exchange, closed in World War I, 438
Nichols, Roy F., 46; *Political Processes and Civil War*, 303-314
Nicolay, John G., 316
Niebuhr, Reinhold, 62
Niles, Hezekiah, 27
Nomini Hall, 83
Norris, George W., 423, 518, 524
North, and states' rights, 306; materialism in, 309
North American Review, 246
North Atlantic Pact, 188
Northern Pacific Railroad, 365, 366, 367
Norway, fall of, 469
Notes on Virginia, 186
Nott, Josiah, 278
Novelist and historian, 39
Nye Committee, 468
Nye, Gerald, 436

OBERLIN COLLEGE, 288
Objectivism, 55-57
Ohio, and sectionalism, 223, 224
Ohio Company of Associates, 224
Ohio Cultivator, 291
Ohio Federation of Labor, 456
Old Virginia and Her Neighbors, 50
Oliver, 119
Olmstead, Frederick, 264
Open Door Policy, 554
Opera, 73
Ordeal of the Union, 11
Oregon and California Railroad, 365
Oregon question, 224
Oregon Railroad and Navigation Company, 365, 366, 367
Oregon and Transcontinental Company, 367
Osgood, Herbert Levi, 25
Osgood, R. E., 515

Osterweiss, Rollin, 282
Otis, Harrison Gray, 423
Otis, James, 96, 98
Owsley, F. L., 62, 260
Oxford Oath, 519
Oxford University, 76

PACIFIC COAST, importance of, 226
Pacificism, 461
Page, Thomas Nelson, 260, 446
Paine, Thomas, 49, 131
Palestine issue, 559
Panic of 1893, 411
Parker, Alton B., 352
Parkman, Francis, 8
Parrington, Vernon L., 31, 32, 37, 49, 50, 51, 98
Parsons, Chief Justice, 196
Party system, 305
Pate, Henry Clay, 296
Paxson, F. L., 35
Peace of 1783, 174
Pearl Harbor, 470, 515, 532; damage at, 534
Peden, William, 43
Peek, George, 507, 510
Pennsylvania, Moravians in, 73; de Liancourt on, 192
People's Party, 344, 348
Perkins, Charles E., 372
Perkins, Dexter, 515
Perlman, Selig, 378
Permanent Court of International Justice, 466
Perry, Ralph Barton, 51
Peru, 74
Philadelphia, society of, 196
Philippine Act, 457
Philippines, 457, 532; World War II in, 529-551
Phillips, Ulrich B., 28, 33
Phillips, Wendell, 254, 295, 322
Pickering, Thomas, 119
Pickering, Timothy, 95, 96
Pilgrims, 68
Pillsbury, Arthur J., 430
Pinckney, C. C., 154
Plantation houses, 86
Plantation life, 82, 83
Plantation owner, 84
Plutocrat, 39

Plymouth Rock, 68
Poetry, puritanism and, 77
Poland, invaded in 1939, 468
Political history, 45-51
Political traditions, 5
Politics, 559; and history, 8, 46; and race, 13; role of Negro in, 354
Polk, Col. L. L., 350
Popular history, 7
Population, growth of, 311
Populism, 133
Populists, 20, 221, 359, 429; and election of 1908, 355; stand on lynching, 345, 348; and Negro vote, 346; and Negro, 347, 349; in 1896, 351; and election of 1904, 352
Poor Richard, 193
Portfolio, 196
Postal systems, 204
Prairie Farmer, 292
Pratt, Julius W., on business attitude toward the Spanish-American War, 406-421
Predestination, 71
Presbyterianism, 69, 77
Prescott, William Hickling, 8
President's Commission on Higher Education, 185
Presidential veto, 140
Prizefighting, 199-200
Proclamation of 1763, 102, 108, 113
Proctor, Senator Redfield, 417
Progressive conferences, 425
Progressive movement, in California, 422-434
Progressivism, 23, 221, 422-434
Prohibition, 493, 512
Propaganda, in World War I, 445
Protestant reformation, 69
Protestantism, 14; and slavery, 308
Province Charter of 1691, 126
Provincialism, 30
Providence, radicalism in, 206
Prynne, William, 78
Psychoanalysis, 49
Psychology, 45, 49
Pulitzer, 407
Puritanism, 387; in New England, 69; economics of, 69; a middle-class movement, 70; intellectual side of, 71, 72; conception of God, 72; and

music, 73; and education, 75; poetry and, 77
Puritans, 13; in New England, 67; in English universities, 77; and liquor, 78; forbid Christmas, 78

QUARLES, 77
Quebec Act of 1774, 108, 113
Quick, Howard, 353
Quincy, Josiah, Jr., 86

RACE CHARACTERISTICS, 13
Radical Reconstructionists, 33
Radicalism, 115-127
Railroads, 365-368, 370-374
Rainbow operation, 534
Randall, James G., 36, 41, 50, 62; *Lincoln and the Governance of Men*, 313-315
Randolph, John, 42, 137, 154, 219
Randolph, Peyton, 80
Ratner, Sidney, 49
Rauch, Basil, 517, 520
Read, Conyers, 57, 58
Reconstruction, 341, 559; "radical," 33; and corruption, 34; Negro and, 34; civil war, 43
Reconstruction Period, 340
Reform Darwinism, 499, 500
Regional history, 55
Regionalism, 310
Regular Democrats, 313
Reizbarkeit, 54
Relativism, 55-57, 58
Religion, and history, 14; and puritan migration, 77; in Middle West, 460; of immigrants, 483
Religion Forward Movement, 430
Renaissance, 54, 76
Republic, 46
Republican Party, 312, 344; and reconstruction, 33; wins first election, 313; in Middle West, 464
Republican Roosevelt, 43
Research Center for Entrepreneurial History, 360
Revolution, American, 152; and currency, 132
Revolution of 1789 (France), 247
Revolutions of 1848, 242-258

Rhodes, Cecil, 345
Rhodes, James Ford, 7, 9, 10, 19, 408
Rhode Island, 76; and puritans, 69; radicalism, 206
Rise of American Civilization, 31
Rise of the City, The, 34
Robber barons, 37, 42, 363, 366
Robinson, James Harvey, 19, 23, 58
Rockefeller, John D., 37, 38
Roman Catholics, and revolution of 1848, 253
Romanticism and slavery, 308
Rosenman, Judge Sam, 517
Roosevelt, Eleanor, 495
Roosevelt, Franklin Delano, 17, 40, 44, 489-513, 514-528, 551; and World War II, 468; governor of New York, 493, 498; first inaugural, 494, 498; fireside chats, 494, 510; family, 496; politics, 496; Assistant Secretary of Navy, 496; nominated Vice President, 496; a nationalist, 497; liberalism, 499; Brain Trust, 502; foreign policy, 516-520; quarantine speech, 519; and Navy, 519; pragmatist, 520-525; and heads of states, 521; and Admiral Darlan, 522; and his policy toward Russia, 527
Roosevelt, Sara Delano, 495
Roosevelt, Theodore, 60, 316, 430, 431, 518
Root Plan, 466, 467
Rossiter, Clinton, 41
Rowell, Chester, 428, 430
Ruef, Abraham, 424
Rum, 78, 110
Rum, Romance and Rebellion, 110
Russell, Bertrand, 180
Russia, 515; expansion in Asia, 250; invades Finland, 524; and Yalta, 526; Roosevelt's policy toward, 527
Rutledge, Ann, 315

SAN FRANCISCO, 424
Sanborn, Frank B., 293
Sanborn, Frederick C., 514
Sandburg, Carl, 331
Santayana, George, 557
Saposs, David J., 378
Scandinavian immigration, 480

Schachner, Nathan, 42, 178
Schafer, Joseph, 30, 35
Schlesinger, Arthur M., 26, 28, 29, 34, 49, 53, 108
Schlesinger, Arthur M., Jr., 6, 42, 43, 44, 45, 50, 57, 60; *Roosevelt and His Detractors*, 514-528
Scholes, Dr. Percy, 75
Schouler, James, 6, 41
Schurz, Carl, 256
Schumpeter, Joseph, 360
Science, and history, 9
Scientific historiography, 10
Scientific history, 10
Scotch-Irish Congress, 480, 486
Scotch-Irish immigration, 480
Scribner's Standard Atlas of the U.S. . . . , 16
Sea power, in World War I, 439
Sectionalism, pre-Civil War, 217-226; in South, 222; in New England, 222-223; and New York, 223; and slavery, 226; attitudes toward, 309
Selective Service Act, 469
Self-government, 186-187
Seligman, E. R. A., 21, 45
Semple, Ellen C., 24
Seward, and Lincoln, 319
Seymour, Charles, 435
Seymour, Governor, 320
Shakespeare, William, 72
Shaler, Nathaniel Southgate, 24
Shanghai, 532
Shannon, Fred, 36
Shays's Rebellion, 121
Sherman, Stuart Pratt, 29
Short, General, 516
Shugg, 33
Shryock, Richard, 30
Significance of the Frontier . . . , 16
Simkins, F. B., 33
Simms, William Gilmore, 249
Simons, Algie M., 21
Singora, 532
Slavery, 253, 254, 308; in Virginia, 83; and sectionalism, 225-226; and liberalism, 262; John Brown on, 288, 289; and Civil War, 303; Jefferson Davis on, 303
Smith, Alfred E., 498
Smith, Harrison, 39

Smith, Hoke, 353
Smith, J. Allen, 21, 31
Smoot-Hawley tariff, 559
Smuggling, colonial, 110
Social life, Colonial, 197
Social reform, in Colonies, 112
Social Science Research Council, 39, 47, 53, 58
Social sciences, history of, 45
Social security legislation, Jefferson's ideas of, 184
Socialism, 377, 378
Socialism in American Life, 32
Socialist Party, 20, 378, 424; in California, 424
Society and history, 18-24
Sociology, 45
Soil Conservation Service, 188
Solge, Reinhold, 250
Sons of Liberty, 120
Sorge, Frederick A., 257, 378
South, lags behind Middle West, 27; Reconstruction Period, 33, 34; corruption in, 34; sectionalism, 222; and Western power, 224; culture in, 264, 307; liberalism and feudalism in, 265; and states' rights, 306; demagoguery in, 340; and white supremacy, 343; and immigration, 478
South Carolina, 75
Southern Historical Association, 478
Southernism, 307, 368
"South in the Building of the Nation," 28
South Pacific Railroad, 424, 427
Soviet historiography, 59
Spain, and cause of Spanish-American War, 410; civil war in, 519
Spanish-American War, 61, 352, 406-421, 453, 559; cause of, 408; and Cuba, 409; and sugar, 419
Sparks, Jared, 10, 27, 144
Spenser, E., 77
Spirit of American Government, 21
Sports, 198-199
Squirearchy, 87
Squires, James D., 436
Stalin, V., 32, 59, 524, 526
Stalingrad, 524
Stalinist historiography, 32

Stamp Act, 112, 113
Standard of living, 192, 193
Stanton, E. M., and Lincoln, 319
Staple Act of 1663, 107
Stark, Admiral Harold C., 516
States' rights, 306
Steamboat, 210
Steam engine, 207-209
Stearns, George L., 295
Steffens, Lincoln, 431
Stephens, Alexander H., 50, 303, 357
Stephenson, George, 221, 473
Stephenson, G. W., 242
Stettinius, Edward R., Jr., 517, 526
Stevens, Aaron D., 299
Stevens, John, 210
Stevens, Thaddeus, 33
Stevenson, Adlai, 40, 60
Stock market, 1929 crash, 491-493
Stoddard, Lothrop, 552
Stowe, Harriet Beecher, 333
Strong, S., 119, 121
Stuart, David, 148
Study of Monopoly Power, 189
Submarine warfare, 435, 441, 462
Sugar, 419
Sugar Act of 1764, 109, 110
Sullivan, Mark, 9, 119
Summary View, 87
Sumner, Charles, 248
Sumner, Helen L., 378
Supreme Court, 181
Sussex crisis, 444, 461
Sutherland, General, 529, 535, 539, 549, 550
Sweden, immigrants, 481; Augustana Historical Synod, 481-485
Swisshelm, Jane, 318

TAFT, WILLIAM HOWARD, 23, 431
Taney, Justice, on Negro, 356
Tansell, Charles, 436, 437
Tarbell, Ida, 37, 316
Tarkington, Booth, 39
Tariff, Alexander Hamilton on, 167, 171
Tariff barriers, 107
Taussig, Charles W., 110
Taverns, 202
Tawney, R. H., 70

Taxes, colonial, 103; pre-Revolutionary, 109; British, and colonial economy, 113
Taxation without representation, 164
Taylor, John, 186
Tea Act, 109
Tennessee, and sectionalism, 223
Tennessee Valley Authority, 508
Territorialism, 308
Teuton, 552
Teutonic hypothesis, 11-15, 17, 28
Teutonists, 45, 53
Thailand, 532
Thanksgiving Day, 78
Thayer, William R., 145
Theater, 197; under Puritanism, 72
Theobald, Admiral R. A., 515
Thermodynamics, 191
Third Provincial Congress, 120
Thirty-nine Articles of the Church of England, 77
This I Do Believe, 180
Thomas, Robert E., 116
Thompson, C. Mildred, 33
Thomson incident, 349
Thoreau, Henry, 294
Thurston, Senator, 410
Ticknor, George, 5-6, 206, 248
Tillman, Benjamin, 346
Tobacco, 82, 103
Tom Jones, 196
Toryism, 120
Townsend, George A., 325
Townshend Acts, 109
Toynbee, Arnold, 62
Trade, English control of, 104; restrictions on, 104; colonial, fostering of, 105; England discourages, 107, 109; colonial, after 1763, 108; and sectionalism, 226; and revolution of 1848, 250; and Spanish-American War, 408; and World War I, 435
Trade regulations, 173
Trade-unionism, 377; in Germany, 383
Traditionalism, 261
Tragic Era, 33
Transcendentalism, 557
Transatlantic commerce, 438
Transportation, 213

Travel, Colonial, 195
Treaty of Paris, 457
Trescot, William Henry, 250
Trevor-Roper, H. L., 524
Trickett, Dean, 129
Triple-A Plowed Under, 32
Triumph of American Capitalism, 38
Troeltsch, E., 69
Trotsky, Leon, 32, 59
Trotting horses, 198
Truman Doctrine, 188, 553
Tucker, N. Beverly, 261
Tugwell, Rexford G., 504-506, 507; on Alexander Hamilton, 158-177
Turner, Frederick Jackson, 15-18, 27, 30, 35, 37, 40, 41, 45, 53, 218, 243, 384, 388, 451, 486, 532; and Teutonism, 16-17; Beard on, 21-22; on pre-Civil War sectionalism, 217-226. *See also* Frontier theory.
Turnpikes, 211
Twentieth Century Fund, 47
Tyler, Moses Coit, 13, 50

UNCONDITIONAL SURRENDER, 522, 523
Unemployment, in World War I, 438; in 1929, 491-493, 499
Unemployment relief, 499
Union Labor Party, 424, 427
United Nations, 557
Union of Soviet Socialist Russia. *See* Russia.
Union, 377

VAGTS, ALFRED, 531
Vallandigham, Clement L., 326, 327, 334
Vardill, John, 162, 164
Venezuela war scare, 411
Veto, presidential, 140
Vice, 196, 198, 202; in California, 432
Viereck, Peter, 61
Villard, Henry, 360-375; early lift, 364; on railroads, 365; as "robber baron," 366-368; wealth of, 369
Virginia, 74, 80-93; population, 79, 81; size, 81; life in, 82; plantation life, 83; slavery in, 83; intermarriage, 86; aristocracy in, 87, 89; squirearchy, 87; Church of England in, 88; church-state rule, 88;

role of justice of the peace in, 89; county officials, 90; class rule in, 91; voting in, 91; and First Continental Congress, 92; political power in, 92; and Constitutional Convention of 1786, 134; ratifies Constitution, 143; racing in, 198; and immigration, 474

Virginia Act for Establishing Religious Freedom, 181

Volney, 194

von Abele, Rudolph, 50

von Erdmannsdorffer, Max, 12

von Holst, Hermann Eduard, 7, 53

von Maurer, G. L., 12

von Ranke, Leopold, 6, 119

von Wolff, Christian Frederick, 99

Vote, Negro and, 346, 354

Voting, in Virginia compared with Massachusetts, 91; Jefferson on, 186-187

WAINWRIGHT, GENERAL JONATHAN, 529

Wake Island, 532

Walker, Frank, 502

Walker, Senator I. P., 252

Wall Street and Spanish-American War, 409

Wallas, Graham, 321

War of 1812, 224

Warranteeism, 264

Washington, George, 48, 80, 91, 136, 144-147, 207; writings, 10; a vestryman, 89; and Constitution, 131; inauguration of, 143, 146; administrative ability, 144-147; biographies of, 144-145; personality and character, 146-148, 155; at Mount Vernon, 149; as military commander, 150; and House of Burgesses, 151; at Constitution Convention, 151; administrative techniques, 152-155; selection of men, 152; and Congress, 153; leadership of, 153; and advisors, 154; and details, 154; as an executive, 155-157; and Whisky Rebellion, 156; and Hamilton, 172

Washington, D.C., design of, 154

Water companies, 210

Watson, Tom, 339-359; early life, 341;

and agrarian rebellion, 342; on Republican and Democratic parties, 344; and People's Party, 344; and emancipation of Negro, 345; and H. S. Doyle, 348; on lynching, 349, 359; benefits to Negroes, 350; and Populists, 350; and Spanish-American War, 352; and election of 1904, 352; seeks Presidency, 355; as "farmer," 356; as political boss, 357; attacks Negroes, 358

Watt, James, 210

Weaver, Col. James Riley, 20, 21

Webb, Walter P., 217

Weber, Max, 69

Webster, Daniel, 21, 249, 250

Webster, Noah, 205

Weed, and Lincoln, 319

Weems, Mason L., 144

Weik, Jesse W., 316

Wertenbaker, Thomas Jefferson, 40, 80, 243

Weitling, Wilhelm, 257

West, and importance of Pacific Coast, 226; railroads in, 366; New England and, 385-386; and frontier, 387; and Cuban independence, 415

Western movements, 219

Weydemeyer, Joseph, 257

Wharton, 33

Wheeler Field, 533

Whig Party, 312, 313

Whisky, 192, 193

Whisky Rebellion, 156

White, Andrew D., 13

White, Leonard, on George Washington, 144-147

White, Morton, 128

White, William Allen, 423, 430

White supremacy, 33, 341, 343, 347, 357

Welfare State principle, 17

Wigglesworth, Michael, 71

Wilmot, Chester, 515

Willard, Charles D., 431

William and Mary Quarterly, 51

Williams, John Chandler, 125

Williams, Roger, 78

Williams, T. Harry, 40, 47

Williamsburg, 92

Willich, August, 257

Wilson, James, 98, 99, 100, 180
Wilson, Prof. Milburn L., 507
Wilson, Woodrow, 23, 60, 136, 138, 202, 463, 496, 498, 516, 557; and submarine warfare, 441; and compromise with Germany, 443; and German aggression, 446; and Henry Cabot Lodge, 464
Wiltse, Charles M., 42, 259
Winsor, Justin, 9
Wisan, Joseph E., 206
Wisconsin and sectionalism, 223
Wisconsin Domesday Book, 30
Wise, Gov. Henry A., 290
Wish, Harvey, 282
Wittke, Carl, 242, 256, 473
Wolfe, Bertram, 58
Woodward, C. Vann, 33, 43; on Tom Watson, 339-359
World Court, 466, 467
World War I, as historical guidepost, 24-28; United States entry in, 435-447; and economics, 436, 437; and neutrality legislation, 436; United States sympathy for Allies, 438, 440; and trade, 438; sea power, 439; and submarine warfare, 441, 462; *Lusitania*, 442; *Sussex* crisis, 444; and Allied propaganda, 445; and severance of diplomatic relations, 445; and profit motive, 446; and Middle Western isolationism, 461
World War II, 46, 61, 514; France blitzed, 38; beginning of, 437, 468; Middle West and, 468-471; and United States foreign policy, 517; in Philippines, 529-551; Japanese attacks, 532
Wright, Benjamin, Jr., 36
Writings of George Washington, 10
Wythe, George, 80; and Declaration of Independence, 95

Yalta Conference, 517, 522, 525-527
Yorktown, 166

Zimmerman note, 463